WEBSPHERE STARTER KIT

WebSphere Starter Kit

Ron Ben-Natan

Ori Sasson

McGraw-Hill
New York   San Francisco   Washington, D.C.
Auckland   Bogotá   Caracas   Lisbon   London
Madrid   Mexico City   Milan   Montreal   New Delhi
San Juan   Singapore   Sydney   Tokyo   Toronto

McGraw-Hill

A Division of The McGraw-Hill Companies

2 3 4 5 6 7 8 9 0   DOC/DOC   0 5 4 3 2 1 0

P/N 0-07-212405-9
PART OF ISBN 0-07-212407-5

The sponsoring editor for this book was Sharon Linsenbach and the production supervisor was Clare Stanley. It was set in Century Schoolbook by D&G Limited, LLC.

Printed and bound by R. R. Donnelly & Sons Company.

Throughout this book, trademarked names are used. Rather than put a trademark symbol after every occurrence of a trademarked name, we use names in an editorial fashion only, and to the benefit of the trademark owner, with no intention of infringement of the trademark. Where such designations appear in this book, they have been printed with initial caps.

This book is not a product of IBM, and IBM is not responsible for the contents of this book. The following terms are trademarks of International Business Machines Corporation in the United States, other countries, or both: IBM, SanFrancisco, and VisualAge.

To all of the amazing people at ViryaNet/RTS Software who make coming to work every day so great.
—RON BEN-NATAN

To my wife Yael, for all her help and support.
—ORI SASSON

Trademarks Owned by IBM

AIX®

AFS

AlphaWorks®

AS/400®

CICS®

CICS Connection®

DB2®

DB2® Universal Database

e-business (logo)

IBM®

MQSeries®

SanFrancisco™

SecureWay®

Top Page™

TXSeries

VisualAge®

WebSphere™

Note: Those trademarks followed by (®) are registered trademarks of IBM in the United States; all others are trademarks of IBM in the United States.

Java and Java-based marks are trademarks or registered trademarks of Sun Microsystems, Inc.

Microsoft, Windows, Windows NT, Windows 95, Windows 98, are trademarks or registered trademarks of Microsoft Corporation.

Netscape and Netscape Navigator are trademarks of Netscape Communications Corporation.

Tivoli is a registered trademark of Tivoli Systems Inc., Tivoli Enterprise Console is a trademark of Tivoli Systems Inc.

Domino Go Webserver is a trademark of Lotus Development Corporation.

NetObjects, SiteStyle, NetObjects Fusion, NetObjects ScriptBuilder, and NetObjects BeanBuilder are trademarks or registered trademarks of NetObjects Inc.

All other trademarks are the property of their respective owners.

Documents Used by IBM

- IBM WebSphere Application ServerPlus for Tivoli product documentation
- IBM WebSphere Application Server Online Documentation Center (part of the product distribution)

Redbooks:

Java Application Development for CICS, SG24-5275-01

Revealed! Architecting Web Access of CICS, SG24-5466-00

Application Development with VisualAge for Java Enterprise, SG24-5081-00

Web Enabling System/390 Applications Using WebSphere for OS/390, Java, and MQSeries, REDP0027

Web Caching and Filtering with IBM WebSphere Performance Pack, REDP0009

Caching and Filtering to Manage Internet Traffic and Bandwidth Demand, REDP0003

IBM WebSphere Performance Pack: Caching and Filtering with IBM Web Traffic Express, SG24-5859-00

IBM WebSphere Performance Pack: Load Balancing with IBM SecureWay Network Dispatcher, SG24-5858-00

IBM WebSphere Performance Pack: Web Content Management with IBM AFS Enterprise File System, SG24-5857-00

Managing Your Java Software with IBM SecureWay On-Demand Server Release 2.0, SG24-5846-00

Java Thin Client Systems: With VisualAge Generator—In IBM WebSphere Application Server, SG24-5468-00

Developing an e-business Application for the IBM WebSphere Application Server, SG24-5423-00

IBM WebSphere and VisualAge for Java Database Integration with DB2, Oracle, and SQL Server, SG24-5471-00

WebSphere Application Servers: Standard and Advanced Editions, SG24-5460-00

Using VisualAge for Java Enterprise Version 2 to Develop CORBA and EJB Applications, SG24-5276-00

IBM WebSphere Performance Pack Usage and Administration, SG24-5233-00

CONTENTS

Contents

Contents

Contents

What Is WebSphere Application Server?

WebSphere is a series of products developed and marketed by IBM. The IBM WebSphere Application Server product series consists of three editions: Standard, Advanced, and Enterprise. WebSphere Application Server is a Java Application Server—that is, a deployment platform for providing Java applications in a server-centric architecture. The three products differ in the breadth of services that are supported and the types of architectural elements that can be used by applications deployed on the IBM WebSphere server.

WebSphere as a product suite is the central and most important element in IBM's e-Business strategy. In fact, the term "IBM WebSphere family" is used by IBM-ers as a synonym for e-Business. The IBM WebSphere family includes much more than the IBM WebSphere server itself—things like development tools, monitoring components, configuration management utilities, and more. This framework is very broad and it is sometimes hard to understand from IBM marketing documents what is truly an integral part of WebSphere as opposed to products that are simply added on. In this book, we will focus in primarily on IBM WebSphere as an application server, but we will also provide quite a lot of information on related products in the IBM WebSphere family. You can use these products to build and deploy true e-Business applications in no time. A perfect example is WebSphere Studio and Visual Age for Java. Both of these products are development environments for Web applications and both have connectors and integration points with the IBM WebSphere server.

In this chapter, we provide an overview of the IBM WebSphere product suite. We will detail the elements comprising each of the three products and mention the audience to which each of the products is targeted. This chapter is the only chapter in the book that is not technical; the purpose of it is to "set the stage" for the rest of the chapters in the book that delve into the various components and services delivered in WebSphere.

Platform Availability

Many IBM WebSphere products are currently offered on Windows NT, Sun Solaris, Linux, and IBM AIX. Support for HP-UX has been mentioned (if not announced). In addition, some of the products are also available on the classic IBM platforms such as OS390 and AS400. Database support varies in IBM WebSphere based on the version of WebSphere you are using and the element of which you make use. You can connect to any relational database having a JDBC driver by including that driver in the paths of the Java server. Because some elements make use of built-in IBM WebSphere features (such as database connection pooling, automated persistence, and so on), it is not enough to plug in the driver in some cases. Version 2.0 has a limitation in one of its main services to DB2 only; this restriction is no longer true starting with version 3.0 of the server. The primary database platform supported besides DB2 is Oracle 8. In this book, our examples will use Oracle and DB2, depending on which element is being discussed.

WebSphere Standard Edition

WebSphere Standard Edition is the entry-level product and one that primarily targets simple, light-weight applications on the Web. One of the great features in the WebSphere product suite is that all editions are upgrade-compatible. This means that any application built and deployed under the Standard Edition will automatically also work in the Advanced Edition and ditto for the Enterprise Edition. Therefore, you may decide to start using the Standard Edition. If (and when) you see that your use of WebSphere is more suited to the Advanced Edition, you can upgrade to a more comprehensive product with very little implication on your development efforts.

Although the Standard Edition is the entry level product, it is still WebSphere. Therefore the core services that are part of the WebSphere Java application server are present in the Standard Edition (as in all WebSphere editions). The Standard Edition includes the Java engine forming the application server. This engine includes support for Java servlets and Java Server Pages (if you are not familiar with these terms, don't worry—by the time you'll finish this book you will be quite an expert). It includes the binding to various Web servers including Netscape, Microsoft, and the Apache servers. It also includes a number of additional services such as database connection pooling for servlet-based applications, XML services, and more. All this is provided from within the Java engine, so the set of services we just mentioned are packaged as sets of Java libraries and APIs that run in a Java *virtual machine* (VM). This makes the Standard Edition (as all other editions) quite portable and is one of the main benefits of basing the server on the Java platform as far as IBM as a vendor is concerned.

WebSphere Advanced Edition

The Advanced Edition is targeted at medium to high-end e-Business applications: applications that may require a high level of transactional support, applications that have high access rates (and therefore stringent requirements on performance and failover), and applications that may involve complex processing. The Advanced Edition includes all the elements in the Standard Edition and is based on fundamentally the same Java engine, although it introduces some important additional services. It is our opinion that the Advanced Edition is the perfect middle ground between the entry level Standard Edition and the sometimes too complex Enterprise Edition. We believe that the Standard Edition will be the right choice for the vast majority of applications and that it will easily dominate the WebSphere landscape.

The two primary additions included in the Advanced edition are support for *Enterprise Java Beans* (EJB—another one of those topics that you will be very familiar with by the end of this book) and support for transactional database connectivity. Because almost all business applications today have transactional requirements serviced by relational databases, this is almost always a mandatory requirement. This is the primary reason for our opinion that serious e-Business solutions require the Advanced Edition and cannot be based on the Standard Edition.

The Advanced Edition differs from the Standard Edition in the deployment environment. The Advanced Edition supports the notion of running a set of physical application servers (on different hosts) while providing the illusion of a single virtual server. This means that you can bring up a set of servers that all cooperatively work as one server. We cannot over-emphasize the importance of this feature in the context of e-Business applications. The whole concept of e-Business application revolves around opening up the business to users on the Web. Although the business implications of this ability are endless, technically this places a heavy burden on the applications. The burden is not only in terms of the performance implications because the user base may be especially high but also because the Web environment is much less controlled than a typical client/server environment. Therefore, the deployment platform on which the e-Business applications run must be highly tolerant and highly scaleable. The best way to do that is to set up multiple hosts (each one possibly with many processors) that can provide the base for the applications. This feature is part of the Advanced Edition.

WebSphere Enterprise Edition

The Enterprise Edition of WebSphere targets e-Business applications that have a very high level of distribution and transaction-related requirements. The Enterprise Edition includes all elements that exist in the Advanced Edition along with the following elements:

- Component Broker
- Encina
- CICS
- MQSeries
- DCE

This is certainly a very impressive list of products. Each one of these is a product (and a fairly complex one at that) that certainly has a life of its own. In this respect, the Enterprise Edition is not truly a coherent product, but rather an "umbrella" for a set of products that IBM makes that target the high-transaction, complex application space. It is hard to envision an environment in which all of these will be used in tandem. For example, Component Broker is a CORBA environment and it is difficult to find an environment in which an application uses both CORBA and DCE. The same is true for CICS and Encina. Finally, MQSeries is a product of its own. Although it is certainly a great middleware product, it is difficult to understand exactly how it links into the other pieces of the puzzle.

Although the previous paragraph seems to be critical of the packaging or branding of the Enterprise Edition, no one can ignore the fact the Enterprise Edition provides products and capabilities that will cover any requirement for high levels of distribution, transaction support, messaging, or practically anything else. This product mix is an impressive combination that should converge in later releases to create a more coherent and integrated product. As is always the case, the problem with such products is the complexity inherent in using it and the high skill sets that must be built within the development organizations. It is our opinion (as we have stated before) that very few organizations and application teams will opt for the Enterprise Edition (or, if they buy it, really use it).

Component Broker is an object engine that supports the CORBA model. As such, it also supports the EJB model (although most developers using EJB will almost certainly use the Enterprise JavaBeans Services in the core WebSphere server). We believe that Component Broker will be mostly used by organizations that have an existing investment in other programming languages such as C++ or by organizations whose environment includes a mix of programming languages and cannot (or do not want to) fully commit to a Java environment.

Apart from being a full-fledged ORB and supporting EJBs, Component Broker also provides support for a large number of services that are useful when building business applications. These services include

- *Concurrency control services*   Help in managing concurrent access to shared resources by multiple threads or transactions

- *Event services*   Provide support for decoupled, asynchronous communication between different entities. Support is provided for both a pull-based model and a push-based model.

- *Notification services*   Sometimes known as a publish/subscribe model, the notification services support a model in which suppliers and consumers interact based on subscription and interests.

- *Externalization services*   Support conversion of object state into a form that can be easily made persistent to be used at a later time

- *Identity services*   Allows each object to have a single identity even when the applications may be highly distributed

- *Lifecycle services*   Defines how objects get created, deleted, moved, or copied in distributed systems

- *Security services*   In addition to the security features available in the Advanced Edition (which focuses on typical Web-related security issues, the security services in the Enterprise Edition provide a set of comprehensive solutions in the areas or authorization, authentication, and encryption.

- *Naming services*   Services similar to DNS or LDAP, allowing you to build named hierarchies of objects for use within your distributed applications

- *Transaction services*   Support an object-oriented API for distributed transactions

- *Session services*   In addition to the session management framework available in the Advanced Edition (which is focused on managing application state for Web applications), the session services provide advanced support for managing state in highly distributed applications.

- *Query service*   Supports the OOSQL standard in which complex search criteria can be phrased in an object-oriented manner and then resolved based on sets of objects

- *Cache service*   Support optimistic and pessimistic models for managing caches of objects

- *Workload management*   A service that allows you to fine-tune and fully control what work gets done by whom, where, and when. This is another one of those important deployment level services that can make or break a successful deployment of a complex application.

The second important addition to the Enterprise product is TXSeries. TXSeries is really two products—TXSeries CICS and TXSeries Encina, both of which are TP monitors and used by applications with extremely high transaction requirements. TXSeries Encina includes the *Recoverable Queues Service* (RQS) supporting transactional queues, the *Structures File Server* (SFS), DCE, AFS, and much more.

The final piece of the puzzle is MQSeries—a highly successful middleware and queuing solution used by many corporate developers. It too is part of the Enterprise Edition. The challenge for IBM is to integrate it in a useful and convenient way into WebSphere.

Now that we have had a high level "marketing" overview of the WebSphere product line, it's time to delve into the product and how it is used to build e-Business applications. Have fun!

Installing and Starting WebSphere

In this chapter, we delve right into WebSphere and run through a typical installation. We will walk you through a complete installation procedure for Windows NT (the other platforms are similar, but with a less pleasing user interface). By the end of this chapter, you should be ready to install WebSphere on your machine with no problems. Later, we will provide more information on different components of the WebSphere server and specifically on things that may go wrong in the installation and how to overcome them.

Figure 2-1 shows the contents of the IBM WebSphere distribution CD (in this case, this is the CD for the Advanced Edition version 2.02). The CD contains the code for all available platforms—that is, Windows NT, Solaris, and AIX. Figure 2-2 shows the contents of the CD for NT and Figure 2-3 shows the contents for the Solaris platform (the contents of the AIX directory are similar to the contents for Solaris).

To begin the installation of WebSphere, perform the following steps:

1. Double-click the install program to start installing it in NT. For Solaris and AIX, run the `install.sh` shell script; this program locates the JDK installation (or lets you point to one) and then uses a Java program to run the installation wizard (a subset of the installation shell is shown in Listing 2-1).

2. For a typical NT installation, double-click the install program to bring up the installation wizard shown in Figure 2-4. The first step of the installation (Figure 2-5) is only relevant if you are installing over an existing WebSphere installation. If you are installing over an older version and need to migrate existing code, view the migration instructions and upgrade your code. For most of you, this will be the first time you're installing WebSphere, in which case you will not even get to this screen. Instead, you will go directly to the setup screen shown in Figure 2-6.

Figure 2-1
Contents of
WebSphere CD

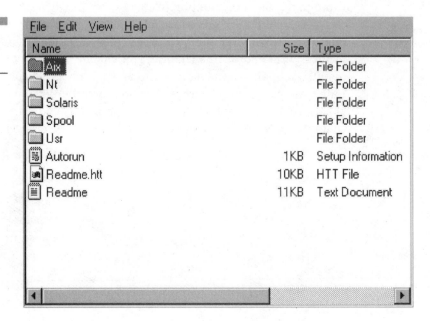

Figure 2-2
Installing for NT

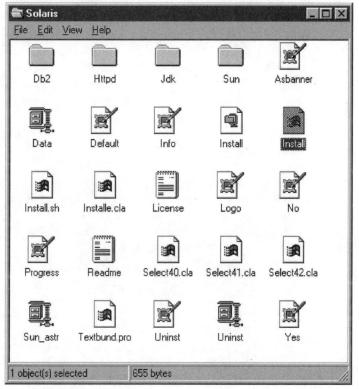

Figure 2-3
Installing for
Solaris (or AIX)

Listing 2-1
Installation Shell
for Solaris

```
#! /usr/bin/sh

CUR_DIR=`pwd`
JDK_PATH=$CUR_DIR/JDK

USERNAME=`/usr/ucb/whoami`

if [ "${USERNAME}" != "root" ]
then
{
  echo "You do not have the privilege neccessary to execute this
function"
  echo "Please login as root and restart "
  exit 1
}
fi

if which java > /dev/null 2>&1
then
{
#   echo "JDK was found on the machine"
  java -version 2>&1 | tee /tmp/abc
  version=`cat /tmp/abc | awk -F\" '{print $2}'`
  if [ "${version}" != "1.1.6" ]
  then
  {
    echo "Version ${version} of JDK was found on the machine"
    echo "The preferred version is JDK1.1.6                   "
    echo "Do you want to install JDK Version 1.1.6 [y/n] "
    read response
    if [ "${response}" = "" ]
    then
    {
       response="y"
    }
    fi

    if [ "${response}" = "y" ]
    then
    {
      ...

    } # response is y
    else
    {
      if [ "${JAVA_HOME}" != "" ]
      then
      {
        echo "JAVA_HOME is set as $JAVA_HOME "
        CLASSPATH=$JAVA_HOME/lib/classes.zip:.:$CUR_DIR/install.jar
        export CLASSPATH
        PATH=$PATH:$JAVA_HOME/bin
        export PATH
      } # JAVA_HOME was found
      else
      {
        ...
      } # JAVA_HOME was not found
```

```
      fi
    } # if response is n
    fi
  } # JDK Version was not 1.1.6
  else
  {
    if [ "${JAVA_HOME}" != "" ]
    then
    {
      echo "JAVA_HOME is set as $JAVA_HOME "
      CLASSPATH=$JAVA_HOME/lib/classes.zip:.:$CUR_DIR/install.jar
      export CLASSPATH
      PATH=$PATH:$JAVA_HOME/bin
      export PATH
    }
    else
    {
      ...
    } # JAVA_HOME not found
    fi
  } # JDK Version is 1.1.6
  fi
}
else
{
  while :
  do
  {
    echo "JDK was not found in your path"
    echo "Please choose one of the following options"
    echo "1. Install the JDK provided on the CD "
    echo "2. Specify the location of your JAVA_HOME"
    echo "3. Quit the installation. "
    read answer
    case $answer in
      1 ) echo "Installing JDK "
          ...
          ;;
      2 ) while :
          do
          {
            echo "Please enter your JAVA_HOME path"
            read JAVA_HOME
            if [ "${JAVA_HOME}" = "" ]
            then
            {
              continue
            }
            fi

            ...
          }
          done
          ;;
      3 ) exit 0 ;;
      * ) continue ;;
```

continued

Listing 2-1
Continued

```
    esac
    break;
  }
  done
}
fi

java -classpath $CLASSPATH Installer
```

Figure 2-4
Installation wizard

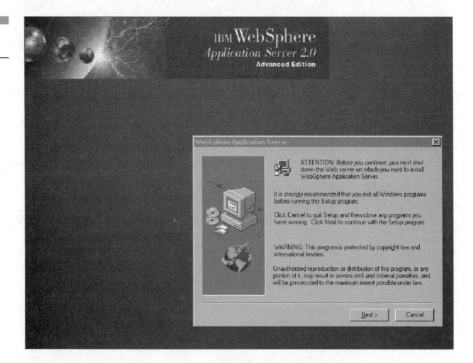

3. After selecting the installation directory (note: this is the installation directory for WebSphere; not the Web server), specify which components to install (Figure 2-7). In case IBM's HTTP Web server is already installed, this option will be left unselected by default.

4. Now you must select the JDK with which you wish WebSphere to work (see Figure 2-8). If you already have a JDK installed and you wish WebSphere to use it, point to it. Otherwise, the WebSphere CD includes a full JDK installation (licensed from Sun) that you may choose to install now to have WebSphere use this JDK. The 2.x release uses JDK 1.1.6, and the 3.x release uses JDK 1.1.8. (Important note: when working with version 2.x of WebSphere we recommend downloading and using Sun's JDK as opposed to IBM's JDK since the latter has numerous bugs.)

Figure 2-5
Detecting a
previous installation

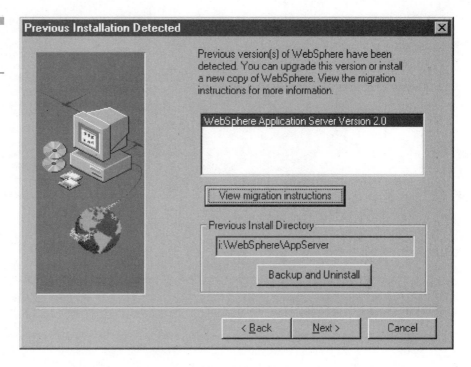

Figure 2-6
Selecting the
installation directory

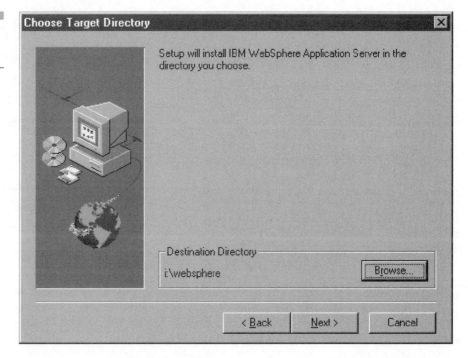

Figure 2-7
Selecting
components
to install

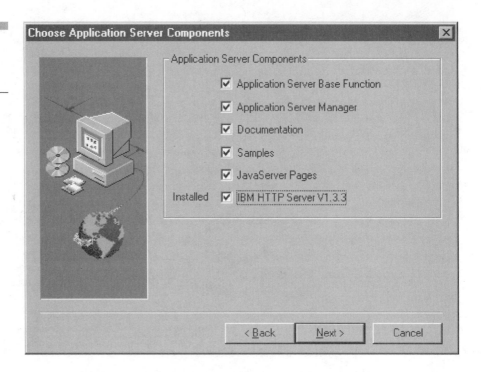

Figure 2-8
Selecting the JDK

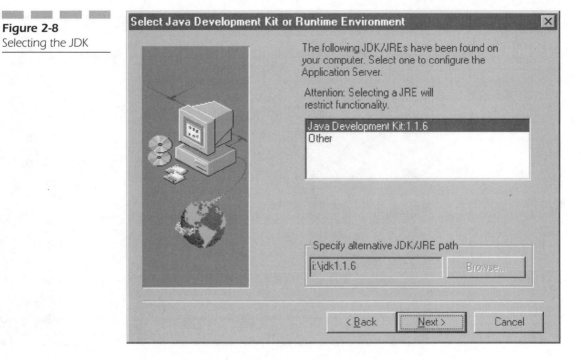

5. Next you must select the Web server with which you will work. As Figure 2-9 shows, you can use a wide variety of servers including Microsoft's IIS (for NT only, obviously), Netscape, Apache, Domino, and IBM's HTTP server, which comes bundled with the WebSphere installation and is based on the Apache server. During the installation, you can choose to install the plugins required to work with any number of these servers. In this book, we will use IBM's HTTP Server because this will be available to all.

6. Next, select the program folder to which you want the server startup links to be added (Figure 2-10). Finally, the installation begins, as shown in Figure 2-11. Note that as part of this installation, DB2 is installed on your machine, so don't fret if this takes quite a while. After all the files have been installed, you will be asked for the Web Server's root (assuming you are installing IBM's Web server) as shown in Figure 2-12. This concludes the installation; you may view the release notes if you like (see Figure 2-13). You must restart your machine before actually activating WebSphere (Figure 2-14).

Figure 2-9
Choosing Web
Server plugins

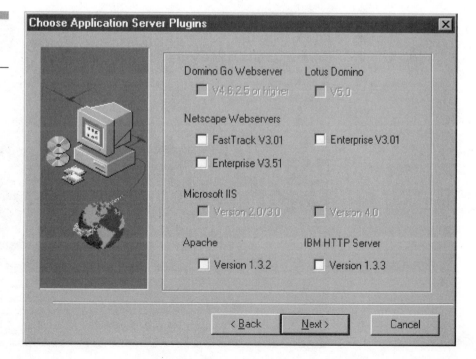

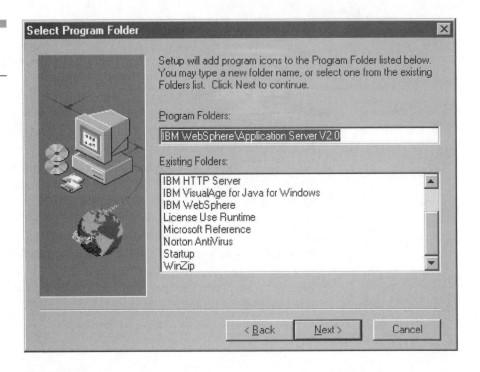

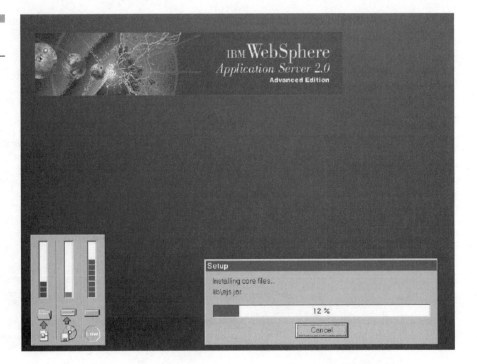

Figure 2-12
IBM Web Server's
root directory

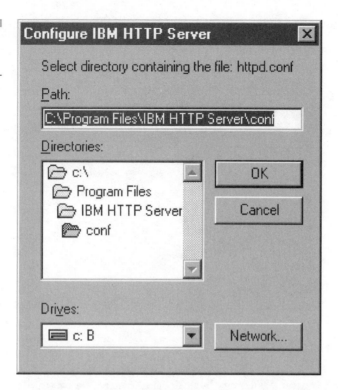

Figure 2-13
Setup complete

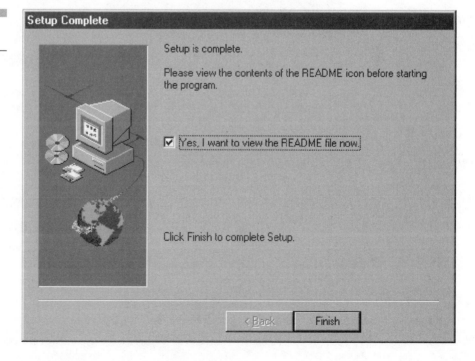

Figure 2-14
Last step of the
installation: restarting
the computer

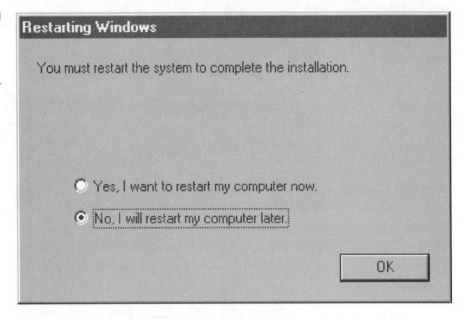

After NT comes back up, make sure the installation completed success-fully.

1. First, try to access the Web server's home page using `http://localhost` or `http://<your machine name and domain name>`. You should see the start page as shown in Figure 2-15.

2. Next, try to bring up the WebSphere administration panel using the program folder created for WebSphere (Figure 2-16). Actually, if this is the first time you are starting the server, give it a few seconds to complete its initialization process or you will get a message telling you that the servlet server has not been properly initialized. If all goes well, you will see the applet shown in Figure 2-17.

3. Finally, if you look at the services panel from the controls panel, you will see two NT services belonging to WebSphere (Figure 2-18). One is the Web server and the second is the servlet server; more on this in Chapter 4. You are now ready for some "Hello World" programs. These will be covered in Chapters 3 through 5.

Figure 2-15
IBM Web server's
start page

Figure 2-16
Bringing up the
administrator panel
from the Start menu

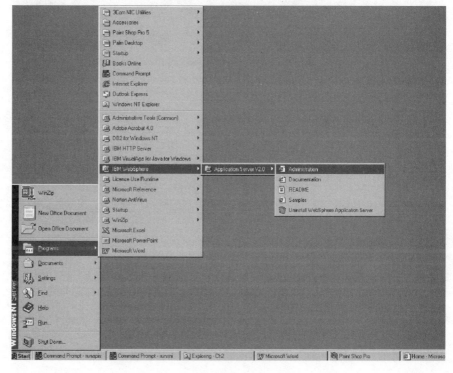

━━ ━━ ━━ ━━

Figure 2-17
WebSphere
administrator panel

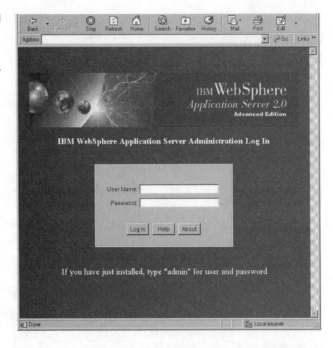

━━ ━━ ━━ ━━

Figure 2-18
NT Services started
by WebSphere

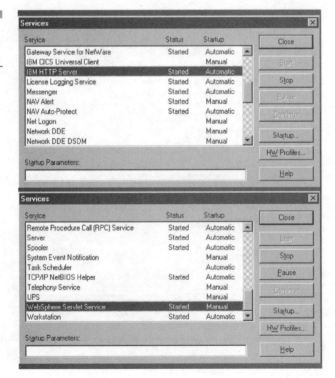

Hello World (Wide Web)

In this chapter, we begin our exploration of WebSphere. Our first stop is the Web server that underlies the Web-Sphere Java Application server. As we shall see in a later chapter, WebSphere can be used with any one of a large number of Web servers such as the Apache server, IBM's HTTP Server, Microsoft's IIS, Netscape servers, and the Domino server. In this chapter, we will be using the IBM HTTP server, which comes bundled with the WebSphere distribution. Because bringing up the HTTP server for viewing files is a trivial task, we will do a bit more in this chapter. We will also bring up a secure server—one that delivers Web pages over a secure connection using the SSL protocol (which will be discussed in Chapter 13, "Java Security and Web Security").

HTTP

Before we begin discussing applications on the Web, we must understand the underlying protocol and delivery mechanism used on the World Wide Web. All Web pages delivered to browsers on end-user machines are a result of a complete request/response cycle in which the browser communicates with the Web server designed to fulfill such requests. The communication protocol used by Web servers and Web browsers to converse with each other and pass data (in the form of requests on the one hand and responses on the other) is called the *Hypertext Transfer Protocol* (HTTP) and is the subject of this chapter.

Because every language, scripting mechanism, and application used on the Web is ultimately packaged into messages as defined by the HTTP specifications, the attributes of this protocol inherently enforce certain limitations and characteristics on any information passed over the Web. These limitations are important to understand before you begin to design applications and services for deployment on the Web.

HTTP is an application-level protocol originally designed for delivering hypertext elements over the Internet and has been in use as the Web protocol since 1990. Although HTTP is now used for much more than just HTML pages, its characteristics as an Internet protocol are still valid and include the lightness and speed required for providing the base for distributed collaborative hypermedia information systems. HTTP is a stateless protocol; this means that each request-response session is independent and does not contain any historical information regarding previous sessions. Stateless protocols are much faster than state-full protocols because less information has to be delivered. Stateless protocols are also relatively simple and straightforward to implement, which naturally simplifies the software required to support it. Finally, HTTP relies on the negotiation of data representation, allowing systems to be built independently of the development of new data representations.

HTTP is based on a request/response paradigm. Each transaction is ended after the server provides a response, thus ensuring stateless operation. An HTTP transaction consists of the following stages:

- *Connection*　The establishment of a connection from the client to the server
- *Request*　The client sends a request message to the server.
- *Response*　The server sends a response to the client.
- *Close*　The connection is closed by the server.

A client request includes a method, a *Universal Resource Identifier* (URI), a protocol version, and a MIME message. The server response includes the protocol version, a status code, and a MIME message.

The HTTP protocol version (sent both as part of the request and as part of the response) is given as

```
<major version number>.<minor version number>
```

Different minor numbers are used when protocol changes do not change the general message parsing algorithm. Message format changes require a change in the major number. This version number will always be a part of the first line on an HTTP version. For example, a response message sent from a server to a client may begin with the line

```
HTTP/1.0 200 OK
```

meaning that the response is of protocol version 1.0 returning a status of 200 (successful completion).

HTTP defines the standard character set to be ISO-8859-1. Because this character set is a superset of US-ASCII, this has no effect on messages defined using 7-bit character sets. The presence of a charset parameter in the content type header overrides the default and is used by the message originator to specify which character set to use.

URIs, URLs, and URNs

Universal Resource Identifiers (URIs) are strings that identify an Internet resource. URIs are best equated with Internet addresses for an object on the Web. *Universal Resource Names* (URNs) also designate a resource on the Internet, but do so using a location-independent name. *Universal Resource Locators* (URLs), on the other hand, identify a resource on the Internet using a scheme based on the resource's location.

All three serve similar purposes and are therefore used interchangeably. URIs are the most abstract and generic; they are therefore usually used in technical specifications. For example, the grammatical definition of URIs provides the basis for the syntactic definition of both URNs and URLs. URNs are very general, but rely on name lookup services and therefore depend on additional services that are not always generally available. URLs are the most commonly used and are the basis for HTTP and Web software.

The syntax of URLs is quite simple. Because URLs reference a resource through a location, they specify the host and the path name on that host where the resource can be found. In addition, the URL can also define the port through which the connection to the host should be made and the protocol used for the connection. A URL therefore takes the form of

```
<protocol> : "//" <host> [:<port>] "/" <absolute path>
```

Documents may reference resources using relative or virtual URLs. These URLs do not specify the protocol or the host but only provide a relative path. This is a convenience offered by Web servers for referencing resources based on their relative location to the resource where this virtual URL is used. These URLs are extremely important in organizing a collection of resources in a cohesive manner so they can be collectively referred to (for example, moved as a single element).

HTTP Transactions

A "round-trip" HTTP transaction consists of a request sent by the client to the server, processing done by the server to satisfy the request, and a response sent from the server to the client. HTTP is a stateless protocol. Each such transaction is therefore completely autonomous; there are no relationships between successive transactions. The HTTP transaction is therefore the largest unit of work and is comprised of messages (the request and the response), each containing a header and a body entity.

HTTP Messages

An HTTP message is a stream of octets transmitted over a connection. The HTTP message is the basic component of an HTTP transaction. Each request sent from a client to a server and each response sent from a server to a client is an HTTP message. Requests and responses can either be simple or full; there are therefore four message types in HTTP (simple request, simple response, full request, full response). Simple requests and responses differ from their full counterparts in that they do not allow the use of any header information.

Message headers contain a series of definitions aimed at describing the message body and providing information pertaining to the HTTP transaction. A header consists of a series of lines having the form:

```
<name> ":" <value>
```

Requests

Requests are HTTP messages that are sent from clients to servers. The request specifies the method to be applied at the server, the resource that this method should be applied to, and the protocol version being used. A typical request line is therefore similar to

```
GET    http://www.entity93.com/docRoot.html    HTTP/1.0
```

(meaning that the resource at the URL should be fetched and returned in a server response). HTTP currently defines the following methods:

- DELETE   Delete the resource at the provided URL.

- GET   Retrieve the resource identified by the URL. If the resource if a program that produces data, the response will contain the output produced by the program and not the program itself.

- HEAD   This method is identical to the process occurring in the GET method, except that the data body returned by the server when this method is in use is empty. Otherwise (for example, headers, meta information, and so on), these two methods are identical. This method is useful, for example, for testing the existence of a resource without actually fetching it.

- POST   In the POST method, the client sends additional information in the message body. This information is used by the server when servicing the request (hence the name—the client is posting information).

- PUT   Create a resource at the specified URL containing the supplied data.

The most commonly used methods are GET, POST, and HEAD. In fact, not all HTTP servers are guaranteed to implement methods other than these three.

In addition, the HTTP definition of requests allows any other token to be placed as a method. This allows dynamic method extensions. When the message arrives at the server, the server will try to apply the method to the resource. If this method is not supported, a response with the appropriate error code is returned by the server. The list of methods acceptable for a given resource on a given server may therefore change dynamically.

Responses

After the server's work is complete and the information to be returned to the client is ready, the server can construct the response. HTTP defines the format of a response to consist of a status line, a header, and a body. The status line records the protocol version, a numeric status code, and a status textual phrase. A status code has three decimal digits. HTTP categorizes the status codes and status phrases to five groups. Each group starts with a different first digit:

- *Informational*   Currently not used: 102 through 199
- *Success*   Returned when the requested action was applied—200 through 299. For example, a 200 status code (meaning OK) means that the requested resource is being returned in the response (for example, when the request applied the GET method).
- *Redirection*   Returned when further action must be taken in order to complete the request—300 through 399. For example, if a resource has migrated and a server side program knows the new URL, a redirection response might be sent back to the client, making the browser navigate to this new URL.
- *Client error*   A syntax error or another error in structure was discovered in the request—400 through 499. If the client has not completed sending the request when a client error status arrives from the server, it should stop the transmission of the request immediately. The server will usually include an explanation of the error as part of the response.
- *Server error*   Returned when a server failure occurs—500 through 599

Message Entities

When a request is made, and when a response is constructed, the contents of the messages are packaged as an entity. An entity consists of meta-information consisting of entity headers and a content segment called the entity body. Entity headers are similar to other headers and consist of names and values. Among other things, a specific entity headers defines the format used for the entity body; this is the Entity-Body header field.

Entity bodies are included in the message when transferring information between client and server. Thus, POST requests will contain an entity body, whereas HEAD and GET requests will not. Responses will usually include an entity body because they are returning some information. Responses to HEAD requests and responses returning with status codes 204 and 304 will not contain an entity body.

When a message includes an entity body, a number of meta-information segments are required. First, the data type and encoding methods should be specified. For example, the entity body and HTML text may be compressed using GZip. A full specification of the form

```
Content-Encoding ( Content-Type ( <entity data> ) )
```

fully informs the receiver of the message how the data should be extracted from the entity body. This information will be included as header fields. The length of the entity body will often also be specified in an additional header field. This is preferable to communication methods based on an EOF because a communication channel may be shut down early for other reasons. For requests, content length is the only possible alternative because if the client were to close down the connection, the server would have no way to return a response.

The HTTP Server

A Web server is simply a service that is registered with the operating system (by default listening on port 80 of the machine) to service HTTP requests. When a Web server is brought up, it defines a set of port numbers on which it will be accepting connections. This set of ports is defined in the server's configuration file (in our case, the file httpd.conf). When a connection is made on one of these ports, the operating system delegates the request to the Web server. Assuming that the request is based on the HTTP protocol, the server will be able to service the request. The simplest request is one that accesses the Web server's root page—the server replies with the default page as defined in its configuration file. The reply provided by the IBM HTTP server is shown in Figure 3-1. Figure 3-2 displays the NT Service Manager showing the service under which the server is running. The most common use of the Web server is to serve up pages that are stored

Figure 3-1
Default Web
server page

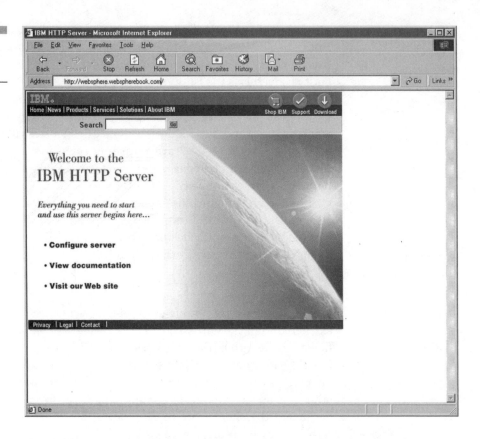

Figure 3-2
Web server as
an NT service

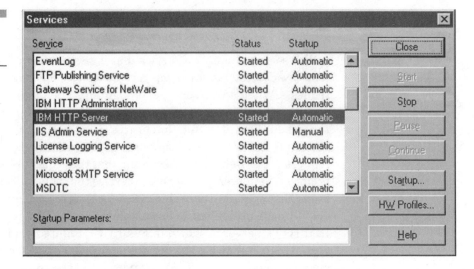

within the Web server's file system; we will describe many other uses of the Web server in building Web applications in later chapters in the book.

Setting Up a Secure Site

Although a Web server is very useful within intranets and for delivering general information to users on the Internet, when we put sensitive information on our Web site or wish to deliver some real applications, the Web server—in its inherent openness—becomes a liability. Luckily, most Web servers can be configured to support secure connections using a protocol called SSL (which we will discuss later in the book). Setting up a secure site is not a trivial thing because it involves not only changing the configuration of the server, but also creating a set of cryptographic keys and a certificate for server authentication. We will discuss all of these concepts in Chapter 13, but at this time it is of value to guide you through a simple process for setting up a secure server using the IBM HTTP server. By the time we complete this process, you will have a regular server listening on port 80 and a secure server listening on port 443 (the default port for SSL).

Before we can set up the secure server, we need to generate a pair of keys. These keys are used for encrypting the session and are based on public-key cryptography (which forms the basis for all modern security protocols). These keys are generated using the key management utility IKEYMAN. This utility can be started from the IBM HTTP server programs as shown by Figure 3-3. The application comes up as shown in Figure 3-4. Select Key Database File, New in order to create a new database file. A dialog box comes up as shown in Figure 3-5. Enter the file name and the location and click OK. Next enter the password as shown in Figure 3-6 (write this somewhere so you do not forget it) and stash the password in a `.sth` file. Click OK to finish this part of the process. The main IKEYMAN window should look like Figure 3-7. If you forgot to mark the checkbox for stashing the password, you can always select this option from the menu as shown in Figures 3-8 and 3-9.

Next we must update the server's configuration file (`httpd.conf` in the server's `conf` directory). In order to do so, we must add some directives to the configuration file as shown in Listing 3-1. Among these configurations are the DLL that implements the security functionality, the port the secure server will be listening on (443), and many directives regarding the attributes of the SSL connections. After we have updates, the configuration file we need to restart the Web server. If for some reason the server fails to

Figure 3-3
Opening
IKEYMAN utility

Figure 3-4
The IKEYMAN
application

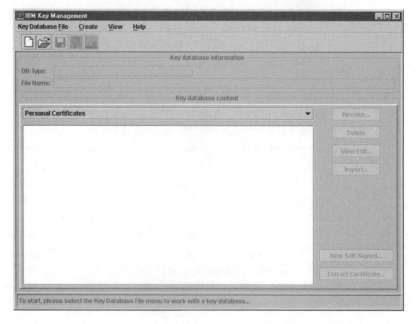

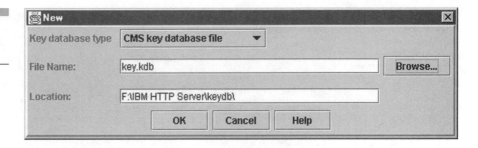

Figure 3-5
Creating a new
key database file

Figure 3-6
Setting the password
for the key database

start, you should inspect your changes to the configuration file; bad values always cause server failure. However, if you've managed to restart the server, you are in business. If, for example, you now access your server using http://<your server name here>, you will be prompted by a dialog box as shown in Figure 3-10. After you receive an acknowledgment, you will be running over a secure connection. It's time to go out there and get some credit card numbers.

Figure 3-7
IKEYMAN view of
the key database file

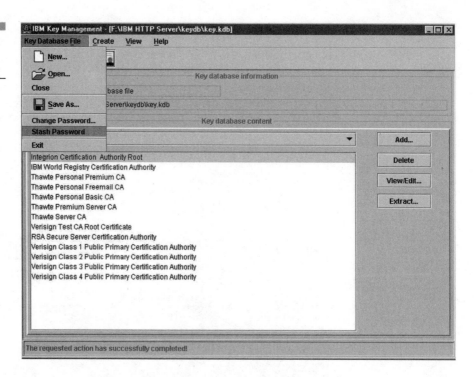

Figure 3-8
Manually stashing
the password

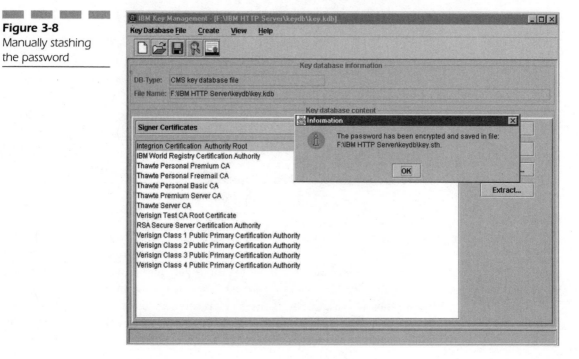

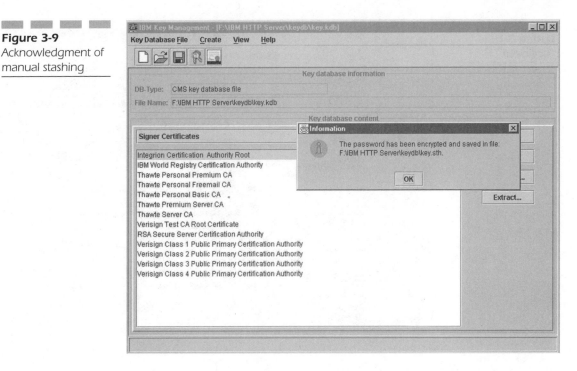

Figure 3-9
Acknowledgment of
manual stashing

Listing 3-1
Directives to be
added to the
httpd.conf file

```
# Load SSL module
# This can be 40,56,128 bit encryption
# For NT
# LoadModule ibm_ssl_module modules/IBMModuleSSL56.dll
# For UNIX
# LoadModule ibm_ssl_module     libexec/mod_ibm_ssl_56.so
LoadModule ibm_ssl_module modules/IBMModuleSSL56.dll

Listen 443
# A virtual host must correspond to a different IP address,
# different port number or a different host
# name for the server, in the latter case the server machine must
be
# configured to accept IP packets for multiple addresses.
<VirtualHost websphere.webspherebook.com:443>
# Enter the Document "root"
DocumentRoot "f:/IBM HTTP Server/htdocs"
ErrorLog logs/error-ssl.log
ServerAdmin ronb@webspherebook.com
SSLEnable
SSLClientAuth none
</VirtualHost>
SSLDisable
##        Keyfile directive:
##
```

continues

Listing 3-1
Continued

```
##        Specify the names of key files that are available, as
defined
##        with the IKEYMAN utility.
##
##        Default:  <none>
##        Syntax:   Keyfile  <filename.kdb>
##        This directive is not allowed inside of a virtual host
stanza

Keyfile "f:/IBM HTTP Server/keydb/key.kdb"

##        SSLV2Timeout and SSlV3Timeout:
##
##        Specify the timeout value for an SSL session. Once the
timeout
##        expires, the client is forced to perform another SSL
handshake.
##
##        Default:  SSLV2Timeout   100
##                  SSLV3Timeout   1000
##        Syntax:   SSLV2Timeout <time in seconds>   range 1-100
##                  SSLV3Timeout <time in seconds>   range 1-86400

SSLV2Timeout 100
SSLV3Timeout 1000
```

Figure 3-10
Security Alert
dialog box

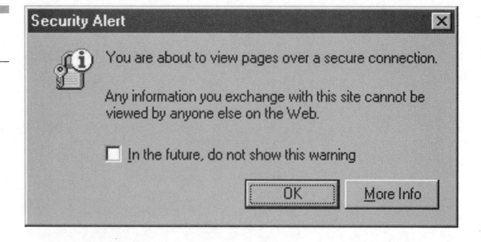

4

Hello Servlets and JavaServer Pages

Two of the primary capabilities that are supported by the WebSphere application server are servlets and *JavaServer Pages* (JSPs). In this chapter, we provide a brief overview of what servlets and JSPs are, and we show a simple set of working examples that use servlets and JSPs. As the name of this chapter suggests, the demonstration programs are simple Hello World programs that are aimed at providing a top-level description of the development cycle for servlets and JSPs. Later chapters focus on the development and deployment of servlets and JSPs and will provide more complete examples.

Servlet Basics

A servlet is a Java code segment that is built following JavaSoft's Servlet API standard. This API defines a set of methods that should be implemented by classes that are to be deployed as servlets. Obviously, this API standard does not say much more than servlet classes should conform to some kind of interface or contract, but this situation is always the case with Java. The servlet API is much more than just another set of interfaces—it defines a certain computational model that is the basis for the servlet life cycle.

The servlet model assumes that code segments called servlets will be maintained and will be managed by a server that conforms to the servlet API. This servlet server is usually coupled in some way with a Web server (i.e., an HTTP server). This coupling is the prevalent configuration, because most servlets are HTTP servlets and are accessed over an HTTP connection (whether by a browser page or by other code fragments). This coupling with the Web server also exists in WebSphere. The WebSphere installation includes both a Web server (be it a Netscape server, a Microsoft server, an Apache server, or the IBM HTTP server that is part of the WebSphere default installation) as well as a server that manages the servlet life cycle. The Web server typically forwards requests to the servlet server, which manages and invokes the servers that are registered with the server. Figures 4-1(a) and 4-1(b) show the NT service window of the Web server and the servlet server.

Figure 4-1(a)
Web server as
an NT service

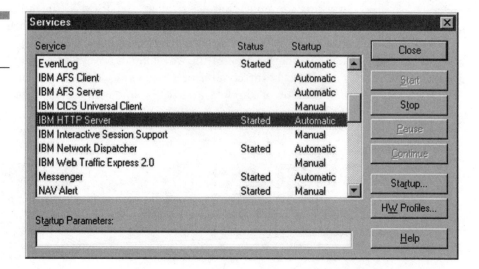

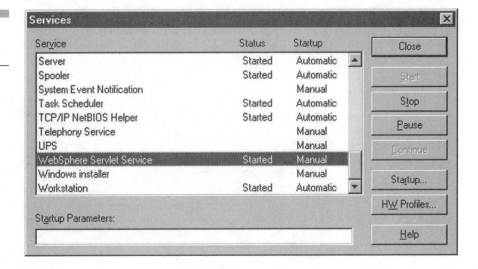

We have a servlet server that can be invoked from the Web server. Now what? Well, there is actually not much more than that. A servlet is simply a piece of Java code that is an entry point for enabling server-side functionality to be invoked through a servlet server. The most common type of servlet (by far) is the HTTP servlet. An HTTP servlet is a Java class that implements a few entry-point methods through which server-side processing can be initiated. Depending on the case at hand, the servlet either implements a simple operation (in which case, it performs something and returns)—while in other cases, the servlet is only the entry point, and most of the work is done in classes that are called by the servlet. Because an instance of a servlet is always invoked within its own thread, the servlet model lends itself to being used for Web applications and inherently scales well.

You will find it easiest to understand what servlets are by comparing them to CGI scripts (refer to the boxed text on the next page). In fact, when servlets were first perceived, they were introduced as a more flexible, portable, and faster alternative to the CGI script. Quite early in the life of the Web, it was clear that static Web pages just would not suffice and that programs were required to perform some computation within a session on the Web. CGI was born as a way to assign programs to certain requests that were coming into the Web server. The two main disadvantages of CGI script are that the scripts run as a separate process to the external server (and such a process has to be created for each request) and that the scripts are coded in various scripting languages such as Perl, Tcl, Pyhton etc. These scripting languages are excellent for system administration scripts and light-weight functionality but are less appropriate for serious applications (and are certainly less portable than Java).

The Common Gateway Interface

The *Common Gateway Interface* (CGI) `http://hoohoo.ncsa.uiuc.edu/cgi/overview.html` defines the communication protocol and the architecture for interactions between HTTP servers and gateway programs on the server providing specialized functionality. The basic premise of the architecture is that the server should perform as little as possible, and delegate responsibilities to specialized components. This allows the server to remain "lean-and-mean", provides greater flexibility in adding new functionality, and provides greater reliability by removing as much code as possible from the server (the most critical component in the architecture). This organization adheres to general Software Engineering concepts of modularity and encapsulation in that functional behavior is packaged in independent components that can then be assembled to provide services.

Figure 4-2 outlines the CGI architecture. Web browsers access Web pages that include components requiring special handling (e.g. clickable maps). A request is sent from the browser to the server. The server, recognizing that a CGI request has arrived, packages the data specified by the client and activates the gateway program. The data is then used by the gateway program to perform the required functionality. When the program completes processing, it returns to the server with data that should be returned to the client. The server completes the cycle by returning to the client with the data.

CGI defines the communication protocols used between the server and the gateway programs. It does not specify what the actual gateway programs should look like, what languages they should be written in, or what they should do. Therefore, gateway programs may be written in any language as long as the final result is an executable that can be registered with the server and invoked upon user request.

Gateway programs fall roughly into two categories: compiled programs and scripts. The first category includes gateway programs that are written in languages such as C, C++, or Pascal. These are compiled and the executables registered with the server (which usually simply means placing them in the appropriate directory). The second category includes scripts that are usually invoked using an interpreter of sorts. Common examples are perl scripts, Unix shell scripts, and tcl scripts. Naturally, each platform has its own scripting languages.

The data passed to the server from the gateway program can be divided into two categories. The first part of the answer includes information passed from the gateway program for the server to use. These are called *server directives* and provide a mechanism for the gateway program to affect the behavior of the server. The second part of the answer is the actual data that should be propagated back to the client.

Figure 4-2
CGI architecture

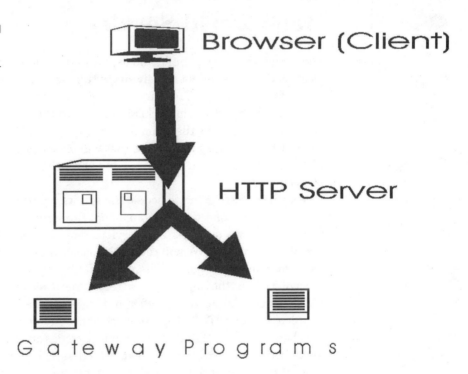

Browser (Client)

HTTP Server

Gateway Programs

Servlets were proposed to overcome these two disadvantages. Servlets are written in Java and can trivially invoke other Java classes to perform serious application processing, such as database access, complex algorithms, document management, etc. This functionality solves the second problem that was mentioned in the previous paragraph. The first problem is solved by the fact that the servlet is run as a separate Java thread but is run under the same Java VM as the servlet server. This process is much more efficient than creating an operating system process for servicing each request (because it requires less memory, no context switching, and little startup delays). Because CGI was so common and because Java as a language is perfect for such development efforts, the servlet concept was an immediate hit and continued to be one of the more successful models in the new world of Web applications. If one reviews the various Java application servers on the market today, the most consistent element in all of them is servlet support, which includes WebSphere, WebLogic, Oracle Application Server, Java Web Server (Sun), NetDynamics, Netscape/Kiva, etc.

Hello World Servlet

The servlet that we will build and deploy in this chapter is probably the simplest servlet. This servlet merely sits within the servlet server and waits for an HTTP request (a GET request, in this case). Once such a request comes in, the servlet writes a small HTML page with the phrase, "Hello World" on it. In order to make the example slightly more interesting, we add servlet support for French so that the servlet will either print "Hello World!!" or "Bonjour tout le monde!!" (our French is certainly not up to par—sorry).

Because we are going to access the servlet functionality from a browser over an HTTP connection, we implement the servlet as an HTTP servlet. In other words, we subclass our servlet from the `javax.servlet.http.HttpServlet` class. We will revisit this class later in the book and will provide many details regarding its usage. Right now, however, the important concept is that the servlet has a set of methods that are invoked when HTTP requests come in. Specifically, the servlet has a `doGet` method that is called when an HTTP GET request comes in and a `doPost` method that is called when an HTTP POST request comes in. Alternatively, one can implement the `service` method, which is called when either type of request comes in (if the `do` methods are not implemented).

The code for the Hello World servlet is shown in Listing 4-1. The main method of interest is the `doGet` method; the other interesting method is the `init` method. The `doGet` method is called when an HTTP GET method comes in to the server that is referencing the servlet. The `init` method is called when the servlet code is first loaded into the servlet server. In our example code, the `init` method is used to initialize the two resource bundles with the strings for the Hello World messages (shown in Listing 4-2), while the `doGet` method outputs the appropriate Hello World message based on the client's locale information. Initialization simply involves reading the two resource bundles that are used in this simple example. These bundles will be maintained in memory for use while the server is running.

Listing 4-1
Code for
HelloServlet1

```
package book.websphere.chapter4;

import javax.servlet.*;
import javax.servlet.http.*;
import java.io.*;
import java.util.*;


public class HelloServlet1 extends HttpServlet {

  Locale usEn;
  ResourceBundle usEnglishMessages;

  Locale frFr;
  ResourceBundle franceFrenchMessages;

  public void init(ServletConfig config) throws ServletException {
    super.init(config);

    Locale usEn = Locale.US;
    usEnglishMessages = ResourceBundle.getBundle(
           "HelloServletsTextMessages", usEn);

    Locale frFr = Locale.FRANCE;
    franceFrenchMessages = ResourceBundle.getBundle(
           "HelloServletsTextMessages", frFr);
  }


  public void doGet(
          HttpServletRequest request, HttpServletResponse
response)
          throws ServletException, IOException {
    response.setContentType("text/html");


    ResourceBundle aBundle;
    if (request.getHeader("Accept-Language").compareTo("FR") == 0
) {
      aBundle = franceFrenchMessages;
      response.setHeader("Content-Language", "FR");
    }
    else {
      aBundle = usEnglishMessages;
      response.setHeader("Content-Language", "EN");
    }
```

continues

```
    PrintWriter out = new PrintWriter (response.getOutputStream());
    out.println("<html>");
    out.println("<head><title>HelloServlets1</title></head>");
    out.println("<body>");


    out.println(aBundle.getString("helloWorld"));


    out.println("</body>");
    out.println("</html>");
    out.close();
  }



  public String getServletInfo() {
     return "This is a simple servlet activated by an HTTP GET
request";
  }
}
```

```
#Property file for HelloServlets1 text messages
#en_US
helloWorld=Hello World!!
```

```
#Property file for HelloServlets1 text messages
#fr_FR
helloWorld=Bonjour tous le monde!!
```

The processing method is activated upon receipt of a GET HTTP request. Based on the URL that is passed from the WebSphere servlet server (in our case, the URL will have the form of http://websphere/servlet/ HelloServlet1, assuming that the host we are running on is called "websphere"), the servlet engine knows which servlet to invoke when a request comes in. Because such a URL is formed within a GET request, the doGet method of the HelloServlet1 servlet will be invoked. The arguments to the invocation are an HttpServletRequest encapsulating the request parameters and an HttpServletResponse encapsulating the objects pertaining to the response (the most important one being the output stream to which the reply should be written).

The first step in the processing method is to set the content type of the response stream. The content type is a MIME type that defines the type of output that will be provided. Because today's browsers and other devices are based on many formats, including HTML, XML, WML, and many other acronyms that will be discussed later in this book, we need to inform the requester what type of output we will be providing. In the code shown in Listing 4-1, we set the content type to HTML by informing the requester that the output will be written out as text, but that the text is an encoding in HTML. The text written out to the output stream that is used later in the code will be HTML.

The next task that the code performs is to inspect the request object to determine what language the browser is using. This action is performed by accessing one of the parameters within the request header. While we will discuss the request header and the request object later in this book, it is interesting to see what kind of information is available to the servlet. One of the servlets that comes with the WebSphere distribution is the snoop servlet (which is invoked by opening a URL of the form `http://websphere/servlet/snoop`). As its name implies, the servlet inspects the request object and writes out the information that it can extract from the request to the output stream. This information then shows up as the resulting HTML page. Figure 4-3 shows the resulting output page. While it

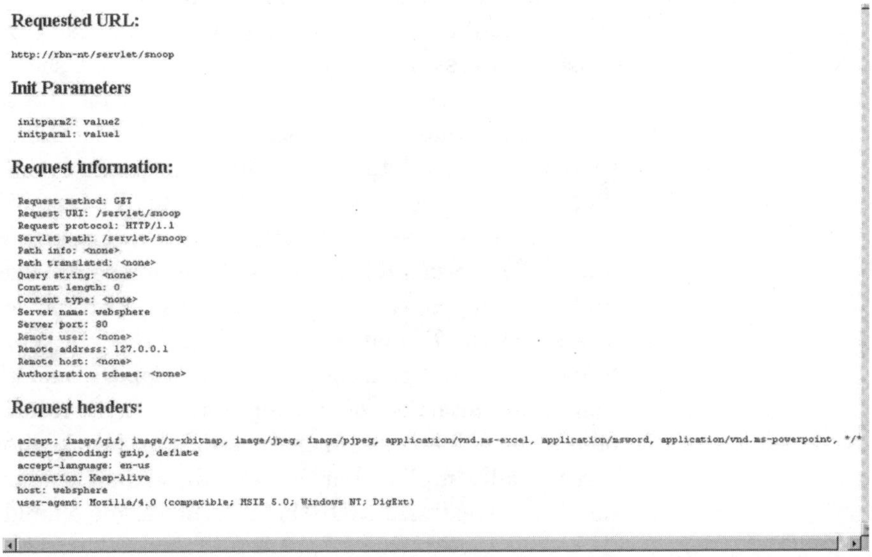

Figure 4-3

The Snoop servlet output

Requested URL:

http://rbn-nt/servlet/snoop

Init Parameters

initparm2: value2
initparm1: value1

Request information:

Request method: GET
Request URI: /servlet/snoop
Request protocol: HTTP/1.1
Servlet path: /servlet/snoop
Path info: <none>
Path translated: <none>
Query string: <none>
Content length: 0
Content type: <none>
Server name: websphere
Server port: 80
Remote user: <none>
Remote address: 127.0.0.1
Remote host: <none>
Authorization scheme: <none>

Request headers:

accept: image/gif, image/x-xbitmap, image/jpeg, image/pjpeg, application/vnd.ms-excel, application/msword, application/vnd.ms-powerpoint, */*
accept-encoding: gzip, deflate
accept-language: en-us
connection: Keep-Alive
host: websphere
user-agent: Mozilla/4.0 (compatible; MSIE 5.0; Windows NT; DigExt)

is not surprising that the HTTP and servlet models require this information (for example, the output can be made sensitive to the user-agent—a concept that we will use in examples later in this book), as a Web user, you might want to be aware that such information is being circulated.

Going back to our Hello World example, determining the language in which the output should appear is based on the Content-Language value in the request object. In our example, we only support French and English. Any language other than French will be displayed in English. Next comes the actual output. The output is written to a `PrintWriter` object that is part of the response object. This `PrintWriter` encapsulates the output stream, and anything that is written on this stream is placed in the HTTP response body. Because we have already declared our output to be an HTML output, we go ahead and issue a number of `println` statements that write the HTML source to be displayed by the browser. Most importantly, we extract the correct Hello World string from the resource bundle that was selected earlier.

So now, we have written the servlet code in our favorite Java IDE (probably VisualAge, because there is a lot to be said for the integration between WebSphere and VisualAge). We are ready to deploy the servlet under WebSphere. We have a set of `.class` files and two property files, and we start the WebSphere administration tool (running as a set of HTML screens and Java applets in the browser and connecting by default to port 9527). On the left-hand side is a navigation menu. Select the *Servlets* option and the *Configuration* option. The servlet configuration tool appears, as shown in Figure 4-4. This tool enables the WebSphere administrator to configure the servlets that are running within the server. Each servlet has a name that is used to access the servlet. For example, when selecting a URL of the form `. . . /servlet/snoop`, we assumed that the servlet was registered under that name (which indeed is the case, as shown in Figure 4-4). Each servlet also has details regarding the path to the class file, parameter names, etc.

Now, on to the `HelloServlet` servlet. Click the *Add* button, and the *Add a New Servlet* dialog appears. Fill in the full class path and the name under which you want the servlet to be registered, as shown in Figure 4-5. Then, click the *Test* button to make sure that the servlet can be run by WebSphere. When clicking *Test*, the WebSphere servlet server first tries to instantiate an object of the appropriate class. If it cannot instantiate this object, you will receive an error similar to the one shown in Figure 4-6. This error usually implies that the class file cannot be found. In other words, you have not copied the files to the right place. You should place your files under

Figure 4-4
Servlet configuration
for the WebSphere
Application Server

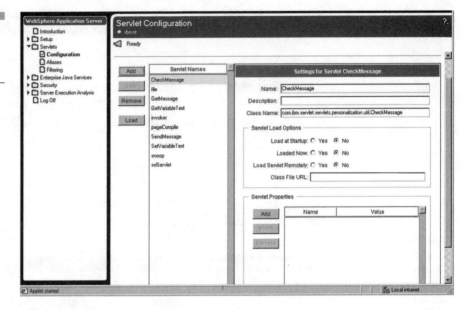

Figure 4-5
Adding a servlet

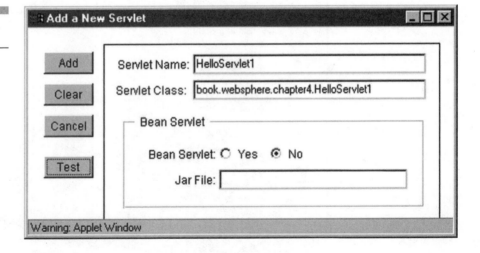

the `servlets` folder in the main WebSphere folder. The correct location for our example is shown in Figure 4-7.

Pressing the *Test* button not only instantiates an object of the appropriate class, but it also calls the `init` method. Because the `init` method is

Figure 4-6
Class Not
Found error

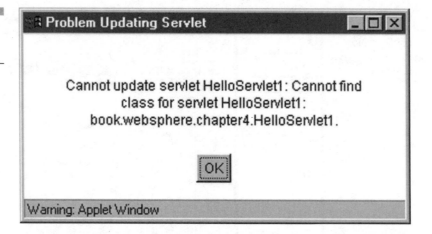

Figure 4-7
Servlet class file
location

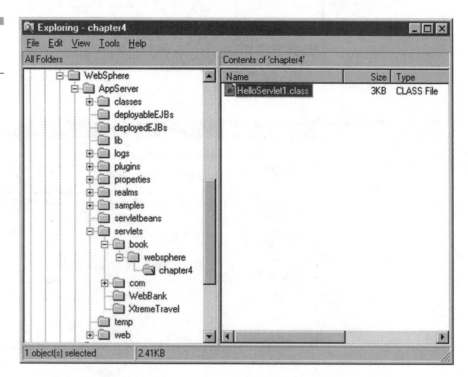

part of the formal servlet API requirement, any servlet can implement this method (or inherit this method from its superclass). In our servlet example, the resource bundles are built. If the files cannot be found, a dialog of the form shown in Figure 4-8 is shown. In this case, you must make sure that

Figure 4-8
Missing Resource
error

the property files are placed anywhere—as long as that folder is in the *Reloadable Servlet Classpath* attribute in the *Paths* tab of the *Java Engine* configuration page.

Hello World JavaServer Page

Now that we know the basics of servlets and have seen how to build and deploy a simple servlet, we can move on to a simple JSP. JSPs follow a relatively new programming model for Java, but this model is not new to the computing industry. This model is similar to Microsoft's successful Active Server Pages model. JSPs aim at providing the same usefulness of servlets but in a way that completely separates the application-processing logic from the presentation logic. JSPs also aim at providing an environment in which it is easy to build relatively simple e-business applications while not sacrificing the full strength of the servlet model. We will not delve into the details of JSPs and the JSP model; instead, this topic will be explored later in this book. Right now, we will focus on building a simple example and deploying it under the WebSphere server. Actually, we will go through a set of four examples—each showing a slightly different variant of JSPs.

Our first example is the simplest possible example, because it includes a simple HTML page that represents our presentation layer and a Java class that represents our model. The JSP file includes the HTML with a reference to the Java class that is providing the data. Obviously, the example only shows the concepts in a simple manner, so you should not scorn the fact that the data is merely the Hello World string.

Listing 4-3 shows the simple bean that represents the model. This bean has one method that we will use: the getTextMessage method that returns the Hello World string. This method is called from the JSP that is shown in Listing 4-4. The example shows a file (which must have a .jsp extension) that includes mostly HTML tags along with two additional elements. The first is a bean element that defines a variable called textProvider that is an instance of the book.websphere.chapter4.HelloJSP1 class. In other words, when the JSP file is processed, an instance of the class is created and can be referenced later in the JSP by using the textProvider variable. The scoping of this variable is defined as an attribute of the bean tag. In our case, the scope is the HTTP request. The part of the JSP file that is making use of this bean is placed within <%..%> delimiters and actually makes the call to the getTextMessage. The resulting HTML (after making a call of the form http://websphere/HelloJSP1.jsp is shown in Listing 4-5, and the screen is shown in Figure 4-9.

Listing 4-3
Java class used from within the JSP

```
package book.websphere.chapter4;

public class HelloJSP1 {

  public HelloJSP1() {
  }

  public String getTextMessage() {
    return "Hello World!!";
  }
}
```

Listing 4-4
Hello World JSP—Example 1

```
<HTML>
<HEAD>
<META HTTP-EQUIV="Content-Type" CONTENT="text/html; charset=iso-
8859-1">
<TITLE>
Hello JSP - Example 1
</TITLE>
</HEAD>
<BODY>
<H1>Hello JSP - Example 1</H1>
<BEAN
        name="textProvider"
        type="book.websphere.chapter4.HelloJSP1"
        scope="request">
</BEAN>
<B><%= textProvider.getTextMessage() %></B>
</BODY>
</HTML>
```

Listing 4-5
Hello World HTML
output—Example 1

```
<HTML>
<HEAD>
<META HTTP-EQUIV="Content-Type" CONTENT="text/html; charset=iso-
8859-1">
<TITLE>
Hello JSP - Example 1
</TITLE>
</HEAD>
<BODY>
<H1>Hello JSP - Example 1</H1>

<B>Hello World!!</B>
</BODY>
</HTML>
```

Figure 4-9
Hello World JSP
output—Example 1

Hello JSP - Example 1

Hello World!!

Now, on to deploying the example (and understanding a little bit about the internals of JSP support in WebSphere). The first question is where to put the bean's class file and where to put the JSP file itself. The bean's class file should go under the *servlets* folder in the *AppServer* folder (the same place where we put our servlet code). The JSP file, on the other hand, should go under the DocumentRoot of the Web server. This scenario is a bit confusing and requires a little more explanation (it is also not clear for Web-Sphere beginners and can cause hours of frustration). The resolution of this issue is based on the *Files* entry in the *Index* tab in the WebSphere documentation, as shown in Figure 4-10). If you have installed the IBM HTTP Web server following the normal installation procedures, this folder is the htdocs folder under the Web server's root folder.

More explanation is in order; the mention of the servlets/pagecompile in Figure 4-10 also requires some explanation. Let's start with the placement of the .jsp file. Because the HTTP request for a file is serviced by the Web server even before it reaches the WebSphere server, the .jsp file needs to be located by the Web server. Hence, the file needs to be placed not within the WebSphere directory structure but rather under the Web server's document root. If, for example, the URL requested is of the form http://host_name/ AAA/BBB/ccc.jsp, then (assuming a standard installation) the file should be placed in <web server installation directory>/htdocs/AAA/BBB (or a \ delimiter in Windows).

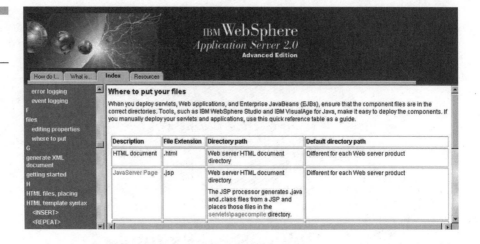

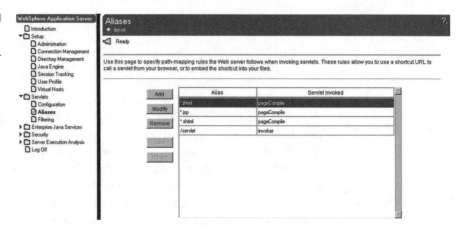

When the Web server receives a request for a URL that ends with a .jsp extension, it locates the file but does not return the file as is. Rather, it calls the WebSphere application server and passes it the JSP file. Then, the magic starts. WebSphere is programmed to invoke a special servlet called pageCompile that is part of the JSP standard distribution from Sun. This feature can be seen in Figure 4-11, which shows the alias definition that causes all requests pertaining to a JSP file to be forwarded to the pageCompile servlet. The pageCompile servlet is registered with WebSphere as any other servlet, as shown in Figure 4-12.

The pageCompile servlet receives the JSP file and goes through the process of parsing it and building a servlet that matches the JSP code. The

Figure 4-12
The pageCompile
servlet

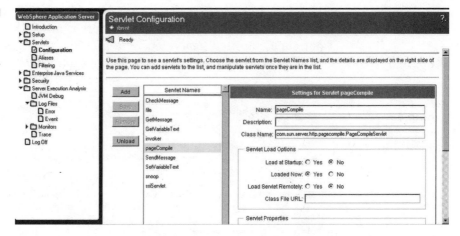

Figure 4-13
pageCompile
servlet code placed
in servlets/
pagecompile

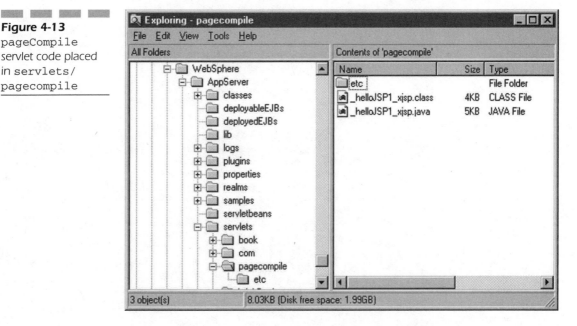

servlet Java code and compiled class file are placed under the servlets/
pagecompile folder in the WebSphere directory structure, as shown in Figure 4-13. This process is only performed once. Additional requests will cause
a quick invocation of the compiled servlet, as long as the JSP file has not
changed. If the JSP file changes, the appropriate servlet is recompiled. JSP
therefore provides a built-in version and configuration control mechanism.

The Java code that was created for our simple JSP by `pageCompile` is shown in Listing 4-6. By the way, if there is an error in the JSP code, output similar to that generated from a compiler will be redirected to your browser. An example is shown in Figure 4-14.

Listing 4-6
pageCompile
generated servlets

```
package pagecompile;

import java.io.*;
import java.util.*;
import javax.servlet.*;
import javax.servlet.http.*;
import java.beans.Beans;
import com.sun.server.http.pagecompile.ParamsHttpServletRequest;
import com.sun.server.http.pagecompile.ServletUtil;
import com.sun.server.http.pagecompile.filecache.CharFileData;
import com.sun.server.http.pagecompile.NCSAUtil;

import book.websphere.chapter4.HelloJSP1;

public class _helloJSP1_xjsp extends javax.servlet.http.HttpServlet
{
    private static final String sources[] = new String[] {
        "c:\\program files\\ibm http
server\\htdocs\\hellojsp1.jsp",
    };
    private static final long lastModified[] = {
        931156442000L,
    };

    public void service(
            HttpServletRequest request,HttpServletResponse response)
            throws IOException, ServletException {
        response.setContentType("text/html");
        PrintWriter out = response.getWriter();
        CharFileData data[] = new CharFileData[sources.length];
        try {
            for (int i = 0 ; i < data.length ; i++)
            data[i] = ServletUtil.getJHtmlSource(this,
                            sources[i],
                            "8859_1",
                            lastModified[i]);
        } catch (Exception ex) {
            ex.printStackTrace();
            throw new ServletException("fileData");
        }
        // com.sun.server.http.pagecompile.jsp.LiteralChunk null-
null
        Object tsxResultObject = null;
        HttpSession tsxSessionHolder = null;
        {
            String url =
HttpUtils.getRequestURL(request).toString();
            if ((request.getAttribute("__XXcallPageXX__") != null)
                && !url.endsWith(".jsp")) {
                out.println("<base href=\"" +
                        url.substring(0, url.indexOf("/", 8)) +
```

```
                             request.getPathInfo() + "\">");
            }
        }

        // com.sun.server.http.pagecompile.jsp.CharArrayChunk
c:/program files/ibm http server/htdocs/hellojsp1.jsp 1,1-
c:/program files/ibm http server/htdocs/hellojsp1.jsp 10,1
        data[0].writeChars(0, 181, out);
        book.websphere.chapter4.HelloJSP1 textProvider=
            (book.websphere.chapter4.HelloJSP1)
            (((com.sun.server.http.HttpServiceRequest) request)
            .getAttribute("textProvider"));
        if ( textProvider == null ) {
            try {
                textProvider = (book.websphere.chapter4.HelloJSP1)
                Beans.instantiate(this.getClass().getClassLoader(),

"book.websphere.chapter4.HelloJSP1");
                if ((Object)textProvider instanceof Servlet) {
                    ((Servlet) (Object)textProvider).
                                init(getServletConfig());
                }
            } catch (Exception ex) {
                throw new ServletException("Can't create BEAN of
class book.websphere.chapter4.HelloJSP1: "+ ex.getMessage());
            }
        ((com.sun.server.http.HttpServiceRequest) request).
                setAttribute("textProvider", textProvider);
    }
    {
    java.util.Properties p = new java.util.Properties();
    java.util.Enumeration e = request.getParameterNames();
    while (e.hasMoreElements()) {
        String name = (String) e.nextElement();
        p.put(name, request.getParameter(name));
    }
    com.sun.server.util.BeansUtil.setProperties(textProvider, p);
    }
    if ((Object)textProvider instanceof Servlet) {
        ((Servlet) (Object)textProvider).service(
                (ServletRequest) request, (ServletResponse)
response);
    }
    // com.sun.server.http.pagecompile.jsp.CharArrayChunk
c:/program files/ibm http server/htdocs/hellojsp1.jsp 14,8-
c:/program files/ibm http server/htdocs/hellojsp1.jsp 15,4
    data[0].writeChars(279, 5, out);
    // com.sun.server.http.pagecompile.jsp.ScriptletChunk
c:/program files/ibm http server/htdocs/hellojsp1.jsp 15,4-
c:/program files/ibm http server/htdocs/hellojsp1.jsp 15,40
    out.print(ServletUtil.toString( textProvider.getTextMessage()
));
    // com.sun.server.http.pagecompile.jsp.CharArrayChunk
c:/program files/ibm http server/htdocs/hellojsp1.jsp 15,40-
c:/program files/ibm http server/htdocs/hellojsp1.jsp 18,1
    data[0].writeChars(320, 25, out);
}
}
```

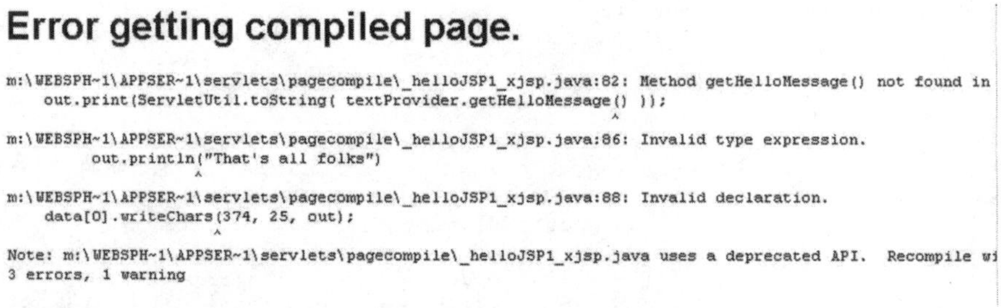

Figure 4-14
pageCompile errors

Error getting compiled page.

```
m:\WEBSPH~1\APPSER~1\servlets\pagecompile\_helloJSP1_xjsp.java:82: Method getHelloMessage() not found in
    out.print(ServletUtil.toString( textProvider.getHelloMessage() ));
                                                                ^
m:\WEBSPH~1\APPSER~1\servlets\pagecompile\_helloJSP1_xjsp.java:86: Invalid type expression.
        out.println("That's all folks")
                ^
m:\WEBSPH~1\APPSER~1\servlets\pagecompile\_helloJSP1_xjsp.java:88: Invalid declaration.
    data[0].writeChars(374, 25, out);
        ^
Note: m:\WEBSPH~1\APPSER~1\servlets\pagecompile\_helloJSP1_xjsp.java uses a deprecated API.  Recompile wi
3 errors, 1 warning
```

Listing 4-7
Hello World JSP—
Example 2

```html
<HTML>
<HEAD>
<%@ language="java" %>
<%@ import="book.websphere.chapter4.*" %>
<%@ content-type="text/html" %>
<%@ extends="javax.servlet.http.HttpServlet" %>
<META HTTP-EQUIV="Content-Type" CONTENT="text/html; charset=iso-
8859-1">
<TITLE>
Hello JSP - Example 2
</TITLE>
</HEAD>
<BODY>
<H1>Hello JSP - Example 2</H1>
<script runat=server>
        String text="Hello World!!";
</script>
</BODY>
<B><% out.println(text); %></B>
</HTML>
```

Before moving on to the next chapter, we want to go through a number of additional examples to show more JSP capabilities. In the previous example, we used JSPs as a mechanism to separate the presentation layer from the model by calling a bean from within a JSP page. Listing 4-7 shows another use of JSP pages as a servlet prototyping mechanism. Because a JSP page is always compiled into a servlet, the tags shown in Listing 4-7 cause a servlet to be created following the specification in the JSP page. This servlet is then used to create the resulting output. Listing 4-8 shows the Java code that was created by pageCompile.

Finally, the use of JSPs as a way to separate presentation from business logic often takes another form. In this form, the request is sent to a servlet. The servlet performs all application-level processing and prepares the output data, irrespective of the presentation to be used. This data is packaged

Listing 4-8

Servlet code created
for Example 2

```
package pagecompile;

import java.io.*;
import java.util.*;
import javax.servlet.*;
import javax.servlet.http.*;
import java.beans.Beans;
import com.sun.server.http.pagecompile.ParamsHttpServletRequest;
import com.sun.server.http.pagecompile.ServletUtil;
import com.sun.server.http.pagecompile.filecache.CharFileData;
import com.sun.server.http.pagecompile.NCSAUtil;

import book.websphere.chapter4.*;

public class _helloJSP2_xjsp extends javax.servlet.http.HttpServlet
{
    private static final String sources[] = new String[] {
        "c:\\program files\\ibm http
server\\htdocs\\hellojsp2.jsp",
    };
    private static final long lastModified[] = {
        931163122000L,
    };
    // com.sun.server.http.pagecompile.jsp.ScriptChunk c:/program
files/ibm http server/htdocs/hellojsp2.jsp 14,1-c:/program
files/ibm http server/htdocs/hellojsp2.jsp 16,10

            String text="Hello World!!";

    public void service(HttpServletRequest
request,HttpServletResponse response)
        throws IOException, ServletException
    {
        response.setContentType("text/html");
        PrintWriter out = response.getWriter();
        CharFileData data[] = new CharFileData[sources.length];
        try {
            for (int i = 0 ; i < data.length ; i++)
            data[i] = ServletUtil.getJHtmlSource(this,
                            sources[i],
                            "8859_1",
                            lastModified[i]);
        } catch (Exception ex) {
            ex.printStackTrace();
            throw new ServletException("fileData");
        }
        // com.sun.server.http.pagecompile.jsp.LiteralChunk null-
null
        Object tsxResultObject = null;
        HttpSession tsxSessionHolder = null;
        {
            String url =
HttpUtils.getRequestURL(request).toString();
            if ((request.getAttribute("__XXcallPageXX__") != null)
&& !url.endsWith(".jsp")) {
                out.println("<base href=\"" +
                        url.substring(0, url.indexOf("/", 8)) +
                        request.getPathInfo() + "\">");
```

continues

Listing 4-8

Continued

```
        }
    }

    // com.sun.server.http.pagecompile.jsp.CharArrayChunk
c:/program files/ibm http server/htdocs/hellojsp2.jsp 1,1-
c:/program files/ibm http server/htdocs/hellojsp2.jsp 3,1
        data[0].writeChars(0, 16, out);
    // com.sun.server.http.pagecompile.jsp.CharArrayChunk
c:/program files/ibm http server/htdocs/hellojsp2.jsp 3,23-
c:/program files/ibm http server/htdocs/hellojsp2.jsp 4,1
        data[0].writeChars(38, 2, out);
    // com.sun.server.http.pagecompile.jsp.CharArrayChunk
c:/program files/ibm http server/htdocs/hellojsp2.jsp 4,42-
c:/program files/ibm http server/htdocs/hellojsp2.jsp 5,1
        data[0].writeChars(81, 2, out);
    // com.sun.server.http.pagecompile.jsp.CharArrayChunk
c:/program files/ibm http server/htdocs/hellojsp2.jsp 5,32-
c:/program files/ibm http server/htdocs/hellojsp2.jsp 6,1
        data[0].writeChars(114, 2, out);
    // com.sun.server.http.pagecompile.jsp.CharArrayChunk
c:/program files/ibm http server/htdocs/hellojsp2.jsp 6,48-
c:/program files/ibm http server/htdocs/hellojsp2.jsp 14,1
        data[0].writeChars(163, 167, out);
    // com.sun.server.http.pagecompile.jsp.CharArrayChunk
c:/program files/ibm http server/htdocs/hellojsp2.jsp 16,10-
c:/program files/ibm http server/htdocs/hellojsp2.jsp 18,4
        data[0].writeChars(393, 14, out);
    // com.sun.server.http.pagecompile.jsp.ScriptletChunk
c:/program files/ibm http server/htdocs/hellojsp2.jsp 18,4-
c:/program files/ibm http server/htdocs/hellojsp2.jsp 18,28
            out.println(text);
    // com.sun.server.http.pagecompile.jsp.CharArrayChunk
c:/program files/ibm http server/htdocs/hellojsp2.jsp 18,28-
c:/program files/ibm http server/htdocs/hellojsp2.jsp 20,1
        data[0].writeChars(431, 16, out);
    }
}
```

in a data bean or is inserted into the request object. The servlet then uses a new API that is part of the JSP release to invoke the processing of a JSP using the data prepared by the servlet. Figure 4-15 shows the scheme of such a process, and Listings 4-9 and 4-10 show the servlet code and the JSP code in a simple example.

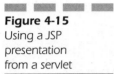

Figure 4-15
Using a JSP
presentation
from a servlet

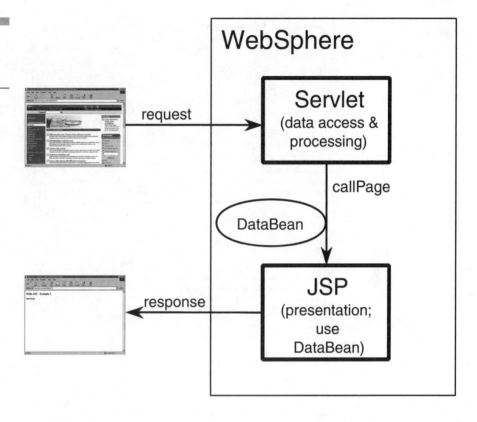

Listing 4-9
Hello JSP—Example 3
—"Model" servlet
code

```
package book.websphere.chapter4;

import javax.servlet.*;
import javax.servlet.http.*;
import java.io.*;
import java.util.*;

public class HelloJSP3Servlet extends HttpServlet {

  public void init(ServletConfig config) throws ServletException {
    super.init(config);
  }

  public void doGet(HttpServletRequest request, HttpServletResponse
                                                             continues
```

Listing 4-10

Hello JSP—Example 3

```
response) throws ServletException, IOException {
    ((com.sun.server.http.HttpServiceRequest)request).
      setAttribute("text", "Hello World!");
    ((com.sun.server.http.HttpServiceResponse)response).
      callPage("/HelloJSP3.jsp", request);
  }

  public String getServletInfo() {
    return "book.websphere.chapter4.HelloJSP3Servlet Information";
  }
}
<HTML>
<HEAD>
<META HTTP-EQUIV="Content-Type" CONTENT="text/html; charset=iso-
8859-1">
<TITLE>
Hello JSP - Example 3
</TITLE>
</HEAD>
<BODY>
<H1>Hello JSP - Example 3</H1>
</BODY>
<B><%= request.getAttribute("text") %></B>
</HTML>
```

Hello EJBs

Much as the previous chapter did, this chapter takes a quick look at one of the WebSphere application server capabilities, *Enterprise Java Beans* (EJBs). The intention of this chapter is to give a quick overview of what EJBs are and what are they are good for, and then provide a simple "Hello World" demonstration program. Chapter 11, "Enterprise Java Beans," looks at the issue of EJBs in more detail and from a broader perspective. Chaper 30 of the book goes through all the aspects of developing and deploying EJBs using the WebSphere application server.

EJB Basics

A JavaBean is a software component conforming to a standard interface that is used for application programming, in particular user interface programming (more on Java Beans in Chapter 10, "JavaBeans"). In the same spirit, *Enterprise JavaBeans* (EJB) are software components for distributed systems. Just like JavaBeans, EJBs conform to a standard interface.

To capture the essence of distributed computing, EJBs are designed with a built-in notion of a client versus a server. The server is an EJB server, which hosts EJB objects. The client accesses these objects to perform certain actions. To make things a little more interesting, the EJBs are not directly contained in the EJB server but rather in "EJB containers." An EJB container is essentially an execution environment for EJBs. An EJB server may well contain several of these containers. The EJB server is of course part of the application server, which in our case is WebSphere.

Client access to EJBs is done using Java *Remote Method Invocation* (RMI). However, client-side code does not directly invoke the bean code. Instead, it goes through two interfaces called the "EJB home interface" and the "EJB remote interface." The home interface is the initial point of contact for the client and acts as a factory for EJBs (that is, creating beans upon request, and removing them when they are no longer needed). The remote interface is a proxy for the EJB itself, used by client-side code to invoke specific methods on the EJB. To summarize, Figure 5-1 illustrates the EJB architecture.

Although this architecture with all its different components might be a little overwhelming at first, it is quite powerful. The nice thing about it is that after you define the remote and home interfaces, you don't have to worry about implementing them because that is the responsibility of the EJB container. When you implement an EJB, all you have to do is define the remote and home interfaces, and then the bean itself.

The home interface for an EJB extends the EJBHome interface. The methods of this interface are listed in Table 5-1. As you can see, the EJBHome interface provides only three mandatory methods. getEJBMetaData(), the first one, returns a reference to an object that contains information about the EJB. This object implements the EJBMetaData interface, the methods of which are listed in Table 5-2. The two other methods of EJBHome are responsible for removing EJBs. Note that there are no methods for creating EJBs in this interface. These should be implemented in the bean-specific extension of EJBHome, as we will see in the next section.

Figure 5-1
The EJB architecture

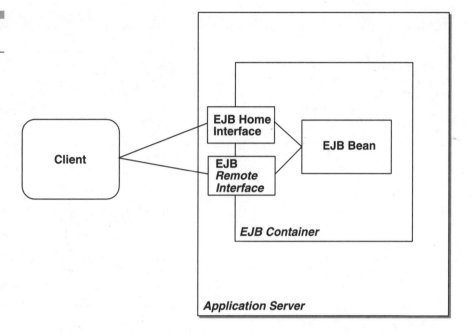

Table 5-1	Method	Signature	Description
Interface EJBHome methods	remove	public void remove (Handle handle)	Removes an EJB object given a handle. A handle is a reference to the bean object that can be serialized by the client.
	remove	public void remove (Object primarykey)	Removes an EJB object by its primary key (primary keys are relevant only to entity beans)
	getEJB-MetaData	public EJBMetaData getEJBMetaData()	Returns the meta-data for the bean object

The remote interface for an EJB extends the EJBObject interface (the methods for this interface are listed in Table 5-3). When you write your own remote interface, include the signatures of all methods you need to invoke remotely.

Now that we've gone through the home and remote interfaces, we can get to the EJB itself. The top-level EJB class is called EnterpriseBean, and

Table 5-2

Interface
EJBMetaData
methods

Method	Signature	Description
getEJBHome	public EJBHome getEJBHome()	Returns a reference to an object implementing the EJB home interface
getHomeInterfaceClass	public Class getHomeInterfaceClass()	Returns the class used for implementing the EJB home interface
getPrimaryKeyClass	public Class getPrimaryKeyClass()	Returns the class used for the primary key for this EJB
getRemoteInterfaceClass	public Class getRemoteInterfaceClass()	Returns the class used for implementing the EJB remote interface
isSession	public Boolean isSession()	Returns a Boolean value indicating if this EJB is a session bean

Table 5-3

Interface
EJBObject
methods

Method	Signature	Description
getEJBHome	public EJBHome get EJBHome()	Returns a reference to an object implementing the EJB's home interface
getPrimaryKey	public Object getPrimaryKey()	Returns the primary key for the EJB object. This is relevant only for entity beans.
getHandle	public Handle getHandle()	Returns a Handle to the object. As previously mentioned, the Handle is a serializable reference to the object.
isIdentical	public boolean isIdentical (EJBObject obj)	This method tests if two EJB object references are referring to the same object. This is useful mostly for entity beans. Note that two beans of the same home interface and with the same primary key are considered to be identical.
remove	public void remove()	This method removes the remote EJB object.

its definition is shown in Listing 5-1. As you can see, there's not much to this definition. When developing an EJB, you obviously do not extend this interface because it contains nothing. Instead, extend either one of the `SessionBean` and `EntityBean` interfaces. These interfaces correspond to two different kinds of EJBs. The first refers to "Session beans," which are usually limited to the scope of a single client session, whereas the other refers to "Entity Beans" that have a longer lifetime, and specifically exist through several separate sessions. In the following sections, we will limit the discussion to Session beans only because our "Hello World" EJB is a Session bean.

Table 5-4 shows the methods of the SessionBean interface. The invocation of these methods is event-driven; that is, they are called to notify the SessionBean about some external event.

Listing 5-1
Interface
EnterpriseBean
definition

```
public interface javax.ejb.EnterpriseBean extends
java.io.Serializable
{
};
```

Table 5-4

Interface Session-
Bean Methods

Method	Signature	Description
setSessionContext	public void setSessionContext (SessionContext ctx)	This method is invoked by the container in order to provide the bean with its context.
ejbRemove	public void ejbRemove()	This method is invoked in order to notify the bean it is going to be removed.
ejbActivate	public void ejbActivate()	This method is invoked in order to notify the bean it is going to be "activated", i.e. moved into main memory from storage.
ejbPassivate	public void ejbPassivate()	This method is invoked in order to notify the bean it is going to be "passivated", i.e. moved into storage.

"Hello World" EJB

The "Hello World" EJB presented in this section is very simple. It provides a method that returns a greeting message string. Client-side code can use this method by finding the bean's home interface, getting access to the bean, and then invoking the method.

Our first step in developing our EJB is defining the remote interface. As mentioned in the previous section, this interface extends the EJBObject interface. Listing 5-2 shows the code for the remote interface. In order to use EJBs, we import the EJB package javax.ejb. We also import the RMI package javax.rmi because we refer to the RemoteException defined there. This exception is thrown whenever there is a network problem, and the client-side code must be prepared to handle it. As a rule, all your EJB methods in the remote interface should throw this exception.

The only method we define in the remote interface is the method of getTextMessage(). The signature for this method should correspond to its definition in the bean itself; the only possible difference is that in the remote interface, its definition must indicate that it throws RemoteException.

After we're done with the remote interface, we can proceed to the home interface. In the home interface, you need to define creation methods for the bean. Such methods should be named create(), and have parameters if needed. The returned value type for the creation method is the type of the remote interface. As with the remote interface methods, the create method must be declared so it throws java.rmi.RemoteException. In addition, it should also throw javax.ejb.CreateException. This exception is thrown when there is a problem in creating the new EJB (for example, when the EJB server is out of memory). Listing 5-3 shows the home interface for our EJB, called HelloHome. We provide a create method

Listing 5-2
Code for remote interface

```
package book.websphere.chapter5;


import javax.ejb.*;
import javax.rmi.*;



public interface Hello extends EJBObject {
        String getTextMessage() throws RemoteException;
}
```

Listing 5-3
Code for home
interface

```
package book.websphere.chapter5;

import javax.ejb.*;
import java.rmi.*;


public interface HelloHome extends EJBHome {
        public Hello create() throws RemoteException,
                                      javax.ejb.CreateException;
}
```

without any parameters. Note that this method must be public because it should be visible outside of the package.

Now that we have the home and remote interfaces, we can move on to the bean implementation class. This is the cool part in writing EJBs; you don't have to provide implementations for the home and remote interfaces—that's the responsibility of the container.

Listing 5-4 shows the code for the bean implementation class, named `HelloBean`. This implements the `SessionBean` interface. Because the requirements are very simple, all implementations of the `SessionBean` interface methods are empty. This means that our bean is oblivious to any calls by the container made when it is active or inactive. Later in this book, we will see more complicated EJB implementations. The only method that actually does anything in the `HelloBean` class is our `getTextMessage()` method, which returns the "Hello World" string. Note that its signature should match the one defined in the remote interface.

Now that we have all the code we need, the next step is to compile it and create a JAR file. This is done with the `javac` and `jar` commands. From your command-line prompt, type

```
javac *.java
jar cmf Hello.jar *.class
```

(This assumes you run both commands from the directory where the source code resides.)

Now we are ready to actually deploy the EJB on our application server. For this purpose, WebSphere provides a tool called "Jet." The batch file for starting it up is in `WebSphere\AppServer\samples\ejs`. Before using this batch file, you might first need to edit it to include the correct settings for your Swing installation. To do that, find the line that states

```
set SWING_ROOT=.
```

Listing 5-4
Code for the bean
implementation class

```
package book.websphere.chapter5;

import javax.ejb.*;


public class HelloBean extends SessionBean {
    public void ejbCreate()
    {
    }

    public void ejbRemove()
    {
    }

    public void ejbActivate()
{
    }

    public void ejbPassivate()
    {
    }

    public void setSessionContext(SessionContext ctx)
    {
    }

    public String getTextMessage()
    {
        return "Hello World";
    }
}
```

Change this line to reflect the location of your own Swing installation.

To run the jet interface, just type "jet" from the command line. The jet window comes up as shown in Figure 5-2. Now you must provide the JAR file where your classes are located, and where you want to place the EJB-JAR file. You put these in the input and output fields respectively. You should place your EJB-JAR file in WebSphere\DeployableEJBs.

After filling out the input and output fields, select the SessionBean tab and click the Build button at the bottom of the page. Figure 5-3 shows the SessionBean tab. After you click the button, the Jet program will generate the EJB-JAR file. This file is the input for the EJB deployment process on WebSphere. To commence the deployment process, log into the WebSphere administration tool. You do that by starting your Internet browser and connecting to a specific predefined port, which is 9527 by default (for example, you open the URL http://my.server.com:9527). On the left side, select

Figure 5-2
The jet window

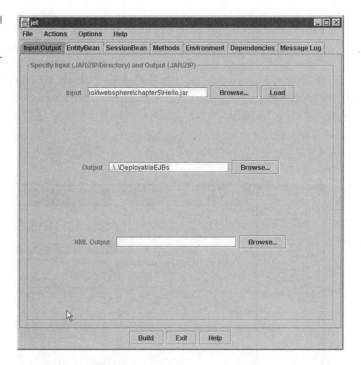

Figure 5-2
The jet window

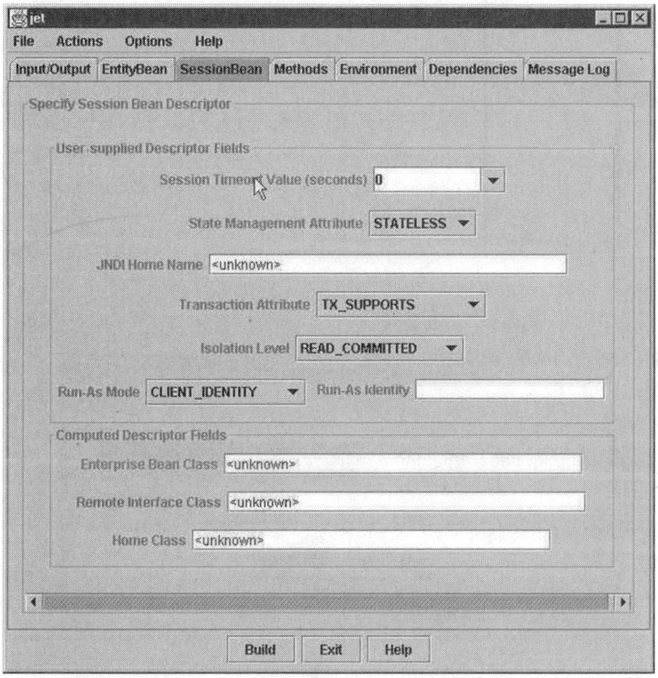

Figure 5-3
The SessionBean
tab

Enterprise Java Services, and then EJB Jar Files. You should be able to see your `Hello.jar` file at the bottom of the list of EJB jar files, as depicted in Figure 5-4. Select this file, and then click Deploy. A dialog box opens up as shown in Figure 5-5. In this dialog box, select the container for your EJB. For this example, select the container called `defaultSessionContainer` and click Deploy.

Figure 5-4
Deploying the EJB under WebSphere

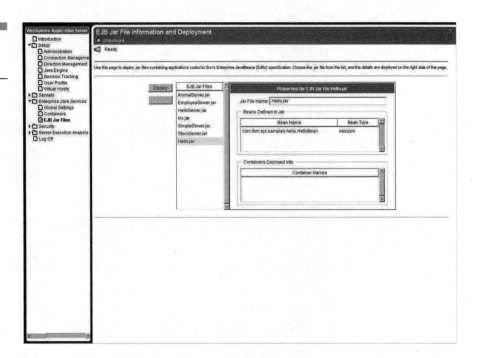

Figure 5-5
The container deployment dialog box

This completes the deployment phase. All that is left is to write a small client-side program to check that this EJB actually works. Listing 5-5 shows the code for this program. Note that the program uses an object of type `javax.naming.InitialContext`. This class provides an interface to the naming service. The properties we set for it are used to hook it up with the WebSphere server. After the `InitialContext` object is initialized, we use it to lookup the home interface of our EJB. Using this home interface, we create a "remote" instance and invoke the `getTextMessage()`.

When you look at this client-side code, you see there is no explicit code for networking. This is all done automatically by the container-created code for the home and remote interfaces. Although the code appears pretty straightforward, behind the scenes there is a lot more going on. When you call the lookup method on the `InitialContext` object, you actually perform a network-wide lookup for the specific bean. In our specific case, the network is limited to one server, but that might be different in a real-world application. Invoking the `create` method on the `HelloHome` reference involves the EJB container, which is responsible for creating a new instance of `HelloBean` instance and connecting it to this session. Finally, when you call `getTextMessage`, this request goes over the network and is executed in the EJB container.

To run the client-side code, all you must do is compile it and run it. The result may look like nothing more than a short message saying "Hello World," but in reality you have created a distributed program running over the network.

Listing 5-5
Client-side code for the Hello bean

```
package book.websphere.chapter5;

import javax.ejb.*;
import java.rmi.*;
import java.util.*;
import javax.naming.*;

public class HelloClient {
    public static void main(String args[])
    {
      try {
        Properties p = new Properties();
        p.put(Context.INITIAL_CONTEXT_FACTORY,
            "com.ibm.jndi.CosNaming.CNInitialContextFactory");
```

continues

Listing 5-5
Continued

```
p.put("java.naming.provider.url","iiop://my.server.com:9020");

        InitialContext ic = new InitialContext(p);
        HelloHome home = (HelloHome) ic.lookup("HelloBean");

        Hello  inc = incHome.create();

        String ret = hello.getTextMessage());
        System.out.println("Returned Message: " + ret);
    } catch (Exception ex) {
        System.out.println("HelloClient Runtime Error:");
        ex.printStackTrace();
    }

  }
}
```

6

Web Servers

WebSphere is a runtime environment for building eBusiness applications. Because an eBusiness application inherently provides access over the Web, WebSphere must be deployed over a Web server (an HTTP server). In this chapter, we discuss some of the Web servers with which the WebSphere product can be deployed. Because HTTP servers are by now quite standard and follow a known pattern, the WebSphere product can be deployed over a large number of HTTP servers. In fact, all major servers are supported, so you should have absolutely no problem deploying WebSphere within your environment. For those who do not have an existing HTTP server infrastructure in place, the WebSphere installation procedure includes an HTTP server called the IBM HTTP server that you can use immediately (and with practically no configuration) upon installation from the WebSphere CD.

The Web servers supported by WebSphere are

- IBM HTTP server
- Apache server
- Domino
- Lotus Domino Go Webserver
- Netscape Enterprise server
- Netscape FastTrack server
- Microsoft Internet Information server

In this chapter, we will briefly discuss the Apache server, the IBM HTTP Server, and the Microsoft Internet Information server.

The Apache Server

The Apache server belongs to a family of products/projects that is a relative newcomer to the software landscape and one that is both remarkable and admirable at the same time. Apache is perhaps the most well-known (or at least one of the two most well-known examples, along with Linux) of software that was developed by a group of people distributed all over the planet with no payment involved. The people doing the work did not get paid for their time and the server does not involve purchasing a license. As software developers, we are in awe of the result. The following snippets are taken from the Apache group distribution and best describe what Apache is all about.

The Apache HTTP Server Project

`http://www.apache.org/`

The Apache Project is a collaborative software development effort aimed at creating a robust, commercial-grade, feature-filled, and freely-available source code implementation of an HTTP (Web) server. The project is jointly managed by a group of volunteers located around the world, using the Internet and the Web to communicate, plan, and develop the server and its related documentation. These volunteers are known as the Apache

Group. In addition, hundreds of users have contributed ideas, code, and documentation to the project.

In February of 1995, the most popular server software on the Web was the public domain HTTP daemon developed by Rob McCool at the National Center for Supercomputing Applications, University of Illinois, Urbana-Champaign. However, development of that HTTPD had stalled after Rob left NCSA in mid-1994, and many Webmasters had developed their own extensions and bug fixes that were in need of a common distribution. A small group of these Webmasters, contacted via private e-mail, gathered together for the purpose of coordinating their changes (in the form of "patches"). Brian Behlendorf and Cliff Skolnick put together a mailing list, shared information space, and logins for the core developers on a machine in the California Bay area, with bandwidth and diskspace donated by HotWired and Organic Online. By the end of February, eight core contributors formed the foundation of the original Apache Group:

Brian Behlendorf	Roy T. Fielding	Rob Hartill
David Robinson	Cliff Skolnick	Randy Terbush
Robert S. Thau	Andrew Wilson	

with additional contributions from

Eric Hagberg	Frank Peters	Nicolas Pioch

Using NCSA HTTPD 1.3 as a base, we added all of the published bug fixes and worthwhile enhancements we could find, tested the result on our own servers, and made the first official public release (0.6.2) of the Apache server in April 1995. By coincidence, NCSA restarted their own development during the same period, and Brandon Long and Beth Frank of the NCSA Server Development Team joined the list in March as honorary members so that the two projects could share ideas and fixes.

The early Apache server was a big hit, but we all knew that the codebase needed a general overhaul and redesign. During May-June 1995, while Rob Hartill and the rest of the group focused on implementing new features for 0.7.x (like pre-forked child processes) and supporting the rapidly growing Apache user community, Robert Thau designed a new server architecture (code-named Shambhala) that included a modular structure and API for better extensibility, pool-based memory allocation, and an adaptive pre-forking process model. The group switched to this new server base in July and added the features from 0.7.x, resulting in Apache 0.8.8 (and its brethren) in August.

After extensive beta testing, many ports to obscure platforms, a new set of documentation (by David Robinson), and the addition of many features in the form of our standard modules, Apache 1.0 was released on December 1, 1995.

Less than a year after the group was formed, the Apache server passed NCSA's HTTPD as the #1 server on the Internet.

The Apache project is a meritocracy—the more work you have done, the more you are allowed to do. The group founders set the original rules, but they can be changed by vote of the active members. There is a group of people who have logins on our server (`hyperreal.com`) and access to the CVS repository. Everyone has access to the CVS snapshots. Changes to the code are proposed on the mailing list and usually voted on by active members—three +1 (yes votes) and no –1 (no votes, or vetoes) are needed to commit a code change during a release cycle; docs are usually committed first and then changed as needed, with conflicts resolved by majority vote.

Our primary method of communication is our mailing list. Approximately 40 messages a day flow over the list, and are typically very conversational in tone. We discuss new features to add, bug fixes, user problems, developments in the Web server community, release dates, and so on. The actual code development takes place on the developers' local machines, with proposed changes communicated using a patch (output of a unified "`diff -u oldfile newfile`" command), and committed to the source repository by one of the core developers using remote CVS. Anyone on the mailing list can vote on a particular issue, but we only count those made by active members or people who are known to be experts on that part of the server. Vetoes must be accompanied by a convincing explanation.

New members of the Apache Group are added when a frequent contributor is nominated by one member and unanimously approved by the voting members. In most cases, this "new" member has been actively contributing to the group's work for over six months, so it's usually an easy decision.

Apache exists to provide a robust and commercial-grade reference implementation of the HTTP protocol. It must remain a platform upon which individuals and institutions can build reliable systems, both for experimental purposes and for mission-critical purposes. We believe the tools of online publishing should be in the hands of everyone, and software companies should make their money providing value-added services such as specialized modules and support, among other things. We realize that it is often seen as an economic advantage for one company to "own" a market—in the software industry, that means to control tightly a particular conduit such that all others must pay. This is typically done by "owning" the protocols through which companies conduct business, at the expense of all those other companies. To the extent that the protocols of the World Wide Web remain "unowned" by a single company, the Web will remain a level playing field for companies large and small. Thus, "ownership" of the protocol must be prevented, and the existence of a robust reference implementation of the protocol, available absolutely for free to all companies, is a tremendously good thing.

Furthermore, Apache is an organic entity; those who benefit from it by using it often contribute back to it by providing feature enhancements, bug fixes, and support for others in public newsgroups. The amount of effort expended by any particular individual is usually fairly light, but the resulting product is made very strong. This kind of community can only happen with freeware—when someone pays for software, they usually aren't willing to fix its bugs. One can argue, then, that Apache's strength comes from the fact that it's free, and if it were made "not free," it would suffer tremendously, even if that money were spent on a real development team.

We want to see Apache used very widely—by large companies, small companies, research institutions, schools, individuals, in the intranet environment, everywhere—even though this may mean that companies who could afford commercial software, and would pay for it without blinking, might get a "free ride" by using Apache. We would even be happy if some commercial software companies completely dropped their own HTTP server development plans and used Apache as a base, with the proper attributions as described in the LICENSE file.

Apache is amazing not only because it is free and open, but because it is so successful. More than half of the world's Web servers are based on Apache. This number is not about to change any time soon. A non-commercial piece of complex software might be synonymous with instability and partial functionality in some people's minds, but this could not be further from the truth where Apache is concerned. It is a mature, stable, and fast product. Support for it (through the Apache group and the hordes of people using it) may not be formal, but is excellent—much better than what we have come to expect from software vendors in general. Simply put, Apache is amazing and we recommend it to anyone who is looking for a Web server.

The Apache server provides a very broad offering in terms of the modules that can be configured to be available. The architecture of the server is modular in nature, providing a distribution that is probably the most comprehensive of all Web servers, at the same time allowing configurations that are slim and simple. The distribution is provided as a set of modules; each module can be compiled and loaded into the server or not. The choice is up to you. The 1.3.x versions of the server dynamically load modules as needed, ensuring that memory utilization is always optimized and that the image size can be small unless many service are provided. Following is a brief description of each available module:

Core

Core Apache features; this module must exist in every deployment of Apache.

mod_access   This module allows an administrator to control access to elements served by the Web server based on the accessing hosts. By using a set of allow and deny directives, the administrator can set up the access rules for directories and files based on the requesting host.

mod_actions   This module allows an administrator to set up CGI scripts to be called whenever a file of a certain MIME type is requested through the Web server.

mod_alias   This module allows files that are not under the Web server root to be served up by the Web server. It allows an administrator to define a sort of symbolic link to the file so, to the Web requester, it would seem that the file resides within the Web server directory structure while maintaining maximal flexibility for setting up the site.

mod_asis   This module can be used by an administrator to specify that files of a certain MIME type are served up by the Web server as is—that is, without slapping on the HTTP response header information.

mod_auth   This module allows an administrator to set up a text file defining authorization groups. Each line in the file names a group and specifies which users belong to this group. This information is used for authorization based on groups.

mod_auth_anon   This module can be used by an administrator to set up the profile of anonymous access (similar to the anonymous user in FTP).

mod_auth_db   This module supports user authentication following the Berkeley DB file style. In this case, a text file defines the groups by having a line per user in which all the groups that the user belongs to are mentioned. An additional file maintains the password per user. These definitions are then used for authorization and authentication.

mod_auth_dbm   This module is similar to the preceding one, except it uses DBM files.

mod_autoindex   This module supports the creation and maintenance of file indexes for the Web server. Both manual index files and automatically generated index files are supported through this module.

mod_cern_meta   This module allows the administrator to set up environment variable values based on the accessing browser. Each request coming in from a browser has a field called `user-agent`. This value identifies the browser. For example, Netscape and IE browsers will have slightly different `user-agent` values, and mobile phones using an HTTP connection will have a drastically different `user-agent` value. It is very typical for software serving up responses to want to behave differently based on the `user-agent` (that is, based on who is making the request). This module provides built-in support for such capabilities at the server level.

mod_cgi   This is the module responsible for invoking CGI scripts for files that have a MIME type of `application/x-httpd-cgi`.

mod_digest   This module allows the administrator to specify a file that contains user names and encoded passwords. The passwords are used for MD5 digest authentication.

mod_dir   This module supports the indexing of directories either manually or through an automatic process.

mod_env   This module allows setting environment variables for the HTTPD process to be passed to CGI scripts called by the server.

mod_example   This module provides some samples and examples of the Apache API; this module is not usually included in a production server.

mod_expires   This module allows the administrator to set a server-wide policy regarding the EXPIRES value sent within the HTTP response. The EXPIRES value is used by the browser to determine when a page that exists in the client cache should be invalidated, causing recurring access to the file from the server. Using this module, the administrator can set the policy for all pages served by the Web server.

mod_headers   This module allows the administrator to set server-wide policies regarding values that should be included as part of response headers. The module allows the use of directives such as set, add, and append for setting name value pairs that are added to every response originating from the server.

mod_imap   This module implements the imagemap facility and is part of the default setup.

mod_include   This module handles server-side includes and is used to handle requests for .shtml files. In this book, we do not use server-side includes because Java Server Pages can be used for any such required processing.

mod_info   This module serves up configuration information regarding the installed server.

mod_isapi   This module provides support for the Microsoft ISAPI API.

mod_log_agent   This module can be used by the administrator to log all user-agent information for all requests coming in to the server. This is a useful auditing capability.

mod_log_config   This module is used by the administrator to customize various aspects of the server log such as where the log file is to be placed and what the format of the log file should be.

mod_log_referer   This module is used by the administrator to customize what is logged. For example, the module supports directives for specifying that requests coming in from a certain domain should not be logged.

mod_mime   This is a very important module that handles attributes to be attached to MIME types (and documents conforming to such types). The module supports directives such as AddEncoding used to associate file extensions with MIME types, `AddHandler` used to map the MIME type with a handling application, and some more advanced directives.

mod_mime_magic   This module can be used by Unix-based servers in a system that uses Unix magic numbers to determine the MIME type of a file.

mod_mmap_static   This module allows bringing a file into memory for faster request handling. This is an experimental module and is not normally used in high-volume production servers (although this is precisely what it is intended for—for example, for keeping the site's default page in memory).

mod_negotiation   This module supports content selection—a feature that allows the server to select the best possible file based on attributes sent in the request header by the client.

mod_proxy   This module implements proxy caching for Apache and is a very important one for production servers. This module is relatively complex and has many features. The Web server administrator should read the documentation regarding this module very carefully in order to achieve the best possible results.

mod_rewrite   Another very important and very powerful module—it allows URL rewriting based on a set of rules that are set up by the administrator.

mod_setenvif   This module allows setup of rules that are evaluated for each request header and, based on the satisfaction of these rules, then sets values of certain environment variables.

mod_so   This module supports loading modules (DLLs on Windows) at runtime. This is an experimental module and should not be used on production servers.

mod_spelling   This module automatically corrects minor typos in URLs.

mod_status   This module serves up various server statistics that are helpful for monitoring how the server is performing. These values are served up as HTML output.

mod_userdir   This module is used to set users' home directories for Web requests.

mod_unique_id   This module creates a unique identifier for each Web request.

mod_usertrack   This module implements tracking of user information using cookies.

As you can see, Apache is very rich in terms of server functionality. With all of the previously mentioned features, you can pretty much do anything your heart desires with the Apache Web server. In addition, Apache supports virtual hosts—a feature that allows you to set up a single server that will answer to requests made using different host names. Apache is also a very open product, providing a fully functional and very convenient API so you can write applications that can interface with the Web server. As we're sure you've realized by now, it is not a coincidence that more that half of all Web servers deployed are Apache servers.

IBM HTTP Server

As mentioned previously, the IBM HTTP server is part of the WebSphere installation CD and is the simplest alternative for those of you who want to be up and running as soon as possible and have no existing server in place. Because this book is meant to be a "starter kit" to help you deploy your first eBusiness application as soon as possible, we suggest that unless you have a very good reason to use another HTTP server, use the IBM HTTP server.

The IBM HTTP server is based on the Apache Web server. It is basically a branding of the Apache server with the IBM name (under a licensing agreement between the Apache group and IBM). Therefore, except for some cosmetic differences (see Figure 6-1), everything said regarding the Apache server applies here. In terms of the installation procedure, this option is the simplest because it is part of the standard installation process (not to say that the other installation procedures are difficult—they are also straight-forward).

As part of the licensing agreement between the Apache group and IBM, IBM makes no effort to hide the fact that it is really the Apache server that is doing the work (see Figure 6-2 for a number of DLLs that form the server code). However, the IBM server does include a few additions to the Apache server. These minor additions mean that although Apache is provided with source code that can be used to port to other platforms, not all of the source code for the IBM HTTP server is available (specifically not the code for the few additional modules). The IBM HTTP server is not truly

Figure 6-1
IBM HTTP server
home page

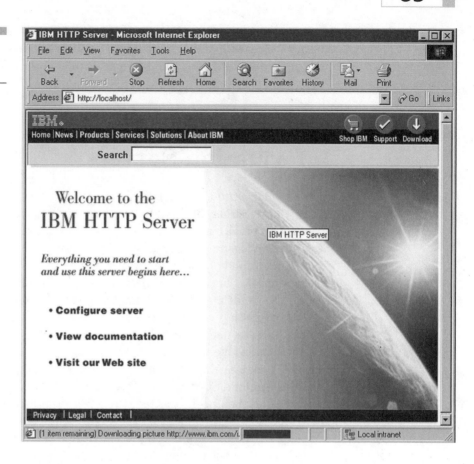

Figure 6-1
IBM HTTP server
home page

Figure 6-2
Some of IBM's
Web server DLLs

Contents of 'modules'		
Name	Size	Type
ApacheModuleAuthAnon.dll	5KB	Application Extension
ApacheModuleCERNMeta.dll	5KB	Application Extension
ApacheModuleDigest.dll	6KB	Application Extension
ApacheModuleExpires.dll	6KB	Application Extension
ApacheModuleHeaders.dll	4KB	Application Extension
ApacheModuleSpeling.dll	6KB	Application Extension
ApacheModuleStatus.dll	10KB	Application Extension
ApacheModuleUserTrack.dll	6KB	Application Extension
IBMModuleSSL.dll	82KB	Application Extension

an open distribution. Another distinction is that whereas Apache is available for Windows 95 and Windows 98 as well as Windows NT, the only Windows platform the IBM HTTP server is available for is Windows NT.

Microsoft Internet Information Server

Internet Information Server (IIS) is a free Web server that is part of the Windows NT Server 4.0 installation. Originally it was part of Microsoft's strategy to break into the Internet product marketplace. Because NT Server is a widespread operating system, quite a few installations of IIS exist. In addition to being free, IIS is a simple product—simple in terms of installation (you basically do not need to do anything) and in terms of its use. All this helps make it the default server for people who run NT Server and who do not have to support a large Web site. Examples include simple intranet servers, departmental servers, and so on.

Another convenience in the IIS offering is that all the server's properties can be set easily using the Service Manager tool. The tool can be started from the Windows Start menu in the IIS category as shown in Figure 6-3. After the tool has been selected, the services that can be managed are shown along with their status (see Figure 6-4). By default, the services managed by the tool are the HTTP service (WWW), the FTP service, and the GOPHER service. Figure 6-4 shows an NT server in which only the HTTP service is available. Each of the services has a set of property sheets that are used to configure the characteristics of the service; Figures 6-5 to 6-8 show the property sheets available for configuring the WWW service.

The main properties are set on the Service tab in the Service Properties dialog box (Figure 6-5). You can set things like the port that the service is listening on (80 by default—other common values include 8080 for test servers), the default timeout, the maximum number of allowed concurrent connections, anonymous account profile, and the authentication schemes supported by the server. The Directories tab (Figure 6-6) allows specifying the directories that participate in forming the content for the site served by the server. The Logging tab (Figure 6-7) allows setting properties that affect what gets logged and where it gets logged to (including the option of logging information stored directly into a SQL/ODBC database). The Advanced tab (Figure 6-8) is used to set the access policy based on grant and deny directives.

Figure 6-3
Starting the IIS
Service Manager

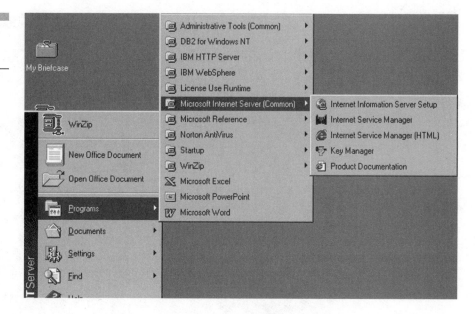

Figure 6-4
The IIS Service
Manager Control
panel

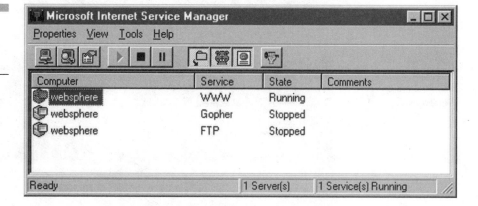

In addition to the main tool used for setting up the service properties, the Key Manager is a tool for managing and adding keys that are attached to certificates and used to set up secure servers that can be used for electronic transactions and ensuring server authentication. The tool is shown in Figures 6-9 and 6-10. Finally, because the setup of the server should be enabled from a remote site and not necessarily by opening the Service Manager on the local host, all tools are available as an HTML version. A sample screen (the main service screen) is shown in Figure 6-11.

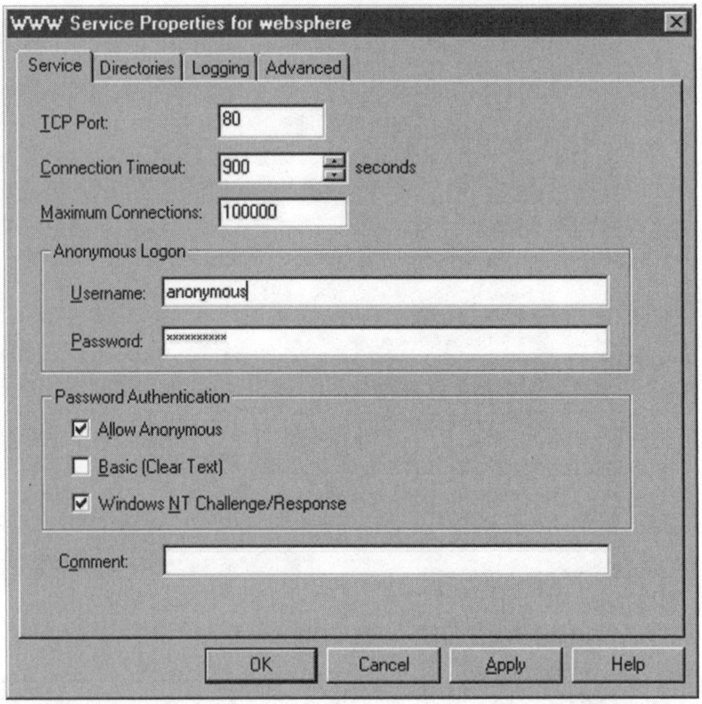

Figure 6-5
WWW Service
Properties dialog box

Figure 6-5
WWW Service
Properties dialog box

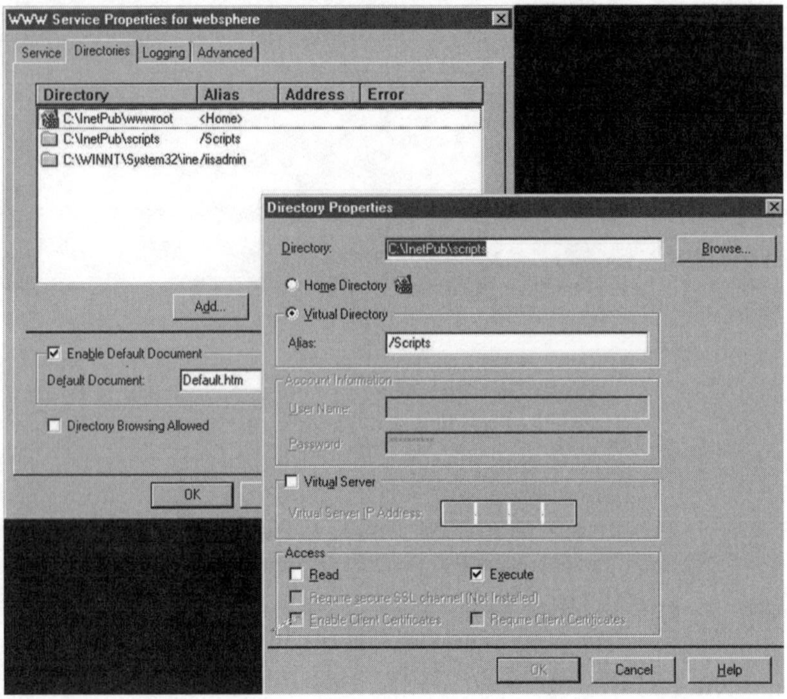

Figure 6-6
WWW Service
Properties
Directories tab

Figure 6-7
WWW Service
Properties
Logging tab

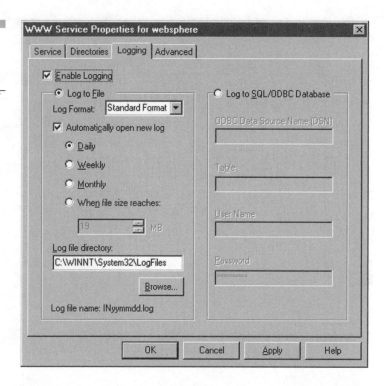

Figure 6-8
WWW Service
Properties
Advanced tab

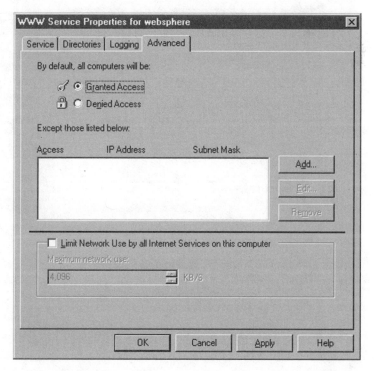

Figure 6-9
IIS Key Manager

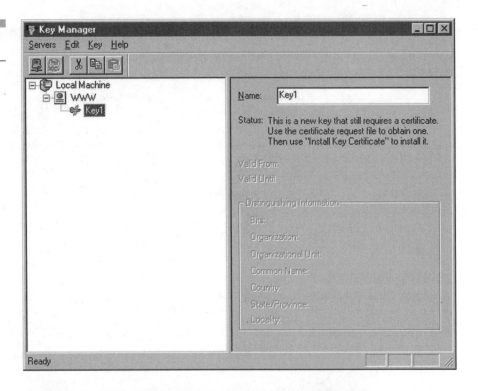

Figure 6-10
Creating a new key

Figure 6-11
HTML version of the
Service Manager

Servlets and JavaServer Pages

This chapter is dedicated to a discussion of the fundamentals of the operational model of servlets and JSPs. We have already briefly seen what servlets and JSPs are and how they work within the WebSphere server, and we will talk about servlets and JSPs much more in Chapters 23 through 28. All of these chapters involve a set of examples that introduce the capabilities of these technological elements. This chapter is slightly different, however, because it provides the theory behind these examples. The model that is specified by the servlet and by the JSP specifications is introduced. This model is important to understand, because it is the unifying thread behind all of the examples involving servlets and JSPs—and as such, this model will facilitate a better understanding of these concepts.

Servlets were introduced by Sun as one of the first instantiations of Java on the server. At the time, the majority of Web server-side processing was performed by CGI programs or by programs that were linked to the Web server via some proprietary API (such as the NSAPI for Netscape servers). Servlets were introduced as a way to provide all of the benefits of server-side processing while making use of the advantages that were inherent to Java (such as portability, access to the large number of Java libraries, etc.). In addition, they were faster than CGI programs and could be deployed under many Web servers. Servlets caught on quickly because they were far superior to the alternatives, but they were also simple to understand. As is often the case, simple things catch on quickly because the "masses" adopt them.

JSPs are relatively new on the Java technology front. In many ways, JSPs can be viewed as the inverse of servlets—kind of a mirror image. When building servlets, we write Java code that outputs HTML. Actually, this statement is not completely accurate. The servlet model is a generic model for processing requests and for creating responses. One kind of a servlet is an HTTP servlet—one that processes HTTP requests and outputs HTML to the response stream. Still, even if the servlet model is far more generic, the vast majority of servlets today are HTTP servlets that generate HTML.

Let's go back to the inverse concept. Servlets usually generate dynamic HTML by running some Java code that accesses databases or performs some other processing and then writes out HTML to the output stream. The HTML tag elements are embedded as strings within the Java code. JSPs reverse the roles. JSPs are fundamentally HTML pages that are served by the Web server. They differ from normal HTML pages in two ways: first, they have a .jsp extension, and second, they have some additional tags that are not HTML tags (these are the JSP tags). These tags enable (among other functions) embedding lines of Java code inside the HTML page. So, the inverse notion is that JSPs are built as HTML with embedded Java (as opposed to servlets that have HTML strings embedded in Java code).

These statements might all sound unimportant, but in fact, they are extremely important. The difference is primarily that JSPs are better at separating the function of the application programmer from the function of the site builder (or the function that is responsible for the presentation and the layout). Therefore, it is quite common for a development team that uses JSPs to include people who build HTML pages with dummy static data and then pass the data on to Java programmers, who replace the dummy data with Java code that builds the real dynamic data when invoked. In some cases, servlets are more appropriate. In other cases, JSPs will work better. The difference involves the role that the HTML plays. If most of the HTML (the presentation layer) is fixed and the Java code is primarily used for dynamically generating data, then JSPs are more appropriate. Until JSPs came to be, many servlet developers simulated what JSPs do by packaging templates of HTML pages and injecting the dynamic data in between the pages.

The Servlet Operational Model

A servlet is a Java class that conforms to the contracts that are defined by the servlet specification. The operational model of a servlet is shown in Figure 7-1. As the figure illustrates, the servlet interacts with the servlet server and goes through a number of stages throughout its life. First, the servlet is registered with the server (i.e., is added to the server's configuration) as part of the capabilities that must be supported by any servlet server. At some point, the server instantiates the servlet by using the registered class. This procedure is usually performed during server startup, although this process might differ depending on the server itself. Next comes the initialization phase, which is defined contractually by the `init` method that a servlet must implement (or inherit). Therefore, after the servlet server instantiates the servlet, it calls the `init` method and passes a `ServletConfig` object that encapsulates information regarding the environment. This information can be used by the servlet in its initialization process. Next comes the actual invocation. Each servlet must implement or inherit a `service` method that is called by the servlet server when a request that needs to be handled by the servlet arrives. Note that HTTP servlets can also implement the `service` method, but they can also implement the `doGet`, `doPost`, or both methods. This statement reflects the fact that an HTTP request uses either a GET or a POST method. Finally, when the servlet server wants to reclaim the servlet, it calls the `destroy` method —another one of those contractual obligations that a servlet has.

We mentioned three contractual obligations: the initialization phase, the servicing of the request, and the finalization stage. Initialization often occurs when you register the servlet with the server. For example, when you run the WebSphere administration utility and add a servlet, you will usually press the Test button. This action instantiates a servlet object and calls the `init` method. The `init` method is the perfect place to put all startup code that is required for the correct operation of the servlet, and that process might take a relatively long time (reading in resources, creating the database connections, etc.). The reason is because instances are often created before the actual requests come in; therefore, time is saved at

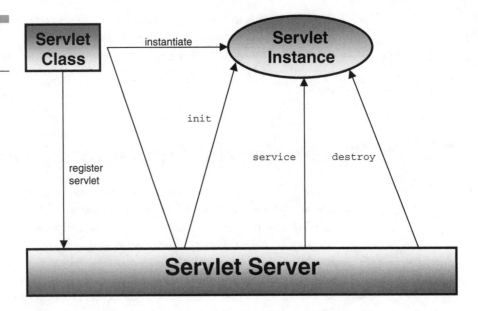

Figure 7-1
Servlet operational
model

the critical phase when the user is looking at the hourglass on the screen. You should note that the `init` method is called for every instance of the servlet. Because (in most real applications) more than one servlet will be instantiated for servicing requests, you should be careful what you do with the `init` method. Typically, the initialization code populates two types of structures. Static structures are used when we do not need an initialization process per instance. In this case, these structures need to only be populated once (i.e., the servlet should check whether they have been initialized or not). A typical example is the creation and population of a resource bundle. Normal instance variables are used when initialization needs to occur for each instance of the servlet. In addition, the model in which a pool of servlets is instantiated before requests actually start coming (with the servlets in the pool often sharing the same resources) is also quite common.

Once the servlet has been initialized, it is ready for processing. The core function of a servlet (its justification for existence) is to take a request that is coming in as a `ServletRequest` (or as an `HttpServletRequest`, in the case of HTTP servlets) and to create a response that is encapsulated in a `ServletResponse` object (or an `HttpServletResponse` object, in the case of HTTP servlets). The servlet model does not say much more, so a servlet is really a generic being that services requests and creates responses. The most common case is obviously that of an HTTP servlet that receives information from an HTML form as parameters in the request object and generates an HTML response that involves some data lookup. Processing is usually based on the parameters that are sent with the request.

As we mentioned, there might be more than one instance of a servlet at any one time. In addition, there might be more than one active thread using the same servlet object. Therefore, unless you specifically implement the `SingleThreadModel` interface in your servlet (marking that you do not want your servlet to be multi-threaded), you must make sure that your code is re-entrant and is thread safe. For example, do not change instance variables or class variables unless they are real global variables (for example, a counter registering the number of hits). Even then, make sure that you access these variables using synchronized methods so that you will not receive errors when multiple threads start running in parallel.

The operational model for servlets involves the contract between them and the servlet server, as phrased in the JavaDoc API description of the following methods (and the objects forming the signatures of the methods):

`javax.servlet.Servlet:`

- `void init(ServletConfig config) throws ServletException` Initializes the servlet. The method is called once (automatically) by the network service when it loads the servlet and is guaranteed to finish before any service requests are accepted. After initialization, the network service does not call the `init` method again unless it reloads the servlet after it has unloaded and destroyed the servlet.

- `void service(ServletRequest request, ServletResponse response) throws ServletException` Carries out a single request from the client. The method implements a request and response paradigm. The request object contains information about the service request, including parameters that are provided by the client. The response object is used to return information to the client. The request and response objects rely on the underlying network transport for quality-of-service guarantees, such as reordering, duplication, privacy, and authentication. Service requests are not handled until servlet initialization has completed. Any requests for service that are received during initialization are blocked until initialization is complete. Note that servlets typically run inside multi-threaded servers; therefore, servers can handle multiple service requests simultaneously. The servlet writer has the responsibility to synchronize access to any shared resources, such as network connections or the servlet's class and instance variables.

■ `void destroy()` Cleans up whatever resources are being held (e.g., memory, file handles, and threads) and makes sure that any persistent state is synchronized with the servlet's current in-memory state. The method is called once, automatically, by the network service when it unloads the servlet. After destroy is run, it cannot be called again until the network service reloads the servlet. When the network service removes a servlet, it calls destroy after all service calls have been completed or when a service-specific number of seconds have passed, whichever comes first. In the case of long-running operations, there could be other threads running service requests when destroy is called. The servlet writer is responsible for making sure that any threads that are still in the service method complete.

■ `void doGet(HttpServletRequest req, HttpServletResponse resp) throws ServletException, IOException` Performs the HTTP GET operation. Servlet writers who override this method should read any data from the request, set entity headers in the response, access the writer or output stream, and write any response data. The headers that are set should include content type and encoding. If a writer is to be used to write response data, the content type must be set before the writer is accessed. In general, the servlet implementer must write the headers before the response data, because the headers can be flushed at any time after the data starts to be written. Setting content length enables the servlet to take advantage of HTTP connection keep alive. If content length cannot be set in advance, the performance penalties that are associated with not using keep alives will sometimes be avoided if the response entity fits in an internal buffer. The GET operation is expected to be safe, without any side effects for which users might be held responsible. For example, most form queries have no side effects. Requests that are intended to change stored data should use some other HTTP method. (There have been cases of significant security breaches reported because Web-based applications used GET inappropriately.)

■ `void doPost(HttpServletRequest req, HttpServletResponse resp) throws ServletException, IOException` Performs the HTTP POST operation. The default implementation reports an HTTP BAD_REQUEST error. Servlet writers who override this method should read any data from the request (for example, form parameters), set entity headers in the response, access the writer or output stream, and write any response data by using the servlet output stream. The headers that are set should include content type and encoding. If a writer is to be used to write response data, the content type must be set before the writer is accessed. In general, the servlet implementer must write the headers before the response data, because the headers can be flushed at any time after the data starts to be written.

- `void doPut(HttpServletRequest req, HttpServletResponse resp) throws ServletException, IOException` Performs the HTTP PUT operation. The default implementation reports an HTTP BAD_REQUEST error. The PUT operation is analogous to sending a file via FTP.

- `void doDelete(HttpServletRequest req, HttpServletResponse resp) throws ServletException, IOException` Performs the HTTP DELETE operation. The DELETE operation enables a client to request a URL to be removed from the server.

- `void service(HttpServletRequest req, HttpServletResponse resp) throws ServletException, IOException` This method is an HTTP-specific version of the `servlet.service` method, which accepts HTTP-specific parameters. This method is rarely overridden. Standard HTTP requests are supported by dispatching to Java methods that are specialized to implement them.

The JSP Operational Model

A JSP page is a text document that includes segments of Java code and other special JSP tags. The document itself can be in any format, such as HTML, XML, or practically anything you wish. Therefore, you can use JSP pages for any application where the response is based on some template (but Java processing is required to build the actual result). As in servlets, where a generic class is provided but the majority of servlets are HTTP servlets, in JSPs, the vast majority of JSPs are HTML pages that include dynamic generation of Java. As time goes on, we envision that JSPs will also be used quite extensively to create XML output.

The JSP operational model is based on the servlet model. JSPs are a Java standard extension that is based on the servlet standard extension. As we already saw, the servlet model defines how a request is processed to create a response and defines what the available main objects are (the request, the response, the output stream, content type, etc.). JSPs are exactly the same (which is what we mean when we say that the JSP operational model is based on the servlet operational model). They, too, define a paradigm by which requests are processed into responses, and the JSP model has precisely the same set of main objects as servlets.

Activating a JSP means pointing the Web server at the file using a `.jsp` extension). The HTTP request is inspected and is the source from which the request object (and everything it encapsulates) is created. Requests might come in from a Web client, from other servlets, or from other Java applications. The core JSP API defines a method called `callPage` from which other servlets can cause a request for a JSP to be issued. Before doing so, they can create or change the request object to make sure that the right input parameters are placed in the request (by using the `setAttribute` method). When the JSP later looks for certain named parameters, it can find them in the request.

Once the request comes in, the processing begins. The process picks up the text file and starts going through the tags. Its role is to create the response stream; hence, the JSP model and the servlet model are quite the same. The process performs this task by traversing the file and looking for JSP tags. Anything that is not a JSP tag is copied as is to the output stream. Anything that is a JSP tag is processed by the engine and usually produces output that is written to the output stream. Some of these tags do not directly write to the output stream but affect how the output stream looks —for example, the content type of the output stream can be set by using a JSP directive.

Most uses of JSPs use embedded Java code in the text file to generate dynamic data. The process through which the JSP engine can take this Java code and produce the data is quite extraordinary (at least, when you first come across the concept). The JSP engine actually generates (codewise) a servlet for each JSP file and generates a `.java` file that is a real servlet, then compiles the file into a `.class` file. Then, it invokes the servlet and thus generates the output stream. The HTML gets to the output stream, because one of the tasks that the servlet performs is to read the `.jsp` file (as text) and copy certain segments from it to the servlet output stream. In later chapters, we will delve into more details regarding how this task is done and how the generated servlets look. At the moment, it is simply important that you know this fact, because it fully explains why the JSP model and the servlet model are so similar. They are actually one and the same. Figure 7-2 illustrates the main process that occurs in the JSP engine. Obviously, this generation and compilation phase takes quite a long time, and it would be unfortunate if we would have to accumulate this overhead every time a JSP is accessed. Luckily, this situation happens only once; after that, the compiled servlet is picked up immediately (so long as the JSP file has not changed since the time it was last compiled).

Figure 7-2
Servlet operational
model

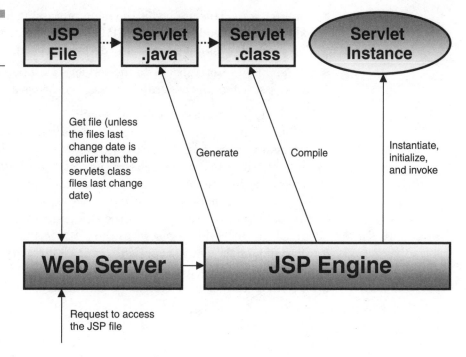

Because the models are identical and the JSP is actually converted into a servlet, anything that is appropriate for a servlet is appropriate for a JSP. For example, you can implement a method called `jspInit()` in your JSP file. If you do so, then when the first request for a JSP comes in (and after the servlet is generated, compiled, and instantiated), your method will be called just like the method in a servlet is called after the servlet is instantiated. Note that any Java code that is not specifically placed in a method by default belongs to the servlet's `service` method.

The contract between the JSP and the JSP engine consists of three methods:

■ `jspInit` Corresponds to the servlet's initialization phase and is called by the JSP engine right after the JSP has been compiled into the servlet and the servlet has been instantiated. By implementing this method as part of your JSP, you can affect what occurs during the initialization phase. Note that this method does not receive any arguments (contrary to the `servlet init` method), and you need to use `getServletConfig` if you need any information regarding the environment.

- `jspService`   This method is the main processing method. All Java code that is embedded into the JSP belongs by default to this method. This method must not be explicitly declared within the JSP.

- `jspDestroy`   Corresponds to the servlet's `destroy` method and is called just before the generated servlet is destroyed

The servlets that are generated by WebSphere's JSP engine are typically placed under the servlets/pagecompile directory in the WebSphere installation structure. Because the servlet is generated based on a JSP file that is placed somewhere under the Web server's root, the location of the generated servlet corresponds to the location of the JSP file. Specifically, if the JSP filename is `CH7.jsp` and is placed under the Web server's root by using a `BOOK/WEBSPHERE/CHAPTER7` path, then the generated servlet (and the compiled `.class` file) will be placed in the `_BOOK/_WEBSPHERE/_CHAPTER7` directory under the `servlets/pageCompile` directory in the WebSphere directory. The servlet's filename, in this case, will be `_CH7_xjsp.java`. Figure 7-3 shows the generated directory structures.

Figure 7-3

Generated servlet file structure

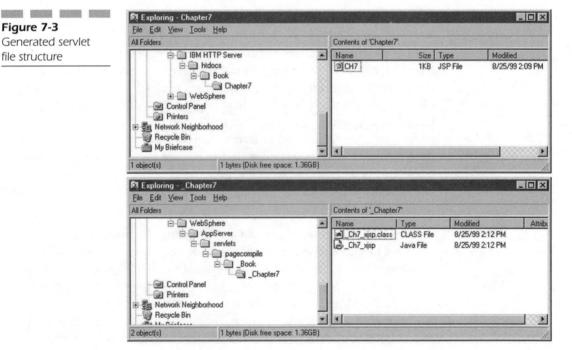

8

CORBA

During the second half of the '80s and throughout the '90s, distributed objects have become a turnkey technology in most *information technology* (IT) organizations. The spawn of distributed objects has its root in three developments: the reliance on networks for connectivity as well as computation, the need for remote access to services and collaboration, and the Internet/Web revolution. Although each of these developments emerged at different times and from different technology clients, they all require distributed access to objects, data, and services to enable truly powerful applications to be constructed.

Although the quest for distributed objects was magnified by the need to integrate disparate applications and services over the Web, it did not start there. In fact, when the Web phenomena was finally recognized as the primary area of growth in IT and solutions geared toward solving Web application problems, the solution to distributed objects was ready. The *Common Object Request Broker* (CORBA), an industry-wide standard for distributed object-oriented architectures developed by the *Object Management Group* (OMG), already fully defined how applications running on different platforms and using different development environments and programming models can interoperate. CORBA is in many respects the global object middleware—perfect for the requirements of Internet applications.

The OMG was founded to work within the software industry to provide an open architecture to support multi-vendor, global, heterogeneous networks of object-based software components. The *Object Management Architecture* (OMA) *Guide* ([OMG1]) was published as an architecture to serve as the foundation for the development of detailed specifications and infrastructure to form the future of object-based systems. The OMA defines many components that together enable the implementation of the OMG's vision. The most important architectural piece defined in the OMA is the *Object Request Broker* (ORB). This component is the main mechanism facilitating the workings of the OMA. The ORB is the facilitator for sending and receiving messages between different objects and components. The ORB environment was defined in the *Common Object Request Broker Architecture* and Specification (CORBA).

CORBA (Revision 1.1) was adopted from a joint proposal produced by Digital Equipment Corporation, Hewlett-Packard Company, Hyperdesk Corporation, NCR Corporation, Object Design, Inc., and SunSoft Inc. It was published as OMG Document Number 91.12.1 and as a book by the OMG and by X/Open [OMG2]. It was the first widely available specification describing the adopted ORB technology. Revision 2.0 was published in mid-1995 and updated in mid-1996 ([OMG4]).

In this chapter, we outline the fundamentals of the CORBA. This includes a description of the common components interacting in a CORBA-based system and their roles. The next chapter then goes on to describe CORBA 2.0 with a focus on ORB interoperability in general and the Internet Inter-ORB Protocol specifically.

The Object Management Architecture (OMA)

The *Object Management Architecture* (OMA) is a general architecture and a taxonomy of necessary components enabling a portable and interoperable environment. The OMA outlines general technical guidelines that should be followed by every component within the OMA. These include the necessity for object-oriented interfaces, distribution transparency, a common object model forming a common base for all components, full support for all stages of the software's life cycle, a flexible and dynamic nature, high performance, robust implementations, and conformance with existing standards within the software industry.

The OMA Reference Model

The OMG reference model for the OMA is shown in Figure 8-1. The reference model provides the underlying framework that guides the OMG technology adoption process. It defines the categories of necessary components to realize the OMG's goals and vision. The reference model is used as a road map to provide a direction for components that must be developed. After this architecture has been defined, the OMG's work can be seen as providing detailed specifications for the components identified within the reference model.

As Figure 8-1 shows, the model comprises of four component categories: the *Object Request Broker* (ORB), Object Services, Common Facilities, and Application Objects. Application Object components represent the actual software being developed for solving domain-specific problems or for providing off-the-shelf products. These objects make use of the other three categories, providing them with a very rich development environment. Using the other three categories, application developers can create portable interoperable code rapidly that can later be reused by other application components. In this respect, the entire architecture is primarily targeted to provide the best possible environment for objects in this category.

The architecture's heart is the ORB, which provides the capabilities for allowing objects to interact and work together to achieve a common goal.

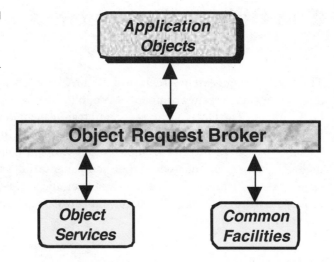

Object Services provide low-level, system-type services that are necessary for developing applications such as object persistence, transaction capabilities, and security. Common Facilities provide higher-level services that are semantically closer to the application objects such as mailing and printing facilities.

Object Services define a collection of services that are necessary for any application to be constructed without requiring the application developers to "reinvent the wheel" for every application. Common Facilities provide an even higher level of functionality that define general capabilities required in many applications. The difference between Object Services and Common Facilities might seem a little obscure; in reality, it is much clearer. Object Services have a system orientation, whereas Common Facilities have an application orientation. Another important difference is that whereas Object Services must be supported by all ORB environments on all platforms, support for Common Facilities is discretionary.

The OMA is composed of objects. Every component in the architecture is defined in terms of an object-oriented interface (although it must not necessarily have an object-oriented implementation). Objects request services from any other object by accessing such object-oriented interfaces. Any object can therefore provide services to any other object. The architecture therefore transcends the client/server architecture because every object is potentially both a client and a server. In fact, every request invocation defines a client and server object in the context of a single invocation. The same object might be required to service a request (making it a server), whereas the implementation invokes a request to get some information from another object (making it a client). Any object (including Application Objects, Object Service objects, and Common Facilities objects) will be involved in such relationships (both as clients and as servers).

Interaction uses object-oriented interfaces. Any implementation, including non object-oriented implementations and "legacy" software, can be made to provide object-oriented interfaces. These are often called object-oriented wrappers or adapters and are easily defined for the vast majority of software. In this way, the OMA can provide an underlying model for all software components; including those that were previously developed or that are not necessarily object-oriented. In addition, because any non-distributed application is a special case of a distributed application (a case that simply uses only one machine), the architecture can truly embed all software developments.

The Object Request Broker (ORB)

The *Object Request Broker* (ORB) is the central component allowing the reference model to function. It provides the basic object interaction capabilities necessary for any of the components to communicate. It is therefore no wonder that this component was the first to be defined by the OMG (as [OMG2]). It allows client objects to issue requests for objects to provide required services. These service requests are issued by the client in a location-, language-, and platform-independent way. The ORB is therefore the primary vehicle delivering interoperability and portability, as well as the enabler of building true distributed applications.

Requests are issued by objects using an object-oriented interface as defined by the service provider. The client constructs a request by specifying a reference to the object the request should be sent to, an operation name, and any other information that is necessary. This will typically include the parameters to be sent, but can also include such things as an environment context.

Object Services

The ORB provides basic interaction capability, but this is insufficient for real applications to be developed. Applications need to assume certain basic services and functionality from the underlying environment; this is the role played by the Object Services layer. For example, the ORB provides ways for a request to be delivered to service providers, but does not define how service providers are found. The Object Services layer may provide a Trader Service, which is similar to the Yellow Pages for locating phone numbers.

The Object Services layer is of primary importance to the success of the OMG reference model. If this layer is not populated with enough functionality, the OMG's vision will not be realized. Even if the ORB is fully functional and usable, applications will be too difficult to build. Too much will have to be developed by the application itself because the support provided by the ORB is low. Most application developers also lack the expertise to develop such functionality on their own.

Object Services are thus a primary component of the OMG reference model. In fact, after an initial ORB-based architecture was in place, the OMG (through the Object Services Task Force) began populating this layer with services such as a Naming service, an Event Notification service, a Relationship service, and a Transaction service.

Following the general concept of separation of interfaces from implementation, Object Services only define interfaces and a semantic specification of functionality. A service definition therefore supplies the developer with an API set and a description of the functional behavior that is provided. This does not place any limitations regarding implementations for the service. In fact, it is assumed that many implementations will be provided for each service. This is absolutely necessary; services are generally complex and may have different characteristics. Stressing one characteristic of the service often leads to lesser support for another. Because different users of the service will require different resolutions of such tradeoffs, different implementations will be necessary. This is formulated in the *Quality of Service* (QOS) notion introduced by the OMG that allows different implementations stressing different attributes of the service to be provided.

Common Facilities

Common Facilities also provide services, but they are typically at a higher level. They are closer to the application levels than are Object Services. Examples of Common Facilities are compound document management, electronic mail, and help systems. Such capabilities are still in the scope of the OMA. They can be used by many applications and can allow applications to be created faster in a portable and interoperable way. Like Object Services, they reduce the complexity of writing software within the OMG framework, thus achieving the overall goal. In fact, because Common Facility services are at a higher level, they will often cover more functionality that is necessary of the application than will lower-level services. For example, a compound document framework would be preferable to a service supporting generic object graph relationships.

The Common Object Request Broker Architecture (CORBA)

This section details the ORB-based architecture that supports portability and interoperability. Figure 8-2 illustrates a client making a request for a service to be provided by an object implementation. The client has an object reference for the object and activates operations for this object. This reference is opaque and the client has no notion as to the location of the object implementation, the language used to implement it, or any other detail about the implementation. It only has a specification for an operation request that is part of the interface. The client issues the request and the ORB is responsible for delivering the request to the object implementation in a format to which the object implementation can respond.

When the client has a handle to an object implementation and desires to issue a request, two possibilities are available. If the interface was defined in IDL and the client has a definition for the type of the object implementation, a static invocation can be issued. The request is made using an IDL stub specific to the interface of the target object. Otherwise, the *Dynamic Invocation Interface* (DII) can be used. This interface is independent of the implementation of the target object and can therefore be used even without thorough knowledge of the target object's implementation specifics. The request is constructed at runtime and makes no use of IDL stubs. Instead the request is handled by the dynamic invocation module using the information stored in the interface repository. Figure 8-3 illustrates the two possible request paths. Note that when the request is delivered to the object implementation, it is not aware and does not care which path was taken.

Figure 8-2
Client request
and object
implementation

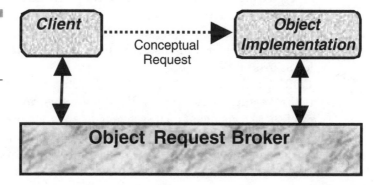

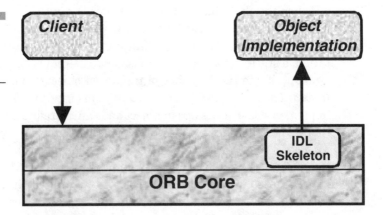

Figure 8-3
Two paths for
forming a request

Figure 8-4
Delivering a request
to an object
implementation

Figure 8-4 shows the delivery of the request to the object implementations. After defining the interface of an object using IDL, an IDL skeleton is generated. Requests are passed from the ORB through this skeleton. An IDL skeleton will be used regardless whether the request was issued through an IDL stub or using the DII. The object implementation is made available using information stored in the Implementation Repository provided at installation time.

CORBA defines a number of ORB sub-components that interact to support this required functionality. Figure 8-5 illustrates a simple schematic view of these components. The schema does not mean to imply a decomposition of the ORB. In fact, CORBA does not make any assumptions or requirements regarding ORB implementations. CORBA only defines the interfaces that must be provided by every ORB.

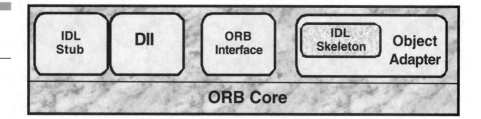

Figure 8-5
Subcomponents
in an ORB

The ORB Core

The ORB Core handles the basic communication of requests to the various components. It can be seen as the underlying transport layer. CORBA is meant to support multiple systems and thus was separated into modular components so different implementations can be used. This allows both different ORB cores to be used by identical layers (while hiding the differences to external components), as well as for different layered components to use the same core. The core provides basic object representation and communication of requests.

IDL Stubs and Skeletons

The Interface definition language is used to define interfaces, types, structures, and modules. The definition of the interfaces is the method by which a client is informed which services are supported by an object implementation. Each interface defined in IDL specifies the operation signatures through which requests are made. It should be noted that the IDL source code is not used at runtime. The IDL definitions are used to create stubs and skeletons and are used to populate the Interface Repository.

Clients issue requests from within their host programming language. IDL is only a definition language; CORBA does not define a manipulation or invocation language. To allow interfaces written in IDL to be used from programming languages, mappings are provided. A mapping will take an IDL definition and generate a stub for each interface within the native programming language. The stubs allow programmers to invoke operations defined as part of the target object's interface.

Implementation skeletons are generated per interface within a programming language. They are the structures that actually invoke the methods implemented as part of the object implementation. They are called

implementation skeletons because they are created from the IDL definitions, yet include no implementation details. The developer of the object
implementation must fill this skeleton with actual code that will be invoked
when a request is received.

An IDL skeleton usually depends on the object adapter; there may be
multiple skeletons for the same interface and the same language—per different object adapters. It is even possible to provide object adapters that do
not make use of IDL skeletons, but rather create implementations on-the-
fly when requests come in.

The *Dynamic Invocation Interface* (DII) allows the dynamic creation of
requests. This allows a client to directly specify an object, an operation, and
a set of parameters and invoke this request. The interface used is common
to all objects and all operations and does not make use of the stub routines
generated for each operation in each interface. Information regarding the
parameters and the operation itself is usually acquired from the interface
repository.

Object Adapters and the ORB Interface

The object adapter provides an interface to ORB services used by the object
implementations. It also provides services that may be required when a
request comes in from the ORB Core and is delivered to the skeleton for
method invocation. Because object implementations can be extremely
diverse in terms of their characteristics, many object adapters are envisioned. This allows support for very diverse cases without changing the
architecture.

Other services used by object implementations are provided directly
through the ORB Interface. This interface is identical for all ORB implementations and does not depend on the object adapter used by the object
implementations. Naturally, this interface will still be mapped to the host
programming language used by the object implementation. These operations are also available to the client objects.

Repositories

The *Interface Repository* (IR) maintains representations of the IDL definitions. These are persistent objects that are available at runtime. The IDL
information is therefore maintained as "live objects" that may be used at
runtime. For example, the DII uses the information maintained in the IR to

allow programs to issue requests on interfaces that were unknown when the program was compiled. The IR service is also used by the ORB. For example, the IR information is necessary for performing marshaling and unmarshaling of parameter values. The IR is also used as a persistent store for additional information pertinent to interfaces such as annotations, debugging information, and so on.

The IR maintains information needed by the ORB to locate and start up object implementations necessary to fulfill a request. It is also used for additional information associated with object implementations such as debugging information, security specifications, and so on. The Interface Repository is specific to an operating environment because it is used in the construction and activation of object implementations—it is not standardized by CORBA.

Object References

An object reference is an opaque representation that is used to denote an object in the ORB-based environment. Both clients and object implementations use object references. An ORB provides a mapping of object references to the programming language used. This mapping must not depend on the ORB representation of object references.

CORBA defines a distinguished object reference used for denoting no object. This reference is guaranteed to be different from any other object reference. In some environments, this maps to a reference of the null (or nil) object.

Clients

A client makes a request from within the application code. The client code uses the IDL stubs as it would use any library routine. When the stub routine is called, the object reference for the target object is mapped to the object reference as represented by the ORB. The stub then calls the ORB. The ORB is responsible for locating the object implementation and for routing the request to the implementations, as well as delivering any results back to the client. If an error occurs during the method invocation or the ORB cannot complete fulfilling the request for any variety of reasons, an exception may be delivered to the client's operating context.

If the client was compiled before the target object's interface was completed, it is possible that the stubs for the target object were not available.

The client code can therefore not access the interface for this object. In this case, the client can name the type of the object and operation to be invoked and use the DII. The client can construct the call programmatically using a sequence of calls for building up the invocation and the parameters, and then invoking the request.

A client uses object references to issue requests and as values for parameters. Clients normally receive object references as output parameters of past requests, or through requests that were sent to the client from other clients. Object references can even be converted into a string format that can be made persistent by simply storing it to disk. The string format can later be turned back to an object reference by the same ORB that converted the reference into the string.

Object Implementations

Object implementations encapsulate the state and behavior of the object. These are internal to the object, but their behavior is used by the skeletons to provide services for the clients. CORBA only defines the necessary mechanisms for invoking operations. It does not define specifically how these objects are activated or stopped, how they are made to persist, how access control is handled, and so on. However, because these object implementations must function in a real environment, all these issues must be addressed. The implemented is free to make choices regarding these issues.

Object Adapters

Object adapters are the primary ORB-related functionality providers to object implementations. The ORB itself also publishes an interface that may be used by the object implementation, but the object adapter provides most of the ORB-related services that are commonly used by the object implementation. Object adapters publish a public interface that is used by the object implementation, as well as a private interface that is used by the interface skeleton. The adapters themselves make use of the ORB-dependent interface. The following are examples for services provided by object adapters:

■ Method invocation used in conjunction with the skeleton

■ Object implementation activation and deactivation

■ Mapping of object references to object implementations, generation of object references

■ Registering object implementations so they may be found when a request comes in

CORBA does not require all object adapters to support the same functionality, nor the same interface. Object adapters may be specialized because they are a primary service provider for object implementations, as well as a major player in the request delivery mechanism. The CORBA specification itself only defines the *Basic Object Adapter* (BOA). Any CORBA-compliant implementation must provide a BOA. However, the CORBA specification does not place any limitations on definitions of additional object adapters; in fact, the specification itself provides some examples where additional object adapters will probably prove useful. Still, because object implementations rely on the object adapter interface, it is not recommended that a very large number of object adapters exist. This is not restrictive because different object adapters should be used only when different services or different quality of service is required. Thus each object adapter will typically be able to support a large set of object implementations.

An example presented in the CORBA specification is the *Library Object Adapter* (LOA). The BOA starts up a processing thread per request or even a separate process per object invocation. This may be unacceptable for library implementations that may be shared by multiple clients. In addition, library objects may actually be running within the client's context so activation and authentication are not required, thus greatly improving performance. If these object implementations were supported through the BOA, all these possible optimizations would not be possible. By providing the LOA, the behavior can be improved.

The Interface Definition Language (IDL)

CORBA is an architecture allowing the development of portable and interoperable applications. It provides for systems to be built using multiple programming languages so objects written in one programming language can make use of objects written in other programming languages. This is transparently handled by the ORB, and none of the participating objects are ever aware that the "other side" talks a different language. It is the universal translator of the objects world.

Translating objects and invocations between different programming languages can be viewed as some sort of bridging—in this case, the bridging involves the translation of the object model in one programming language to the (same) object model in another programming language. Bridging can involve two fundamental architectures: immediate bridging and mediated bridging. In the context of programming language interoperability, immediate bridging implies translation of each relevant programming language directly into every other relevant programming language. Mediated bridging introduces a single language (and runtime format) that describes the object model and is used as the intermediate format into which every other programming language is translated.

CORBA was intended to be ubiquitously available and to support interoperability from a large set of programming languages. Already, products are available that allow CORBA interoperability in C, C++, Smalltalk, Ada, Objective-C, Java, and COBOL. Due to the size of this large (and constantly growing) set of programming languages, the fact that a programming language may change, and the fact that different development environments may support slightly different dialects of the language, it is impossible to support programming language immediate bridging.

Mediated bridging is the only possible solution. But what is this intermediate language? The IDL is the language used to specify the interfaces that are used by clients to issue requests. Object implementations provide methods that provide the necessary services defined by the interfaces. Interfaces are defined in IDL and used by the client programs. IDL is not used for writing code, only specifications. The client will therefore not be written in IDL; it will use the IDL interface specifications, whereas the actual call will be done in the native programming languages. These calls will be a result of a mapping of the IDL interfaces to the programming language. The object implementations are also not written in IDL, but in a (possibly other) programming language. The interface operations then map to the implementation methods.

Mapping from IDL involves the creation of stubs on the client side and skeletons on the server side. The stubs are programming language functions (or methods) that may be called by the client code. Calling such a stub (using a CORBA object) will cause an invocation to occur, even when the real object is remote and implemented in a different programming language. All this is transparent to the client. When such a call takes place, the object implementation skeleton is invoked. This is the skeleton that was created as a result of mapping the IDL to the object implementation's programming language. Because such invocations require application-specific behavior to be performed, it is the developer's task to provide programming language implementations for each of the skeletons created as a result of the IDL mapping. All this is performed within the normal development environment used by the object implementation developer.

As defined in the CORBA specification, any mapping of the IDL to a host programming language must include the following:

■ *A mapping of all IDL data types, constants, and object references* This includes providing a means of expressing basic data types, constructed data types, and constants in the target programming language. The mapping must also specify how an object is represented in the target programming language. Because the mapping must respect the host programming language semantics, the object representation is not dependent on the ORB's representation. The representation can either use an opaque handle to the ORB representation or as a real programming language object. In the second case, the mapping must support identical object semantics of inheritance, operation signatures, and so on.

■ *A mapping of operation signatures and invocations* The mapping includes definitions for how input parameters are handled, how return values are handled, how operations map to the programming language functions, and so on. The mapping not only has to define how IDL constructs are mapped, but also how they are used. This may involve dealing in memory management and lifecycle issues.

■ *A mapping of the exception model* If the target programming language's exception handling mechanism (when such a mechanism exists) is being used, the mapping should describe how this mechanism is used for implementing IDL exceptions. Otherwise, the mapping should describe how operations are extended to support exceptions and what management functions are required.

■ *A mapping of IDL attributes* Attributes are modeled by two accessor operations (that is, a get and a set function).

■ *A mapping of the ORB interface and other pseudo-interfaces* This is necessary to allow programmers using the target programming language to access interfaces implemented by the ORB or one of the related components (the *Interface Repository* [IR], the object adapter, the *Dynamic Invocation Interface* [DII], and so on). One approach might be to define these as a set of services packaged as a library. Another approach could involve pseudo-objects. A pseudo-object has an interface defined in IDL, but is not implemented as an ORB-managed object. Operations can only be invoked using the *Static Invocation Interface* (SII), and the ORB may intercept such calls and handle them. In this approach, the ORB interfaces would actually be defined as IDL interfaces. These interfaces would be part of a pseudo-object. The advantage is that the ORB interfaces can then be mapped into many programming languages using the same mechanisms developed for application interfaces. Because it is just another interface, it is handled by the mapping procedures, and the case of ORB interfaces defaults to the general case.

The Dynamic Invocation Interface (DII)

The *Dynamic Invocation Interface* (DII) allows requests to be built up and invoked dynamically by clients. The client need only know interface-related information at the invocation time; no prior knowledge (for example, at compile time) is necessary. Although the structure and the process of performing requests is very different, the semantics of DII requests is identical to the semantics of requests issued using mapped IDL stubs. A DII request, like a static request, is composed of an operation name, an object reference, and a parameter list. Parameters are inserted into a name-value list that is then used in the invocation. Because the DII always accepts a parameter list (as an object), it doesn't care how many parameters there are; this allows the DII interface to support any invocation. These structures are built and used at runtime. (These parameters may still be type checked at runtime, as well as compared to the information in the *Interface Repository* [IR].)

The basic structure supporting the DII is the NamedValue structure (used to associate a name with a value of type *any*). This structure represents a single parameter. An NVList is used to hold all the parameters sent in an operation invocation. An instance of the NamedValue structure contains the argument name, an argument value, the length of the argument, and mode flags (which are similar to the mode specifiers in-out-in-out in IDL and are called ARG_IN, ARG_OUT, and ARG_INOUT). The value is inserted into a variable of type any consisting of a type code and the actual data.

A Request pseudo-object is used for the actual construction and invocation of requests. The operations available in the Request interface are

```
Interface Request {
    ORBStatus    add_arg(......);
    ORBStatus    invoke(......);
    ORBStatus    delete();
    ORBStatus    send(......);
    ORBStatus    get_response(......);
};
```

ORB Interoperability and IIOP

Although CORBA 1.0 and CORBA 1.1 were a big success in defining a standard architecture for distributed object-oriented systems, they did not achieve all the goals related to interoperability their creators had envisioned. Users were reluctant to select ORBs as the central middleware component in their mission-critical systems. Although this was partly due to the relative immaturity of some of the products and to non-technical issues such as the users' lack of familiarity with these products, the initial version of the CORBA specification has a fundamental flaw.

In their effort to create a flexible and open specification, the creators of CORBA 1.x did not address the issue of *interORBability*—that is, the notion of interoperability among different ORBs. One of the main goals of CORBA as an architecture is to define mechanisms by which application and service objects can be constructed in such a way that any object can be used by any other object. The ORB is defined as the primary enabler of this architecture by delegating requests between objects. However, CORBA 1.x did not address issues regarding how ORBs interact with other ORBs. Therefore, the result of CORBA 1.x was an open architecture so long as a single ORB type was used. Systems utilizing ORBs from a single vendor could indeed accomplish what CORBA intended; unfortunately, if one attempted to use multiple ORB products within the system, interoperability was not achieved.

This fact was a major hurdle in the adoption of CORBA as an enterprise-wide solution by many corporations (and hence in the adoption of CORBA in general because CORBA primarily targets the corporate market). This was not only because CORBA 1.x was perceived as incomplete, but for many other pragmatic reasons as well. Because ORBs could not interoperate and an ORB-based architecture could only be constructed using a single vendor, corporations felt that they would not be achieving a vendor-independent and open solution (which, as you might recall from the previous chapter, was one of CORBA's goals). Also, because different ORB products stressed support for different programming languages and environments (for example, Iona's Orbix initially for C++ and HP's DST for Smalltalk—now owned by ParcPlace), it was only natural to have a mix of ORBs.

When CORBA 2.0 was published, ORB vendors immediately embraced the standard and CORBA 2.0 products began to appear at an impressive rate. CORBA 2.0 was also the turning point as far as corporate (user) adoption was concerned. There is no doubt that CORBA has truly taken off as a primary enabler of distributed object-oriented systems over the past couple of years. It is difficult the assess how much of this was due to CORBA 2.0 and how much was due to the simple fact that CORBA, like any technology, had a maturing period. In addition, the phenomenal growth of the Internet and the *World Wide Web* (WWW) was an important catalyst in the use of CORBA as a foundation for application-level communication.

First-generation applications offered on the Web were no more than form-based information accessors with little to no application functionality. The Web as a delivery platform, however, quickly proved that it had infinite possibilities as far as audience and client base was concerned. This made IT organizations think of using the Web to deliver applications to a very large client base. The emergence of the corporate intranet as *the* application delivery mechanism accelerated this trend, giving CORBA a tremendous boost.

CORBA, and specifically CORBA 2.0, emerged as an obvious candidate to fill this gap. CORBA as an architecture was, from the outset, meant to solve precisely such interoperation problems. Luckily, the battle over CORBA 2.0 was won by the TCP/IP–Internet backers. (It is quite certain that had CORBA interoperability been based on DCE, CORBA would not be where it is today—in fact, it would probably have become one more good, unused technology.) This positioned CORBA perfectly for use as *the* interoperable architectural standard for Web-based systems and allowed CORBA to ride the Internet wave.

CORBA 2.0 deals with many issues not handled by CORBA 1.x. Among these topics, interoperability is not only the most important issue, but also the area in which the most work has been invested, producing more results than any other. The CORBA 2.0 specification not only defines the GIOP and IIOP protocols, but also addresses DCE-based interoperability and interoperation with the Microsoft Component Object Model and OLE Automation.

In addition to being a concrete specification, CORBA 2.0 also addresses interoperability architectures as a design-level abstraction. By providing an in-depth discussion on what interoperability architectures should provide, how bridges should work, and what solutions should be used in different cases, CORBA 2.0 becomes central to the underlying technologies of distributed systems (no matter whether these are locally distributed systems or systems being distributed on the *Wide Area Network* (WAN)). The CORBA 2.0 specification is certainly one of the cornerstone documents in the field of distributed computing.

CORBA 2.0 addresses interoperability between objects running in different ORB environments (after all, even CORBA 1.x addressed interoperability of objects running within an ORB environment). ORB interoperability is defined as " . . . the ability for a client on ORB A to invoke an OMG IDL-defined operation on an object on ORB B, where ORB A and ORB B are independently developed" (see Figure 9-1). ORB interoperability is a difficult task (as seen by the set of solutions that were required of CORBA 2.0). The inherent complexity of ORB interoperability is the result of the following points:

■ CORBA is a specification defined at the behavioral and architectural level. It does not enforce implementation-level properties. Different ORBs can therefore be very different in terms of their inner workings. Because the definition of ORB interoperability makes no assumptions on the participating ORBs, the specification ensuring interoperability must take into account any possible implementation of the spec.

Figure 9-1
ORB interoperability

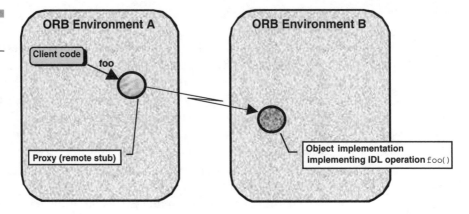

■ The CORBA world (that is, the core ORB, object services, and object facilities) is a very complex environment supporting a lot of functionality. The set of properties forming the semantic context of an object and of a request can therefore be very large and complex. These semantics must be correctly managed and maintained when a request or object reference passes an ORB boundary. In addition, CORBA as an architecture is continuously evolving. The specifications for interoperability must ensure that future services or facilities are supported with little or no additional work—and certainly must make sure that future additions are in no way compromised by a limited architectural view taken today.

■ Interoperability is and must be bi-directional. It is not enough for one ORB environment to have access to another. An invocation often includes an object reference that is passed as an argument and is then used by the object implementation to invoke another operation on the referenced object (thereby reversing the role of client and server). An invocation in which an object in one environment has access to an object in a second environment implies that every reference passed into the first environment is available to the second environment.

Because interoperability between ORBs must handle many cases, the CORBA 2.0 specification defines two distinct approaches to bridging between two environments. The first, called *mediated bridging* and shown in Figure 9-2, asserts that each internal ORB environment may adhere to its own internal representations and requires that an interoperable format be used externally to communicate between the two ORB environments.

Elements that need to cross ORB boundaries are transformed into the interoperable format and then into the other ORB's representation. IIOP, for example, (for ORBs that do not use IIOP internally) is an example of a protocol used for mediated bridging.

In the second approach, called *immediate bridging* and illustrated in Figure 9-3, entities are converted directly between the two internal forms. Naturally, immediate bridging is more efficient but less flexible because transformation routines are required for each pair of differing environments.

Figure 9-2
Mediated bridging

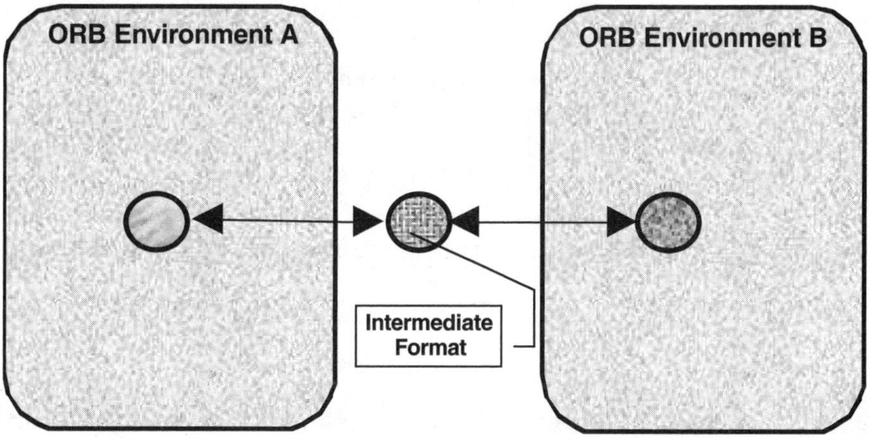

Figure 9-3
Immediate bridging

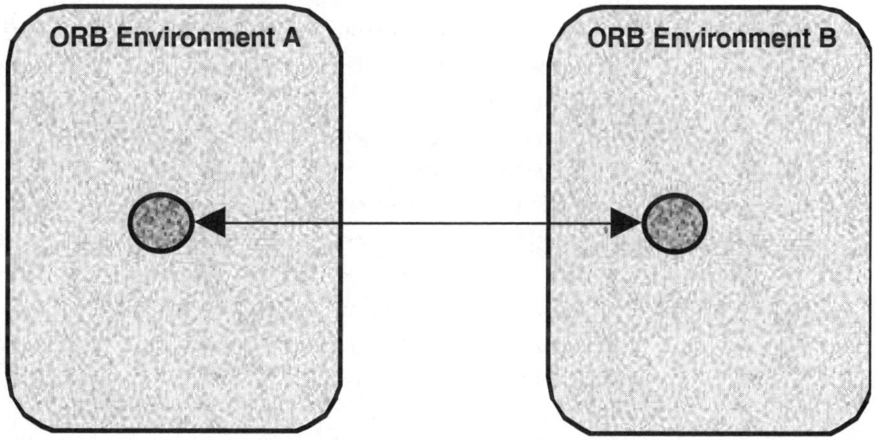

Domains

A domain is an organizational unit aggregating a set of components with similar characteristics. This is a very broad term that can be used both for physical partitioning as well as for functional-related partitioning. Characteristics of domains are important when interoperability is concerned because bridging between domains requires a mapping from one set of characteristics to another. It is not always possible to define a mapping between two domains that will not lose information because some domains are semantically richer than others.

Physical or administrative domains are relatively well understood. The focus of this chapter is interoperability between domains defined as separate ORB environments. The notion of domain bridging is limited to bridging between two different ORB environments.

When defining domain bridging, the CORBA 2.0 specification distinguishes between two bridging levels. The first, called *request level bridging*, uses public CORBA APIs to perform the required translations. ORB and ORB-based components are used to perform the translations. *In-line bridging,* on the other hand, encapsulates the entire translation process within the ORB.

The Dynamic Skeleton Interface (DSI)

A major component defined in CORBA 2.0 for use in request-level bridging is the *Dynamic Skeleton Interface* (DSI). The DSI resides alongside implementation skeletons generated by IDL as shown in Figure 9-4. The difference between the DSI and an IDL-skeleton is that the DSI can serve as a skeleton for any object implementation without knowing what the actual interfaces are.

The DSI magic is somewhat similar to the DII magic. The DII allows a client to create a request by specifying the target object reference, the operation name, and the parameters. It provides a mechanism by which this request can be fired off after its construction. The DSI provides the implementation-side counterpart to this process, but in reverse. No matter which request comes in, the DSI is invoked with the same method. This method is called the *Dynamic Implementation Routine* (DIR) and receives the same structures created within the DII that represent any operation request (that is, a structure that specifies the target object, the operations, and the parameters). The DSI is defined as a pseudo-object (that is, its

Figure 9-4
The Dynamic
Skeleton Interface

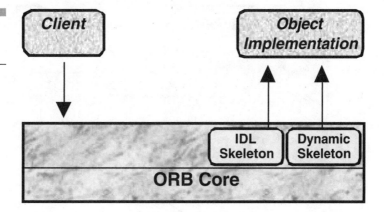

interface is defined using an IDL interface, but not necessarily implemented as a CORBA object—for example, it can be embedded as part of the ORB). The *pseudo-IDL* (PIDL) representing a server request is shown by the following IDL:

```
module CORBA {

        pseudo
interface ServerRequest {

                Identifier  op_name();
                Context     ctx();
                void        params(inout NVList params);
                any         result();

};

};
```

Just as the object implementation is not aware of how a request was generated when servicing it (that is, whether the DII or an IDL stub was used), a client issuing a request (and receiving results) is oblivious to whether a request was serviced through an IDL skeleton or through the DSI.

This transparency allows the DSI to be used for request-level bridging. In such a scenario, the request (issued on an object reference managed by another ORB) is delivered to the bridge using the DSI (which can handle any request without requiring any compile-time information). On the other side of the bridge, the DII will be used to deliver the request to the real object in the second ORB environment. This is shown in Figure 9-5. The combination of these two components dealing with an abstract and generic model of a request makes such bridges relatively simple to build.

Figure 9-5
Request-level
bridging

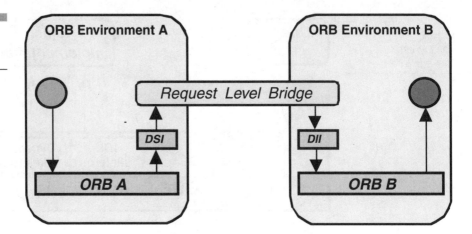

Inter-Domain Referencing

The issue of how object references are represented is perhaps the single most important issue in interoperability. As long as both the client and the object implementation reside within the same ORB environment, references are legal—but what happens if they reside in different domains and use different representations? The notion of reference representation is not only relevant for the target object reference used in a call made on an object implementation in another ORB environment. Observe the scenario depicted in Figure 9-6. The client invokes an operation on an object in another ORB environment. The operation call has another object as a parameter; the actual object used is within the client's environment. When the object implementation services the request, it may need to use the object reference passed as an argument—that is, send it a message. This implies that the inter-domain call (the first one in our example) must manage the object reference translation so the object implementation may transparently use the argument to make additional calls. As an even more elaborate example, the object reference serving as the operation argument could reside in a third (different from both the client's and the object implementation's) ORB environment.

The CORBA 2.0 specification identifies the following information as necessary for object reference representation and translation:

- Is the object being referenced a `null` object?
- What is the object's type?
- What protocols are supported within the environment?
- What ORB services are available?

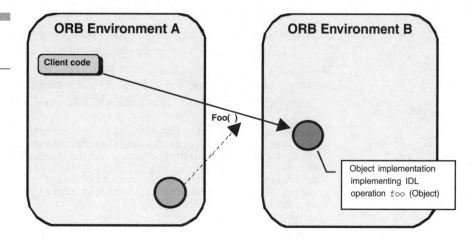

Figure 9-6
Inter-domain
referencing

This data, which is required to correctly represent an object reference, comprises the structure of the *Interoperable Object Reference* (IOR), which is so critical to ORB interoperability.

Interoperable Object References (IORs)

IORs represent object references as a data structure useful to bridges in order to support ORB interoperability. The data structure is defined in IDL for convenience, but should not be used by components other than bridges.

An IOR consists of a type specifier and a set of tagged profile specifiers, one per supported protocol. Although many cases will have a single protocol (for example, ORB environments that use IIOP as the internal protocol), the specification supports multiple environments with multiple protocols. A tagged profile contains an identifier and an octet stream, which holds all the information required to identify the object being referenced within that particular protocol (that is, hold the "opaque" representation of the object in the appropriate protocol). The fact that an IOR holds this identifying information for multiple protocols allows the same IOR to be passed around even when the underlying protocol changes (as long as the underlying profiles have corresponding octet streams defined within the IOR). Null objects are represented by an IOR with a special type ID as well as an empty set of profiles.

IORs may be stringified (that is, a string representing the IOR can be created) using the `object_to_string` operation defined in the ORB interface. This string representation can be later used to create an IOR for direct usage using the `string_to_object` call. This implies that the string representing the IOR is encoded with all the data contained in the IOR. A typical stringified representation will therefore be quite a long string similar to

```
IOR:000000000000002849444c3a4a4f4d6573736167696e674c617965722f4a4f4
d6573736167655175657565653a312e300000000000020000000100000064000000000000
0000040000000a000000107d48e77d8ceb000002500312cd00000000000000b00000
0107d48e77d8ce6000002500312cd000000008104000000000c4453543a352e363a
0113057b081040030000001038302e332e31382e3230353b3334363000000000000
0002c000100000000000c38302e332e31382e323035000d840000000000107d48e7
7d8ceb000002500312cd000000
```

The stringified representation of an IOR is very important to allow systems to have a common starting point. The first object reference from which others are accessed has always been problematic to agree upon. Although name services are already prevalent, the fact that simply passing a string in some way can create a common starting point is used extensively. For example, a string that can be embedded in an applet parameter is a very convenient way to start an ORB-based interaction.

ORB Services

The ORB service is a new concept defined by the CORBA 2.0 interoperability specification and should not be confused with the term CORBA services or Object services (although they are related). ORB services are ORB-level modules supporting special interoperability transformations required to support CORBA services.

CORBA services provide various application-level functionalities such as support for transactions, security, relationships, and more. These services can be partitioned into two groups (relevant to the discussion of ORB Services): those that require no support at the ORB level and are completely defined through a set of IDL interfaces, and those that do require ORB-level awareness. In order to support this second group, ORB Services were defined.

For example, the transaction service and security services both require ORB-level support. Transactions bracket code that must be atomically performed (that is, either all code is performed or nothing is). Because a transaction may include a remote invocation, the transaction bracket may span more than one process on more than one machine. It is therefore necessary for the transaction context information to be passed along with the remote invocation. This management of transaction context, however, must not be visible to the application programmer and must therefore be supported by the ORB service.

Assume now that the environment in which the application runs is different than the environment in which the object implementation resides. In such a case, the call is made in one ORB environment and must be transformed into the second ORB environment. Because this call must include appropriate transaction context information, this part of the request must also be translated into the new environment; the ORB service created to provide interoperability support for the transaction service is the component responsible for performing such translations.

The security service is another good example for the necessity of ORB services. Security information (such as authorization, signatures, and so on) is propagated along with a request in a secure environment. This information must be transformed when a call crosses domain boundaries —a transformation handled by the appropriate ORB service.

Because the CORBA specification does not directly deal with CORBA services, ORB services are defined as architectural components. The specification does not address any particular service and how it can be supported; rather, it puts a framework in place for dealing with these services with the intent that such support can be extended later to any other service that will be added. It tries to identify the various areas in which such support may be required and what hooks are required from within the ORB layers. It also defines how negotiation between different ORBs occurs when each supports a (possibly) different set of ORB services.

In order to support translation for any service-related information that might be required for various services, the interoperability specification defines an IDL type that encapsulates service-related information in a sequence of structures, each one composed of a service identifier and an octet stream holding onto the service-related context information:

```
module IOP {

    // Each CORBA Service will define its own constant
    typdef unsigned long ServiceID;

    struct ServiceContext {

        ServiceID          context_id;
        sequence<octet>    context_data;

};

    typedef sequence<ServiceContext> ServiceContextList;

};
```

These additional context structures are sent by the communicating ORBs as part of the requests, thus allowing the propagation of service context.

The General Inter-ORB Protocol (GIOP)

The *General Inter-ORB Protocol* (GIOP) is an ORB interoperability protocol that can be mapped onto any connection-oriented transport layer. The GIOP associates a request with a connection and assumes that the connection provided by the transport layer is reliable and maintains message ordering. It also assumes that the transport layer provides some form of connection-less notification and acknowledgment of delivery. Although the GIOP is a generalized protocol and these assumptions are not very limiting as far as connection-based transport protocols, the GIOP was constructed with TCP/IP as the reference transport level model. The mapping to TCP/IP—code-named IIOP—is therefore very natural.

The GIOP specification consists of the *Common Data Representation* (CDR) and the GIOP message specifications. The CDR maps IDL types into a wire-level representation forming the GIOP transfer syntax. The GIOP also defines which set of messages may be exchanged between the participants in a session and how these messages are formatted.

The Common Data Representation

The CDR defines how IDL types are packaged into byte streams. CDR was designed to be simple, efficient, and flexible (yes, these do contradict each other, but we have to try). The CDR is a wire-level transfer syntax that defines what actually goes over the wire and how IDL is packaged into these byte streams.

CDR not only maps IDL types; it maps the entire contents that will have to be passed in order for a request to be performed correctly. For example, CDR also defines the mapping of pseudo-objects such as typecodes, as well as data types that are not fully specified by the CORBA core specification.

CDR places everything in an octet stream (that is, a byte stream for our purposes). It deals with how these streams are created and how they may be unpacked. In doing so, it distinguishes between two types of streams; streams that are used to package a GIOP message and streams that package *encapsulations*. An encapsulation is a stream that packages any IDL data structure into an independent byte stream (having an IDL type of `sequence<octet>`). This can later be used as a module for insertion into other streams, whether they are message streams or other encapsulations. Encapsulations are useful in creating a containment hierarchy of streams and supporting a "divide-and-conquer" approach for marshaling and unmarshaling data onto streams.

CDR's approach to byte ordering is called *receiver-makes-right*. CDR does not enforce and maintain a certain byte ordering (that is, big-endian or little endian). Instead, CDR packaging of data types may be either way. The CDR stream encodes which of the two byte orderings were used when the stream was packaged. It is the receiver's responsibility to use the bytes as they are packaged or to reverse them if the packaging ordering does not match its own ordering. This approach has the advantage that if the two endpoints use the same byte ordering, no conversions are necessary. Note that encapsulation streams also have an ordering tag and that it is quite possible for an enclosing stream to have a different byte ordering than an encapsulation stream embedded in it.

Other than IDL data types and typecodes, the CDR also defines how the following are encoded:

■ *Context*   The context is a list of name-value pairs that holds information that forms the context in which a request was made. The context is passed to the object implementation by writing it to a CDR stream as a sequence of strings—a sequence in which there must be an even number of strings.

■ *Principal*   The principal identifies a caller and is used in security-related mechanisms. CDR merely defines that the principal is packaged as a byte stream; it does not associate any semantics with this stream at this level.

■ *Exceptions*   Exceptions are packaged as a string identifying the exception followed by members of the exception structure.

■ *Object references*   Object references are packaged using the IOR structure.

GIOP Messages

GIOP supports all functionality required by CORBA using a small set of simple messages. The core set consists of only seven messages; these support all invocation models, exception raising and propagation, context passing, and reference management.

A typical GIOP session starts out with a `Request` type message being sent from the client to the server (the client being the ORB through which the application client holding the object reference invokes the operation and the server being the ORB through which the object implementation will be activated). If all is well, the server will respond with a `Reply` message. To close the session, the server sends the `CloseConnection`. At any time, both the client and the server may issue a `MessageError` message.

`Request` messages are used by clients to encode an operation invocation. The request message contains a header and a body. The header contains such information as the service context (see the section entitled "ORB Services"), an indication of whether the request requires that a response to be sent back to the client, and the name of the operation for which the request message was issued. The body of the request message encapsulates the in and `inout` parameters (that is, the parameters that are passed from the client to the object implementation) and an optional encoding of the context object.

Replies are sent in response to a request (where appropriate—for example, one way operations do not require a response). `Reply` headers contain a context list, a request id, and a reply status. The reply status can be one of the following:

- ▪ NO_EXCEPTION   The request processing was completed normally. In this case, the reply message body encodes the return value and values for the `out` and `inout` parameters.

- ▪ USER_EXCEPTION or SYSTEM_EXCEPTION   An exception occurred while processing the request. In this case, the body of the message will encode the exception that occurred.

- ▪ LOCATION_FORWARD   The server is indicating to the client that the operation should be resent to a different object reference (for various possible reasons—for example, the object may have been relocated). The message body will encode the IOR that should be used for resending the message.

`CancelRequest` messages are sent by clients to their servers, and they encode within their headers the request ID that should be canceled. `LocateRequest` and `LocateReply` are useful for querying about a particular object reference. A client can issue a `LocateRequest` for determining whether the object packaged in the message is legal, whether it is managed by the server, and so on. The server replies with a `LocateReply` message in which the locate status is either UNKNOWN_OBJECT, OBJECT_ HERE, or OBJECT_FORWARD. When the status is LOCATE_FORWARD, the body of the message contains the new IOR to be used for accessing the object.

During a request session, both server and client may send MessageError message to indicate inconsistencies in version number or unrecognized message structures. The last message type, CloseConnection, is sent by the server to indicate that it will not respond to further requests.

The Internet Inter-ORB Protocol (IIOP)

The *Internet Inter-ORB Protocol* (IIOP) is a specific version of the GIOP mapped to the TCP/IP transfer protocol. Because TCP/IP is so ubiquitous, the name IIOP has become a code-name for CORBA 2.0 and for GIOP. TCP/IP and the Internet (which is mostly comprised of networks running TCP/IP) have made IIOP the ORB protocol.

The IIOP can serve two roles in ORB environments. The IIOP was built as an interoperability protocol in that it can be used as the common representation to which ORB environments convert when crossing ORB boundaries. Because the IIOP is a published format owned by the OMG, it is a perfect candidate for the various ORB vendors to convert to.

Although the IIOP's goal was to serve as the common interoperability protocol over the most common transport protocol (TCP/IP), it is being used in a far more encompassing way. IIOP is an interoperability protocol; however, it is also an ORB protocol that can represent all that is required within an ORB environment. Therefore, IIOP is not only being used as an interoperability protocol; it is also being used as an ORB protocol for many of today's commercial ORBs. IIOP is not only being used within ORB boundaries; it is also being used internally to an ORB's domain.

Because IIOP is merely an implementation of GIOP over TCP/IP, it only requires a specification of the IIOP profile that will be the "IIOP representative" in IORs. Because TCP/IP supports the abstraction in which a communication channel is formed using a host identifier and a port number, the profile body contains these along with the additional byte stream representing an opaque data structure used by the managing ORB to denote the object. This structure is put within request messages by the ORB software; because the receiver ORB is the owner and creator of the opaque structure, it can interpret it and service the request.

JavaBeans

JavaBeans is a component model that defines the structure of Java components. Software component models in general —and JavaBeans in particular—aim at defining a simple yet powerful model that will enable the creation of reusable pieces of code and their packaging in a way that others can easily use the functionality that is provided by these components. Component models aim at specifying a strict structure that is well known by creators of software components, as well as by users. By adhering to such structures, developers can guarantee that their components will be well understood and will be compatible with development environments, frameworks, etc.

The purpose of any component model is to enable a component-based industry to evolve. In order for that to happen, it is not enough to create a component model; rather, it is also necessary to achieve a certain critical mass in terms of *Integrated Development Environments* (IDEs), packaging tools, and third-party components. While JavaBeans is certainly not the first component model to be created (among the prestigious list of component models, we can find Microsoft's highly successful *Component Object Model* (COM) and Apple/IBM's not-so-successful OpenDoc), JavaBeans certainly holds the record in terms of the rate at which it has been embraced. Java-Beans is currently part of the base JDK distribution (the package `java.beans` is part of the JDK 1.1.x) and forms the base for almost any Java library on the market today. This application also forms the base for the *Enterprise Java Beans* (EJB) specification, which will be the topic of the next chapter.

This chapter provides an overview of the JavaBeans specification, as defined in [JB]. The JavaBeans component model specifies the structure of Java components in terms of properties, events, and methods. In addition to this basic structure, the issues of persistence, introspection (which is akin to Java reflection), customization, and packaging will be discussed. Readers who are familiar with JavaBeans can skip this chapter.

Definition of a JavaBean

A JavaBean (or bean) is a reusable Java component that has a specific structure as defined by the JavaBeans specification. This structure forms a common ground between components that are developed by many organizations, that perform different tasks, and that use different resources. As such, this bean can be manipulated both at development time and at run time by tools and programs that were written well before the bean was written (and without any specific knowledge of the bean's particulars). These tools do not have to know anything special about our bean; instead, they can handle *all* beans, because all beans will have the same fundamental structure. The abstraction level at which these tools and programs can perform is at the component-abstraction level. Much like software hierarchies in object-oriented programming enable many different implementations to be viewed by external users as being similar by providing a common inheritance root, JavaBeans does this task as well—and to a greater extent—by defining a common structure. The fundamental principle behind JavaBeans (and any component model) is as follows:

JavaBeans defines an abstraction level that unifies software entities and that enables each such entity to become a *component*. By enabling disparate code from multiple origins to look the same in terms of its handling—both at the time of development and at run time—JavaBeans elevates software reuse within the Java world.

The structure that defines the common base for all beans includes the following three categories:

- *Properties*   Properties are the attributes of a bean. Each attribute has a name and a type and is accessed through accessors (get and set methods). Attributes usually map to the functionality that the bean implements, and much can be learned about a bean by its set of properties. Examples of properties can include attributes such as size, color, and shading for visual beans or domain-specific attributes such as pager type, pager number, and retry policy in a `PagerRequest` bean. (You might be asking why we would want to package such an object as a bean.) Packaging objects as beans enables tools that are being used within your system to be used with all of these objects. For example, property editors can be written—or even bought—that can be used to edit any bean, so that we can use the editor for creating page requests, part orders, or almost any other domain object. In other words, you can often create extremely generic software by doing little else but following the standard.

- *Methods*   Methods are an object's main functional interface. A bean's public methods comprise its normal API, which reflects what this object knows to do. A bean developer might decide to export only a partial set of the public methods as the bean's API, in which case he or she will have to build a special descriptor for the bean.

- *Events*   The third category that affects how a bean behaves in a run time environment is the set of events that the bean might raise. Events are the preferred mechanism for one software component to notify another, thereby supporting component interaction by enabling one component to react to events that are created by another component. The JDK 1.1 (and onward) relies heavily on the notion of components raising events and other components being registered on these events using listeners. JavaBeans stresses this architecture by requesting that each bean define the set of events that it might raise by a set of subscription methods, through which other components can be notified of the bean's events.

A bean's life is slightly more complicated than the life of an ordinary piece of reusable Java code. This complication arises from the fact that a bean is built to be very reusable. A bean is reusable because it knows how to behave within an IDE during development time. The bean must therefore not only provide a set of APIs for use at run time but also must provide APIs and structures that are useful during development time. For example, the bean must work with the IDE so that the IDE can know the bean's properties, methods, and events. The bean must also provide enough information about itself so that it can plug into the tools that are available within an IDE (e.g., property editors and visual connection managers). The bean must provide developers with the opportunity to customize and set the bean's attributes and must provide the mechanisms for saving itself once it has been customized. All of these additional complexities are necessary for a component to be a true bean. Once this complexity has been managed, the bean's value grows as a reusable component, because the effort involved in using the bean in a program is much smaller.

A bean developer must be aware of the following issues in order for the bean to behave correctly at development time as well as at run time:

- *Persistence* A bean must provide the functionality required so that it can be serialized and deserialized. This feature is required because a bean user will typically set some of the bean's properties and then will want to save these settings until run time. The mechanism that is afforded to beans under the JavaBeans model is that of serialization; i.e., a bean should provide methods for writing itself on a stream and reading itself from a stream. These methods are then used by IDEs and/or by programs that are using the bean.

- *Introspection* A bean must provide enough information about itself so that an IDE can help a developer understand what the bean can do and define how it interacts with other code segments in the system. JavaBeans defines two ways in which this task can be done. The first relies on a set of conventions. For example, if a `PagerRequest` bean has a property called `TelephoneNumber` of type `String`, then the bean developer should provide two methods in the following format:

```
String getTelephoneNumber()
void setTelephoneNumber(String aString)
```

These are the canonical accessors for a property. Often, a bean developer will not need to do much more than follow these conventions in order for the bean to perform correctly within an IDE. This situation is not true in cases of complex beans, however. For example, the naming conventions imply that all public methods are viewed as the JavaBeans methods of the component. If a bean developer wants to shield some of these methods (yet cannot change the access category to anything but public), he or she will have to work a little harder. In this case, a `BeanInfo` object must be defined and implemented. This object describes the bean structure and is used by the IDE in the introspection process (the object is a metadata object).

■ *Customization* Beans can define customizers, which are specialized editors that are tailored to enable the bean to be more easily used within an IDE. Customizers often involve building wizards and attractive user interfaces that guide a bean user through the process of customizing and using a bean.

■ *Packaging* Because beans are components that are written by one party and are used by another, the JavaBeans specification defines how beans are packaged by bean developers so that users of the bean are not faced with unnecessary difficulties when trying to use the bean within their development environment.

Before delving into the details of JavaBeans, we will offer a simple example. In this example, we will look at a simple Juggler bean and a simple button bean and how they look inside Sun's BeanBox. (The BeanBox is part of the *Bean Developer Kit* (BDK), and is available at `http://java.sun.com: 80/beans/software/bdk_download.html`). We will create a simple application involving two buttons that control the juggler: one starts the juggling, and one stops the juggling. All of the programming will be done within the BeanBox by visually hooking events. Both of the beans used are part of the BeanBox distribution and are provided as examples for bean development.

The BeanBox is composed of three tools. The canvas shown in Figure 10-1 is the work area in which beans are placed. The ToolBox shown in Figure 10-2 is the palette from which beans can be dragged. Upon startup, the BeanBox startup procedure analyzes a set of JAR files (the package format for beans) and places all available beans in the ToolBox. All you have to do in order to add a new bean to your palette is to place the JAR file in the right directors (`%BDK_HOME%jars` by default). Finally, Figure 10-3 shows the property editor. The editor enables you to set the values of a bean's properties. The editor will always reflect the properties of the current selection. In Figure 10-3, the editor shows the property of the default container that is also part of the BDK distribution.

First, we drop the three beans on the canvas (as shown in Figure 10-4). Then, we notice that the juggler is juggling too fast, so we want to change the rate at which the juggling is performed. We click the Juggler bean and look at the property sheet for the Juggler (refer to Figure 10-5). One of the

Figure 10-1
The BeanBox canvas

Figure 10-2
The BeanBox ToolBox

Figure 10-3
The BeanBox
Property Editor

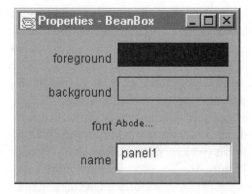

Figure 10-4
Placing the beans
on the canvas

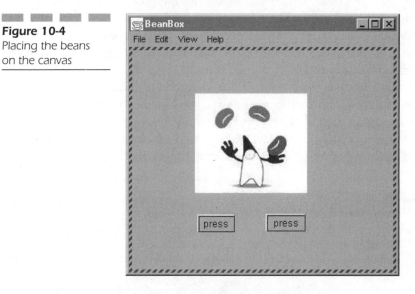

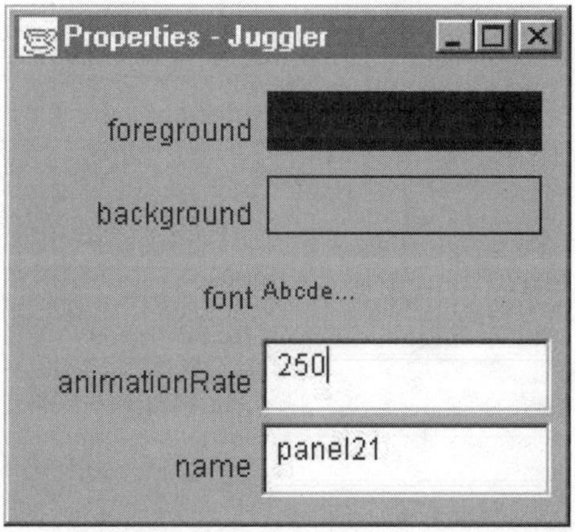

Figure 10-5
Juggler
property sheet

juggler's properties is the juggling rate. The introspection mechanism enables the BeanBox to know this information and to place this property in the editor. Because we want to slow the rate down, we select 125 instead of the original 250. Also, we need to set the labels of the button to Stop and Start, respectively. One of the button bean's properties is its label, so we use the property editor to set the right labels.

Now, we need to hook up the events. Buttons can be pressed. When a button is pressed, an action event is generated. What we would like to do is hook up this event (which occurs within the buttons) to call methods in the juggler (specifically, the `startJuggling` and `stopJuggling` methods). The BeanBox enables us to perform all of these actions visually (as do many other modern IDEs). Under the covers, an adapter is placed between the juggler and the button. The adapter is added as a listener on the action-performed event (that is generated by the button), and when fired, the adapter calls the appropriate juggler method (which is part of the API that is defined by the juggler).

For us, the job is much simpler. The BeanBox enables us to perform all of these actions without writing a line of code. First, we select the button that we have designated to be the start button. Then, we select Edit→button push→actionPerformed, which defines the event in which we are interested (refer to Figure 10-6). Then, we drag the line to the juggler bean. A list

Figure 10-6
Selecting the Push button event

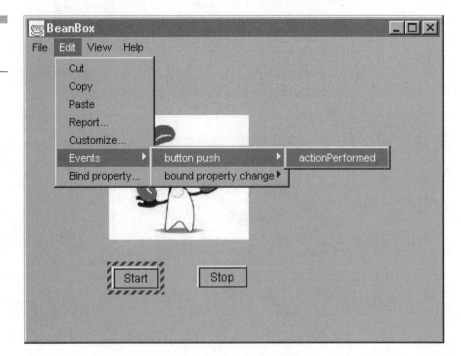

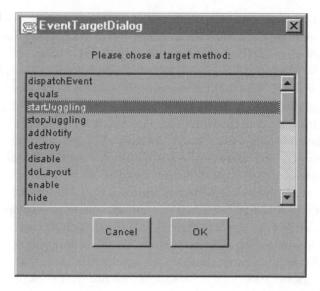

of methods forming the juggler's public interface pops up (refer to Figure 10-7). We select `startJuggling`, and the adapter is created and compiled. The process is repeated for the Stop button. That concludes our experiment. We have a small working application that we can save and run.

Introspection

Introspection is the process through which a development environment discovers which properties, events, and methods a bean supports. In the example in the previous section, we saw the effect of this discovery process. By knowing a bean's properties, the BeanBox can provide the correct property sheet listing the events—enabling us to choose an action on which to be registered and to know the methods that we can select—controlling what happens when the event occurs. The BeanBox uses introspection for both the button bean and for the juggler bean in order to enable this visual programming.

The fundamental purpose of JavaBeans introspection is to provide a means through which a bean's capabilities can be inspected. This concept is not totally new. There are many environments in which a definition or specification language is used for defining capabilities. For example, IDL is a specification language, and the information embodied within an IDL specification is stored as live objects within the IR (and is accessible to tools that provide browsing capabilities). JavaBeans introspection makes use of the Java language itself so as not to introduce a new language and cause the entire definition to be completely phrased in Java.

Java introspection can be achieved through one of two mechanisms. The low-level approach relies on conventions. The JavaBeans specification defines a set of conventions (which we will discuss later on in this chapter) for naming methods that provide access to properties, events, and methods. The low-level introspection mechanism uses Java reflection to access these names, and based on the set of conventions, it ascertains which properties, events, and methods a bean supports.

The default low-level mechanism is useful for most simple beans. For more complex beans, it is often not enough—because a complex bean might have been built to provide different services in different environments, or it might contain too rich an interface to be useful for simple programming tasks. Java-Beans introspection defines a second mechanism that, while requiring more work from a bean developer, provides fine control over what a bean will show to the outside world. JavaBeans defines a `BeanInfo` interface that provides methods for describing properties, events, and methods of a bean. A bean developer can create a class that implements the `BeanInfo` interface for describing the capabilities of his or her bean. Listing 10-1 shows a simple class that is implementing the `BeanInfo` interface for our `PagerRequest` bean. The `PagerRequestBeanInfo` class extends `SimpleBeanInfo`—a utility class in the `java.beans` package that has a null implementation for each of the required methods. Our bean will have three simple properties: telephone number, *Personal Identification Number* (PIN), and message and will have a method for paging the number and an event that will be raised when the pager receives the message. Note that we did not explicitly define the methods, which shows that you can use an explicit `BeanInfo` definition for some aspects of the bean yet rely on the default naming conventions for others.

Listing 10-1
The
PagerRequestInfo
class

```
import java.beans.*;


public class PagerRequestBeanInfo extends SimpleBeanInfo {


    public BeanDescriptor getBeanDescriptor() {
            BeanDescriptor _descriptor =
                    new BeanDescriptor(PagerRequest.class);
            return _descriptor;
```

```
        }
        public PropertyDescriptor[] getPropertyDescriptors() {
                try {
                        PropertyDescriptor _propertyDescriptors[] = {
                                new PropertyDescriptor(
                                        "Telephone Number" ,
                                        String.class),
                                new PropertyDescriptor(
                                        "PIN" ,
                                        String.class),
                                new PropertyDescriptor(
                                        "Message" ,
                                        String.class)
                        };
                        return _propertyDescriptors;
                } catch (IntrospectionException e) {
                e.printStackTrace();
                        return null;
            }
        }


        public int getDefaultPropertyIndex() {
                return 0;
        }


        public EventSetDescriptor[] getEventSetDescriptors() {
                try {
                        EventSetDescriptor _eventDescriptors[] = {
                        new EventSetDescriptor(
                                PagerRequest.class,
                                "Acknowledge Received",
                                java.awt.event.ActionEvent.class,
                                "acknowledgeReceived"
                                )};
                        return _eventDescriptors;
                } catch (IntrospectionException e) {
                e.printStackTrace();
                        return null;
            }
        }


        public int getDefaultEventIndex() {
                return 0;
        }


        public java.awt.Image getIcon(int iconKind) {
            java.awt.Image img = loadImage("PagerRequest.gif");
            return img;
        }


}
```

Because beans take the form of classes, and because a class can inherit from another class, the introspection process is a multi-phased process that walks up the inheritance tree. For every superclass of a bean, JavaBeans introspection will try to determine whether a `BeanInfo` object can be retrieved. If so, it will merge this information into the bean's complete description. If not, it will activate the low-level reflection mechanism and will add the convention-based definitions to the bean-merged description.

Properties

Properties are named attributes of beans that have a name and a type and are defined by providing accessor methods in a bean. If the property is read/write, two accessors (a `get` and a `set`) will be implemented. Read-only properties only require a `get` method. Just as in CORBA IDL attributes, a property does not necessarily imply that the bean has a data member (although typically it does). A property might be derived (or computed) and can involve complex business logic.

The convention regarding properties for low-level introspection is that for a property by the name of `<PropertyName>` of type `<PropertyType>`, two accessors should be defined:

```
public <PropertyType> get<PropertyName>()
public void set<PropertyName>(<PropertyType> arg)
```

If the property is read-only, only the `get` accessor should be defined. When a `BeanInfo` class is not provided and the low-level introspection mechanism discovers a pair of public methods as described earlier, it will know about the bean's property.

Special handling is defined for a number of common cases. If a property is of a Boolean type (which is common), then the `get` method should be defined as follows:

```
public boolean is<PropertyName>()
```

If a property has an array type (i.e., `<PropertyType>[]`), then the pattern to be followed is as such:

```
public <PropertyType> get<PropertyName>(int index)
public void set<PropertyName> (int index, <PropertyType> arg)
```

JavaBeans defines two more categories of properties called bound and constrained properties. Bound properties support automated notification upon a property value change, and constrained properties enable subscribers to perform validation on property value changes. Bound and constrained properties will be described in full detail later, because they require a complete understanding of events.

Methods

By default, all public methods of a bean are exposed as the bean's API, which also includes all property accessors and event-listener subscription methods. Therefore, it is usually wise to define the method signatures within a `BeanInfo`.

Events

The JavaBeans event model follows the JDK 1.1 event model and defines a framework for propagating notifications from a source object to a set of listeners. Propagation means the activation of Java methods defined in the listener objects that follow a set of naming conventions. The Java methods that handle the events are grouped in interfaces called event listener interfaces, whose signatures correspond to the naming conventions.

Hooking up an event subscriber to an event producer requires that both the source (the producer) and the listener (subscriber) follow the JavaBeans event pattern. The source must provide methods that the subscriber can use to register interest in a certain event. These are the `add` and `remove` methods. For example, if an object wishes to support publishing an `ActionEvent`, then that object should implement an `addActionListener` and a `removeActionListener`. Using these methods, subscribers can register their interest on this event type on the source object. In order to complete the cycle, the subscribers must implement a method defined in the appropriate listener interface (the argument to the `addActionListener` method). This method is the one that will be called by the source object when firing the event.

The implementation specifics of how an event is raised and how it is propagated to the listeners is less important and is not limited to one implementation by the JavaBeans specification. For example, most implementations of beans will maintain a collection of dependents (subscribers) and will use the `add` and `remove` methods to manage this collection. Firing an event, in this case, implies iterating over this collection and calling each subscriber. Nothing in the JavaBeans specification requires such a collection to be managed, however, and many alternative implementations are possible. The only truly important specification is the protocol between the publisher and the subscriber.

Firing an event by a source object means creating an event object (an instance of a class that is inheriting from `java.util.EventObject`), inserting information regarding the state change into this event object, and invoking a method in every one of the interested listeners. Event objects are immutable and should not be changed by individual listener objects. Because the same event object will be passed to all listeners, any such change might affect correct processing in other listeners.

As in properties and methods, low-level JavaBeans introspection uses reflection and naming conventions to determine which events can be fired by a source object. A pair of methods of the following format,

```
public void add<EventListenerType>(<EventListenerType> ev)
public void remove<EventListenerType>(<EventListenerType> ev)
```

implies that the bean creates <EventType> events that notify listeners who are implementing the <EventListenerType> interface. A special case supported in JavaBeans defines the naming convention to be used for Unicast event sources. The default event-handling paradigm enables handling multiple subscribers on a single-event source. If the event-source model should only support a single listener, then the method definition should be of the following form:

```
public void add<EventListenerType>(<EventListenerType> ev)
throws java.util.TooManyListenersException
```

Finally, when an event source raises an event, it iterates over all of the subscribed listeners. For each one, it calls a method of the form

```
Public void <EventOccurenceMethodsName>(<EventStateObejctType> ev)
```

The event object that is used encapsulates the information regarding the state change.

The event-delivery semantics that are defined in the JavaBeans model are one of synchronous delivery with respect to the event source. The call that is made by the source object on the subscriber is performed within the caller's thread. If one listener fails (in a way that fails the thread), the following listeners will not get notification.

The synchronous event delivery semantics are fundamental to the notion of constrained properties. Constraint properties are an enhancement of bounds properties; both are constructs that couple properties with events and are so common that they receive special status in JavaBeans. A bound property is a property that is of interest to another object—usually, the container of the bean. This feature is useful for binding customized behavior to a change in property value. Constrained properties are similar to bound properties in that an object might be interested in a property change, but it goes even farther in supporting validation by enabling the interested object to reject the change if deemed inappropriate. Synchronous semantics are important for implementing constrained properties, because a listener might reject a change by simply raising an exception—thereby stopping normal processing of the event-handler thread.

Bound Properties

As mentioned, bound properties enable coupling a property with an OnChanged notification type. In order to provide a bound property, a bean supports a pair of multicast listener registration methods for the PropertyChangeListener type:

```
public void addPropertyChangeListener(PropertyChangeListener l)
public void removePropertyChangeListener(PropertyChangeListener l)
```

When a change occurs, the bean calls the listener's propertyChange method and passes it a PropertyChangeEvent object. The property name that has changed, its old value, and its new value are included in the PropertyChangeEvent object. If one wants to register precisely on a single named property, the following methods are also supported by JavaBeans (and are preferred):

```
public void addPropertyChangeListener(
String propertyName, PropertyChangeListener l)
public void removePropertyChangeListener(
String propertyName, PropertyChangeListener l)
```

The call to the listeners' propertyChange methods is performed only after the change has been made. The subscribers have no say regarding the change. Listing 10-2 shows a simple example of using a bound property of internal frame in the Swing (JFC) library (com.sun.java. swing.JInternalFrame). When an internal frame is maximized, the property will change—and we will be notified of the change.

Listing 10-2
Using a bound
property

```
//
// When the screen is opened set up the listener to get
// notified when the internal frame's properties change.
// One of these properties is the isMaximized property which
// is of interest.
//

public void postOpenWindow(com.sun.java.swing.JInternalFrame win) {

        OnMaximizeOrMinimize aListener = new OnMaximizeOrMinimize();
        win.addPropertyChangeListener(aListener);

}



//
// When called, check whether this is the property of
// interest to us in and if so, call the handling routine
// (not showed here)
//

class OnMaximizeOrMinimize implements
java.beans.PropertyChangeListener {

        public void propertyChange(java.beans.PropertyChangeEvent
ev) {
            if (ev.getPropertyName().compareTo(
          com.sun.java.swing.JInternalFrame.IS_MAXIMUM_PROPERTY) ==
0) {
                boolean aBoolean =
                    ((Boolean)ev.getNewValue()).booleanValue();
                            setBasedOn(aBoolean);
                }
        }

        public void setBasedOn(boolean aBoolean) {
                // ....
        }

}
```

Constrained Properties

Constrained properties extend bound properties with support for validation. Instead of being called after the property changes, subscribers are
called before the change is made and are given a chance to veto the
change. A subscriber can stop the change from being made by raising a
PropertyVetoException. Due to the synchronous event semantics,
however, it is possible for the bean to ensure that the change will not be
performed until all listeners have been called and have been given a

chance to veto the change. The naming conventions used for constrained properties include add and remove methods of the following format:

```
public void addVetoableChangeListener(VetoableChangeListener 1)
public void addVetoableChangeListener(VetoableChangeListener 1)

public void addVetoableChangeListener(
String propertyName, VetoableChangeListener 1)
public void addVetoableChangeListener(
String propertyName, VetoableChangeListener 1)
```

The handling method in the listener interface is defined to throw a PropertyVetoException.

One of the complexities involved with a constrained property is the fact that if one subscriber vetoes the change, it is possible that other subscribers might have already been notified of the change and might have already taken some actions accordingly. Because this situation might cause incorrect application behavior, the subscribers must be notified when the property is being changed back to the old value (when a veto occurs). Therefore, when a bean handles a veto exception that is raised by one of its subscribers, it must fire another vetoable change event for reverting back to the old value.

Event Adaptors

Event adaptors are objects that interpose between the source objects and the subscribers (or between the event producer and the event consumer). Event adaptors are not necessary for the correct propagation of events, but they are often convenient to use. This convenience might be attributed to two issues:

1. Event adaptors enable decoupling the subscriber from the source. Instead of forcing the subscriber to implement the correct set of methods necessary for the event to be passed from the source, the adaptor can form a translator of sorts, enabling the source and subscribers to remain unaware of each other. Because the different components are often developed by third parties, it is even possible that such a coupling might not be possible. In this case, event adaptors are a must. Figure 10-8a shows the basic setup of an event adaptor, and Figure 10-8b shows what happens at run time. In this example, the paging system is a subscriber that has been purchased by a third party. The system has an API for paging, using a phone number and a PIN. Our source is a dispatch queue that raises an event whenever a

Figure 10-8-a
Event Adaptor setup

Figure 10-8-a
Event Adaptor setup

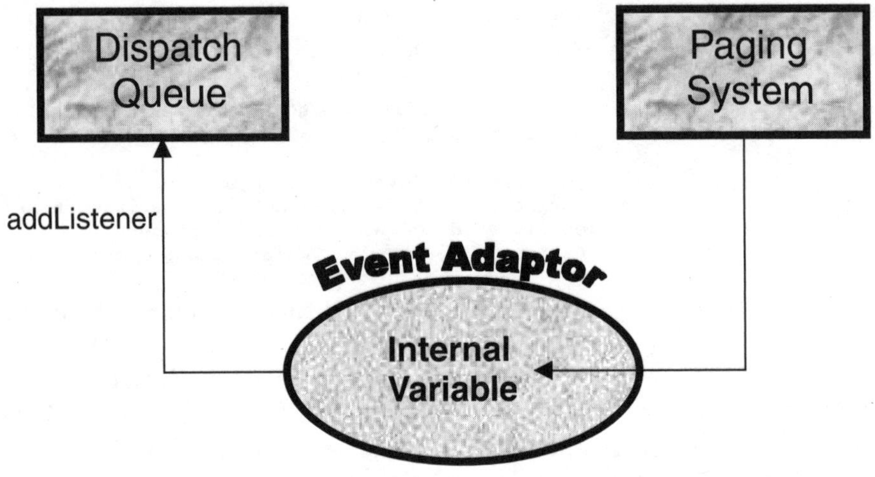

Figure 10-8-b
Event Adaptor at
run time

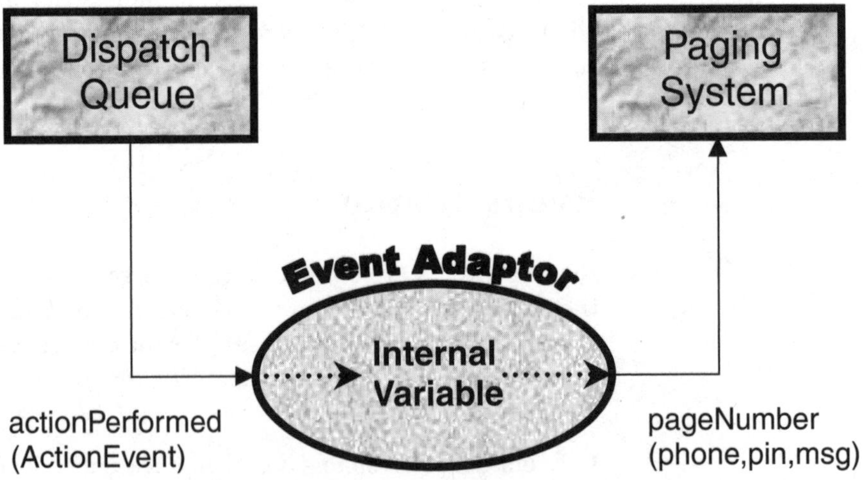

dispatch request should be issued. The event adaptor implements the listener API that is required in order for the API to be added as a listener and calls the API translation for the paging system.

2. Event adaptors might perform additional operations that are required by the application, such as filtering events, implementing security policies, implementing queuing (for example, the CORBA Event Service has a notion called the Event Channel, which could be partially implemented within an application as an event adaptor), etc. Another example of the usefulness of adaptors involves transactions.

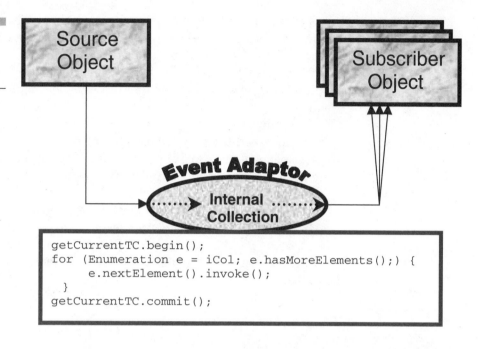

Figure 10-9
An Event Adaptor
as a transaction
coordinator

```
getCurrentTC.begin();
for (Enumeration e = iCol; e.hasMoreElements();) {
      e.nextElement().invoke();
   }
getCurrentTC.commit();
```

Suppose that we have multiple subscribers on the same node that must all perform some operation when the source fires an event. Also, suppose that all of these operations need to occur within the same transaction bracket (i.e., either they all complete successfully, or none are performed). Someone must coordinate this transaction. The coordinator will usually not be the source object (either because the source object was not developed internally; i.e, its source cannot be changed—or because other users of the same component care nothing about transactions). This person certainly cannot be one of the subscribers, because we cannot rely on notification ordering (any implementation trying to make use of one of the subscribers for this coordination will almost surely be messy and non-reentrant). This job is obviously perfect for an adaptor. As Figure 10-9 depicts, the adaptor can manage the transaction for its subscribers.

Customization

Property editors such as the one shown in Figure 10-3 are useful for simple beans. For complex beans or for beans that have complex data types as properties, the default property editors might not be enough. For such cases, JavaBeans defines the notion of a customizer for a class. A customizer is a class that provides a way for a user of a bean to provide values for properties of a bean at design time. This customization can include wizards, specialized user interfaces, or editors that enable complex data types to be entered.

Customizers need to inherit (directly or indirectly) from `java.awt.Component` because they are used by the bean IDE as a GUI. They must also implement the `java.beans.Customizer` interface. These methods are used for managing the interaction with the rest of the IDE (using property-change events, obviously).

Attaching a customizer to a certain bean involves going through the `BeanInfo` object. The customizer for a bean is retrieved by calling the `getCustomizerClass()` method that is called after getting the bean description from the `BeanInfo` object (by using the `getBeanDescriptor()` method).

Persistence

When using a bean within an IDE, the user will typically customize the bean by setting properties, attaching events, etc. This information must be externalized to some persistent store in order for the system to function correctly at run time. JavaBeans use Java-object serialization as the mechanism for storing out and reading in beans. While the specification defines other alternatives for making a bean persistent (including enabling the tool to control the process and enabling specialized formats to be used), the current state of the market is such that you should only use serialization and/or externalization.

Packaging

JavaBeans are packaged within JAR files. JAR files were introduced in JDK 1.1 as a generic and useful packing and distribution mechanism. JAR files were not produced specifically for beans; rather, they were used to solve issues involving cohesive packaging of code, bitmaps, help information, etc. Because JAR files can contain Java bytecodes, serialized objects, help files, icons, and more, however, JAR was an obvious candidate for packaging beans. Details regarding the JAR manifest file and the precise use of JAR files for bean packaging are beyond the scope of this book and can be reviewed in [JB].

11

Enterprise Java Beans

In the push toward a balanced thin client, Java plays an important role. Java's characteristics as a language, however, make it an ideal candidate for building both Web-based clients as well as servers. Java's strengths are as important to the server side of applications as they are to the client side, and as the language matures, we will find it more and more on the server, rather than with the client. Its strengths as a good object-oriented language, such as its security capabilities, portability, and networking features, have made it an important player in the enterprise software market (on the server). However, due to Java's immaturity, application server developers were hesitant to use Java in this central role. It was clear by the end of 1997 that unless some structure was put in place for supporting issues such as transactions, security, and distribution, Java was going to become a language for writing applets (after which it was certain to disappear).

Enter *Enterprise Java Beans* (EJB). Just like building client software requires frameworks and standards to ensure that one can make use of others' tools and services, so do server-side components. Business logic on the server should focus on building domain functionality and not of systemic features such as transaction management and coordination or security policy enforcement. Since no serious application can do without a solution to each of these issues, a standard and API set was required to ensure that application components on the server can select solutions for system and architecture problems without limitations and without being locked into a single solution. This is what EJB is all about.

EJB defined a component model for the development and deployment of Java applications based on a multi-tier, distributed object architecture . . . Java currently has a component model called JavaBeans. Enterprise JavaBeans extends the JavaBeans component model to support server components. Server components are components that run on the server. In a multi-tier application architecture, most of an application's logic is moved from the client to one or more servers. A server component model simplifies the process of moving the logic to the server. The component model implements a set of automatic services to manage the component.

Enterprise JavaBeans
Server Component Model for Java
By Anne Thomas, Patricia Seybold Group, December 1997
Prepared for Sun Microsystems, Inc.

The importance of EJB stems from the fact that when building real systems, the work can be partitioned into two primary categories: domain-level application programming and system-level issues. Every software system developed at the department or enterprise level has two types of programmers: developers faced with the need to implement business logic and domain-specific functionality and developers who build an "infrastructure" that deals with issues such as transactions, security, and naming. EJB tries to separate these two categories and provides a framework in which application developers can focus on the domain functionality while using servers and containers built by specialists to solve their needs at the system level. In this form, not only can enterprise software developers save a lot of time, but they can also find solutions that are potentially far superior to those they would have received had they built the entire system themselves. EJB enables an "infrastructure" developed by "infrastructure vendors" to have a standard API and standard framework so that it can be used by multiple domain-level applications. The goals of the EJB architecture, as defined in the EJB specification, are as follows:

- To define a component architecture for the development of Java-based distributed business applications

- To enable the mixing of components built by different vendors to provide an enterprise-level solution

- To facilitate scenarios in which experts provide solutions for transactions, security, distribution, multi-threading, and other system-level issues in a way that can be easily used by domain experts building business applications

- To address the entire software lifecycle and provide definitions by which EJB components can be used within tools during development time (much like JavaBeans addresses both the runtime and the design time issues)

- To define aspects of interoperability. Specifically, EJB relies on CORBA for distributed object interoperability; this does not mean that EJB interoperability is only related to CORBA. Many other API mappings and transports are possible.

EJB Components

The EJB architecture provides a framework for building distributed, transaction-oriented components. Like JavaBeans, EJB is a component model and, as such, defines what the structure of an EJB component is as well as the world in which it lives. This second point is extremely important. A well-known thesis in philosophy is that in order to fully describe an entity, one must describe its surroundings and how it interacts with its environment. This is also the approach taken by the EJB architecture. An EJB component is a Java component that implements business logic. As a component living within the EJB world, it must assume a well-defined environment and a set of interactions in which it must participate. For example, the EJB architecture defines the notion of a container. In describing containers, the EJB specification defines the responsibilities of containers and EJB components in the context of components. It also fully defines the interaction between the container and the EJB component, thereby defining a structured world on which an EJB builder can rely. This brings the task of building EJB components and EJB-based systems a little closer to being an engineering discipline than an art, the ultimate purpose of the computer science field called software engineering.

The EJB architecture is inherently difficult in that it attempts to create a balance between various contradictory requirements. On the one hand, it attempts to create a strict framework for distributed, object-oriented systems so that many components can be easily created and assembled into larger systems. In this respect, the framework must be simple, clear, concise, and easy to use. On the other hand, the EJB architecture aims at large, robust, mission-critical systems that often have very specialized requirements and that push the envelope in many issues such as customization, performance, and throughput.

The balance afforded by the EJB architecture relies on the divide-and-conquer approach. The EJB architecture divides responsibilities typically found in systems into a number of roles. It then defines a modular architecture in which different entities fill these roles (the word "entities" is used instead of "components" simply because this is an overloaded word in the context of this chapter). Finally, it defines the interaction between these entities and the contracts each must conform to in order for the entire architecture to function correctly. The fundamentals of the definition of an EJB component's environment are as follows:

■ An enterprise bean is developed to implement business functionality.

■ An enterprise bean is not an island of its own. An enterprise bean lives within a container deployed within a server. The enterprise bean is never accessed directly; the container manages access to the enterprise bean's functionality. This enables the responsibility of managing things like transactions and security to be moved from the enterprise bean to the container and the server. For example, instance creation of the enterprise bean type is performed exclusively by the container. This allows the container to manage lifecycle and transaction issues for this class. Figure 11-1 illustrates the high-level relationships between an enterprise bean and a container.

■ Enterprise beans and containers are fully decoupled. This means that multiple EJB-compliant containers can be used to manage instances of an enterprise bean. All services provided to the enterprise bean by the container are well defined in the EJB specification. The specification allows for EJB containers and EJB servers to provide extended

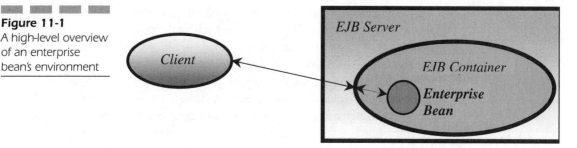

Figure 11-1
A high-level overview of an enterprise bean's environment

services. Enterprise beans that rely on such services may be limited in the range of EJB containers and servers they may run in.

■ An enterprise bean defines sets of properties that affect its runtime behavior. These properties are separated as metadata or descriptors in order to enable customization at setup and deployment time. This is similar in nature to the notion of design time customization in JavaBeans; the difference is mostly in the nature of the properties. Although JavaBeans properties are usually user interface-related, enterprise beans' properties involve control over transaction, distribution, security, and persistence.

In order for an EJB component to be used by client software, it must provide support for the following implementation issues:

■ *Object identity* The unique identifier that can be used to identify an object (not all enterprise beans have an object identity visible at the application level).

■ *Method invocation* Business methods form the contract between the enterprise bean and, ultimately, the client. The methods are grouped into an interface that forms the contract that must be satisfied by the bean developer.

■ *Home interface* Home interfaces are defined according to EJB type. Within a home, each bean can be identified using the primary key (if the bean has an application-level identity). Object lookup therefore involves two stages: locating the home interface and then using the primary key for locating a specific object. The home interface is stored by a naming service and the client can access it using the standard *Java Naming and Directory Interface* (JNDI). An enterprise bean's home interface extends the `javax.ejb.EJBHome` interface.

Client software never actually uses the enterprise bean directly and never accesses the bean's functionality without first going through an intermediary container. The container is involved since it is responsible for managing most of the system-level issues and must therefore constantly know what is happening to the enterprise bean. The effect is that each container of an enterprise bean must also support the API categories mentioned. This support usually requires some work of the container (for example, determining what the transaction bracket is and possibly changing it) and then delegating to the appropriate method in the enterprise bean.

A client using an enterprise bean can rely on the fact that it has a unique identifier. The responsibility for actually creating this identifier is sometimes that of the enterprise bean and sometimes that of the container. For example, if the bean represents a persistent domain object, it will provide the object identifier and the container will simply propagate this identity to the client's when asked. On the other hand, a bean can be a transient object that is used by the client for performing some tasks. Such an enterprise bean may be an extension of the client on the application server and may expire when the client is no longer using it. In this case, the bean's lifetime is cohesive with the client's and its identity is undefined as a property of the bean itself; the container may generate the object identity for use by the client (usually when it constructs the bean for the client).

Home interfaces define one or more `create` methods and zero or more `find` methods. Creation methods enable clients to create new instances of EJB components, and finder methods enable clients to look up a specific EJB. Both of these sets of methods must obviously be supported by the enterprise bean itself; for example, an enterprise beans developer must provide an `ejbCreate` method for each of the `create` methods, and an `ejbFind` method for each of the `find` methods defined by the home interface. In addition, the container provides system-level functionality that is accessed by the client; some of these require work to be done by the enterprise bean developer.

Since an enterprise bean lives within an EJB container, the EJB specification also precisely defines the APIs used by the container when managing the enterprise bean. The notion of a container is an important part of EJB since it enables an enterprise bean developer to rely on standard services that are taken care of by the container. The most important of these is lifecycle management. Although lifecycle management is the container's responsibility, it cannot do this without the full cooperation of the enterprise bean. This cooperation (or contract between the enterprise bean and its container) is defined in a set of interfaces that must be implemented by the enterprise bean. Specifically, an enterprise bean must implement a set of state management callbacks that is called by the container in order to notify the enterprise bean of important changes made as part of lifecycle operations. These interfaces are either `javax.ejb.SessionSynchronization` or `javax.ejb.EntityBean`, depending on whether the enterprise bean is a session bean or an entity bean. Other elements of this contract between an enterprise bean and its container include APIs through which a container can inform a bean on what its current context and environment are.

Finally, since EJB aims at the high-end market for component development, a standard mapping of enterprise beans' interfaces to CORBA exists. This opens up the EJB architecture, making it truly a multi-vendor, multi-language, and multi-platform architecture. The mapping for EJB to CORBA includes a number of important categories: the mapping of interfaces to CORBA IDL, the propagation of an EJB transaction bracket as an *Object Transaction Service* (OTS) transaction context, support for the naming service, and the propagation of security information within a security context. By defining the mapping in terms of these categories, EJB elevates itself to full semantic as well as wire-level interoperability.

Session Enterprise Beans

Enterprise beans are categorized into two groups: session enterprise beans and entity enterprise beans. The major distinguishing feature between these two groups is the notion of persistence. Session beans represent server-side components that implement business logic but are not persistent, while entity beans guarantee full persistence of their state. This section focuses on session beans; the next section discusses entity beans at length.

A session bean implements business logic on behalf of a client. The session bean is not persistent and is not shared by multiple clients; in this respect, it is a convenience mechanism for providing correct application partitioning. Application partitioning is an important concept in distributed computing that recognizes that business logic should often be performed at differing locations while continuing to support location transparency to the client software. A primary example of this is application partitioning as a facilitator of improved performance. Assume, for example, that a certain business function receives a small set of inputs and produces an output, but is very database-intensive while performing the function. Obviously, the

Figure 11-2a
Application
partitioning,
option 1

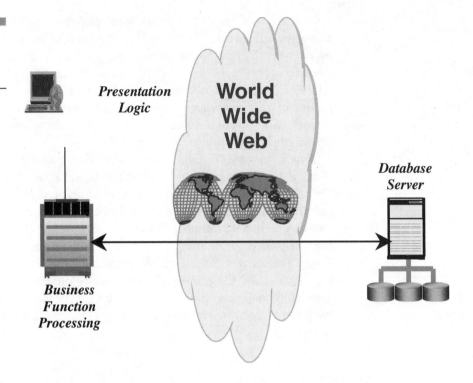

application partition shown in Figure 11-2a will not perform as well as the partition shown in Figure 11-2b. Session beans enable an application developer to partition the application in a way that some of the business logic processing occurs on the server *on behalf* of the client. The session bean is therefore a logical extension of the client process.

A session bean has an object identity, but as a non-persistent entity, its object identity is also not persistent. A session bean might therefore live for a while, providing service to some client, and later be reborn with a different identity. The object identity of a session bean is therefore never an application-meaningful descriptor; at best, it could be used by the client for temporary convenience functions (such as placing it within a hash table managed by the application). Please note that while the session bean may logically be reborn to provide services to the same client, it is in fact a different object with a different identity; it should not be confused with an entity object that can support a complex lifecycle. The session bean's identity cannot be used as a key and should, in principle, not be exposed to the client.

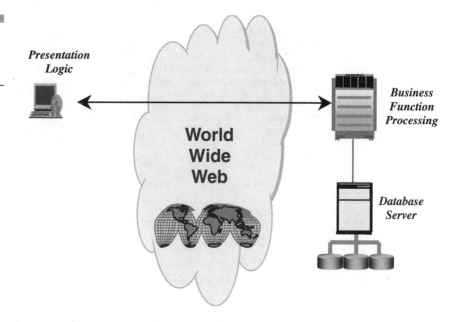

Figure 11-2b
Application
partitioning,
option 2

Access to a session bean's functionality is always through an object called an *EJB Object*. The EJB Object exposes a session bean's interface as a remote interface using Java RMI, possibly layered over CORBA IIOP. All calls made on the EJB Object are delegated to the enterprise bean. A user of a session bean's functionality does not have to be concerned about the precise location of the bean; RMI and CORBA will make the remote nature of the invocations transparent. In addition to delegating the domain-level method calls to the enterprise bean, an EJB Object provides a few methods for managing the EJB Object itself, such as object comparison.

Like all enterprise beans, a session bean too lives within an EJB container. The container manages the bean's lifecycle, access to the bean's methods, security, transactions, and more. The container also supports lookup via JNDI. Using a container's lookup function, a client can access the home interface of the enterprise bean. The home interface provides functions for creating new EJB Objects, removing an EJB Object, and accessing metadata information (implementing the `javax.ejb.EJBMetaData` interface) of the enterprise bean that is useful for tools during design time (similar to the `BeanInfo` object). For example, the code fragment required to create a new `PartOrder` object is shown in Listing 11-1. Note that the actual creation method (the constructor) is specific to the part order, but that all

Listing 11-1

Creating a new
PartOrder object

```
Context clientContext = new InitialContext();

PartOrderHome partOrderHome =
javax.rmi.PortableRemoteObject.narrow(
    clientContext.lookup("applications/services/parts/orders"),
    PartOrderHome.class);

PartOrder aPartOrder = partOrderHome.create(
    new Date(),                    // creation date
    "AT&T",                        // company name
    "Jane Doe",                    // person ordering
    ...);
```

creation methods are called using the home interface; the actual creation is always managed by the EJB container.

Figure 11-3 depicts a schematic view of the states a session bean will typically go through during its lifetime. A session bean is created when one of the home interface's creation methods is invoked. The enterprise bean is created on the server and an object (possibly remote) reference is returned to the caller (this is the EJB Object). The client can then start invoking methods using the bean's handle.

When the client is through with using the bean and wants to release it, one of the removal methods should be called to destroy the bean. Removal methods can be called using either the EJB Object or the home interface. In both cases, the result is the state in which the enterprise bean no longer exists but is still referenced by the client; the client should then release the reference. If the client uses the handle when the enterprise bean no longer exists, a NoSuchObjectException will be raised. If the client releases the reference before it calls one of the removal methods, then the enterprise bean will continue to exist until the server exits (either through a normal shutdown or a system crash). During that time, the client can reclaim the handle using a getEJBObject call to the EJB Object (the handle) that returns our state machine to the state in which the enterprise bean exists and is referenced.

Calls made through the EJB Object and through the container will ultimately reach the enterprise bean. A session enterprise bean should implement the following methods defined in the SessionBean Java interface:

- setSessionContext, which is used by the container to set a bean's context. The context is managed by the container. The

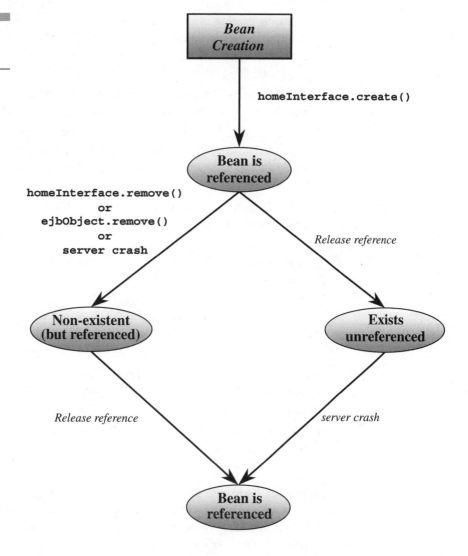

Figure 11-3
A session bean's
life cycle

SessionContext object provides the following functions that are used by the enterprise bean:

- getEJBObject, which returns the handle object
- getHome, which returns the home interface
- getEnvironment, which returns the environment properties
- getCallerIdentity, which returns the identity of the invoking client. This is a convenient function, allowing the bean to possibly configure its reply based on the identity of the calling object. For

example, pricing information may differ based on whether the ordering entity is an internal or external customer. A price book bean may therefore want to know details regarding the object that requested the pricing information.

- `isCallerInRole`, which provides a bean with a testing method for matching a caller with a certain role

- `setRollbackOnly`, which enables the bean to guarantee that the current transaction will not be committed and that any changes made within this transaction bracket must eventually be discarded by a rollback

- `getRollbackOnly`, which is a testing method returning a Boolean value indicating whether the transaction is marked as rollback only

- `getUserTransaction`, which returns the `javax.jts.UserTransaction`, providing direct access to the transaction and enables manual handling of transaction bracketing

■ `ejbRemove`, which is called by the container when it removes a bean, allowing the bean to perform any cleanup or finalization procedures. The container is responsible for managing the lifecycle for a bean. Since a session bean is not a persistent entity, such cleanup is usually simple.

■ `ejbPassivate`, which is called by the container when it intends to passivate a bean, allowing it to close resources or do miscellaneous preparations so that after reactivation its state will be correct

■ `ejbActivate`, which is called by the container when a bean is activated. The bean can then perform any inverse operations required to prepare its state.

A session bean can also implement additional methods defined in the `SessionSynchronization` interface. These methods provide synchronization hooks, allowing a session bean to tune its behavior with the context of a transaction. They are as follows:

■ `afterBegin`, which is called when a transaction begins

■ `beforeCompletion`, which is called before the commit stage begins but after the client has completed its work. This enables the bean to do any preparations before the commit.

■ `afterCompletion`, which is called after the transaction completes, whether by rollback or by successful commit (a flag is passed as an argument)

Although a session bean is not a persistent entity, it can still manage a state on behalf of its client; its non-persistent nature simply implies that this state will not persist after the bean is destroyed. Distributed object applications can be generally classified as conforming to one of two models: the stateless model and the stateful model. In a stateless model, the server does not maintain state on behalf of the client; during each invocation, the client must pass enough information to the server in order for the server to successfully perform the operation on behalf of the client. The HTTP Web model is stateless; each request made by a browser for information served by a Web server is independent and does not rely on previous requests. In a stateful model, the server maintains a session for the client and is aware of some state parameters regarding this client. Both models of distributed interaction are legitimate, each being more appropriate in different cases. Enterprise JavaBeans therefore supports both models.

When a session bean is deployed, it defines how it should be managed by its container. By specifying that the bean is stateless, the container is told that no conversational state needs to be maintained and that it is possible for the same bean to be used by multiple clients (none of the clients need to be aware of this fact since no state is managed within the server). Alternatively, the container may be told that the bean is stateful, in which case the container will manage the bean's conversational state on behalf of the client. Conversational state is defined as the bean's field values and every object that is reachable from one of these fields. Obviously, since object-based applications manage quite complex object graphs, this definition of the conversational state can easily include a large number of objects. Therefore, conversational state is not coupled with transaction support. A session bean's conversational state is not transactional and is not rolled back when a bean's transaction is rolled back. The bean developer is responsible for correctly managing conversational state in the context of transactions.

Please note that while session beans are not persistent, they may be transactional in the sense of operations being atomic. The only difference being that the transaction outcome is not guaranteed to be persistent (or durable, the fourth word in the transaction-defining acronym ACID: Atomicity, Consistency, Isolation, and Durability).

Stateless beans should be viewed as workers belonging to a pool of service providers. The assignment of workers to clients is arbitrary, and creating a new instance of a stateless bean will simply add to the pool. The only allowed creation method in the home interface for a stateless session bean is a creation method taking no arguments. The size of the worker pool is controlled by the container and is based on load parameters and availability times.

Stateful session beans have a much more elaborate lifecycle, as shown in Figure 11-4. A bean is created when a client invokes a `create` method on the home interface. The container then calls `newInstance` to create the

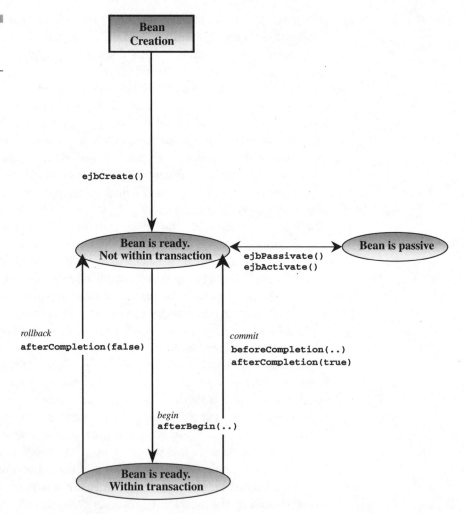

Figure 11-4
The lifecycle of a
stateful session bean

bean and sets the context using `setSessionContext`. Finally, `ejbCreate` is called and an EJB Object is returned to the client. The bean is then ready for use by the client.

As long as the client makes non-transactional calls, the bean stays in a non-transactional state. When a transactional method is called, the bean is included in a transaction and `afterBegin` is called, allowing the bean to perform any bean-specific handling. As long as other transactional methods are called, the bean stays in the transactional state. If a non-transactional method is called while the bean is in the transactional state, an error is flagged.

If the transaction is about to commit, the container makes the call `beforeCompletion` (which is guaranteed to be delivered before the actual commit). The same is true when the transaction is about to be rolled back. The end transaction status is passed as an argument to the `afterCompletion` call.

While the bean is in a non-transactional state, the container may decide to evict the bean from memory. In this case, it will call `ejbPassivate` to enable the bean to free up any resources it may be currently holding and prepare for its eviction. When the client later requests a service to be provided by this bean (recall that we are talking about stateful beans), the container will reactivate the bean and call the `ejbActivate` method, giving the bean a chance to prepare itself.

Entity Enterprise Beans

Entity enterprise beans represent an object stored in some form of persistent storage. Entity beans include states that can be saved between different uses of the object. As a persistent object, an entity bean has an object identity that is created at the same time that the object is created and is fixed throughout the object's lifetime. The identity can be used to lookup the object and serves as a primary key through which objects can be identified and compared.

Entity beans live within EJB containers that manage lifecycles, transactions, and security. In addition, containers manage the entity bean's persistence. Multiple clients may use the same entity bean concurrently. Synchronization is managed by the container in which the entity bean lives. A client accesses the entity bean by using the home interface that returns an EJB object that serves as the handle to the bean. In this respect, the framework for entity beans is identical to session beans. The rest of this section will therefore focus on the differences introduced by entity beans and will not reiterate on what is common to session beans.

Like session beans, entity beans require a home interface that provides access to creation methods and finder methods. Unlike session beans, a home interface of an entity beans must implement the method `findByPrimaryKey`. This method provides access to entity beans using a primary key; this is possible since an entity bean is a persistent object that is uniquely identified by the primary key. Typical examples include an account number, a part order number, and a country name. A key is itself an object and can made be of any type so long as it is serializable. Please note that a primary key is unique only within a home interface. The combination of a home interface and a primary key value is what uniquely identifies an object; in fact, if two objects have the same home interface and have the same key value, they are considered to be identical. The key is accessible by calling the getPrimaryKey() method implemented by the EJB object. Given two EJB objects, one can use obj1.isIdentical(obj2) to determine if they are identical.

As mentioned previously, an entity bean represents a persistent entity and is an application extension to an object residing in another system that takes care of the persistence details. Examples include an object that is stored within a relational database as a set of records or an object that interfaces with a legacy application that is responsible for the persistence details.

Two possibilities for entity bean persistence exist: bean-managed persistence and container-managed persistence. In the case of bean-managed persistence, the bean itself is responsible for implementing object persistence. For example, the bean developer may use JDBC or JSQL calls to implement load and save capabilities directly into the bean. In container-based persistence, the container performs database access on behalf of the bean. In order for the container to construct the appropriate data access calls, it requires descriptive metadata from the bean. The entity bean protocol calls for a containerManagedFields deployment descriptor to be provided by the entity bean.

Each of the persistence mechanisms have advantages and disadvantages. Bean-based persistence is obviously simpler to implement and conceptually clearer (anything involving two entities is inherently more complex than tasks that are performed by one party). However, bean-based persistence is hard-coded into the bean and cannot remain persistence-neutral. Container-based persistence delays the coupling with the data store until the bean is deployed in some container, thus making the entity bean inherently more reusable.

Figure 11-5 depicts the lifecycle of an entity enterprise bean. An entity bean is created when the container calls the newInstance method (after which the context is set by calling the setEntityContext method). At this point, the instance is part of a pool. It has been created but has not been associated with an EJB Object, nor does it have any distinguishing data; all instances in the pool are equivalent.

The next transition is to the ready state. This can be performed either by using an ejbCreate method or by calling an ejbActivate method, following an ejbFind method invocation. Immediately after calling an ejbCreate method, the container calls the ejbPostCreate method. At the time the ejbPostCreate method is called, the object identity is

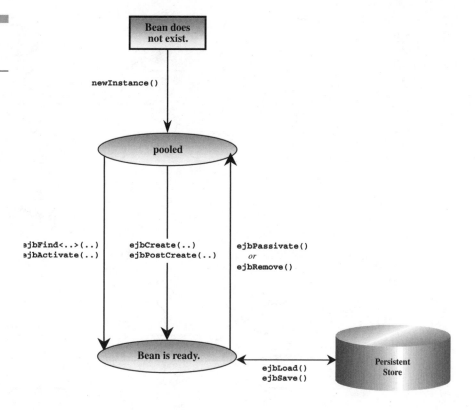

Figure 11-5
The lifecycle of an
entity bean

already available; the call enables the bean to take further action that may require the object identity. The first case discussed creates a new object to service the client, while the second enables using an existing object. Once entering the ready state, the container activates the `ejbLoad` method to retrieve the bean's data from its persistent store; after that, the container can periodically save the data using `ejbStore` or refresh the data using `ejbLoad`. When the work is complete, the bean transitions back to the pooled state using `ejbPassivate` or `ejbRemove`. Once back in the pool, the entity bean no longer has the object identity; the next time around it may be assigned to a new object.

Since entity beans represent domain objects, an entity bean can be accessed by two concurrent clients. Synchronization of concurrent access is one of the services provided to the bean user and bean developer by the container. It is the responsibility of the container to ensure correct synchronization between concurrent clients using the same entity bean.

Figure 11-6 illustrates the two possible management strategies. In the first case, the container manages two entity beans accessed through the

Figure 11-6
Managing
concurrent access to
an entity bean

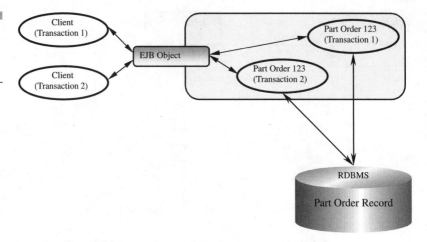

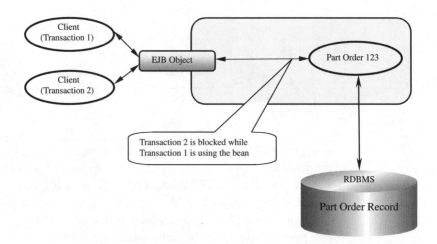

same EJB object. Each of the two beans lives within a different transaction context; each transaction belongs to a different client. Ultimate synchronization is performed by the data store when calling the `ejbLoad` and `ejbStore` methods. In the second case, the container manages exclusive access to the bean through the EJB Object. Only one bean exists and access to its functionality through the EJB Object is serialized. In most cases, the first scenario is preferable due to the following reasons:

- Better performance can be achieved.
- Database synchronization is usually more robust and has more features than container synchronization.

- In complex applications, the database is often used by additional modules, such as the reporting module and data extraction procedures. It is therefore much safer to rely on transaction and locking management at the database level than within the EJB world.

- Containers do not need to incorporate complex locking and serialization code.

The EJB Transaction Model

Support for distributed transaction is perhaps the primary feature making EJB attractive to enterprise software developers. Building support for distributed transactions into an application is a difficult task that is alleviated when using EJB. By moving the responsibility for managing transactions from the bean developer to the container and server provider, EJB simplifies application development and ensures that the difficult issues involving transactions are handled by experts.

EJB transaction support mirrors the CORBA *Object Transaction Service* (OTS) and supports the flat transaction model. OTS defines required support for a flat transaction model and optional support for nested transactions. Nested transactions enable transactions to be started within the context of another transaction. Each transaction manages its own change set. When a nested transaction is rolled back, all changes made within that nested transaction are discarded. If the nested transaction is committed, the changes made within the nested transaction become part of the enclosing transaction's change set (to be committed or rolled back by the enclosing transaction). In a nested model, the top-level transactions often correspond to the database transactions. In this case, the nested transactions are limited in that they are often not durable (that is, persistent), since right up until the moment when a top-level commit occurs, the information is not stored in the database. EJB transaction support stays with the flat transaction model; this decision is based on the fact that today's database systems and transaction monitors support the flat transaction model.

EJB uses the *Java Transaction Service* (JTS), and specifically the Java Transaction API. JTS maps the OTS API to the Java programming language (that is, it maps the OTS IDL definitions to Java using the IDL-to-Java language mapping). In addition, JTS is a Java mapping for the X/Open XA interface standard. The Java Transaction API provides a convenient set of Java interfaces to be used for transaction processing. Such conformance to standards ensures that JTS will remain the standard as far as transaction handling in Java.

The JTS `javax.transaction` package defines the application-level demarcation APIs, allowing transaction bracketing to be defined by the application developer. EJB relies on this interface, and more specifically on the `javax.transaction.UserTransaction` interface (the EJB container provider only needs to implement this interface). Bean developers and clients make demarcation calls using APIs in this package.

Transaction demarcation can be performed by the client, the bean, or the container. Demarcation performed by the container is the simplest, since both client and bean are oblivious to transactions. Obviously, the container must use policy information defined by the bean, since the container is a generic entity that must adapt its behavior to the bean. In the case of transactions, the bean defines a demarcation policy through the transaction attribute. The container uses the fact that access to bean functionality must go through the container in order to manage transaction demarcation. The actual decision of what to do is based on the transaction attribute defined by the bean. Note that the policy can be defined globally for the entire bean or for one bean method at a time; it is therefore possible for different transactional behaviors to occur for different methods. For example, a bean can set its transaction attribute to say that every method invocation must reside within its own transaction. In this case, the container will start up a new transaction for every call made on the bean and manage the propagation of that transaction context if the bean makes additional calls during the processing of the original invocation. This scenario is shown in Figure 11-7.

Possible transaction attribute values are as follows:

- `TX_NOT_SUPPORTED` By using this value, the bean notifies the container that it does not support transactions. Invocations coming through the container will not be within a transaction. The container guarantees this by suspending any transaction active during calls made on the bean.

- `TX_BEAN_MANAGED` This attribute is used by the bean when it intends to use explicit demarcation and wants to notify the container that it should not manage transactions on its behalf.

- `TX_REQUIRED` This is used by beans that want to ensure that any processing is performed within a transaction. If the call is made within a transaction started by a client, the bean invocation is performed within this transaction. Otherwise, the container is responsible for starting a transaction before handing control over to the bean. The container is also responsible for committing the transaction before returning control over to the caller.

Figure 11-7
An example of
container
demarcation

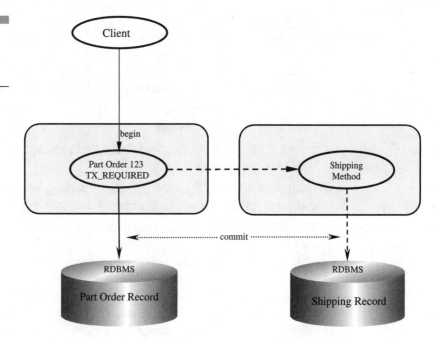

- TX_SUPPORTS   This is used by beans that want to be invoked within the same scope as the client. If the client has a transaction open when calling the bean, the bean performs within the transaction of the caller; otherwise, it will perform without an active transaction.

- TX_REQUIRES_NEW   Beans using this value inform their container that they need to be invoked within the scope of a new transaction. No matter what the transaction state of the client, the container will always open a new transaction that will be active throughout the operation of the bean. When the bean completes, the container commits the transaction and resumes the suspended client transaction.

- TX_MANDATORY   This is similar to TX_SUPPORTS in that the bean is activated within the transaction of the client. However, if a client without an open transaction tries to make the call, the exception TransactionRequired is raised. This attribute is used by beans that need to be invoked within the context of the client transaction but want to guarantee that they cannot be invoked without a transaction.

Another attribute that must be defined by beans in order for the container to manage transactions on its behalf is the transaction isolation level that controls the locking options for reads. These values mirror the options available in the `java.sql.Connection` interface. Possible values for transaction isolation levels are as follows:

- `TRANSACTION_READ_UNCOMMITTED` It is possible to read data that is marked as dirty (dirty reads); uncommitted data can be read.
- `TRANSACTION_READ_COMMITTED` Dirty reads are prevented; only committed data can be read.
- `TRANSACTION_REPEATABLE_READ` Dirty reads and non-repeatable reads are prevented.
- `TRANSACTION_SERIALIZABLE` Transactions are serialized; one transaction must complete in order for another to proceed.
- `TRANSACTION_NONE` No transaction is used.

Although container demarcation is certainly the simplest model for the client and bean developers, sometimes the set of possible values allowed as transaction attributes does not provide fine enough control over transaction demarcation. Both bean-managed and client-managed demarcation is allowed under the EJB transaction model. For bean-managed demarcation, the bean will be defined using the `TX_BEAN_MANAGED` transaction attribute (which will inform the container that it should not manage transactions on behalf of the bean). The bean can then use the `javax.transaction.UserTransaction` interface. Beans that do not define `TX_BEAN_MANAGED` as their transaction attribute are not allowed to make direct calls to the underlying transaction manager. Alternatively, the client itself can use the `javax.transaction.UserTransaction` interface to begin, commit, and rollback transactions.

Because the container and server can manage transactions, exceptions related to transactions can be raised—`TransactionRolledbackException`, `TransactionRequiredException`, and `InvalidTransactionException`. Any exception-handling mechanism is in general a mechanism designed for situations in which the error detector (the object that raises the exception) is a different object than the error handler (the object that catches the exception and can possibly try to take corrective measures). Therefore, raising an exception within the context of a container-managed transaction cannot automatically mean that the transaction must be marked for rollback only. It is quite possible that the client having caught the exception can fix the problem and continue with a follow-up call to the business method. The only case in which the client can assume that the current transaction has been marked for rollback is if the `TransactionRolledbackException` exception is raised. Alternatively, the exception handler can use the explicit test of `getRollbackOnly()` to verify the status of the active transaction. Beans that manage their own transaction processing (that use TX_BEAN_MANAGED) should use the setRollbackOnly() call before raising the exception, depending on whether the error that they have discovered is such that it should not allow the changes made thus far to commit.

The EJB Distribution Model

EJB targets large-scale distributed object applications. Distribution is therefore fundamental to the definition of EJB. Application programming in the EJB world involves building the enterprise beans and the clients using the business functionality implemented by the beans. The containers, servers, and other EJB infrastructure objects are provided by vendors and are used to simplify building the distributed applications. The EJB distribution model must therefore be simple enough so that applications programmers can use it, yet powerful enough to build mission-critical and large-scale applications.

In order to do so, the EJB distribution model uses a proven distribution technology based on proxies and object stubs. The EJB distribution model is not a new model; it uses standard Java RMI based on the CORBA distribution model. Distribution transparency is complete from both sides. Enterprise bean functionality can be accessed locally or remotely and clients can access enterprise beans with no regard to their actual physical location. Neither the client nor the enterprise bean is aware of its peer's location.

The Java RMI stubs created involve the EJB Object and the home interface object. Since the EJB Object is the interface object through which functionality is accessed, it is only natural for it to be the object for which a Java RMI stub is created. In addition, the home interface gets its own RMI stub; this is necessary to initiate the connection with the enterprise bean (either through creation or a finder process). Using Java RMI as the stubs and interfaces for supporting distribution in EJB does not infer the underlying wire-level protocol. In fact, the preferred solution for EJB in terms of the network protocol is CORBA IIOP. By using IIOP, EJB ensures that its distribution model remains interoperable and open to interfacing with non-Java objects and legacy systems. The basing of EJB on CORBA IIOP is quite natural; after all, the distribution model is identical, EJB transactions are based on the CORBA OTS model, and both use the same object model. Even the naming issue is resolved by mapping the CORBA naming service, which is part of the *Common Object Services* (COS), to the JNDI API. Finally, EJB security (discussed in the next section) is mapped to CORBA security using CORBA::Principal for mapping the user ID, IIOP over

SSL for client authentication and encryption, and the SECIOP-Secure IIOP for mapping to a specific security mechanism, such as GSSKerberos.

EJB Security

As in transactions, the primary goal of EJB in terms of its security infrastructure is to provide a set of interfaces that enable the responsibility of implementing security to be moved from the enterprise bean developer to the container and server implementor. This does not mean that an enterprise bean cannot control security; it means that mechanisms are provided so that the typical enterprise bean can declaratively define what its security attributes are, allowing the implementation details to be handled by the server and container. As in transactions, this is achieved through a set of security attributes used at deployment time.

Through the `AccessControlEntry` attribute, a bean defines rules for defining an access control policy. An `AccessControlEntry` can be defined per method or for the entire bean. Methods that do not have their own access control entries assume the access control value associated with the bean as a whole. Each access control entry defines a list of authorized users; each authorized entry being of type `java.security.Identity`, the standard interface in Java used for access control identification and authorization.

Additional deployment attributes related to security include the attributes `RunAsMode` and `RunAsIdentity`. The `RunAsMode` defines the security identity that will be propagated when the bean makes additional calls while servicing a client request. Possible values that may be assumed by this attribute are as follows:

- `CLIENT_IDENTITY`   This value is used when the call made by the bean should assume the security information of the client making the original call; the bean servicing the second call will think that the original client made the call (in terms of security). This is shown in Figure 11-8.

Figure 11-8
CLIENT_IDENTITY

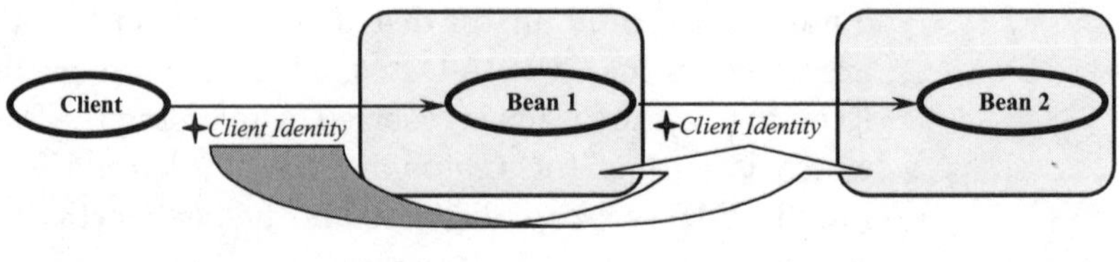

- ■ SYSTEM_IDENTITY   The call will use the identity of a privileged system account.
- ■ SPECIFIED_IDENTITY   The call will be made using a specific user account.

The RunAsIdentity attribute is relevant only when the RunAsMode attribute has a SPECIFIED_IDENTITY; in this case, it defines the actual user identity to be used when making the second call.

12

The Extensible Markup Language (XML)

The *eXtensible Markup Language* (XML) is one of the most important developments in the IT world that is taking the world by storm today. Everywhere you look you see vendors and developers scurrying to XML, and for good reason. XML is a standard developed by the W3C to forward the notion of data sharing and formatting over the Web. In general, it supports the notion of tagged data in a way that preserves the semantics of the domain. XML is an application (or subset) of the *Standard Generalized Markup Language* (SGML), but is much simpler to deal with. It is more powerful than HTML and, in fact, HTML can be phrased as an application (or subset) of XML (hence XHTML). Therefore, XML is just the right combination of SGML's powerful expression options with HTML's simplicity and is already slated to become the "lingua franca" of the Web. Obviously, this will take time, but we are quite certain that it will be a dominant player in the future of the Web. In addition, it also promises much in other areas such as business-to-business applications, EDI, document management, and so on.

XML is the center of intensive research and development both within the W3C and throughout the industry. As a standard, it is the basis for many other standards that are being developed by the W3C, standards such as the *eXtensible Linking Language* (XLL), the *Document Object Model* (DOM), the *Simple API for XML* (SAX), and the *eXtensible Style Language* (XSL). All of these specifications can be found in the W3 site at www.w3.org.

XML is already an important technology used for e-business applications and we are sure this trend will accelerate very quickly to the point where XML and e-business are almost synonymous. Even today, the number of applications of XML is pretty amazing. The sources for the applications of XML include not only the W3C and even go well past the vendors.

For example, the *Financial Products Markup Language* (FpML) is an application of XML that deals with descriptions of financial products such as derivatives, swaps, and so on. It is being developed by J.P. Morgan and PricewaterhouseCoopers and is being distributed under the Mozilla license. An obvious question is why J.P. Morgan would publish work that it has invested in internally (in order to create a technological advantage) and that could be now picked up by its competitors. The answer is obviously not because the people involved are "nice" (although in this specific case, this is very true). It is all about the new paradigm that is being created by the Web and e-business, a paradigm that is based on open standards than enables services and systems that were never possible before. XML is leading this charge and it is therefore not surprising that the number of applications of XML to various markets is growing every day. Therefore, we feel it is an important technology to cover in this book. Apparently, the WebSphere creators felt the same way, since they packaged IBM's XML technology with the WebSphere server.

This chapter provides a review of what we feel to be the most important XML-related technologies to e-business applications. We will cover XML, DOM, SAX, and XSLT (the subset of XSL that deals with transformations, as opposed to the second part that deals with format objects). We hope to provide a solid understanding of these issues so that in Chapters 34 through 36 we can cover some specific examples.

XML

The beginning of XML occurred way back in 1996 with a working group chaired by Jon Bosak of Sun. XML was designed as a subset of SGML with the following goals in mind:

- XML needs to be simple to use on the Internet.
- XML needs to support a wide variety of applications.
- XML must be such that building software to process XML documents should be a simple task.
- XML documents must be readable to humans in its native form.
- Creating an XML document should be a simple task.

In fact, one may say that the design goal of XML is to be a subset of SGML (and therefore maintain its powerful feature set), but be simple to use.

XML is a format in which documents are structured. Therefore, the primary entity described by the XML standard is the XML document. Each XML document has a physical structure and is composed of entities. Each XML document has exactly one entity called the *root entity*; all other entities must belong to the root entity. Entities are defined by a start tag and an end tag much like many elements in HTML. When one entity is embedded in another, the start and end tags of the embedded entity must both reside within the start and end tags of the embedding entity. For example, if we want to describe a contact that has a phone number, then the entities can be embedded as follows:

```
<contact>
    <name>Jane Doe</name>
    <phone>201-861-7533</phone>
</contact>
```

An empty tag, an element in which there is no data, can be specified either using start and end tags with nothing in between or using a simple self-closing start tag. For example, a contact can have two alternative phone numbers, and if they are empty, we can use the following XML entity:

```
<contact>
    <name>Jane Doe</name>
    <phone>201-861-7533</phone>
    <altPhone1></altPhone1>
    <altPhone2/>
</contact>
```

XML documents include entities of many types. Most entities reflect the information embedded within the XML document and the semantics of the domain being described by the document.

Many other elements comprise a typical XML document. For example, comments can be embedded into XML documents using a syntax familiar to HTML developers:

```
<!- note that the <contact> here is not really a tag; it
is part of the comment and will be ignored by applications,
parsers, and other XML tools (except to view it as a comment) ->
```

The most fundamental concept of XML (and where its name comes from) is that the tag set in XML is not fixed, but rather extensible (duh!). What this means is that different applications of XML define their own tag sets and in effect create a new language for describing elements in a certain domain. This is a powerful notion since it means that instead of trying to box every type of information using the same set of descriptive rules, we are now free to build "languages" that are well fitted for that particular domain. Still, if we "invent" a new language every time, we must make sure that the rules of this language are well known to anyone trying to use this XML document (just as we need to learn grammar and vocabulary before we can start using a language).

XML has also introduced the notion of a *Document Type Declaration* (DTD). A DTD describes the rules of the tag set used by an XML document. It specifies the available tags and how they may or may not be composed together. A typical XML document can then include the DTD in the document so that readers (especially tools and programs) know how to interpret and validate the document. Note that DTDs are not mandatory and many XML documents do not include DTDs. In fact, there is a movement away from DTDs in which the description of the new language is itself phrased in XML, but this is outside the scope of this chapter.

Elements have attribute sets. An attribute is associated with an element by adding the attributes and their values as part of the start tag. Attributes are used to describe the element, or define its inherent properties. This is sometimes confused with additional tags that are embedded in the entity. It is easy to understand the difference between these two if one views the XML as a description of an object model. In this case, the equivalent difference is that between the properties of an object and the other objects it references. Attributes are defined as part of the DTD and can be defined to be mandatory, have default values, and much more. For example, if we need to add an attribute to the contact entity specifying a "VIP level," we could use the following XML:

```
<contact vipLevel="6">
        <name>Jane Doe</name>
        <phone>201-861-7533</phone>
        <altPhone1></altPhone1>
        <altPhone2/>
</contact>
```

The Document Object Model (DOM)

The *Document Object Model* (DOM) is an API for HTML and XML documents. It provides a programmatic paradigm to access the objects represented by the document. Interfaces are provided for building documents, navigating documents and entities within the documents, view and edit attributes, and practically anything that you might require in a document. DOM is also a standard defined and supported by the W3C. By promoting it as a standard, the W3C wants to assure a standard API for managing XML and HTML documents that will enable developers to build portable code and further promote XML.

Each XML (and HTML) document can be parsed and broken down into a hierarchical structure of objects. This is fundamentally what DOM does; it defines how forests (sets of trees) are created from XML documents (and vice versa). Since the tree structures are objects defined by DOM, an API is provided for manipulating these trees and the document. Since DOM is primarily an API for manipulating these objects, it is phrased in CORBA IDL. Since IDL is a specification language that can then be mapped to multiple programming languages, the DOM APIs can be processed to create sets of libraries in many programming languages, all the while maintaining a single consistent API.

DOM originated from HTML. It was originally built to provide an object model that could be used by developers building client-side applications (in JavaScript, for example) for browsers. It has since evolved considerably, but still has very extensive definitions for HTML objects and objects that are common in the browser. Therefore, the DOM specification has two main parts: the definition of a set of core interfaces (which match XML) and a set of interfaces specifically for HTML objects. Some of the main interfaces provided by DOM for XML are as follows:

■ Document   This represents the entire XML or HTML document. This interface has attributes such as `docType`, `implementation`, `documentElement`, and methods such as `createElement`, `createDocumentFragment`, `createTextNode`, `createComment`, `createCDATASection`, `createAttribute`, `createEntityReference`.

- Node   The primary object for the entire DOM. Recall that the DOM is fundamentally a tree; each element is therefore a node. A node has attributes such as nodeType, parentNode, childNodes, firstChild, lastChild, previousSibling, nextSibling, ownerDocument, and methods such as insertBefore, replaceChild, removeChild, appendChild, and hasChildNodes.

- Attr   This represents an attribute in an element (those things that are inserted into the start tag when building the XML). Attributes in DOM are also nodes, so the tree that is created in DOM is one that includes both the elements and the attributes. Therefore, an element having embedded elements and attributes will be mapped into a node in the DOM tree that has child nodes for the embedded elements, but will also have an additional relationship with nodes that represent the attributes.

- Element   This is a node that represents the tagged objects in the document. This is by far the most common type of node encountered when traversing the tree structure. The element interface inherits from the node interface and adds methods such as getAttribute, setAttribute, removeAttribute, getAttributeNode, setAttributeNode, removeAttributeNode, and getElementsByTagName.

- Comment   This represents a comment in the document.

In addition, there is a set of interfaces that is specific to HTML objects. These include the following:

- HTMLDocument, which adds attributes such as title, URL, body, images, applets, links, forms, anchors, cookie, and methods such as open, close, getElementById, and getElementsByName

- HTMLElement, which inherits from Element (from the first category) and adds attributes such as id, title, lang, dir, and className

- HTMLHeadElement, which inherits from HTMLElement and represents the HEAD for the HTML document

- HTMLLinkElement, which adds attributes such as href, rel, rev, target, and type

- HTMLTtitleElement

- HTMLStyleElement

- HTMLBodyElement, which adds attributes such as aLink, background, bgColor, link, text, and vLink

- ■ `HTMLFormElement`, which adds attributes such as `action`, `method`, and `target` and methods such as `submit` and `reset`
- ■ `HTMLSelectElement`, which adds attributes such as `selectedIndex`, `value`, `form`, `options`, `disabled`, and `name` and methods such as `add`, `remove`, `blur`, and `focus`
- ■ `HTMLInputElement`, which adds attributes such as `defaultValue`, `defaultChecked`, `form`, `accept`, `align`, `checked`, `disabled`, `value`, and methods such as `blur`, `focus`, `select`, and `click`
- ■ `HTMLTextElement`, which adds attributes such as `form`, `disabled`, `rows`, `tabIndex`, `type`, and `value` and methods such as `blur`, `focus`, and `select`
- ■ `HTMLButtonElement`, which adds attributes such as `form`, `name`, `disable`, and `value`
- ■ `HTMLLabelElement`, which that adds attributes such as `form` and `htmlFor`
- ■ `HTMLUListElement` for UL elements
- ■ `HTMLOListElement` for UL elements
- ■ `HTMLDListElement` for DL elements
- ■ `HTMLLIElement` for LI elements
- ■ `HTMLHeadingElements` for H1 to H6 elements
- ■ `HTMLPreElemement` for PRE elements
- ■ `HTMLBRElement` for BR elements
- ■ `HTMLFontElement` for FONT elements in HTML 4.0
- ■ `HTMLHRElement` for HR elements
- ■ `HTMLAnchorElement` for A elements and adds attributes such as `href` and `target`
- ■ `HTMLImageElement` for IMG elements adding attributes such as `name`, `align`, `alt`, `height`, `isMap`, `src`, and `width`
- ■ `HTMLAppletElement` for APPLET elements adding attributes such as `archive`, `code`, `codebase`, `height`, `object`, and `width`
- ■ `HTMLMapElement` for MAP elements
- ■ `HTMLScriptElement` for SCRIPT elements in HTML 4.0 with attributes such as `event`, `src`, and `type`
- ■ `HTMLTableElement`, which adds attributes such as `tHead`, `tFoot`, `rows`, `align`, `bgColor`, `border`, and `frame` and methods such as

createTHead, deleteTHead, createTFoot, deleteTFoot, createCaption, insertRow, and deleteRow

- A bunch of elements such as HTMLTableCaptionElement, HTMLTableColElement, HTMLTableSectionElement, HTMLTableRowElement, and so on
- HTMLFrameElement for FRAME elements
- HTMLFrameSetElement for FRAMESET elements

The Simple API for XML (SAX)

DOM provides the capabilities for processing any XML document. You, as the programmer, can use the DOM APIs to build the tree structures for the XML document and then traverse the trees to manipulate the elements, extract information, or do any other kind of processing. However, this can sometimes be highly inefficient. For example, if the XML document represents all the contacts that the company has, the XML will certainly be a very large document. If we need to parse this document, build the trees, and then traverse them, we might be in for a long wait. If we really need to go through all of the elements in the XML document, we have no choice and the solution provided by DOM is probably as efficient as any. However, if all we need to do is do some processing for a subset of the elements (and potentially a much smaller set), then there is another better alternative.

SAX is an event-based API for processing XML documents. Being event-based means that SAX provides a way for an application developer to express interest in certain elements without requiring all elements to be pre-built before beginning the application-level processing. This has the benefit that structures that are not necessary will not be built; instead, a callback into the application code will be called whenever any interesting event occurs. Note that SAX is not only much more efficient when we need to process a subset of the elements, but it can be a useful tool if we need to process very large XML documents (for example, tens or even hundreds of MBs). In this case, even if we do need to process all elements, we may run into memory problems because building so many objects can be very memory-intensive. SAX, on the other hand, does not need to build anything; processing is done in real-time, as opposed to a number of passes.

Using SAX is simple. It involves two stages. First, we need to use the SAX APIs to define what we are interested in. For example, we may say that we are interested in the contact names only, or, in a larger context, in the contacts that should be renewed this month. Once we've defined this, we can go ahead and fire up the parser that will parse the XML document. As the parser goes through the XML document, it comes across the element tags and generates events (such as START ELEMENT CONTRACT, END ELEMENT CONTRACT, START ELEMENT CONTACT, and so on). Some of these events will be of no interest to us and so nothing will happen; the parser will continue with its job. When an event occurs that we have expressed an interest in, the event will cause the application callback to be called and processing of that particular element can begin.

As is clear from the previous description, using SAX is only possible if we use a SAX-enabled parser. Since the parser will need to traverse the tree and generate events, it must obviously know how to do this. SAX defines a package called `org.xml.sax` that has a number of interfaces such as `Parser`, `AttributeList`, and `Locator`. A SAX-enabled XML tool needs to implement these interfaces in this package in order to support SAX processing.

SAX defines another set of interfaces in the `org.xml.sax` package that needs to be implemented by the application developer. This set includes the following:

- `DocumentHandler` An interface that defines the methods and through which the parser notifies the application of events that have occurred. This is the most important interface from the point of view of the application developer.

- `ErrorHandler` An interface that is used for calling application-level code when some error occurs while processing the document

XSL Transformations (XSLT)

XSL Transformations (XSLT) is a subset of XSL (actually one half, the second half being the formatting language) that defines a language for transforming XML documents into other XML documents. XSLT is very important in the XML grand scheme. XML documents are based on a certain tag set defined by the creator of the XML document. It will often be the case that two parties that want to exchange data in the form of XML documents do not completely agree on the tag set. In this case, it is often feasible to perform a mapping between the two XML tag sets using XSLT.

XSLT is itself an application of XML that defines a tag set, allowing the definition of transformation rules. These rules define how a source tree constructed from an XML document is processed into a result tree that can then be used to generate the resulting XML document. Each transformation rule has a pattern and a template. The pattern is matched up with the source tree to identify the constructs that are identified by this rule, the base for the transformation. Once the pattern has been matched, the template is applied to the source tree to create an element of the result tree. Obviously, all this is performed recursively, so while applying the template, other transformation rules can also be involved. Templates can be quite involved and XSLT has a lot of expressive power when it comes to the templates. Tree elements can be created either independently or based on the source tree. Apart from the large number of element types that XSLT defines, one can always use processing instructions that are also supported by XSLT.

Each rule has a pattern. This pattern defines when the rule is valid and can be applied to the source tree to create the result tree. Patterns have expressions that are based on the XPath specifications. These expressions select the node that is appropriate for processing. For example, an expression can include conditions on nodes (for example, the type of node), on attributes of the node, on the ancestors of the nodes, on the descendants of the nodes, or any combination.

Once an expression has been evaluated, causing the template to be matched, processing of the template begins. When the expression is matched, a current node is always identified. This node is the one matched by the pattern. All processing of the template is based on this node. For example, if we include a directive to traverse all subnodes, then this will apply to the node matched by the expression.

XSLT is a complex language and one that takes a long time to fully understand and learn. We will not go over all features of this language, since XSLT deserves a book itself. The interested reader is referred to www.w3.org/TR/WD-xslt where more details can be found.

We will conclude this chapter with a simple example in which we transform a XML document describing trade counterparts (using a simple document based on FpML, shown in Listing 12-1) to an HTML table. The XSLT stylesheet is shown in Listing 12-2 and the resulting HTML in Listing 12-3. The output page is shown in Figure 12-1.

Listing 12-1
The FpML example

```xml
<?xml version="1.0" standalone="no"?>
<!- Copyright (c) 1999 by J.P.Morgan and PricewaterhouseCoopers.
PricewaterhouseCoopers refers to the individual member firms of
the world
wide PricewaterhouseCoopers organization. All rights reserved.
->
<!- version 1.0b2 : August 6, 1999 ->
<fpml:FpML xmlns:fpml="urn:fpml-FpML"
 xmlns:t="urn:fpml-type"
 xmlns:d="urn:fpml-date"
 xmlns:m="urn:fpml-money"
 xmlns:r="urn:fpml-rate">

<fpml:Trade>
 <fpml:tradeIDs>
  <tid:TradeIDs xmlns:tid="urn:fpml-TradeID">
   <tid:TradeID>
    <tid:partyReference>ABC Trust</tid:partyReference>
    <tid:transactionReferenceNumber>237732</
tid:transactionReferenceNumber>
   </tid:TradeID>
   <tid:TradeID>
    <tid:partyReference>XYZ Group</tid:partyReference>
    <tid:transactionReferenceNumber>1230</
tid:transactionReferenceNumber>
   </tid:TradeID>
   <tid:TradeID>
    <tid:partyReference>CDF Inc.</tid:partyReference>
    <tid:transactionReferenceNumber>237732</
tid:transactionReferenceNumber>
   </tid:TradeID>
   <tid:TradeID>
    <tid:partyReference>TUV Ltd.</tid:partyReference>
    <tid:transactionReferenceNumber>1230</
tid:transactionReferenceNumber>
   </tid:TradeID>
   <tid:TradeID>
    <tid:partyReference>MNO LLC</tid:partyReference>
    <tid:transactionReferenceNumber>237732</
tid:transactionReferenceNumber>
   </tid:TradeID>
   <tid:TradeID>
    <tid:partyReference>HIJ.com</tid:partyReference>
    <tid:transactionReferenceNumber>1230</
tid:transactionReferenceNumber>
   </tid:TradeID>
  </tid:TradeIDs>
 </fpml:tradeIDs>
</fpml:Trade>


</fpml:FpML>
```

```xml
<?xml version="1.0"?>

<xsl:stylesheet
    xmlns:xsl="http://www.w3.org/XSL/Transform/1.0"
      xmlns="http://www.w3.org/TR/REC-html140"
    xmlns:fpml="urn:fpml-FpML"
    xmlns:tid="urn:fpml-TradeID"
    result-ns=""
      indent-result="yes">


<xsl:template match="fpml:Trade">
  <HTML><BODY>
  <H3>Trade Counterparts</H3>
  <TABLE BORDER="1">
   <TR align="center" bgcolor="CCCCCC">
    <TD>Party Name</TD>
    <TD>Ref.#</TD>
   </TR>
    <xsl:apply-templates/>
  </TABLE>
  </BODY></HTML>
</xsl:template>

<xsl:template match="fpml:TradeIDs">
    <xsl:apply-templates/>
</xsl:template>

<xsl:template match="tid:TradeID">
  <TR>
   <xsl:apply-templates/>
  </TR>
</xsl:template>

<xsl:template match="tid:transactionReferenceNumber">
  <TD>
   <xsl:apply-templates/>
  </TD>
</xsl:template>

<xsl:template match="tid:partyReference">
  <TD>
   <xsl:apply-templates/>
  </TD>
</xsl:template>

</xsl:stylesheet>
```

Figure 12-1
The resulting
HTML page

Listing 12-3
The resulting HTML
code

```
OCTYPE html PUBLIC "-//W3C//DTD HTML 4.0 Transitional//EN">


<HTML>
<BODY>
<H3>Trade Counterparts</H3>
<TABLE BORDER="1">
<TR align="center" bgcolor="CCCCCC">
<TD>Party Name</TD>
<TD>Ref.#</TD>
</TR>


<!D    <TR>
    <TD>ABC Trust</TD>
    <TD>237732</TD>
  </TR>
  <TR>
    <TD>XYZ Group</TD>
    <TD>1230</TD>
```

continues

Listing 12-3
Continued

```
   </TR>
   <TR>
    <TD>CDF Inc.</TD>
    <TD>237732</TD>
   </TR>
   <TR>
    <TD>TUV Ltd.</TD>
    <TD>1230</TD>
   </TR>
   <TR>
    <TD>MNO LLC</TD>
    <TD>237732</TD>
   </TR>
   <TR>
    <TD>HIJ.com</TD>
    <TD>1230</TD>
   </TR>


</TABLE>
</BODY>
</HTML>
```

13

Java Security and Web Security

This chapter is meant to be a very high-level introduction to Java security and other security schemes common in e-business applications. The issue of security is a very broad one and is very central to the very existence of Web applications. Our intent in including this chapter in this book is merely to make you familiar with some of these concepts. If this topic sparks your interest, the number of good books dealing exclusively with this matter abound.

Recall that Java was described as a "portable and interpreted, distributed, reliable, robust and *secure*, high-performance and threaded, simple, dynamic, and object-oriented programming language supporting run-time environments." We will therefore start with a discussion of the security features that are built into the Java programming language.

Java was designed from scratch to be secure. As a language that was intended for building robust distributed systems that could be deployed over the Web, it had to be designed with security in mind—anything else would have rendered Java useless for real over-the-Web systems. Java supports security from the ground up. Coupled with an extensive set of security-related services provided by newer releases of either the JDK or of support packages, Java is uniquely capable in terms of making distributed Web objects a reality.

Java security is made up of many features. First off, Java as a programming language is defined in a way that eliminates using language features to break into systems written in Java. Java eliminates the notion of pointers and hides the physical layout of memory and constructs from the programmer. Programmers may therefore not use the language itself to break the language. Java is type-safe and casting exceptions are flagged, thus eliminating hacking within the type system. Such properties of the Java programming language are not only crucial to eliminating bugs and making the programming model simpler to use, they also help to make Java safer from hackers.

Although such language features are helpful in making the language more secure, they certainly cannot ensure security on their own. In fact, probably no set of features, services, or capabilities can guarantee security in a Web environment—attackers are ingenious, innovative, and motivated. However, as we shall see in this chapter, Java supplies extremely useful and all-encompassing security features that, together with sets of conventions and human intervention, can certainly make Web applications a reality.

The Java Security Model

Security is an inherent part of the Java programming environment. Security features were incorporated into the first release of the Java JDK. Apart from the type safety enforcement of the Java compilers and the decoupling of the logical structure from the physical implementation, the basic Java model enforces security through four primary enablers:

- *The sandbox model* The sandbox model is perhaps the most well known part of the Java security model, and certainly one of the most important ones. Java takes an approach that is very different from conventional operating environments. In most operating systems, for example, applications have access to all resources in the systems— files, printers, the network, and so on. In Java, untrusted code that is downloaded from the Web runs within a very confined environment called the *sandbox*. By confining the untrusted code and severely limiting the resources to which it has access, any malicious behavior can be contained to doing harm only within this sandbox. Note that the ability to support such a model is made possible by Java's virtual machine approach.

■ *The class loader*　Java dynamically loads class files as required by a running program. When working on the Web, these class files are downloaded from the originating Web site and dynamically added to the working environment (similar in some respects to dynamic loading of DLLs). However, this loading is performed by a specific object—the class loader. This object forms the first line of defense because it controls and limits what is being loaded, from where, and when. Class loaders enforce name space rules and ensure that inappropriate classes are not loaded (for example, they do not allow other class loaders that may incorporate security breaches in them to be loaded).

■ *The byte code verifier*　The verifier is used before the code is actually executed. Untrusted code that is loaded by the class loader must go through a verification process that "proves" that the bytecodes loaded represent Java code that adheres to all rules of the language. Because bytecodes are the "machine language" of the JVM, and because the party loading the code does not know who created the bytecodes (nor how), the security model must make sure that the bytecodes do not hide a dangerous breach of the internal Java type enforcement. The verifier ensures that access restrictions are maintained, that illegal casting is not performed, and that memory access is not forged.

■ *The security manager*　The security manager controls runtime access to resources including the internal objects that form the security framework in Java. For example, the security manager will not allow for untrusted code to create class loaders that may potentially be used to circumvent the security provided by that layer. Access to physical resources such as sockets, files, and so must all be okayed by the security manager. The security manager is the sandbox's watchdog.

The Java Sandbox

The Java sandbox is the "playground for untrusted code." It defines the environment in which untrusted code runs and ensures that the code (for example, a downloaded applet) cannot break out of this confined space and do harm to the client machine. It gives the applet or other downloaded code all the capabilities it might require without allowing it to access external components in the system. This sandbox metaphor makes the JVM (and only parts of the JVM) the entire world of the applet.

The sandbox model is enforced by the class loader, the byte-code verifier, and the security manager. It defines the invariants and assertions that must always exist within the JVM state machine. Any state that might be reached when handing control over to untrusted code must remain within the confines of the Java sandbox model. The Java sandbox model defines the following transitions of the JVM state machine as fundamental to Java security:

- When a class loader's constructor is called, the security manager object is called to verify that the thread can create a class loader. This ensures that untrusted code cannot create additional class loaders (even if bytecodes were tampered with).
- The next state is entered when the JVM calls the class loaders method to load a class. First, any system classes are found using the class loader's findSystemClass method—thereby ensuring that untrusted code cannot masquerade as system code.
- After the code is loaded, the verifier is called to validate the code. The verifier makes sure that the code conforms to syntactic and structural rules. Static members are initialized with default values.
- The class loader then maps the loaded class into the namespace it is maintaining.

Obviously, the notion of the sandbox (assuming there are no bugs and security holes in the implementation of the sandbox) is an excellent idea. It allows you as a user to download untrusted applets and run them on your client with no worries. This is drastically different than other models, for example, ActiveX, in which you must rely on the creator of the downloaded code and its digital signature. In all fairness, it is important to mention that the sandbox model is sometimes overly restrictive. In these cases, digital signatures are used to allow some code to be "more trusted than others." In such cases, the security model is is many respects similar to that of ActiveX.

The sandbox as defined in JDK 1.0x is extremely restrictive. For example, applets downloaded from untrusted sources do not have access to system resources, system properties, and so on. These restrictions may cause such programs to be almost useless. If this occurs, developers and users will be faced with the option of either bypassing the sandbox model (thus making their system extremely insecure) or depriving applications of necessary functionality.

Luckily, there is a solution to this dilemma. The solution is based on the notion of defining a model in which finer control is provided in determining what is and what is not allowed. Specifically, JDK 1.1 (to some extent) and JDK 1.2 allow for different levels of trust to be defined. Such levels can be defined at the client side based on digital signatures, thus allowing signed downloaded code to run within various virtual sandboxes—each with a different set of available resources and permissions.

The Class Loader

Class loaders are responsible for mapping class names to Java bytecodes, loading the appropriate bytecodes from the class files, and calling the verifier if necessary. These responsibilities are crucial to maintaining the security invariants, thus making class loaders part of Java's first line of defense.

The JDK defines the class loader as an abstract class (that is, it cannot be instantiated). Subclasses define the concrete manner in which classes are dynamically loaded. The default behavior is that of loading from the CLASSPATH in a platform-dependent manner in addition to the network access allowing bytecodes to be downloaded and instantiated.

The Verifier

The verifier is responsible for validating downloaded code before it can be run by the JVM. It is called by the class loader upon loading of the bytecodes and before the class object is returned. Clearly, the verifier works at a very low level and only makes sure that the bytecodes conform to the Java rules—it does not perform any application level analysis or heuristic security validation.

If we could be sure that Java bytecodes were always created with a legal Java compiler, the verifier would not be necessary. Bytecodes created by legal Java compilers (for example, the compiler that is part of the JDK distribution) always adhere to the Java language rules. Although it is true that the vast majority of Java bytecodes out there are created using such compilers, we cannot rely on this fact—unfortunately, this seems to be a flaw rooted deep in human nature. The verifier is used specifically to block the possibility that bytecodes were created in a malicious way in order to break the JVM. For example, bytecodes can be artificially formed in such a way that if run, they will cause a stack underflow in the JVM, thus crashing the JVM. The verifier is the security component responsible for ensuring that such behavior is blocked before it is allowed to run.

The Security Manager

The final component in the JDK 1.0 security model is the security manager. The security manager is the component responsible for limiting what untrusted code can do, or, in the case of JDK 1.0, what an applet can do. In simple terms, it is the component responsible for enforcing that untrusted code does not leave the sandbox at runtime.

The security manager is both active and passive. It performs runtime validation on certain methods and is also used by other security-related components who ask the security manager to approve a requested operation. If the security manager does not want to OK the operation, it raises a security exception, thereby not allowing the operation to occur. Among other tests, the security manager limits the following features:

- Access to the operating system
- Access to sockets
- Access to the file system
- Access to Java packages
- Access to the security model—for example, the security manager ensures that new class loaders are not installed
- Access to threads and thread groups
- Access to the clipboard (JDK 1.1)
- Access to printers and spoolers (JDK 1.1)

Applet Security

Security restrictions imposed on applets are fairly extensive. This is clearly necessary because downloaded applets may incorporate malicious code. The sandbox must therefore be, by default, as restrictive as possible. However, supporting enterprise applications on the Web often implies that downloaded code requires a less restricted runtime environment—JDK 1.1 and

JDK 1.2 introduce a richer model that provides more selective control based on digital signatures.

Applets are prevented from reading and writing files on the local (or for that matter—any) file system. They cannot check for the existence of a file, rename a file, create a directory, check file attributes, and so on. This eliminates the danger of a downloaded applet deleting your hard drive or reading confidential information and broadcasting it over the net. In more advanced versions of the JDK, this restriction is relaxed and more advanced features are introduced. For example, Sun's applet viewer in JDK 1.1 uses access control lists as a mechanism to provide finer control in limiting file access (using the `acl.read` property in the `properties` file).

Applets are also restricted in the network connections they may create. Applets can only make a network connection to the host from which it was downloaded. For example, a socket may only be opened to the host on which the Web server that supplied the applet resides.

Applets are also restricted as to which system properties they can access. System properties provide information about the environment in which a piece of Java code runs and includes the name of the operating system, the host, and other environment attributes. Access to system properties is provided through the `getProperty`, `getProperties`, and `setProperties` methods—all implemented by the `System` class.

JDK 1.1 Security

JDK 1.0 defined the basic security model used by early Java applets, but was far from adequate as far as real-world applications deployed over the Web were concerned. JDK 1.1 extends the basic security model with a large set of features providing greater control and finer granularity levels for associating security properties with Java code.

The JDK 1.1 security API and packages include supports for the following security-related concepts:

- *Digital signatures* JDK 1.1 introduces digital signatures in the Java world. Signatures, keys, certificates, providers, and algorithms are all formulated in Java, allowing applets to be signed by their creators. Clients running this Java code can then decide to relax security restrictions for code signed by a certain party. JDK also introduces the notion of jar files. Jar files are archive files that can package together class files, images, locale-specific data, and so on. These jar files can be used to form a standalone representation of all that is required from a download site in order to run an application. In terms of security, JDK 1.1 provides for signing of a jar files with a digital signature and using this signature to uniquely identify the source of the jar file, thereby eliminating man-in-the-middle attacks.

■ *Access control*   JDK 1.1 introduces *access control lists* (ACLs) as a mechanism for managing principals and their permissions.

■ *Message digests*   Support for creating message digests as a digital fingerprint is provided in JDK 1.1.

■ *Key management*   Initial support is provided for allowing management of keys and certificates in a security database.

JDK 1.2 Security

JDK 1.2 has an even richer and more complete security architecture. The JDK 1.2 security model not only has more features, it is a more consistent, well organized model that uses a very small number of primitive concepts in order to define a reference model. As for features, the JDK 1.2 security model improves the JDK 1.1 model in the following areas:

■ *Fine-grained access control*   Although applications may define and implement their own class loaders and security managers even today, this is hard work. JDK 1.2 provides a much easier way for an application to modify security-related control mechanisms.

■ Configurable security policies

■ *Extensible access control*   The JDK 1.2 allows extensions to the access control model without requiring `check` methods to be added to the `SecurityManager` class.

■ *Consistency in terms of checking*   Trusted and untrusted code (applets and applications) move closer to one another and are managed in similar ways—different security attributes are implemented by using different security domains. These domains are the primitive security enabler that determines what kind of sandbox (if any) is used.

The central concept in the JDK 1.2 security architecture is the notion of a protection domain. A protection domain aggregates code and has a set of

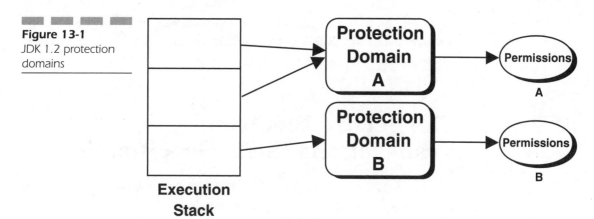

Figure 13-1
JDK 1.2 protection
domains

permissions associated with it (see Figure 13-1). Every segment of code is contained within a protection domain and assumes the security attributes from the permissions associated with that domain. A single thread of execution may be completely embedded in a single protection domain or may have different segments each belonging to different domains. Naturally, moving from one domain to another (especially if the second has more permissions) involves some security restrictions altering the permissions available to the caller.

Protection domains in general can either be system domains (which include system code that has more permissions associated with it) or various application domains. Naturally, the system domain will be accessible to application code only under very limiting restrictions.

Secure Multipurpose Internet Mime Extensions (S/MIME)

The *Secure Multipurpose Internet Mime Extensions* (S/MIME) is a specification for secure electronic mail that introduces security options to electronic mail messages in MIME format. S/MIME is an RSA Data Security initiative offering authentication using digital signatures and privacy using encryption. S/MIME has been submitted to the IETF and is the *de facto* standard for secure electronic mail. S/MIME uses a public-key algorithm for setting up a symmetric key, after which encryption is performed using this symmetric key. X.509 digital certificates are used for authentication and certification.

The Secure Electronic Transactions (SET) Specification

The *Secure Electronic Transactions* (SET) specification is an open industry standard developed by MasterCard International, Visa International, GTE, Microsoft, Netscape, SAIC, Terisa Systems, and VeriSign. SET was conceived to allow consumers and merchants to make secure bank card purchases on the Web.

SET is a technical specification for securing payment card transactions over open networks (specifically the Internet). SET's goal is to allow bank card transactions to be as simple and secure on the Internet as they are in retail stores today. Because there are currently more than 80 million users of the Web (most having above average income), making this a reality is of great interest to everyone. The specification itself is comprised of three parts: a business requirements document, a developer information document, and a protocol specification document. The SET core is a payment protocol designed to protect consumers' bank card information when they use bank cards to pay for goods and services on the Internet.

The SET initiative is designed to form an open specification that will ensure both a correct security model and an open interoperable standard. SET uses cryptographic concepts to ensure payment integrity and to authenticate both the buyer and the merchant. In terms of standardization, the forming of a standard specification is designed to ensure that applications developed by one vendor will interoperate with applications developed by other vendors. SET therefore not only defines the semantics of operations, but also the wire-level protocol to be used.

The business requirements addressed by SET and defined in the SET Business Description (Book 1) are to

- Provide confidentiality of payment and order information
- Ensure data integrity
- Authenticate that a cardholder is a legitimate user of the account
- Authenticate that a merchant has the financial relationship with the card brand company

- Secure the transaction information in transit
- Ensure flexibility and extensibility for security mechanisms
- Ensure interoperability

It is interesting to note that a system supporting SET transactions is not a digital cash system. The cardholder communicates card information to the merchant. This information is used by the merchant to communicate with the financial institution and get an authorization for the transaction. The payment itself is not within the scope of SET.

Certificates are heavily used by SET both for certifying a cardholder (effectively the certificate is the electronic replacement for the piece of plastic we have gotten so used to) and for certifying that the merchant has a relationship with the financial institution (similar to that sticker on the merchants window informing us which cards we can use there). SET certificates are verified through a hierarchy of trust. Each certificate is linked to the certification organization, allowing the trust tree to be traversed in a hierarchical manner.

The Secure Socket Layer (SSL)

The *Secure Socket Layer* (SSL) is a security protocol supporting private, authenticated communication over the Web. The protocol is layered between application-level protocols such as HTTP or CORBA invocations and the TCP/IP transport-level protocol and is designed to prevent eavesdropping, tampering, or message forgery. The protocol provides data encryption, authentication capabilities, and data integrity verification. Because the protocol is layered under application-level protocols, it may be used for any TCP/IP-based application-level protocols (for example, FTP, IIOP, and so on). In addition, it is transparent to the application level, a property that makes it very easy to integrate and add SSL into currently available Web software. SSL is the *de facto* industry standard.

SSL has three main security-related features:

- *Privacy*   An application session using an SSL connection is private. The SSL initiation phase allows the two parties to negotiate a secret key that is then used for encrypting the data stream. SLL data encryption uses algorithms such as DES and RC4 (see [DES] and [RC4]).

- *Authentication*   Each party in an SSL connection can authenticate the counterpart's identity using public key algorithms (see [RSA] and [DSS]).

■ *Reliability*   An SSL connection is assured to be reliable and includes integrity checks countering malicious tampering attacks.

In addition, SSL is designed to be efficient and extensible. SSL includes a caching mechanism allowing a number of sessions to use the same connection, thus saving the initial set-up time. Extensibility is provided by designing SSL as a framework into which additional encryption algorithms can be integrated (as long as both sides support them).

Naturally, for an SSL transaction to occur, both sides of the session must be using it. In a Web session, this means that both the browser and the Web server must be SSL-aware in order for a secure HTTP session over SSL to occur. In a distributed CORBA-based system, this implies that both ORBs must be SSL-enabled.

SSL operations in a session consist of two main stages: the initiation and the data transfer. In addition, various alert handlers ensure that various security attacks do not disrupt the session or compromise the participants' security. Initiation of a TCP/IP connection involves a security handshake process in which the client and the server agree on the security attributes of the session and in which authentication (both of the client to the server and of the server to the client) may occur. During the data transfer itself, one of a number of possible symmetric key encryption algorithms are used. In addition, data integrity mechanisms are used to ensure that data is not corrupted either by a mishap or due to a malicious attack.

The SSL Protocol

SSL is designed primarily to provide privacy and reliability for application-level communication over the Internet. SSL is designed as two interacting layers. The low level, which is layered on top of TCP/IP, is the *SSL record protocol,* providing low-level services to the second layer, which is called the *SSL handshake protocol*. This protocol provides the application-level protocols with the access to required security mechanisms. The SSL handshake protocol allows the two interacting applications to authenticate each other (if necessary) and to negotiate an encryption algorithm and cryptographic keys.

SSL provides data encryption security for message transfer as well as client and server authentication. The technology used in SSL for data encryption is mostly RSA Data Security technology. For transactions occurring with one endpoint outside the United States, the RC4 stream encryption algorithm with a 40-bit key is used. A message encrypted with this algorithm will take a typical workstation approximately a year of brute force computation to crack. Inside the United States, a 128-bit key is used, which effectively cannot be broken using brute force computation. SSL authentication is based on digital certificates issued by trusted certificate authorities using a public key to perform a cryptographic test.

SSL supports four encryption operations:

- *Digital signatures*   SSL uses either RSA signing in which a 36-byte structure is encrypted with a private key (that is, digitally signed) or DSS, which activates a digital signing algorithm on a 20-byte structure.

- *Block cipher encryption*   In this mode, every block of data (plaintext) is encrypted into a block of ciphertext.

- *Stream cipher encryption*   The data stream is XOR-ed with a cipher stream, which is generated from a cryptographically-secure generator.

- *Public key encryption*   A one-way function with a "trap door" is used to encrypt a data segment. The public key is not private to the connection (that is, it is available to all), but the decryption of the delivered segment requires the private information.

The first phase of an SSL connection involves setting up an SSL session. SSL is not a stateless protocol and information is maintained throughout a connection and even between multiple connections (allowing SSL to provide increased performance). Session state includes

- Session identifier
- Peer certificate
- Compression method
- Cipher spec—Specifies the data encryption algorithm used
- Master (symmetric) secret key used between the parties
- A flag indicating whether the session can be used to support multiple connections

Connection state includes

- Random byte sequences each chosen by one party of the connection
- Server secret key used for MAC operations
- Key used for data encrypted by the server
- Client secret key used for MAC operations

- Key used for data encrypted by the client
- A set of initialization vectors
- Sequence numbers used for ensuring correct order of messages

The first and most important phase in an SSL connection is the handshake phase. In this phase, the client and the server communicate in order to set up the session and connection state. If the two parties cannot come to an agreement regarding encryption and authentication, no transfer of data will occur. The handshake defines the protocol version used and the encryption algorithms to be used. In addition, any one of the participating parties may require the counter party to authenticate itself as part of the handshake. Finally, the handshake phase creates a set of shared secret keys using public-key encryption techniques. After the handshake is complete, the session will usually only involve direct data communication (other than handling of exceptional events).

The handshake phase begins with the client sending a CLIENT_HELLO message to the server. The server responds with a SERVER_HELLO message. Each of these messages includes a random value generated by one party and delivered to the other. In addition, a public key algorithm is negotiated using these two messages. The next part of the handshake involves the optional authentication of each party. Assuming authentication has been successfully performed (or that it is not required in the first place), the server sends the SERVER_HELLO_DONE message. The client then sends the CLIENT_KEY_EXCHANGE message using the public key that has been chosen previously. Finally, the client selects a ciphering algorithm and sends the CHANGE_CIPHER_SPEC message to the server, thereby installing the new encryption algorithm in place of the (until now) NULL algorithm. Note that this message may also be used later to replace one encryption method with another. Before actually replacing the cipher spec, the server will send a CHANGE_CIPHER_SPEC to the client—only then will it replace the spec. When the server has successfully replaced the old spec with the new one, it sends a FINISHED message to the client, this time using the new cipher spec. This is done to coordinate the precise moment at which the new spec should be used in both the client and the server.

Apart from encryption, SSL compresses all data passing over the wire. SSL records are compressed using an algorithm that is part of the session definition. The default algorithm does not change the stream (that is, no compression is performed), but any compression and the matching decompression algorithm to which both the client and the server agree can be used. In terms of structures, SSLPlainText structures are replaced by SSLCompressed structures.

The compressed structures are then converted into SSLCiphertext structures using the encryption functions and message authentication codes. This is possible because keys have already been negotiated in the handshake phase. These structures are then transmitted over the wire along with a sequence number used to monitor packets that do not arrive or that arrive in the wrong order. Note that encryption is performed after compression and not vice versa. On the receiving side the order is reversed: First decryption is performed, and then decompression.

The SSL protocol defines some advanced features, making it suitable for Web transactions and as a basis for IIOP sessions. SSL supports a cipher change protocol allowing the client and the server to re-negotiate a cipher spec. This could be used when either one of the communicating parties feels that security might have been compromised. A special SSL message is then used by one of the parties to notify the other party of the cipher change. Another example of an advanced SSL message is the Alert protocol. Alert messages can be used to inform a communicating party of an exceptional condition. In some cases (for example, when the alert level is fatal), this will cause a termination of the communication session. Other exception conditions include

- Unexpected message
- Record contains an incorrect message authentication code
- Decompression function failure
- Handshake failure
- No certificate is available to fulfill a certification request
- Corrupt certificate
- Expired certificate

14

WebSphere Studio

WebSphere Studio is an integrated tool for developing Web sites. It simplifies the tasks of design, development, and maintenance of sites. WebSphere Studio has a blend of powerful tools with seamless integration with external tools. In addition to the standard HTML page design features, WebSphere Studio allows you to create JavaBeans, applets, database queries, and servlets using special wizards that don't even require programming knowledge. In addition, it allows you to group together and manage the different files used for your Web site. The actual work of editing and displaying different files can be done either with WebSphere studio or with external tools, some of which will be discussed in the following chapters.

Installation

The WebSphere Studio installation can be downloaded directly from the IBM Web site at `http://www.software.ibm.com/websphere/studio`.

The actual installation process is simple and should not pose any difficulty. Unzip the installation if you downloaded it from the Internet. Next run the setup.exe program, which takes you through the installation. The only thing you should check before starting the installation process is that you have a Java Runtime Environment (JRE) installed on your machine, and that you know where it is located. During the installation process, the WebSphere Studio installation program will prompt you for the JRE location, in case it cannot be found through environment settings.

Getting Started

Much like tools used for software development, WebSphere studio uses Project to manage a collection of files, which are used to build a Web site. To start a new project, select New Project under the File menu, and then select the project name, for instance "demo," and a folder to place it in. The dialog box for a new project includes the option to select a project template, but for the purpose of our example, just select "<none>" (the default) in the project template field.

Figure 14-1 shows the main window display for the new project. The main window contains a menu bar on top. Just below it there is a toolbar

Figure 14-1
WebSphere Studio
Workbench

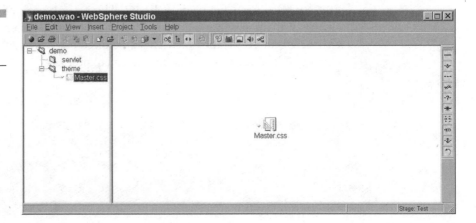

that contains shortcuts to various menu entries, and below that is the work area. Finally at the bottom of the window there are several status bars. The work area is divided into two parts. On the left side there is a hierarchy view that shows all open projects, along with their different components that are grouped into folders. Each project is composed of folders, which in turn are composed of folders and files. Files are the objects that actually contain data such as pictures, HTML pages, scripts, and so on. Each project and folder therein can be expanded or collapsed, similar to Windows Explorer. On the right side, the Details view shows details for the item selected on the Hierarchy view. On the far right edge of the window is the Links Filter toolbar. This toolbar can be used to filter out certain kinds of links. The filter categories are shown in Table 14-1. Using this filtering can allow you to focus on items of interest. For example, by turning off the embedded links you can focus on interpage relationships.

On the right side of the toolbar are filter buttons that control the files that are on display in the details frame, based on file extensions. These buttons can be displayed at will by selecting Files Filter toolbar under View. Table 14-2 details the different filter categories. Filtering can be imported when the details view is cluttered with a lot of elements, some of which might be irrelevant for the task being done. For example, when reviewing the logic of a JSP, you might want to turn off the image files for all the buttons in a page and concentrate on Java files.

In order to beef up our new project, we need to add some files and folders. Folders are easily added in using the Folder option under the Insert menu. For example, add a new folder called Images under the project. To add a new file into this folder, select the folder, and then select File under the Insert menu. The Insert File dialog box shown in Figure 14-2 allows you to insert either new files, existing files, or files from an external source.

When creating a new file, you may select the file type on the left side of the dialog box, and then choose a name on the right side. For example, add a new file called MyPicture of type Picture.gif. Now add an existing file, `image\anim\flower.gif`, from the samples provided with WebSphere Studio.

An important feature of WebSphere Studio is the capability to import files over the Web. If you select Import under the File menu, you will see the dialog box shown in Figure 14-3. Here you can import stuff from published Web sites. For the purpose of our example, we select `www.rtssoftware.com` (see Figure 14-4). The Import Wizard then prompts you (as shown in Figure 14-5) to select whether you want to follow links (that is, HTML links) or recursively iterate over folders. The latter requires

Table 14-1

Link filter options

Icons	Meaning
	Show links to other files in the same project ("inside" links)
	Show links to files embedded in the page
	Show outside links which go outside of the project ("outside" links)
	Show links to files which do not exist or cannot be opened ("broken" links)
	Show links which cannot be verified
	Show custom links, specified by the user for files not recognized by WebSphere Studio
	Show links between files which are generated out of other files ("source" links)
	Show links created by WebSphere Studio based on the parameters of code files
	Show link to locations inside the same file (anchor links)
	Show links to the same page ("self links")

FTP access. Similarly, you can select whether you want to import only pages and files provided to the browser or scripts and other files residing in the Web site. Again, the latter required FTP access. The next dialog box enables you to select whether you want to follow outside links and whether to limit the number of links followed in a chain. Both selections are important in order to avoid infinite or very long retrieval time. If you follow outside links and do not limit the chain, you might as well try to import half the Web into your project. In the next step, you can determine the action taken upon encountering password-protected pages and encountering files already imported. Finally, the wizard shows you a summary of your selections and allows you to select whether a report should be created for this action.

Table 14-2

File filter options

Icons	Meaning
	Show files which are non-publishable
	Show files owned by other users
	Show image files
	Show audio files
	Show executable files

Figure 14-2
Insert File dialog box

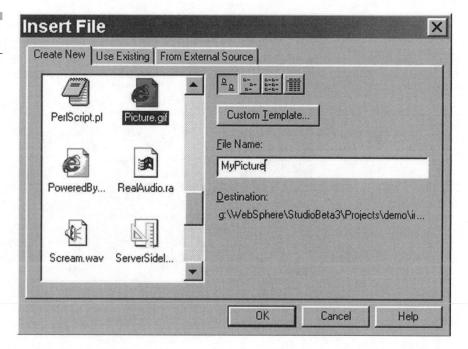

Figure 14-3
Insert Existing File
dialog box

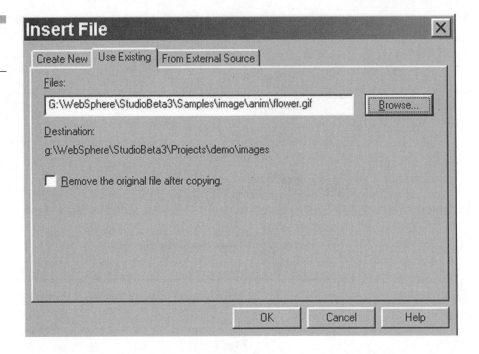

Figure 14-4
Import Wizard dialog
box

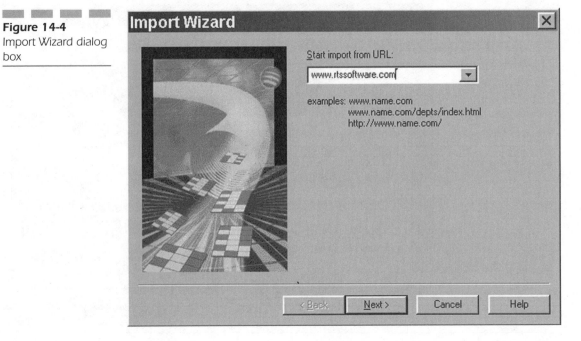

Figure 14-5
The second page of
the Import Wizard
dialog box

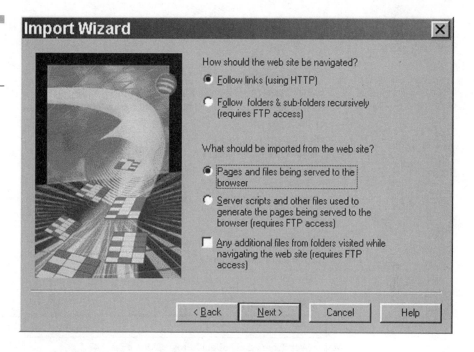

Figure 14-6
Import Progress
window

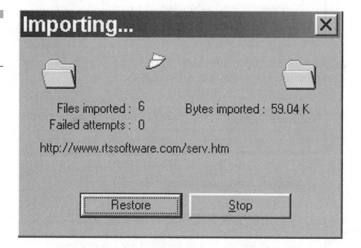

When the import begins, you will see a window showing its progress, as shown in Figure 14-6.

At the end of the process you get the report, if you asked for it. The report output is shown in Figure 14-7.

Figure 14-7
Import Report

Import Report for Project demo
20/09/99 13:45:45

Import Summary:

Starting location	http://www.rtssoftware.com
Completion	Import completed without interruption
Folders created	1
Files imported	87
Deepest nesting of folders	1

By MIME type

image	47
text	40

Files Found with Errors and Warnings

Sets of duplicate file names	0
Orphaned File	0

Folder Summary

Folder	Files imported	Size* (KB)	Time (min.)
g:\WebSphere\StudioBeta3\Projects\demo\pix	47	605.00	6.10
g:\WebSphere\StudioBeta3\Projects\demo	40	302.00	3.45
Totals:	**87**	**907.00**	**9.55**

Inaccessible Links
Imported from Location: http://www.rtssoftware.com/

Inaccessible Links	In File
http://www.rtssoftware.com/contact/cfm.servlet	\contact.htm

Imported from Location: http://www.rtssoftware.com/

Inaccessible Links	In File
http://www.rtssoftware.com/pix/callavod.jpg	\support.htm

Figure 14-7
Continued

Imported from Location: http://www.rtssoftware.com/

Inaccessible Links	In File
http://www.rtssoftware.com/pix/stock2.jpg	\stock.htm

Imported from Location: http://www.rtssoftware.com/

Inaccessible Links	In File
http://www.rtssoftware.com/corp1.htm	\servplan.htm
http://www.rtssoftware.com/corp1.htm	\support.htm
http://www.rtssoftware.com/corp1.htm	\report.htm
http://www.rtssoftware.com/corp1.htm	\repair.htm
http://www.rtssoftware.com/corp1.htm	\spare.htm
http://www.rtssoftware.com/corp1.htm	\call.htm
http://www.rtssoftware.com/corp1.htm	\mobile.htm

Imported from Location: http://www.rtssoftware.com/

Inaccessible Links	In File
http://www.rtssoftware.com/pix/fsm_rem.pdf	\support.htm

Imported from Location: http://www.rtssoftware.com/

Inaccessible Links	In File
http://www.rtssoftware.com/pix/hierachy.jpg	\contract.htm

Imported from Location: http://www.rtssoftware.com/

Figure 14-7
Continued

Inaccessible Links	In File
http://www.rtssoftware.com/KSDesigns/RTS WEB PAGE/About BO Template.txt	\part1.htm

Imported from Location: http://www.rtssoftware.com/

Inaccessible Links	In File
http://www.rtssoftware.com/www.calicotech.com	\part.htm

Imported from Location: http://www.rtssoftware.com/

Inaccessible Links	In File
http://www.rtssoftware.com/home.htm	\part6.htm
http://www.rtssoftware.com/home.htm	\support.htm

Imported from Location: http://www.rtssoftware.com/

Inaccessible Links	In File
http://www.rtssoftware.com/plan.htm	\news11.htm
http://www.rtssoftware.com/plan.htm	\news10.htm
http://www.rtssoftware.com/plan.htm	\news6.htm
http://www.rtssoftware.com/plan.htm	\news7.htm
http://www.rtssoftware.com/plan.htm	\spare.htm

Sets of duplicate file names
None

Orphaned File
None

Getting Acquainted with WebSphere Studio

Our first step of getting to know WebSphere Studio is reviewing the menu bar composition.

- File Menu
  - *New Project* Create a new project, as explained previously
  - *Open Project* Open an existing project. Note that several projects can be open concurrently.
  - *Import* Activate the import wizard as discussed previously
  - *Save as Archive* Save the whole site in archive format
  - *Open Archive* Open a project previously saved in archive format/
  - *Print, Print Preview* Standard printing options
  - *Open Saved Report* Open a previously saved report in Web browser
  - *Exit* Quit WebSphere Studio
- Edit Menu
  - *Cut, Copy* Ordinary clipboard operations
  - *Copy As* Copy an object as URL Text, HTML Tag, or HTML script so it can be pasted later on
  - *Paste to replace link* Paste over an existing link
  - *Delete* Remove selected item
  - *Edit Link* Edit the URL for the link
  - *Bookmarks* Add, Remove, or Go To previously added bookmarks
  - *Start Page* Set or go to start page
  - *Set Status* Set status of an item, based on a customizable set of color-codes
  - *Set as Publishable* Make the selected item to be considered publishable (if not publishable, the file is not published even when the folder containing it is published)
  - *Use Default Publishing Path* Indicate whether the default publishing path should be used
  - *Find File* Find a file given its name
  - *Find and Replace Text* Find and replace a text string in all files or selected files only

- *Rename* Rename a file or folder. You cannot rename a file used in links.

- *Properties* View file properties. These include General (name, path, size, type, creation date, ownership, and comments), Version Control data, Relationships (that is, incoming and outgoing links), and Publishing Properties (that is, is publishable, publish path, and when published).

■ View Menu

- *Main Toolbar* Toggle display of main toolbar

- *Files Filter Toolbar* Toggle display of file filter toolbar

- *Links Filter Toolbar* Toggle display of links filter toolbar

- *Status Bar* Toggle display of status bar at the bottom of the window

- *Sort Relations View By* Allows sorting relations view by different attributes

- *Show Files* Filter files (same as Files Filter toolbar)

- *Show Links* Filter links (same as Links Filter toolbar)

- *Refresh* Refresh the display

- *Relations* Toggle details view to show relations display (showing links)

- *Publishing* Toggle Details view to show publishing display (showing hierarchy in folders when publishing)

- *Keep Views in Sync* Indicates whether different views should be synchronized

■ Insert Menu

- *File* Insert a new or existing file, as explained in the previous section. Note that you may also create files using the Wizards under Tools below.

- *Folder* Insert a new folder under the currently selected project or folder

- *Server* Insert a new server

- *Custom Link* Insert a new custom link, i.e. a link which has a user defined meaning

- *Source Link* Insert a new source link, i.e. a link between two files, one of which is created from the other

■ Project Menu

- *Check In* Check in a previously checked-out file

- *Check Out*   Check out a file (automatically done when editing a file)
- *Undo Check Out*   Undo a previous check-out operation
- *Check Out Info*   List of check out information for all checked out files (that is, when checked out and by whom)
- *Version Control*   Activate external version control tools
- *VisualAge for Java*   Direct link to VisualAge for Java. Allows you to send files to VisualAge for Java or receive an updated version of them from VisualAge for Java.
- *Compile*   Compile a file with the compiler specified under Preferences in the Tools menu below
- *Debug*   Activate debugger
- *Publishing Stage*   Set the publishing stage for an item. This in turn affects the server to which it is published, as set under Publishing Options below.
- *Copy Publishing Stage*   Collective change of publishing stage from one to another. Useful when you finish the one phase and want to change all items from this phase to another.
- *Customize Publishing Stages*   Allows you to add or remove publishing stages

- Tools Menu
  - *Edit With*   Edit the selected file with one of the editors designated for it (using Tool Registration below), or by a different editor specified by you
  - *Preview File With*   Preview file with one of the preset viewers (one of which is the system default Web browser). You may add viewers using the Preferences entry below.
  - *Wizards*   Activate one of the wizards, which are the SQL Wizard, Database Wizard, and JavaBean Wizard
  - *Check Project Integrity*   Perform a static check of the project integrity. This includes verification of all links to make sure they are not broken (including external links to remote sites).
  - *Tools Registration*   A dialog box enabling you to customize the way different file extensions are handled. For each extension, you can determine its MIME type, the associated editor, and whether or not it is published. As shown in Figure 14-8, the dialog box indicated which extensions are currently customized (that is, were modified from the default).

Figure 14-8

Tools Registration
dialog box

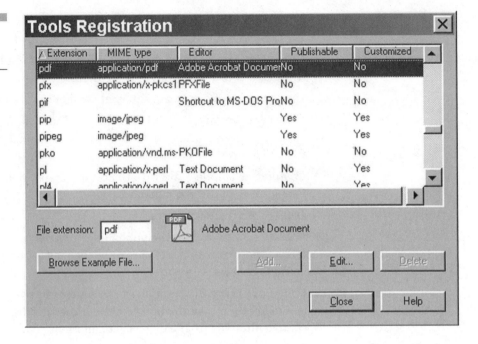

- *Publishing Options* Dialog box used to set publishing options. The same dialog box pops up when selecting Publish this file under File menu. The tabs in the dialog box are:
    - *General* Publish only modified files or all, style of links (absolute or relative path), and other options
    - *Prompts* Define in what events the user should be prompted for a response (for example, before overwriting files, before creating folders, and so on)
    - *Warning* Define when to issue warnings (for example, when unable to publish a file)
    - *Advanced* File extensions for which FTP ASCII mode should be used (this should be updated if you are using some new ASCII file type not in the list), Default servers (for publishing)
- *Preferences* Configure WebSphere Studio according to your needs. The following tabs are provided:
    - *General* File templates location. This is useful when you want to create your own templates in order to ensure that some common structure and content exist in all your projects.
    - *Check Out* Path of checked out files for current project

- Java compiler and CLASSPATH settings
- Previewing applications
- *Advanced*   Parser configuration file and FTP DLL. These should usually not be changed.
- Help Menu
  - *Help Topics*   Listing of help topics
  - *Studio Guide*   Users Guide
  - *About*   Program information dialog box

WebSphere Studio Editors

In addition to being able to edit files with external editors, WebSphere Studio does include several document editors. When double-clicking an HTML file, you open the WebSphere Page Designer, as shown in Figure 14-9. The Page Designer is composed of a menu bar and numerous tool bars. The work area includes a file browser that can be used to insert elements into

Figure 14-9
WebSphere Page
Designer

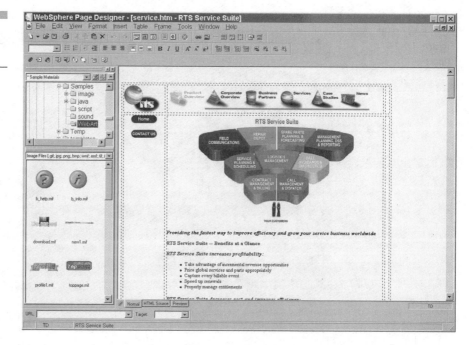

the HTML page and a large document display that can be either one of the following:

- *Normal*   Allowing visual editing
- *HTML source*   Showing HTML source file
- *Preview*   Preview of Web-browser display

At first glance, the Page Designer looks like any other HTML editor. It includes a lot of features for formatting text and pictures, inserting links and frames, and so on. However, in addition to all these standard options, the WebSphere Page Designer allows you to easily incorporate dynamic elements in your pages. Under the Insert menu you are able to insert into pages your own scripts, Java applets, and servlets.

When selecting an image you may ask for editing it (the same effect can be achieved by selecting Edit Image in the popup menu that appears after right-clicking an image). The Image Editor provides several simple services and is shown in Figure 14-10. In order to use more sophisticated services, you can configure WebSphere Studio to launch external editors.

Similar to the way you edit an image, you may edit the image map (that is, the way it is mapped to links). The Image Map Editor provides this functionality, as shown in Figure 14-11.

Figure 14-10
Image editor

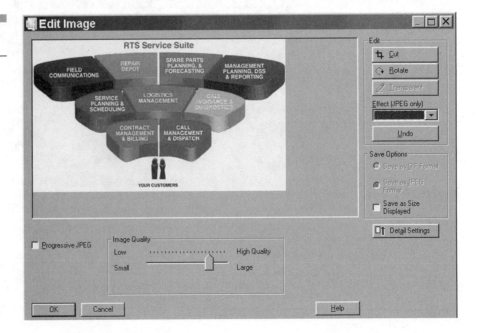

Figure 14-11
Image Map Editor

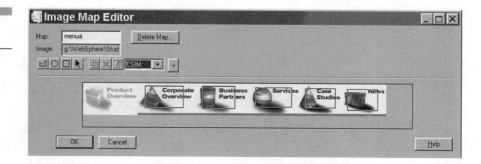

Figure 14-11
Image Map Editor

Figure 14-12
WebSphere WebArt
Designer

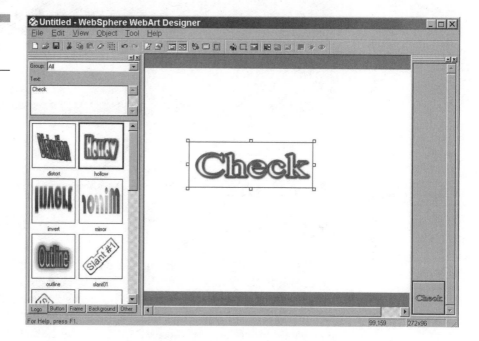

Under the Tools menu, you can activate the WebSphere WebArt designer, shown in Figure 14-12. This tool allows you to design different forms of text art. Yet another tool is the WebSphere AnimatedGif Designer, shown in Figure 14-13. This tool allows you to create animated GIFs to be transplanted in HTML pages.

Figure 14-13
WebSphere
AnimatedGif
Designer

WebSphere Studio Wizards

SQL Wizard

The SQL wizard can be used to create SQL statements without being an expert on SQL syntax. After this wizard is started, the Welcome page is shown. Here, you can key in the logical name for your SQL statement. In the next page, the Logon page (shown in Figure 14-14), you must specify the database connection parameters. After you do that, click the Connect button. Then you may choose the output data, choosing the names of database tables, column containing the data, and which join operations should be performed. You may provide a condition for data selection (that is, a SELECT clause), and you may also specify a sort criteria. All these operations are done using a GUI, not by keying the actual SQL statement.

Finally, the complete SQL statement is shown so you can copy it for later use. You may also save it or execute it to see the results.

Figure 14-14
Database Wizard
Logon page

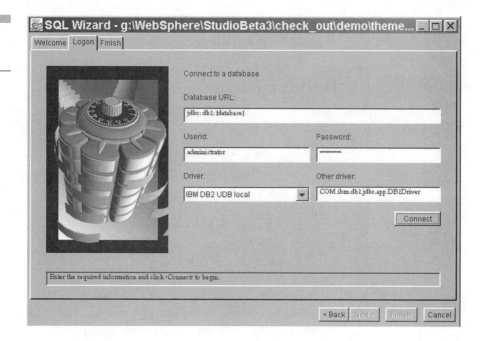

Database Connectivity Wizard

The Database Connectivity Wizard takes an SQL statement created with the SQL Wizard and creates a Java Servlet. This servlet retrieves data from the relational database and displays the result in an HTML page. This wizard automatically creates an input HTML page invoking the servlet, JavaBean files that include the logic for accessing the database and performing the SQL statement, a servlet configuration file to configure the servlet, and finally a JSP file that contains the JSP and HTML output tags for the selected database columns. Note that you may later on manually modify the servlet configuration file to change the database URL, driver, userID, or password.

When you start this wizard, you should indicate the SQL statement to use. Then you select the servlet name, the package qualification, and the output folder in which to place the HTML and JSP files created. After this step is finished, you need to select the input parameters to be used and the output fields (you might not need to display all of them). Before completing the creation of the servlet, you are required to confirm the filenames for the created files, and you may edit them at will. All the files can be edited by you later on. For example, the HTML files can be edited for the purpose of formatting them according to the required style and form.

Servlet Wizard

The basic servlet wizard allows you to quickly generate a servlet that uses a JavaBean for input processing or output. This can be any JavaBean you write yourself or acquire elsewhere. This wizard, similar to the previous one, prompts you to specify the bean and the operations to perform and creates an input HTML page, servlet files, servlet configuration files, and an output JSP file.

After you start this wizard, you are prompted to select the JavaBean to be used. Note that you must first add the bean (and compile it) under the Servlet folder under your project. After you select the bean, you are prompted to select whether you want an input page, an output page, and an error result page (see Figure 14-15). Each of these is optional because you might be operating an input-only or output-only bean. Next you need to select the fields to be shown on your input page, out of the bean attributes, and then the fields to be shown on the output page. In the next step, you

Figure 14-15
Servlet Wizard Web pages

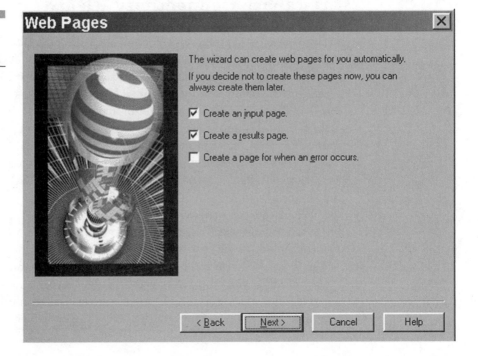

Figure 14-16
Servlet Wizard session

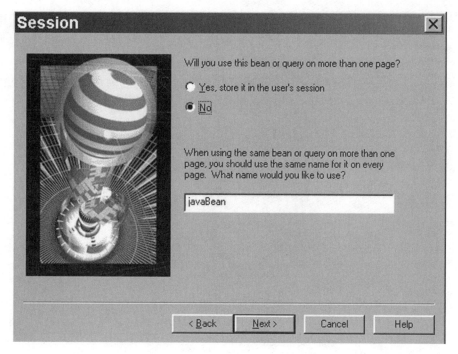

need to select the methods to be performed on the JavaBean out of the list
of exported methods. Then, you need to select whether you want to use your
bean on more than one page (see Figure 14-16). Finally you need to confirm
the filenames before they are created, as shown in Figure 14-17. As with the
previous wizard, you may later on edit the files and use them in your Web
site as needed.

Figure 14-17
Servlet Wizard
confirmation window

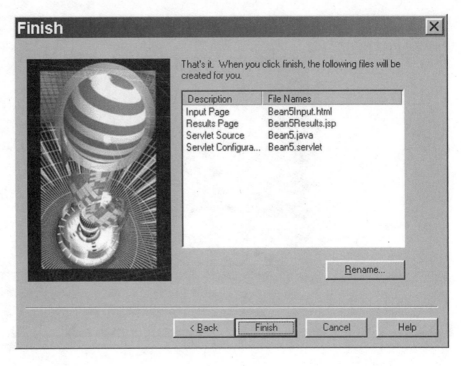

Finish ✕

That's it. When you click finish, the following files will be created for you.

Description	File Names
Input Page	Bean5Input.html
Results Page	Bean5Results.jsp
Servlet Source	Bean5.java
Servlet Configura...	Bean5.servlet

Rename...

< Back   Finish   Cancel   Help

15

VisualAge for Java

VisualAge for Java is IBM's *Integrated Development Environment* (IDE) for Java Development. This chapter provides a quick glance at this product and its main features. With working knowledge of Java, you should be able to master VisualAge for Java in no time. The advantage of using VisualAge for Java when developing WebSphere-based applications is the seamless integration between VisualAge and other WebSphere components. VisualAge for Java is a first-class Java development environment that provides an all-in-one solution for code editing, browsing, execution, and debugging. In addition, it provides numerous wizards and tools that support the development of EJB, JSP, and other Java software components that are used in WebSphere applications.

Installation

The VisualAge for Java installation can be downloaded from the IBM Web site at `http://www.software.ibm.com/ad/vajava`. Note that this product comes in three different levels: Entry Edition, Professional Edition, and Enterprise Edition. For the purpose of developing Enterprise applications for WebSphere, you obviously need the last one.

The actual installation process is straightforward and similar to most other installations. If you downloaded the installation from the Internet, unzip it first. Then (or immediately if you have the VisualAge for Java CD) you should run the setup.exe program to take you through the installation. The only aspect that might be a little tricky is the Web browser configuration. VisualAge for Java requires that the proxy exceptions for the browser will include localhost: 49213, 127.0.0.1. The installation program will prompt you to update this automatically. This update process might not succeed if your proxy configuration is automatic (that is, set by the system administrator). In that case, you should verify with your system administrator that the aforementioned settings are included in the proxy configuration.

After you have VisualAge for Java up and running, you can start writing code. However, in order to develop WebSphere applications, you should first make sure you are using a few of the VisualAge for Java features. These features should be added into your work environment. To add features, go to the WorkBench, and then select Quick Start under File menu. In the dialog window that appears, select Features on the left side and Add Feature on the right size, as shown in Figure 15-1. The window that comes up next shows the list of features to select from, as depicted in Figure 15-2.

Hello VisualAge for Java

Creating a new application is VisualAge for Java couldn't be simpler. The process and the outcome should feel familiar to you if you have any previous experience with any IDE for Java or even C++, such as Microsoft Visual C++. To get things started, go to the Quick Start button and select Create Applet on the right side (while Basic is selected on the left). As shown in Figure 15-3, you need to select the Project, Package, and Class names. Because the default application created for you includes a multitude of controls such as menu bars and buttons, you are provided with the option whether you want them to be based on AWT or Swing components. This option is quite convenient because forcing you to use one or the other might

Figure 15-1
QuickStart dialog box

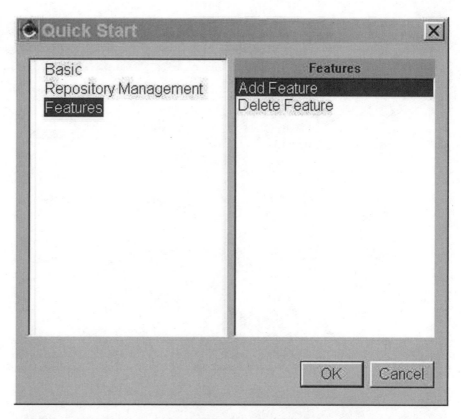

Figure 15-2
Add New Features
dialog box

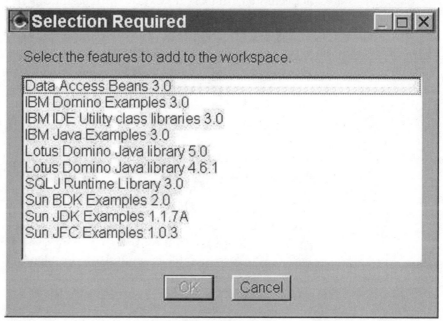

Figure 15-3
Create Application
dialog box

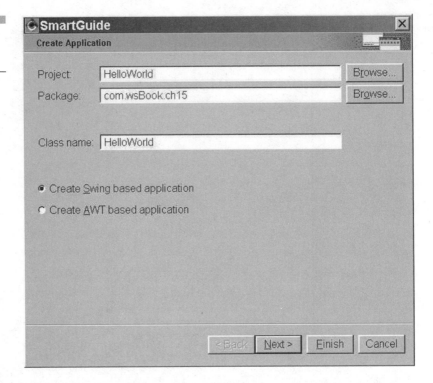

not comply with existing code or with standards in your project or organization.

Anyway, after you select Next in this dialog box, you should see the dialog box shown in Figure 15-4. In this dialog box, you can select which components to include in your application. This selection determines what menu-bars and other bars should be included, the text for the title bar, and also the inclusion of additional dialogs (for example, the About dialog box). For the sake of this example, we won't change anything here—just click Finish.

This completes the creation of our new application. Before continuing with this application, let's get acquainted with the VisualAge WorkBench, shown in Figure 15-5. As with most Windows-based applications, you have a menu bar on top, and then a toolbar below it, a work area which takes most of the window, and at the bottom a couple of status bars. Inside the work area there is a tab control that allows you to go between Projects, Packages, Classes, Interfaces, and All Problems. The menu bar on top changes as you make your selection in the tab control. The following menus are fixed for all selections:

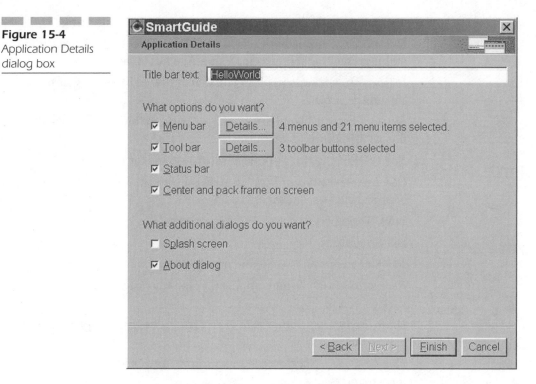

Figure 15-4
Application Details
dialog box

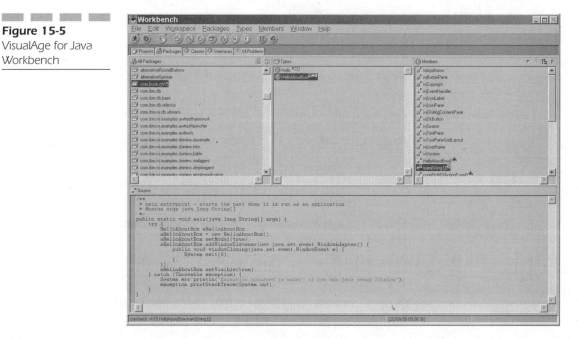

Figure 15-5
VisualAge for Java
Workbench

- *File*   Controls file creation, loading and saving, and quitting
  - *Quick Start*   Immediate access to different creation wizards, and adding/removing features for VisualAge for Java
  - *Import*   Insert code in a directory, JAR file, or repository into a VisualAge project
  - *Export*   Save a VisualAge project or package into a directory, JAR file, or repository
  - *Print Setup*   Customary page setup options for printing
  - *Quick access to recent files*   Entries shown the names of recently accessed classes, packages, and projects
  - Save Workspace
  - Exit VisualAge
- *Edit*   Controls source code and other editing
  - *Revert to Saved*   Where applicable, you may revert to a saved version of a file
  - *Undo, Redo, Cut, Copy, Paste, Select All*   The usual clipboard operations
  - *Format Code*   Fix the code indentation, braces location, and other formatting issues
  - View Reference Help
  - Open on Selection
  - Find/Replace
  - Print Text
  - Save
  - Save Replace
  - *Breakpoint*   Place a breakpoint for debugger tracing
- Workspace
  - *Open Project Browser*   Open a specific project, selected from a list, possibly using a search string
  - *Open Package Browser*   Open a specific package, selected from a list, possibly using a search string
  - *Open Type Browser*   Open a specific type, selected from a list, possibly using a search string
  - *Search*   Search for a given string in the workspace
  - *Text Search / Replace*   Search and replace a string in the workspace

- *Search Again*   Quick access to searches previously made
- *Search Results*   Show the search results window
- *Tools*   Invoke workspace tools such as Fix Manager or SQLJ tool
- *Window*   Window manipulation; this menu is the second on the right.
  - *Clone*   Create a duplicate of the current active window
  - *Switch to*   Make a different window active
  - *Refresh*   Refresh the current window
  - *Lock Window*   Make sure the window remains open; this feature is useful to prevent you from closing it by accident.
  - *Maximize Pane*   Maximize the selected pane to take up all the work area (once selected, this entry changes to Restore Pane)
  - *Flip Orientation*   Flips the alignment of components in the work area from vertical to horizontal and vice versa
  - *Show Edition Names*   Show the version names for components (projects, packages, classes)
  - *Workbench*   Make the Workbench window the active window
  - *Scrapbook*   Open the Scrapbook which can be used to review and edit code fragments, including imported code
  - *Repository Explorer*   Browse through the class repository in an Explorer-like fashion
  - *Console*   Show Java console for programs using text I/O
  - *Log*   Show execution log and error log window
  - *Debug*   Access debugger, breakpoints and exceptions
  - *Options*   Customize the display of and behavior of VisualAge for Java through a multitude of options
- *Help*   Online help

In addition to these menus, which are fixed and available on all VisualAge for Java windows, the following menus depend on the selected tab on the tab control.

When selecting the Projects tab, the work area shows the project hierarchy, allowing you to expand and contract each folder. When this tab is selected, the following menu appears between the Workspace and Window menus:

- *Selected*   Manipulate the currently selected project
  - *Open*   Open the selected project

- *Open To*   Open the selected project and go to a specific tab there, which could be any one of Packages, Classes, Interfaces, Editions, Resources, and Problems

- *Go To*   Jump to a Project, Package, or Type, which is selected from a list, possibly using a search string. This submenu also includes bookmarks, which can be manipulated directly from this menu.

- *Add*   Add a new element: Project, Package, Class, Applet, Application, Interface, Method, Field. This submenu is used in different context, and not all entries are applicable in all instances. For example, under the Selected menu for Projects, the last two entries are grayed out because you cannot add methods or fields to a project.

- *Attribute filters*   A dialog window allowing you to select the qualifications of elements that are on display. This would apply to classes, methods, and members. You may filter by visibility (`public`, `protected`, `private`) and other modifiers (`final`, `static`, and so on).

- *Import*   Import code into the selected project

- *Export*   Export code out of the selected project

- *Replace with*   Replace the current version of the project with the previous edition or a different edition

- *Delete*   Remove this project

- *Reorganize*   Copy, move, or rename this project

- *Manage*   Control the way version names are given

- *Compare With*   Compare with a previous or different edition

- *Run*   Execute Project; Entries are available for running in applet viewer where applicable, running main where applicable, checking the `CLASSPATH` environment (in order to be sure it is set correctly so everything will indeed run).

- *Document*   Print out source code or create JavaDoc

- *Tools*   Gain access to external tools such an external Source Control Management system or SQLJ

- *Properties*   Show properties of the selected project, including its name, status, creation time, and version

When you select the Packages tab, you get a more interesting view. The upper half of the work area is now split into three parts: Packages, Types, and Members. You may browse through the packages. After you select one, all the types (that is, interfaces and classes) contained in it are shown in the middle part. If you select a specific type, you will get its members on the right side and the code for it on the lower half of the work area. Figure 15-6

Figure 15-6
Packages view

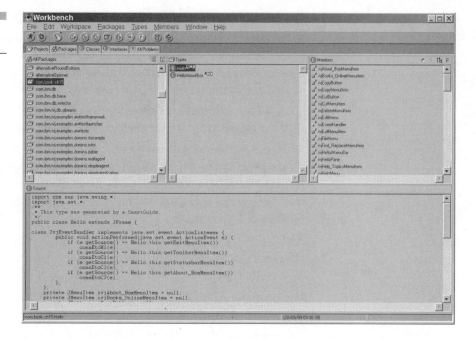

shows this view. Note how the Types area indicates whether the class is an interface or a type (by a C or I icon before the name). Also, graphic icons at the end of the name indicate if the class can be run and if it can be visually composed. Similarly, for members, a small M or F indicates whether this member is a method or a field, and a graphic icon at the end of the name shows the access mode if it is not public. When the Packages tab is selected, the menu bar shows the Packages, Types, and Members menu between the Workspace and Window menus. These menus are quite similar to the Selected menu for projects, so we will just focus on the differences. One difference is that each of these menus has a Go To entry (specific to the kind of object) that is manipulated in this menu (for example, Go To Member in the Members menu). The Packages menu has a Layout entry that allows you to switch between a tree or a list layout for packages. The Attribute Filters entry appears only in the Members menu.

The Types menu allows you to manipulate types. It differs from the Selected menu for Projects in the specific support for types. It has the following special entries:

- *Generate*   Automatic code generation for accessors or required methods

- *Method Template*   Create a new method

- *References to* Find references to this type or a specific field in it
- *Externalize Strings* Take strings that are hard coded or are bean properties in this class and externalize them into resource bundles. This is useful for internationalization and localization or just for externally customizing the titles and captions on controls.
- *Tools* This submenu includes more entries here, such as Generate RMI for generating remote method invocation stubs

The Members menu allows you to manipulate menus. The following entries are provided in this menu in addition to the standard ones:

- *Inheritance Filters* Allows you to filter the display of inherited members and methods based on where they are declared in the inheritance hierarchy
- *References* References to the selected member in the Workspace, Hierarchy, or Working Set (which is a user-defined collection of Java code elements)
- *Declarations* Declarations of the selected member in the Workspace, Hierarchy, or Working Set
- *References to* This entry is available only for methods. It shows references made by the selected method to methods, fields, and types.
- *Declarations of* This entry is available only for methods, and it shows the declarations of methods, fields, or types that are accessed by this method.

- The Packages, Types, and Members menus can be accessed by right-clicking a package, type, or member, respectively.

- The Classes and Interfaces tabs allow you to see all the classes or interfaces, respectively, without regard to the package or project to which they belong. In these views, the upper half of the work area is divided into two parts only, the left showing the class or interface hierarchy, and the right showing the methods. The Classes and Interfaces menus, which become available, are virtually identical to the Types menu previously discussed.

- The All Problems tab allows quick access to all errors encountered in all components. This is an aggregated view of problems that can be viewed in specific packages/classes.

This completes our review of the Workbench, which is the main window. Obviously, when working on a specific class, you can open a window for it. For example, double-click our Hello class to see a window focusing on it. This

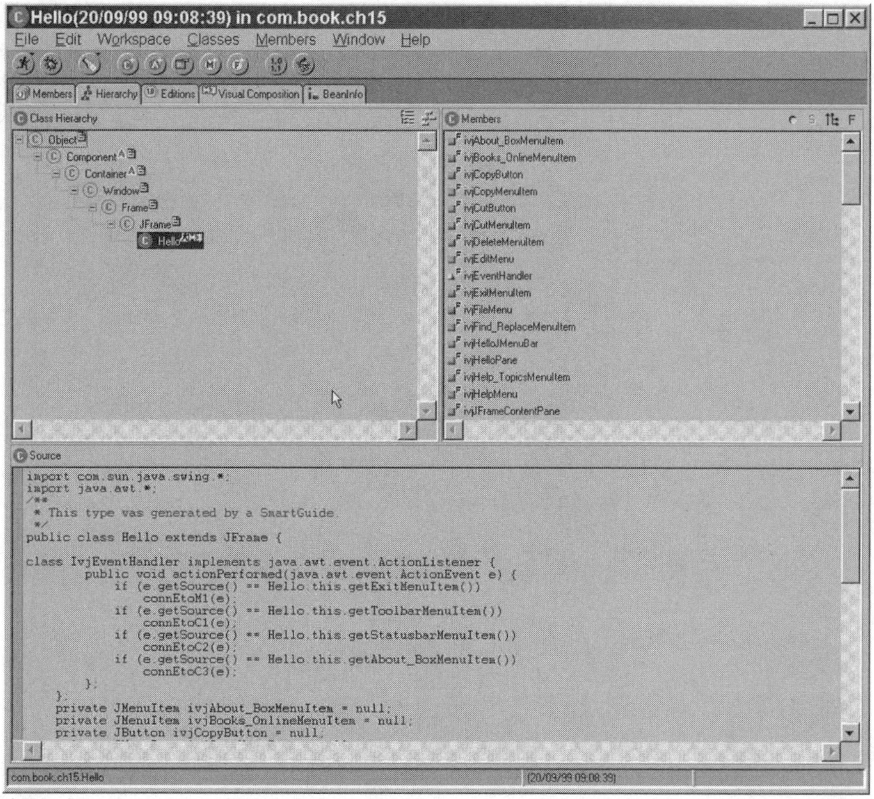

Figure 15-7
Class hierarchy view

window is shown in Figure 15-7. Here also you have a tab control that determines the kind of view of the class you get. The Members view focuses on the members, whereas the Hierarchy view shows the class hierarchy along with the members. In the latter, the members displayed correspond to the class selected in the hierarchy. The Classes and Members menus available in both tabs are identical to the ones in the Workbench. The Editions tab allows you to review the history of the class in either list or graph form. When this tab is selected, the Editions menu appears. It has some entries that are similar to ones already discussed.

The Visual Composition tab allows you to review this class from a visual perspective. As shown in Figure 15-8, you see the layout of visual components in the class, including menus and callbacks. On the left side is a toolbar that contains JavaBeans you may drag and drop into the main work area. At the top of this bar is a pulldown menu that allows you to

Figure 15-8
Visual Composition
View: Class Hello

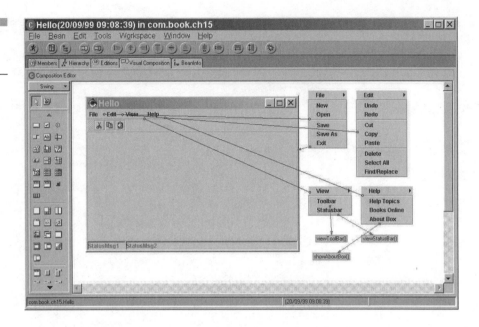

select the set of beans to use (for example, Swing, AWT). This list can be customized to include new elements to support different libraries you are using. For example, an entry can be added for San Francisco GUI components (see Chapter 18, "NetObjects BeanBuilder,"). Below the pulldown menu is an option to select beans graphically by icons or textually by name. This is useful for instantiating a bean without making it available on the toolbar.

The last tab, BeanInfo, allows you to browse through and edit the BeanInfo for the class, assuming that it is a JavaBean.

The visual composition is done in an intuitive manner, as are other tasks in VisualAge for Java. For example, select the HelloAboutBox class in our sample program and go into visual mode, as shown in Figure 15-9. Now double-click the Hello label to get the properties for this components. You can easily edit them. For example, change the label from Hello to Hello World, as shown in Figure 15-10.

Now, run this class (by clicking the Run button, which is the leftmost one on the toolbar). Alternatively, you can run the Hello program and select About from the Help Menu.

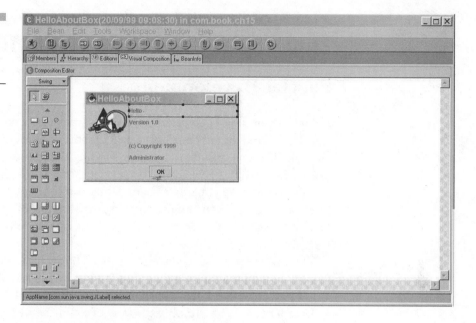

Figure 15-9
Visual Composition
View: Class
HelloAboutBox

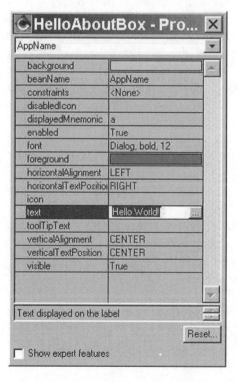

Figure 15-10
Property Editor

Using VisualAge for Java for Developing WebSphere Applications

Servlet Development

VisualAge for Java includes a Java Web server and a servlet engine inside the IDE JVM. You may perform servlet testing directly from VisualAge for Java. Just run your Web browser for sending the request: The servlets then execute in the IDE. Executing the servlets from within VisualAge for Java has the advantage of being able to debug the servlets easily, which is usually not the case when you are running a full-scale HTTP server. Moreover, you may modify the code on the fly, and the new code is linked to the running servlet.

To activate the servlet, you should select Launch Servlet under Run. This in turn activates the Web server (if it is not already running) and opens the Web browser with a URL pointing to the specific servlet.

In order to further simplify the task of coding servlets, the visual composition mode for servlets includes a set of HTML JavaBeans. This allows you to drag and drop these elements to design the servlet much as you would an HTML editor. The only difference is that after the visual editing, you can go on and add the logic behind.

Chapter 28, "Debugging Servlets and ISPs Using VisualAge," goes into more detail regarding the development and debugging of servlets in VisualAge for Java.

Java Server Pages Development

As previously discussed in Chapter 4, WebSphere supports JSPs through the `pageCompile` servlet, which translates the JSP into a servlet. Using VisualAge for Java, a special Execution Monitor enables you to step through JSP code and track its correspondence with the generated servlet. This generated servlet can actually be debugged with the usual IDE debugger. You can even debug JSP code. While running, you can step into any JavaBeans called by the JSP. If you find an error is detected in the JSP source, you can fix it using an external editor such as NetObjects ScriptBuilder, described in detail in Chapter 17, "NetObjects ScriptBuilder." After the JSP source is rectified, it can be reloaded into WebSphere, which then repeats the translation process of the JSP into a servlet. Debugging can then take place with the new source code.

Enterprise Java Beans Development

For EJBs, VisualAge for Java has a special creation wizard that takes care of creating the bean according to your specifications. In order to simplify the process of tracing and degugging, a unit-test environment is provided. This environment runs an Enterprise JavaBean Server reference implementation within the IDE, saving the trouble of deploying the EJBs when doing initial testing. You simply edit the EJB and run it in the IDE, making full use of the debugger. The IDE uses multiple JVMs internally in order to execute EJBs. VisualAge for Java also includes support for container-managed persistence using the Persistence framework. When development is complete, the EJB can be exported as an EJB JAR file that can be installed into the WebSphere application server.

Remote Debugger

VisualAge for Java installation includes the IBM distributed debugger. This is a remote debugger tool that can be used for debugging programs remotely. For our purposes, it is useful for debugging code running inside a servlet engine or an EJB server.

In order to use it, you need to start the debugger, and then select the Interpreted (Intel/AIX) tab in the Load Program dialog box. There you need to specify the language (Java is default), the program parameters, JVM argument, and finally whether to execute locally or remotely. If the program is to execute remotely (for example, on WebSphere Application Server), you need to specify the host name and port. Note that for remote debugging you must have the debugger back end installed on the remote machine too.

In general, using the remote debugger is very cumbersome. You are better off testing your programs inside the VisualAge for Java IDE. However, when deploying a real-life application, you will occasionally (well, always) encounter some problems. Remote debugging can help you track down the causes of these problems.

16

NetObjects Fusion

NetObjects Fusion is a tool for building Web sites. It helps you design HTML pages quickly and conveniently and is the natural choice of page designer to complement WebSphere Studio. As opposed to the tools described in the last couple of chapters, NetObjects fusion is very intuitive and easy to learn and use. One of the reasons why it is so is that NetObjects opted to support more complex activities relating to scripting in their ScriptBuilder product, described in the next chapter.

The main advantage of NetObjects Fusion that is immediately apparent is that it provides a powerful visual composition mode.

Installation

A trial version of NetObjects Fusion can be downloaded from www. netobjects.com/fusion. The actual installation process is very easy. When you execute the installation program, it unzips the installation files and takes you through the installation.

Getting Started

After you start NetObjects Fusion, you get the Welcome to NetObjects Fusion dialog box. In this dialog box, you are prompted to decide if you want to create a new blank site, create a site from an existing template, or open an existing one. Select Blank Site and then click OK. The next dialog box prompts you for the filename and the directory path.

The NetObjects Fusion main window now opens, as shown in Figure 16-1. Below the standard menu bar containing entries for File, Edit, View, Go, and Help, there is a toolbar. On the left side of this toolbar are buttons for controlling the view. NetObjects Fusion has five different views: The one selected initially is Site. On the right side of the same bar are navigation buttons. Below the toolbar are tabs that are view-specific. Below that is the actual view. To the left is a select tool and a zoom tool. Inside the view area is one icon that represents a page, which is the default home page. This page is currently selected, as indicated by the bold blue borderline. The properties dialog window shows the properties of this selected page.

To actually edit the page content, select the Page view (the second from the right). The result is shown in Figure 16-2. In this view, there is no tab control at the top. Instead there is a caption showing the page name. Below it there is the MasterBorder label, to the right is a banner showing the page name. On the left side is a button navigation bar that is also part of the MasterBorder. The MasterBorder is essentially a collection of objects that are repeatedly used in several correlated pages. The remainder of the view contains the page layout, which is currently empty. NetObjects Fusion includes a useful online help facility, which can be invoked by right-clicking an element and then selecting What's This? For example, right-clicking the

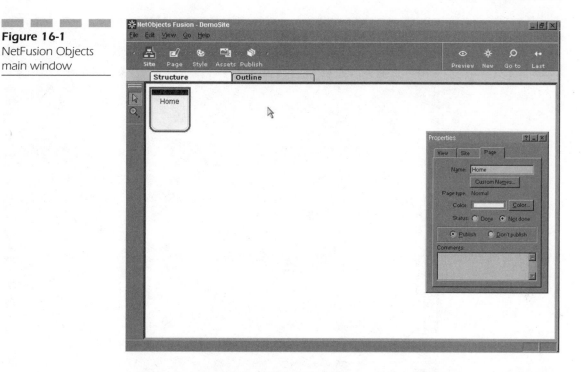

Figure 16-1
NetFusion Objects
main window

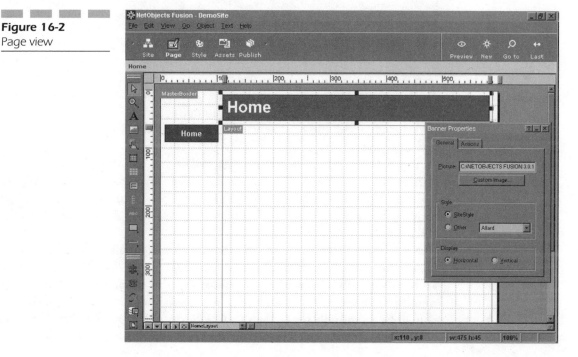

Figure 16-2
Page view

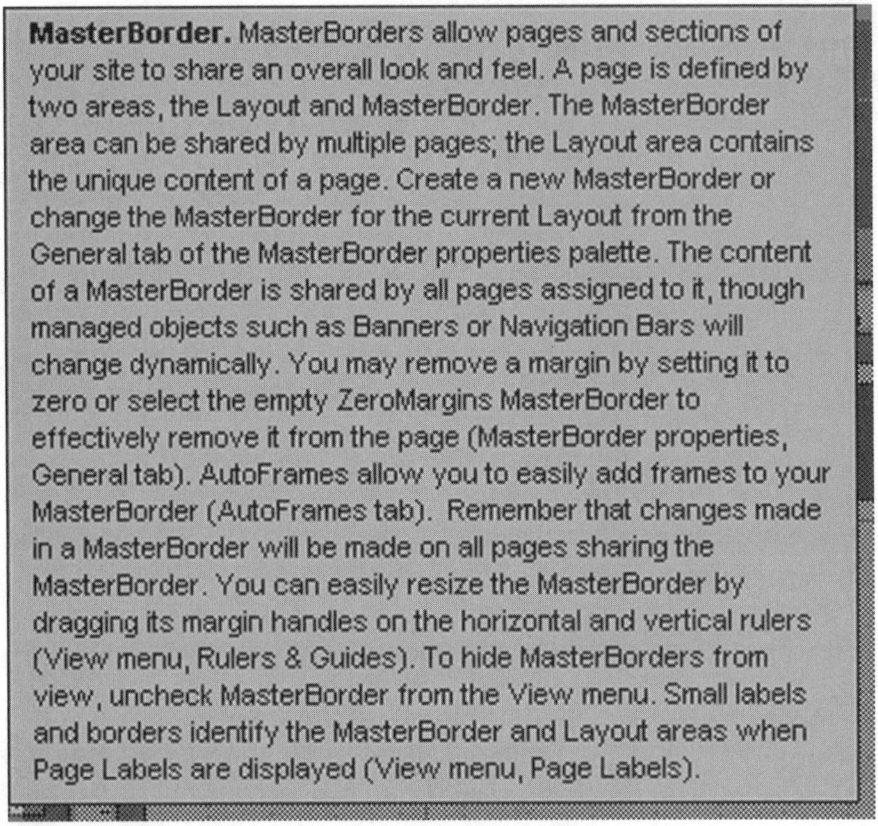

Figure 16-3
MasterBorder
online help

MasterBorder. MasterBorders allow pages and sections of your site to share an overall look and feel. A page is defined by two areas, the Layout and MasterBorder. The MasterBorder area can be shared by multiple pages; the Layout area contains the unique content of a page. Create a new MasterBorder or change the MasterBorder for the current Layout from the General tab of the MasterBorder properties palette. The content of a MasterBorder is shared by all pages assigned to it, though managed objects such as Banners or Navigation Bars will change dynamically. You may remove a margin by setting it to zero or select the empty ZeroMargins MasterBorder to effectively remove it from the page (MasterBorder properties, General tab). AutoFrames allow you to easily add frames to your MasterBorder (AutoFrames tab). Remember that changes made in a MasterBorder will be made on all pages sharing the MasterBorder. You can easily resize the MasterBorder by dragging its margin handles on the horizontal and vertical rulers (View menu, Rulers & Guides). To hide MasterBorders from view, uncheck MasterBorder from the View menu. Small labels and borders identify the MasterBorder and Layout areas when Page Labels are displayed (View menu, Page Labels).

MasterBorder label and requesting help produces the message shown in Figure 16-3. Left of the view itself are two toolbars: the standard (on top) and the advanced (just below it). These toolbars are discussed in detail in the following text.

To get things going, select the Text tool on the left side, click in the layout, and type some text. The Properties palette now shows the text properties, which you may edit, as shown in Figure 16-4. Note that you may place the properties palette wherever you want by dragging it. The same goes for the toolbars on the left side.

Now return to the Site view and select New Page under Edit. Repeat this operation several times to create several new pages, as shown in Figure 16-5. Select the new pages and rename them by double-clicking their names to highlight them and then typing in the new name. The result should be something similar to the one shown in Figure 16-6. Now double-click on the first page that is not Home (Page1 in our example). This opens

Figure 16-4
Inserting a text label
to a page

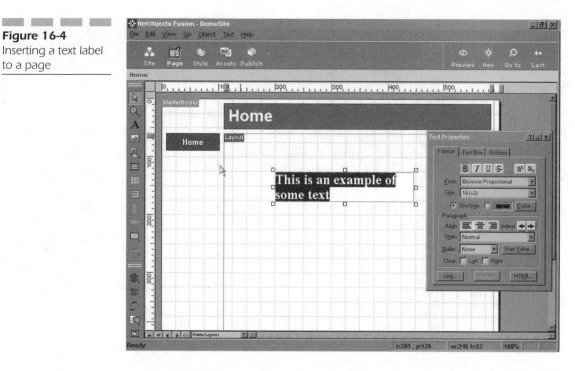

Figure 16-5
Adding new pages

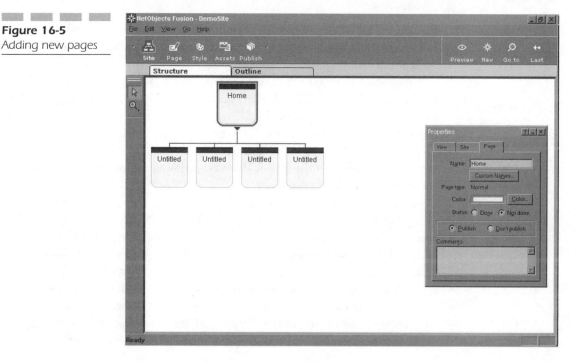

Figure 16-6
Renaming pages

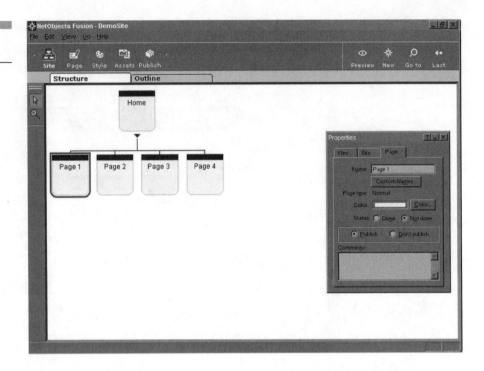

the Page view (this is basically equivalent to clicking on the Page view). Notice that the MasterBorder is extended to include navigation buttons for each of the new pages.

Now select the Style view. This allows you to select a different style for your page components. The style is just a collection of settings that together provide a certain look and feel. For example, select the Remote style. The page style now resembles a VCR remote control, as shown in Figure 16-7. To actually set your pages to this style, you must select the Set Style button on the top bar to the left of the navigation buttons. Figure 16-8 shows the resulting effect on our Page 1.

At this point we have to prepare a simple site. In order to see it in your default Web browser, all you need to do is click Preview in the navigation tools bar. This is a good time to explain the other navigation buttons. The New button creates a new item, usually a new page. In the Style view it creates a new site, in the Assets view (explained in the following text) it creates new files, links, data objects, or variables, and in the Publish view (also explained later), it creates new folders. The Go To button allows you to jump to an object given its name or part of its name, as shown in Figure 16-9. If there are several objects that meet your search criteria, a list is

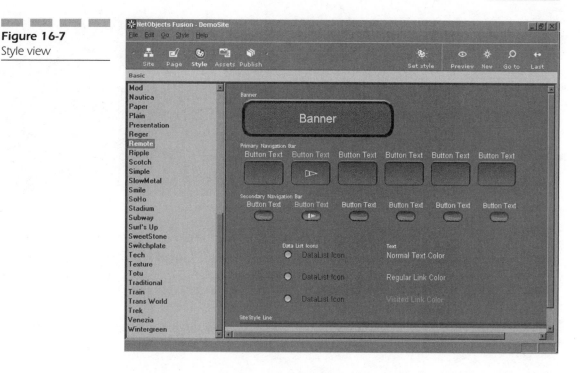

Figure 16-7
Style view

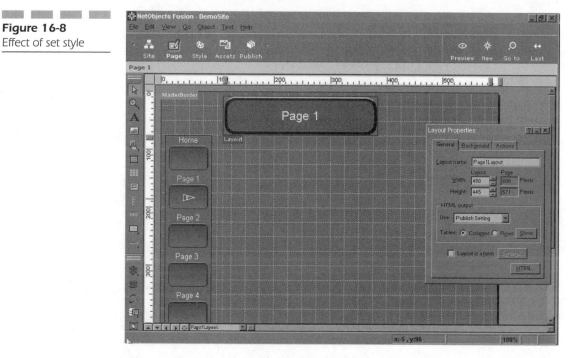

Figure 16-8
Effect of set style

Figure 16-9
Go To navigation
dialog box

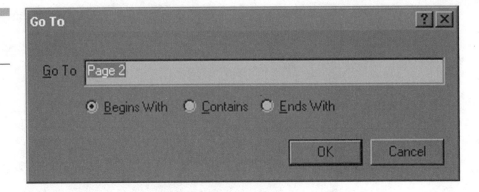

shown for you to select from. The Last button does much the same thing as the Back button in your Web browser. (It takes you back to the previous view or item you were editing.)

Before completing this section, you may save your sample site using the Save Site option under the File menu.

In the next section, we will delve into the features offered by NetObjects Fusion by going over all the different menus.

NetObject Fusion Menus and Toolbars

Menu Bar for Site View

The NetObjects Fusion Menu bar is quite standard. When in the Site view, it contains the following menus:

- *File*   File Manipulation
    - *New Site*   Creates a new site, which may be either blank, from a template, or is an existing local or remote site (stored as HTML files)
    - *Open Site*   Opens an existing NetObjects Fusion Site File (with suffix .nod)
    - *Save Site*   Saves the current site file
    - *Save Site as . . .*   Saves the site file, possibly under a new name
    - *Import Site*   Imports a local or remote site. The dialog box for importing a remote site is shown in Figure 16-10. Just like the WebSphere Studio import facility, you are required to specify here

Figure 16-10
Import Remote Site
dialog box

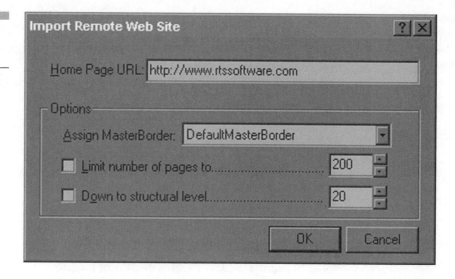

limits on the page numbers and number of levels imported. Levels numbering is based on the hierarchical structure of folders in the Web site.

- *Import Template*   Imports a previously saved template
- Reference HTML
- *Export Site*   Saves the site as a template for future use
- Page Setup
- Print Preview
- Print
- *Quit*   Exits NetObjects Fusion
- *Edit*
  - *Cut, Copy, Paste*   Standard clipboard operations
  - *Delete Page*   Deletes the currently selected page
  - *Select Section*   Selects a whole section
  - *New Page*   Adds a new page
  - Custom Names   This is the equivalent of pressing the Custom Names button on the Page Properties Palette. As shown in Figure 16-11, this dialog box allows you to place different names on the page title, navigation button, and banner. It also allows you to change the file extension for this page.
  - *Preferences*   Edits preferences

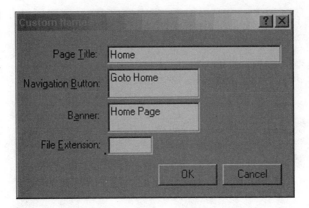

Figure 16-11
Custom Names
dialog box

- *View*   Used to turn on and off different components in the display
  - *Standard Tools*   Toggles display of toolbar
  - *Properties Palette*   Toggles display of properties palette
- *Go*   Provides navigation features
  - *Site, Page, Style, Asset, Publish*   Changes to the corresponding view
  - *Next Page, Previous Page*   Page navigation
  - *Parent, First Child*   Traverses the pages tree
  - *Follow Link*   Follows a link to a new page
  - *Go To*   Same as the Go To navigation button discussed in the previous section
  - *Last*   Same as the Last navigation button discussed in the previous section
  - *Recent*   Selects from a list of recently used views and pages
  - *Preview*   Launches the browser and display site preview, as explained earlier
- *Help*   Online help
  - *Help Topics*   List of help topics
  - *NetObjects Web Site*   Opens a Web browser on the NetObjects Web site
  - *About*   Product information window

Menu Bar for Page View

In the Page view, the View menu gets a few more entries that allow you to control the display of the following components:

- *Toolbars*
  - *Standard Tools*   Toggles display of Standard Tools toolbar
  - *Advanced Tools*   Toggles display of Advanced Tools toolbar
  - *Component Tools*   Toggles display of Component Tools bar
  - *Form Tools*   Toggles display of Form Tools toolbar
- *Palettes*
  - *Properties Palette*   Toggles display of Property Palette mentioned previously
  - *Object Tree*   Toggles display of Object Tree for the current page, as shown in Figure 16-12
- *MasterBorder*   Toggles display of MasterBorder
- *Page Labels*   Toggles display of page labels
- *Object Outlines*   Toggles display of object outlines
- *Rulers and Guides*   Toggles display of rulers and guides
- *Grid*   Toggles display of grid

Figure 16-12
Object tree display

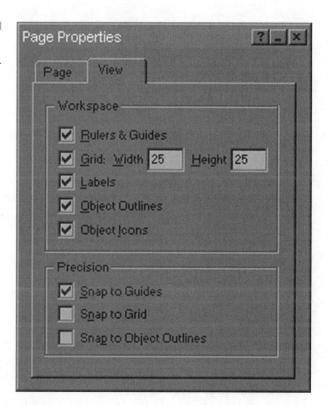

- *Snap To Guides* Forces improved precision by snapping mouse clicks to Guides

- *Snap To Grid* Forces improved precision by snapping mouse clicks to Grid

- *Snap To Object Outlines* Forces improved precision by snapping mouse clicks to Object Outlines

- *Page View Options* Selects the View tab on the Page Properties Palette. This tab allows you to select precision policy (that is, the Snap To . . . items mentioned previously) and the different items displayed on the page. This dialog box is shown in Figure 16-13.

- *Zoom* Selects zoom level out of several options available

In the Page view, there are a few other changes in the menu bar:

- The Edit menu includes some new entries:

  - *Find* Finds text

  - *Replace* Searches and replace text in page

Figure 16-13
Page Properties
display

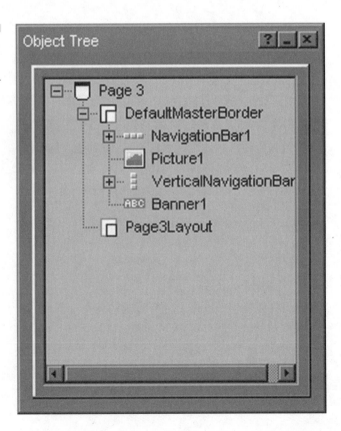

- *Word Count*   Provides word count statistics for page
- *Spell Checking*   Provides spell-checking for page
- *Select All*   Selects all items
- *Select*   Allows selecting specific items such as MasterBorder, Layout, and Whole page

- New Text menu for manipulating text objects

- Edit Text
- *Show Text Invisibles*   Toggles the display of text invisibles
- *Edit Text Style*   Modifies the text style out of a set of predefined styles as shown in Figure 16-14. These styles can be customized.
- *Insert Object*   Allows the insertion of a new object into a textbox that has been selected out of a multitude of possible objects, including tables, pictures, and active objects.
- *Insert HTML*   Keys in HTML source code directly into the textbox
- *Insert Symbol*   Inserts a special symbol (for example, the copyright symbol)
- *Insert Field*   Inserts a date/time or site-related variable (for example, creation date, modification date, author, and so on) or a user-defined and set variable

Figure 16-14
Text Styles dialog box

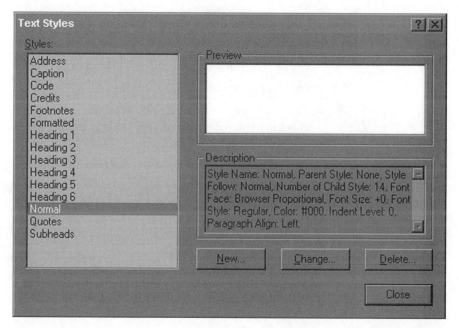

Menu Bar for Style View

In the Style view, it is possible to create new style or select existing ones. The Style menu includes the following entries:

- *New Style* Creates a new style (equivalent to clicking the New button)
- *Add Style to List* Opens a new style stored in a file on disk
- *Remove Style from List* Removes a style from the current list of styles
- *Update Style List* Refreshes the list from disk. Useful if you add new styles directly to the folder in which the styles are stored.
- *Set Style* Sets the site style. Equivalent to clicking the Set Style button, which was previously discussed.

Menu Bar for Assets View

The Assets view is used to review and edit files, links, data objects, and variables. These are traversed using the tab control on top of the work area when in this view, as shown in Figure 16-15. The Assets menu contains the following entries:

- *New . . .* Creates a new file, link, data object, or variable. It is equivalent to clicking the New button.
- *Delete All Unused File Assets* Deletes all files that are not in use in pages. Available only under the Files tab.
- *Open Asset* Opens the selected asset
- *Verify Assets* Verifies all assets in the current tab. This includes checking the existence of files and that links are not broken.

Figure 16-15
Assets view

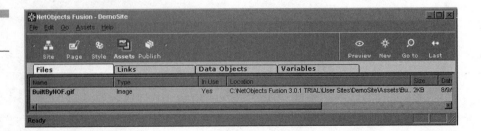

Figure 16-16
Publish view

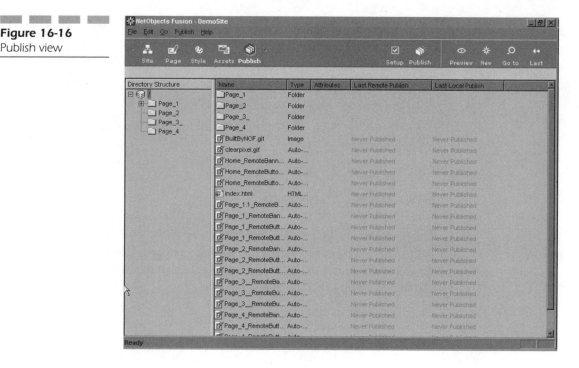

Menu Bar for Publish View

The Publish view, shown in Figure 16-16, is used to review the site before publishing it, and for actually publishing it. The Publish menu available in this view provides the following options:

- *Publish Setup* Shows dialog box controlling publishing. It contains the following tab-controls:

  - *Directory Structure* Uses flat structure (that is, no folders), by file types (that is, pictures in a separate directory, and so on), or by site sections (that is, following the page hierarchy in the site view)

  - *HTML output* Indicates the character set to be used, whether to include comments in HTML output, and what kind of HTML output to generate as far as tables are concerned (this relates to compatibility problems, and the dialog box explains each option)

  - *Server Location* Local and remote server locations can be reviewed, added, and edited under this tab.

- *Properties* Publish properties such as last publish date, need to publish, read-only, and so on.

- *Clear all customizations*   Removes all changes made to the publish directory; that is, re-creates it based on the site.
- *New Folder*   Creates new folder, equivalent to clicking the New button
- *Rename Folder*   Renames the selected folder
- *Delete Folder*   Deletes the selected folder
- *Publish Site*   Does the actual publishing; that is, posts the files on a local or remote site

Standard Toolbar

The standard toolbar allows you to insert so-called standard items into your pages. Table 16-1 summarizes the options on this toolbar. Note that some of these options actually include more options under them: These are indicated by a small arrow on their tool icon.

Advanced Toolbar

The advanced toolbar allows you to utilize more complex and usually dynamic items in your Web pages. Such items include media (sounds and video), Java applets, ActiveX controls, Data Lists, and External HTML files imported directly into your page. The advanced toolbar items are summarized in Table 16-2.

Components Toolbar

The Components toolbar (mentioned in the View menu for the Page view) allows you to place special dynamic objects in your page. These are essentially prepared mini-applications with a specific functionality. The available components are summarized in Table 16-3.

Form Tools

Forms are created using the Form Area tool in the standard tool box. After it is created, you can add objects to it using the Form Tools toolbar, the content of which is summarized in Table 16-4.

Table 16-1

Standard toolbar
buttons summary

Icon	Meaning
	Select Selects an object
	Zoom In / Out Changes the level of zoom for the display of the page
	Text Inserts Text
	Picture Inserts Picture object
	Hotspot Creates a link attached to a portion of a picture. The hotspot can be rectangular (default), circular, or polygonal.
	Layout Region Creates a layout region within an existing layout region.
	Table Adds a table
	Form Area Creates a form area
	Navigation Bar Inserts a navigation bar, which is an object that automatically generates and updates internal links for the site.
	Banner Inserts a banner showing text or an image. Banners are usually generated automatically and are automatically updated as the site changes. By default, the banner name is based on the page name.
	Draw Draws a shape. Options are Rectangle (default), Rounded Rectangle, Ellipse, Polygon.
	Line Draws a line. Options are: *HR Rule (default)* A line that uses the HTML tag for "Horizontal Rule" (<HR>) *Draw* A freestyle line or arrow *SiteStyle* A line conforming to the currently selected site style. This line can be used to divide a page into sections.

Properties Palette

The Properties palette allows you to edit the different attributes associated with objects such as button and text boxes. The attributes that can be

Table 16-2

Advanced toolbar
buttons summary

Icon	Meaning
	Media Inserts a media object. Options are: Plug-in (default), Shockwave, QuickTime, Video, Sound.
	Java Inserts a Java applet
	ActiveX Inserts an ActiveX control
	Data Inserts Data List or new External Data Source. Data Lists show data which is extracted from an external data source. External data sources are usually ODBC complaint database systems.
	External HTML Inserts external HTML

Table 16-3

Components
toolbar buttons
summary

Icon	Meaning
	Forms Button Inserts a button inside a form
	Forms CheckBox Inserts a checkbox inside a form
	Forms Radio Button Inserts a radio button inside a form
	Forms Edit Field Inserts an editable field inside a form
	Forms Multi-Lines Inserts a multi-line field inside a form
	Forms Combo Box Inserts a combo-box into a form

modified include background colors, spacing, alignment, and location. For
selected text, it is possible to modify the text formatting, but more importantly, it is possible to link it. Links (or hypertext links) are the essence of
Web browsing because they are the ones allowing you to jump between
pages. You might want to define anchors for your links (these are just pieces
of text on your page and can be set by clicking the Anchor button on the
Properties palette after selecting the text). NetObjects Fusion supports four
kinds of links.

Table 16-4

Form toolbar
buttons summary

Icon	Meaning
	DynaButtons Inserts a "Dynabuttons" object, which is a Java button linking to another page or a file.
	TickerTape Inserts a "ticker tape" object which shows a text message
	SiteMapper Inserts an object which shows a navigation map for the site
	MessageBoard Inserts a fully-blown "bulletin board"
	Picture Rollover Adds a picture which "rolls over"
	Time Based Picture Adds a picture display which depends on the time of day
	Picture Loader Inserts a picture which is to be loaded from a different site
	Rotating Picture Adds a set of pictures which appear sequentially in predefined intervals. This can be used to provide simple "animation."
	NetObjects Fusion Components Inserts other components (possibly your own or third-party components)

- *Internal Links*   Links to pages and anchors in your site.
- *Smart Links*   Links to pages in your site, based on relative position in the site structure rather than on the name of the page. This allows structural linking that is oblivious to changes in page names.
- *External Links*   These are essentially URLs on remote sites. These should include the protocol, host name, path name, and possibly filename. For example, `http://quote.yahoo.com`.
- *File Links*   Links to local files that are to be included in your site.

After you add a new link, you select the appropriate tab for the type of link you want and key in the specifics of the link.

The Deployment Phase— Publishing Your Site

In order to actually put your site online, you need to publish it. For this purpose, you use the Publish View, which as explained previously includes the Publish menu. In this view, you arrange the directory structure as you want it, the HTML output required, and the server profiles to be used (all these are under Publish Setup). You may manually customize your directory structure further as needed by creating folders and moving files and folders around.

To publish your site, click the Publish button or select Publish from the Publish menu. Note that if your site is behind a firewall or stored on a proxy server, you may not publish directly. Instead, you need to publish the site to a local folder, and then copy it using FTP or any other means.

17

NetObjects ScriptBuilder

NetObjects ScriptBuilder is a script editor that provides full support for the vast variety of scripting languages available on the Web. ScriptBuilder focuses on script editing rather than on HTML page design. In this respect, it complements NetObjects Fusion, which is described in the previous chapter. The main advantages of ScriptBuilder are that it is easy to develop scripts with it using a visual interface, and that it provides an execution environment for testing your scripts. Another useful feature is the built-in reference manual for language elements. It is easy to get confused with all these different scripting languages out there.

The last section in this chapter focuses on the JavaScript scripting language, which is one of the languages supported by ScriptBuilder.

Installation

The NetObjects ScriptBuilder can be downloaded from the NetObjects Web site at `http://www.netobjects.com/scriptbuilder`. The installation is straightforward and hassle-free. Just run the installation executable, and it will guide you through the installation.

Getting Started

When you start NetObjects ScriptBuilder, you see the following three elements on your screen, as shown in Figure 17-1:

Figure 17-1
ScriptBuilder
main window

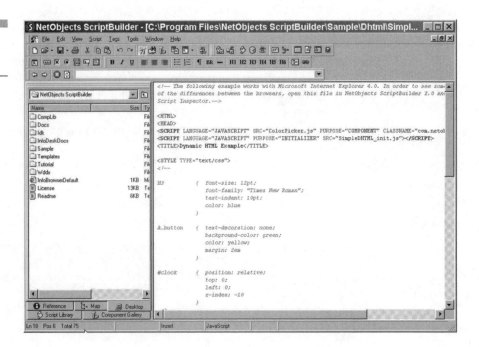

1. *Toolbars*   Directly under the menu bar. For each toolbar, we specify the button from left to right. Note that toolbars can be displayed or removed using the Toolbars option in the View menu.

- *Standard Toolbar*   Includes entries for the most common operations: New, Open, Save, Print, Cut, Copy, Paste, Undo. In addition, it has a control for showing the currently highlighted language and for toggling the display of the ToolBox and of the Results View. The last four buttons in this toolbar are responsible for opening the component inspector window (detailing the current component), toggling between edit/preview modes, opening external preview on any browser outside of ScriptBuilder, and deploying the current document.
- *Search*   Standard items for Find, Replace, Find Previous, Find Next, and Find in Files
- *Script*   A toolbar for working with scripts that contains the following elements:
  - **a.** *Syntax Checker*   Checks syntax of the current document
  - **b.** *Script inspector*   Inspects the script and places results in the results view. Inspection includes testing compatibility with Netscape and Microsoft browsers.
  - **c.** *Script block*   Inserts a <SCRIPT> block into the current document
  - **d.** *Server block*   Inserts a server block into the current document
  - **e.** *Servlet*   Inserts a servlet block into the current document
  - **f.** *Comment Block*   Inserts a comment block into the current document
  - **g.** *Function Block*   Inserts a function block into the current document
  - **h.** `Window.open()`   Inserts a `window.open()` method to the current document
  - **i.** `Document.write()`   Inserts a `document.write()` method to the current document
  - **j.** *Message Box*   Displays the Message Box dialog box
  - **k.** *Custom Objects*   Displays the Customer Objects dialog box
- *Form Elements*   Used for managing forms. Includes the Form, Button, CheckBox, RadioButton, Select, Text, and TextArea, each showing the respective dialog box.
- *HTML Tags*   This provides WordPad-like buttons for HTML tags. These buttons include Bold, Italic, Underline, Align Left, Center, Align Right, Unordered list (items), Ordered list, Paragraph, Line

Break, Horizontal Line, Heading 1 to Heading 6, the Image button for inserting an image, and the Link button for inserting or editing hypertext links.

■ *InfoBrowser*   Back, Forward, Stop, and Refresh, used the same way they are used in a Web Browser. This toolbar also includes a text area for typing a URL. The InfoBrowser essentially provides you a miniature Web browser within ScriptBuilder.

■ *Window List*   Previous Document, Next Document—Select a new window from the list of open documents

2. *ToolBox*   This is the area on the left side of the window. It has a tab control with five different tabs:

■ *Map*   A visual tree of the current document (as shown in Figure 17-2)

■ *Desktop*   Windows Explorer-like access to your desktop (as shown in Figure 17-1).

■ *Reference*   Online reference manual for the different scripting languages

■ *Script Library*   A list of predefined scripts that can be used

■ *Component Gallery*   A collection of predefined components that can be included in a document

3. *Main WorkArea for Editing*   This area shows the currently edited document. The different tags and code fragments are color-coded for

Figure 17-2
ScriptBuilder Main
Window with Map
Display on ToolBox

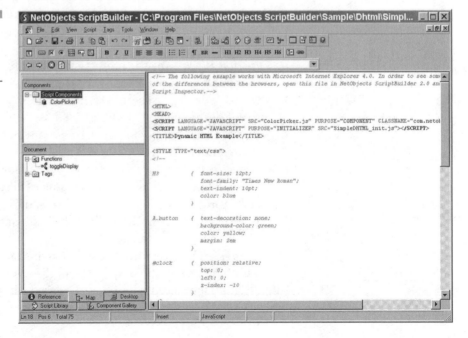

easy identification. The status bars at the bottom of the window indicate the location in the file, the current edit mode, and the currently edited language (based on the current cursor location).

To get started with ScriptBuilder, select the New entry under the File menu. You are presented with the New file menu dialog box, as shown in Figure 17-3. Select Default HTML File. The empty file created is shown in Listing 17-1. Go into the Body section and select the comment indicating where to add the HTML, as shown in Listing 17-2. Remove this comment and click the Bold button instead. This would add two tags, `<B>` and `</B>`. Between them type `This is a test`, as shown in Listing 17-3. Now click the Toggle Edit/Preview to see the preview for this, as shown in Figure 17-4.

So far, we have created a very simple HTML file. This is of course a very simple task for which we do not need ScriptBuilder, but we started with it just to get the feel of this tool.

Figure 17-3
New File dialog box

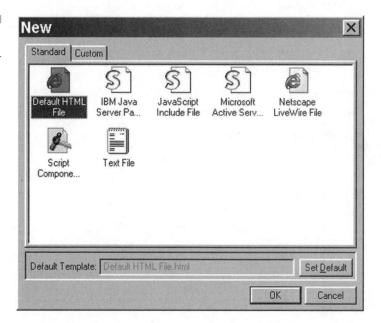

Listing 17-1
New file source

```
<HTML>
<HEAD>
<META NAME="GENERATOR" Content="NetObjects ScriptBuilder 3.0">
<TITLE>Document Title</TITLE>
</HEAD>
<BODY>
<!-- Insert HTML here -->
</BODY>
</HTML>
```

Listing 17-2
New file source with
comment selected

```
<HTML>
<HEAD>
<META NAME="GENERATOR" Content="NetObjects ScriptBuilder 3.0">
<TITLE>Document Title</TITLE>
</HEAD>
<BODY>

<!-- Insert HTML here -->
</BODY>
</HTML>
```

Listing 17-3
File source with
bold text added

```
<HTML>
<HEAD>
<META NAME="GENERATOR" Content="NetObjects ScriptBuilder 3.0">
<TITLE>Document Title</TITLE>
</HEAD>
<BODY>
<B>This is a test</B>
</BODY>
</HTML>
```

Figure 17-4
New file preview

This is a test

The next section goes into building scripts. Before continuing, it is important to note that when using the various buttons to insert script components, it is imperative to place the cursor in the right place. ScriptBuilder has no inherent consistency-checking to prevent you from adding an element inside a different tag where it is not allowed, or even in a manner that breaks a different tag.

The Options entry under the Tools menu allows you to customize the display and colors used in the editor. In addition, it allows you to select the browsers used, the default folder for scripts, default file format (Windows, UNIX, or Macintosh), file extensions to be recognized by ScriptBuilder, location of ToolBox Reference files, and optional settings for code, such as a username to include automatically in functions.

Writing Scripts

Continuing our previous example, place the cursor below the label we inserted and add a Script block. In this block, type `for`. As shown in Listing 17-4, ScriptBuilder automatically completes this to a fully blown `for` statement in JavaScript. This is thanks to the AutoScripting feature under the Tools menu. Note that this feature can be customized so that any keyword prompts any desired statement. Change the variable value in the `for` statement to 100. Inside the `for` loop block, add a `document.writeln()` statement as shown in Listing 17-5. The `<U>` and `</U>` indicate the underlining and can be created by clicking the Underline button. You only need to wrap them with quotes. The result of executing this script is shown in Figure 17-5.

Now, remove the `for` loop and add instead a new script using the Script button. Into this script, add the `DisplaySource` script in the Script library on the ToolBox. To add the script, place the cursor inside the new script you

Listing 17-4
Adding a `for` loop

```
<HTML>
<HEAD>
<META NAME="GENERATOR" Content="NetObjects ScriptBuilder 3.0">
<TITLE>Document Title</TITLE>
</HEAD>
<BODY>
<B>This is a test</B>
<SCRIPT LANGUAGE="JavaScript">
<!--
for ( var i=0; i<value; i++ ) {

}

//-->
</SCRIPT>
<INPUT TYPE="button" NAME="button" HREF="javascript:toggleDisplay('clock');">
</BODY>
</HTML>
```

Listing 17-5
Finalizing the
for loop

```
<HTML>
<HEAD>
<META NAME="GENERATOR" Content="NetObjects ScriptBuilder 3.0">
<TITLE>Document Title</TITLE>
</HEAD>
<BODY>
<B>This is a test</B>
<SCRIPT LANGUAGE="JavaScript">
<!--
for ( var i=0; i<100; i++ ) {
    document.writeln("<U>" + i + "</U>");
}

//-->
</SCRIPT>
</BODY>
</HTML>
```

Figure 17-5
For loop preview

This is a test 0 1 2 3 4 5 6 7 8 9 10 11 12 13 14 15 16 17 18 19 20 21 22 23 24 25 26 27 28 29 30 31 32 33 34 35 36 37 38 39 40 41 42 43 44 45 46 47 48 49 50 51 52 53 54 55 56 57 58 59 60 61 62 63 64 65 66 67 68 69 70 71 72 73 74 75 76 77 78 79 80 81 82 83 84 85 86 87 88 89 90 91 92 93 94 95 96 97 98 99

added and then drag the new component into your editing area. In addition, add in the page body a new script calling the function DisplaySource(). This function should show the source of the HTML file. The code is shown in Listing 17-6.

Now execute the script. We get the This is a test message as before, except now a new window with the HTML page source pops up.

Because it is beyond the scope of this chapter (or of this book) to cover the syntax of all scripting languages supported by ScriptBuilder, the remainder of this chapter focuses on one scripting language, JavaScript.

Listing 17-6
DisplaySource
function

```
<HTML>
<HEAD>
<META NAME="GENERATOR" Content="NetObjects ScriptBuilder 3.0">
<SCRIPT LANGUAGE="JavaScript">
<!--
function DisplaySource()  {
   var This_URL = "";
   This_URL = document.location;
   window.location = "view-source:"+This_URL;
}
//-->
</SCRIPT>
<TITLE>Document Title</TITLE>
</HEAD>
<BODY>
<B>This is a test</B>
<SCRIPT LANGUAGE="JavaScript">
<!--
DisplaySource();
//-->
</SCRIPT>

</BODY>
</HTML>
```

Figure 17-6
ScriptInspector
output

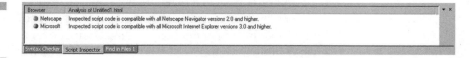

An important feature of ScriptBuilder that is very useful in writing scripts is the Script Inspector, which provides information relating to the compatibility of your scripts with both Netscape and Microsoft Explorer browsers. Figure 17-6 shows a sample output of such an inspection.

JavaScript Primer

JavaScript is a scripting language that has its roots in a joint development effort between Sun and Netscape and that has become Netscape's Web scripting language. JavaScript is a very simple programming language that supports client-side scripting allowing HTML pages to include functions and scripts. These scripts can help implement complex Web page behavior with relatively little programming effort. In addition, Netscape offers the JavaScript language for server programming in the form of the *LiveWire* package.

The primary attribute of JavaScript distinguishing it from Java is its simplicity. JavaScript (which was originally called *Java-lite* and then *Mocha*) is not a scaled-down version of Java. Rather, it is a scripting language with relatively few programming primitives, a very flexible type-less system, and limited functionality. The language is somewhat object-based, providing a model based on objects and object naming. However, it is certainly not an object-oriented programming language and provides very limited support as far as software engineering concepts are concerned. In general, JavaScript is most appropriate for creating scripts that add functionality to form elements and other interactive capabilities to HTML pages. Its primary claim to fame relies on the fact that JavaScript code can directly interact with HTML elements, getting and setting their properties.

JavaScript syntax resembles those of C and C++. It is probably closest to C syntax because of its heavy utilization of structures. Most of the operators, expressions, and statements are identical to those found in C. The primary difference is that there are no pointers and that objects (which resemble C structure syntax) can be created and methods invoked. In these, JavaScript syntax is similar to C++ (once more—without pointers).

In order to give you a brief introduction to JavaScript programming, we first look at one detailed example and then continue to discuss the JavaScript object model and JavaScript event handling. Because JavaScript is a primary contender for the title of Web scripting language, many reference texts have been published on JavaScript (for example, [Fea], [NeRe], [Rit]) and a number of Web sites provide JavaScript documentation (`http://home.netscape.com/eng/mozilla/Gold/handbook/javascript/index.html` to name just one).

Example: Unit Conversion

The example presented in this section is a simple conversion tool. The tool converts between inches and centimeters, between pounds and kilograms, and between miles and kilometers. The HTML page definition including the JavaScript code is shown by Listing 17-7. Figure 17-7 shows the resulting screen in Netscape Navigator where values have been entered in one field in each of the three lines (conversion units). Figure 17-8 shows the result after the Convert button is pressed. Note that we can enter a value in either of the two input fields in each line. The scripts produce the value for the matching (not entered) unit (that is, conversion is allowed both from and to the metric units). If both values are entered, the script will use the nonmetric unit as the primary and will create the metric value.

Listing 17-7
Unit conversion code

```
1    <html>
2
3      <head>
4
5        <title>Simple JavaScript Example</title>
6
7        <script language="JavaScript">
8          <!- For old browsers
9
10           // This functions receives two input fields and performs
the actual
11           // conversion based on which field is the empty one.
12           // The function receives the factor which would be
required to
13           // convert the units of the first field into units of
14           // the second field.
15           // If the first filed is not empty the second is
converted according
16           // to the parsed value in the first filed. If the first
field is
17           // empty and the second one isn't then the first field
is converted
18           // according to the value in the second field (using the
19           // inverse factor). If both fields are empty do nothing.
20           function performConvert(field1, field2, factor) {
21             var aValue
22             if (field1.value != '') {
23               aValue = parseFloat(field1.value)
24               field2.value = aValue * factor
25             } else {
26               if (field2.value != '') {
27                 aValue = parseFloat(field2.value)
28                 field1.value = aValue / factor
29               }
30             }
31           }
32
33           // This function invokes the conversion functions
defined above.
34           // Use the generic conversion function performConvert()
sending
35           // in the fields pairs and the appropriate conversion
factors.
36           function convert(form) {
37             performConvert(form.pounds, form.kilograms, 0.45)
38             performConvert(form.inches, form.centimeters, 2.5)
39             performConvert(form.miles, form.kilometers, 1.6)
40           }
41
42       // ->
43     </script>
44
45   </head>
46
47   <body>
48
```

continues

Listing 17-7
Continued

```
49      <form name="convForm">
50          These widgets are used to provide conversion between
various metric
51          and non-metric units.<br> Please fill in at most one
value in each line.
52      <p>
53
54      <input type="text" name="pounds" size=10> Pounds
55      =
56      <input type="text" name="kilograms" size=10> Kilograms
57      <br>
58
59      <input type="text" name="inches" size=10> Inches
60      =
61      <input type="text" name="centimeters" size=10>
Centimeters
62      <br>
63
64      <input type="text" name="miles" size=10> Miles
65      =
66      <input type="text" name="kilometers" size=10> Kilometers
67
68      <p>
69      <input type="button" value="Convert"
onclick="convert(this.form)">
70
71      </form>
72
73    </body>
74
75  </html>
```

Figure 17-7
Unit conversion;
before activating
the script

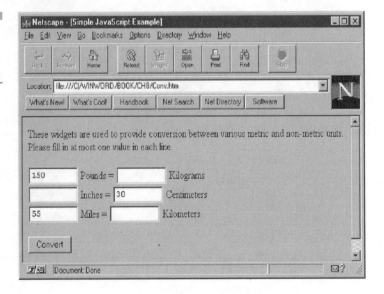

Figure 17-8
Unit conversion; after
activating the script

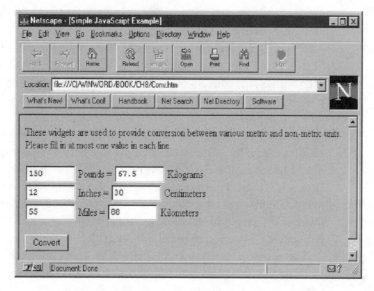

The HTML page shown in Figure 17-7 has two main parts—the *head* and the *body*. In our case, all JavaScript code is placed in the *head* section of the page. Although JavaScript can be placed in the *body* part (and cases do arise in which it is preferable to do so), JavaScript code is usually placed in the *head* portion of the page. Because HTML is read from top to bottom (we will discuss this at length in a later section), placing the code in the *head* section ensures that the scripts are available for use by any HTML element defined in the *body* of the page. To inform the browser that we are defining a script (using the JavaScript language), we use the SCRIPT HTML element with the LANGUAGE attribute set to JavaScript as shown in lines 7 and 43. Note that the JavaScript code is embedded within an HTML comment (starting on line 8 and ending on line 42). This assures that old browsers that do not support scripting in general and JavaScript specifically will ignore the code and not display it.

The *body* of the page consists of the form in which the different values are entered. Each line consists of two input elements of type text (see lines 54-56, 59-61, and 64-66). In addition, an input element of type button is used to activate the conversion code. Please note that every element is explicitly named, including the form itself. Besides being a good habit in general, this allows the JavaScript code to easily reference the elements on the page by using that name (for example, line 37 references the input element for pounds in the form as `form.pounds` because the element's name is pounds and it is scoped by the form; in this case, *form* is the argument sent to the function). The names given to the elements using the NAME attribute allow easy references using a standard hierarchical scoping (the hierarchy being the instance hierarchy).

The most interesting part of the *body* definition is the attributes for the button input element. Apart from the TYPE and VALUE attributes, a new attribute is introduced—ONCLICK. The value of this attribute in line 69 is a JavaScript function call specification. It defines what should happen when the button is clicked. Because JavaScript follows the event based model used in Navigator and other GUI systems, function calls and script segments can be associated with events. Input elements of type button can always handle the click-on event; the ONCLICK attribute is the specifier through which a programmer can define what should happen when this event occurs. In our case, we want the `convert` function (defined in the *head* of the page) to be called passing in the form as an argument. Chapter 8 discusses JavaScript events at length.

The convert function that is invoked when a button is clicked is defined in lines 37-40. It accepts a single argument—the form in which the fields are defined. We chose to pass the form as an argument even though we could have hardcoded the hierarchical name (that is, used `document.convForm.pounds`). Because JavaScript provides several mechanisms for referencing an HTML element, programmers often have a certain degree of flexibility regarding the function signatures. It is usually a good habit to make the functions as generic and decoupled from the actual document and form structures as possible.

The convert function makes use of a utility function, `performConvert`, which performs the actual conversion. This function (defined in lines 20-31) can perform any conversion that is based on a single multiplier (for example, one kilogram = 2.2 pounds. More complicated conversions cannot be handled by this function. For example, the function cannot be used to convert Celsius to Fahrenheit because this involved a multiplier as well as an additive value). The convert function makes three calls to this helper function. In each call, it passes in three arguments: the input element for the non-metric unit, the input element for the metric unit, and the conversion factor required to convert a value of one of the non-metric unit to metric units. Because inside the `convert` function, the form variable is bound to the HTML form in the page, and because each of the elements is explicitly named, each call to `performConvert` can be made with the appropriate elements.

The `performConvert` function receives three arguments: two fields and a conversion factor. Note that JavaScript is not a typed language, so typing information is nowhere to be found. Thus, only the argument variable names are specified in the function definition in line 20, and the temporary variable `aValue` is defined using the `var` statement on line 21 with no type specification. The function then branches on whether a value has been entered in the non-metric field. (Recall that this field is the primary, so if both fields have been given a value, the non-metric value takes precedence.) If there is a non-metric value (line 22), the value in the field (referenced by `field1.value` in line 23) is converted from a string to a float using the built-in JavaScript `parseFloat` function and is assigned to the `aValue` variable. This value is then multiplied by the conversion factor and assigned to the value of the metric input element as shown in line 24. If the non-metric field has no value and the metric field has one, the inverse conversion is performed in lines 27 and 28.

The JavaScript Object Model

As we have already mentioned, JavaScript is not an object-oriented language. It fails to satisfy some basic features available in all object-oriented programming languages such as inheritance and polymorphism. It also provides no explicit handling of encapsulation and object structure definition. However, JavaScript provides a very simplistic mechanism that allows creating object structures along with object properties and functions (called methods). This mechanism is based on a flexible non-typed object model that resembles slot-based model such as those found in the CLOS and Self programming languages ([CLOS], [SELF]).

Objects may have attributes (or properties). We have already seen a number of such examples in the previous two examples. A property has a name and a value. The value of a property can be any JavaScript value or object; no typing information is associated with the property. In this respect, a property is similar to a slot in which some value may be placed. This can also be recognized from the two ways available for referencing a property. For example, if an object `aList` has a property named `size`, we can reference that property (for retrieval or assignment) using one of the following three forms:

```
aList.size
aList["size"]
aList[2]
```

The second and third forms of property access exemplify some of the reflective capabilities of JavaScript. This specific reflective capability allows an object to be viewed as an array composed of the object's properties. The third form shows the relationship between objects and arrays even more explicitly. In our example, the assumption is that the `size` property is the second attribute in the object definition. This perspective of properties allows us to, for example, iterate over all of the object's properties as we would iterate over all the elements of an array. This iteration is completely decoupled from the actual object definition and will work on any object because we are taking the view of an object as a collection of properties. For example, we could use the following code for iterating over all properties in an object:

```
for (var propIndex in anObject)
// Do something using anObject[propIndex]
```

The duality of objects and arrays can also be used for handling arrays. JavaScript does not provide an explicit array type; instead, arrays are simply objects that have a size and a number of slots that can reference values and objects. Because these properties may be accessed using the array operator, we have effectively defined an array without explicit language support for the array concept. This makes the number of primitives in the language very small, allowing it to remain simple for understanding and for implementation.

Like any object-based language, objects in JavaScript can be associated with behavior as well as state. JavaScript supports a notion of methods that are functions associated with an object. This is done be explicitly naming a reference to the JavaScript function. For a JavaScript function called `aFunctionName` that has already been defined, we can name a method in the object `anObject` called `aMethodName` using the form:

```
anObject.aMethodName = aFunctionName
```

This allows us to make calls of the form

```
anObject.aMethodName()
```

(assuming that the function takes no arguments). Note that the function is associated with the object in terms of naming and context. This implies that this variable will reference the object for which the method has been invoked inside the function. Therefore, if the function includes a reference to

```
this[1]
```

it will reference the property at slot number one in the object for which the method was called. Note that methods only imply a context and a calling format; no encapsulation is enforced and the function may be called independently of the object.

Functions can have any number of arguments. In fact, functions can even have a variable number of arguments. Like properties, function arguments may be accessed by either using their names as defined in the function prototype or using an array-like mechanism making use of the arguments properties array. For example, if a function is defined as

```
aFunction(firstArg, secondArg, thirdArg) {
.....
}
```

we can reference the value of the second argument either by using the explicit name secondArg or by using the form arguments[1] (because the argument array starts with an index of zero). This form allows us to define functions with a variable number of arguments. The arguments pseudo-variable has a length property allowing us to reference all variables without knowing how many are available using

```
for (var argIndex = 0 ; argIndex < arguments.length; argIndex++)
            // Do something using arguments[argIndex]
```

Objects are created by defining a function that populates properties and method associations and then using the new keyword. For example, if we want to create a new object that represents a bond with a maturity and a coupon value, we define a function of the form

```
function Bond(aMaturity, aCoupon) {
        this.maturity = aMaturity
        this.coupon = aCoupon
    }
```

and then make the call

```
aBond = new Bond(20, 6.5)
```

This will create a new object (a Bond object) with two properties initialized to 20 and 6.5. The function being used is similar to a constructor in languages such as C++ in which the members may be initialized to certain values. However, these functions are more important in JavaScript because they are actually the JavaScript programming construct with which objects structures are defined (as opposed to the class construct in C++ for example). It is good practice, for example, to include any association of functions as methods of the object inside these constructor methods.

As mentioned, JavaScript does not have an array data type and arrays are viewed as objects with properties that are referenced using an index instead of a name. The following piece of code shows a definition of a function named MakeArray in which the duality between objects and arrays is used for creating an array.

```
// Create an array with n elements.
// JavaScript has not explicit array type but just like
// objects that can have a constructor-like function,
// we can have a function creating an array. All we have
// to do is populate the array's properties.
function MakeArray(n) {
this.length = n;
for (var i = 0; i < n; i++) this[i] = 0
return this
}
```

The length property is used to set the size of the array. The properties for the actual array values may or may not be initialized (in the example, they are initialized). These slots may later be accessed using the index-based property access. This is the preferred access method for arrays because the properties are not named.

JavaScript Built-In Objects

Programming JavaScript is a simple task due not only to the simplicity of the JavaScript programming language but also to the fact that the environment includes a number of built-in objects and functions that are extremely useful in any HTML-related task. This built-in support can be broadly categorized to two categories:

- Browser objects
- Miscellaneous objects and functions

Browser objects include object definitions and instantiations of commonly used HTML objects such as forms, documents, windows, and frames. When a browser session is initiated, a number of objects are created automatically by the browser for the HTML page. The following objects are automatically available for any JavaScript script:

- *document* Represents the page's document and can be used to access all components in the page. As shown in the previous sections, any HTML element can be scoped through the document object.
- *history* An object representing the list of visited URLs as shown by the Go button in Navigator
- *location* An object representing the current URL
- *window:* An object representing the current window that can be used to control attributes such as frames, parent, and child windows

Figure 17-9
Built-in browser
objects instance
hierarchy

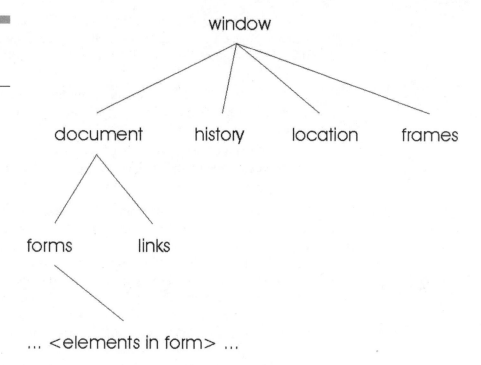

Each of these objects are organized in a hierarchy as shown in Figure 17-9. The top level object is always the window object. Using this object, the document, history, and location objects may be accessed (although they may also be accessed directly named because the default scoping is the window scope).

Each element in the HTML *body* section is accessible from the document object. Access relies on the name given to the element using the NAME attribute. In addition, some elements may be accessed through helper structures. For example, forms are normally accessed using the forms' names as shown in previous examples. In addition, Navigator defines an array by the name of forms that are scoped by the document object and may be used to access any form (whether it is named or not). If the HTML page has two forms, the second (in order of appearance in the HTML page definition) can be accessed using

```
document.forms[1]
```

(once more, the array is 0-indexed).

In addition to browser objects, JavaScript implements the following objects:

- *Date*   The Date object implements various functionalities related to dates and times. These include methods for accessing dates, displaying dates, printing dates, deriving differences between different dates and times, and so on.

- *Math*   The Math object implements a number of mathematical constants and functions such as trigonometric, exponential, and logarithmic functions.

- *String*   String objects are implicitly created as quoted literals. JavaScript implements a number of support methods for these objects such as substring() and case conversions.

Finally, JavaScript defines a number of specialized functions that are not associated with any particular object, but rather provide general capabilities useful in any context. These include functions such as parseInt and parseFloat that are useful for converting a string into an integer or a float (as used for example in Listing 17-7), and the eval function that can be used to evaluate an expression. The eval function receives a string and invokes the interpreter to evaluate the expression, simulating a scenario in which this was explicitly part of the page definition. This provides a dynamic model in which code can be dynamically generated and invoked and is similar to the perform construct found in languages such as Smalltalk and Objective-C.

JavaScript Events

Like most programming environments today, JavaScript is event-based. As an environment managed by an Internet browser, scripts can be associated with events that are signaled by the browser. These include events such as button clicks, field entry, and selection changes. In addition, specialized events are signaled upon loading and unloading, which is useful for initialization and finalization.

Listing 17-7 shows how JavaScript code is associated with a combination of an element and an event. The string associated with the event/element pair is usually a JavaScript function call, but can also be a short JavaScript code segment. When the browser signals such an event, the code table is inspected and the function (or code) invoked. Table 17-1 lists the available events in JavaScript and the HTML elements for which they are allowed. It is not an error to use a wrong event for a wrong element, but it will have no effect.

Table 17-1	**Event**	**HTML Elements**	**Event Description**
JavaScript Event Handlers and HTML Elements	blur	Field, Select	Remove focus from element.
	change	Field, Select	Value change.
	click	Button (all kinds), Checkbox, Link	Click on element.
	focus	Field, Select	Focus given to element.
	load	Page	Navigator has completed loading the page.
	mouseover	Link	Mouse moves over link.
	select	Field	Element is selected.
	submit	Submit button	For submission
	unload	Page	Navigator exits from page.

It is important to understand that pages are loaded by the HTML client (typically an Internet browser) top-down. Code that is activated must only reference elements that have been previously loaded (that is, that are defined before it is in the page definition). This does not apply to function definition because the functions are not invoked during the loading process; this applies only to JavaScript code and event specifications. This is the primary reason for placing JavaScript function definitions in the *head* segment of the page; event handler in the *body* section can then use these functions because the *head* segment is completely loaded before the *body* segment is.

Programmatic Window Control

One of the built-in object types in JavaScript is the Window object. The Window object is an example of an instance of the Window type and is the root of the instance hierarchy in any Internet browser session. Like any built-in object, these objects have properties and methods associated with them. Using these methods, one can create and control additional browser windows and frames.

One of the most interesting capabilities afforded by window methods is the open method allowing one to open additional browser windows. Listing

17-8 shows a code segment in which the user enters a number in an input field and clicks on the *Open* button. A JavaScript function is then called that causes a number of windows to be opened. The code segment shows the use of the open method as well as the `writeln` *document* method allowing HTML to be dynamically generated. Figure 17-10 shows screen snapshots of the initiating window and two resulting windows (two because this is the number entered in the input field).

Listing 17-8

JavaScript code for opening browser windows using the open method

```
1   <html>
2
3     <head>
4
5       <title>A Simple JavaScript Example with Programmatic Window
Opening</title>
6
7       <script language="JavaScript">
8
9         // Open a number of windows and display a bit of text in
them
10
11        function openWindows() {
12          var aNumber =
parseInt(document.aForm.numberToOpen.value)
13          var newWindow
14          for (var i = 1 ; i <= aNumber ; i++) {
15            newWindow = window.open()
16            // Let's create some HTML dynamically.
17            // Notice the automatic coercion of integer to string.
18            newWindow.document.writeln(
19              "<center><h1>Hi, I'm New Window Number " + i +
"</h1></center>")
20                }
21          }
22
23      </script>
24
25    </head>
26
27    <body>
28
29      <form name="aForm">
30
31        <h3>Enter Number of Windows to open:</h3>
32        <input name="numberToOpen" type="text">
33        <input name="clickToOpen"
34              type="button"
35              value="Open"
36              onClick="openWindows()">
37
38      </form>
39
40    </body>
41
42  </html>
```

Figure 17-10
Resulting browser windows

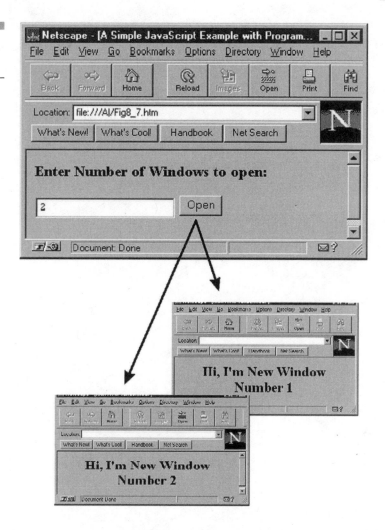

The open method accepts three argument strings. The first string specifies an HTML document on which the window should be opened. The second string specifies the name provided to the window. This name can later be used when referring to the window as a target of a form submit or a hyperlink. The third argument allows specifying various window properties such as height, width, scrollbars, and so on. The open call may also be used with no arguments as shown in Figure 17-9.

In addition to the open method, windows may be closed using the close method (which can be sent by owning windows), frames may be accessed using the frames array, and window properties may be controlled. Together with the document object, these allow JavaScript programmers to fully control a browser session at runtime.

NetObjects BeanBuilder

The last NetObjects product we will look at is BeanBuilder. NetObjects BeanBuilder is aimed at rapid and painless development of Web-based applications. This product is based on a former IBM product called Lotus BeanMachine. BeanBuilder allows you to use JavaBeans to create Java-Beans, Java applets, and Java applications virtually without any coding by using a point-and-click interface. This can come in handy when you want to develop relatively simple applications quickly and without significant effort. For more complicated tasks, you would probably need to use a different tool, such as VisualAge for Java.

Getting Started

NetObjects BeanBuilder is available for download at `http://www.netobjects.com/products/html/nbb1.html`.

The installation process is quick and smooth. At the end of it, you are presented with a dialog box asking if you want to start BeanBuiler. To verify your installation, start BeanBuilder.

After the program is up and running, it automatically starts its Applet Wizard, as shown in Figure 18-1. This wizard allows you to quickly create Java applets. Click Next several times until you get to the Ticker Tape tab. Here you can create a ticker tape effect in your applet. Indicate that you want such an effect and type the text you want to be displayed by the ticker tape. Figure 18-2 shows how the dialog box should look. Note that you have an option to have the ticker tape take the text from a file. Now, all you have to do is press Next a couple of times and then Finish, and the applet is ready.

Figure 18-1
BeanBuilder Applet
Wizard

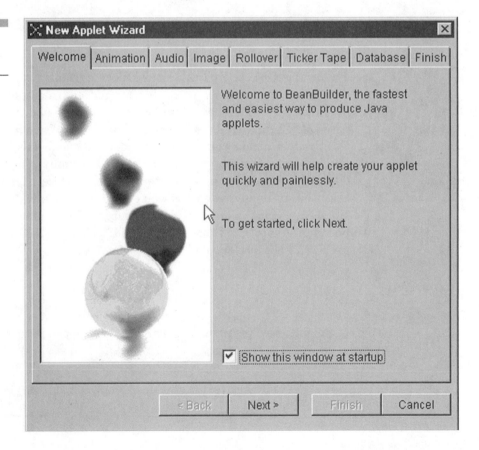

Figure 18-2

Applet Wizard Ticker Tape tab

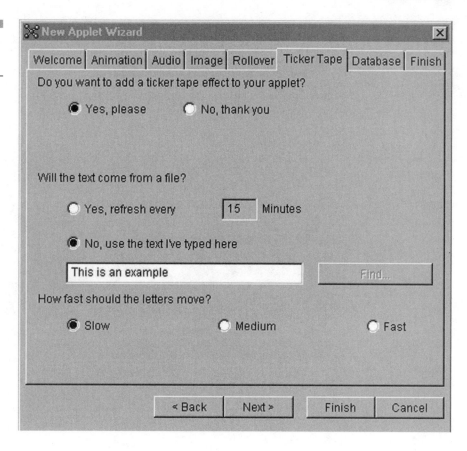

To check it out, select Run under File. After a quick preparation phase, you get to see the applet running, and it shows the ticker tape (see Figure 18-3). That was easy, wasn't it?

Using BeanBuilder

Now that we have a running applet, let's get acquainted with the surroundings. The main window is called BeanBuilder Composer and is shown in Figure 18-4. This window has a menu bar, toolbar, and a work area that

Figure 18-3
Ticker Tape applet

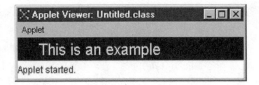

Figure 18-4
BeanBuilder main window

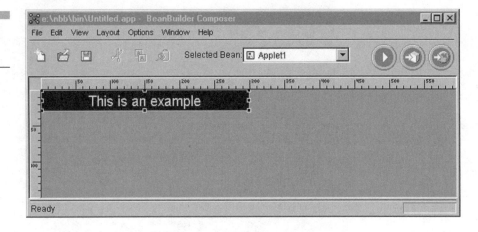

shows our applet. The tools palette shown in Figure 18-5 provides many components that can be readily used. The components are grouped into the following groups: Accessories, Controls, Multimedia, and Networking. The two buttons at the bottom of the palette allow you to add new components to the palette and to customize it.

The Gallery window shown in Figure 18-6 provides quick access to pictures and audio files that can be incorporated into the beans you create. Animations can be represented by a series of image files. When using objects from this gallery, you are implicitly using JavaBeans from the palette.

The Details window shows the properties of the currently selected bean. For example, select the TickerTape1 bean (you can change the selected bean using the Selected Bean entry on the toolbar, as shown in Figure 18-7). The Details window shows the different properties of the ticker bean. These properties can be easily modified. Select the Foreground Color entry (see

Figure 18-5
BeanBuilder palette

Figure 18-6
BeanBuilder Gallery

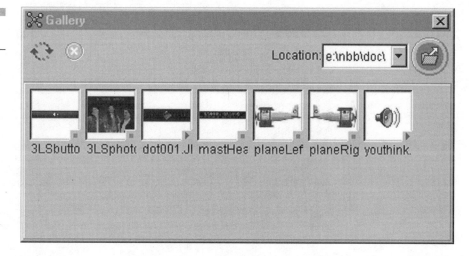

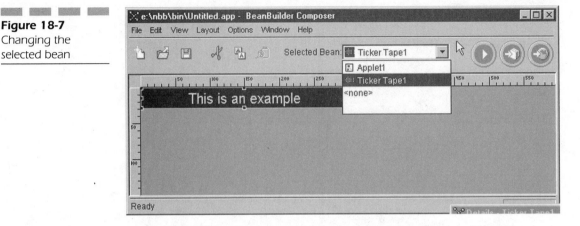

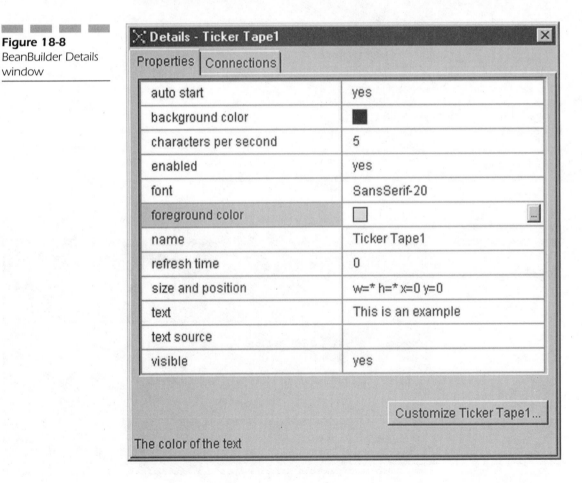

Figure 18-8) and change it using the dialog that opens up (see Figure 18-9). The change is immediately reflected both on the Details window and on the visual representation of the applet in the work area on the main window. If you run the applet, you can see the color change. The Details window includes, in addition to the Properties tab, a tab labeled Connections. This tab allows you to define the connections between different components in an event-driven manner.

To demonstrate the use of connections, select the Timer bean from the Multimedia palette and place an instance of it into the applet. To do so, click on the timer icon (which looks like an alarm clock) and then click the work area in the main window to place the timer. Select the newly created Timer1 bean and review the Connections details, as shown in Figure 18-10. Now click the Connections Wizard button (the rightmost button on the toolbar for the Details window). This wizard helps you define the connections between different beans (see Figure 18-11). Click Next on the Welcome tab to go to the next tab. This tab, labeled Source Bean (see Figure 18-12), allows you to select the bean that initiates the connection (in other words, the bean that is the source of the event or action that takes place). Select Timer1. In the next tab (labeled What Happens), select timer elapsed. This

Figure 18-9
Color Selection
dialog box

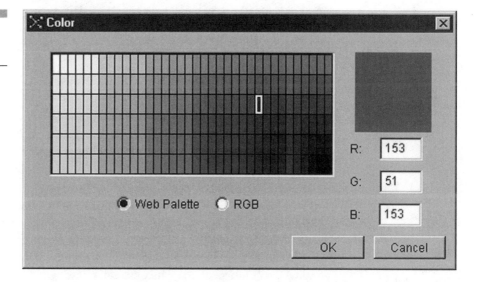

Figure 18-10
Connections tab in
Details window

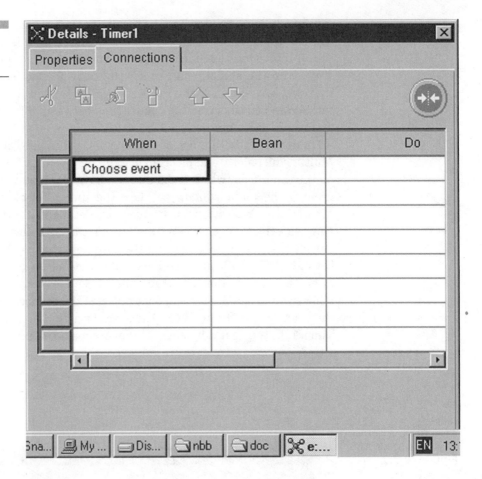

is the only option here, as shown in Figure 18-13. Now we select the Target
bean. This is the bean on which we want to perform an operation after the
event occurs. In other words, we want to invoke a certain operation on a
specific bean after the timer elapse event occurs. Select TickerTape1 in this
window (see Figure 18-14). The next tab allows you to specify the operation.

Figure 18-11
Connection Wizard
Welcome tab

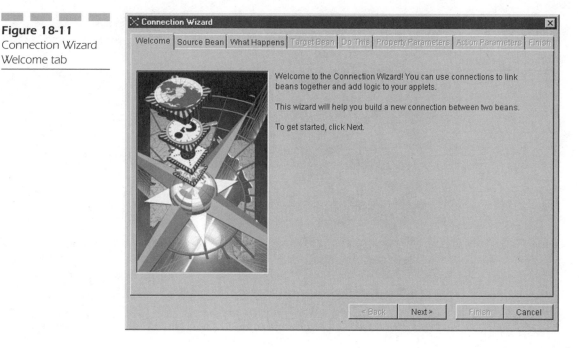

Figure 18-12
Connection Wizard
Source Bean tab

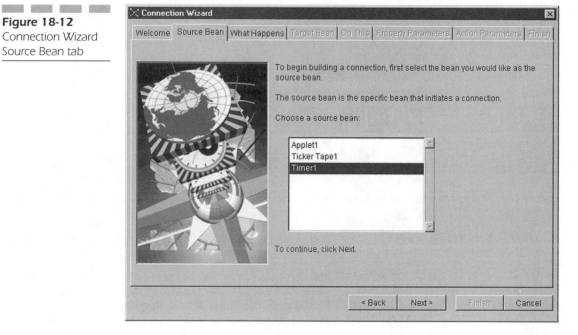

Figure 18-13
Connection Wizard
What Happens tab

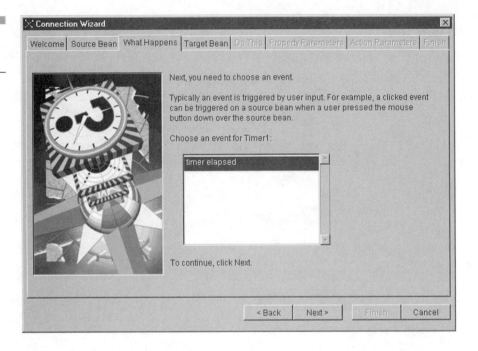

Figure 18-14
Connection Wizard
Target Bean tab

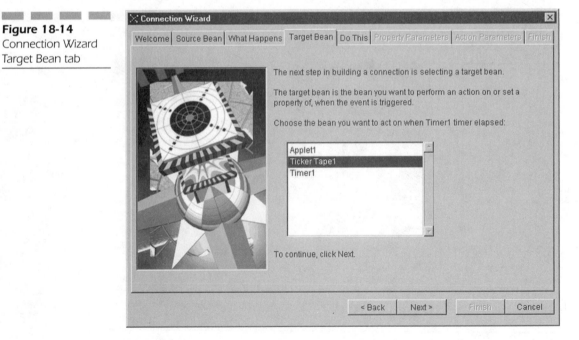

In this tab, select Set Foreground Color. Now select the desired color in the next Property Parameters tab, shown in Figure 18-15. To keep things simple, click the Set Value button and select a new color (using a dialog box that opens up, which is identical to Figure 18-9). Now go to the Finish tab and complete this connection.

Well, generating this connection was a long process, but quite a simple one. To summarize, we indicated that when the timer elapses, we want to change the foreground color of the ticker. The timer bean has a property that determines its interval in milliseconds. After this time passes, we expect the color to change. You can run the applet now to see that this actually works. You can play with the interval length (shown in the Details) to see it determines how much time passes before the color changes. This example is obviously very simple, but it illustrates the way you can program interactions between your beans without writing any code at all.

Figure 18-15
Connection Wizard
Property Parameters
tab

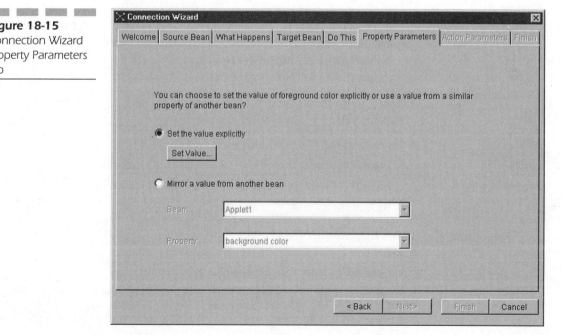

Quick Reference

This section briefly reviews the different features of BeanBuilder.

Menu Bar

The menu bar is quite standard, and contains the following entries:

- File
  - *New*   Create a new bean/applet/application
  - *New Applet Wizard*   Invoke the Applet Wizard
  - *Open*   Open a file
  - Close
  - Save, Save As
  - *Run*   Run an applet
  - *Stage*   Perform local publishing, which includes compiling the Java code, optimizing it, and placing it in the destination location (specified using the Publish option explained below).
  - *Publish*   Starts the Publish Wizard, which allows you to select the different options for publishing. Namely, you can select if you want to create an applet, application, or a bean, and you can select the publishing destination (local or remote).
  - Quit
- *Edit*   Includes the standard entries Undo, Redo, Cut, Copy, Paste, Delete, Select All, Deselect All
- *View*   Controls the display of
  - Standard toolbar
  - Layout toolbar (provides options from the Layout menu)
  - Rulers
  - Status bar
- Layout
  - *Grid*   Controls the display of a grid
  - *Snap to Grid*   Indicates whether clicks should be snapped to the grid
  - *Set to Preferred Size*   Resizes the selected object to the preferred size

- *Fix Size* Fixes the size of the selected object to the current size
- *Align* Allows aligning groups of objects (to left, center, right, top, middle, and bottom)
- *Space Evenly* Allows placing objects that are part of a group in a manner where spaces are even
- *Match Width, Match Height* Used to correlate the width and height of different objects in a group
- *Move To Front, Move Forward, Move Backward, Move To Back* Controls the layering of different objects which overlap each other

- Options

  - *Preferences* Controls settings such as grid width and height
  - *Clear Gallery* Clears the gallery (that is, de-selects the current gallery directory)
  - *Bean Wizard* Starts the Bean Wizard, which helps you create new JavaBeans
  - *Connection Browser* Starts the Connection Browser, which shows all the currently available connections (in other words, a concatenation of the connections available in the Connections section of each of the Details windows)

- *Window* Allows viewing or hiding each of the following windows:

  - *Details* Shows Properties and Connections
  - Gallery
  - Palette
  - *Java* A window showing Java code. This is useful for making some modifications by hand or adding specially designed pieces of code.
  - *Log* Runtime log

- Help

  - Documentation
  - About

Toolbars

The toolbar on the main window is quite simple and contains buttons for New, Open, and Save from the File menu and Cut, Copy, and Paste from the

Edit menu. On the right end are round buttons for Run, Stage, and Publish from the File menu. In addition, there is a control for changing the currently selected bean.

The toolbar on the Connections tab in the Details window contains entries for Cut, Copy, Paste, Delete, Move Up, Move Down, and for invoking the Connection Wizard.

Built-in Components

Most of the BeanBuilder's power is in its built-in component palette. This palette can be customized to include any JavaBeans. In this section, we will cover the different components available. The way these components are used is identical to the way the Ticker Tape and Timer beans were used previously. In other words, beans are placed on work area, and then connections are established using the Connection Wizard.

The controls are divided into four groups by default:

- *Accessories*
  - *Boolean Evaluation*   A Boolean expression bean. This bean encapsulates two Boolean values (x and y). The operations you can perform on it (for example, through the Connection Wizard) are Set X, Set Y, or calculate the value to be X OR Y or X AND Y.
  - *Math*   This bean also has two variables x and y, but it supports a large number of mathematical operations.
  - *Numeric Evaluation*   This bean allows the comparison of two variables (x and y) that have numeric values and is used much the same way the Boolean evaluation bean is used.
  - *Text Source*   This bean allows storing a piece of text that may originate from another bean.
- *Controls*   This palette entry contains standard GUI controls. Each of these controls has properties that can be edited and actions that can be invoked through Connections.
  - Button
  - Checkbox
  - Choice
  - Label
  - List

- Panel
- TextArea
- TextField

■ *Animation*   This palette entry provides several animation and multimedia features.

- *Animation*   A bean that displays several image files (for example, JPEG) sequentially and repeatedly
- *Audio*   Play an audio file
- *Clock*   Show the current time
- *Image*   Show an image file (for example, JPEG, GIF)
- *Motion*   Generate a motion that can be repeated in a loop
- *Nervous Text*   Show a string of jumpy characters
- *Rollover*   Create a special button that shows three different pictures: one by default, one when rolled-over, and one when clicked
- *Shadow Text*   Text display with shadowing
- *Teletype*   Text display with a teletype effect
- *Text*   Plain text display
- *Ticker*   Ticker Tape as used above
- *Timer*   A timer bean as used above

■ Networking

- *Database*   A bean that allows connection to the database. You specify the database URL, userID, and password to connect to the database, and then you can specify the query.
- *Email*   A bean that sends e-mail to a specified recipient
- *Headline*   A bean that can show a banner with several other texts, each associated with a URL link
- *HTML Parameter*   Bean for a simple HTML parameter field
- *Email link*   Simple mail link bean (that is, an HTML link that sends email when clicked upon)
- *URL link*   Simple HTML link bean

19

IBM
San Francisco

IBM San Francisco is structured as a set of object-oriented frameworks. Object-oriented frameworks are the latest trend in object-oriented programming, and they promise to dramatically improve the software development process by integrating a set of reusable and extensible classes that provide well defined sets of functionalities. Frameworks are not building blocks. They are fully functional out-of-the-box applications, yet they can be extended through delegation or sub-classing. Frameworks provide infrastructure and design. The internal wiring between the reusable components making up the framework ensures that the architectural model and the design of the framework are preserved. As opposed to the use of class libraries in which the application controls the flow and calls the library components, a framework controls the main application processing and calls out to the custom code added by the extending developer. The code added by the application developer must conform to the framework design, ensuring that the end result is a well designed system.

Installation

With San Francisco being the largest object-oriented framework commercially available today, it contains quite a lot of code, and has quite an intricate installation process.

You should be sure you have the right JDK version and the right JFC version. Take a look at the Environment tab under the System icon in the control panel. You should confirm that the CLASSPATH and PATH environment variables are correctly set. Note that if either the JDK or JFC are not installed and included in the CLASSPATH, the installation will fail.

After you complete installation, proceed to check if the installation was successful. For this purpose, the San Francisco environment provides a simple sample application that can be executed; if the installation is correct, the sample should run properly. The sample is GUI CheckBook and is located off the San Francisco programs category. When started, a window should come up, allowing you to create an account by typing in your name and an account number. Next, click Submit. An account will be created for you (assuming this is the first time you are running the program). After an account exists, you can start depositing and withdrawing, each within a San Francisco transaction. After you are finished, exit the sample—you have successfully completed the San Francisco installation and are ready to start working.

The Layers of San Francisco

Although San Francisco includes many frameworks, services, and utilities, the core of the environment are three software layers with increasing proximity to business applications: the foundation layer, the *Common Business Objects* (CBO) layer, and the *Core Business Processes* (CBR) layer. Each of these layers relies on the previous layer (see Figure 19-1). The foundation layer implements the infrastructure and services available for all objects participating in the San Francisco environment. It supports the notion of object persistence, transaction processing, distribution and location transparency, naming, security, ownership, and so on. It is the largest layer and the one providing context-free infrastructure-related support that is surely useful for all applications. The CBO layer implements a set of elementary business objects that are common to a very large set of business

Figure 19-1
San Francisco
framework layers

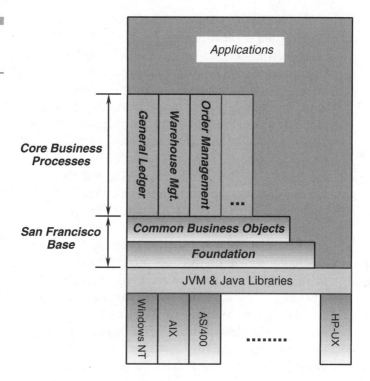

domains. These objects include addresses, money-related objects, customer and location, and so on. The final layer, the CBR, provide complete sets of business objects and processes that form sets of mini-application and include working functionality useful in the relevant domains. This layer is actually not one layer but rather a set of vertical layers, each one providing support in a certain domain. Naturally, the first verticals to be selected were those most relevant to IBM customers. As time goes on, additional verticals will be added. By understanding and using both the CBR and the CBO, one can customize the San Francisco frameworks either through derivation or composition (or a combination of both), making the end result extremely attractive. The simplest reuse scenario involves the use of business objects and processes out of the box while setting properties that are built-in parameters of the business objects. The next level of complexity allows you to alter the way in which objects are created and define which class should be used for instantiating a certain business concept. By supplying your own extension to the business class, you can customize behavior while remaining within the framework. Alternatively, you can fully extend a domain's class through substitution or through derivation and modification of functionality.

As shown in Figure 19-1, the foundation layer and the Common Business Objects layer form the San Francisco Base. The base layers provide the services and underlying object support required for building multitier, distributed, object-oriented applications along with a fundamental set of objects that conform to the San Francisco patterns. This not only allows the application builder to be somewhat oblivious to the difficulties involved with complex application architectures, it also helps to jump-start the development process. The CBRs complement the base with rich functionality in various domains, all while building on the base. As Figure 19-1 shows, an application builder is not limited in how the frameworks may be used. Applications can be built within one (or more) of the CBRs (in which case San Francisco can provide the most bang for the buck). If the domain is not covered by one of the process frameworks or the functionality provided is too different from the one required, the application can make use of the CBO layer as a set of reusable business objects that functions within the San Francisco environment. This use will save a lot of development time and even more testing time, but it will still require more work than a use of the CBR layer. Finally, new business objects will be sometimes created directly over the foundation. In this case, the new business objects will make use of the underlying services only—which solves the most complex of issues in the system architecture. Obviously, any combination of the described alternatives are possible. An application may use parts of the CBR, some of the CBOs directly, combined with a set of objects using foundation services. After all pieces of the application use the foundation services, the objects will work in tandem.

We mentioned that as long as objects are built over the foundation layer, they form a coherent application structure. Building objects that are external to the foundation to work at the application level is much more difficult and is not suggested. As long as objects use the foundation services and conform to the San Francisco patterns, they can participate in the San Francisco world and thus make use of the benefits. Objects not built in this way need to solve many difficult problems such as persistence, transactions, and so on. Even worse, if you do decide to do so, you will have to synchronize and maintain the two models. For example, if you have a single business transaction that includes objects using the base and objects that require self-management for transactions, you will somehow have to synchronize all of this into one transaction—something you really should not attempt without serious "adult" supervision.

The San Francisco base, and especially the foundation layer, are extremely important for implementation neutrality and may be viewed as an exten-

Figure 19-2
Levels of
independence

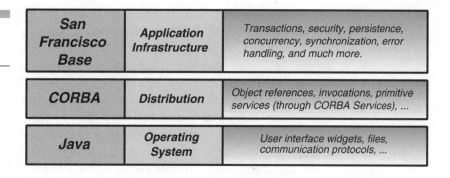

San Francisco Base	Application Infrastructure	Transactions, security, persistence, concurrency, synchronization, error handling, and much more.
CORBA	Distribution	Object references, invocations, primitive services (through CORBA Services), ...
Java	Operating System	User interface widgets, files, communication protocols, ...

sion to Java and CORBA in terms of the level in which neutrality may be achieved (see Figure 19-2). Java provides hardware and operating system neutrality by basing all application code on Java bytecodes that drive the Java virtual machine. By building your application using Java, you attain one level of platform neutrality and portability. CORBA provides an additional level of portability and interoperability by supporting location transparency. By using CORBA, you can hide details regarding physical location and support application functionality that can be distributed across various configurations. The San Francisco foundation layer allows you to achieve another level of portability by encapsulating capabilities and services in application infrastructure areas such as persistence, transactions, security, and so on. By building on the San Francisco base, you ensure that any vendor product conforming to San Francisco and supporting its APIs will be an option in your application. The extent to which neutrality and independence is achieved is considerably greater because the abstractions you can rely on are closer to the application level.

The Foundation Layer

The foundation layer is part of the San Francisco base and is perhaps the layer that is functionally the most important. It supplies the underlying infrastructure necessary for building San Francisco applications including a set of services and utilities. The foundation layer is the lowest level at which San Francisco may be used. In most practical scenarios, some application components will be built directly over the foundation (as opposed to a reuse of higher levels of the framework).

The foundation layer encapsulates application services. This means two things: It provides these services, but it hides many implementation details regarding these services. Therefore, by basing the entire application over the foundation layer, an application can remain independent from the implementation of these services. In a world that is constantly moving towards standards-based products (be they formal standards or *de facto* standards), this is of great benefit to the application developer.

Services provided by the foundation layer are encapsulated and abstracted within a set of base classes called the object model classes. These classes form an object model that is the basic structure of San Francisco objects and provide the consistent programming model within San Francisco applications. The object model classes include a number of classes that form the basic types in the systems—types not in terms of a certain application domain but rather in terms of structural types. These types categorize objects into a set of fundamental behaviors that differ in how they are managed within the application frameworks and especially in the overall lifecycle. For example, objects can be categorized into objects that represent a distinguished entity and may be referenced by many other objects or to objects that are contained in other objects and have no existence outside their container. The object model classes include a base class called Entity for the first category and a base class called Dependent for the second. The most important classes forming the object model classes are

■ Entity *and* Dependent   These base classes represent the business objects in the system. Domain level business objects and support objects used for managing a user interface will typically be implemented by a class that inherits from one of these two classes. These two classes form the primary hierarchy for business objects and objects supporting application functionality. A common base class is very common in object libraries because it allows definition of framework functionality at the root level. Both classes can be used for persistent or transient object and for objects used primarily to manage a user interface process. The difference between the two classes involves the notion of ownership and dependence. Entity objects are objects that have an independent being and do not depend on another object for their existence. Dependent objects on the other hand live within another object (typically within an Entity object) and have no existence outside their owner. This may seem like a philosophical discussion but it has many practical consequences. A dependent object is not referenced from any object other than the dependent's container. The dependent object's lifecycle is completely dependent on the container's lifecycle; for example, when the container ceases to exist, so does the dependent. Finally, a dependent that is persistent will define its mapping to persistent storage through the container; for example, if persistence uses a mapping to a relational database, the dependent object will be mapped to the container's tables.

The answer to the question of which classes are dependents and which classes are entities is a complex one that sometimes has an objective answer and is sometimes specific to the domain or application in question. Most classes that represent important concepts in the real world will be entities. Thus, many classes of the *Common Business Objects* (CBO) and the *Core Business Processes* (CBR) layer are already categorized as either dependent classes or entity classes (or both—through two classes). It is almost certain that this categorization will fit almost all applications (which is very fortunate because if it wasn't so, these classes would be useless for many application developers). On the other hand, the fact that the conceptual difference between dependents and entities is based on the subjective notion of existential, it is very possible that a concept will be a dependent in one application and an entity in another. For example, the notion of a ZIP code is usually represented simply as a string in many applications and may be modeled as a dependent of a containing address object. On the other hand, in an application that manages addresses and ZIP codes and performs geographical inferences based on those ZIP codes (such as various systems offered by Lucent Technologies or Bellcore), a ZIP code will certainly be an entity.

Figure 19-3 shows the root of the San Francisco class hierarchy including the classes `Entity`, `Dependent`, and `DynamicEntity` (along with snippets from the javadoc documentation pages). `DynamicEntity` is an `Entity` class that also support runtime binding of named properties. This provides additional flexibility because attributes can be dynamically attached at runtime without requiring code changes to the class definition. Addition of property values is not only supported at runtime but supported per object—therefore, different objects of the same type can have different properties associated with them (allowing some form of instance-based programming). Note that the API for binding property values is defined in the `PropertyContainer` interface.

■ `BaseFactory` Factory objects are responsible for lifecycle operations. They are used to create objects, delete them, and so on. Factories are certainly not a new concept in object-oriented systems and are present in Java and in CORBA. The `BaseFactory` interface denotes objects in San Francisco that are responsible for lifecycle issues, in addition to

Figure 19-3
The San Francisco
base hierarchy

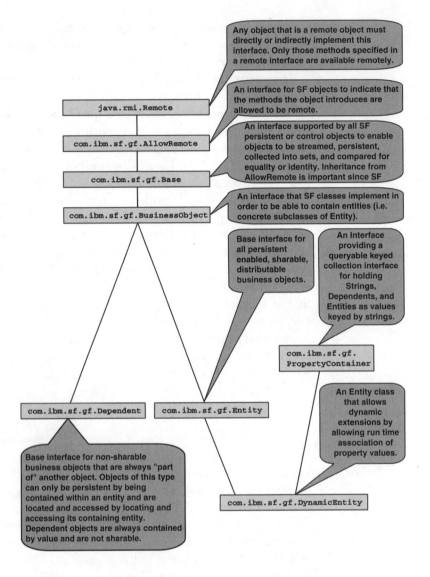

many other issues—it is also involved with handling transactions, security policies, distributed access, and more. BaseFactory as an interface does not directly define APIs—it is merely an aggregation of numerous other interfaces each responsible for an important aspect of object management—this is shown in Figure 19-4. Each of the interfaces in this figure represents a system-level category supported by the foundation layer.

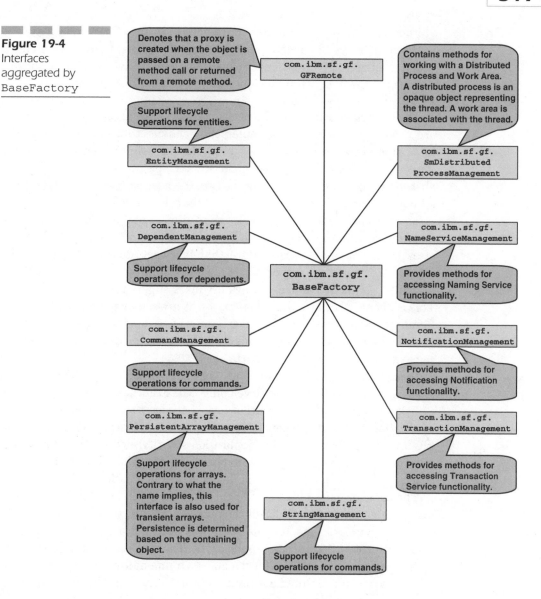

Figure 19-4
Interfaces aggregated by `BaseFactory`

- `Collection/Iterator` Like any object-oriented type system, San Francisco supports collections of objects and iterators used to traverse these collections.

- `Command` The command object encapsulates a set of operations on an object or a group of objects that are to be performed together. It is an important feature of San Francisco both in terms of performance (if the set is moved to a remote process and performed there) as well as in terms of an abstraction of business logic that involves more than one object or more than one operation.

The base classes forming the object model classes are inherited from and are used in two ways. They implement behavior that is assumed by the inheriting class. In addition, the base classes define interfaces that are implemented by the inheriting classes as specific implementations of abstract concepts. By supporting the two, the base classes provide the overall object architecture assumed by each San Francisco application (something that is crucial in any development project and always very hard to accomplish) while leaving enough flexibility for customization. The benefits of a consistent object architecture that has been designed and built by experts are enormous. A good object model (assuming it is used correctly) is difficult to build but almost always produces superior application designs. This is not only because the design patterns are somewhat embedded in the fundamental object models but also because decisions that are always hard to make (and therefore may be made with little or no understanding of the consequences) are made by experts.

In addition to the services and base classes provided within the foundation layer, a set of utilities aid in developing San Francisco applications. These utilities are part of the foundation layer because they are useful for every application and do not depend on certain business objects or domains. Utilities are provided for managing application security, managing configuration information, synchronizing between operations that should not be performed concurrently, creating installation procedures, and creating audit trails.

The basic premise of the San Francisco foundation layer is that of creating a robust environment for developing large scale, transaction-oriented, distributed applications. It is not a development environment for small user interface-centric data access applications. The architectural requirements for supporting applications in such an environment are stringent and complex. It is now an accepted assumption that "normal" application programmers cannot provide "correct" architectures without the assistance of experts. The goal of the foundation layer architecture is to capture this expertise and provide a solid architecture on which all applications can rely. As such, the foundation layer creates an architectural structure that inherently takes care of the following issues:

- Persistence
- Transactions

- Distribution
- Naming
- Notification
- Queries
- Security

Persistence

We already mentioned that San Francisco supports persistence of object state in both relational databases and POSIX files. The intent is that storage mechanism independence will be one of the features of the San Francisco foundation layer (as you know, in software the "0,1, many" rule implies that you either don't support a feature, you support it in one certain way, or you support it in many ways). Although this is all very nice, the POSIX file feature is only useful for demos and for proof-of-concepts. It is not a mechanism that can serve as the underlying data storage for any real application. The relational database layer, on the other hand, abstracts away the details of different RDBMSs and provides for application-independence of the actual product used. At this time, San Francisco supports DB2 for Windows NT, Oracle for Windows NT, and DB2 Common Server for AIX. We are assuming that in the event San Francisco becomes widely used, more RDBMS vendors will provide adapters. Because the interface to RDBMS is based on ODBC and because almost all vendors provide ODBC interfaces, this should be a no-brainer.

As documented by the San Francisco manuals:

> "It is important to understand that choosing the persistence model is a purely administrative task that can be performed without influencing the application coding. You can configure your persistent data stores with an administrative utility. If you later need to modify your choices in terms of persistent stores, you can later do it without modifying a single line of code. This extremely powerful feature allows you to configure the same application in completely different ways as far as persistence is concerned. Install an application for a small customer who only uses a single database server, and later install the same application at a larger customer's site where multiple distributed databases are used. In the first case, you may choose to concentrate all the persistent data on a single database; in the latter case, you can distribute objects across multiple data stores. All this does not require a single change to the application code."

Figure 19-5
Database
independence

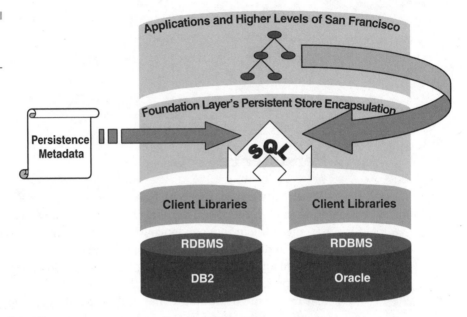

The concept is depicted in Figure 19-5. Database independence in San Francisco means two things: vendor independence and deployment configuration independence. Vendor independence is a common feature in today's tools and is almost assumed of a new framework like San Francisco. It is accomplished by adding an abstraction layer that is product-independent and forms the interface to the application levels. This abstraction layer uses sets of product-specific interfaces to the product client libraries.

The configuration independence is part of a more complex feature that uses persistent metadata. This metadata contains data regarding the mapping between objects to tables as well as data regarding the actual database deployment. This independence is much harder to support and can, theoretically, produce very elegant system architectures. So why "theoretically," and why did we quote the San Francisco manual instead of simply explaining the notion of configuration independence? Our experience has shown that the issues involving the mapping between object structures and database schemas as well as the issues involving how the databases are used by the application have extensive effect on application performance. This effect on performance can be so radical that it can make the difference between an application being viable and being a joke. In our opinion, the decoupling of object models and database schemas is a very nice academic exercise that does not hold up in the real world. In real applications, the tension between the object model and the relational model is something that has to be balanced—meaning that the relational schema must sometimes give way to the object model, and the object model will sometimes have to be changed to accommodate efficient use of the database.

Transactions and Locking

Transactions allow concurrent access to objects. They form the backbone of any system that needs to service multiple clients (or requesters). Without transactions, we could not have multiple processing threads that are shielded from one another—any processing would be non-deterministic and unusable. The fact that transactions provide a protected environment for completing operations is mandatory to any multiuser application sharing data. In addition, transactions ensure persistence of changes made within a transaction scope.

The foundation layer supports object-level transactions that map to database level transactions. The San Francisco transaction model is flat—nested transactions are not supported. Changes made to business objects should be made only within a transaction context. The notion of attaching an object to a transaction context relies on locking policies that define the constraints placed on the shared business objects and affects their behavior in other transactions. The foundation layer defines an extensive set of locks to provide for numerous access methods controlling object locking.

San Francisco transactions follow the conventional transaction API. The API can be used programmatically by accessing a `BaseFactory` object (using the `Global.factory()` call) and then using the interface methods defined in `com.ibm.sf.gf.TransactionManagement`, which is one of the base interfaces of `com.ibm.sf.gf.BaseFactory`. In addition, the `Command` object may be activated using the `doTransaction()` method, which performs all the operations of the `Command` object within a transaction block.

Although most changes and accesses to business objects will be made from within a transaction, San Francisco also provides a feature for accessing business objects outside of a transaction. This mode, called the NO_LOCK mode, creates a copy of the business object. Any change made to the copy will not be performed on the real object, so this feature is useful in cases where read-only access is performed and we want to minimize overhead. This mode is also useful in another pattern that we call the draft pattern. This pattern supports changes made to business objects using short-lived transactions, while allowing work to be performed on an object that appears to be the real object. Instead of opening a transaction, making changes directly on the object, and then either performing a commit or a rollback based on whether the user accepts the changes, we actually work on a copy (effectively making a draft of the changes). Because changes made in the NO_LOCK mode will not persist, we need to perform all the changes on the real object when asked to accept the changes made—this time within a transaction bracket.

Lock options are defined in the class LockMode. This class has static values used to specify the desired lock when accessing an Entity through the factory. The lock types provided are

- NO_LOCK   Provides access to the Entity with no lock by making a copy of the object. During creation of the copy, a READ lock is acquired and released after the copy has been created. Thus, this mode will conflict with WRITE locks while those are being held on the entity.

- OPTIMISTIC   Synchronization is performed at commit time, at which point the transaction may fail if the object has been changed since the entity was locked. When the lock is acquired, the entity is copied using a READ lock and may conflict with any existing WRITE locks. The READ lock is released after the copy has been made. When the transaction is committed, Entity version-checking is performed to determine if the Entity has changed since the optimistic lock was acquired; if so, an OptimisticLockException is raised.

- OPTIMISTIC_CLEAN   This lock type is a variation on the optimistic lock in that checks performed on entities at transaction commit time are performed even on objects that have not been changed inside the current transaction. This can be useful when you wish to signal that the processing of the current transaction relies on the value of the entity.

- READ   Pessimistic read lock conflicting with existing write locks

- WRITE   Pessimistic write locks conflicting with existing read or write locks

Distribution

Every entity in San Francisco may be distributed anywhere in the logical San Francisco network, and every object may be remotely referenced from any other object in a location-transparent manner using a handle to the object (handle is one of the infrastructure classes the foundation layer provides). Any object may be uniquely situated at any node in the logical network.

However, the notion of distribution in San Francisco does not stop with providing location transparent access to objects (as do most environments supporting distributed processing). The foundation layer supports both the reference model and the replication model. When creating an object, one can pass an `AccessMode` object to the `BaseFactory`. `AccessMode` objects allow programmers to control characteristics of the object created in the local address space—one of them is a specification of whether local mode or home mode is desired (other characteristics include lock types and lock wait timeout). When selecting home mode, the Foundation layer is told that we want to use the object in its home environment. If the object lives in a separate address space other the caller, a proxy will be created pointing at the real object. If, on the other hand, local mode is specified, we are telling the foundation that we want a local copy of the object to be created in our address space. Using the locking specification, we can even request any changes committed on the local object to be propagated to the real object—in effect, supporting a replication model. Obviously, the fact that the Foundation layer supports both models for distributed computing is a very important advantage for enterprise software developers.

Naming

The Naming service is one of the cornerstones of the San Francisco architecture in allowing distribution and location transparency as well as supporting correct application structure. The primary functions of the Naming Service are defined in `com.ibm.sf.gf.NameServiceManagement` interface. This interface allows

- Binding, unbinding, and replacing user aliases with `Entity` objects (that is, associating a name—a string—with a handle to an entity)
- Retrieval of a handle to a container of a class that can then be used for creating entities
- Access to special factories associated with classes
- Control over which concrete instance will be created when a factory is used. This is performed using class replacement that allows a class name to be mapped to the concrete instance that will be created. This mapping can be changed dynamically using configuration tools, thereby allowing the software to follow a design that can have multiple

installed deployments—each with slightly different behavior based on the concrete class used for instantiation.

Notification

In the past five years, the notification function has become central to many modern applications. The publish/subscribe model (in which one party defines what they are interested in and one party publishes information that is ultimately dispatched to all parties that expressed interest in that information type) solves many application problems. The decoupling afforded by this model is extremely important for robust scaleable application architectures. The foundation layer fully supports notification using two possible delivery mechanisms—asynchronous or on-demand. Asynchronous notification follows the Observable pattern (also knows as the Model-View pattern). On-demand notification used a mailbox paradigm.

Asynchronous notification is supported by the interface com.ibm.sf. gf.NotificationManagement that provides an API for adding and removing Observers. A typical interface call includes the following arguments:

- observerEntity   The entity expressing interest (to be notified upon events)
- notificationInterest   An Interest object (part of the foundation layer), which is an abstract class that should be inherited from by application-specific classes to define the events that cause notification
- access   For application control over how the asynchronous notification is performed
- observable   A handle to the entity upon which the interest is being expressed

On-demand notification is supported by the interface com.ibm.sf. gf.NotificationMailbox that acts as an intermediary between the observer and the observable and serves as a "mailbox" in which events (placed by the observable) wait until they are pulled by the observer. The two notification patterns follow the CORBA Event Service in that the functionality supported by the com.ibm.sf.gf.NotificationManagement interface resembles conventional event dispatch, whereas the functionality supported by the `com.ibm.sf.gf.NotificationMailbox` interface is similar to the features of the Event channel.

Queries

Queries are central to any business application. As a result, the San Francisco foundation layer provides mechanisms for phrasing queries in the object world. Generally, queries have historically been associated with relational databases and SQL—queries are certainly what they do best. SQL databases form the benchmark for querying in terms of ease-of-use, availability, and performance.

The San Francisco approach to querying is based on the notion of query commands that are applied to collections of objects. Each application of the query command acts as a filter that determines whether the object in the collection satisfies the query; if so, it will be part of the collection returned from the call applying the query command to the original collection.

The syntax for defining a query command in San Francisco is a subset of the SQL92 syntax with additions allowing accessors to objects to be used. Therefore, it is easy to retrieve all part orders that include more than ten-part order lines using a syntax that is close to the object world; one would simply phrase it as `getLineNumber() > 10` and be done with it. In general, most collections can be used as starting points for queries. As much as possible, the resulting collection (the collection of the objects satisfying the query) will have the same attributes (for example, applying a query to a set will in general produce a set). The one important difference is that the resulting collection is always transient and never owns the objects it contains. In addition, because the `EntityOwningExtent` collection is closely related with the underlying relational database—it can provide important performance enhancements by using the underlying store's query engine and optimizer.

The Foundation layer provides two interfaces for creating query commands—the `com.ibm.sf.gf.QueryCmd` interface and the `com.ibm.sf.gf.AdhocQueryCmd` interface that extends the `QueryCmd` interface. `QueryCmd` defines the query activation mechanism, requiring subclasses to implement the specifics for performing the query as a command object. The actual work is performed by the subclasses of the abstract class `QueryCmdImpl`. Another class that is of use is the `AdHocQueryCmdFactory`, which creates `AdHocQueryCmd` objects. These ad hoc query objects take any select statement and perform queries on collections of objects following the San Francisco syntax.

Security

Support for application level security is built into the foundation layer. Features supported include user management, user passwords, and authorization. User logins and passwords are managed through a security policy that controls authentication in San Francisco. Although an installation of San Francisco can disable authentication, a user will have to provide a login and a password with which authentication is performed before accessing any resource on the San Francisco network if the system administrator defines that authentication is to be performed. This authentication process will usually also involve authentication at the database level—although specifics may change through the usage of specialized security policy objects that can be configured to be used by any San Francisco installation. The default LogonController object in San Francisco ensures that only a single logon is necessary from any client using resources within the same LSFN—as long as all accesses are performed from within a single JVM.

Authorization in San Francisco follows a paradigm of actor-resource-action. An *actor* represents a user of the system who has been authenticated and therefore can be given a system identity (to which authorization specifications may be linked). *Resources* can be one of two things—servers in the LSFN or functional entities controlled by the Company object (part of the *Common Business Objects* [CBO]). The Company object is a central manager for all systemwide entities—one of the categories being the secure entities. An *action* is any usage that may be attempted using a resource by an actor. Authorization in such a model is naturally defined by associating access right definitions with linkages between actors and actions on resources.

Authorization to functional entities is managed through a concept called *secure tasks*. Secure tasks are built into the foundation layer. Forming a secure task involves the following steps:

■ An application developer creates a SecureTask instance. Code that needs to be performed before or after authentication is performed is placed within the beginSecureTask method and the endSecureTask method respectively. Note that the secure task bracketing is performed by the application developer—the secure task merely provides a placeholder for associating access control information.

- Access control lists specifying which actors can perform which secure tasks are defined.

- At runtime, when a secure task begins, the `beginSecureTask` verifies that the user has the appropriate access rights; if not, an authorization exception is called.

Localization

San Francisco targets the global market. As such, it supports the notion of internationalization and localization. Internationalization means building software in such a way that location-specific and cultural-specific issues are decoupled from the code. If this is performed, the software can be localized according to local conventions at deployment time.

Well known examples of internationalization and localization include date formats, number formats, and language. A program that has been internationalized (or globalized) will have displays pertaining to dates and numbers that are formatted based on external policy objects (which are called locales, as we will shortly see). Texts and messages are displayed using an additional level of indirection. Instead of having code that hard-codes the message text to be shown to the user, the code uses a symbolic name (or a numeric code) that is then mapped to various message texts in various languages based on the localization of the program. Obviously, there are many other issues pertaining to localization—some of them much more difficult to deal with (for example, languages that are written from right-to-left or top-to-bottom, sorting of strings, maintaining application data in various languages, and so on).

The foundation layer supports locales as a specifier for a geographic and cultural selection. Many classes in the San Francisco distribution are locale-sensitive. A class is locale-sensitive if its behavior is affected by the locale used when that class's functionality is invoked. Thus the locale is merely a specifier, whereas the locale-dependent behavior is encapsulated in a set of classes forming the foundation. For example, date objects are locale-sensitive because their formatting features depend on the current locale.

San Francisco follows the accepted representation of locales as strings of the form:

```
LA_CO_XXX
```

where LA is a two-letter encoding of the language (such as EN for English and FR for French), CO is an encoding of a country name (such as US or CA for Canada), and XXX is the variant code (such as WIN for Windows or MAC for Macintosh).

Locales are managed within an LSFN by the `LocaleController` and `LocaleContext` classes. The `LocaleController` maintains all the available locales in the LSFN—starting with the locales available in the native JDK1.1. There is only one instance of the `LocaleController` possible in a LSFN, maintained by the `LocaleContext`. Trying to create an additional `LocaleController` will result in an error. All applications running in a LSFN share the same controller through the `LocaleContext` used for retrieving locales.

San Francisco provides very broad support in terms of locale-sensitive classes. Obviously, time zones are fully supported, as are date and time formats. Message catalogs are used to implement string mappings based on locales. Message catalogs include both `StaticMessageCatalogs` and `DynamicMessageCatalogs`—the latter allowing runtime modifications. Static message catalogs are normally used for error and informative messages that are fully bound at development time. Dynamic message catalogs are usually used for maintaining messages encapsulated with a `DescriptiveInformation` object. A `DescriptiveInformation` is returned by objects implementing the `Describable` interface.

Although this may sound confusing, it is actually very simple. Most classes in the *Common Business Object* (CBO) and the *Core Business Process* (CBR) layers implement the `Describable` interface (or an interface extending it, such as `DynamicDescribableEntity`). As such, the implement a method returning a `DesciptiveInformation`:

```
public abstract DescriptiveInformation
getDescriptiveInformation() throws SFException
```

This is then used as an entry point into the dynamic message catalogs, allowing entities to describe themselves differently based on differing locales.

Foundation Class Architecture

Apart from supporting the infrastructure services described previously (and certainly no less importantly), the foundation layer defines the basic software architecture assumed by applications using San Francisco by providing the base classes that must be used by all applications. These classes ensure that applications conform to the architectural rules defined by the foundation layer. They also introduce a few fundamental concepts such as dependency, ownership, and references.

Dependency is an important notion that was already covered in the previous chapter (a class inheriting from the `Dependent` class is wholly contained and has no existence outside its container). Dependency is somewhat related to another important notion of the San Francisco foundation called *ownership*. One object is owned by another if its lifecycle fully depends on the lifecycle of its owner. For example, a part order object may be modeled as a part order header and a collection of part order. The part order header and the part order lines are fully owned by the part order. This means, for example, that when a part order is deleted, the part order header and the part order lines are as well. The notion of ownership is wider than the notion of dependents. Instances created from a dependent class are always fully contained—they are always fully owned. On the other hand, objects created from an entity class can be wholly owned or not. There will be cases where they will be shared and have multiple references to them, whereas in other systems they may be fully owned. In our example, a part order line may be fully owned by the part order object in a Help Desk system (which only cares about the customer's view of the part order) and as an independent entity driving the supply process in a Warehouse/Logistics application. The notion of ownership allows more flexibility because control over lifecycle is based on how the objects are used, not on how they are defined.

Common Business Objects (CBO)

The *Common Business Objects* (CBO) layer provides classes that are useful in almost any domain. Examples include `Company`, `Currency`, `Address`, `BusinessPartner`, `FiscalYear`, `PaymentMethod`, `PaymentTerms`, `Project`, `UnitOfMeasure`, and so on. Although it is clear that such entities are certainly common to many domains and applications, it is also clear that different systems will have slightly different data structures and behavior associated with these concepts. The CBO layer therefore defines the interfaces and APIs to these entities and how they interact with other central entities. However, in order to support differing functionality in different systems, San Francisco patterns allow for the common portions to be provided by the CBO layer while allowing application segments to extend and provide custom structures and behavior.

Even within one concept, there are a number of classes and interfaces involved. For example, com.ibm.sf.cf.Company is an interface defining the behavior of the basic organization structure of the "owning" entity of the application (the company providing the service in a customer service application, the bank in a financial application, or the manufacturing company in a manufacturing application). com.ibm.sf.cf.CompanyImpl is class implementing the Company interface, which can be used to instantiate Company objects. com.ibm.sf.cf.CompanyFactory is the factory object for the Company class. com.ibm.sf.cf.CompanyController and com.ibm.sf.cf.CompanyControllerImpl are an interface and a class used for creating a singleton (a single object of that type) used for managing the extent of all Company objects. com.ibm.sf.cf.CompanyContext adds some static methods that help clients to work with companies, the controller, and the active Company. These form the basic Company-related classes and interfaces (a few more exist but are of no interest at this point).

You may have noticed that the classes and interfaces forming the examples of the CBO layer have all been in the com.ibm.sf.cf package—CF for common functions. The CBO layer includes an additional package—the com.ibm.sf.cffi—which includes all the common financial objects. Examples include the bank abstraction, accounts, invoices, and so on.

Architecturally, the CBO are organized as an object library. This layer provides reusable classes used by application code as well as by the various CBRs. Following is a partial list of interfaces in the Common Business Objects layer:

- com.ibm.sf.cf.Address   Encapsulates an address for San Francisco objects

- com.ibm.sf.cf.Area   Structurally, this interface merely provides accessors for a code and a description, but semantically, it represents an arbitrary area such as a geographic area, a shipping area, or an organizational area.

- com.ibm.sf.cf.BusinessPartner   Represents a business partner of the Company in a San Francisco application. The concept of a business partner is an important one in the San Francisco framework and additional support classes (such as business partner types representing a supplier, customer, sub-contractor, and so on).

- com.ibm.sf.cf.BusinessPartnerBalance   Maintains a balance of a business partner

- com.ibm.sf.cf.BusinessPartnerCachedBalances   Encapsulates the mechanism of caching a balance for business partners—useful when many transactions affect the bottom line. Although we can always recalculate the result from the individual transactions, the balance will often be cached. This is an important mechanism used by almost every business application for performance and convenience reasons.

- `com.ibm.sf.cf.BusinessPartnerController` Manages the accessing of business partners for a company

- `com.ibm.sf.cf.BusinessPartnerGroup` Supports the grouping of business partners

- `com.ibm.sf.cf.CalendarPeriod` Encapsulates a period within a calendar. Many operations in the business world must be associated with a period. Examples include services provided to customers, arrivals on site, and so on. Other San Francisco operations—such as transactions in the General Ledger Core Business Process—require an association with a calendar period.

- `com.ibm.sf.cf.Company` Encapsulates any part of the organization structure for the organization for which the application is written (for example, in a field service management system, the company is the service company as opposed as the customers of the service companies). Each independent organizational unit may be represented by such an object, and these objects may be grouped in some structure.

- `com.ibm.sf.cf.Country`

- `com.ibm.sf.cf.Currency` Encapsulates all attributes for currencies in the system; these are referenced by monetary values in the system

- `com.ibm.sf.cf.CurrencyController` The manager for currency objects

- `com.ibm.sf.cf.DatedCalendarPeriod` A *from-to* type calendar period

- `com.ibm.sf.cf.DatedFiscalPeriod` Encapsulates a fiscal period covering a specific date range

- `com.ibm.sf.cf.Day`

- `com.ibm.sf.cf.DocumentLocation`

- `com.ibm.sf.cf.Enterprise` The root of the company organizations

- `com.ibm.sf.cf.ExchangeRateType` Used for conversion between currencies

- `com.ibm.sf.cf.FiscalCalendar`   Encapsulates the fiscal calendar and is used by the General Ledger and Accounts Payable/Receivable Core Business Processes

- `com.ibm.sf.cf.FiscalPeriod`   The primitive element comprising the fiscal calendar

- `com.ibm.sf.cf.FiscalYear`   A fiscal year that can be separated into mutually exclusive periods

- `com.ibm.sf.cf.HierarchyLevelInformation`   One of the various interfaces and classes useful for creating and using hierarchical structures

- `com.ibm.sf.cf.Initials`   Represents a signature of a person or a group

- `com.ibm.sf.cf.NaturalCalendar`

- `com.ibm.sf.cf.NumberSeries`   Used for creating number series such as system-generated numbering of application objects

- `com.ibm.sf.cf.PaymentMethod`   Defines details relevant to verification and validation performed in payment processes

- `com.ibm.sf.cf.PaymentTerms`   Involved in defining payments for items

- `com.ibm.sf.cf.PeriodizedCalendar`   A calendar that is made up of years, which are themselves made up of periods

- `com.ibm.sf.cf.Project`   Used as a handle to projects and used for associating properties with a project

- `com.ibm.sf.cf.SupplementaryCharge`   Encapsulates additional charges that may be associated with contracts, quotes, and so on

- `com.ibm.sf.cf.UndatedCalendarPeriod`   A calendar period with no dates associated with it

- `com.ibm.sf.cf.UnitOfMeasure`   Encapsulates the properties of a physical unit used to measure items

Core Business Processes (CBR)

The *Core Business Process* (CBR) frameworks provide the highest abstraction levels in San Francisco by supplying not only classes and services for certain domains, but by providing processes and collaborations that supply

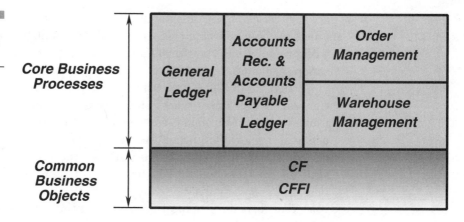

Figure 19-6
Layering of the Core
Business Processes

working application structures. The CBR frameworks rely on the *Common Business Objects* (CBO)—including the financial objects—as depicted in Figure 19-6.

The core processes are impressive because they are working sets of behaviors that provide real application structures while incorporating enough extension points in order to allow application developers to customize behavior with business rules, country-specific requirements and functions, user interface, and so on.

The current release of San Francisco provides the General Ledger (`com.ibm.sf.gl` package), Warehouse Management (`com.ibm.sf.whs` package), Order Management (`com.ibm.sf.om` package), and the Accounts Receivable and Accounts Payable Ledger processes (`com.ibm.sf.le` package). The General Ledger framework provides behavior common in application managing the general ledger of sets of companies such as journaling operations and book closing. The Account Ledger framework supports functions for processing accounts receivable and accounts payable items including all payments and item transfers to business partners. The Warehouse Management frameworks supports stock logistics and inventory management including replenishments, stock movements between warehouses, and both bin and bin-less management of inventory tracking. The Order Management frameworks builds on the Warehouse Management framework and provides for sales order management, sales order quotes and contracts (including pricing, costing, and discounts), purchase order management (including back-to-back processing), and more.

The San Francisco CBRs form the top-most layer in the San Francisco architecture. The CBRs are a set of domain-specific frameworks that provide very high abstraction levels for application developers. These frameworks are very close to being quasi-applications out of the box in that they not only provide sets of reusable classes but rather complete sets of classes along with processes and structural information that can support complete application segments.

Version 1.3 of San Francisco provides four high-level frameworks: The General Ledger framework, the Account Payable/Accounts Receivable framework, the Warehouse Management framework, and the Order Management framework. Each of these frameworks provides functionality specific to a certain domain. As such, these frameworks are not architected with the goal of providing building blocks to be used for building applications in other domains. For example, the Warehouse Management framework provides interfaces and classes supporting costing policies and costing calculations. Among other interfaces, it defines the `com.ibm.sf.whs.DCostingPolicy` interface for defining handling common to various costing policies. Although it would be reasonable to think that costing as a concept is not specific to warehouse management and could be used in other types of applications (such as field service dispatching, service outsourcing, and so on), this is contrary to the San Francisco architecture. The positioning of the CBRs is such that they are not constructed to provide reusable objects used in multiple application domains—this is the intent of the CBO. Each of the CBRs provides a complete set of classes that operate together, aiming to completely solve a certain application domain. So while the CBRs do not add to the number of common reusable objects, they can focus on providing higher reusability levels than could have been achieved using CBOs.

CBRs are architected to allow for multiple implementations in the specific domain to use the same base code. So although each CBR is fully functional out of the box, it has many built-in customization features (called extension points) that are used to customize and adapt the framework to the specific need of the application developer. In other words, the CBRs were designed and developed to be a cross between a shrink-wrapped application and a template for applications. The formidable goal of the CBRs is to allow the creation of applications extremely quickly with very limited changes or code additions while allowing for advanced usage of these frameworks in more elaborate schemes. Therefore, the CBRs will typically be used in one of three methods:

- The CBR may in some cases provide the complete functionality required by your application. In this case all you will need to do is study the framework and make use of its structures (but make no mistake about it—this in itself can be a very lengthy task).

- The CBR definitely supports the general functionality, but there are differences between how your application handles various issues and how the framework does. In this case, you will use the framework extension points to adapt the framework, making it compliant with your functionality requirements.

- The CBR provides only a limited set of the functionality you require. In this case, you will need to make use of all architectural tools at your disposal using perhaps some of the CBRs together with CBOs, and even homegrown objects directly above the foundation layer. You may need to subclass some classes or create delegation structures—in any case, your task will obviously be more complex and require a higher skill level.

Because a CBR usually requires some customization to allow for differences between different applications and business rules, the use of a CBR involves two stages:

- Setup
- Activities

Setup is the process in which an application designer uses the built-in classes and extensions points provided by the framework to define the correct structures and data required for correct operation of the framework in the context of the specific application. Any application framework implementing functionality in a way that can accommodate multiple implementations will have many parameters (both in terms of values as well as algorithms). These extension points are necessary in order to support the customization of the framework. However, in order to customize the framework, the correct structures and parameters must be set up before the framework can be used within the application. This setup stage is often the most difficult part in a reuse process because it assumes a good understanding of the semantic structures used by the frameworks—after this is understood, the rest is easy.

Activities are the actions or business transactions performed in the system. They form the dynamic entities that are responsible for moving the system from one state to the next—they are the lifeline of the system. Any information regarding the system can be attained through analysis of the activities. Generally, activities are classified as either being day-to-day or periodic. For example, in the context of a field service management system, a day-to-day activity may be a part order, or a service fix—anything that needs to be recorded in the context of a service call. A periodic activity may be the creation of invoices to be mailed to the customers every month for collecting payments for services and contract maintenance.

The General Ledger Framework

The purpose of the General Ledger framework is to track and report on the flow of money within a company. The General Ledger framework—as other CBRs—requires a setup phase in which the structures are formed. In the case of the General Ledger, the structures being created are the "Chart of Accounts"—basically this is the collection of accounting structures that will later be used as buckets to aggregate transactions. Setting up the account structure involves four steps (bottom-to-top):

- Setting up analysis codes
- Setting up analysis groups
- Setting up posting compositions
- Setting up accounts

Analysis codes and analysis groups form the primitive elements of a Chart of Accounts. `AnalysisCodes` form validation structures that define the appropriate values, types, and units of measures for each primitive piece of the accounting structure. `AnalysisGroups` aggregate `AnalysisCodes` into higher level structures; the codes themselves are owned by `AnalysisGroupCodeController` objects, which are themselves aggregated in a hierarchical structure with a root of type `AnalysisGroupCodeControllerRoot`. This hierarchy forms the analysis structure for the Chart of Accounts for the entire company. Because the creation of the structure is completely data driven, it can accommodate differences in companies, countries, and so on.

The next concept used in the General Ledger framework is that of a posting combination and a dissection. A `PostingCombination` is usually an account in the General Ledger—it forms one of the serialized categories managed by the Ledger. The term `PostingCombination` is a generalization of the account because it represents the basic entity for which activities or transactions can be reported. It therefore allows a very high degree of flexibility in that no restrictions are placed on what can aggregate transactions. Structurally, a `PostingCombination` holds sets of `AnalysisCodes` from one or more `AnalysisGroups`. A dissection is the actual object that associates a value with a `PostingCombination`.

After the valid structures for posting combinations and dissections have been defined, the accounts for the company may be defined. Valid account types and the account structures for the company are all that is required for activities to be reported within the General Ledger.

After the setup has been defined for the application, activities may be reported. Activities are categorized as being either day-to-day activities or as periodic activities. Day-to-day activities are the business transaction recordings that detail money transfers involving the company, whereas periodic activities include accounting operations that occur when closing a year or generating reports. After a chart of accounts has been set up, the journal will be continuously updated with transactions that associate value with a transaction. It will even been updated with transactions that associate quantities (with an arbitrary unit of measure) with dissections (using a `com.ibm.sf.gl.DQuantityDissection`), thereby documenting the transfers recorded by the journal. Obviously, individual transactions may invalidate a journal temporarily. Additional offsetting transactions will normally correct the journal, making it a valid one for posting. Day-to-day activities normally end with an activity that makes the journal valid and ready for posting. Note that the definition of the validation business rule for a journal in a Core Business Process extension point allows different applications to redefine what is a valid journal. In fact, almost any entity in the framework has some validation policy, and these policies may be changed by different application—for example, the interface `com.ibm.sf.gl.DDissectionValidationPolicy` defines how dissections and quantity dissections are deemed to be valid, allowing different applications to provide their own concrete implementation of the validation rules.

Finally, the General Ledger framework supports all periodic processes regarding journals. This includes activities related to the end of a fiscal year, activities run when a period is closed, and the generation of reports such as *profit and loss* (P&L) statements and balance sheets. Support for reports includes only the processing of the data and not the formatting—this should be handled by the application using an external report generator. The fact that the CBRs are based on CBOs and on the Foundation layer are very apparent and provide a very clear and convenient structure, helping to understand and become proficient in the frameworks.

The Accounts Payable/Accounts Receivable Framework

The Accounts Payable/Receivable framework records transactions between parties in the context of sets of accounts, ledgers, and logs in order to provide an accurate and up-to-date snapshot of a company's assets and liabilities. This framework is an important addition to the General Ledger framework in the management of a company's financials. It includes support for the following topics:

- Enter values for payments and receipts
- Assign a payment or a receipt to an account or accounts
- Validate a value of a payment or receipt in the context of assigning it to an account or set of accounts
- Support for the full lifecycle of a payment of receipt, including logging, canceling, and so on
- Support for all aspects of payment and receipts in the context of a debt, including adjustments, discounts and fines, and currency rates
- Management of associations between various documents and Accounts Payable/Receivable objects such as ledgers, transactions, payments, debts, accounts, and so on

Following the general spirit of the CBRs, the Accounts Payable/Receivable framework also involves initial setup for use within an application after which activities (both day-to-day and periodic) manipulate the defined structures. The setup stage involves setting up business partners, account structures, analysis codes and groups, dissections, payments types, and so on. Day-to-day activities involve payments and receipts, all performed as transactions that affect accounts, ledgers, and logs. Posting combinations and dissections are fully supported—making use of similar concepts from the General Ledger framework. Periodic activities include ledger reconciliation, debt management and collection, and re-evaluations. The objects of the framework are ready-built, allowing information to be extracted for periodic reports and letters to business partners.

The Warehouse Management Framework

The Warehouse Management Framework supports the management of inventory and stock items. Processes supported include product and part ordering, sourcing, replenishment, warehousing (both binned and not), transfer of inventory between warehouses, creation of follow-up activities, and so on. The primary entities forming the Warehouse Management Framework include

- Warehouse   The `com.ibm.sf.whs.Warehouse` interface represents the warehouse abstraction in the system, associating inventory with a location. Organization of inventory within a warehouse is also supported using stock zones (`com.ibm.sf.whs.StockZone`), which can contain multiple stock locations (`com.ibm.sf.whs.StockLocation`). Each stock location may contain more than one product type. Lots are also fully supported by the Warehouse Management framework.

- `Inventory`   Inventory represents goods that are in stock. An instance of an implementation class for `com.ibm.sf.whs.Inventory` holds the balance of one product in a warehouse. The inventory may be maintained for serialized or non-serialized inventory; if the goods are serialized, the collection of serial numbers may be maintained.

- `Product`   `Product` is the main entity managed by the framework. Structurally, a product maintains the descriptive information of the entities in the warehouse. Functionally, many of the methods required to manipulate goods in a warehouse are implemented either directly on the `Product` hierarchy or are related to its methods.

- `Stock Transaction`   Stock transactions form the lifeline of a warehouse application and record all stock movements in a warehouse. Obviously, the types and effects of stock transactions are important extension points of the framework.

The Order Management Framework

The Order Management framework implements functionality related to order processing systems including creation and processing of orders, order types, purchases, prices, and so on. The framework provides many extension points allowing any order types to be processed and allowing customization of the processes used. Products on order and business partners performing the order are encapsulated by the `com.ibm.sf.om.OrderProduct` and the `com.ibm.sf.om.OrderPartner` interfaces respectively. Prices and discounts are fully supported along with various extension points for different calculation methods. The entire framework is built around sets of policy objects that make the framework very flexible in the processing of orders; in fact, of approximately 350 interfaces comprising the framework, almost 150 are policy- and extension-related.

As for the actual business processes supported by this framework, the Order Management framework builds on (and uses classes from) the Warehouse Management framework. In addition, the framework supports invoicing and supplementary charges using CBO support, and new business processes involving order capture, order acknowledgment, and details requests.

WebSphere Applications Using San Francisco

Although San Francisco is a little difficult to master, considering the sheer size of the frameworks, it is quite a powerful tool for developing business applications. San Francisco supports EJB from version 1.3 onwards. Through this support, it is possible to develop WebSphere applications that make use of the frameworks. Using San Francisco allows you to have a strong basis for developing large enterprise applications. The San Francisco object model blends into the WebSphere application server in a seamless manner through the EJB abstraction.

20

Connection Pooling and Data Access Beans

The issue of database connectivity is central for Web-based applications. Whether the application is a search engine, online shopping ("e-tailing"), or just a plain business application holding records of customers and suppliers, it almost always requires handling large amounts of information.

This chapter focuses on issues of database connectivity. Database connectivity in Java applications is almost synonymous with *Java Database Connectivity* (JDBC). JDBC is a Java extension API focusing on providing programmers with data access capabilities based on SQL queries. It is an open API that enables different vendors to provide their own implementations of the API, implying that code based on JDBC is completely portable between databases. Providing a detailed introduction to JDBC is beyond the scope of this book, and actually has been the subject of several books. A good place to find out more about JDBC is Sun's JDBC Web page at `http://java.sun.com/products/jdbc`.

Two aspects of database connectivity are covered in this chapter, and both are part of the WebSphere Application Server package. The first is connection pooling, which is aimed at improving the performance of database-reliant Java servlets. The other one targets programmer performance or, in other words, provides an alternative to the JDBC API in an attempt to simplify the programmer's work when developing database-reliant servlets. This is done using a set of JavaBeans called *data access beans*.

Connection Pooling

One of the most common paradigms for developing WebSphere applications (or Web based applications in general), and a recurring theme in this book, is a three-tier application. The first tier is responsible for user interaction and presentation, and is actually a Web browser. The second (or middle) tier is the Web server (or application server), which takes care of the business logic of the application. The third tier is responsible for managing the data used by the application. This third tier could be a relational database system (such as Oracle or DB2) or some other system capable of managing data.

One of the main drawbacks in this three-tier architecture is the communication overhead between the middle tier and the third tier. The problem is that "connecting" to a database is a relatively expensive operation, due to considerations such as security. In a non-Web-based environment, this does not pose much of a problem, since a typical user logs into the system to do his work and is willing to wait the extra second for the connection. In contrast, Web-based applications are expected to handle large volumes of users whose access patterns are much less predictable and are usually composed of short interactions. In such cases, it is possible that the time spent in connecting and disconnecting to the database will exceed the time spent in the act of retrieving data.

Since performance is a critical aspect for Web applications (as the patience of users easily wanes), WebSphere includes a built-in capability for connection *pooling*. Pooling is essentially a form of sharing resources. Instead of having each user request incur the overhead of a connect operation, a pool of connections is prepared in advance (or created dynamically on demand) and is shared by all servlets processing requests. This way, the servlets might not have to wait for a database connection. If there is an available connection, it can be readily used. If there is no such connection, a new connection might be created. This would incur some overhead for the connection, but in subsequent requests, we would have one more connection pooled. In the worst case, which occurs when the maximum allowed size for the connection pool is reached, the requesting servlet needs to wait for a connection to be freed by the servlet using it and returned to the pool. Because most database interactions are quite short, this waiting period shouldn't amount to much. Another important advantage of such pooling is that it enables limiting the maximum number of connections to the database. This can come in handy if the database product or its licensing terms might impose some restrictions on the number of concurrent users.

The implementation of this pooling mechanism in WebSphere is transparent to the using servlet. Actually, this is part of the JDBC 2.0 Standard Extension API. An abstraction called `DataSource` is provided in order to get connections, and this hides the details of pooling. This stands in contrast to the way connections are handled in JDBC 1.0, where a connection is established using the `getConnection` method of the JDBC driver manager (and the same connection is explicitly closed after use). Listing 20-1 shows an example of establishing a connection in the JDBC 1.0 API.

Listing 20-1
The sample servlet using JDBC 1.0 API

```
package book.ws.ch20.example;

import javax.servlet.*;
import javax.servlet.http.*;
import java.io.*;
import java.util.*;
import java.sql.*;
import java.text.*;

public class JDBCServlet extends HttpServlet {

    // Other methods

    public void doGet(HttpServletRequest request,
HttpServletResponse response) throws ServletException,
```

continues

Listing 20-1
Continued

```
IOException {
      response.setContentType("text/html");
      PrintWriter out = new PrintWriter
(response.getOutputStream());

      out.println("<HTML>")
      out.println("<HEAD><TITLE> Table </TITLE></HEAD>");
      out.println("<BODY>");
      try {
            Class.forName("com.ibm.db2.jdbc.app.DBDriver");
            Connection con = DriverManager.getConnection(
                  "jdbc:db2:myDb:5001",
                  "db2admin",
                  "db2passwd");
            Statement stmt = con.createStatement();
            ResultSet rs = stmt.executeQuery("select * from Tbl")
            While (rs.next()) {
                  // Assume we have two column in the table
                  out.println("<P> " + rs.getString(1) + "," +
                                    rs.getString(2));
            }
            con.close();
      } catch (Exception ex) {
        ex.printStackTrace();
      }
    out.close();
  }
}
```

In order to use connection pooling, the DataSource object is looked up. Listing 20-2 shows an example, based on the previous example, of how that can be done. First of all, note that in order to use connection pooling, you need the following two import statements:

```
import com.ibm.db2.jdbc.app.stdext.javax.sql.*;
import com.ibm.ejs.dbm.jdbcext.*;
```

Listing 20-2
Sample servlet using
JDBC 2.0 API and
exploiting connection
pooling

```
package book.ws.ch20.example;

import javax.servlet.*;
import javax.servlet.http.*;
import java.io.*;
import java.util.*;
import java.sql.*;
import java.text.*;
import com.ibm.db2.jdbc.app.stdext.javax.sql.*;
import com.ibm.ejs.dbm.jdbcext.*;
public class JDBC2Servlet extends HttpServlet {

  // Other methods
```

```
   public void doGet(HttpServletRequest request,
HttpServletResponse response) throws ServletException,
IOException {
    response.setContentType("text/html");
    PrintWriter out = new PrintWriter (response.getOutputStream());

    out.println("<HTML>")
    out.println("<HEAD><TITLE> Table </TITLE></HEAD>");
    out.println("<BODY>");
    try {
        Hashtable parms = new Hashtable();
        parms.put(Context.INITIAL_CONTEXT_FACTORY,
        "com.ibm.ejs.ns.jndi.CNInitialContextFactory");
        Context ctx = new InitialContext(parms);
        DataSource ds = (DataSource)ctx.lookup("jdbc/mydb");
        Connection con = ds.getConnection(
                "db2admin",
                "db2passwd");
        Statement stmt = con.createStatement();
        ResultSet rs = stmt.executeQuery("select * from Tbl")
        While (rs.next()) {
            // Assume we have two column in the table
            out.println("<P> " + rs.getString(1) + "," +
                            rs.getString(2));
        }
        con.close();
    } catch (Exception ex) {
      ex.printStackTrace();
    }
    out.close();
  }
}
```

As you can see, the difference from the previous example is that the code takes care of looking up the DataSource object. Note that it is also possible (and more efficient) to do the data souece lookup in the servlet init method, as done later on in Listing 20-3. For this to work, the DataSource object should have been created in advance by the Web administrator and stored in the naming service using the WebSphere Administrative Console (see Chapter 40). For the lookup, we need to create a JNDI naming context with parameters provided via a hash table. JNDI is explained in more detail in Chapter 22. What happens in the doGet method of this servlet is that the connection is retrieved from the data source and not from the driver manager. Although it looks quite similar, there is a huge difference. If the data source object has the right settings, it will implement connection pooling in a transparent manner, hence improving performance. Although we invoke the close method on the connection, it doesn't actually disconnect from the database, since the data source might need to use it later on.

To summarize, the idea is to access the `DataSource` in the `init` method and subsequently use it to get the connections, implicitly making use of pooling.

When using the connection obtained from the data source, you might want to treat two possible exceptions:

- `ConnectionPreemptedException` This occurs if the servlet doesn't use a connection for a long period of time. In this case, the underlying mechanism grabs the connection back to make better use of it.

- `ConnectionTimeoutException` This occurs if the pool is empty when a `getConnection` request is made; in other words, no connections are available at the time of the call, nor are any made available during the specified timeout.

An important caveat is that `DataSource` doesn't support pooling by its definition, and this support is implementation-dependent. So, when using other implementations of JDBC 2.0, you cannot count on having this feature.

While on the subject of different implementations, note that WebSphere Application Server version 2.0 implements its own mechanism for connection pooling through the "connection manager" implemented in the `com.ibm.servlet.connmgr` package. The connection manager is still partly supported in version 3.0, but only in deprecated form, and it might not be supported in future versions. If you have some old WebSphere applications implemented using the connection manager, it shouldn't be difficult to upgrade them to use `DataSource` objects. The reason is that the underlying design model is identical, so what was previously called `IBMConnSpec` can now be replaced with a `DataSource` object.

As already discussed, one of the main motivations for connection pooling is performance. Setting the size of the connection pool is a tricky issue. Having a large connection pool would improve service time, since it increases the chances of a servlet getting a free connection from the pool upon request. On the other hand, maintaining a large connection pool might load the system and hence degrade performance. The WebSphere Administrative Console provides a few parameters that can be set in order to control the behavior of the pooling mechanism. Although a detailed discussion of how to use the Administrative Console will be covered in Chapter 40, it is worth mentioning the parameters related to connection pooling:

- *Maximum connection pool size* The maximal number of connections in the pool. If this size is reached and all connections are in use, a `ConnectionTimeoutException` is thrown, as explained previously.

■ *Idle timeout*   How long an idle connection remains in the pool before being freed

■ *Orphan timeout*   How long a connection can be owned by a servlet not using it before taken from it

■ *Connection timeout*   How long a request for connection waits until an exception is thrown. Again, this happens when the maximal pool size is reached.

■ *Minimum connection pool size*   The initial number of connections in the pool

Data Access Beans

This section focuses on a different aspect of the relationship between the middle tier (business logic in the Web server) to the third tier (data source). In order to access the data source, the middle tier application code typically uses the JDBC API (assuming that the data source is JDBC-compliant). Data access beans are essentially IBM's alternative to JDBC (also known as a `java.sql` package).

The idea of not using JDBC is a little surprising, since it has already gained stature as the defacto standard for Java database connectivity. The motivation for replacing JDBC is implied by the name of IBM's data access beans. The JavaBeans programming model provides numerous benefits, not the least of which is the ability to use beans in IDEs (such as VisualAge for Java) in a process of visual composition. Visual composition reduces the amount of code that needs to be written and that can't be too bad. Other features of data access beans are as follows (note that some of the following material appears in the "Data Access JavaBeans" article of the Version 3 IBM WebSphere Application Server Documentation Center, published by IBM):

■ *Caching of query results*   When making an SQL query, the results are retrieved all at once and placed in a cache. This enables the servlet (or application) to freely move forward and backward through the cache or to jump to arbitrary rows in the cache. When making SQL queries in JDBC, which are retrieved one by one, only forward iteration is supported.

■ *Updates through cache*   The cache holding query results can be manipulated to add, remove, or modify rows. These changes can be then written back to the relational database. When using this feature, there is no need to use SQL to update the database.

■ *Parameterized query*   In many situations, the SQL query submitted to the database includes some parameters that are available only at runtime. Instead of composing the string at runtime explicitly, the data access beans enable defining a "base" SQL query string with "variables" in place of some of the actual values. Before the query is actually executed, these variables are replaced with the values. The base query is an ordinary SQL query with some of the elements replaced by question marks ("?").

■ *Metadata*   Taking the idea of parameterized query one step further; consider having parameters, which are not necessarily strings but arbitrary Java objects. Metadata specifications define how to convert Java objects into SQL datatypes. These specifications work in the other direction too, converting SQL datatypes to JAVA datatypes. This prevents the need to spend time and code performing type conversions and string construction when manipulating database information.

Listing 20-3 shows an example of a simple servlet using the data access beans. This example introduces the different data access beans. This example is a little more complicated than the previous ones. However, compared to the example in Listing 20-2, there is no change in the way DS is generated in the `init` method. The obvious reason is that in order to enjoy the benefits of connection pooling, we make use of the `DataSource` object. The data access JavaBeans are contained in the `com.ibm.db` package, so we need to import it. You should also make sure that CLASSPATH includes the `databeans.jar` file in which the relevant classes are kept (this file is in the WebSphere Application Server `lib` directory). In this example, we use the `DataBaseConnection` bean called `dconn`, which establishes the link between the data access beans layer and the actual database. Then we create a `StatementMetaData` bean that stores metadata information for the query. This includes the SQL query string, the database column used in the

Listing 20-3
The sample servlet using IBM data access beans

```
package book.ws.ch20.example;

import javax.servlet.*;
import javax.servlet.http.*;
import java.io.*;
```

```
import java.util.*;
import java.sql.*;
import java.text.*;
import javax.naming;
import com.ibm.db2.jdbc.app.stdext.javax.sql.*
import com.ibm.ejs.dbm.jdbcext.*;

public class DataBeanServlet extends HttpServlet {

     private static DataSource ds = null;

  // Other methods

  public void init(JDBC2Servlet js) throws ServletException {
      super.init(js);
      Hashtable parms = new Hashtable();
      parms.put(Context.INITIAL_CONTEXT_FACTORY,
               "com.ibm.ejs.ns.jndi.CNInitialContextFactory");
      Context ctx = new InitialContext(parms);
      ds = (DataSource) ctx.lookup("jdbc/mydb"
  }
  public void doGet(HttpServletRequest request,
HttpServletResponse response) throws ServletException,
IOException {
      response.setContentType("text/html");
      PrintWriter out = new PrintWriter
      (response.getOutputStream());

      out.println("<HTML>")
      out.println("<HEAD><TITLE> Table </TITLE></HEAD>");
      out.println("<BODY>");
      try {
           Connection con = ds.getConnection(
                   "db2admin",
                   "db2passwd");
           DatabaseConnection dconn = new
           DatabaseConnection(conn);
           String query = "select PRODUCT, QTY, PRICE from Tbl"+
                          "where PRICE >= ?";
           metaData = new StatementMetaData();
           metaData.setSQL(query);
           metaData.addParameter("minPrice", Integer.class,
                                           Types.SMALLINT);
           metaData.addColumn("PRODUCT",
           String.class,Types.VARCHAR);
           metaData.addColumn("QTY",
           Integer.class,Types.SMALLINT);
           metaData.addColumn("PRICE",
           Integer.class,Types.SMALLINT);
           metadata.addTable("Table");

           SelectStatement stmt = new SelectStatement;
           stmt.setConnection(dconn);
           stmt.setMetaData(metaData);
           // Here we set the minPrice parameter
```

continues

Listing 20-3
Continued

```
            // we omit the details of how this price
            // is determined. The point is it is not fixed
            selectStatement.setParameter(minPrice, getMinPrice());
            selectStatement.execute();

            SelectResult rs = stmt.getResult();
            while (rs.nextRow()) {
                    // Assume we have two column in the table
                    out.println("<H1> " +
                            (String)rs.getColumnValue("ID")
                            + "," + (Integer)
                            rs.getColumnValue("QTY")
                            + "</H1>");
            }
            stmt.close();
            con.close();
            out.println("</BODY></HTML>");
        } catch (Exception ex) {
          ex.printStackTrace();
        }
        out.close();
    }
}
```

query, their respective Java datatypes and SQL datatypes, the query parameters (represented by question marks in the query itself), their Java and SQL datatypes, and the table name. In case of multiple parameters, the parameters are associated with question marks in the query string in the order in which they are introduced into the StatementMetaData bean.

The SelectStatement bean represents an actual instantiation of the parameterized query defined by the StatementMetaData. To this end, it requires the connection, the metadata bean, and an assignment of a value to the parameter. Once the execute method of the SelectStatement is invoked, a SelectResult bean is used to extract the results. This bean provides the nextRow and previousRow (not used in this example) for traversing the result rows, as well as getColumnValue and setColumnValue for getting and setting column values.

To summarize, data access beans provide an attractive way to program database interaction. They enable efficient traversal of the database and easy construction of queries that contain parameters not known at compilation time. Note that the caching of query results doesn't necessarily take place literally in cases where table queries are very large. In this case, it is broken down into blocks that are fetched individually, but in a manner transparent to the programmer using the data access beans.

WebSphere Security Services

Security is an important aspect of contemporary network computing. It wasn't such a long time ago when physical security of computer mainframes implied the security of data. The rapid adoption of the Internet as a vehicle for business places a lot of sensitive information on computers that are connected to the Internet. Although this is done in order to boost productivity by sharing information inside the organization or with select business partners, it does expose data and system to risks of misuse. Other technological advances (floppy disks, CD-ROMs, laptops, and data-enabled cell phones) make it easy to extract and move information, hence increasing the importance of security.

In broad terms, the issues of security for Web-based applications can be divided into four different categories:

- *Server security* Server security involves both physical security (which is still important) and mechanisms working at the operating system level aimed to control access to the server. On top of the security services of operating systems, numerous products offer host access control or intrusion detection capabilities.

- *Client security* Securing the client machine is not necessarily an issue, but it is facilitated through some of the Java security mechanisms, described in Chapter 13.

- *Network security* An effective way to protect servers (or clients, for that matter) is to prevent or limit access to the network. That is the idea of firewalls, or in their more powerful version, *Virtual Private Networks* (VPNs). Security in the network level is also achieved through the use of encryption, such as when using SSL. Encryption is quite important when running applications over long haul networks, where data is routed through unknown (thus non-trusted) sites.

- *Application security* This is concerned with controlling and limiting the actions of application users. Once inside the application, different users are not necessarily treated equally. Some users have different permissions and privileges, and these must be enforced.

Although a brief overview of Java and Web security was provided in Chapter 13, this chapter focuses on WebSphere security features. The purpose of these features is to minimize the risk of unauthorized access to data. WebSphere security features are mainly in the application level, with the exception of SSL support. This implies that WebSphere by itself does not provide enough protection against malicious actions and should be complemented with other security-related capabilities of the kinds mentioned previously.

The main features of any security service, including WebSphere's are *authentication* and *authorization*. Authentication is the process of identifying a user or process, and it takes place when the user (by user here we mean either a human user or a computer process) first attempts to access the system associated with the security service. The most common authentication scheme is a combination of user ID and password. Authentication is the first step toward accessing resources within the domain of the system. In addition, access to individual resources requires authorization. Authorization is usually handled by maintaining *Access Control Lists* (ACLs) for each resource or resource group. These lists define which users are allowed what kind of access to the resource.

In the case of WebSphere, the resources are Web pages, JSP files, servlets, and EJBs. WebSphere provides a uniform way of handling both authentication and authorization for these resources, as detailed in Chapter 42. In order to work correctly, the underlying Web server (HTTP server) requires a security plug-in in order to interact with the WebSphere security services on issues of authentication and authorization. The plug-in is deployed as part of the WebSphere installation process.

It is possible to disable all security services in WebSphere through the administration console. This setting is not really recommended for a Web site. However, it is quite useful for application development and for local testing.

Authentication

Authentication of users in WebSphere is based on external user registry. In other words, there is no database of users in WebSphere. Instead, one of two alternatives is available:

- Using the underlying operating system for authorization, usually with a username and password
- Using *Lightweight Third-Party Authentication* (LTPA), which is essentially a protocol to retrieve authentication data from an LDAP server

An LDAP server could be though as a "directory" of users for the purpose of LTPA (LDAP is explained in Chapter 22). Authentication is required prior to accessing protected information. Applications can define different authentication requirements:

- *None*   No authentication required
- *Basic*   User is prompted for user ID and password (most likely based on HTTP authentication supported by Web browsers)
- *Certificate*   The client must provide a digital certificate. A digital certificate is a stream of bytes (or an "electronic document") for proving the identity of a certain party.
- *Custom*   Tailor-made servlets can be used to perform authorization.

Using certificates might have some advantages beyond providing plain access security. Since these certificates prove the identity of the client, they can be used to ensure non-repudiation (that is, avoid denial of a certain transaction by an involved party). Clearly, certificate security and management is an important issue to tackle when using digital certificates. Several products help in managing and issuing certificates, such as Verisign (see `www.verisign.com`).

In order to make authentication effective, it is recommended to make authentication over SSL. If you use plain HTTP, there is a substantial risk of the password being exposed, which increases as the "distance" between the client and the server grows. Distance here refers to the distance in the network topology, measured as the number routers and switches passed on the way between the client and server. At each such point, a person with basic know-how can pick up your passwords and certificates. SSL is provided through the `javax.net.ssl` Java extension package and is supported by virtually all up-to-date Web browsers and servers, as well as by the WebSphere application server.

Authorization

Once a user is authenticated, it is still important to limit his access to the system based on predefined permissions. The WebSphere administration console enables detailed definitions of access permissions to various resources, namely EJBs, JSPs, servlets, and HTML pages. Permissions can be defined in a rather fine-grained manner, going to the level of individual methods.

The mechanics of WebSphere authorization are based on ACLs. The idea is to attach to each action a list of users allowed to perform it (corresponding to a method invoked on a resource). In order to promote efficiency (and brevity), it is possible to group together actions that are handled together. It is also possible to group resources into "applications" that share common security-related attributes.

For EJBs, there is a little more to the issue of authorization. Using the security attributes in the deployment descriptor of EJBs, it is possible to have the EJB execute using different permissions than those available to the user. This is relevant mainly to EJBs that are invoked from other EJBs on the server (hence, there is less likelihood of misuse by clients). It is also possible to maintain the same user identity across multiple invocations, even when crossing EJB server boundaries (this is referred to as *delegation*).

It is important to point out that the EJB server in WebSphere does not use the "access control" and "run-as identity" attributes in the deployment descriptor. It only uses the "run-as mode" attribute.

22

Naming
Service and
LDAP Support

When programming in any distributed environment, one issue that must be addressed is naming. When clients need to gain access to a resource, they must have a way to translate a "logical" name to an actual object reference and to do so transparently in case the object is on a remote machine. The WebSphere naming service provides this capability and is used primarily for locating EJBs by prospective clients. In WebSphere, the actual implementation of the naming service is of no importance to the programmer because it is masked through the use of JDNI. JNDI is the Java extension API for using naming and directory services. LDAP is an example of a directory service of the kind JNDI to which should interface. This chapter introduces LDAP and describes the JNDI API.

LDAP stands for *Lightweight Directory Access Protocol*. It is an open industry standard aiming at providing a way to manage information pertaining to files, users, printers, and other resources that can be dispersed over several different networks.

The WebSphere Application Server, Advanced Edition allows storing the user registry (for authentication purposes) on an LDAP server (or servers). However, in order to use LDAP, you must install an LDAP server, which is not part of the WebSphere Application Server distribution. (Note that Version 3.0 does include a complimentary LDAP server on the CD in the Advanced Edition).

What Is LDAP?

The growing popularity of computers as a tool for supporting business, alongside the advent of the Internet as a business vehicle, gives rise to the necessity of a directory service that allows users to look up people or resources on a certain network. A directory would be used in much the same way a library catalog or a telephone directory would be used.

LDAP was born during the early 1990s as a lightweight alternative to a protocol called *Directory Access Protocol* (DAP), which was part of the specification for a protocol called X.500. X.500 was developed as part of the standardization efforts initiated by several international organizations (notably among the *International Standards Organization* (ISO). These efforts resulted in what is known as *Open Systems Interconnect* (OSI), which was once considered an alternative to Internet protocols. The OSI model is a reference model that defines a seven-layer model of data communication that starts with the physical layer as the lowest layer and works its way up to application protocols as the highest layer. The OSI reference model and subsequent protocols were developed from scratch, usually resulting in a cleaner design. However, the relatively slow development and even slower deployment and installation process doomed the OSI protocols to failure, especially with the rapid development of the Internet, based on the TCP/IP protocol.

Similar to other Internet standards, LDAP went through several stages of evolution before reaching its current state. On the way, it became an industry-wide standard, and most vendors provide some support for it.

LDAP is essentially based on the client/server paradigm. Although it seems at first that LDAP is a "directory" protocol, it actually defines the protocol of communication between LDAP clients to LDAP servers. Through this protocol, and the structure of the messages involved, a directory model is induced. In other words, the communication protocol implies certain restrictions imposed on designers of LDAP servers, and these restrictions define what an LDAP directory is in abstract terms.

LDAP is implemented on top of TCP/IP and as such, the way clients interact with servers resembles other TCP/IP-based protocols such as HTTP or FTP. A session that "binds" to the server is initiated by the client (this corresponds to a TCP/IP operation that requires specifying the host IP address and TCP/IP port number for the LDAP server is listening). Following an optional authentication procedure based on username and password, the actual session commences. Without authentication, the client can assume "anonymous" identity with default access rights. The session itself consists of a series of operations on directory data, namely search and update operations. Operations are conducted by the client issuing a request and the server responding. When the client is done, the session is closed.

All search and update operations requested by the LDAP client revolve around the basic data structure in which the LDAP server stores information, referred to as directory entry. A single directory entry describes a real-world object such as a person, a printer, or a computer. The entry is identified by a name called a *distinguished name* (DN), which is composed of smaller parts called *relatively distinguished names* (RDN). This situation is strikingly similar to the way files are organized (in a hierarchy of directories) in most modern operating systems (such as UNIX or Windows). Consider a file named `E:\WebSphere\AppServer\readme.txt`. This name is composed of four smaller names delimited by backslashes. Each of these smaller names, referring to drive, directory, or file names are the equivalents of RDNs. In addition to the entry name, each entry contains one or more attributes that comprise the description of the entry. For example, a directory entry for a computer could include its type, operating system, IP address, physical location, and so on. The list of attributes, along with the type of each attribute and possible syntax restrictions, are described in a schema. The relationship between the schema and a directory entry is identical to the relationship between a class and an object in an object-oriented language; that is, the directory entry can be thought of as an instance of the schema. New schemas can be derived from existing ones, just like class inheritance in an object-oriented language. A special attribute called `objectClass` exists in each directory entry and identifies the schema to which it belongs. This attribute is defined in the "top" object class, which essentially is a root class from which all schemas are derived.

In a specific directory entry, zero or more values are associated with each attribute. Zero values mean that nothing is associated with it, and this is possible for optional attributes (their being optional is part of the schema definition). The usual case is one value, but one attribute can have several values. Multiple values are useful for attributes such as phone numbers, where several of them are associated with one object (a person, in the case of phones).

Attribute types or syntaxes are used to define the kind of value the attribute takes. The typing system is flexible enough to allow general purpose binary data as well as printable strings that can be either case-sensitive or not. It is possible to define new types of attribute syntaxes, limiting the length of the value or its content.

Attribute names and values are used to specify RDNs. Recall that entry names, DNs, are composed of smaller names called RDNs. These are usually of the form `<attribute name>=<value>`, but in general you can specify an RDN as a set of plus-sign delimited pairs of attributes and values. For example, in the case of two pairs:

```
<attribute1 name>=<value1>+<attribute2 name>=<value>.
```

Directory entries are organized in a tree-like structure called the *Directory Information Tree* (DIT), starting from a virtual root node. For a given entry, the RDNs composing its DN corresponds to the path from the virtual root to the node of the entry on the tree. The DN is a list of comma-separated RDNs, except that unlike file system pathnames, the order in which the RDNs are specified is from the node up to the root. Figure 22-1 shows an example of a simple DIT. In this example, a directory composed

Figure 22-1
A simple DIT

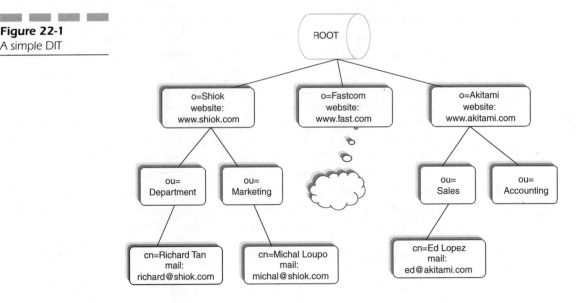

of people who belong to departments and organizations. So for example, the DN for Ed Lopez in the Sales department of Akitami is `cn=Ed Lopez,ou=Sales,o=Akitami`. The directory root shown in the figure is virtual, and there is no corresponding directory entry.

Inside the DIT, it is possible to create aliases, which can be thought of as links between nodes. These aliases are the reason for the DIT being a tree-like structure and not really a tree. Aliases can be used to represent cases where a certain entity belongs to two categories (like a person belonging to two departments in our example shown in Figure 22-1). Another motivation to use aliases is to ensure "backward compatibility"; that is, although we make changes in the DIT, we would like old DNs to remain valid (at least temporarily). This can be achieved easily by moving the directory entry to its new location, but leaving behind an alias with the old DN.

Considering the kinds of applications for which LDAP is intended, scalability is an important issue. Specifically, this means that a single server is not sufficient to maintain the entire DIT. In order to provide the support for scalability, the DIT can include "referrals" to other servers. This allows creating a distributed DIT with multiple servers. The topmost node in a server is called the *server suffix*. The reason for this name is that this is the longest common suffix for all DNs in this server. Actually, a single server can have several suffixes, corresponding to several "sub-trees" of the DIT. Referrals to other servers are represented by a special kind of entry. Referrals can be handled in one of two ways: either the requesting client receives the referral and can access the referred server, or "server chaining" takes place. In the latter case, the server originally contacted by the client makes a request to the referred server.

After reviewing the structure of the DIT, let's look at how operations are performed on it. The most important operation supported in the LDAP protocol is the "search" operation. LDAP is designed under the (reasonable) assumption that most operations performed are search operations. Only a small minority of requests are updates. If that is not the case, any standard database system might do better than an LDAP server. The search operation allows a client to perform a search on a certain part of the DIT looking for certain entries. The parameters for a search operation are as follows:

- *Base*   A node in the DIT from which the search shall commence
- *Scope*   How deep within the DIT the search should go. There are three options here:
  - *BaseObject*   Only the base node will be searched
  - *SingleLevel*   Only the immediate sub-nodes of the base node will be searched
  - *WholeSubTree*   All descendants of the base node are to be searched.

■ *Search Filter* A search criteria to be met by returned entries. The search criteria is composed of a series of assertions relating to an attribute. These assertions are of the form attribute operator value. Operators are =, >=, <=, =*, ~=. The first three comparison operators have the obvious meaning, the =* operator is used without a right operand and returns all entries which have a value set for the attribute, and the ~= operator provides an approximate match. If more than one assertion is provided, they should be accompanied by a Boolean operator (&, |, or !, meaning AND, OR and NOT respectively). The operators are specified in "prefix" notation; that is, the operator precedes the arguments. For example:

```
"&(cn=Ed Lopez)(website=www.akitami.com)".
```

■ *Returned Attributes* List of attributes to return
■ *Alias Dereferencing* Whether or not aliases should be followed. (If they are not followed, the "alias" itself is examined and might be returned. If they are followed, the search continues at wherever the link is pointing at.)
■ *Size and Time Limit* Maximal number of entries to be returned and maximal search time. These can be specified in order to limit the amount of load imposed by the search.

The update operations that are supported are adding a new entry to the directory, deleting entries (which must be leaf nodes), and modifying existing entries. A special variant of modifying entries is modifying DNs, which could either mean changing the first (least significant) component of the DN or changing the location of the node to a different sub-tree.

All operations, and especially update operations, might require authorization. LDAP has support for various levels of user authentication (corresponding to the desired level of security) ranging from no authorization, basic authorization (similar to the one used in HTTP), to a more powerful authentication scheme, possibly using SSL and similar security mechanisms.

Java Naming and Directory Interface (JNDI)

Although LDAP has a C/C++ API, we focus here on the Java-based API called JNDI. JDNI is a generic API that is not specific to LDAP, but rather applies to other naming and directory services such as *Domain Naming Service* (DNS). The motivation for JNDI is the desire to have a consistent model for accessing different resources. Basically, this sounds a little like the motivation for having LDAP. In some senses, JNDI is "bigger" because it can accommodate other ways of managing resources such as CORBA or DNS. However, JDNI is just an API and does not contain the logic for directory management.

JNDI is a Java extension API and is contained in the following packages:

- `javax.naming` The basic API used to look up objects and values in a naming service

- `javax.naming.directory` A more sophisticated API used for filtered searching and updates

- `javax.naming.spi` Interfaces for use by service provider developers. These are rarely of any interest for application developers because they are intended for developing support for specific services (for example, LDAP).

WebSphere includes a built-in implementation of a JNDI server for the purpose of providing a naming service for EJBs. The "Hello EJB" example of Chapter 5 made use (albeit very basic use) of JNDI.

The Naming Package

The `javax.naming` package provides a set of interfaces and classes aimed at representing a generic naming service. The most basic abstraction in the naming package is a context. A *context* can be viewed as the name space in which your operations will take place. Examples of a context are an LDAP node (along with the associated sub-tree) or a file system directory (and all directories inside it). An important attribute of contexts is that they can contain other contexts; that is, this is a recursive construct. For example, in the domain of file systems, consider directories that can contain other directories. When working with JNDI, there is also a notion of initial context. This initial context is considered the root of all naming operations that use it. So for example, if the initial context in a file system were set to be `E:\WebSphere\AppServer`, the path to the file `E:\WebSphere\AppServer\readme.txt` would be `\readme.txt`.

In order to work with JNDI, the first thing to do is create a context on which operations are made. Contexts are represented in the naming package by the Context interface. In order to create a context, you must set up the environment variables for JNDI. Table 22-1 lists some of the properties

Table 22-1

JDNI environment

Environment Property	Definition Constant	Description
java.naming.factory.initial	Context.INITIAL _CONTEXT_FACTORY	Class name of the initial context factory to use. In the WebSphere Server Advanced Edition, this should be set to com.ibm. ejs.ns.jndi.CNInitial ContextFactory.
java.naming.provider.url	Context. PROVIDER_URL	Specifies configuration information for the provider to use. When using WebSphere AE, this should be iiop:// servername:portnum. The port number can be determined with the WebSphere Administration Client and is 900 by default.
java.naming.dns.url	Context.DNS_URL	Specifies the DNS host and domain names to use for the JNDI URL context

used by JNDI. These properties are the relevant ones when creating a context for use by a WebSphere client. JNDI supports numerous other environment variables defining security, internationalization, and service-related parameters. For all those properties not set explicitly, the system default is used. In order to set properties, you may either read them from a file (using the load method of the Properties object, providing it an InputStream opened on the property file) or specify them during runtime using the properties object put method.

The class javax.naming.InitialContext implements the Context interface and can be used to create context objects. With the context at hand, you can retrieve naming information. The retrieval methods of the Context interface all take either a String or a Name as parameters. Name is an interface that represents an ordered sequence of zero or more elements and is useful in cases where multiple namespaces are required. The Context interface supports four retrieval methods (each has two variants, one for a String and one for a Name):

■ list   Returns a NamingEnumeration (an extension of Enumeration) of the names and the class names of the objects bound to them in the context passed as parameter (The parameter is a name of a context within the current context.) The returned collection consists of `NameClassPair` objects, from which the name and class name can be retrieved.

- `listBindings` Returns a `NamingEnumeration` of names and the actual objects bound to them in the parameter context. The returned collection consists of `Binding` objects, from which the name and object can be retrieved.
- `lookup` Returns the named object
- `lookupLink` Returns the named object, following links

Management of the objects inside the context is done using binding objects. The Context interface provides the following bind-related methods:

- `bind` Binds the name to the object in the context (an exception occurs if the name is already in use)
- `createSubcontext` Creates and binds a new context to the name (the equivalent of `mkdir` in a file system such as MS-DOS)
- `destroySubContext` Destroys the context and removes it from the name space (the equivalent of `rmdir` in a file system such as MS-DOS)
- `rebind` Binds the name to the object, overwriting any existing bind
- `rename` Takes the object bound to one name and binds it to a new name
- `unbind` Unbinds the named object from the namespace (the equivalent of a `delete` operation)

The Directory Package

The `javax.naming.directory` extends the naming package to provide functionality of accessing and managing directory services. The main feature supported by it is object attributes, which can be used as the basis for search operations. The directory package draws its notion of a directory search concepts from the LDAP specification.

In order to search for objects in a directory, you need to create an object implementing the `javax.naming.directory.DirContext` interface. This interface extends the `Context` interface so all naming package operations are applicable here too. The class `InitialDirContext` is an implementation of the `DirContext` interface.

In order to represent attributes, the directory package introduces the following two interfaces:

- `Attribute` Represents an attribute associated with a named object. The attribute itself is a sequence of zero or more objects. The attribute can provide a schema in the form of a `DirContext` in order to describe the structure of the attribute. Yet another `DirContext` can be provided, holding the syntax of the values in the attribute (the syntax definitions are provider-dependent; that is, they might just be strings whose meaning depends on the underlying service).

- `Attributes` Represents a collection of `Attribute` objects associated with a named object

These two interfaces provide methods for adding and removing values and attributes respectively.

The `DirContext` interface provides four flavors of the search method. The simplest one just takes a name along with an `Attributes` object. It searches for objects that contain the provided set of attributes. The result of the search is a `NamingEnumeration` just like in the naming package. The elements inside the `NamingEnumeration` are of a subclass of Binding class `SearchResult`, which provides access to search attributes. Listing 22-1 provides a schematic example of a directory search, using the classes `BasicAttribute` and `BasicAttributes`, which implement the respective interfaces. A more efficient search method allows you to specify in advance which attributes to fetch (for example, if you are searching a directory of people, you might be looking just for their phone numbers).

The last two search methods allow you to search with filtering and search controls. Both ideas were already described in the previous section as part of the description of LDAP. For the purpose of filtering, the search method is provided with a filter string of the same format of LDAP search filters.

Search controls are represented by a `SearchControls` object that defines the following:

- *Search scope* OBJECT_SCOPE, ONLEVEL_SCOPE, or SUBTREE_SCOPE (corresponding to base object, single level, or whole sub-tree, respectively)

- *Maximum number of entries* A limit on the number of returned entries

- *Maximum Time* Time limit in milliseconds for the search

- *Dereference Flag* Indicating whether links should be dereferenced during the search

- *Returned Attributes* Indicates what attributes to return (again, promoting efficiency when only part of the attributes are needed)

- *Return object values* Flag indicating whether object values or only name and class should be returned

Listing 22-1
A simple JNDI
Directory Search

```
.
.
.
Properties props = new Properties;
props.put(Context.INITIAL_CONTEXT_FACTORY,
"com.ibm.jndi.LDAPCtxFactory");
props.put(Context.PROVIDER_URL, "ldap://host");
try {
      // Create Search Context
      DirContext ctx = new InitialDirContext(props);

      // Define attributes
      Attributes attrs = new BasicAttributes(true);
      attrs.put(new BasicAttribute("cn"));
      attrs.put(new BasicAttribute("website"));


      // Perform search
      Naming Enumeration result = ctx.search("ou=shiok", attrs);

      // Iterate over results
      While (result.hasMore()) {
      .
      .
      .
      }
}
catch (NamingException ex) {
.
.
.
}
.
.
.
```

Listing 22-2 shows a schematic example of a search using filtering and search controls.

The directory package allows modifying attributes via the `DirContext` interface. This is important in order to place the attributes on objects so the search methods have something with which to work. This is done with the `modifyAttributes` method, which takes a name, an attributes array, and the operation to perform. The operation can be one of the following:

- `DirContext.ADD_ATTRIBUTE`

- `DirContext.REPLACE_ATTRIBUTE`

- `DirContext.REMOTE_ATTRIBUTE`

Alternatively, it is possible to call `modifyAttributes` with a name and an array of `ModificationItem` objects, which are just pairings of such an operation with an `Attributes` object.

```
.
.
.
Properties props = new Properties;
props.put(Context.INITIAL_CONTEXT_FACTORY,
"com.ibm.jndi.LDAPCtxFactory");
props.put(Context.PROVIDER_URL, "ldap://host");
try {
     // Create Search Context
     DirContext ctx = new InitialDirContext(props);

     String[] attrs = { "email" };
     String filter = "(&(cn=E*)(website=www.shiok.com))"

     // Define Search Controls
     SearchControls sc = new SearchControls(SUBTREE_SCOPE, 1000,
0, attrs, false, false);

     // Perform search
     Naming Enumeration result = ctx.search("ou=shiok", filter,
sc);

     / Return results
     While (result.hasMore()) {
        .
        .
        .
     }
}
catch (NamingException ex) {
```

One last feature of the JNDI directory package is that it allows the user to retrieve the schema of a directory using the getSchema and getSchemaClassDefinition methods, both returning DirContext objects (similar to the schema methods in Attribute mentioned previously).

LDAP in WebSphere

As explained in the beginning of this chapter, in order to use LDAP in WebSphere, an LDAP server is required. One option is the IBM SecureWay Directory, which has the advantage of being an IBM product, thus providing better integration with other IBM products. More information on this LDAP server can be found in the IBM Web site at http://www.ibm.com/software/network/directory.

The main use of LDAP in the context of WebSphere is to maintain the user registry, which is the basis for the authentication procedure. In other words, the WebSphere security services are capable of using an LDAP-based user database. In order to look up users, a search filter is used. Pre-defined filters exist for the common defaults used in Netscape LDAP server, Domino 4.6, Domino 5.0, and of course SecureWay Directory. The configuration of the user registry is described in more detail in Chapter 42, "Administering WebSphere Security."

HTTP Servlets

Now that you are now familiar with what servlets are and how they work (having gone over servlet lifecycle and seen a simple "Hello World" example), you are ready to tackle the next stage. In this chapter, we will describe two full servlet examples. Because the most common servlets are HTTP servlets (that is, servlets that are accessed through an HTTP connection), this chapter focuses on two such examples. The purpose of this chapter is both to show you some "real world" examples so you are familiar with how servlets are usually used, and to give you a chance to get a bit of "flight time" on WebSphere servlets. Both examples illustrate an end-to-end process including the generation of some form of user interface and access to data stored in a RDBMS.

The Configuration Servlet

Our first example is taken from the world of part configurations. In this example, we are requested to provide a display of a configuration of a complex piece of machinery. Such a part is usually composed of a hierarchical structure in which each part may be broken down into a set of smaller parts that themselves may be broken down into yet smaller parts. Due to limitations of human abstraction, almost all objects in the real world are broken down into such hierarchical structures. Each level is manageable in its own right and the observer can decide at which level the part should be viewed. For example, computer hardware is broken down into the motherboard, the network card, the disk, and so on. The motherboard itself is further broken down into the CPU, the memory chips, the controller, and so on. Just like computer hardware, software is also broken down into modules, procedures, and functions. But such a hierarchical view is not limited to IT-related issues. Everything from projects to power plants to aircraft to cities and practically everything else is maintained in some hierarchical structure.

We have a breakdown that is usually maintained in a database of some sorts and we are asked to provide a view of this configuration. Obviously, we want to display it as a hierarchy. What better way to do so than to use a tree widget?

Our job is quite simple—given some data model representing a hierarchical structure, we are asked to build a Web-enabled interface that will display the hierarchies as trees in a browser. This will allow anyone with authorized access to our Web site to view the configurations in a convenient manner. Because we must provide this service from any browser, we will build an HTTP servlet to service these requests. Our HTTP servlet will receive the request, access the data in the database, and return some user interface to display the hierarchical information.

We need to make a couple of decisions. First, we need to decide what our server model will be. This part is quite simple (especially if you know the title of this chapter). The best fit is an HTTP servlet (surprise, surprise). We will build a servlet that will accept GET requests. Upon receiving this request (along with a set of parameters we require to identify the root of the configuration), we will access the database and get the information regarding the entire tree. We will then write this information to the output stream.

That was easy enough. But how should we write the information? As straight HTML? That would be very ugly. Maybe we can put it in an HTML table and indent the lines based on the depth in the tree? That would be slightly better—but not by much. Actually, because we were asked to provide a dynamic user interface, we need some code to be passed to the browser so the tree can be displayed and manipulated (that is, nodes collapsed, opened, and so on). Our selection is therefore much narrower—we can either go with a combination of JavaScript and DHTML or with a Java applet. Because we are much more experienced with Java, we opt for that choice.

Next comes the fun part. Being lazy in nature, whenever we need to write something, we always spend a little time on the Web looking for examples or even code to buy. After spending half an hour (isn't the Web great?), we come up with a list of 10 applets that do precisely what we need. After a little more time comparing the available packages, we zoom in on a package called TreeControl by `cdare-edwards@mcsoftware.com.au` available at `http://www.mcsoftware.com.au/java/TreeControl/treeControl.html`. It is a superb applet that is small, fast, pleasant to look at, and easy to use. After 15 minutes spent downloading it and reading the instructions, we are ready to go.

First, we build the servlet class and the `init` method of the servlet. This method will be called whenever the servlet is loaded—that is, when the application server is started. Because our servlet accesses the database, we need an open connection to the database. Because creating a connection is a very lengthy process (one of the operations that consumes the longest time), it only makes sense that we open the connection during servlet startup (when there are no users waiting on this operation). We also do other things that must happen only once, such as reading the property files and setting all constants to be used later in the actual processing. The code for the servlet variables and the `init` method is shown in Listing 23-1. Note that the database connection is performed through a very simplistic connection class shown in Listing 23-2; in a later chapter, we will show a more appropriate solution to database connectivity. For now, it is good enough. By the way, in this example, we use the JDBC thin driver from Oracle. Be sure to include this in the CLASSPATH specified in the Java Engine administration screen. If you don't, you will get an exception while trying to register the servlet with the application server.

```java
package configurations.ui;

import javax.servlet.*;
import javax.servlet.http.*;
import java.io.*;
import java.util.*;
import java.sql.*;
import java.text.*;
public class ConfigServlet extends HttpServlet {

  static ResourceBundle aBundle = null;
  static String serialFormat;
  static String nonSerialRootFormat;
  static String serialRootFormat;
  static String nonSerialFormat;
  static String bgImage = "";
  static String codebase;
  static String fontString;

  public void init(ServletConfig config) throws ServletException {
    super.init(config);
      aBundle = ResourceBundle.getBundle("ConfigServlet");
      serialFormat = aBundle.getString("serialFormat");
      nonSerialFormat = aBundle.getString("nonSerialFormat");
      serialRootFormat = aBundle.getString("serialRootFormat");
      nonSerialRootFormat =
aBundle.getString("nonSerialRootFormat");
      codebase = aBundle.getString("codebase");
      fontString = aBundle.getString("font");
      bgImage = aBundle.getString("bgImage");
      DBConnection.init(
        aBundle.getString("dburl"),
        aBundle.getString("dbuser"),
        aBundle.getString("dbpass"));
      try {
        Connection conn = DBConnection.getConnection();
        CallableStatement stmt = conn.prepareCall(
            "alter session set NLS_DATE_FORMAT = 'DD MON YYYY'"
);
        stmt.execute();
        stmt.close();
      } catch (Throwable ex) {
        ex.printStackTrace();
      }
  }
```

Listing 23-2
Simple database
connection class

```
package configurations.ui;

import java.sql.*;

public class DBConnection {
  static Connection conn = null;
  static String aURL;
  static String aUserName;
  static String aPassword;

  public static void init(String url, String userName, String
password) {
    // Load the JDBC driver.
    if (conn == null) {
      try {
        DriverManager.registerDriver(new
oracle.jdbc.driver.OracleDriver());
      } catch (Exception e) {
        System.err.println("Could not load driver ");
        e.printStackTrace();
      }
      aURL = url;
      aUserName = userName;
      aPassword = password;
    }
  }

  public static Connection createConnection() {
    try {
      // Establish the connection to the database.
      conn = DriverManager.getConnection(aURL, aUserName,
aPassword);
    } catch (Exception e) {
      System.err.println("Could not create connection " +
e.getMessage());
      e.printStackTrace();
      conn = null;
    }
    return conn;
  }

  public static Connection getConnection() {
    Connection toRet = null;
    if (conn == null)
      toRet = createConnection();
    else toRet = conn;
    return toRet;
  }


}
```

The next step is to build the method doing all the work. Because we want the service to be available in the most flexible way, we implement the doGet method of the servlet. The method accepts a number of arguments from the request object and proceeds to build the configuration tree. The code for the method is shown in Listing 23-3. Note that we have omitted some of the database access code because it is not of much interest here; it is sufficient to understand that the arguments passed in through the request object are used to invoke a database operation that builds the tree. The tree is then read from the database and used to produce the arguments to the applet.

Listing 23-3
doGet method of the configuration servlet

```
public void doGet(
HttpServletRequest request,
HttpServletResponse response)
throws ServletException, IOException {

    response.setContentType("text/html");
    PrintWriter out = new PrintWriter (response.getOutputStream());

    String nodeKey = request.getParameter("nodeKey");
    String rootSerialId = request.getParameter("serialsT");
    String rootPartId = request.getParameter("partId");
    String rootPartDesc = request.getParameter("partDesc");
    String rootRevision = request.getParameter("rev");
    String quantity = request.getParameter("qty");

    out.println("<html>");
    out.println("<head><title>Configuration View</title></head>");

    out.println("<applet code=\"TreeApp.class\" codebase=\"" +
codebase + "\" name=\"Tree\" width=\"700\" height=\"500\">");
    out.println("<param name=\"baseURL\" value=\"" +
request.getHeader("Referer") +"\">");
    out.println("<param name=\"expanded\" value=\"true\">");
    out.println("<param name=\"font\" value=\"" + fontString +
"\">");
    out.println("<param name=\"dotted\" value=\"true\">");
    out.println("<param name=\"showURL\" value=\"false\">");
    out.println("<param name=\"bgColor\" value=\"white\">");
    out.println("<param name=\"bgImage\" value=\"images/" +
bgImage + "\">");
    out.println("<param name=\"bgHighlight\" value=\"black\">");
    out.println("<param name=\"fgColor\" value=\"black\">");
    out.println("<param name=\"textColor\" value=\"black\">");
    out.println("<param name=\"textHighlight\" value=\"white\">");

    Stack displayStringStack = new Stack();
    Stack levelStack = new Stack();
    String rootName = formatRootBySerial(
```

```
        rootPartId,rootPartDesc, rootRevision, rootSerialId);
    out.println("<param name=\"rootTitle\" value=\"Root
Configuration;images/fold.gif,images/fold2.gif\">");
    out.println("<param name=\"item1\" value=\"" + rootName +
                    ";images/fold.gif,images/zoom.gif\">");
    displayStringStack.push(rootName);
    levelStack.push(new Integer(1));

    // ... Build the tree in the database and read it in
    // rs is the result set object returned from the
    // database query - holding the nodes that need to
    // go into the tree structure

    while (rs.next()) {
        // read in the data per row and place it in variables
        // to be used in the following code
        // then, based on the level and the values on the stack
        // decide where in the tree the node belongs
        if (configLevel == atTop) {
            String itemString = "item" +
Integer.toString(itemNum++);
            String dispString = ((String)displayStringStack.peek())
+
                            "/" + dString;
            out.println("<param name=\"" + itemString + "\"
value=\"" +
                            dispString + ";images/" + gifString +
                            ",images/zoom.gif\">");
        } else if (configLevel < atTop) {
            while (configLevel <
                    ((Integer)levelStack.peek()).intValue()) {
                displayStringStack.pop();
                levelStack.pop();
            }
            String itemString = "item" +
Integer.toString(itemNum++);
            String dispString = ((String)displayStringStack.peek())
+
                            "/" + dString;
            out.println("<param name=\"" + itemString + "\"
value=\"" +
                            dispString + ";images/" + gifString +
                            ",images/zoom.gif\">");
        } else {    // configLevel > atTop
            String itemString = "item" +
Integer.toString(itemNum++);
            String dispString = ((String)displayStringStack.peek())
+
                            "/" + dString;
            out.println("<param name=\"" + itemString + "\"
value=\"" +
                            dispString + ";images/" + gifString +
                            ",images/zoom.gif\">");
            displayStringStack.push(dispString);
```

continues

Listing 23-3
Continued

```
            levelStack.push(new Integer(configLevel));
        }
    }
    stmt.close();
} catch (Throwable ex) {
    ex.printStackTrace();
}

out.println("</applet>");
out.println("</body></html>");
out.close();
}
```

The method starts by reading in the arguments sent to the servlet. This determines what node forms the root of the configuration tree. The servlet then proceeds to set the output stream's content type (an HTML page) and write out the applet tag. The TreeControl applet receives the parameters affecting its display through a set of PARAM tags. It also receives the data forming the tree using PARAM tags. The servlet therefore needs to write to the output stream both the general display parameters (done in the first part of the method) and the parameters encapsulating the data (the rest of the method).

After the general parameters have been written, the database is accessed to get the nodes. The database call returns the nodes in the order they should be displayed as opposed to a tree ordering (such as depth first search or breadth first search). A stack object is used to build the tree structure based on a config level value marked in each of the rows coming back from the database. Then, a PARAM tag is added to the applet with a name of itemX where X is incremented by one each row. The tree structure is attained by concatenating the complete path to each node name (the prefix is managed by the stack). The resulting HTML source for an example is shown in Listing 23-4, and a sample Web page is shown in Figure 23-1.

Listing 23-4
HTML page
generated by
configuration servlet

```html
<html>
<head>
<title>Install Base Configuration</title>
</head>
<body>
<applet
     code="TreeApp.class"
     codebase="http://websphere/conf/tc"
     name="Tree"
     width="700" height="500">
<param name="baseURL" value="null">
<param name="expanded" value="true">
<param name="font" value="TimesRoman-plain-12">
<param name="dotted" value="true">
<param name="showURL" value="false">
<param name="bgColor" value="white">
<param name="bgHighlight" value="black">
<param name="fgColor" value="black">
<param name="textColor" value="black">
<param name="textHighlight" value="white">
<param
  name="rootTitle"
  value="Root Configuration;images/fold.gif,images/fold2.gif">
<param
  name="item1"
  value="Serial #EEE (PPP (HHH) Rev:
1);images/fold.gif,images/zoom.gif">
<param
  name="item2"
  value="Serial #EEE (PPP (HHH) Rev: 1)/RPART (R part) Rev: 0 Qty:
1;images/doc_web.gif,images/zoom.gif">
<param
  name="item3"
  value="Serial #EEE (PPP (HHH) Rev: 1)/RPART (R part) Rev: 0 Qty:
1/PRINTER (PRINTER FOR MF SYSTEMS (SERIALIZED)) Rev: 1 Qty:
1;images/doc_web.gif,images/zoom.gif">
<param
  name="item4"
  value="Serial #EEE (PPP (HHH) Rev: 1)/RPART (R part) Rev: 0 Qty:
1/CPU (CPU FOR NDMF) Rev: 1 Qty:
1;images/doc_web.gif,images/zoom.gif">
<param
  name="item5"
  value="Serial #EEE (PPP (HHH) Rev: 1)/RPART (R part) Rev: 0 Qty:
1/PENTIUM3-400 (PENTIUM III 400 MHZ CPU) Rev: 1 Qty:
1;images/doc_web.gif,images/zoom.gif">
<param
  name="item6"
  value="Serial #EEE (PPP (HHH) Rev: 1)/RPART (R part) Rev: 0 Qty:
1/PENTIUM3-400 (PENTIUM III 400 MHZ CPU) Rev: 1 Qty: 1/MODEM
(MODEM) Rev: 1 Qty: 1;images/doc_web.gif,images/zoom.gif">
</applet>
</body>
</html>
```

Figure 23-1
Web page result from
the configuration
servlet

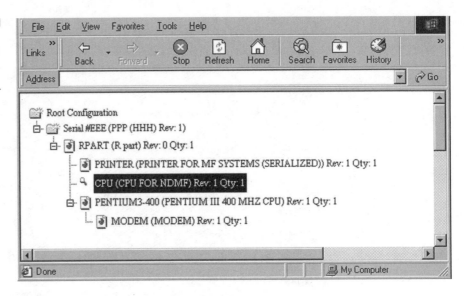

The Ticker Servlet

We now move on to our second example of a servlet. In fact, this example is a little more elaborate and includes a servlet forming the front-end and a back-end server process. The example is taken from a completely different domain—that of financial services.

The example involves a hypothetical company called `Ticker.com` (at least, it was hypothetical when we wrote this chapter) that provides an on-line stock notification service. There are many examples of such services; in this chapter, you will see just how simple it is to build such software (and maybe question why Internet companies are so successful on Wall Street). Obviously, it won't have any fancy bells and whistles, but it will be fully functional.

The service allows users to define a profile. A profile consists of a set of stock symbols that the user wants to track as well as a definition of a set of thresholds. For each stock symbol that the user wants to track, a lower bound and an upper bound can be defined. If a lower bound is defined and the stock price drops below that threshold, the user should be notified. If an upper bound is defined and the stock price goes over that threshold, the user should be notified. Notification is based on sending e-mail to the user —which is also part of the profile. Because today's pager and cellular technology enables us to send a message to a pager or phone (through SMS) via e-mail, e-mail notification is useful for reaching almost anyone at any time. The final part of the profile is an interval that the user sets up for checking stock prices and notification. Note that the "no frills" implementation shown here mandates that if the user specifies an interval of five minutes and the stock price is above the upper limit but does not change, a notification is sent every five minutes. It is true that there is no apparent reason to keep sending a message if the stock doesn't move, but hey—no one is making money off this implementation.

The implementation comprises of two pieces—the maintenance of the user profiles and the process checking stock values and performing the notification. We start with the description of the profile maintenance.

Because user profiles will be updated on the Web, we need a servlet to generate and manage the user profile. We will keep this servlet simple, so the user interface will be fairly ugly. The first access to the system is through a login form shown in Figure 23-2. This form then connects to our servlet using a GET request. The doGet method proceeds to lookup the user in the database. If the user is found (and the password is correct), it proceeds to read the user's profile and create an HTML form with the values of the user. This is written out to the servlet output stream. An example form created by this servlet is shown in Figure 23-3 and the HTML created by the doGet method is shown in Listing 23-5. Note that the form's action accesses the same servlet but uses the POST method. This is because in this example, the servlet is used for two purposes: The GET method is used to retrieve the user profile, whereas the POST method is used for updating the user profile.

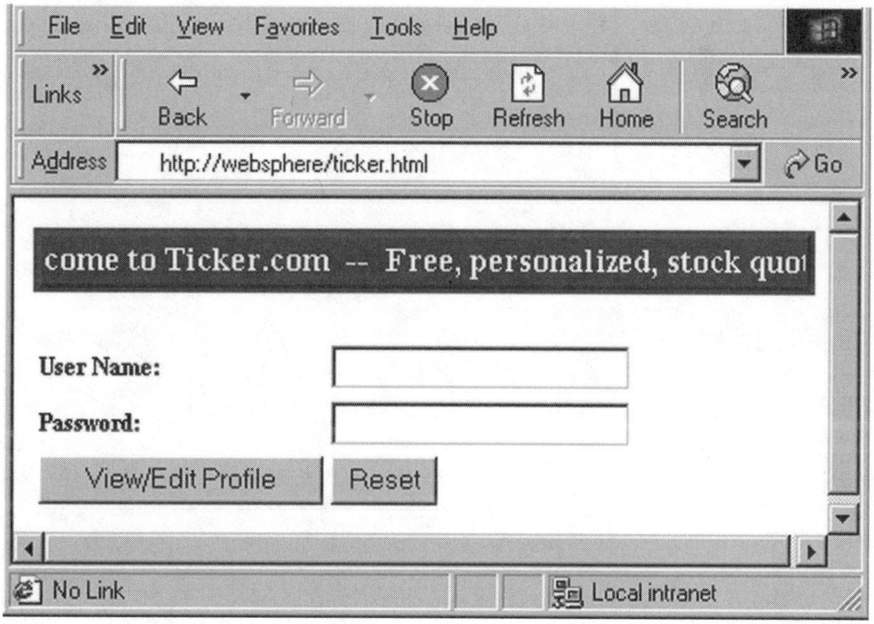

Figure 23-2
Login to
Ticker.com

Figure 23-3
Web page result from
the doGet method
of the ticker servlet

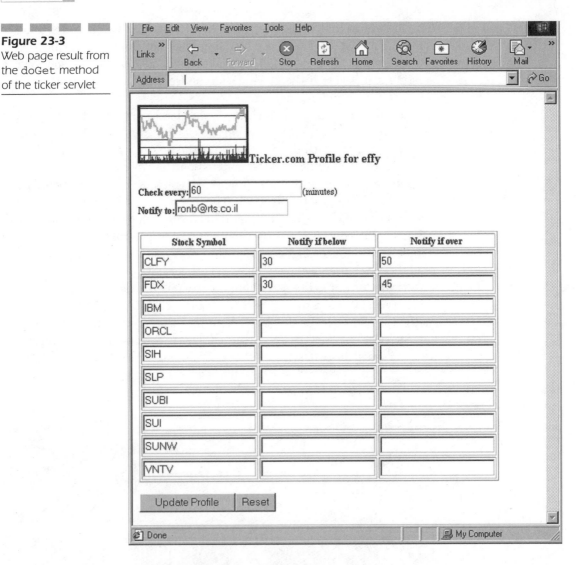

Listing 23-5
HTML generated
from the doGet
method of the ticker
servlet

```
<HTML>
<HEAD>
<TITLE>Ticker.com Profile
</TITLE>
</HEAD>
<BODY>
<H2><IMG SRC="http://websphere/ticker.gif" BORDER>Ticker.com
Profile for effy</H2>
<FORM ACTION="http://websphere/servlet/Ticker" METHOD=POST>
<INPUT TYPE="HIDDEN" NAME="userName" VALUE="effy">
<B>Check every:</B><INPUT NAME="frequency" VALUE="60">(minutes)
```

```
<BR><B>Notify to:</B><INPUT NAME="email" VALUE="effy@effy.coml">
<P><P><TABLE BORDER>
<TR><TH>Stock Symbol</TH><TH>Notify if below</TH><TH>Notify if
over</TH></TR>
<TR>
<TD><INPUT NAME="symbol0" VALUE="CLFY"></TD>
<TD><INPUT NAME="low0" VALUE="30"></TD>
<TD><INPUT NAME="high0" VALUE="50"></TD>
</TR>
<TR>
<TD><INPUT NAME="symbol1" VALUE="FDX"></TD>
<TD><INPUT NAME="low1" VALUE="30"></TD>
<TD><INPUT NAME="high1" VALUE="45"></TD>
</TR>
<TR>
<TD><INPUT NAME="symbol2" VALUE="IBM"></TD>
<TD><INPUT NAME="low2" VALUE=""></TD>
<TD><INPUT NAME="high2" VALUE=""></TD>
</TR>
<TR>
<TD><INPUT NAME="symbol3" VALUE="ORCL"></TD>
<TD><INPUT NAME="low3" VALUE=""></TD>
<TD><INPUT NAME="high3" VALUE=""></TD>
</TR>
<TR>
<TD><INPUT NAME="symbol4" VALUE="SIH"></TD>
<TD><INPUT NAME="low4" VALUE=""></TD>
<TD><INPUT NAME="high4" VALUE=""></TD>
</TR>
<TR>
<TD><INPUT NAME="symbol5" VALUE="SLP"></TD>
<TD><INPUT NAME="low5" VALUE=""></TD>
<TD><INPUT NAME="high5" VALUE=""></TD>
</TR>
<TR>
<TD><INPUT NAME="symbol6" VALUE="SUBI"></TD>
<TD><INPUT NAME="low6" VALUE=""></TD>
<TD><INPUT NAME="high6" VALUE=""></TD>
</TR>
<TR>
<TD><INPUT NAME="symbol7" VALUE="SUI"></TD>
<TD><INPUT NAME="low7" VALUE=""></TD>
<TD><INPUT NAME="high7" VALUE=""></TD>
</TR>
<TR>
<TD><INPUT NAME="symbol8" VALUE="SUNW"></TD>
<TD><INPUT NAME="low8" VALUE=""></TD>
<TD><INPUT NAME="high8" VALUE=""></TD>
</TR>
<TR>
<TD><INPUT NAME="symbol9" VALUE="VNTV"></TD>
<TD><INPUT NAME="low9" VALUE=""></TD>
<TD><INPUT NAME="high9" VALUE=""></TD>
</TR>
</TABLE><BR>
<INPUT TYPE="SUBMIT" VALUE="Update Profile"><INPUT TYPE="RESET">
</FORM>
</BODY>
</HTML>
```

The doGet method itself is shown in Listing 23-6. After the user name and password has been verified, the servlet proceeds to read all the rows for that user. For each such row, a set of fields in the HTML form is generated with the appropriate values as initial values. The form itself is built in such a way that the servlet's doPost method is called when Submit is clicked. The doPost method (shown in Listing 23-7) updates the user profile in the database.

Listing 23-6
doGet method of the ticker servlet

```
public void doGet(
HttpServletRequest request, HttpServletResponse response)
    throws ServletException, IOException {
  try {
    String loginName = request.getParameter("loginName");
    String passwd= request.getParameter("passwd");

    PrintWriter out = response.getWriter();
    response.setContentType("text/html");
    out.println("<HTML><HEAD><TITLE>Ticker.com
Profile</TITLE></HEAD>");
    out.println("<BODY>");
    out.println("<H2><IMG SRC=\"http://websphere/ticker.gif\"
BORDER>Ticker.com Profile for " + loginName + "</H2>");
    Statement stmt = null;
    try {
        Connection conn = DBConnection.getConnection();
        stmt = conn.createStatement();
        ResultSet rs = stmt.executeQuery(
            "select passwd__t, frequency_c, email_c from
monitor_users where user__t = '" + loginName + "'");
        if (rs.next()) {
          String p = rs.getString(1);
          int f = rs.getInt(2);
          String email = rs.getString(3);
          if (email == null)
            email = "";
          if (p.compareTo(passwd) != 0)
            out.println("<H3>Incorrect password. Please back up
and try again</H3>");
          else {
            stmt.close();
            stmt = conn.createStatement();
            rs = stmt.executeQuery(
              "select symbol__t, low_c, high_c from monitors
where user__t = '" +
              loginName + "' order by symbol__t");
            String[][] profileValues = new String[10][3];
            for (int i = 0; i < 10 ; i++)
              for (int j = 0 ; j < 3 ; j++)
                profileValues[i][j] = "";
            int i = 0;
            while ((i < 10) && rs.next()) {
```

```
                    profileValues[i][0] = rs.getString(1);
                    profileValues[i][1] = rs.getString(2);
                    profileValues[i][2] = rs.getString(3);
                    if (profileValues[i][1] == null)
                      profileValues[i][1] = "";
                    if (profileValues[i][2] == null)
                      profileValues[i][2] = "";
                    i++;
                  }
                  out.println("<FORM
ACTION=\"http://websphere/servlet/Ticker\" METHOD=POST>");
                  out.println("<INPUT TYPE=\"HIDDEN\" NAME=\"userName\"
VALUE=\"" + loginName + "\">");
                  out.println("<B>Check every:</B><INPUT
NAME=\"frequency\" VALUE=\"" + f + "\">(minutes)");
                  out.println("<BR><B>Notify to:</B><INPUT
NAME=\"email\" VALUE=\"" + email + "\">");
                  out.println("<P><P><TABLE BORDER>");
                  out.println("<TR><TH>Stock Symbol</TH><TH>Notify if
below</TH><TH>Notify if over</TH></TR>");
                  for (int k = 0 ; k < 10 ; k++) {
                    out.println("<TR>");
                    out.println("<TD><INPUT NAME=\"symbol" + k + "\"
VALUE=\"" + profileValues[k][0] + "\"></TD>");
                    out.println("<TD><INPUT NAME=\"low" + k + "\"
VALUE=\"" + profileValues[k][1] + "\"></TD>");
                    out.println("<TD><INPUT NAME=\"high" + k + "\"
VALUE=\"" + profileValues[k][2] + "\"></TD>");
                    out.println("</TR>");
                  }
                  out.println("</TABLE><BR>");
                  out.println("<INPUT TYPE=\"SUBMIT\" VALUE=\"Update
Profile\"><INPUT TYPE=\"RESET\">");
                  out.println("</FORM>");
              }
            }
            else
              out.println("<H3>No user named " + loginName + ".
Please back up and try again</H3>");
        } catch (Throwable ex) {
          out.println("<H3>Server error; please try again
later</H3>");
          ex.printStackTrace();
        }
        if (stmt != null)
          stmt.close();

        out.println("</BODY></HTML>");
        out.close();

      } catch (Exception e) {
        e.printStackTrace();
      }
    }
```

```java
public void doPost(
HttpServletRequest request, HttpServletResponse response)
      throws ServletException, IOException {
      response.setContentType("text/html");
      PrintWriter out = response.getWriter();
      out.println("<HTML><HEAD><TITLE>Ticker Profile
Updated</TITLE></HEAD>");
      out.println("<BODY>");

      String[] symbols = new String[10];
      String[] lows = new String[10];
      String[] highs = new String[10];
      String frequencyS = request.getParameter("frequency");
      String emailS = request.getParameter("email");
      String userName = request.getParameter("userName");
      for (int i = 0 ; i < 10 ; i++) {
        symbols[i] = request.getParameter("symbol" + i);
        lows[i] = request.getParameter("low" + i);
        highs[i] = request.getParameter("high" + i);
      }
      Statement stmt = null;
      try {
          Connection conn = DBConnection.getConnection();
          stmt = conn.createStatement();
          ResultSet rs = stmt.executeQuery(
            "update monitor_users set email_c = '" + emailS +
"',frequency_c = " + frequencyS + "where user__t = '" + userName +
"'");
          rs.next();
          stmt.close();
          System.out.println("delete from monitors ");
          stmt = conn.createStatement();
          stmt.executeUpdate(
            "delete from monitors where user__t = '" +
            userName + "'");
          stmt = null;
          for (int i = 0 ; i < 10 ; i++)
            if (symbols[i].trim().length() > 0) {
            System.out.println("Inserting for symbol " +
symbols[i]);
            stmt = conn.createStatement();
            StringBuffer sqlString = new StringBuffer(100);
            sqlString.append(
              "insert into monitors(user__t, symbol__t");
            if (lows[i].trim().length() > 0)
              sqlString.append(", low_c");
            if (highs[i].trim().length() > 0)
              sqlString.append(", high_c");
            sqlString.append(") values ('" + userName +
              "','" + symbols[i].trim() + "'");
            if (lows[i].trim().length() > 0)
              sqlString.append("," + lows[i]);
            if (highs[i].trim().length() > 0)
              sqlString.append("," + highs[i]);
            sqlString.append(")");
            String sqlS = sqlString.toString();
            System.out.println(sqlS);
```

```
                    stmt.executeUpdate(sqlS);
                    stmt.close();
                    stmt = null;
                }
            out.println("<H3>Profile successfully updated</H3>");
        } catch (Throwable ex) {
            out.println("<H3>Error while updating profile</H3>");
            ex.printStackTrace();
        }

        out.println("</BODY></HTML>");
        out.close();
    }
```

The second part of the system is the process of doing the actual stock lookup and notifications (shown in Listing 23-8). The process is implemented as a runnable class. It is invoked from the init method of a second servlet—this is merely a convenience allowing us to register this process for startup after the WebSphere application server starts up. The process manages a worker thread pool so it can handle many users for whom profiles need to be tracked. For each such user, the database information is constantly read. We must reread the information because it is quite possible that while the worker thread is running, the user has logged into the system and changed the threshold values. Next, the stock prices need to be retrieved. The servlet accesses the Nasdaq Web site. As avid investors, we have found the Nasdaq site at www.nasdaq.com an excellent source for stock quotes (including NYSE quotes), and we have used that site in this example. The site is convenient in that the actual price lookup is performed using a URL. It is simple for us to build this URL based on the user's profile.

Listing 23-8

The ticker notification daemon

```
package com.ticker;

import java.util.*;
import java.sql.*;
import java.net.*;
import java.io.*;
import javax.mail.*;
import javax.mail.internet.*;

public class TickerDaemon implements Runnable {

    final static int dbPollingInterval = 30000; // 30 seconds

    Hashtable workerThreads;
```

continues

Listing 23-8
Continued

```java
void updateWorkerThreads() {
  Statement stmt = null;
  try {
    Connection conn = DBConnection.getConnection();
    stmt = conn.createStatement();
    ResultSet rs = stmt.executeQuery(
      "select user__t, frequency_c, email_c from monitor_users");
    while (rs.next()) {
      String uName = rs.getString(1);
      int f = rs.getInt(2);
      String email = rs.getString(3);
      if (email != null) {
        if (!workerThreads.contains(uName)) {
          System.out.println("Adding worker thread for " +
uName);
          WorkerThread nt = new WorkerThread(uName, f, email);
          workerThreads.put(uName, nt);
          (new Thread(nt)).start();
        }
      }
    }
  } catch (Throwable ex) {
    ex.printStackTrace();
  }
}

public TickerDaemon() {
  workerThreads = new Hashtable(100);
}

public void run() {
  updateWorkerThreads();
  try {
    Thread.currentThread().sleep(dbPollingInterval);
  } catch (Throwable ex) {
    ex.printStackTrace();
  }
}

public static void main(String[] args) {
  DBConnection.init("jdbc:oracle:thin:@websphere:1521:ORCL",
"ws", "ws");
  Thread t = new Thread(new TickerDaemon());
  t.start();
}
}

class WorkerThread implements Runnable {

  String userName;
  String email;
  int frequency;

  public WorkerThread(String uName, int f, String e) {
    userName = uName;
    frequency = f;
```

```
      email = e;
  }

  void updateBaseData() {
    try {
      Connection conn = DBConnection.getConnection();
      Statement stmt = conn.createStatement();
      ResultSet rs = stmt.executeQuery(
        "select frequency_c, email_c from monitor_users where
user__t = '" + userName + "'");
      rs.next();
      frequency = rs.getInt(1);
      email = rs.getString(2);
      stmt.close();
    } catch (Throwable ex) {
      ex.printStackTrace();
    }
  }

  void checkQuoteData() {
    updateBaseData();
    StringBuffer urlBuf = new StringBuffer(1000);
    urlBuf.append("http://quotes.nasdaq-
amex.com/Quote.dll?mode=stock");
    Vector values = new Vector(10);
    try {
      Connection conn = DBConnection.getConnection();
      Statement stmt = conn.createStatement();
      ResultSet rs = stmt.executeQuery(
        "select symbol__t, low_c, high_c from monitors where
user__t = '" + userName + "' order by symbol__t");
      while (rs.next()) {
        String[] aValue = new String[3];
        aValue[0] = rs.getString(1);
        aValue[1] = rs.getString(2);
        aValue[2] = rs.getString(3);
        values.addElement(aValue);
        urlBuf.append("&symbol=");
        urlBuf.append(aValue[0]);
      }
    } catch (Throwable ex) {
      ex.printStackTrace();
    }
    urlBuf.append("&quick.x=71&quick.y=9");
    String urlString = urlBuf.toString();
    String urlResponse = getHTMLFor(urlString);
    if (urlResponse != null)
      parseAndNotify(urlResponse, values);
  }

  String getHTMLFor(String url) {
   try {
   URLConnection aConnection = (new URL(url)).openConnection();
   aConnection.setDoInput(true);
   aConnection.setDoOutput(true);
```

continues

Listing 23-8
Continued

```
     aConnection.setUseCaches(false);
     InputStream inS = aConnection.getInputStream();
     StringBuffer buffer = new StringBuffer(4096);
     boolean atEnd = false;
     while(!atEnd) {
       int len = inS.available();
       byte[] buf = new byte[len];
       if (inS.read(buf, 0, len) == -1)
       atEnd = true;
       if (len > 0)
         buffer.append(new String(buf));
       Thread.sleep(10);
     }
     String retString = buffer.toString();
     return retString;
   } catch (Throwable ex) {
     ex.printStackTrace();
   }
   return null;
 }

 void notifyQuote(String messageText) {
   Vector messagesToSend = new Vector(5);
   int beginAt = 0;
   while (beginAt < messageText.length()) {
     int endAt = beginAt + 150;
     if (endAt > messageText.length())
       endAt = messageText.length();
     messagesToSend.addElement(messageText.substring(beginAt,
endAt));
     beginAt = endAt + 1;
   }
   for (int i = 0; i < messagesToSend.size() ; i++) {
     String partS = (new Integer(i + 1)).toString() + "/" + (new
Integer(messagesToSend.size())).toString();
     sendEmail((String)(messagesToSend.elementAt(i)), partS);
   }
 }

 void sendEmail(String messageText, String part) {
   Properties props = new Properties();
   props.put("mail.smtp.host", "mail.ticker.com");
   try {
     Message msg = new
MimeMessage(Session.getDefaultInstance(props, null));
     InternetAddress from = new InternetAddress("ticker.com");
     msg.setFrom(from);
     InternetAddress[] to = { new InternetAddress(email) };
     msg.setRecipients(Message.RecipientType.TO, to);
     msg.setSubject("Stock quote from Ticker.com for " + userName
+ " " + part);
     msg.setContent(messageText, "text/plain");
     Transport.send(msg);
     System.out.println("Sent email to " + email);
   } catch (MessagingException ex) {
     ex.printStackTrace();
   }
 }
```

```
void parseAndNotify(String urlResponse, Vector values) {
  Hashtable prices = new Hashtable(values.size());
  Vector symbolLocations = new Vector(50);
  Vector symbols = new Vector(50);
  int beginAt = 0;
  int endAt = 0;
  while (beginAt != -1) {
    beginAt = urlResponse.indexOf("symbol=", beginAt);
    if (beginAt != -1) {
      symbolLocations.addElement(new Integer(beginAt + 7));
      endAt = urlResponse.indexOf("\"", beginAt);
      symbols.addElement(urlResponse.substring(beginAt + 7,
endAt));
      beginAt = endAt + 1;
    }
  }
  beginAt = 0;
  endAt = 0;
  for (int i = 0 ; i < values.size() ; i++ ) {
    beginAt = urlResponse.indexOf("$", endAt);
    endAt = urlResponse.indexOf("<", beginAt);
    int indexFirstLargerThan = 0;
    int j = 0;
    while ((j < symbolLocations.size()) && (indexFirstLargerThan
== 0)) {
      if (((Integer)symbolLocations.elementAt(j)).intValue() >
beginAt)
        indexFirstLargerThan = j;
      j++;
    }
    if (indexFirstLargerThan == 0)
      indexFirstLargerThan = symbols.size();
    prices.put(symbols.elementAt(indexFirstLargerThan-
1),urlResponse.substring(beginAt+2, endAt));
  }
  StringBuffer messageText = new StringBuffer(200);
  for (int i = 0 ; i < values.size() ; i++ ) {
    String[] aValue = (String[])values.elementAt(i);
    boolean sendQuote = ((aValue[1] == null) && (aValue[2] ==
null));
    double aPrice = (new
Double((String)(prices.get(aValue[0])))).doubleValue();
    if (aValue[1] != null)
      if ((new Double(aValue[1])).doubleValue() >= aPrice)
        sendQuote = true;
    if (aValue[2] != null)
      if ((new Double(aValue[2])).doubleValue() <= aPrice)
        sendQuote = true;
    if (sendQuote) {
      messageText.append(aValue[0]);
      messageText.append("=");
      messageText.append(prices.get(aValue[0]));
      messageText.append(" ");
    }
  }
```

continues

Listing 23-8

Continued

```
      String text = messageText.toString();
      if (text.length() > 0)
        notifyQuote(text);
    }


    public void run() {
      while(true) {
        checkQuoteData();
        try {
          Thread.currentThread().sleep(frequency*60*1000);
        } catch (Throwable ex) {
          ex.printStackTrace();
        }
      }
    }

  }
```

After hitting the Nasdaq Web site using a URL connection, we read in the returning HTML page and extract the pricing values based on crude parsing—obviously any real application would need to perform this in a much better way. Then we compare the prices with the threshold values. If need be, we create and send an e-mail message using the javax.mail package. We think it is quite phenomenal that the entire example, performing a service of real value, took less than one day to build and deploy!

Servlet Sessions

In this chapter, we continue our discussion of servlets and focus on the issue of session management within servlets. WebSphere as an application server supports two primary application models—that of servlets (and therefore JSPs) and EJBs. Although it is true that EJBs are more appropriate for complex applications and servlets are more appropriate for Web-deployed, short-lived transaction-oriented applications, servlets are certainly also used in scenarios in which managing application state is mandatory. Servlets form the basis for many of today's Web-enabled applications. As such, most development projects using servlets must manage application state in some way.

A servlet sits within a WebSphere application server and waits for HTTP requests (or requests coming over some other protocol). Because the HTTP servlet model is inherently related to the Web server model, each request coming in will usually have no history associated with it. This is usually called the statelessness of the Web model—that is, the Web is inherently stateless. The fact that the Web model is stateless is important and has enabled the Web to become what it is. A stateless model performs better than a model that is required to manage state. Software performing in a stateless model is also simpler to build because it does not need to address issues such as how many sessions one can manage, how to know that someone has broken off communication, how multiple servers are used for load balancing, and so on. Hence, the stateless model fits well with the basic requirements of the Web.

However, an application often *does* need to manage state on behalf of the clients using its services. Because an application can span multiple screens, software modules, and sometimes even machines, there must be a way to manage a connecting thread for all these occurrences. It would be impossible to build even the simplest of applications without some form of session management. Luckily, just as a connectionless communication model is more fundamental than a connection-based one and can be used to build a connection-based implementation, so can a stateless model be used as the foundation for a model that must maintain state. It is quite possible (and even simple) to add some application-level handling that uses the stateless model in such a way that application state can be maintained. In fact, because this is such a fundamental need for all applications, this additional layer has been added in all application servers. WebSphere is no exception.

In this chapter, we will describe a number of schemes for managing state on behalf of an application and provide examples for the use of each scheme. We will focus on the session management API introduced into the servlet specification because it is the most appropriate solution for servlets. In the next chapter, we will see more examples related to the management of sessions when we provide examples of WebSphere-specific servlets.

HTTP Cookies

Before we actually delve into servlet session management, we must understand what cookies are. HTTP cookies are state objects that are created by a server and passed to the client (typically a browser). These state-encapsulating entities were first supported by Netscape Navigator and have since become common in most browsers. As such, cookies are now the most common way in which state information created by a server program can be passed back to the client so future invocations from the client can include this information. This allows sessions to be demarcated—a session can be defined by the existence of the cookie. All interactions between client and server involving a certain cookie can be identified to be a single session.

Cookies have a number of attributes. A cookie has a name and a value. The value is a sequence of characters that is most commonly used as an opaque structure (for example, an identity). A cookie can have an expiration date that defines a timeout after which the cookie's value is no longer meaningful. A cookie also has two attributes that define its scope—a domain and a path. The domain defines the Internet domain for which the cookie is relevant. The default value is the server name on which the cookie was created (from whence the cookie arrived to the client), but the server can specify a broader domain if need be. In addition, the cookie can have a path attribute, which is useful when the scope should be narrowed.

Finally, a cookie can be marked as a secure cookie by an additional attribute. This defines that the cookie should only be transmitted between the client and the server over a secure connection. This is an important feature without which the existence of applications over secure connections would be impossible. Consider a scenario in which the information we pass over the wire should be encrypted—for example, an online trading application. If the application is very simple and involves only one screen, perhaps we don't need secure cookies. However, the typical online trading application is quite complex and involves first logging into the system and then continuing within the secure application. One possible scheme for managing the application state is a cookie. In a sense, the cookie encapsulates the identity of the user and the application may be built in such a way that anyone holding onto the cookie can proceed with a session and, for example, perform trades. In this case, the application must protect the cookie value as fanatically as it protects the user name and password.

Although cookies are almost ubiquitously used these days, they have had their share of controversy. These controversies revolved around two issues —privacy and security. The major one is that of privacy. Cookies allow applications to track state. However, they can be used to do many other things. For example, they provide a mechanism by which a Web site can track users that come again and again to the Web site. In time, an advanced Web site may customize the information it provides to different users based on this tracking information. Although in our opinion this is a good thing, it is apparent that such tracking can be misused and is certainly a mechanism that works against the basic anonymity that used to characterize the Web. As an example, Listing 24-1 shows an example cookie file that we found on disk—apparently from `barnesandnoble.com` (cookie files on Windows NT are placed in a folder called *Cookies* under the user's profile folder. The second cookie—the one called *userid*, was placed there by the Web site—this is not an id created explicitly by the user. From now on, whenever we revisit this site, we will be identified using that ID. It is quite possible that this information may be used for purposes we are not aware of (and have not given consent to). In order to allow "private people" to use the Web without compromising their beliefs (or their company's policies), all browsers have capabilities for disallowing cookies. Figure 24-1 shows the preference setting screen in which cookie support can be disabled. Note that disabling this may affect your ability to use many of today's Web applications.

The other objection that has been voiced regarding cookies is that cookies are stored on disk so they may be used in later visits to a Web site. This kind of use of cookies is slightly different than managing an application's session or state—it is customarily used to identify returning users, maintain a user's state, and so on. Therefore it is meaningful to distinguish between cookies used within a session from cookies stored on disk. Figure 24-2 shows the section devoted to cookies in Internet Explorer's option

Listing 24-1

A sample cookie file

```
SITESERVER
ID=da4fcbc400eeb9b3d9190a88570eb57a
barnesandnoble.com/
0
642859008
31887777
3660024432
29271958
*
userid
3MMN8PH9NX
barnesandnoble.com/
0
358989312
29785928
3660324432
29271958
*
browserid
BITS=2&OS=3&VERSION=5%2E0&AOLVER=0&BROWSER=2
barnesandnoble.com/
0
1841121280
29308070
3660724432
29271958
*
```

Figure 24-1
Enabling/Disabling
cookies in Netscape
Navigator

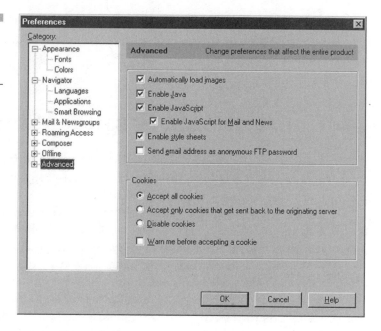

Figure 24-1
Enabling/Disabling
cookies in Netscape
Navigator

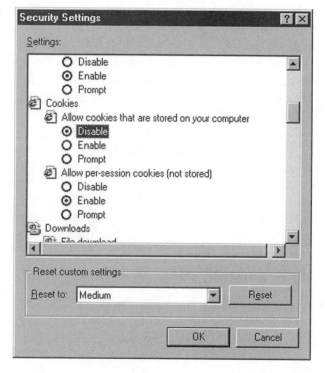

Figure 24-2
Enabling/Disabling
cookies in Microsoft
Internet Explorer

panel. As you can see, one can allow cookies that are used for session management (that is, within a browser session) while disallowing persistent cookies.

Conventional Session Management

Because session management is so fundamental to the very nature of an application, it has been around since the first applications on the Web—much longer than servlets. And because it has been around for such a long time, many methods for maintaining sessions have evolved. We do not propose to provide an overview of all such methods for two reasons. The first reason is that it is not within the scope of this book. The second reason is that we do not wish to encourage bad habits. Although we do not oppose any such methods, we believe that those who write servlets should use the session management capabilities built into the servlet API. For completeness, we mention some of the conventional session management mechanisms before proceeding with our mainstream discussion.

Probably the oldest method for tracking session state involves hidden fields within forms. We have actually used this in the previous chapter when we embedded the user name into the `Ticker.com` profile update screen. This field was inserted by the servlet's GET processing and used by the POST update. In a typical scenario using hidden fields, the session and state information is passed around by a set of hidden fields within forms. Because all fields, whether they are hidden or not, are propagated from the client to the servlet in any submit operation, this information is effectively passed around from one server process to the other. The primary benefits of this method is that it is simple, it is supported by all browsers, and it makes no assumptions regarding the operating environment (and is thus safest in the sense that it will always function correctly).

Another method that is similar (it also piggy-backs state information using a mechanism originally designed for something else) is URL rewriting. In this method, the state information is appended to the servlet path and later retrieved using the `getPathInfo` method of the request object. Although this method is similar in many ways to hidden form fields, we personally prefer hidden fields.

The final method we would like to mention before moving on to describe the built-in support for session management provided by servlets is the use of cookies. Servlets provide a way to create and use cookies manually. This is provided through the `javax.servlet.http.Cookie` class, the addCookie method in HttpServletResponse, and the getCookies method in HttpServletRequest. This simple API provides an approach that is simple to use and quite elegant (certainly more elegant than hidden fields, but still less elegant than what we'll learn in the next session).

We proceed with a simple example of the use of cookies. In this example, we provide a testing service on the Web. The user is presented with a question and asked for an answer. Each time a user submits an answer, it is compared with the right answer. If a wrong answer is received, the question is returned to the user along with a cookie value maintaining the number of wrong answers received and cookies for all wrong answers. This session information is used to score the question (because the grade is inversely proportional to the number of attempts) as well as produce the final output (in our code we will omit the actual scoring of the test). Figure 24-3 shows the screen presented to the user. This screen is created by the servlet's GET handling method. In the doGet method, besides generating the HTML, a

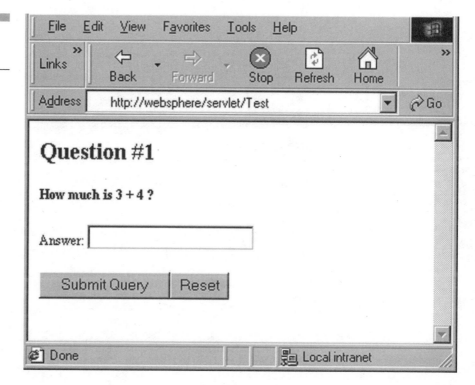

Figure 24-3
Initial form for
test servlet

cookie named FAILED_ATTEMPTS is added with a value of 0. If the user enters the answer 5, the `doPost` method increments the value of the cookie and resets the value for the failed attempts. It also adds an additional cookie with the wrong answer. Figure 24-4 shows the resulting output and Figure 24-5 shows the output after an additional mistake has been entered. Note that each such output writes out the number of attempts—this is possible because the cookie information comprising the application state always includes the number of failed attempts. Figure 24-6 is displayed when the user finally gets the answer right—all erroneous answers can be displayed because they are part of the session's state. Listing 24-2 shows the servlet code for this example.

One important point about sessions and cookies is that if you run the example in your browser and open an additional browser window (through the File menu—not by opening an additional instance of the application), both browser windows share the same session context. In our case, the number of attempts are counted as a sum of all attempts made in both windows. If, on the other hand, you open a new instance of the browser, the two resulting windows do not share a session and two series of attempts are tracked. (Note: This depends on the type of browser you are using.)

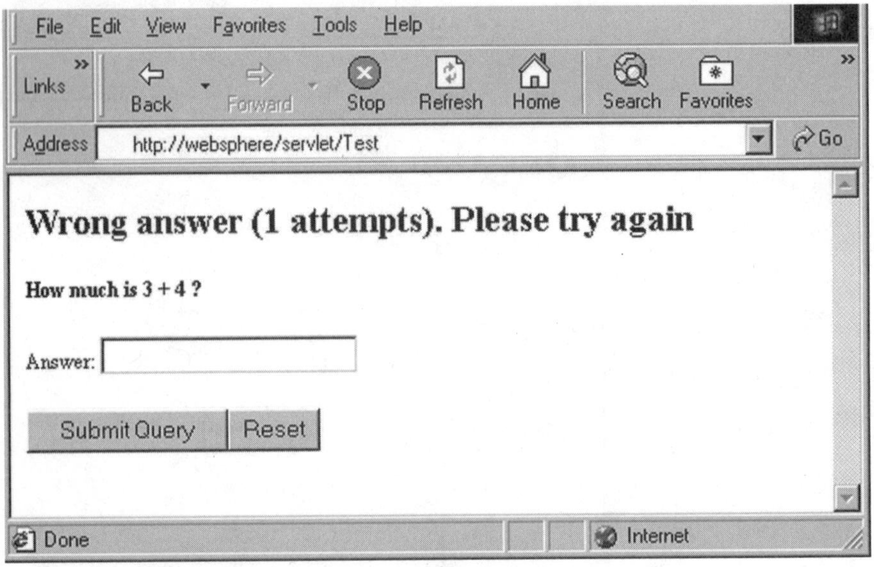

Figure 24-4

Test servlet form after one wrong answer

Figure 24-5
Test servlet form after
two wrong answers

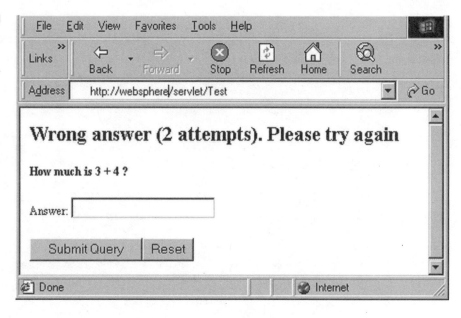

Figure 24-6
Test servlet form after
correct answer

Listing 24-2

Test servlet code
using cookies

```
package book.websphere.chapter24;

import javax.servlet.*;
import javax.servlet.http.*;
import java.io.*;
import java.util.*;

public class TestServlet extends HttpServlet {

  public void init(ServletConfig config) throws ServletException {
    super.init(config);
  }

  public void doGet(
      HttpServletRequest request,
      HttpServletResponse response)
      throws ServletException, IOException {
    response.setContentType("text/html");
    PrintWriter out = new PrintWriter (response.getOutputStream());

    Cookie myCookie = new Cookie("FAILED_ATTEMPTS", "0");
    response.addCookie(myCookie);

    printOutForm(out, "Question #1");
    out.close();
  }


  void printOutForm(PrintWriter out, String extraString) {
    out.println("<html>");
    out.println("<head><title>TestServlet</title></head>");
    out.println("<body><H1>" + extraString + "</H1>");
    out.println("<B>How much is 3 + 4 ?</B>");
    out.println("<FORM ACTION=\"http://websphere/servlet/Test\"
METHOD=POST>");
    out.println("Answer: <INPUT TYPE=\"TEXT\"
NAME=\"answer\"><P>");
    out.println("<INPUT TYPE=\"SUBMIT\"><INPUT
TYPE=\"RESET\"></FORM>");
    out.println("</body></html>");
  }

  public void doPost(
      HttpServletRequest request,
      HttpServletResponse response)
      throws ServletException, IOException {
    response.setContentType("text/html");
    PrintWriter out = new PrintWriter (response.getOutputStream());

    int currentNumberOfWrongAnswers = 0;
    Vector wrongAnswers = new Vector();
    Cookie[] myCookies = request.getCookies();
    for (int i = 0 ; i < myCookies.length; i++) {
      String name = myCookies[i].getName();
      String value = myCookies[i].getValue();
      System.err.println("Cookie named " + name + " has value " +
value);
      if (name.compareTo("FAILED_ATTEMPTS") == 0)
```

```
            currentNumberOfWrongAnswers = Integer.parseInt(value);
        else
            wrongAnswers.addElement(value);
    }
    System.err.println("Finished reading cookies");
    int currentAnswer =
Integer.parseInt(request.getParameter("answer"));
    if (currentAnswer != 7) {
      currentNumberOfWrongAnswers++;
      Cookie anotherWrongAnswer = new Cookie(
        "WRONG_ANSWER_" + currentNumberOfWrongAnswers,
        request.getParameter("answer"));
      response.addCookie(anotherWrongAnswer);
      Cookie myCookie = new Cookie(
        "FAILED_ATTEMPTS",
        Integer.toString(currentNumberOfWrongAnswers));
      response.addCookie(myCookie);
      printOutForm(out,
        "Wrong answer (" + currentNumberOfWrongAnswers +
        " attempts). Please try again");
    } else {
      out.println("<html>");
      out.println("<head><title>TestServlet</title></head>");
      out.println("<body>");
      out.println("<B>Hurray!! This is the right answer.</B><BR>");
      if (currentNumberOfWrongAnswers > 0) {
        out.println("Unfortunately, you had " +
currentNumberOfWrongAnswers +
          " wrong answers:<BR>");
        out.println("<UL>");
        for (Enumeration e = wrongAnswers.elements() ;
e.hasMoreElements() ; ) {
          out.println("<LI>");
          out.println(e.nextElement());
        }
        out.println("</UL>");
        out.println("</body></html>");
      }
    }
    out.close();
  }

  public String getServletInfo() {
    return "book.websphere.chapter24.TestServlet Information";
  }
}
```

The Session Tracking API

Now we can finally move on to the preferred way to track and manage session state in servlet-based applications. Our discussion of cookies was important not only because of its common use in Web applications, but also because cookies form the underlying foundations for servlet session tracking. The difference between the servlet session tracking mechanism and cookies can be summarized in one sentence. Cookies allow a server to attach a dictionary of values (a set of name-value pairs) to the messages passed between the server and the browser. The servlet session tracking mechanism maintains this dictionary on the server only and provides a unique identifier that can be used to retrieve this dictionary; this identifier is placed in a cookie that is sent off to the browser. What this provides is the best of both worlds. The supported capabilities are similar to the full power of cookies but there is less communication, more privacy, simpler maintenance, and better encapsulation.

Listing 24-3 shows the code for a testing servlet that uses session capabilities instead of cookies. It provides the same functionality as the example in Listing 24-2 and aims only at demonstrating how the code changes when you want to use session tracking. We have `highlighted` the code that has changed.

Listing 24-3
Test servlet code using session tracking

```
package book.websphere.chapter24;

import javax.servlet.*;
import javax.servlet.http.*;
import java.io.*;
import java.util.*;

public class TestServlet2 extends HttpServlet {

  public void init(ServletConfig config) throws ServletException {
    super.init(config);
  }

  public void doGet(
      HttpServletRequest request,
      HttpServletResponse response)
      throws ServletException, IOException {
    response.setContentType("text/html");
    PrintWriter out = new PrintWriter (response.getOutputStream());

    HttpSession aSession= request.getSession(true);
    aSession.putValue("FAILED_ATTEMPTS", new Integer(0));

    printOutForm(out, "Question #1");
    out.close();
  }


  void printOutForm(PrintWriter out, String extraString) {
    out.println("<html>");
    out.println("<head><title>TestServlet</title></head>");
    out.println("<body><H1>" + extraString + "</H1>");
    out.println("<B>How much is 3 + 4 ?</B>");
```

```
    out.println("<FORM ACTION=\"http://websphere/servlet/Test2\"
METHOD=POST>");
    out.println("Answer: <INPUT TYPE=\"TEXT\"
NAME=\"answer\"><P>");
    out.println("<INPUT TYPE=\"SUBMIT\"><INPUT
TYPE=\"RESET\"</FORM>");
    out.println("</body></html>");
  }

  public void doPost(
      HttpServletRequest request,
      HttpServletResponse response)
      throws ServletException, IOException {
    response.setContentType("text/html");
    PrintWriter out = new PrintWriter (response.getOutputStream());

    int currentNumberOfWrongAnswers = 0;
    Vector wrongAnswers;

    HttpSession aSession = request.getSession(true);
    currentNumberOfWrongAnswers =
      ((Integer)(aSession.getValue("FAILED_ATTEMPTS"))).intValue();
    if (aSession.getValue("WRONG_ANSWERS") == null)
      wrongAnswers = new Vector();
    else
      wrongAnswers = (Vector)(aSession.getValue("WRONG_ANSWERS"));
    int currentAnswer =
      Integer.parseInt(request.getParameter("answer"));
    if (currentAnswer != 7) {
      currentNumberOfWrongAnswers++;
      wrongAnswers.addElement(request.getParameter("answer"));
      aSession.putValue(
        "FAILED_ATTEMPTS", new
Integer(currentNumberOfWrongAnswers));
      aSession.putValue(
        "WRONG_ANSWERS", wrongAnswers);
    printOutForm(out,
        "Wrong answer (" + currentNumberOfWrongAnswers +
        " attempts). Please try again");
    } else {
      out.println("<html>");
      out.println("<head><title>TestServlet</title></head>");
      out.println("<body>");
      out.println("<B>Hurray!! This is the right answer.</B><BR>");
      if (currentNumberOfWrongAnswers > 0) {
        out.println("Unfortunately, you had " +
          currentNumberOfWrongAnswers +
          " wrong answers:<BR>");
        out.println("<UL>");
        for (Enumeration e = wrongAnswers.elements() ;
          e.hasMoreElements() ; ) {
          out.println("<LI>");
          out.println(e.nextElement());
        }
        out.println("</UL>");
        out.println("</body></html>");
      }
```

continues

Listing 24-3
Continued

```
    }
    out.close();
  }

  public String getServletInfo() {
    return "book.websphere.chapter24.TestServlet Information";
  }
}
```

The example in Listing 24-3 makes very simple usage of the session tracking API. In the example, the session object is used to hold onto a set of data structures. Because the objects are maintained within the WebSphere application server, any object can be stored within the session. In the cookies examples, we had to store each wrong answer in a string on its own; in the example shown by Listing 24-3, we can store all wrong answers in a vector and store the vector in the session as a single entity. This eliminates the need to use the artificial names for the information to be tracked as we had to use in Listing 24-2.

The code using the session tracking API is very simple. First, the session object is retrieved using the request's getSession method. The argument passed to this method specifies (in our case) that if a session object has not yet been created, one should be created as a result of the call. The session object is then used as a storage container using the getValue and setValue methods.

The session tracking API is obviously more functional than what we just saw. Still, the important parts are simply the fact that the session object can be used to maintain the objects on the server and a single cookie passed to the browser is used to provide an index into this structure. This can be seen in Figure 24-7, where the snoop servlet is activated after using the test servlet. Because cookies are maintained by the browser using the sessionid cookie, this cookie still exists even after the test servlet has completed. This is why we can view it by activating the snoop servlet.

Obviously, there are more to sessions than just maintaining a dictionary of objects. Additional methods supported by the HttpSession object in the JSDK 2.0 are

- getCreationTime()   Used to retrieve the time at which the session was created
- getId()   Each session is assigned an identifier. This method retrieves this identifier. This identifier is unique within WebSphere and is precisely the identifier that is passed along in the cookie to the browser.

Figure 24-7
Session ID sent
as cookie

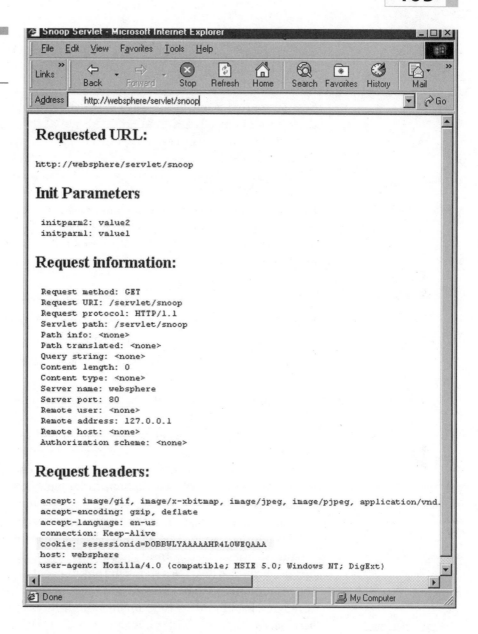

Figure 24-7
Session ID sent
as cookie

Also, the session context object (an object of type `HttpSessionContext` that can be retrieved using the `getSessionContext` method discussed below) can be queried for all possible identifiers (`HttpSessionContext.getIds()` and then using an identifier a session can be retrieved using `HttpSessionContext.getSession(String sessionId)`). Note this means that every servlet can have access to all sessions of all servlets running in WebSphere. Although this may be shocking to the security-sensitive among us, it is very useful for such operations as session invalidation.

Session context is one of the ways in which WebSphere does more than the standard JDSK from Sun. The actual class for the object representing the session context is `com.ibm.servlet.personalization.sessiontracking.IBMSessionContextImpl`. This class knows how to handle the fact that in a WebSphere deployment, multiple servers may be used for scaleability and fault tolerance. These servers all form one conceptual server and need to work in tandem. We will discuss this issue further in the next chapter. This implementation of the session context also handles a number of other WebSphere-specific enhancements such as user authentication and additional data fields.

- `getLastAccessedTime()` Returns the last time the client sent a request carrying the identifier assigned to the session

- `getSessionContext()` Returns NULL

- `getValueNames()` This method returns all keys of the objects associated with the session.

- `invalidate()` This is an important method that is used to tell WebSphere that a session should no longer be maintained. All objects maintained for that session are discarded and the session should no longer be used. This method is very important given the working model of the Web. The Web model is such that browser uses the server and at some point goes away. This can happen for many reasons. For example, the user may close the browser and go do something else or the connection may be lost. In the meantime, we may still be holding on to objects maintained for that session. Unless we want our server's memory footprint to constantly grow (until we're out of space or until our performance degrades so much that a reboot is necessary), this information needs to be discarded at appropriate intervals. One way is through a logoff routine that among other things invalidates the session. Another is a background process that periodically invalidates sessions that have not been used for a while. In the next chapter, we will see yet another way to manage such cleanup.

- `isNew()` A session is considered to be "new" if it has been created by the server, but the client has not yet acknowledged joining the session.

Caveat: Sessions and JSPs

Before we conclude our discussion about servlet sessions, we want to briefly mention sessions in the context of servlets compiled from JSPs. If you've read this book in order without skipping around, you have no idea what we're talking about—JSPs are only covered in Chapter 26, "JSP Syntax and Lifecycle," and Chapter 27, "IBM JSP Support." Still, we've opted to discuss this here because it really is about servlet session tracking. Therefore, you might consider putting a flag at the top of this page and coming back to it after Chapter 27.

Because JSPs are compiled into servlets, eventually anything that happens in the JSP really happens in the servlet. One of the features available to JSP builders is that of embedding a Java object using the BEAN tag. As we'll see in Chapter 28, "Debugging Servlets and JSPs Using VisualAge," the BEAN tag can define that the Java object is available in the context of the request or in the context of the session. I'm sure you are beginning to get the picture now. When a BEAN is defined to be available in the context of a session (as in Listing 24-4), the object is actually placed in the session object by the servlet that is automatically generated by the JSP engine (shown in Listing 24-5). Then, when another page uses the same bean name (as in Listing 24-6), the session object is used to look for the bean (shown in Listing 24-7). Figure 24-8 shows the output after navigating to the JSP shown in Listing 24-4. While this page is processed, the date object is stored in the session object. Then, when we navigate to the second JSP (the one shown in Listing 24-6), the date object is extracted from the session object as shown in Listing 24-7, and the output produced is Figure 24-9.

Listing 24-4
Defining a JSP BEAN
in a session

```
<HTML>
<BODY>
<bean
        name="beanInSession"
        varname="myDate"
        type="java.util.Date"
        create="yes"
        scope="session">
</bean>
The first page was executed at
<%= myDate.toString() %>
</BODY>
</HTML>
```

```
<HTML>
<BODY>
<bean
        name="beanInSession"
        varname="hisDate"
        type="java.util.Date"
        create="no"
        scope="session">
</bean>
The first page was executed at
<%= hisDate.toString() %>
and the second page at
<%= (new java.util.Date()).toString() %>
</BODY>
</HTML>
```

```
tsxSessionHolder = request.getSession(true);
java.util.Date myDate = (java.util.Date)
tsxSessionHolder.getValue("beanInSession");
        if ( myDate == null ) {
            try {
                myDate = (java.util.Date) Beans.instantiate(
                            this.getClass().getClassLoader(),
                            "java.util.Date");
                if ((Object)myDate instanceof Servlet) {
                    ((Servlet) (Object)myDate).
                                init(getServletConfig());
                }
            } catch (Exception ex) {
                throw new ServletException(
                    "Can't create BEAN of class java.util.Date: "+
                    ex.getMessage());
            }
tsxSessionHolder.putValue("beanInSession", myDate);
```

```
tsxSessionHolder = request.getSession(true);
java.util.Date hisDate = (java.util.Date)
tsxSessionHolder.getValue("beanInSession");
        if ( hisDate == null )
            throw new ServletException(
                "Invalid BEAN name: beanInSession");
```

Figure 24-8
Output from first JSP

Figure 24-9
Output from
second JSP

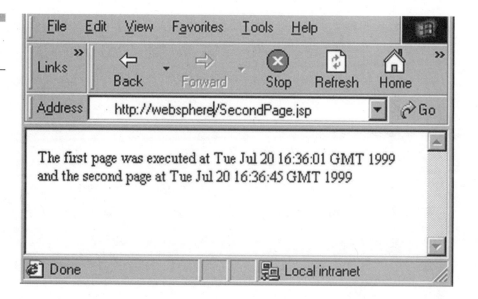

WebSphere-Specific Servlet Issues

In this chapter, we continue with our discussion of servlets and focus on WebSphere-specific servlet support. We will provide more details regarding WebSphere session management and will describe two servlets that are part of the WebSphere distribution. We will also provide built-in support for some simple groupware operations.

WebSphere Session Tracking

As already mentioned in the previous chapter, the WebSphere distribution replaces the JSDK2.0 classes for servlet-session management with its own set of classes. We have already mentioned the fact that the class that is used to implement the notion of a session context is `com.ibm.servlet.` `personalization.sessiontracking.IBMSessionContextImpl`, and while we have briefly noted that this class enhances normal session tracking with support for multiple WebSphere servers, this class requires more explanation.

In a typical e-business scenario that supports a large number of users, no one processor will ever be powerful enough for any job. Therefore, in order to support high-performance sites that scale well, the typical installation will include multiple WebSphere servers that all need to function as though they were a single server instance. This setup can be configured on a multiprocessor machine with each processor running a server—or on multiple machines, each possibly running a number of servers. Apart from the performance and scaleability issue, fault-tolerance requirements typically demand that we run multiple WebSphere instances—preferably on more than one machine. This way, even if a machine crashes, we are not dead in the water.

Whatever the case might be, the outcome is that we need to run multiple WebSphere servers that behave as one logical server. Such a logical scheme is called a cluster. In WebSphere, such a cluster of WebSphere instances work within an installation of the WebSphere Performance Pack, and the WebSphere instances are managed by an IBM eNetwork Dispatcher. The dispatcher manages the delegation of requests to the cluster instances. One of the implications when we say that the configuration must run as one logical server is that session management must be conceptually centralized. Therefore, it must be possible for all sessions to be available to all servers in the cluster.

WebSphere supports three possible schemes for sharing session information between cluster instances. The first scheme is one in which there is no sharing of session information—i.e., each WebSphere instance manages its own session information, and no sharing is available. This scheme is obviously not too useful if session tracking is truly used. The second scheme enables the central cluster server to store all session information. In this scheme, the cluster server acts as a central repository for all session information. When one of the session instances invokes the getSession method (or any other session-tracking method, for that matter), the cluster instance communicates with the cluster server to retrieve this information. Because the session-tracking API enables event-based functionality in which a subscriber can register interest in a session-related event, the cluster server must maintain such registrations and must notify the subscriber in case of events that are related to that session. This complex interaction between possibly three address spaces (e.g., the instance invalidating a session, the cluster server, and the subscriber) is managed by the IBM session-tracking classes.

The third scheme is the most scaleable and fault tolerant, because it maintains the distributed nature of session tracking and does not create a bottleneck (as does the previous scheme with the cluster server). This scheme also supports complete availability of all session information to all instances. In this scheme, each instance maintains the sessions that were created by that instance. When an instance creates a new session, however, it notifies the cluster server of that event, and the cluster server records the session identifier and the instance in which it is stored. Then, when an instance needs to access a session, it contacts the cluster server—and the server forwards the session to the cluster instance that is managing that session. This scheme has the best characteristics and is available as of version 2.0.

Obviously, session management is available to Java programs by using the session-tracking API and the IBM session-tracking extensions. In addition, the WebSphere administration tool provides convenient tools for setting session-tracking information and for viewing the status of WebSphere sessions. Figure 25-1 shows the Session Tracking page. The page is part of the Setup item in the main navigation panel.

The session-tracking tool has a number of attributes that can be modified and is organized as a set of tabs on a notebook. In the first tab (shown in Figure 25-1), you can enable or disable sessions completely and enable or disable URL rewriting, cookie support, and protocol switching rewriting. Protocol switching rewriting tells WebSphere whether it should propagate the session information when it needs to switch between a secure and a non-secure connection (or vice-versa).

Next comes the cookie tab, as shown in Figure 25-2. This tab enables you to set the defaults pertaining to the cookie that is holding the session identifier. You can set its name, restrict the domains to which such a cookie will be sent (e.g., if you know that your application server supports the application only on your intranet). The maximum age field is an integer value in milliseconds that defines the duration after which the cookie will be invalidated by the browser. Do not be confused with session invalidation that can

Figure 25-1
Session Tracking
administration tool

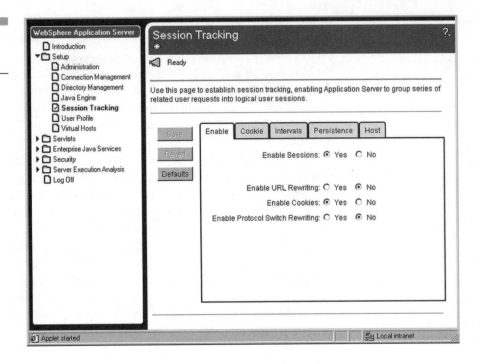

Figure 25-1
Session Tracking
administration tool

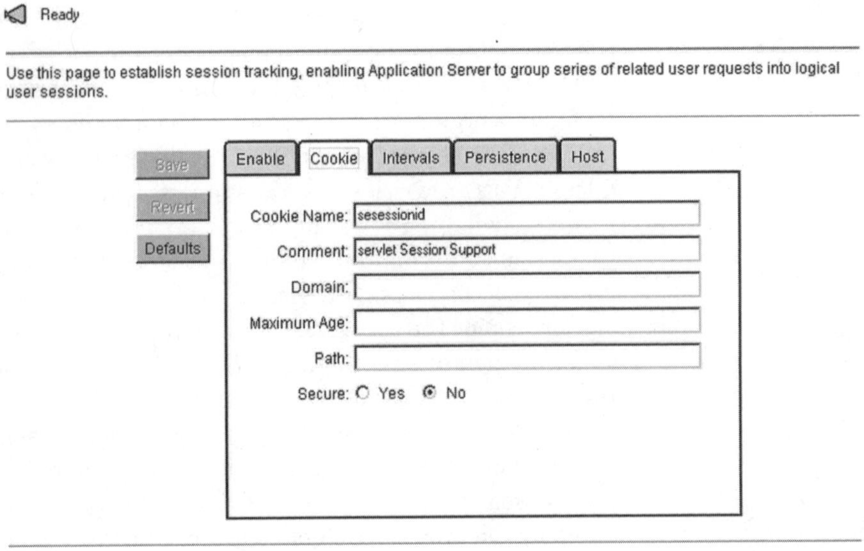

Figure 25-2
Cookie tab

happen on the server. This value goes into the response header as part of the cookie information (as was described in Chapter 24, "Servlet Sessions"), and invalidation is performed by the browser. Finally, the Path field enables you to restrict the paths on the server to which the session cookie will be sent.

Figure 25-3 shows the Intervals tab that defines the default values for built-in session tracking. These values are used by the session tracker to determine when a session should be invalidated and how many sessions can coexist in memory. The values come in pairs, with one pair controlling session invalidation and one pair controlling the swapping of session information from memory to disk. Each pair specifies the value that tells WebSphere what to do (in other words, how many sessions should be kept in memory and how long a session is assumed to be active after the last time it was last used) and specifies the interval that defines how often WebSphere should check these values (in other words, how often the server should check the number of in-memory sessions and the last time each session was used).

Next comes the Persistence tab, as shown in Figure 25-4. The values in this tab determine whether the session information should be made persistent by the server. For example, if a server goes down and comes back up again, turning on this option enables the server to resume from where it left off without having to break off client sessions. Finally, the Host tab, as shown in Figure 25-5, defines the clustering properties for session tracking.

Figure 25-3
Intervals tab

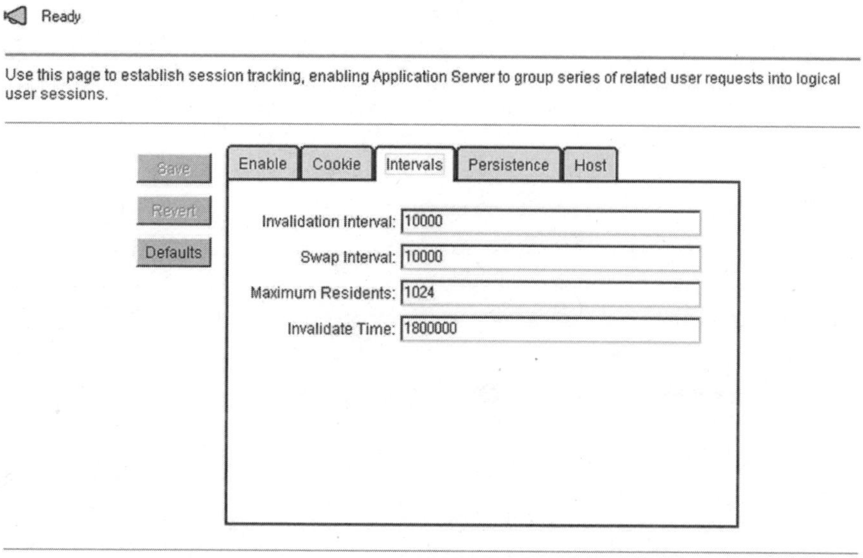

Figure 25-4
Persistence tab

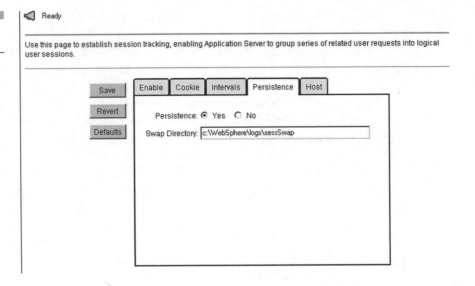

Figure 25-5
Host tab

Site Bulletins

WebSphere has a number of built-in servlets that can come in handy
when building a Web site. One of these is the site bulletin servlet, which
enables you to disseminate information among the users of your site. This
feature is provided through two servlets called SetVariableText and

GetVariableText. Figure 25-6 shows the Servlet Configuration screen with the built-in WebSphere servlets, marking the mentioned servlets.

When you want to create a site bulletin, you activate the SetVariableText (as shown in Figure 25-7). This form enables you to enter a text message and to specify a topic name (called the queue name) on which you want the message to be added. As a site builder, you can build any number of queues simply by defining this property of the servlet. The topics for which bulletins can

Figure 25-6
Site bulletin servlets

 Ready

Use this page to see a servlet's settings. Choose the servlet from the Servlet Names list, and the details are displayed on the right side of the page. You can add servlets to the list, and manipulate servlets once they are in the list.

Add	Servlet Names	Settings for Servlet SetVariableText
Save	CheckMessage	Name: SetVariableText
Remove	file	Description:
	GetMessage	Class Name: com.ibm.servlet.servlets.personalization.util.SetVariableText
Load	GetVariableText	
	invoker	Servlet Load Options
	pageCompile	Load at Startup: ○ Yes ⊙ No
	SendMessage	Loaded Now: ○ Yes ⊙ No
	SetVariableText	Load Servlet Remotely: ○ Yes ⊙ No
	snoop	Class File URL:
	ssiServlet	

Figure 25-7
The
SetVariableText
Page

| File | Edit | View | Favorites | Tools | Help |

Links   Back   Forward   Stop   Refresh   Home   Search

Address http://websphere/servlet/SetVariableText   Go

Site Queue Name : [   ]

Site Message : [   ]

[Submit Request]

Done   Local intranet

be created are created dynamically by requests to the servlet. Figure 25-8 shows a Web page with two references to the `GetVariableText` servlet— each with a different queue name. This situation ensures that all messages that are added to the appropriate queue appear on the page. Listing 25-1 shows the HTML code that is used to display this information. Note that you

Figure 25-8
Displaying the bulletins

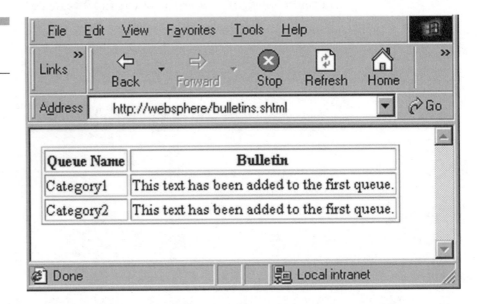

Listing 25-1
HTML code using the built-in bulletin support

```
<HTML>
<BODY>
<TABLE BORDER>
        <TR>
                <TH>Queue Name</TH>
                <TH>Bulletin</TH>
        </TR>
        <TR>
                <TD>Category1</TD>
                <TD>
                <SERVLET name="GetVariableText"
queueName="category1">
                </SERVLET>
                </TD>
        </TR>
        <TR>
                <TD>Category2</TD>
                <TD>
                <SERVLET name="GetVariableText"
```

```
queueName="category2">
              </SERVLET>
              </TD>
         </TR>
</TABLE>
</BODY>
</HTML>
```

need to name this file with a .shtml or a .jsp extension so that the Web server will know that it needs to perform some server-side processing and replace the SERVLET tag with the appropriate call to the servlet.

Person-to-Person Messages

Other servlets (shown in Figure 25-9) that come as part of the standard distribution are the SendMessage, CheckMessage, and GetMessage servlets. These servlets enable users to send messages directly to one another, and they use the IBM implementation of the session-context object to store the messages directly in the session for the users. In other words, the only people who can communicate with one another by using these servlets are those who have session objects. The text itself is stored in the com.ibm.servlet. personalization.sessiontracking.IBMSessionData class that replaces the conventional session object in WebSphere. To retrieve this object, simply call request.getSession() with the appropriate cast.

As an example, we used the previous chapter's testing servlet to enable anyone who is taking the test to communicate with one another (and maybe share ideas about the answers to the difficult questions). We started by building a page with three parts: the actual test area, a place from which messages are sent, and a place from which messages are retrieved. We built the page as three frames, because that enabled us to reuse the testing servlet code as is. Listing 25-2 shows the code for the frameset and for each of the individual frames (in order). Each frame is itself an SHTML file that is processed by the server to create the output from the appropriate servlet (three servlets, in this case). The Test2 servlet inserts the testing form; the SendMessage servlet inserts the button that enables us to send a message; and the CheckMessage servlet displays an icon that provides a visual cue telling us whether we have any outstanding messages or not.

Figure 25-9

User-to-user message servlets

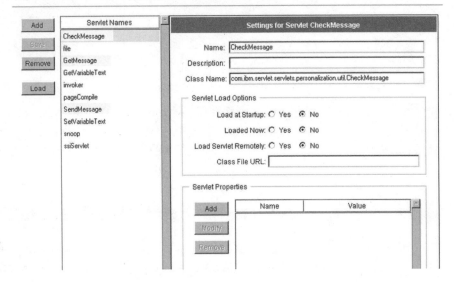

◁ Ready

Use this page to see a servlet's settings. Choose the servlet from the Servlet Names list, and the details are displayed on the right side of the page. You can add servlets to the list, and manipulate servlets once they are in the list.

Listing 25-2

Frameset code

```
<HTML>
<FRAMESET rows="40%,30%,30%">
<FRAME src="testFrame.shtml">
<FRAME src="sendMessageFrame.shtml">
<FRAME src="readMessageFrame.shtml">
</FRAMESET>
<NOFRAMES>
<H2>Frame Alert</H2>
This document is designed to be viewed using the frames feature.
If you see this message, you are using a non-frame-capable web
client.
</NOFRAMES>
</HTML>

<HTML>
<BODY>
<SERVLET name="Test2">
</SERVLET>
</BODY>
</HTML>

<HTML>
<BODY>
```

```
<B>Send a message by clicking this button </B>
<SERVLET name="SendMessage">
</SERVLET>
</BODY>
</HTML>

<HTML>
<BODY>
<SERVLET name="CheckMessage">
</SERVLET>
</BODY>
</HTML>
```

This result is at least what we thought would happen, based on the WebSphere documentation. When we performed this action, however, we came across a whole sleuth of problems. The first problem is that when we open this page, we get the output shown in Figure 25-10. As you can see, there is something wrong with the icon showing us whether we have messages or not. So, we looked at the source file for this frame (refer to Listing 25-3), and obviously something is wrong. Where did this path originate? After a bit of investigation, we found out that the servlet is not written well, and these paths are hard coded into the constructor of the servlet. We were almost about to give up when we remembered that WebSphere has a feature called `XMLServletConfig`.

At this point, we will introduce you to one more aspect of WebSphere's built-in support for servlets. WebSphere enables us to create a setup file for each servlet that defines the information required to configure the servlet. This feature is supported in a convenient manner. For each servlet, we can define a configuration file that follows an XML syntax. This configuration file can be used to define all of the servlets' attributes. Specifically, this feature enables us to define the attributes that will be used later in the servlet initiation. When WebSphere loads a servlet called `CheckMessage` from the administration tool (or at startup), it looks for a file called `CheckMessage.servlet`. If this file exists, the file is used to determine the class of the servlet—as well as the attributes. Then, in the `init` method of the servlet, the parameters defined in the file can be retrieved by using `getInitParameter`. So, in our examples, we would use `config.getInitParameter("messageWaiting")`.

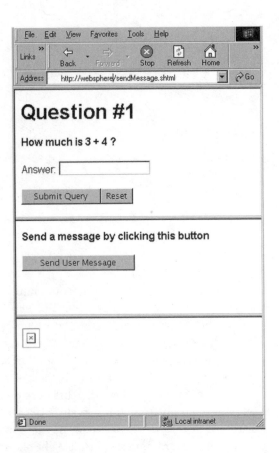

```
<HTML>
<BODY>
<img src="/IBMWebAS/samples/XtremeTravel/phonflat.gif" BORDER=0 >

</BODY>
</HTML>
```

Listing 25-4 shows the XML file that we created for the `CheckMessage` servlet. With this file in hand (and after having unloaded and reloaded the servlet by using the administration tool), we anxiously loaded our page. To our dismay, we saw what is shown in Figure 25-11 (HTML for the bottom frame is shown in Listing 25-5). What is wrong now? Well, instead of having the string in the configuration file interpreted as the actual GIF file to be displayed, the servlet simply plugs the string as HTML code.

Listing 25-4
XML configuration
file for
CheckMessage

```xml
<?xml version="1.0"?>
<servlet>
  <code>
    com.ibm.servlet.servlets.personalization.util.CheckMessage
  </code>
  <description>
    Generates the appropriate page showing whether there
    are messages or not
  </description>
  <init-parameter
    name="messageWaiting"
    value="messageWaiting.gif"
  />
  <init-parameter
    name="noMessageWaiting"
    value="noMessageWaiting.gif"
  />
</servlet>
```

Figure 25-11
Second-try test page
with messages

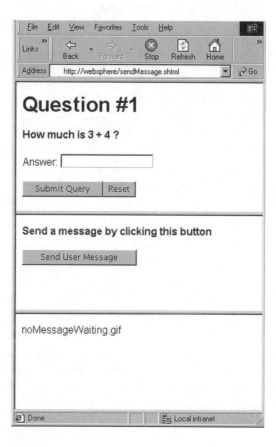

## Chapter 25

Listing 25-5
Second-try source for
frame-checking mes-
sage availability

```
<HTML>
<BODY>
noMessageWaiting.gif

</BODY>
</HTML>
```

Listing 25-6
Code for
OurCheckMessage

```
package book.websphere.chapter25;

import javax.servlet.*;
import javax.servlet.http.*;
import java.io.*;
import java.util.*;
import
com.ibm.servlet.personalization.sessiontracking.IBMSessionData;

public class OurCheckMessage extends HttpServlet {

  private String gifNameForMessage;
  private String gifNameNoMessage;

  public void init(ServletConfig config) throws ServletException{
    super.init(config);
    gifNameForMessage = config.getInitParameter("messageWaiting");
    gifNameNoMessage = config.getInitParameter("noMessageWaiting");
  }

  public void doGet(
      HttpServletRequest request,
      HttpServletResponse response)
      throws ServletException, IOException   {
    response.setContentType("text/html");
    PrintWriter out = new PrintWriter (response.getOutputStream());
    out.println("<html>");
    out.println("<head><title>OurCheckMessage</title></head>");
    out.println("<body>");
```

At this point, we resorted to coding. We decided to create our own version
of CheckMessage, so we created OurCheckMessage, as shown in Listing
25-6. Then, we changed the XML file to point at our class (Listing 25-7).
Note that we do not even have to change the class definition used in the
administration tool, because when the .servlet file is found, it is the only file
used for the servlet configuration. At this point, we can finally bring up the

```
    IBMSessionData aSession =
(IBMSessionData)request.getSession(false);
    if ((aSession != null) && (aSession.getMessage() != null))
      out.println(
        "<a href=\"/servlet/GetMessage\"><img src=\"" +
        gifNameForMessage + "\">");
    else
      out.println("<img src=\"" + gifNameNoMessage + "\">");

    out.println("</body></html>");
    out.close();
  }

  public String getServletInfo() {
    return "book.websphere.chapter24.OurCheckMessage Information";
  }
  }
}
```

Listing 25-7
Second XML
configuration file

```
<?xml version="1.0"?>
<servlet>
  <code>
    book.websphere.chapter25.OurCheckMessage
  </code>
  <description>
    Generates the appropriate page showing whether there
    are messages or not
  </description>
  <init-parameter
    name="messageWaiting"
    value="messageWaiting.gif"
  />
  <init-parameter
    name="noMessageWaiting"
    value="noMessageWaiting.gif"
  />
</servlet>
```

page, as shown in Figure 25-12. Now, if we send a message (to ourselves, for example) by using the pop-up created by the SendMessage servlet (shown in Figure 25-13) and refresh the CheckMessage frame, we will see the page shown in Figure 25-14. Finally, Figure 25-15 shows the result after clicking the image—the output that is created by the GetMessage servlet.

Figure 25-12
Final test page with
messages

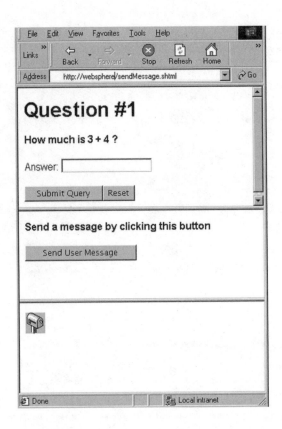

Figure 25-12
Final test page with
messages

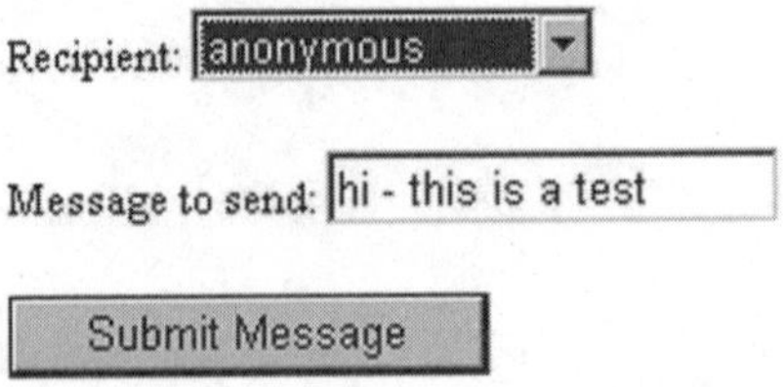

Figure 25-13
Send message
pop-up

Figure 25-14
OurCheckMessages
indication of message
arrival

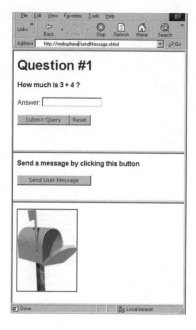

Figure 25-15
Getting the message
text

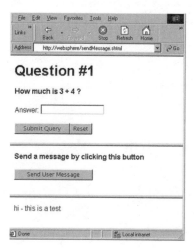

26

JSP: Syntax and Life Cycle

JSP is the Java technology best-suited for building dynamic Web-based applications. Such applications use presentation technologies such as HTML, DHTML, XML, and Java applets while using Java server-side code for business processing. JSP is specifically designed to support a convenient and smooth integration between these technologies by allowing dynamic content to be generated using Java server code in a way that can be easily embedded in template-based user interfaces. We have already covered the functional model and processing foundations of JSPs in previous chapters; in this chapter and the next we will delve into the gory details of JSPs and of deploying JSPs in WebSphere. We will start with a detailed discussion and examples illustrating the JSP tag set and functional capabilities while discussing how the JSP engine performs its feats of magic. We will continue with a description of additional support for JSP within WebSphere and additional helper libraries provided by IBM.

Apart from the discussion of the JSP tag set, the next chapter focuses on describing two sets of extensions to JSP that considerably help when building JSP-based applications. The first is a set of elements added by IBM and implemented by WebSphere that allows iterations and grouping of information. The second is the JSP format bean library developed by IBM, which makes common functionality very simple to code in JSP.

JSP Syntax

JSP files are text files that include HTML tags, scripts, and any other tag sets in addition to a set of elements conforming to the JSP syntax. The syntax described here conforms to the implementation of JSP on WebSphere 2.x (WebSphere 3.x supports both this version as well as 1.0). The JSP specification version 1.0 defines a syntax that is slightly different. (Note that WebSphere Application Server 3.0 supports JSP 1.0). It also defines the tag set as an application of XML and uses XML namespaces. In XML syntax, most tags look slightly different. For example, a tag following the JSP format defined in the JSP specification 1.0 may look like the following:

```
<%@ include file=" . . . " %>
```

whereas the WebSphere syntax is slightly more compact:

```
<%@ include=" . . . " %>
```

The JSP XML syntax in this case will look like

```
<jsp:directive.include file=" . . . " />
```

Although there are some distinct advantages in phrasing JSP files as XML documents, there are also a number of disadvantages. For example, an XML document must have a single root element, whereas JSPs do not have such a natural root. Such a node can be defined, but it is somewhat artificial. In addition, the XML syntax is more cumbersome to use, and because one of the fundamental reasons for JSPs is the fast and easy coding of Web presentations, this formality can be a serious drawback. Therefore, although the XML syntax may be more useful for tools and programs, the JSP syntax is simpler for programmers. The specification therefore does not abandon the JSP syntax, and neither will we. In this book, we use the JSP syntax exclusively—specifically, the WebSphere 2.x JSP format.

The JSP syntax defines a number of possible elements. Anything that does not fall into one of these categories is not processed by the JSP engine and passes unchanged to the resulting page. These elements are normally called template elements because they usually form the presentation code into which dynamic content is injected. Each JSP element falls into one of the following categories:

- Comments
- Standard objects
- Directives
- Declarations
- Scriptlets
- Expressions
- Bean references

Comments

Comments in the JSP file follow the general pattern of comments in HTML. By embedding a line of the form

```
<!- put comment here ->
```

we can pass a comment all the way to the browser page. If we require the comments to appear in the JSP but not be passed to the resulting page, we can embed a comment following Java conventions in a scriptlet; that is, write the code as

```
<% /* put comment here */ %>
```

Note that this does not mean that the comment is passed into the Java file that is created on your behalf by the JSP engine. Also note that you need to end the comment within the line and start a new comment if you wish to have a comment span more than one line.

Standard Objects

Because the JSP model follows the servlet model (and JSPs are actually compiled into servlet code), there is a standard set of objects that are always available. These objects can be referenced without being explicitly declared. These objects form the "environment" one would expect in a servlet.

Listing 26-1 shows the simplest such use of standard objects. The `request` object is an object of type `javax.servlet.HttpServletRequest` (assuming the JSP is accessed through HTTP). The object referenced by `out` is defined by the specification to be of type `javax.servlet.jsp.JspWriter` and is similar to a servlet's print writer object. Figure 26-1 shows the result of accessing this code. Listing 26-2 shows an equally simple example that uses the `response` object (of type `javax.servlet.ServletResponse`) to redirect the client to another URL. The types mentioned previously are defined in the JSP specification. Because WebSphere is an implementation of the JSP standard, the actual classes used are different, as shown in Listing 26-3 and Figure 26-2.

Listing 26-1
Using the `request` and `out` standard objects

```
<HTML>
<BODY>
The query string passed into this URL is:
<%
        out.println(" " + request.getQueryString());
%>
</BODY>
</HTML>
```

Figure 26-1
Resulting output when accessing the JSP shown in Listing 26-1

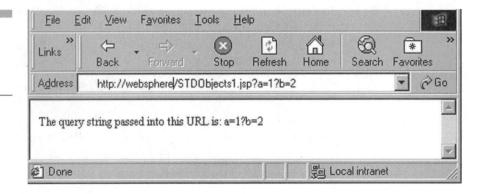

Listing 26-2
Redirection using the response object

```
<HTML>
<BODY>
<%
        response.sendRedirect("http://www.ibm.com/developer/java");
%>
</BODY>
</HTML>
```

Listing 26-3
Printing out standard object types

```
<HTML>
<BODY>
<%
        out.println("Request is of type " + request.getClass());
%>
<BR/>
<%
        out.println("Response is of type " + response.getClass());
%>
<BR/>
<%
        out.println("Out is of type " + out.getClass());
%>
</BODY>
</HTML>
```

Figure 26-2
Standard object type printout

Directives and Declarations

Directives are instructions to the JSP engine. They comprise a set of specifications that enables the JSP engine to be compiled into the generated servlet. Listing 26-4 shows a JSP page using directives. The resulting Java servlet code (created by the JSP engine) is shown in Listing 26-5. In Listing 26-5, we have `highlighted` all values defined in the directives of Listing 26-4.

All directives are enclosed between a `<@%` and a `%>`. The *language* directive specifies which language is being used for the scripting. For JSP, the only legal value is `"java"`; anything else will cause the JSP engine to fail. The *import* directives tells the JSP engine what import statements to include in the generated code. Because the JSP engine first processes the JSP file (creating a Java class for the servlet) and only then compiles it, the import statements are useful so code inserted later in the JSP file can use shorthand when referencing Java classes. Similarly, the *extends* directive

```
<HTML>
<%@ language="java" %>
<%@ import="com.ibm.xml.parser.*,org.w3c.dom.*" %>
<%@ extends="javax.servlet.http.HttpServlet" %>
<%@ content_type="image/gif" %>
<%@ method="doGet" %>
<%@ implements="org.xml.sax.DocumentHandler" %>

<script runat=server>
   public void startDocument() {
      /* do nothing */
   }
   public void setDocumentLocator(org.xml.sax.Locator l) {
      /* do nothing */
   }
   public void endDocument() {
      /* do nothing */
   }
   public void startElement(
java.lang.String s,
org.xml.sax.AttributeList a) {
      /* do nothing */
   }
   public void endElement(java.lang.String s) {
      /* do nothing */
   }
   public void characters(char[] c, int i, int j) {
      /* do nothing */
   }
   public void ignorableWhitespace(char[] c, int i, int j) {
      /* do nothing */
   }
   public void processingInstruction(
java.lang.String s1,
java.lang.String s2) {
      /* do nothing */
   }
</script>


<BODY>
</BODY>
</HTML>
```

```
package pagecompile;

import java.io.*;
import java.util.*;
import javax.servlet.*;
import javax.servlet.http.*;
import java.beans.Beans;
import com.sun.server.http.pagecompile.ParamsHttpServletRequest;
import com.sun.server.http.pagecompile.ServletUtil;
import com.sun.server.http.pagecompile.filecache.CharFileData;
import com.sun.server.http.pagecompile.NCSAUtil;
```

```
import com.ibm.xml.parser.*;
import org.w3c.dom.*;

public class _JSPDirectives_xjsp extends
javax.servlet.http.HttpServlet
  implements org.xml.sax.DocumentHandler {
    private static final String sources[] = new String[] {
        "c:\\program files\\ibm http
server\\htdocs\\jspdirectives.jsp",
    };
    private static final long lastModified[] = {
        931331396000L,
    };
    // com.sun.server.http.pagecompile.jsp.ScriptChunk c:/program
files/ibm http server/htdocs/jspdirectives.jsp 9,1-c:/program
files/ibm http server/htdocs/jspdirectives.jsp 34,10

        public void startDocument() {
         /* do nothing */
        }
        public void setDocumentLocator(org.xml.sax.Locator l) {
         /* do nothing */
        }
        public void endDocument() {
         /* do nothing */
        }
        public void startElement(
         java.lang.String s,
         org.xml.sax.AttributeList a) {
         /* do nothing */
        }
        public void endElement(java.lang.String s) {
         /* do nothing */
        }
        public void characters(char[] c, int i, int j) {
         /* do nothing */
        }
        public void ignorableWhitespace(char[] c, int i, int j)
{
         /* do nothing */
        }
        public void processingInstruction(
         java.lang.String s1,
         java.lang.String s2) {
         /* do nothing */
        }

    public void doGet(HttpServletRequest
request,HttpServletResponse response)
        throws IOException, ServletException
    {
        response.setContentType("image/gif");
        PrintWriter out = response.getWriter();
        CharFileData data[] = new CharFileData[sources.length];
        try {
            for (int i = 0 ; i < data.length ; i++)
            data[i] = ServletUtil.getJHtmlSource(this,
```

continues

Listing 26-5

Continued

```
                                  sources[i],
                                  "8859_1",
                                  lastModified[i]);
        } catch (Exception ex) {
            ex.printStackTrace();
            throw new ServletException("fileData");
        }
        // com.sun.server.http.pagecompile.jsp.LiteralChunk
null-null
        Object tsxResultObject = null;
        HttpSession tsxSessionHolder = null;
        {
        String url =
HttpUtils.getRequestURL(request).toString();
            if ((request.getAttribute("__XXcallPageXX__") != null)
&& !url.endsWith(".jsp")) {
                out.println("<base href=\"" +
                        url.substring(0, url.indexOf("/", 8)) +
                        request.getPathInfo() + "\">");
            }
        }


        // com.sun.server.http.pagecompile.jsp.CharArrayChunk
c:/program files/ibm http server/htdocs/jspdirectives.jsp 1,1-
c:/program files/ibm http server/htdocs/jspdirectives.jsp 2,1
        data[0].writeChars(0, 8, out);
        // com.sun.server.http.pagecompile.jsp.CharArrayChunk
c:/program files/ibm http server/htdocs/jspdirectives.jsp 2,23-
c:/program files/ibm http server/htdocs/jspdirectives.jsp 3,1
        data[0].writeChars(30, 2, out);
        // com.sun.server.http.pagecompile.jsp.CharArrayChunk
c:/program files/ibm http server/htdocs/jspdirectives.jsp 3,51-
c:/program files/ibm http server/htdocs/jspdirectives.jsp 4,1
        data[0].writeChars(82, 2, out);
        // com.sun.server.http.pagecompile.jsp.CharArrayChunk
c:/program files/ibm http server/htdocs/jspdirectives.jsp 4,48-
c:/program files/ibm http server/htdocs/jspdirectives.jsp 5,1
        data[0].writeChars(131, 2, out);
        // com.sun.server.http.pagecompile.jsp.CharArrayChunk
c:/program files/ibm http server/htdocs/jspdirectives.jsp 5,32-
c:/program files/ibm http server/htdocs/jspdirectives.jsp 6,1
        data[0].writeChars(164, 2, out);
        // com.sun.server.http.pagecompile.jsp.CharArrayChunk
c:/program files/ibm http server/htdocs/jspdirectives.jsp 6,22-
c:/program files/ibm http server/htdocs/jspdirectives.jsp 7,1
        data[0].writeChars(187, 2, out);
        // com.sun.server.http.pagecompile.jsp.CharArrayChunk
c:/program files/ibm http server/htdocs/jspdirectives.jsp 7,48-
c:/program files/ibm http server/htdocs/jspdirectives.jsp 9,1
        data[0].writeChars(236, 4, out);
        // com.sun.server.http.pagecompile.jsp.CharArrayChunk
c:/program files/ibm http server/htdocs/jspdirectives.jsp 34,10-
c:/program files/ibm http server/htdocs/jspdirectives.jsp 42,0
        data[0].writeChars(925, 36, out);
    }
}
```

tells the JSP engine which class to subclass from and the *implements* directive defines which interfaces the servlet class should implement. Note that when the *implements* directive is used, the JSP must include an implementation for the methods of the mentioned interfaces. This is shown in Listing 26-4 within the `script` tags. If these implementations are not provided, an error of the form shown in Listing 26-6 is produced. This is only natural because if the implementations are not provided, the generated servlet is a class implementing an interface without implementations for the interface's methods. Finally, the *method* and *content_type* directives inform the JSP engine which servlet method should be implemented and what content type to use for the response stream.

Listing 26-6

Compiler errors due to missing method implementations

```
m:\WEBSPH~1\APPSER~1\servlets\pagecompile\_JSPDirectives_xjsp.java:
16: class pagecompile._JSPDirectives_xjsp must be declared
abstract. It does not define void
setDocumentLocator(org.xml.sax.Locator) from interface
org.xml.sax.DocumentHandler.
public class _JSPDirectives_xjsp extends
javax.servlet.http.HttpServlet
                 ^
m:\WEBSPH~1\APPSER~1\servlets\pagecompile\_JSPDirectives_xjsp.java:
16: class pagecompile._JSPDirectives_xjsp must be declared
abstract. It does not define void startDocument() from interface
org.xml.sax.DocumentHandler.
public class _JSPDirectives_xjsp extends
javax.servlet.http.HttpServlet
                 ^
m:\WEBSPH~1\APPSER~1\servlets\pagecompile\_JSPDirectives_xjsp.java:
16: class pagecompile._JSPDirectives_xjsp must be declared
abstract. It does not define void endDocument() from interface
org.xml.sax.DocumentHandler.
public class _JSPDirectives_xjsp extends
javax.servlet.http.HttpServlet
                 ^
m:\WEBSPH~1\APPSER~1\servlets\pagecompile\_JSPDirectives_xjsp.java:
16: class pagecompile._JSPDirectives_xjsp must be declared
abstract. It does not define void startElement(java.lang.String,
org.xml.sax.AttributeList) from interface
org.xml.sax.DocumentHandler.
public class _JSPDirectives_xjsp extends
javax.servlet.http.HttpServlet
                 ^
m:\WEBSPH~1\APPSER~1\servlets\pagecompile\_JSPDirectives_xjsp.java:
16: class pagecompile._JSPDirectives_xjsp must be declared
abstract. It does not define void endElement(java.lang.String) from
interface org.xml.sax.DocumentHandler.
public class _JSPDirectives_xjsp extends
javax.servlet.http.HttpServlet
                 ^
```

continues

Listing 26-6
Continued

```
m:\WEBSPH~1\APPSER~1\servlets\pagecompile\_JSPDirectives_xjsp.java:
16: class pagecompile._JSPDirectives_xjsp must be declared
abstract. It does not define void characters(char[], int, int) from
interface org.xml.sax.DocumentHandler.
public class _JSPDirectives_xjsp extends
javax.servlet.http.HttpServlet
                ^
m:\WEBSPH~1\APPSER~1\servlets\pagecompile\_JSPDirectives_xjsp.java:
16: class pagecompile._JSPDirectives_xjsp must be declared
abstract. It does not define void ignorableWhitespace(char[], int,
int) from interface org.xml.sax.DocumentHandler.
public class _JSPDirectives_xjsp extends
javax.servlet.http.HttpServlet
                ^
m:\WEBSPH~1\APPSER~1\servlets\pagecompile\_JSPDirectives_xjsp.java:
16: class pagecompile._JSPDirectives_xjsp must be declared
abstract. It does not define void
processingInstruction(java.lang.String, java.lang.String) from
interface org.xml.sax.DocumentHandler.
public class _JSPDirectives_xjsp extends
javax.servlet.http.HttpServlet
                ^
8 errors
```

As shown in Listing 26-4, Java declarations—variables or methods—can be added to the JSP file and enclosed by a `script` tag. All such code will be added to the servlet class generated from the JSP and thus available anywhere within the class. The `runat` attribute of the `script` tag informs the JSP engine that this is server-side code and should be inserted into the servlet class.

Scriptlets and Expressions

JSP includes a convenient syntax in which Java code can be written. By enclosing Java code within `<% . . . %>`, we tell the JSP engine to copy this code into the servlet processing method (that is, into the `service` method when there is no method directive or into the method defined by the method directive). A very simple example is shown by Figure 26-3 and Listings 26-7 and 26-8. Such code segments are called *scriplets*. In addition, a similar syntax allows defining expressions that are evaluated by the servlet and written out to the output stream. The difference from scriptlet syntax is that the opening tag uses `<%=` and the embedded code is viewed as an expression. Because the expression is embedded in Java code writing to the output stream (see Listing 26-9), the expression should not be terminated with a semicolon.

Figure 26-3
Output from the
simple scriptlet

Listing 26-7
Simple scriptlet

```
<HTML>
<BODY>
<% int i = 6; %>
<% i = i + 1; %>
The value of <B>i</B> is
<%= i %>
</BODY>
</HTML>
```

Listing 26-8
Generated servlet
for simple scriptlet
example

```
package pagecompile;

import java.io.*;
import java.util.*;
import javax.servlet.*;
import javax.servlet.http.*;
import java.beans.Beans;
import com.sun.server.http.pagecompile.ParamsHttpServletRequest;
import com.sun.server.http.pagecompile.ServletUtil;
import com.sun.server.http.pagecompile.filecache.CharFileData;
import com.sun.server.http.pagecompile.NCSAUtil;


public class _JSPScriptlets1_xjsp extends
javax.servlet.http.HttpServlet {
    private static final String sources[] = new String[] {
        "c:\\program files\\ibm http
server\\htdocs\\jspscriptlets1.jsp",
    };
    private static final long lastModified[] = {
        931333918000L,
    };

    public void service(HttpServletRequest
request,HttpServletResponse response)
```

continues

Listing 26-8

Continued

```
        throws IOException, ServletException
    {
        response.setContentType("text/html");
        PrintWriter out = response.getWriter();
        CharFileData data[] = new CharFileData[sources.length];
        try {
            for (int i = 0 ; i < data.length ; i++)
            data[i] = ServletUtil.getJHtmlSource(this,
                            sources[i],
                            "8859_1",
                            lastModified[i]);
        } catch (Exception ex) {
            ex.printStackTrace();
            throw new ServletException("fileData");
        }
        // com.sun.server.http.pagecompile.jsp.LiteralChunk null-
null
        Object tsxResultObject = null;
        HttpSession tsxSessionHolder = null;
        {
        String url =
HttpUtils.getRequestURL(request).toString();
            if ((request.getAttribute("__XXcallPageXX__") != null)
&& !url.endsWith(".jsp")) {
                out.println("<base href=\"" +
                        url.substring(0, url.indexOf("/", 8)) +
                        request.getPathInfo() + "\">");
            }
        }


        // com.sun.server.http.pagecompile.jsp.CharArrayChunk
c:/program files/ibm http server/htdocs/jspscriptlets1.jsp 1,1-
c:/program files/ibm http server/htdocs/jspscriptlets1.jsp 3,1
        data[0].writeChars(0, 16, out);
        // com.sun.server.http.pagecompile.jsp.ScriptletChunk
c:/program files/ibm http server/htdocs/jspscriptlets1.jsp 3,1-
c:/program files/ibm http server/htdocs/jspscriptlets1.jsp 3,17
                int i = 6;
        // com.sun.server.http.pagecompile.jsp.CharArrayChunk
c:/program files/ibm http server/htdocs/jspscriptlets1.jsp 3,17-
c:/program files/ibm http server/htdocs/jspscriptlets1.jsp 4,1
        data[0].writeChars(32, 2, out);
        // com.sun.server.http.pagecompile.jsp.ScriptletChunk
c:/program files/ibm http server/htdocs/jspscriptlets1.jsp 4,1-
c:/program files/ibm http server/htdocs/jspscriptlets1.jsp 4,17
                i = i + 1;
        // com.sun.server.http.pagecompile.jsp.CharArrayChunk
c:/program files/ibm http server/htdocs/jspscriptlets1.jsp 4,17-
c:/program files/ibm http server/htdocs/jspscriptlets1.jsp 6,1
        data[0].writeChars(50, 28, out);
        // com.sun.server.http.pagecompile.jsp.ScriptletChunk
c:/program files/ibm http server/htdocs/jspscriptlets1.jsp 6,1-
c:/program files/ibm http server/htdocs/jspscriptlets1.jsp 6,9
        out.print(ServletUtil.toString( i ));
        // com.sun.server.http.pagecompile.jsp.CharArrayChunk
c:/program files/ibm http server/htdocs/jspscriptlets1.jsp 6,9-
c:/program files/ibm http server/htdocs/jspscriptlets1.jsp 8,7
        data[0].writeChars(86, 18, out);
    }
}
```

One interesting thing to note regarding scriptlets is that you can truly mix HTML output and Java source together to a surprising level. For example, Listing 26-9 shows another simple JSP file about which you should note two things. The first is that when you compare the JSP to the resulting HTML page (shown in Listing 26-10; the actual output is in Figure 26-4), the lines almost completely match but there are blank lines where the scriptlets were originally. The second interesting thing is that the `if` clause is actually written using a set of scriptlets, but the actual output to be done in both the `then` and the `else` are in HTML. Therefore we are writing one piece of code that combines not only programming languages in one clause but also two completely different processing models.

The key to understanding how such a thing works is in the generated Java servlet code shown in Listing 26-11. Let's look at the implementation of the `service` method—the method that performs the action on behalf of the JSP and writes the output. The first thing that the method does after writing out the content type is to read in the JSP source file and store it in

Listing 26-9
JSP scriptlet example

```
<HTML>
<BODY>
This is an example of what happens to a scriptlet in the output.
Notice how the line will be missing when we observe the resulting
HTML's source.
<% int i = 1; %>
<BR/>
This is an even better example.
Based on how the scriptlet code segments evaluate
we get different lines that are really part of the HTML:
<BR/>
<% if (i == 1) { %>
i really does equal 1
<% } else { %>
i does not equal 1
<% } %>
</BODY>
</HTML>
```

Figure 26-4
Output from scriptlet of Listing 26-9

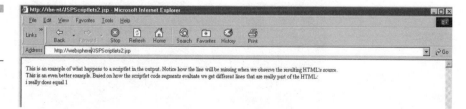

the data array. Then it goes through a series of commands that are a mix of Java commands (the code within the scriptlets in the JSP) and calls to writeChars. These other calls effectively write out the HTML (from the JSP source file) to the output stream of the servlet. This combination of Java code and copy-code is the most important aspect of the code generation process performed by the servlet engine. It is interesting to note that the Java servlet code generated for the JSP is in many ways a mirror image of the JSP. In the JSP, the scriplets embed the Java code that is an "outsider" to the HTML code, whereas in the generated servlet, the Java code from the scriptlets forms the "native" code. The HTML code is copied in from the JSP source.

Listing 26-10
HTML page sent as a result of the JSP in Listing 26-9

```
<HTML>
<BODY>
This is an example of what happens to a scriptlet in the output.
Notice how the line will be missing when we observe the resulting
HTML's source.

<BR/>
This is an even better example.
Based on how the scriptlet code segments evaluate
we get different lines that are really part of the HTML:
<BR/>

i really does equal 1

</BODY>
</HTML>
```

Listing 26-11
Java servlet code generated for JSP in Listing 26-9

```
package pagecompile;

import java.io.*;
import java.util.*;
import javax.servlet.*;
import javax.servlet.http.*;
import java.beans.Beans;
import com.sun.server.http.pagecompile.ParamsHttpServletRequest;
import com.sun.server.http.pagecompile.ServletUtil;
import com.sun.server.http.pagecompile.filecache.CharFileData;
import com.sun.server.http.pagecompile.NCSAUtil;


public class _JSPScriptlets2_xjsp extends
javax.servlet.http.HttpServlet {
    private static final String sources[] = new String[] {
        "c:\\program files\\ibm http
server\\htdocs\\jspscriptlets2.jsp",
```

```
    };
    private static final long lastModified[] = {
        931355714000L,
    };

    public void service(HttpServletRequest
request,HttpServletResponse response)
        throws IOException, ServletException
    {
        response.setContentType("text/html");
        PrintWriter out = response.getWriter();
        CharFileData data[] = new CharFileData[sources.length];
        try {
            for (int i = 0 ; i < data.length ; i++)
            data[i] = ServletUtil.getJHtmlSource(this,
                            sources[i],
                            "8859_1",
                            lastModified[i]);
        } catch (Exception ex) {
            ex.printStackTrace();
            throw new ServletException("fileData");
        }
        // com.sun.server.http.pagecompile.jsp.LiteralChunk null-
null
        Object tsxResultObject = null;
        HttpSession tsxSessionHolder = null;
        {
            String url =
HttpUtils.getRequestURL(request).toString();
            if ((request.getAttribute("__XXcallPageXX__") != null)
&& !url.endsWith(".jsp")) {
                out.println("<base href=\"" +
                        url.substring(0, url.indexOf("/", 8)) +
                        request.getPathInfo() + "\">");
            }
        }


        // com.sun.server.http.pagecompile.jsp.CharArrayChunk
c:/program files/ibm http server/htdocs/jspscriptlets2.jsp 1,1-
c:/program files/ibm http server/htdocs/jspscriptlets2.jsp 5,1
        data[0].writeChars(0, 165, out);
        // com.sun.server.http.pagecompile.jsp.ScriptletChunk
c:/program files/ibm http server/htdocs/jspscriptlets2.jsp 5,1-
c:/program files/ibm http server/htdocs/jspscriptlets2.jsp 5,17
                int i = 1;
        // com.sun.server.http.pagecompile.jsp.CharArrayChunk
c:/program files/ibm http server/htdocs/jspscriptlets2.jsp 5,17-
c:/program files/ibm http server/htdocs/jspscriptlets2.jsp 11,1
        data[0].writeChars(181, 159, out);
        // com.sun.server.http.pagecompile.jsp.ScriptletChunk
c:/program files/ibm http server/htdocs/jspscriptlets2.jsp 11,1-
c:/program files/ibm http server/htdocs/jspscriptlets2.jsp 11,20
                if (i == 1) {
        // com.sun.server.http.pagecompile.jsp.CharArrayChunk
c:/program files/ibm http server/htdocs/jspscriptlets2.jsp 11,20-
c:/program files/ibm http server/htdocs/jspscriptlets2.jsp 13,1
        data[0].writeChars(359, 25, out);
        // com.sun.server.http.pagecompile.jsp.ScriptletChunk
```

continues

Listing 26-11
Continued

```
c:/program files/ibm http server/htdocs/jspscriptlets2.jsp 13,1-
c:/program files/ibm http server/htdocs/jspscriptlets2.jsp 13,15
                } else {
        // com.sun.server.http.pagecompile.jsp.CharArrayChunk
c:/program files/ibm http server/htdocs/jspscriptlets2.jsp 13,15-
c:/program files/ibm http server/htdocs/jspscriptlets2.jsp 15,1
        data[0].writeChars(398, 22, out);
        // com.sun.server.http.pagecompile.jsp.ScriptletChunk
c:/program files/ibm http server/htdocs/jspscriptlets2.jsp 15,1-
c:/program files/ibm http server/htdocs/jspscriptlets2.jsp 15,8
        }
        // com.sun.server.http.pagecompile.jsp.CharArrayChunk
c:/program files/ibm http server/htdocs/jspscriptlets2.jsp 15,8-
c:/program files/ibm http server/htdocs/jspscriptlets2.jsp 17,7
        data[0].writeChars(427, 18, out);
    }
}
```

Bean References

The BEAN tag allows a JSP to access a bean and use it as a reusable component encapsulating business logic processing. The BEAN tag takes a large number of attributes, allowing it to be used in a variety of ways. The attributes of the BEAN tag are

- *Scope* A bean created in a JSP can be created either in the scope of a request, a session, or a userprofile. When a bean is created in the scope of a request, it exists only during that request. When a bean is created in the scope of a session, the same bean may be reused across multiple requests all performed within a single session of a browser. Actually, the session scope is based on the host. The final scope, userprofile, is a WebSphere-specific feature that provides direct access to the user profile in the session—an object of type com.ibm.servlet.personalization.userprofile.UserProfile.

- *Type* The Java class of the bean

- *Create* An attribute with a value of "yes" or "no" determining whether to create a new bean if the JSP engine can't find the bean in scope. If the JSP engine does find a bean by the specified name (next bullet point), this attribute is not used.

- *Name* We just said that the JSP checks if a bean exists in the scope of the call and, in some cases, creates one if it can't find the bean.

Determining whether the bean exists is done by looking up the bean using the value of the name attribute.

- *Varname*   A name given to the bean through which other scriptlets and expressions can access the bean. This name is only good for the scope of the JSP.

- *BeanName*   Because the bean may be stored in a serialized file and be reconstructed from a file rather than instantiated based on the specified class name, this parameter is used to define from where to reconstruct the bean.

- *Param*   A list of name value pairs that are used to set properties inside the bean using the reflection mechanism.

- *Introspect*   This attribute can be set to "yes," in which case the JSP engine will try to match the set of properties of the request in which the call is made with the set of properties of the bean. This is a shorthand by which we can say that we want the bean's properties to be set based on the request properties. It is a very convenient form, as we will see shortly.

In the final example of this chapter, we will put together some of the bean tag concepts to illustrate a number of the features supported by the tag's attribute set. First we build an HTML form in which a user can enter a user name, a password, and an e-mail address. The form's HTML source is shown in Listing 26-12 and the form in the browser is shown in Figure 26-5.

Listing 26-12
HTML source for a simple form

```
<HTML>
<BODY>
<FORM
  ACTION="http://websphere/JSPBeanInput.jsp"
  METHOD=GET>
  <TABLE>
  <TR><TD><B>User Name:</B></TD>
<TD><INPUT TYPE="TEXT" NAME="username"></TD></TR>
  <TR><TD><B>Password:</B></TD>
<TD><INPUT TYPE="TEXT" NAME="password"></TD></TR>
  <TR><TD><B>Email:</B></TD>
<TD><INPUT TYPE="TEXT" NAME="email"></TD></TR>
  <TR><TD><INPUT TYPE="SUBMIT" VALUE="Insert To Bean"></TD>
<TD><INPUT TYPE="RESET" VALUE="Reset"></TD></TR>
  </TABLE>
</FORM>
</BODY>
</HTML>
```

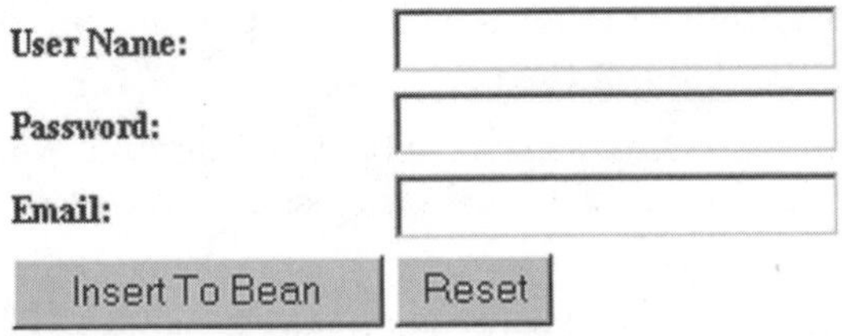

Figure 26-5
Entering user name,
password, and e-mail

User Name:

Password:

Email:

| Insert To Bean | Reset |

Listing 26-13
JSP storing the
form data in bean

```
<HTML>
<BODY>
<bean
     name="userProfile"
     type="book.websphere.chapter27.ExampleBean"
     introspect="yes"
     create="yes"
     scope="session">
</bean>
<B>The parameters have now been inserted!</B>
```

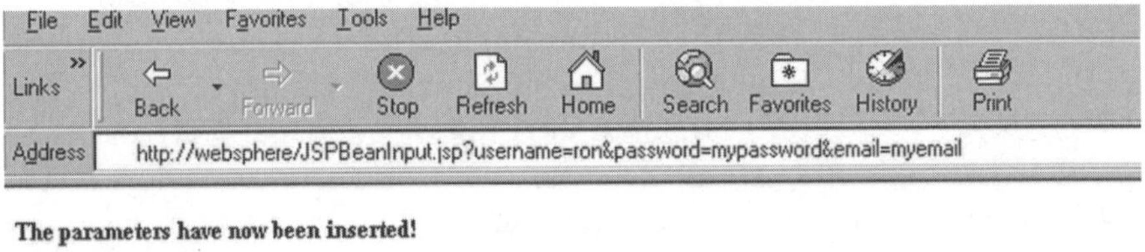

Figure 26-6
Browser after
injecting values
nto the bean

File   Edit   View   Favorites   Tools   Help

Links   »   Back   Forward   Stop   Refresh   Home   Search   Favorites   History   Print

Address   http://websphere/JSPBeanInput.jsp?username=ron&password=mypassword&email=myemail

The parameters have now been inserted!

The form's action URL is a JSP whose source is shown in Listing 26-13. This JSP uses the introspection mechanism to take parameters from the request and inject them into a bean. When the button on the form is pressed, the browser hits the server and the resulting page on the browser is shown in Figure 26-6. Let's run the process in slow motion. Pressing the form's Submit button causes the browser to hit the server using the URL shown on the Address line in Figure 26-6. Recall what we learned about servlets: This URL means that there are three parameters sent into the servlet. Now let's look at the BEAN element again. What we learn from it is that we are asked to search the session (because the bean is in the session scope), looking for a bean by the name of userProfile. Because it is not there, it will be created (see the create tag?). Now, because of the introspect tag and that fact that the bean (shown in Listing 26-14) has properties by exactly the same names as those used by the form (surprise, surprise), the values sent in the URL are stored within the bean—and look, no hands! (In other words, there is no code doing this explicitly.)

Listing 26-14
Input JSP

```
package book.websphere.chapter27;

public class ExampleBean {

  String username;
  String password;
  String email;

  public ExampleBean() {}

  public String getUsername() {
    return username;
  }

  public void setUsername(String u) {
    username = u;
  }

  public String getPassword() {
    return password;
  }

  public void setPassword(String p) {
    password = p;
  }

  public String getEmail() {
    return email;
  }

  public void setEmail(String e) {
    email = e;
  }

}
```

Finally, because the bean's scope is "session," whenever we want to see these values again (so long as we're in the same session), we can access the JSP shown in Listing 26-15 and see the output shown in Figure 26-7. Note that in this second JSP we give the bean a variable name; this enables us to access it later in the JSP.

Obviously, the magic is performed in the servlet code generated by the JSP engine. The first servlet instantiates the bean and puts it into the session object. It then iterates over the request's parameters and injects the values into the bean. The interesting part of the generated code is shown in Listing 26-16. The second servlet code generated by the JSP engine retrieves this object through the session object as shown in the code fragment in Listing 26-17.

```
<HTML>
<BODY>
<bean
      name="userProfile"
      varname="theData"
      type="book.websphere.chapter27.ExampleBean"
      create="no"
      scope="session">
</bean>
<B>Bean parameters all the way from the initial form:</B>
<BR/>
<B>Parameter values are:</B><BR/>
<%
   out.println("Username: " + theData.getUsername() + "<BR/>");
   out.println("Password: " + theData.getPassword() + "<BR/>");
   out.println("Email: " + theData.getEmail() + "<BR/>");
%>
<BR/>
<B>That's all folks!</B>
```

Bean parameters all the way from the initial form:
Parameter values are:
Username: ron
Password: mypassword
Email: myemail

That's all folks!

```
      tsxSessionHolder = request.getSession(true);
      book.websphere.chapter27.ExampleBean userProfile =
        (book.websphere.chapter27.ExampleBean)
        tsxSessionHolder.getValue("userProfile");
      if ( userProfile == null ) {
            try {
               userProfile =
(book.websphere.chapter27.ExampleBean)

Beans.instantiate(this.getClass().getClassLoader(),

"book.websphere.chapter27.ExampleBean");
                if ((Object)userProfile instanceof Servlet) {
                    ((Servlet) (Object)userProfile).
                         init(getServletConfig());
                }
            } catch (Exception ex) {
                throw new ServletException(
 "Can't create BEAN of class book.websphere.chapter27.ExampleBean:
"+
```

```
ex.getMessage());
    }
    tsxSessionHolder.putValue("userProfile", userProfile);
}
{
java.util.Properties p = new java.util.Properties();
java.util.Enumeration e = request.getParameterNames();
while (e.hasMoreElements()) {
    String name = (String) e.nextElement();
    p.put(name, request.getParameter(name));
}
com.sun.server.util.BeansUtil.setProperties(userProfile, p);
}
if ((Object)userProfile instanceof Servlet) {
    ((Servlet) (Object)userProfile).
     service((ServletRequest) request, (ServletResponse)
response);
}
```

Listing 26-17
Output from Bean

```
tsxSessionHolder = request.getSession(true);
book.websphere.chapter27.ExampleBean theData =
    (book.websphere.chapter27.ExampleBean)
    tsxSessionHolder.getValue("userProfile");
if ( theData == null )
    throw new ServletException("Invalid BEAN name:
userProfile");
```

27

IBM JSP Support

In this chapter, we continue with our detailed examples of JSP. Specifically, we focus on building JSPs within the WebSphere environment. Because JSP is one of the primary technologies of WebSphere and of building e-business applications in general, IBM has placed great efforts into making JSP as productive an environment to work in as possible. As such, JSP not only provides great tools such as WebSphere Studio and Visual Age for Java with a JSP add-on, but it has also provided some built-in extensions to JSP and provides a rich set of libraries to speed up JSP development. In this chapter, we will describe the built-in WebSphere extensions to JSPs and will introduce the JSP Format Bean Library by IBM.

## Chapter 27

The HTML Template Extensions

This section describes the built-in WebSphere extensions called the HTML Templates for Variable Data. This extension consists of two simple, additional elements that are supported by the IBM JSP engine and are specifically aimed at making the generation of tabular data simpler. Because most business applications make heavy use of repeating data—often from a relational table placed in some tabular presentation structure—such an extension is of much use to many WebSphere developers.

The HTML Template extensions consist of three additional tags. The <INSERT> tag enables the user to insert a value based on a property name and an object specifier. This object specifier can either be a bean name (of a bean previously declared in a BEAN tag) or a reference to an object in the request object. The <REPEAT> tag enables a user to write a for loop within a JSP page (as an HTML element, not as a Java loop). This tag defines an index that can then be used inside the REPEAT tag—by, for example, INSERT tags.

Before we proceed to our examples, let's look at Listing 27-1. This listing shows the data bean that we will be using throughout these examples. This bean is simple and simulates access to rows of data. Given an index, the bean provides four sets of data: an ID, a name, a string based on the index modulus 10, and a string based on the index divided by 100. While this data is not especially meaningful, it serves to illustrate the concepts that we wish to show, because it is not too different from data retrieved from some data store.

Listing 27-1
Data bean

```java
package book.websphere.chapter28;

public class ExampleBean1 {

  public ExampleBean1() {
  }

  public String getId(int i) {
    return "ID" + (new Integer(i)).toString();
  }

  public String getName(int i) {
    return "Name " + (new Integer(i)).toString();
  }

  public String getModulus(int i) {
    return "Modules Bucket " + (new Integer(i % 10)).toString();
  }
```

```
    public String getDivide(int i) {
      return "Div Bucket " + (new Integer(i / 100)).toString();
    }

  }
```

Figure 27-1
Output from the JSP
from Listing 27-2

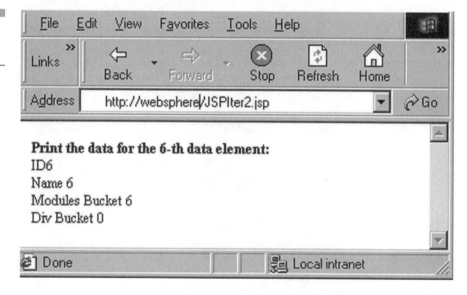

Listing 27-2 shows a JSP making use of the INSERT tag. JSP defines a bean using the BEAN tag and then proceeds to use a set of INSERT tags to print out the data values of the sixth element in the data bean. The output is shown in Figure 27-1.

The INSERT tag enables a user to insert a value from a bean in a way that is similar to what can be done with scriptlets and other basic JSP features. In this respect, this tag is not too interesting. The tag is useful, however, when used with the REPEAT tag. The next example illustrates this fact. In this example, we iterate through the first 20 elements from the data bean and display them in an HTML table. The JSP source code is shown in Listing 27-3, and the resulting output is shown in Figure 27-2. Note that the capability to iterate and display an appropriate data set makes use of both the REPEAT tag and the INSERT tag. This form is so common in business applications that it is truly an added benefit provided by WebSphere. As always, the magic is in the generated servlet code. The IBM JSP engine converts the tags in the extension to Java code, as shown in Listing 27-4.

Listing 27-2
Using the INSERT
tag

```
<HTML>
<BODY>
<bean
      name="dataBean"
      varname="theData"
      type="book.websphere.chapter28.ExampleBean1"
      introspect="no"
      create="yes"
      scope="request">
</bean>
<B>Print the data for the 6-th data element:</B><BR/>
<insert
      bean="theData"
      property=id(6)>
</insert>
<BR/>
<insert
      bean="theData"
      property=name(6)>
</insert>
<BR/>
<insert
      bean="theData"
      property=modulus(6)>
</insert>
<BR/>
<insert
      bean="theData"
      property=divide(6)>
</insert>
</BODY>
</HTML>
```

The JSP Format Bean Library

The rest of this chapter is devoted to the JSP Format Bean Library. At the time of this writing, this package was available through the IBM Alpha-Works projects within the AlphaBeans site at `http://www.alphaworks.ibm.com/alphabeans`. This package, while not a part of the JSP standard and still in its alpha stage, is so useful for building business-oriented JSP-based applications that we have decided to provide a detailed description of it, along with many examples of how to use this package. We certainly recommend that anyone who is planning to do serious business applications in JSP should have a look at the library, and we are sure that with time, this library will find its way into the standard WebSphere distribution.

The library is a set of JavaBeans that is meant to be used from within JSPs. As such, they are meant to be referenced from within JSPs and to output HTML that is used on the resulting page. In many cases, using the

Figure 27-2
Output from the JSP
from Listing 27-3

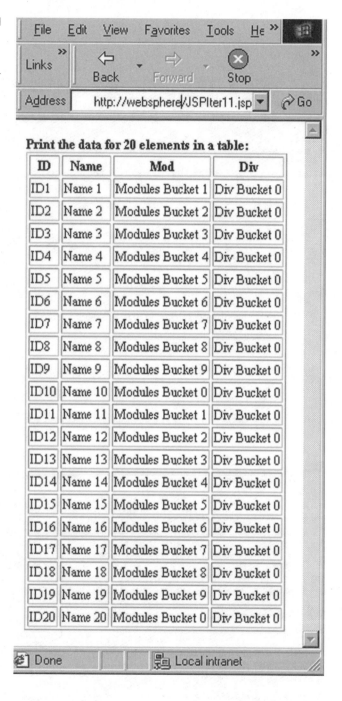

Print the data for 20 elements in a table:

ID	Name	Mod	Div
ID1	Name 1	Modules Bucket 1	Div Bucket 0
ID2	Name 2	Modules Bucket 2	Div Bucket 0
ID3	Name 3	Modules Bucket 3	Div Bucket 0
ID4	Name 4	Modules Bucket 4	Div Bucket 0
ID5	Name 5	Modules Bucket 5	Div Bucket 0
ID6	Name 6	Modules Bucket 6	Div Bucket 0
ID7	Name 7	Modules Bucket 7	Div Bucket 0
ID8	Name 8	Modules Bucket 8	Div Bucket 0
ID9	Name 9	Modules Bucket 9	Div Bucket 0
ID10	Name 10	Modules Bucket 0	Div Bucket 0
ID11	Name 11	Modules Bucket 1	Div Bucket 0
ID12	Name 12	Modules Bucket 2	Div Bucket 0
ID13	Name 13	Modules Bucket 3	Div Bucket 0
ID14	Name 14	Modules Bucket 4	Div Bucket 0
ID15	Name 15	Modules Bucket 5	Div Bucket 0
ID16	Name 16	Modules Bucket 6	Div Bucket 0
ID17	Name 17	Modules Bucket 7	Div Bucket 0
ID18	Name 18	Modules Bucket 8	Div Bucket 0
ID19	Name 19	Modules Bucket 9	Div Bucket 0
ID20	Name 20	Modules Bucket 0	Div Bucket 0

Listing 27-3
Using the REPEAT
and INSERT tags

```
<HTML>
<BODY>
<bean
      name="dataBean"
      varname="theData"
      type="book.websphere.chapter28.ExampleBean1"
      introspect="no"
      create="yes"
      scope="request">
</bean>
<B>Print the data for 20 elements in a table:</B><BR/>
<TABLE BORDER>
<TR><TH>ID</TH><TH>Name</TH><TH>Mod</TH><TH>Div</TH></TR>
  <repeat
      index="anIndex"
      start=1
      end=20>
            <TR>
            <TD><insert bean="theData" property=id(anIndex)>
            </insert></TD>
            <TD><insert bean="theData" property=name(anIndex)>
            </insert></TD>
            <TD><insert bean="theData" property=modulus(anIndex)>
            </insert></TD>
            <TD><insert bean="theData" property=divide(anIndex)>
            </insert></TD>
            </TR>
  </repeat>
</TABLE>
</BODY>
</HTML>
```

Listing 27-3
Using the REPEAT
and INSERT tags

Listing 27-4
Generated servlet
code supporting
iteration

```
for (int anIndex = 1; anIndex <= 20; anIndex++)
        {
            try
            {
    // com.sun.server.http.pagecompile.jsp.CharArrayChunk
c:/program files/ibm http server/htdocs/jspiter11.jsp 17,9-
c:/program files/ibm http server/htdocs/jspiter11.jsp 19,7
    data[0].writeChars(347, 16, out);
        // com.sun.server.http.pagecompile.jsp.LiteralChunk c:/program
files/ibm http server/htdocs/jspiter11.jsp 19,7-c:/program
files/ibm http server/htdocs/jspiter11.jsp 19,60
            if (theData.getId(anIndex) != null)
    out.print(theData.getId(anIndex));
                else
                    out.print("");
    // com.sun.server.http.pagecompile.jsp.CharArrayChunk
c:/program files/ibm http server/htdocs/jspiter11.jsp 19,60-
c:/program files/ibm http server/htdocs/jspiter11.jsp 20,7
    data[0].writeChars(416, 13, out);
    // com.sun.server.http.pagecompile.jsp.LiteralChunk c:/program
```

```
files/ibm http server/htdocs/jspiter11.jsp 20,7-c:/program
files/ibm http server/htdocs/jspiter11.jsp 20,62
            if (theData.getName(anIndex) != null)
    out.print(theData.getName(anIndex));
                else
                    out.print("");
    // com.sun.server.http.pagecompile.jsp.CharArrayChunk
c:/program files/ibm http server/htdocs/jspiter11.jsp 20,62-
c:/program files/ibm http server/htdocs/jspiter11.jsp 21,7
    data[0].writeChars(484, 13, out);
    // com.sun.server.http.pagecompile.jsp.LiteralChunk c:/program
files/ibm http server/htdocs/jspiter11.jsp 21,7-c:/program
files/ibm http server/htdocs/jspiter11.jsp 21,65
            if (theData.getModulus(anIndex) != null)
    out.print(theData.getModulus(anIndex));
                else
                    out.print("");
    // com.sun.server.http.pagecompile.jsp.CharArrayChunk
c:/program files/ibm http server/htdocs/jspiter11.jsp 21,65-
c:/program files/ibm http server/htdocs/jspiter11.jsp 22,7
    data[0].writeChars(555, 13, out);
    // com.sun.server.http.pagecompile.jsp.LiteralChunk c:/program
files/ibm http server/htdocs/jspiter11.jsp 22,7-c:/program
files/ibm http server/htdocs/jspiter11.jsp 22,64
            if (theData.getDivide(anIndex) != null)
    out.print(theData.getDivide(anIndex));
                else
                    out.print("");
    // com.sun.server.http.pagecompile.jsp.CharArrayChunk
c:/program files/ibm http server/htdocs/jspiter11.jsp 22,64-
c:/program files/ibm http server/htdocs/jspiter11.jsp 24,3
    data[0].writeChars(625, 18, out);
    // com.sun.server.http.pagecompile.jsp.LiteralChunk c:/program
files/ibm http server/htdocs/jspiter11.jsp 24,3-c:/program
files/ibm http server/htdocs/jspiter11.jsp 24,12
        }
            catch(ArrayIndexOutOfBoundsException ae)
            {
                break;
            }
            catch(Exception e)
            {
                out.println("Exception: " + e);
            }
        }
    // com.sun.server.http.pagecompile.jsp.CharArrayChunk
c:/program files/ibm http server/htdocs/jspiter11.jsp 24,12-
c:/program files/ibm http server/htdocs/jspiter11.jsp 27,7
    data[0].writeChars(652, 28, out);
```

beans in this library saves hours of coding that aims to produce the appropriate HTML output. This library is especially useful for creating business applications, because it focuses on issues such as formatting based on locale information, creating useful tabular representations, and (in general) providing a set of reusable components that alleviate the necessity of writing and fine-tuning repetitive JSP code.

In order to get up and running, you will need to download the package from the AlphaBeans site and unpack the files. Then, you need your server to include the two archive files (`collections.zip` and `JSPFormatBeans.jar`) in the `classpath` so that when the `pagecompile` program tries to compile the generated Java code based on your JSPs (which will include references to the formatting beans), these beans will be found. Unfortunately, WebSphere 2.x has a bug. The JSP compilation engine does not read archive files when looking for classes. When trying to run the examples that follow in this chapter, you will know that you are being affected by this program if you receive messages from the JSP engine claiming that the classes in `com.ibm.jsp.*` cannot be found or that an import of this package does not succeed. In this case, what you need to do is unpack the two archives into a directory-tree structure under the servlets directory.

Date and Time Formats

One of the features provided in the JSP Format Library is a set of beans for formatting dates. Formatting is supported for different locales so that internationalized applications can be easily written. Listing 27-5 shows a JSP that is making use of the `JSPDateFormat` formatting bean for producing an output of the date in various formats, based on two locales. The output of this JSP is shown in Figure 27-3. Listing 27-6 and Figure 27-4 show the corresponding examples for formatting time values.

Numeric Formats

The library supports a wide variety of numeric formats, including percentage and currency formats. Once more, the library supports locale-based formatting through the standard Java methods. Listing 27-7 and Figure 27-5 illustrate this point.

Formatting Lists

List-formatting beans are useful when we need to create an *Unordered List* (UL) or *Ordered List* (OL) in HTML. The list-formatting beans work with

Listing 27-5
Formatting dates
in a JSP

```
<HTML>
<BODY>
<%@ import="java.util.*,com.ibm.jsp.*" %>
<%
      DateaDate= new Date();
%><B>Todays date in various formats according to the default locale
is: </B><BR/>
<%=
      JSPDateFormat.format("com.ibm.jsp.DateFormatFull", aDate)
%>
<BR/>
<%=
      JSPDateFormat.format("com.ibm.jsp.DateFormatLong", aDate)
%>
<BR/>
<%=
      JSPDateFormat.format("com.ibm.jsp.DateFormatMedium", aDate)
%>
<BR/>
<%=
      JSPDateFormat.format("com.ibm.jsp.DateFormatShort", aDate)
%>
<P>
<B>Todays date in various formats according to a French locale is:
</B><BR/>
<%=
      JSPDateFormat.fullFormat(Locale.FRANCE, aDate)
%>
<BR/>
<%=
      JSPDateFormat.longFormat(Locale.FRANCE, aDate)
%>
<BR/>
<%=
      JSPDateFormat.mediumFormat(Locale.FRANCE, aDate)
%>
<BR/>
<%=
      JSPDateFormat.shortFormat(Locale.FRANCE, aDate)
%>
</BODY>
</HTML>
```

either a list object or an iterator (both from the collections package) and have a set of attributes that control the formatting itself. This set of parameters is controlled using set methods in the JSPListFormat class.

Listing 27-8 shows a number of uses for the list-formatting bean. The first scriptlet defines three lists: a list of strings, a list of integers, and an empty list. We define the list of integers so that we can demonstrate the combination of the list-formatting bean with the numeric-formatting bean

Figure 27-3

Formatted date
results

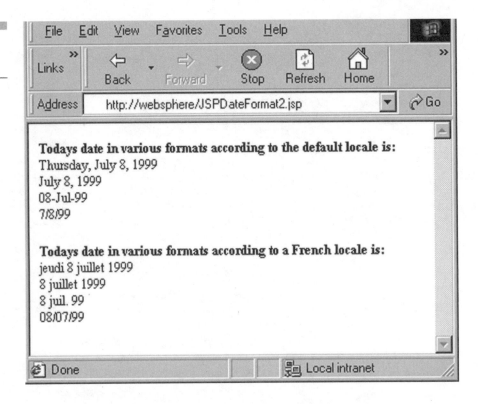

Address http://websphere/JSPDateFormat2.jsp

Todays date in various formats according to the default locale is:
Thursday, July 8, 1999
July 8, 1999
08-Jul-99
7/8/99

Todays date in various formats according to a French locale is:
jeudi 8 juillet 1999
8 juillet 1999
8 juil. 99
08/07/99

Listing 27-6

Formatting times
in a JSP

```
<HTML>
<BODY>
<%@ import="java.util.*,com.ibm.jsp.*" %>
<%
     Date aDate = new Date();
%>
<B>Todays date in various formats according to the default locale
is: </B><BR/>
<%=
     JSPTimeFormat.fullFormat(request, aDate)
%>
<BR/>
<%=
     JSPTimeFormat.longFormat(request, aDate)
%>
<BR/>
<%=
     JSPTimeFormat.mediumFormat(request, aDate)
%>
<BR/>
<%=
     JSPTimeFormat.shortFormat(request, aDate)
```

```
%>
<P>
<B>Todays date in various formats according to a French locale is:
</B><BR/>
<%=
        JSPTimeFormat.fullFormat(Locale.FRANCE, aDate)
%>
<BR/>
<%=
        JSPTimeFormat.longFormat(Locale.FRANCE, aDate)
%>
<BR/>
<%=
        JSPTimeFormat.mediumFormat(Locale.FRANCE, aDate)
%>
<BR/>
<%=
        JSPTimeFormat.shortFormat(Locale.FRANCE, aDate)
%>
</BODY>
</HTML>
```

Figure 27-4
Formatted time
results

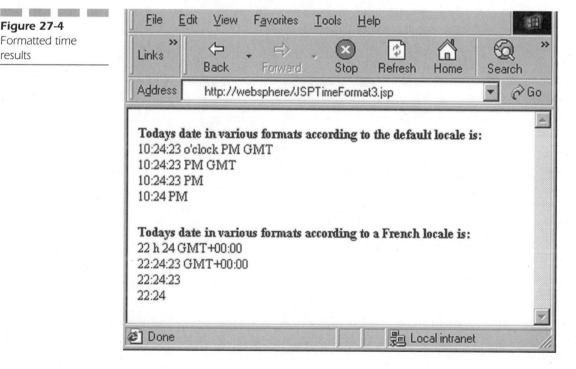

Listing 27-7
Numeric formats
in a JSP

```
<HTML>
<BODY>
<%@
import="java.util.*,com.ibm.jsp.*,com.sun.java.util.collections.*"
%>
<%
        List stringList = new ArrayList();
        for (inti = 1 ; i <= 10 ; i++)
                stringList.add("Element " + i);
        List intList = new ArrayList();
        for (inti = 1 ; i <= 10 ; i++)
                intList.add(new Integer(i));
        List emptyList = new ArrayList();

        JSPListFormat orderedFormat = new JSPListFormat();
        orderedFormat.setOrdered(true);
        orderedFormat.setEmptyListString("The list is empty!!");
        orderedFormat.setItemPrefix("- ");
        orderedFormat.setItemSuffix(" -");

        JSPListFormat unorderedFormat = new JSPListFormat();
        unorderedFormat.setOrdered(false);
        unorderedFormat.setGenerateListTag(true);
        unorderedFormat.setListPrefix("<B>");
        unorderedFormat.setListSuffix("</B>");
        unorderedFormat.setItemFormatBean("com.ibm.jsp.NumberFor-
matCurrency_US");
%>
<B>Ordered list with 10 string elements:</B><BR/>
<%=
        orderedFormat.format(request,stringList)
%>
<P>
<B>Unordered list with 10 number elements: </B><BR/>
<%=
        unorderedFormat.format(request, intList)
%>
<BR/>
<B>Empty list: </B><BR/>
<%=
        orderedFormat.format(request, emptyList)
%>
</BODY>
```

Figure 27-5
Formatted numbers, percentages, and currencies

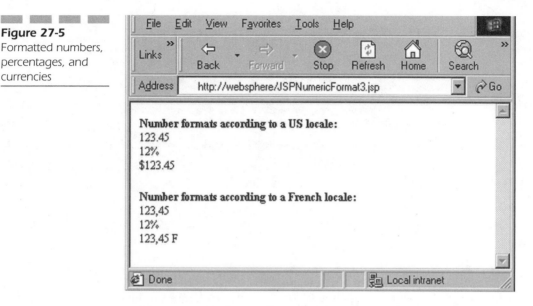

Number formats according to a US locale:
123.45
12%
$123.45

Number formats according to a French locale:
123,45
12%
123,45 F

Listing 27-8
Formatting lists

```
<HTML>
<BODY>
<%@ import="java.util.*,com.ibm.jsp.*,book.websphere.chapter28.*"
%>
<%@ implements="com.ibm.jsp.JSPTableRawDataGetter" %>
<bean
        name="dataBean"
        varname="theData"
        type="book.websphere.chapter28.ExampleBean1"
        introspect="no"
        create="yes"
        scope="request">
</bean>
<script runat=server>
        public Object[][] getTableRawData(Object object, Vec-
tortableFieldTokens) {
                ExampleBean1 myData = (ExampleBean1)object;
                Object[][] toRet = new Object[20][5];
                for (inti = 0 ; i < 20 ; i++) {
                        toRet[i][0] = myData.getId(i);
                        toRet[i][1] = myData.getName(i);
                        toRet[i][2] = myData.getModulus(i);
                        toRet[i][3] = myData.getDivide(i);
                        toRet[i][4] = new Integer(i);
                }
                return toRet;
        }
        public String[] getTableRawDataHeader(
                Object object, Vector tableFieldTokens, String
preferHeaders[]) {
                String[]myHeaders = {"ID", "Name", "Modulus",
"Divide", "Seq"};
                return ,myHeaders;
```

continues

Listing 27-8
Continued

```
        }
        public boolean acceptType(Class aClass) {
                return aClass == book.websphere.chapter28.Example-
        Bean1.class;
        }
</script>
<%
        JSPTableFormat aTableFormat = new JSPTableFormat();
        aTableFormat.setTableRawDataGetter(this);
        aTableFormat.setTableAttributes("BORDER");
        aTableFormat.setCaption("This HTML was generated by the JSP
Format Library");
        aTableFormat.setCaptionAttributes("align=bottom");
%>
<%= aTableFormat.format(request, theData) %>
</BODY>
</HTML>
```

to format each line in the list. Obviously, we can also use other formatters to format lines in the list. Once the lists are defined, we go ahead and create the list formatters and set their properties. The most important property is the one defining whether the list should be formatted as an OL or as a UL. The properties of the list-formatting beans are fairly self-explanatory. Note that when using setItemFormatBean in this example, we are defining the formatting bean that will be responsible for the formatting of each of the elements in the list. In our case, we are using a serialized bean. In the distribution of the library, there is a file called NumberFormatCurrency_US.ser that is a dump of a numeric-format bean with a set of parameters, enabling us to directly format each item in the list. Figure 27-6 shows the resulting list output.

Formatting Tables

At this point, we finally get to the apex of the formatting library. Because business applications rely on tabular representation of data probably more than any other representation, the formatting bean library has a thorough solution for creating HTML tables from JSP. This support is so comprehensive that the package even supplies a tool for generating the JSP code that later generates the HTML code. The rest of this chapter is devoted to the table-formatting bean.

The purpose of the table-formatting bean is to provide an object through which all attributes of an HTML table can be defined. Because a table (along with all of its cells, headers, columns, rows, and captions) has many

Figure 27-6
Formatted list output

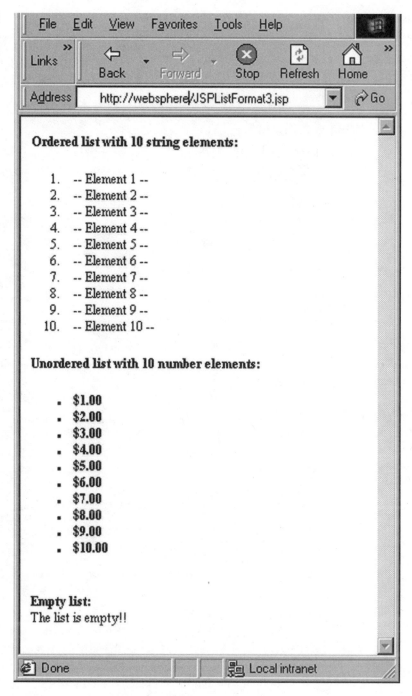

Listing 27-9
Using a
JSPTableFormat

```
<HTML>
<BODY>
<%@ import="java.util.*,com.ibm.jsp.*,book.websphere.chapter28.*"
%>
<%@ implements="com.ibm.jsp.JSPTableRawDataGetter" %>
<bean
        name="dataBean"
        varname="theData"
        type="book.websphere.chapter28.ExampleBean1"
        introspect="no"
        create="yes"
        scope="request">
</bean>
<script runat=server>
        public Object[][] getTableRawData(Object object, Vector
tableFieldTokens) {
                ExampleBean1 myData = (ExampleBean1)object;
                Object[][] toRet = new Object[20][4];
                for (int i = 0 ; i < 20 ; i++) {
                        toRet[i][0] = myData.getId(i);
                        toRet[i][1] = myData.getName(i);
                        toRet[i][2] = myData.getModulus(i);
                        toRet[i][3] = myData.getDivide(i);
                }
                return toRet;
        }
        public String[] getTableRawDataHeader(
                Object object, Vector tableFieldTokens, String
        preferHeaders[]) {
                String[] myHeaders = {"ID", "Name", "Modulus",
        "Divide"};
                return myHeaders;
        }
        public boolean acceptType(Class aClass) {
                return aClass == book.websphere.chapter28.Example-
        Bean1.class;
        }
</script>
<%
        JSPTableFormat aTableFormat =
(JSPTableFormat)JSPLookup.lookup(
        "book.websphere.chapter28.CustomizerExample");
%>
<%= aTableFormat.format(request, theData) %>
</BODY>
</HTML>
```

potential attributes, this formatter is quite complex. Let's look at a simple example. Listing 27-9 shows a JSP that is making use of the table-formatting object. We start the JSP with a number of directives that make the rest of the coding slightly simpler. Then, we include a BEAN tag for creating the data bean (a class that we have already used earlier in this chapter). Then, we implement a set of methods so that the servlet class itself will be the extractor of the data from the bean. The table formatter can work with a data object in a number of ways—one of which is through a `List` or `Iterator` object, and the other is through a *getter* object that returns an `Object[][]` from the data bean passed into the format method of the `JSPTableFormat`. Think of this getter object as an adapter that adapts between the data bean representation and the generic data model with which the `JSPTableFormat` object works. In our case, we simply build an array with 20 objects, each one being an array of five data items. This getter object also returns the set of strings to be used for the table headings. All of this part is embedded in a `SCRIPT` tag, because we want it included as a method of the generated servlet.

Next comes the actual formatting. We instantiate a formatting object and attach it to the getter—which is the generated servlet itself, in our case— hence, the `this`. Then, we set a few attributes that will affect the output. Finally, we call the format method, and (drum-roll...) up comes the browser showing Figure 27-7. While we definitely have worked harder now than when we constructed a similar output using the `REPEAT` tags, you should not be discouraged. The `REPEAT` tag is a simple solution, but it can only provide a primitive outcome. The `JSPTableFormat` can produce absolutely any possible output that is conceivable using an HTML table while still maintaining a simple API. In fact, the `JSPTableFormat` has `set` methods in which you can add ad-hoc HTML tags and thus fully control any presentation attribute of the table. Table 27-1 shows the possible `set` methods of the formatter so that you can appreciate to what extent you can fine-tune the result.

As is obvious from the detailed API that is provided by the formatting object, creating a good HTML table interface can be complicated. Also, the development cycle here is long (making a change involves changing your JSP file, saving the file, and reloading your browser with the page). You can understand why tables are not always all that pretty in HTML pages. In order to solve this inconvenience, the creators of the library at IBM went one step further. They include a tool in the package that you can use to build the table and customize it to your heart's content, then use your results in your JSP.

Let's look at this tool and use it to build a table that is more pleasant than the one in the previous example. In order to start the tool, make sure that the `collection.zip` and the `JSPFormatBeans.jar` archives are in your classpath, and start the tool in a DOS window (or in any other command-line window) by using the following command:

```
java com.ibm.jsp.customizer.FormatBeanCustomizer
```

The tool appears as shown in Figure 27-8. The tool divides the table into its individual elements, such as a `TableInfo`, a `HeaderRow`, a `HeaderName`,

Figure 27-7
Output generated
from a
JSPTableFormat

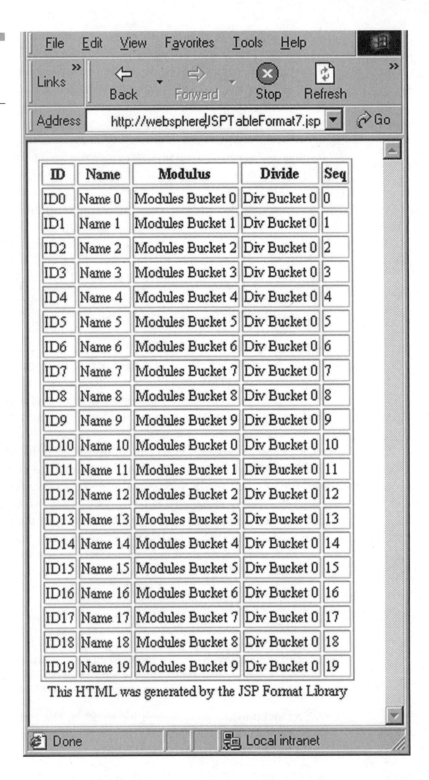

Table 27-1

JSPTableFormat
set methods

Method Signature	Used For
setCaption(String)	Defines the string for the table caption
setCaptionAttributes(String)	A string that is attached to the HTML caption tag. This string should be a legal HTML string, because it is attached as a part of the HTML.
setCaptionPrefix(String)	This string is embedded into the HTML page just before the table caption.
setCaptionSuffix(String)	This page is embedded into the HTML page just after the table caption.
setCellAttributes(int, int, String)	For a row and a column, set a string that is appended to the HTML that is defining the cell attributes.
setCellAttributes(String[][])	Same purpose as above, but instead of setting a single cell attribute, pass in a two-dimensional array for all cells
setCellPrefix(String[][])	For a row and a column, set a string that is appended to the HTML before the cell attributes.
setCellPrefix(String[][])	Same purpose as above, but instead of setting a single cell attribute, pass in a two-dimensional array for all cells
setCellSuffix(int, int, String)	For a row and a column, set a string that is appended to the HTML after the cell attributes.
setCellSuffix(String[][])	Same purpose as above, but instead of setting a single cell attribute, pass in a two-dimensional array for all cells
setColumnAttributes(int, String)	The string is added to the HTML, defining the attributes for the column at the index.
setColumnAttributes(String[])	Same as above, but pass in an array for all columns
setColumnPrefix(int, String)	The string defines the HTML that is inserted before the column definition at the index.
setColumnPrefix(String[])	Same as above, but for all columns

continues

Table 27-1

Continued

Method Signature	Used For
setColumnSuffix(int, String)	The string defines the HTML that is inserted after the column definition at the index.
setColumnSuffix(String[])	Same as above, but for all columns
setFields(String)	When the data bean supplies the data by using a set of indexed properties, this string can be used to define which properties to access. For example, if we could use the data bean of the previous figures, we could have used a string of the form *id,name,modulus, divide*, but we would not have had a sequence because the bean does not have such a property.
setFormatBeans(int, String)	Define what bean should be used to format entries at a certain column
setFormatBeans(String[])	Same as above, but for all columns
setFormatString(String)	Same as above, but using a single comma-delimited string
setHeaderAttributes(String)	This string is appended to the header tab for the table.
setHeaderCellAttributes (int, String)	This string is appended for the header cell at the specific location.
setHeaderCellAttributes(String[])	Same as above, but for all headers cells
setHeaderCellNames(int, String)	Set the name for the specific header.
setHeaderCellPrefix(int, String)	Set the prefix for the specific header.
setHeaderCellSuffix(int, String)	Set the suffix for the specific header.
setHeaderCellSuffix(String[])	Set all header suffixes.
setHeaderOn(boolean)	Set whether there should be a header or not. The default is yes.
setHeaderPrefix(String)	Set the prefix string.
setHeaderRepeatDistance(int)	Set the integer that determines how many rows before the header are repeated.
setHeaderSuffix(String)	Set the suffix string.

Method Signature	Used For
setMaximumUnexpressedHeader	Set the maximum number of rows Distance(int) that would be left at the end if we included a last header. For example, if we set this number to 2 and set the repeat distance to 4 and have 10 rows, we would only have two headers—one at the top, and one after 4 rows (the last chuck would be comprised of 6 rows). If, on the other hand, we have 11 rows, we would have 3 headers—one at the top, one after 4 rows, another after 4 more rows, and at the end, we would have 3 rows.
setOptionalHeaderNames(String)	A comma-delimited string for the header names
setRowAttributes(int, String)	A string appended to the TR tag at the specified location
setRowAttributes(String[])	Appended to all TR tags
setRowPrefix(int, String)	A string placed before the <TR> tags
setRowPrefix(String[])	Same as above for all rows
setRowSuffix(int, String)	A string placed after all the </TR> tags
setRowSuffix(String[])	Same as above for all rows
setTable Attributes(String)	A string added to the TABLE tag
setTablePrefix(String)	A string placed before the TABLE tag
setTableRawDataGetter (JSPTableRawDataGetter)	Set the object serving as the adapter between the data bean and the formatter.
setTableStyle(int)	Determines whether the headers are at the top, right, bottom, or left
setTableSuffix(String)	A string placed after the TABLE tag
setVectorFields(Vector)	Use the vector to specify the property names to use when extracting the data bean information.

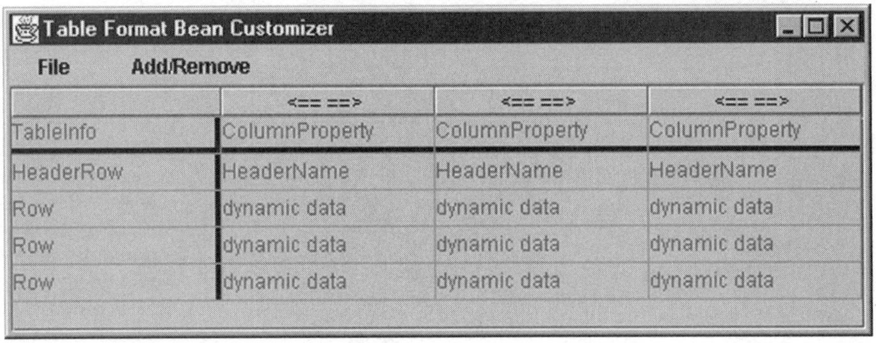

Figure 27-8
Starting the
customizer

a `ColumnProprty`, a `Row`, and `dynamic data`. Each of these elements can be customized by setting the properties. In addition, you might change the order of the columns or their sizes by using the row at the top (the labels of the Swing table). Finally, you can add a column or a row by using the actions on the menu bar of the application.

Most of the customization is done by changing properties of the elements. In order to open the property editors for each of the elements comprising the table, double-click the appropriate element in the table. Because each of the elements has slightly different properties, property editors do not always look the same. Some parts of the editors are common, such as the editors for defining colors associated with the elements.

Figure 27-9 shows the property editor for the `TableInfo` element. Through this editor, you can set all of the attributes that we already saw in the API that have to do with the table as a whole, including both visual and model-related properties. For example, you can set the header location for the table and set which data bean and data elements are used. You perform this action by pressing the Browse button and pointing the editor to the class file for your data bean. The tool then uses reflection to figure out the indexed properties of the data bean. Then, if you open the property editor for the columns, you can select which column will display which data element—as shown in Figure 27-10, which uses the data bean from earlier in the chapter.

Finally, once you have set all properties and have customized the table to look exactly the way you want it to look on the HTML page (refer to Figure 27-11), you are ready to make the table ready for deployment. From the main menu, select `Save as .ser file`. This option saves the formatter bean (along with all of your customizations) in a bean that is ready for use in a JSP. Place the file under the WebSphere servlets directory so that you can use the file later. Let's take our JSP from Figure 27-9 and modify it to use the serialized bean. This example is shown in Listing 27-10. The output is shown in Figure 27-12. This method is much simpler, right? Finally,

Figure 27-9
Property editor for
the `TableInfo`

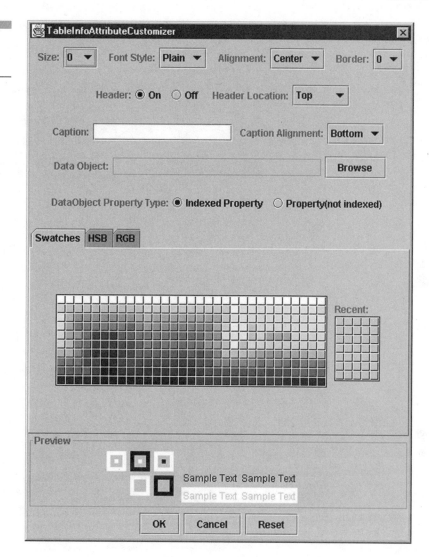

selecting "Verbose Save" from the tool's main menu generates a JSP that comments out the table attributes as JSP code, instead of creating a formatter. Part of the generated JSP (the part that is setting all of the table attributes) is shown in Listing 27-11.

Figure 27-10
Selecting the indexed
property from the
data bean

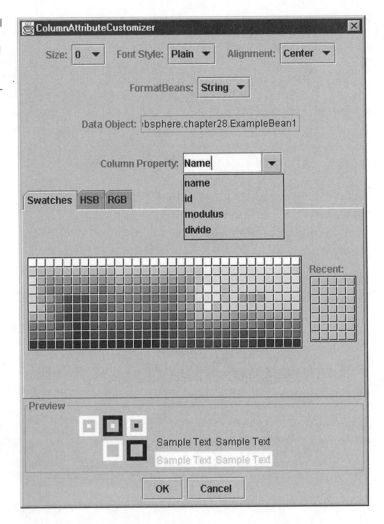

Figure 27-11
The Table Format
tool display

Table Format Bean Customizer

File	Add/Remove			
	<== ==>	<== ==>	<== ==>	<== ==>
TableInfo	id	name	modulus	divide
HeaderRow	HeaderName	HeaderName	HeaderName	HeaderName
Row	dynamic data	dynamic data	dynamic data	dynamic data
Row	dynamic data	dynamic data	dynamic data	dynamic data

Listing 27-10
Using the Formatter
bean in a JSP

```
JSPTableFormat jspTableFormat = new JSPTableFormat();


jspTableFormat.
        setTableAttributes(" BGCOLOR=#c8c8c8 ALIGN=CENTER
BORDER=0");
jspTableFormat.setHeaderOn(true);
jspTableFormat.setTableStyle(JSPTableFormat.DEFAULTHEADER_TABLESTYL
E);

jspTableFormat.setHeaderAttributes(" BGCOLOR=#c8c8c8
ALIGN=CENTER");
jspTableFormat.setHeaderRepeatDistance(2147483647);
jspTableFormat.setMaximumUnexpressedHeaderDistance(1);
jspTableFormat.setHeaderPrefix("<B>");
jspTableFormat.setHeaderSuffix("</B>");

String[] headerCellAttributes = new String[4];
headerCellAttributes[0]=" BGCOLOR=#c8c8c8 ALIGN=CENTER";
headerCellAttributes[1]=" BGCOLOR=#c8c8c8 ALIGN=CENTER";
headerCellAttributes[2]=" BGCOLOR=#c8c8c8 ALIGN=CENTER";
headerCellAttributes[3]=" BGCOLOR=#c8c8c8 ALIGN=CENTER";
jspTableFormat.setHeaderCellAttributes(headerCellAttributes);


String[] headerCellNames = new String[4];
headerCellNames[0]="HeaderName";
headerCellNames[1]="HeaderName";
headerCellNames[2]="HeaderName";
headerCellNames[3]="HeaderName";
jspTableFormat.setHeaderCellNames(headerCellNames);


Vector fields = new Vector();
fields.addElement("id");
fields.addElement("name");
fields.addElement("modulus");
fields.addElement("divide");
jspTableFormat.setVectorFields(fields);

String[][] cellAttributes = new String[2][4];
cellAttributes[0][0] = " BGCOLOR=#c8c8c8 ALIGN=CENTER";
cellAttributes[0][1] = " BGCOLOR=#c8c8c8 ALIGN=CENTER";
cellAttributes[0][2] = " BGCOLOR=#c8c8c8 ALIGN=CENTER";
cellAttributes[0][3] = " BGCOLOR=#c8c8c8 ALIGN=CENTER";

cellAttributes[1][0] = " BGCOLOR=#99ffff ALIGN=CENTER";
cellAttributes[1][1] = " BGCOLOR=#99ffff ALIGN=CENTER";
cellAttributes[1][2] = " BGCOLOR=#99ffff ALIGN=CENTER";
cellAttributes[1][3] = " BGCOLOR=#99ffff ALIGN=CENTER";

jspTableFormat.setCellAttributes(cellAttributes);
```

Figure 27-12
HTML table created
by Formatter bean

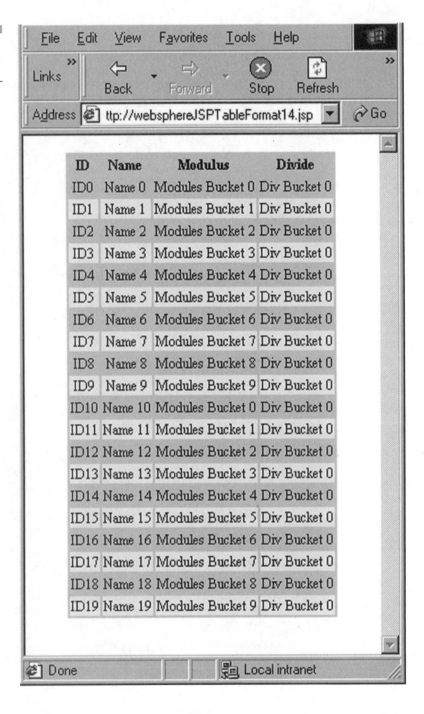

```
<HTML>
<BODY>
<%@ import="java.util.*,com.ibm.jsp.*" %>
<B>Number formats according to a US locale: </B><BR/>
<%=
        JSPNumberFormat.numberFormat(Locale.US, new Float(123.45))
%>
<BR/>
<%=
        JSPNumberFormat.percentFormat(Locale.US, new Float(0.12))
%>
<BR/>
<%=
        JSPNumberFormat.currencyFormat(Locale.US, new Float(123.45))
%>
<P>
<B>Number formats according to a French locale: </B><BR/>
<%=
        JSPNumberFormat.numberFormat(Locale.FRANCE, new
Float(123.45))
%>
<BR/>
<%=
        JSPNumberFormat.percentFormat(Locale.FRANCE, new
Float(0.12))
%>
<BR/>
<%=
        JSPNumberFormat.currencyFormat(Locale.FRANCE, new
Float(123.45))
%>
</BODY>
</HTML>
```

Debugging Servlets and JSPs Using VisualAge

The WebSphere runtime platform supports servlets and JSPs as one of the two primary application server models (the other being EJB). We have already seen quite a few examples of how servlets and JSPs are deployed under WebSphere. However, we have said very little regarding the development of these servlets and JSPs.

Although it is true that it is possible to develop servlets and JSPs using any development environment and even plain JDK (with TextPad or another good text editor), IBM's Java development environment, VisualAge for Java, offers a better environment for developing servlets and JSPs. The major difference is that VisualAge for Java has a built-in WebSphere test environment that can be activated from within the VisualAge *integrated development environment* (IDE); therefore, the program-test-debug cycle is all done from within the VisualAge IDE. The alternative is to build the servlets in some other Java IDE or using a text editor (or building the JSP pages using a site builder), and then install it in the WebSphere environment and view the results. The difference in development productivity can be considerable. In fact, in many cases, the difference in development time can be an order of magnitude.

Two main reasons for this difference exist: a unified environment and debugging tools. As we shall shortly see, when using VisualAge for Java's WebSphere test environment, the entire development cycle is done from within the VisualAge IDE. The coding, running, and testing can all be completed from the IDE without ever starting up the real WebSphere server or the administration tool. This means that everything is simpler and there is less overhead. In addition, if you are using the Enterprise edition of VisualAge for Java, the whole issue of version control and configuration management is automatically activated on the development cycle for the servlets.

The second major difference when using the WebSphere test environment is the set of debugging tools that is available. Normally, if you use another environment or an editor, the only way to know what is happening is to use a series of print commands that are then inspected to see what code is reached, what the variables' values are, and so on. When using the VisualAge IDE with the WebSphere test environment, the entire set of debugging tools available for any Java programs (and more) is available to the servlet and JSP developer. This means that we can insert breakpoints in the servlet code and have the WebSphere test environment stop at this breakpoint, allowing us to perform any action that we did when building a plain old Java application. Also, a new tool is added to the environment— the JSP execution monitor, which we will see later in the chapter.

Installing and Loading the Tools

The WebSphere test environment is an add-on to VisualAge for Java. If you are using Version 2 of VisualAge for Java, you must be sure Rollup2 is installed in your environment before you install the WebSphere test environment. If you are using Version 3, you will already have all you need. The installation process for Version 2 is not so trivial. First you must install Rollup2. After downloading the patch, unzip it *over* the files in the IDE directory (a little scary). Next, start up VisualAge—instead of starting up the IDE, this brings up a small dialog box informing you that the installation procedure will now continue. This takes quite a long time, so don't panic and end the task or halt the system. After the rollup is installed, install the enterprise update, including support for servlets and JSPs.

The next part of the installation involves the update including the WebSphere test environment. This installation is much simpler, quicker, and follows a normal installation procedure (with an installation wizard). As part of this second installation process, you will be asked to identify your Web server root. Because the WebSphere test environment knows how to serve up HTML and JSP pages in addition to running servlets, it must know where you want the document root to reside. If you have installed the regular WebSphere environment or plan to do so, we strongly recommend you use the same document root for the two environments. If you don't, you will constantly have to copy files back and forth. In fact, if you plan on installing both environments at approximately the same time, we suggest you first install WebSphere and install the update to VisualAge only when you know where the document root will be.

Next, you must load the appropriate projects into your environment. This is especially true if you are a developer in a team using the Enterprise product, in which case you need to load the projects from the main repository. Go ahead and select all projects that begin with "IBM JSP" or "IBM Servlet." Most importantly, don't forget to mark the project named "IBM WebSphere Test Environment." After you've completed the load, your workbench browser should include at least the projects marked in Figure 28-1. In addition, various menu items in your IDE will have changed, reflecting that you now have some additional tools at your disposal. Figure 28-2 shows such an example.

Figure 28-1
Workbench after
loading the
WebSphere test
environment

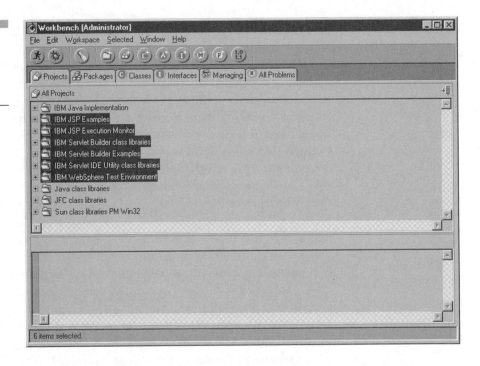

Figure 28-2
Additional tools
added to the IDE

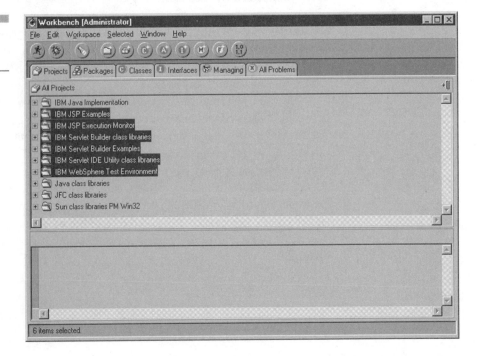

The WebSphere Test Environment

The WebSphere test environment is a slim Web server and application server that is integrated with the Visual Age for Java IDE. It allows you to deploy servlets under a Web server, serve up HTML pages, and process JSP pages, creating HTML pages that are propagated to the browser. It includes all the components necessary to be sure your servlet/JSP e-business application works correctly before you deploy it under WebSphere. The tools are conveniently packaged into the IDE, so activating them is very simple.

Although the WebSphere test environment is used for debugging both servlets and JSPs, the tools differ and the startup process is not always the same. In order to activate the servlet tool, you need only mark the servlet class in one of your IDE browsers and, using the right-button menu, select the Tools, Servlet Launcher, Launch option as shown in Figure 28-3. This starts the process of bringing up the server test environment.

Figure 28-3

Launching a servlet in the WebSphere test environment

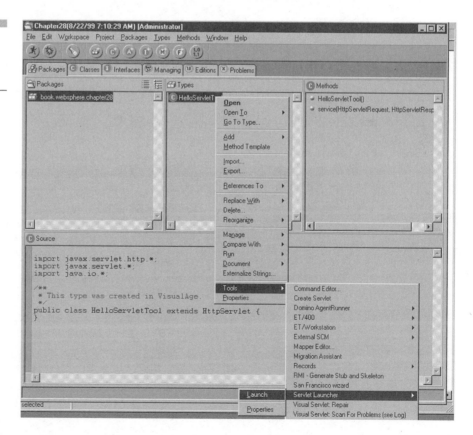

The first window to appear is the servlet launch parameter dialog box shown in Figure 28-4. This dialog box simulates the session that would typically occur when accessing a servlet from a browser and allows you to set the URL and the parameters passed into the servlet. Note that the port is set to 8080—the default port used by the test environment. Note that because a WebSphere deployment usually uses port 80, it is no problem to simultaneously run both a WebSphere server and the test environment.

Figure 28-4
Servlet launch
parameters

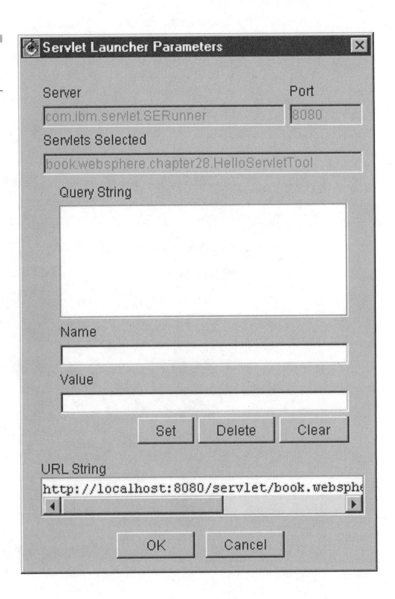

Next, the test environment window comes up as shown in Figure 28-5. There is not much you can do with this window except to stop the test server. In addition, the console is brought up and a lot of information is written to it (Figure 28-6). A lot is printed out to the console—practically any property that the server assumes. Therefore, this printing takes a while and you should not be concerned that something is wrong. Because you have asked to launch a servlet, the test environment goes one step further—it launches a browser window that accesses the servlet, as shown in Figure 28-7. This in turn causes more output specific to the servlet invocation to appear in the console (Figure 28-8). Once again, this takes a long time, so don't be alarmed—wait patiently. Note that in Figure 28-7, the URL used is `http://127.0.0.1:8080/servlet/book.websphere.chapter28.HelloServletTool`. There are three things that deserve mention. First, note that the address used is always the one assigned to the local host— that is, the machine running the IDE. This does not mean you cannot access a servlet running in someone else's IDE, but it is not typical. As mentioned, the server is accessed on port 8080. Finally, note that because the test environment does not require registration with the server (similar to the process that we usually do in the servlet configuration page of the Web-Sphere administration tool), the path to the servlet always uses the package qualified class name—assuring a unique mapping to our servlets.

Figure 28-5
The WebSphere test environment window

Figure 28-6
Test environment
printout to the
console

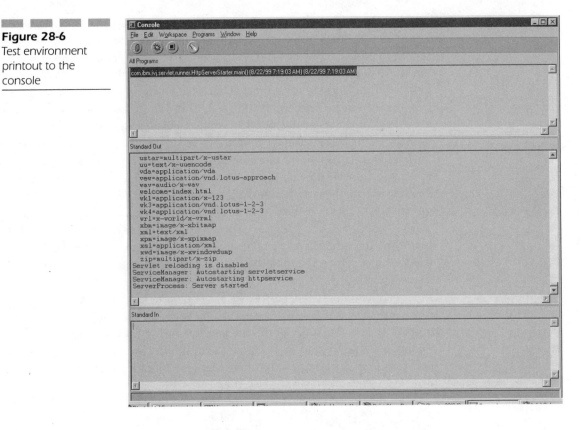

Figure 28-7
Automatic invocation
from browser

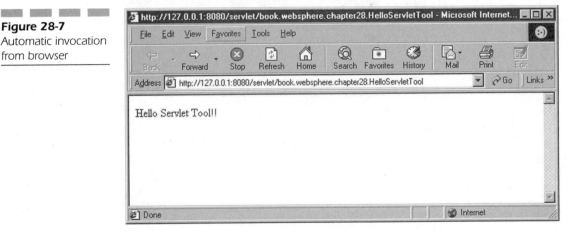

Figure 28-8

Servlet activation
printout to the
console

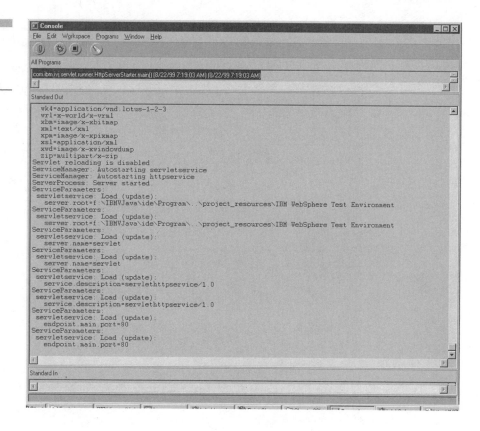

Note that it is possible to start up the test environment without launching a servlet. This is done by running the `main` method of the `SERunner` class in the `com.ibm.servlet` package in the IBM WebSphere Test Environment project, as shown in Figure 28-9.

Debugging Servlets

After you've managed to install, load, and start up the test environment, the rest is easy. The beauty of this environment is that all the IDE tools are now available for debugging the servlet. Most importantly, you can insert breakpoints, inspect variables, and so on. Figure 28-10 shows the browser after a breakpoint has been inserted in the `service` method. The next time the servlet is accessed (for example, by clicking the Refresh or Reload button on

Figure 28-9

Starting the test
server using
SERunner

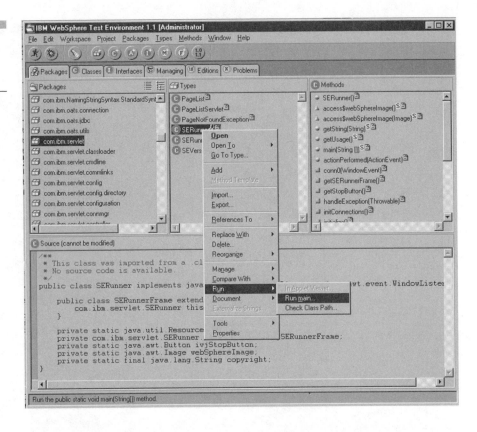

Figure 28-10

Breakpoint inserted
into the service
method

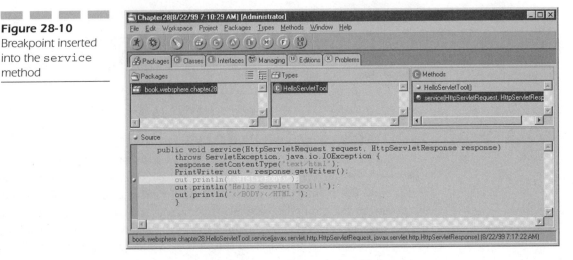

Figure 28-11
Debugger opened
following servlet
access

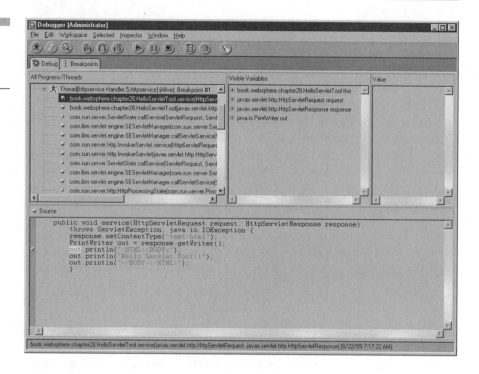

the browser), the test environment starts executing the servlet and comes across the breakpoint, immediately bringing up the debugger, as shown in Figure 28-11. While in the debugger, you are free to do anything you usually do in the IDE—for example, you can inspect any object reachable from the debugger. Figure 28-12 is an example, showing the request object.

Debugging JSPs

Now for the tools available for JSP debugging. The first thing to do when debugging JSPs is to start the test server. In this case, the simplest way is to start the server from the SERunner class (unless the server is already up because of a previous debugging session). Next, start up the execution monitor from one of your IDE browsers, as shown in Figure 28-13. A dialog box shown in Figure 28-14 will prompt you for an internal port number and will allow you to decide whether you want to enable JSP execution and whether

Figure 28-12
Inspector on the
HTTP request object

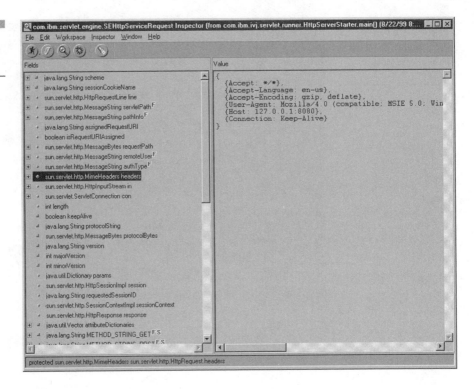

you want syntax error to be trapped. After the test server is up and running, you may open up your browser and access the JSP. Don't forget that the URL must include the 8080 port. Yes—it is a bit confusing; after all, we did use 8082 when starting the JSP execution monitor. However, the test server is listening on port 8080, so access must be performed through that port. The test server then delegates to the JSP execution monitor using the internal port.

Figure 28-13
Starting the JSP
Execution Monitor

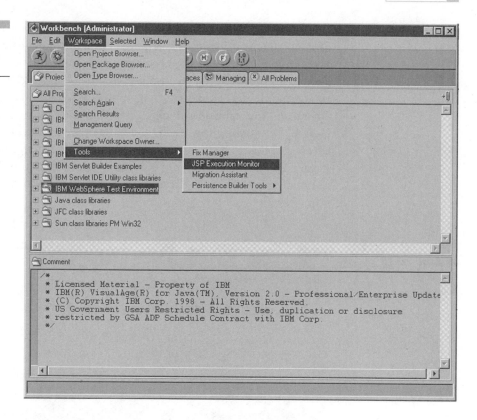

Figure 28-14
JSP Execution
Monitor startup
dialog box

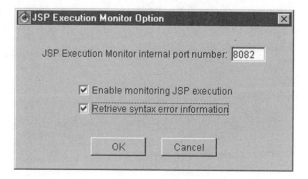

Figure 28-15 shows the JSP Execution Monitor window with our trivial JSP. The monitor includes four panes—a pane showing the JSPs that have been launched through the browser, a pane showing the JSP source, a pane showing the Java code compiled by the JSP engine (pageCompile— remember?), and a pane showing the HTML generated after invoking the Java code. You can control which panes are actually visible and which are closed. The monitor is itself a debugger of sorts, allowing you to step through the Java code and see how the HTML is generated as a result (see Figure 28-16). Although this monitor is nowhere as complete as the VisualAge debugger, it beats the trial-and-error approach we would need to use otherwise.

Figure 28-15
JSP Execution
Monitor

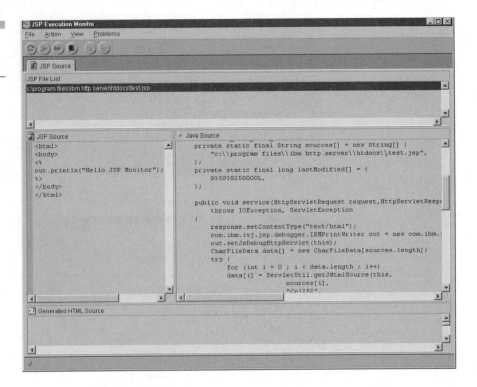

Figure 28-16

Stepping through
the JSP

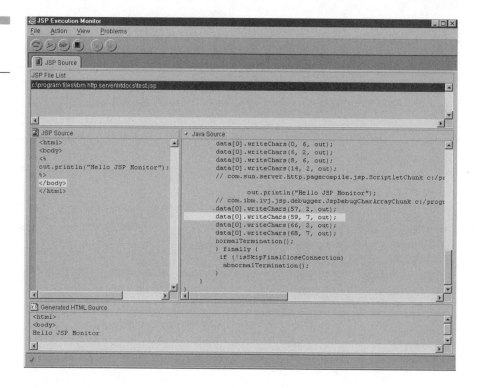

29

WebSphere EJB Server

In previous chapters, we became acquainted with EJBs. The WebSphere EJB server is where EJBs live. This server is essentially a middle tier in WebSphere's own multi-tier architecture, acting as a bridge between the EJB clients (whether these are JSPs, servlets, or Java applications) and the actual data source, which is usually an RDBMS.

The Bigger Picture

Before focusing on the EJB server, let's take a step back to see how this server fits into the bigger picture. The typical usage scenario for a WebSphere-based application would be one where the end user uses an HTTP-based client. This client would usually be a standard Internet browser (such as Microsoft Internet Explorer®. The client would connect to the WebSphere application server, which would do the processing-interacting with some database server that holds the relevant data. Figure 29-1 shows a schematic view of this three-tier architecture.

The rationale behind having a three-tier architecture was already reviewed in previous chapters. As a reminder, we will note that the main advantage of this architecture is that it enables separating the business rules from the user-interface logic and from the database. Obviously, the architecture shown in Figure 29-1 does not enable separating business rules from user-interface logic, because both are actually part of the WebSphere application server. In reality, the WebSphere Application Server itself is multi-tiered, with one of these tiers being the EJB server. Figure 29-2 provides a zoomed-in view of the architecture shown in Figure 29-1. Figure 29-3 shows a different architecture, where the client is not HTTP-

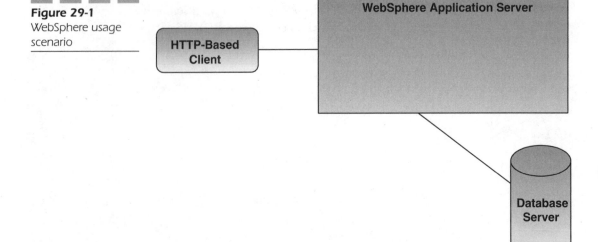

Figure 29-1
WebSphere usage scenario

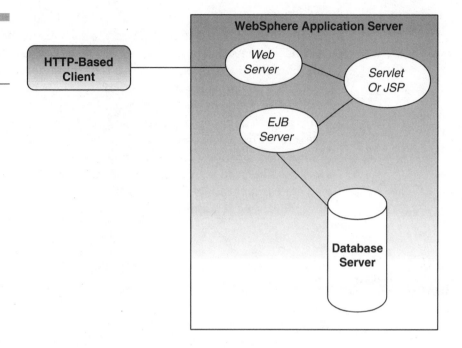

Figure 29-2
WebSphere usage
scenario zoomed-
in view

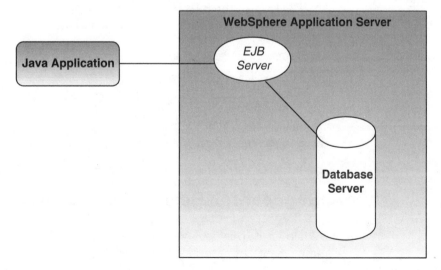

Figure 29-3
Three-tier architecture
with Java Application

based and instead is a Java application. As you can see in both figures, the players in the EJB environment are the EJB client, EJB server, and the database. As mentioned in Chapter 5, "Hello EJBs," the EJB server contains one or more EJB containers. An EJB container holds and runs one or more EJBs and provides the execution environment for them.

Obviously, when developing a WebSphere application, you do not necessarily have to go through the trouble of using EJBs. You can use the database directly from your JSP or servlets (which is actually what we did in the examples in previous chapters when illustrating the use of JSP and servlets). The need for EJBs stems from the inherent complexity of large distributed applications, which require three-tiered or *n*-tiered architectures. This issue is addressed in the next chapter.

EJB Server Roles

WebSphere includes two variants of the EJB server. The WebSphere Advanced Application Server product includes the basic EJB server, while the Enterprise Application Server includes both this basic EJB server and a slightly more advanced EJB server that is part of Component Broker. Following the convention of IBM's WebSphere documentation, we will refer to the basic server as *AE EJB Server*, and we will refer to the more advanced server as *CB EJB Server*.

The roles of the EJB server are as follows:

- Support for Bean deployment
- Support for transactions
- Support for persistence
- Support for workload management
- Support for pooling and caching
- Support for security

Support for Bean Deployment

When an EJB is deployed, the EJB container creates several classes that implement the interfaces required for the bean, along with any stub or skeleton classes that are required for RMI. For entity beans, the deployment process also includes treatment of the bean persistency.

In order to facilitate the deployment process, the bean developer must create a deployment description that defines the properties of the specific bean. This deployment descriptor is packaged along with the other components of the bean into the EJB JAR file, as briefly reviewed in Chapter 5.

The deployment descriptor and an in-depth review of the deployment process are provided as follows later in this chapter.

Support for Transactions

Transactions are useful abstractions when designing and implementing distributed applications. EJBs have built-in transactional support that is provided by the EJB container. The author of the EJB can specify the kind of transactional support required (one of the options is no transactional support), and this decision is communicated to the EJB container through the deployment descriptor that is associated with the bean. Chapter 31, "EJB Persistence and Transactions in WebSphere," explores the details of support for transactions.

Support for Persistence

As explained in Chapter 11, "Enterprise Java Beans," there are two kinds of EJBs: session beans and entity beans. The former are short lived and are intended to encapsulate data related to a single session with a single client, whereas the latter are relatively long lived and encapsulate data that is persistent (i.e., is stored in a database).

Persistence support is required only for entity beans. The WebSphere EJB makes sure that the data associated with entity beans mirrors the current state of the database. To that end, it makes use of the transactional support to retrieve data from the database and modify the data as needed. Chapter 31 goes into more detail relating to EJB persistence.

You should note that entity beans have two kinds of persistency: *Container-Managed Persistency* (CMP) and *Bean-Managed Persistency* (BMP). Entity beans with CMP do not need to specify how to manipulate the underlying database; instead, the EJB container manages this task automatically. In contrast, entity beans with BMP contain code that interacts with the underlying database.

Support for Workload Management

In order to promote scalability, the WebSphere EJB server enables you to group several EJB servers into a server group. A server group appears to be a single EJB server as far as clients are concerned, while in reality, the workload is distributed as evenly as possible among the EJB servers that are participating in the group.

The definition of server groups is handled by the WebSphere administration tools and is covered in Chapter 40, "The WebSphere Administration Console."

Pooling and Caching

The EJB server provides two mechanisms aimed at boosting the performance of single EJBs: pooling and caching.

Pooling is essentially sharing resources. Database connection pooling is used to minimize the overhead of a database connection for a single operation by reusing a pool of existing connections. By doing so, when an EJB requires database connection, the EJB avoids the overhead of establishing the connection. This feature is particularly useful, because in the context of EJBs, database connections are made frequently-but the transactions are typically short. Another advantage of connection pooling is that it enables you to control the maximum number of concurrent database connections. This feature can come in handy if your database product places some limit on the number of connections.

In the same way, the EJB server implements thread pooling (and in some cases, EJB instance pooling)-both of which are performed in order to improve efficiency.

Another technique used to improve efficiency is caching. Caching is a well-known concept that essentially involves trading memory for time. The EJB server caches the state information of EJBs to speed up their creation.

In order to have more memory, the EJB server can temporarily swap out an EJB. In order to do so, it performs instance passivation. Note that for entity beans, the same mechanism is used for synchronizing the bean with the underlying database.

Security

Security considerations play a central role in enterprise computing, and EJBs are no exception. In many cases, EJBs are used to encapsulate sensitive data; therefore, security aspects are critical.

Access to EJBs in the EJB server depends on the security settings that are made by the administrator. A detailed discussion of these settings is described in Chapter 42, "Administering WebSphere Security."

To complete our discussion here, you should note that the EJB server requires authentication of users, and a user can only invoke EJB methods for which he or she has the required permissions.

Tiered Applications in WebSphere

As explained in the first chapter, the WebSphere Application Server Advanced Edition is aimed at medium to high-end eBusiness applications. Such applications require transactional support (including graceful handling of failures) as well as complex processing. In order to meet this requirement, as well as others, the application server provides support for EJBs.

Although virtually any Web-based application is multitiered (just the Web browser and the server provide two tiers, and usually there is some database involved as well), using EJBs, it is possible to go even further with the idea of multiple tiers. Although EJBs are server-side entities, they can at the same time be clients of other EJBs.

A typical tiered application in WebSphere is composed of the following elements:

- *Presentation*   HTML pages, JSP, servlets
- *Business Logic*   EJBs
- *Data Repository*   A relational database

User interaction is handled through the presentation layer. This is not necessarily to say there are no "business rules" encapsulated in this layer. The presentation layer can channel user interaction in some ways in order to make it comply with the needs of the application.

The middle tier is implemented through EJBs. The flexibility of the EJB architecture allows us to generate multiple middle tiers by using several layers of EJBs. This is suitable for complex applications, where multiple layers are required either for modularity, reliability, or performance. In the case of complex logic, which would produce an EJB class to large to handle, it makes sense to promote modularity and break it up into several EJBs. Using several EJBs doesn't imply multiple layers, but in order to simplify client-side programming, it is convenient to provide a well-defined entry point; that is, one or a small number of EJBs providing the interface to the middle tier.

In order to illustrate this idea, recall the ticker servlet example from Chapter 23, "HTTP Servlets." In continuation of the hypothetical scenario stated in that chapter, let's say that Ticker.com decides to go into the business of online trading, leveraging the success of the stock notification service.

Given the fact that this kind of service must provide high reliability, a simple architecture such as the one used for the ticker servlet is not sufficient. Instead, we'll look at an EJB-based solution that will be laid out in the following chapters. Before delving into its details, let's define the problem more accurately.

The online trading program allows the user to feed orders and to review his portfolio. An order is made up of the following components:

- *Stock*   Given by its ticker symbol
- *Quantity*   The amount of stocks to be purchased or sold (a positive number indicates buying, and a negative number indicates selling)
- *Price limit*   A price at which to make the trade or "market" (which means take whatever price the market is at the time of execution)
- *Time limit*   Date and time until which the order is valid

After the user confirms his orders, they go into the system. After a trade is carried out, the result is registered in the user portfolio, which he can review later on.

The application implementation will be based on two servlets: the first `OrderServlet` is responsible for placing orders, whereas the second `PortfolioServlet` allows the user to review its current portfolio. In a real-world application, these two servlets should be wrapped by a lot of fancy HTML interfaces, but we'll omit those in the interest of brevity.

The actual "business logic" is implemented by several EJBs:

- *Trade*   An entity bean representing the trade
- *Portfolio*   An entity bean representing a customer portfolio
- *Quote*   A session bean that provides a quote service (that is, gives the current price on a stock)

One more component should be a daemon server that goes over the trades and initiates them when the limit is reached. We encapsulate the actual placement of the trade in the Trade bean.

The diagram in Figure 30-1 shows the structure of the application. Note how the `OrderServlet` interacts with the Trade bean and with the Portfolio bean in order to place a trade, whereas the `PortfolioServlet` uses the Portfolio bean, which in turn uses the `Quote` bean, to show the customer the current value of his portfolio.

The data repository tier for this application consists of two database tables, one for trades and one for portfolios. The portfolio table has the following columns:

- CUSTNAME—Customer name
- TICKER—Stock ticker symbol
- QUANTITY—Number of stocks
- LASTTRADE—Date of last trade

Figure 30-1
Online trading
application
architecture

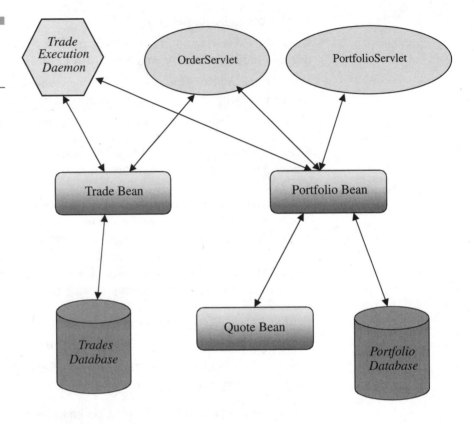

The trade table has the following columns:

- CUSTOMER—Customer requesting the trade
- TICKER—Stock ticker symbol
- QUANTITY—Number of stocks
- PRICELIMIT—Price limit (0 represents "market")
- TIMELIMIT—Time of day limit
- DATELIMIT—Time limit date

Note that these tables need not be created unless we are using what is called "bean-managed" persistency. Otherwise, the EJB container implicitly creates the tables.

In the following three chapters, this sample application is used to provide examples. Chapter 31, "EJB Persistence and Transactions in WebSphere," focuses on persistency and transactional aspects. Chapter 32, "EJB Server-Side Code" reviews EJB implemention, and Chapter 33, "EJB Client Code," goes into the details of client-side programming with EJBs.

EJB Persistence and Transactions in WebSphere

This chapter focuses on two important aspects of EJB programming; namely, persistence and transactional support. These two issues are central to bean programming. In most cases they go hand in hand because more often than not, transactions are used for performing database updates. For both persistence and transactions, the EJB specification allows leaving the details to the EJB container. In the case of persistency, there is the notion of *Container Managed Persistence* (CMP), which allows the bean programmer to delegate the task of managing persistent data to the EJB container. This is in contrast to *Bean Managed Persistence* (BMP), in which the bean itself manages persistent data. Similarly, it is possible to delegate transactional behavior to the container using the attributes in the deployment descriptor for transactions. Conversely, the bean programmer can manage transactions at the bean level or even have the EJB client involved in management transactions.

EJB Persistence

By definition, entity beans are used to encapsulate and maintain persistent data. In order to store data, entity beans store their data in a "data source," which usually is a database.

In order to illustrate the issue of persistency in WebSphere, we will consider two examples of beans, one with CMP and one with BMP.

Example of Container-Managed Persistence

For the purpose of this example, consider the Trade bean from the Ticker online trading application described in the previous chapter. For simplicity, assume that each customer can only place one trade on one stock. This guarantees that the combination of the customer and the stock name constitutes a unique key for trades. The `TradePK` class defined in Listing 31-1 represents this key.

Listing 31-1
Class TradePK

```
package com.ticker;

public class TradePK implements java.io.Serializable
{
```

```
        public String customerName;
        public String tickerSymbol;
}
```

Listing 31-2
Trade remote
interface

```
package com.ticker;

import java.util.*;
import java.rmi.RemoteException;
import javax.ejb.*;

public interface Trade extends EJBObject
{
        public String    getCustomerName() throws RemoteException;
        public String    getTickerSymbol() throws RemoteException;
        public int  getQuantity() throws RemoteException;
        public int  getPriceLimit() throws RemoteException;
        public Date getDateLimit() throws RemoteException;
        public Time getTimeLimit() throws RemoteException;

        public void setPriceLimit(int plimit) throws
                                        RemoteException;
        public void setQuantity(int qty) throws RemoteException;
        public void setDateLimit(Date dlimit) throws
                                        RemoteException;
        public void setTimeLimit(Time tlimit) throws
                                        RemoteException;
}
```

The remote interface to the Trade bean, shown in Listing 31-2, provides standard JavaBean `get` and `set` methods. We do not provide set methods for the attributes comprising the key because modifying them changes the identity of the bean.

Listing 31-3 shows the home interface for the Trade bean. This interface includes the `create` method. Note that the `ejbCreate` method defined later in the implementation class returns a different value; namely, an instance of the bean's primary key class (in this case `TradePK`). Another method in this interface is `findByPrimaryKey`. This method finds an instance of the bean given the primary key, and its implementation is the container's responsibility. For the last method, the situation becomes more interesting. The purpose of this method is to find trades given the associated customer. The returned value is a `java.util.Enumeration` because

Listing 31-3
Trade home interface

```
package com.ticker;

import java.util.*;
import java.rmi.RemoteException;
import javax.ejb.*;

public interface TradeHome extends EJBHome
{
        public Trade  create(String customerName, String tickerSym,
                int qty, int plimit, Date dlimit, Time tlimit)
                        throws RemoteException, CreateException;
        public Trade  findByPrimaryKey(TradePK key)
                        throws RemoteException, FinderException;
        public Enumeration findByCustomerName(String customerName)
                        throws RemoteException, FinderException;

};
```

Listing 31-4
Trade finder logic

```
public interface TradeBeanFinderHelper
{
        String findByCustomerNameQueryString =
            "select * from ejb.tradebeantbl where customerName = ?";
}
```

there might be more than one object returned. The container cannot understand that from the method signature, so we must provide some more information. This information is supplied in the form of a "finder helper" interface, which essentially spells out to the container the finder logic. Listing 31-4 shows the finder helper class for our example. This example demonstrates that the finder logic is specified through an interface called `<bean-name>BeanFinderHelper`, and that it should be contained in a string constant called `<find-method-name>QueryString`. This string contains question marks that represent variables. These are to be replaced with the actual values of the finder method arguments. The fields of the implementation class can be used in the query string. The query string in the example uses `customerName` defined in the implementation class shown in Listing 31-5. Note that the table name is `ejb.<bean-name>tbl` with the bean name given in lower-case letters.

Listing 31-5
Trade
implementation class

```
package com.ticker;

import java.util.*;
import java.rmi.RemoteException;
import javax.ejb.*;
import java.io.Serializable;

public class TradeBean implements EntityBean
{
    transient protected EntityContext context;
    public String customerName;
    public String tickerSymbol;
    public int    priceLimit;
    public int    quantity;
    public Time   timeLimit;
    public Date   dateLimit;

    public void ejbActivate()
    {
    }

    public void ejbPassivate()
    {
    }

    public void ejbLoad()
    {
    }

    public void ejbStore()
    {
    }

    public void ejbRemove()
    {
    }

    public void setEntityContext(EntityContext ctx)
    {
        context = ctx;
    }

    public void unsetEntityContext()
    {
        context = null;
    }

    public void ejbPostCreate(String cname, String tsym,
                    int qty, int pl,
                    Date dlimit, Time tlimit)
    {
    }

    public TradePK ejbCreate(String cname, String tsym, int qty,
                    int pl,
                    Date dlimit, Time tlimit)
    {
```

continues

Listing 31-5
Continued

```
        customerName = cname;
        tickerSymbol = tsym;
        quantity = qty;
        priceLimit = pl;
        dateLimit = dlimit;
        timeLimit = tlimit;

        TradePK key = new TradePK();
        key.customerName = cname;
        key.tickerSymbol = tsym;

        return key;
}

public String      getCustomerName()
{
        return customerName;
}

public String      getTickerSymbol()
{
        return tickerSymbol;
}

public int        getPriceLimit()
{
        return priceLimit;
}


public int        getQuantity()
{
        return quantity;
}

public Date        getDateLimit()
{
        return dateLimit;
}

public Time        getTimeLimit()
{
        return timeLimit;
}

public void        setPriceLimit(int limit)
{
        priceLimit = limit;
}

public void        setQuantity(int qty)
{
        quantity = qty;
}

public void        setDateLimit(Date dlimit)
{
        dateLimit = dlimit;
```

```
        }

        public void      setTimeLimit(Time tlimit)
        {
            timeLimit = tlimit;
        }
}
```

The bean implementation class must define the bean fields as public so the container can access them. This class includes several methods that have empty implementations because the actual work they are intended to do is done by the EJB container. These methods are `ejbActivate`, `ejbPassivate`, `ejbRemote`, `ejbLoad`, `ejbStore`, and `ejbPostCreate`. Just in case you were wondering, you can add code there because these methods are called when the respective events take place.

As you can see for yourself, the persistence code for this bean is very easy to come by because it is just a handful of empty methods. When you opt for BMP, you have to provide special-purpose code, as shown in Listing 31-6.

Listing 31-6
Trade
implementation class
for BMP

```
package com.ticker;

import java.util.*;
import java.rmi.RemoteException;
import javax.ejb.*;
import java.io.Serializable;

public class TradeBean implements EntityBean
{
    transient protected EntityContext context;
    private String customerName;
    private String tickerSymbol;
    private int    priceLimit;
    private int    quantity;
    private Time    timeLimit;
    private Date    dateLimit;

    private DataSource ds;

    public void ejbActivate()
    {
    }

    public void ejbPassivate()
    {
    }

    public void ejbLoad()
```

continues

Listing 31-6
Continued

```
{
        TradePK key = (TradePK) ctx.getPrimaryKey();
        customerName = key.customerName;
        tickerSymbol = key.tickerSymbol;

        String query =  "select * from TRADES set " +
                "where CUSTOMER = '", + customerName + "','" +
                "TICKER = '" + tickerSymbol + "'";
        Connection con = ds.getConnection("db2admin",
                                        "db2passwd");
        Statement stmt = c.createStatement();
        ResultSet rs =  stmt.executeQuery(query);
        boolean more = rs.next();
        if (more) {
            quantity = rs.getInt(2);
            priceLimit = rs.getInt(3);
            dateLimit = rs.getString(4);
            timeLimit = rs.getString(5);
        }
        rs.close();
        stmt.close();
        con.close();
}

public void ejbStore()
{
        String query =  "update TRADES set " +
                "QUANTITY = ", + quantity + ",PRICELIMIT = " +
                priceLimit + ",TIMELIMIT = '", timeLimit +
                "',DATELIMIT = '",  + dateLimit + "'";
                "where CUSTOMER = '", + customerName + "','" +
                "TICKER = '" + tickerSymbol + "'";

        Connection con = ds.getConnection("db2admin",
                                        "db2passwd");
        Statement stmt = c.createStatement();
        int count = stmt.executeUpdate(query);
        stmt.close();
        con.close();
}

public void ejbRemove()
{
        String query = "delete from TRADES where " +
                "CUSTOMER = '", + customerName + "','" +
                "TICKER = '" + tickerSymbol + "'";

        Connection con = ds.getConnection("db2admin",
                                        "db2passwd");
        Statement stmt = c.createStatement();
        int count = stmt.executeUpdate(query);
        stmt.close();
        con.close();
}

public void setEntityContext(EntityContext ctx)
{
```

```
        context = ctx;
        ds = (DataSource) ctx.lookup("jdbc/mydb");
}

public void unsetEntityContext()
{
        context = null;
        ds = null;
}

public void ejbPostCreate(String cname, String tsym, int qty,
                int plimit, Date dlimit, Time tlimit)
{
}

public TradePK ejbCreate(String cname, String tsym, int qty,
                int plimit, Date dlimit, Time tlimit)
{
        customerName = cname;
        tickerSymbol = tsym;
        quantity = qty;
        dateLimit = dlimit;
        timeLimit = tlimit;
        priceLimit = plimit;

        TradePK key = new TradePK();
        key.customerName = cname;
        key.tickerSymbol = tsym;

        String query =  "insert into TRADES (CUSTOMER, TICKER, "
                +"QUANTITY, PRICELIMIT, TIMELIMIT, DATELIMIT)"
                +"values ('" + customerName + "','" +
                tickerSymbol + "'," + quantity + "," +
                priceLimit + ",'", timeLimit + "','",  +
                dateLimit + "')";

        Connection con = ds.getConnection("db2admin",
                                          "db2passwd");
        Statement stmt = c.createStatement();
        int count = stmt.executeUpdate(query);
        stmt.close();
        con.close();

        return key;
}

public TradePK ejbFindByPrimaryKey(TradePK key)
{
        String cName = key.customerName;
        String tSymbol = key.tickerSymbol;

        String query =  "select * from TRADES set " +
                "where CUSTOMER = '", + cName + "','" +
                "TICKER = '" + tSymbol + "'";
        Connection con = ds.getConnection("db2admin",
                                          "db2passwd");
```

continues

Listing 31-6
Continued

```
    Statement stmt = c.createStatement();
    ResultSet rs =  stmt.executeQuery(query);
    boolean more = rs.next();
    boolean toomany = false;
    if (more)
        boolean toomany = rs.next();;
    rs.close();
    stmt.close();
    con.close();
    if (more)
    {
        if (toomany) {
            throw new FinderException("Too many rows");
        }
        else {
            return key;
        }
    }
    else {
        throw new FinderException("Not found");
    }
}

public Enumeration ejbFindByCustomerName(String cName)
{
    String query =  "select * from TRADES set " +
            "where CUSTOMER = '", + cName + "'";
    Connection con = ds.getConnection("db2admin",
                                    "db2passwd");
    Statement stmt = c.createStatement();
    ResultSet rs =  stmt.executeQuery(query);

    Vector v = new Vector;
    TradePK key;
    boolean more = rs.next();

    while (more) {
        key = newTradePK;
        pk.customerName = cname;
        pk.tickerSymbol = rs.getString(1);
        v.addElement(key);
        more = rs.next();
    }
    rs.close();
    stmt.close();
    con.close();
    reutrn v.elements();
}

public String      getCustomerName()
{
    return customerName;
}

public String      getTickerSymbol()
{
    return tickerSymbol;
```

```
    }

    public int      getPriceLimit()
    {
        return priceLimit;
    }

    public int      getQuantity()
    {
        return quantity;
    }

    public Date     getDateLimit()
    {
        return dateLimit;
    }

    public Time     getTimeLimit()
    {
        return timeLimit;
    }

    public int      setPriceLimit(int plimit)
    {
        priceLimit = plimit;
    }

    public void     setQuantity(int qty)
    {
        quantity = qty;
    }

    public void     setDateLimit(Date dlimit)
    {
        dateLimit = dlimit;
    }

    public void     setTimeLimit(Time tlimit)
    {
        timeLimit = tlimit;
    }
}
```

One last thing to keep in mind is that during bean deployment, you should specify all the fields of the bean as container-managed in order to inform the container this is indeed a CMP.

Example of Bean-Managed Persistence

In order to demonstrate the implementation of a bean with bean-managed persistence, we will take the Trade bean from the previous example and modify it. A possible motivation for using BMP in this case might be that we want to control the database structure in order to make it compatible with a different (possibly not even Java-based) application.

In the process of changing the Trade bean to one with BMP, the home and remote interfaces remain unchanged and only the implementation class needs to be revised. Note that the finder helper class is not needed in this case because all finder methods are coded manually.

In general, BMP can be implemented in a variety of ways, ranging from plain serialization into files to complex industrial-strength transactional systems. In our example, we look at a JDBC connection to a relational database, which is a typical scenario for Java-based persistency.

The following points highlight the difference in implementation compared to the previous example, which used CMP:

- Each of the methods `ejbLoad`, `ejbStore`, `ejbRemove`, and `ejbCreate` had to be implemented at length.
- The finder methods were coded manually to look up rows in the database. It is important to throw the `FinderException` in the `findByPrimaryKey` method if nothing is found.
- The fields of the bean are not required to be declared public.

Note that during deployment of such a bean, there is no need to specify any fields as container-managed nor to supply any information regarding finder methods because these are implanted in the implementation.

EJB Transactions

As explained earlier in Chapter 11, the EJB specification defines two attributes in the deployment descriptor that determine the transactional behavior of a bean. The first is the transaction attribute, which informs the container what kind of transactional behavior applies to method invocation. The other attribute is the transaction isolation level, which indicates how transactions for this bean should be isolated from each other inside the container.

Both transaction attributes can be defined at the time of deployment, either for the bean as a whole or for individual methods, as described in Chapter 29, "WebSphere EJB Server." The only exception is that the `TX_BEAN_MANAGED` specification cannot be applied to any individual method, but only to the bean as a whole. When using the `TX_BEAN_MANAGED` setting, the bean is able to obtain the transaction from the `SessionContext` object provided to it in the `setSessionContext` method.

In the WebSphere Enterprise Edition (CB), there are some special restrictions on EJB transactions:

- If a stateful session bean is set to be TX_BEAN_MANAGED, any method that starts a transaction must complete it.
- TX_MANDATORY must be used for entity beans with CMP that are used to connect to CICS applications (see Chapter 39).
- TX_REQUIRES_NEW is not supported.
- Entity beans with CMP must be accessed with a transaction; that is, TX_NOT_SUPPORTED cannot be used.

It is possible to make a bean reentrant as part of its deployment process. This is useful when a bean needs to be accessed from within a transaction already in use in the transaction. This can happen if the bean invokes another bean, which invokes the first bean. Such implementation is strongly discouraged even by the EJB specification. If the described scenario takes place for a non-reentrant bean, a RemoteException is thrown. If the bean is specified (during its deployment) as reentrant, the method invocation is allowed. This is really at the risk of the bean developer because programming reentrant code is much more tricky.

One last thing to note about EJB transactions is that in a stateful session bean, the bean state is not transactional. In other words, if a transaction is started within a stateful EJB, and later a rollback is performed, the EJB state is unchanged. The state must be modified explicitly to reflect the state before the transaction started.

EJB
Server-Side
Code

This chapter focuses on the implementation of EJB server-side code. The previous chapter already provided a glimpse into EJB coding through the examples illustrating persistence. In this chapter, we provide some practical guidance relating to the restrictions of the EJB programming model and to the question of choosing the right kind of bean.

EJB Restrictions

Basically, EJB code is plain Java code. However, there are numerous constraints imposed by the EJB specification. To a large extent, these constraints are intended to allow the EJB container to do his job uninterrupted. In addition to the obvious constraints relating to the fact you need all the pieces of the bean (remote interface, home interface, and bean implementation), the following constraints apply:

- EJBs cannot start new threads, or use thread synchronization primitives.
- EJBs must not be abstract.
- EJBs cannot directly access the transaction manager, unless declared TX_BEAN_MANAGED.
- EJBs are not allowed to have mutable static variables (that is, ones that are not declared "final").
- EJBs that have any sort of transactional support from the container (that is, not declared TX_NOT_SUPPORTED) must never use the JDBC commit and rollback operation. That is the responsibility of the container.
- Fields of container managed EJBs must be declared public.

Choosing the Right Type of Bean

The difference between entity beans and session beans lies in the notion of persistence. Session beans are intended to be short-lived and are supposed to be used only by one client, lasting only as long as the session with the client lasts. Specifically, session beans are not able to survive a server crash, or even a session disconnection (this is tunable through the session timeout defined in the descriptor). In contrast, entity beans can be used concurrently by multiple clients and are intended to have a long lifetime (their lifetime is completely independent of specific clients). Being long-lived, entity beans are supposed to survive server crashes and other failures. It is important to realize that although session beans are not stored into databases, this does not mean they cannot manipulate databases. Similar to other pieces of Java code (such as servlets), session beans are perfectly capable of making queries or updates to databases.

The aforementioned characteristics distinguish session beans from entity beans. When designing an application, the choice between those kinds of bean should prove to be quite simple. The reason is that the persistence requirements of an application tend to be evident. For example, consider a typical business with a group of customers. Because a lot of records are associated with a customer, it makes sense to use an entity bean to represent a customer.

A session bean could never actually represent a customer, although it could change customer records. Specifically, session beans can represent business processes and procedures, implementing business logic in the middle tier. For example, in our abstract example, consider an action of checking whether the customer's account is currently balanced. This action can be encapsulated in a session bean because it is purely procedural (that is, there is no state information). Of course, this kind of action doesn't necessarily require a bean in the first place. You can implement it in client code (for example, in a servlet). However, the advantages of separating business logic from the presentation layer are substantial, both in terms of modularity and in terms of performance. Modularity is promoted because properly designed session beans become reusable components that can be used by different clients. Performance can be improved in case the actions performed require multiple method invocations on entity beans that are in the same container as the session bean.

When developing session beans, there is the question of state. A session bean can be either stateless or stateful. The motivation for having state in the session bean is to provide the client with some context, thus steering clear of the need to send over the whole history of the session (which is pretty much what happens when you use cookies for the same purpose). The drawback of stateful beans is a separate instance that must be created for each client, which might burden system resources. Stateless beans do not take up a lot of resources because in reality, the server can share them between clients.

The corresponding dilemma when developing entity beans is whether to use bean-managed or container-managed persistence. It is unquestionably more convenient to use CMP, so BMP should only be used in cases where there are compelling considerations involving the data repository. Such considerations could be related to connectivity to other systems or to performance. Bean-managed persistence has the advantage of allowing the developer to optimize the usage of resources in general and databases in particular. In cases where performance is not critical, or in simple cases where there is not much to optimize, CMP should be preferred.

It should be noted that the savings achieved by not implementing the persistency methods could grow as the development cycle progresses. Using bean-managed persistence means that the persistence methods must be maintained as modifications are made to the bean definition. Furthermore, the bean becomes much more portable between platforms.

Example: Quote Bean

In order to illustrate the different alternatives for developing a bean, consider the Quote bean in the online trading application. Listing 32-1 shows the remote interface for this bean. The interface contains one method, which retrieves the last price in which the stock passed as parameter was traded. To keep things simple, we assume the price is an integer (that is, we drop fractions), and a value of 0 is returned if the bean is provided with an invalid stock ticker symbol. Listing 32-2 shows a simple implementation of this bean, based on the code used for the ticker servlet back in Chapter 23. Listing 32-3 shows the home interface of this bean.

Listing 32-1
Quote bean remote interface

```
package com.ticker;

import javax.ejb.*;
import javax.rmi.*;


public interface Quote extends EJBObject {
     int getPrice(String ticker) throws RemoteException;
}
```

Listing 32-2
Quote bean implementation

```
package com.ticker;

import javax.ejb.*;
import java.util.*;
```

```java
import java.sql.*;
import java.net.*;
import java.io.*;

public class QuoteBean extends SessionBean {
    public void ejbCreate()
    {
    }

    public void ejbRemote()
    {
    }

    public void ejbActivate()
    {
    }

    public void ejbPassivate()
    {
    }

    public void setSessionContext(SessionContext ctx)
    {
    }

    int getPrice(String tickerSym) {
        StringBuffer urlBuf = new StringBuffer(1000);
        urlBuf.append("http://quotes.nasdaq" +
"amex.com/Quote.dll?mode=stock");
        urlBuf.append(tickerSym);
    urlBuf.append("&quick.x=71&quick.y=9");
    String urlString = urlBuf.toString();
    String urlResponse = getHTMLFor(urlString);
    if (urlResponse != null) {
    int beginAt = 0;
    int endAt = 0;
    beginAt = urlResponse.indexOf("$", endAt);
    endAt = urlResponse.indexOf("<", beginAt);
    double price = new Double(urlResponse.substring(beginAt+2,
endAt));
    return int(price);
        }
    return 0;
    }

    String getHTMLFor(String url) {
        try {
    URLConnection aConnection = (new URL(url)).openConnection();
    aConnection.setDoInput(true);
    aConnection.setDoOutput(true);
    aConnection.setUseCaches(false);
    InputStream inS = aConnection.getInputStream();
    StringBuffer buffer = new StringBuffer(4096);
    boolean atEnd = false;
    while(!atEnd) {
      int len = inS.available();
```

continues

Listing 31-2
Continued

```
            byte[] buf = new byte[len];
        if (inS.read(buf, 0, len) == -1)
        atEnd = true;
        if (len > 0)
                buffer.append(new String(buf));
        Thread.sleep(10);
      }
      String retString = buffer.toString();
      return retString;
      } catch (Throwable ex) {
      ex.printStackTrace();
      }
      return null;
        }
}
```

Listing 32-3
Quote bean home
interface

```
Package com.ticker;

import javax.ejb.*;
import java.rmi.*;


public interface QuoteHome extends EJBHome {
      public Hello create() throws RemoteException,
                                  javax.ejb.CreateException;
}
```

Listing 32-4 shows a slight variation of the remote interface, that requires an implementation of a stateful bean. A new method is added, which is intended to provide the price of the stock most recently requested. Such an interface might be useful in a case where some verification process is made on the first time a quote is requested. On subsequent requests, this verification process can be skipped. This is hardly the case for our implementation, since we use an external website for obtaining quotes. Nonethess, it provides a valid example of a stateful session bean. Listing 32-5 outlines the implementation of such a bean.

Finally, consider implementing the same bean as an entity bean. This could be relevant if we happen to have a relational database holding all current stock prices, and this database is constantly updated with recent prices.

Listing 32-4
Stateful quote bean
remote interface

```
package com.ticker;

import javax.ejb.*;
import javax.rmi.*;

package com.ticker;

import javax.ejb.*;
import javax.rmi.*;
```

Listing 32-5
Stateful quote bean
implementation

```
package com.ticker;

import javax.ejb.*;
import java.util.*;
import java.sql.*;
import java.net.*;
import java.io.*;

public class QuoteBean extends SessionBean {

    String lastTicker;

    public void setSessionContext(SessionContext ctx)
    {
        lastTicker = null;
    }

    public int getPrice()
    {
        if (lastTicker == null) {
            return null;
        }
        else
        return getPrice(lastTicker);
    }


    public int getPrice(String tickerSym)
    {
        lastTicker = tickerSym;
    //
    // The remainder of this method remains unchanged
    //
    }

    //
    // Other methods remain unchanged
    //
}
```

To implement the entity bean, a primary key could be defined as containing the stock ticker symbol. The bean itself would have methods for extracting the ticker symbol and the most recent price; for example, `getPrice` and `getTickerSymbol`. In addition, it should have persistency methods that access the underlying database. The implementation details here would be quite similar to the Trade bean discussed in the previous chapter.

Now consider a slightly different scenario, in which the process of updating the database with current prices is also done through the entity bean. In this case, we need to add methods for setting the bean attributes, `setPrice`, and `setTickerSymbol`. Then it is possible, using EJB security definitions, to allow some users only read access (that is, to get quotes), while allowing other clients to set the updated price. The security setup is part of the deployment and administration process (see Chapter 42). Note that if updates are done through the bean, we can use container-managed persistence and simplify the bean implementation.

33

EJB Client Code

This chapter addresses the issue of EJB client-side programming. The first step in EJB client-side programming is gaining access to the bean. Because EJBs are objects whose natural habitat is a distributed environment, the most common way to look them up is with JNDI. This method is used when working with WebSphere.

EJB client-side programming is basically general-purpose Java programming. It imposes fewer restrictions than server-side programming, so it is much easier to master. The tricky aspects are those resulting from the underlying model of distributed objects, which is susceptible to network and server failures. In terms of client-side programming, this means that objects might suddenly become invalid (or disappear) without any warning.

Client Programming Basics

EJB can be used by a variety of different client types:

- Java servlets
- Other EJBs
- *Java Server Pages* (JSP)
- Java applications and applets

Regardless of the kind of client developed, the procedure for accessing EJBs is pretty much the same. To gain access to a bean, you must go through the EJB home interface for that bean. The EJB home is retrieved using JNDI. With the bean home at hand, the client can either create or search for beans. Searching for beans is relevant only for entity beans because session beans are not persistent.

When a client requests the creation of a new session bean, the server creates a new bean and returns to the client an EJBObject referring to the bean. As mentioned in the previous chapter, the EJB server might do some optimizations here, such as reusing stateless beans for several clients.

For entity beans, the situation is slightly different. The client can create entity beans too. However, because the primary key must be unique, you should make sure no bean already exists for this key (this can be done using the findByPrimaryKey method on the home interface).

Consider the example shown in Listing 33-1. To understand the process of bean creation, this example shows part of the implementation of the Portfolio bean, which belongs to our hypothetical Ticker.com online-trading application. In this case, the EJB client is an EJB itself. The client code should have import statements for java.rmi, javax.ejb, and javax.naming. In this case, the first two are there although the code is an EJB client because they are required for defining the bean. The JNDI lookup uses several properties, which should be set in the InitialContext object. At the risk of slightly repeating Chapter 22, we'll look at these properties:

- `java.naming.Context.PROVIDER_URL`. Specifies a URL used to access the name server. This should take the form `iiop://` `hostname:port`. The port used by a WebSphere server can be set in the administrative client. By default, it is 900.

- `javax.naming.Context.INITIAL_CONTEXT_FACTORY`. Identifies the name service to be used by the client. In the WebSphere AE environment, this should be `com.ibm.ejs.ns.jndi.` `CNInitialContextFactory`. This value is EJB server-dependent. For example, in the CB environment, you should use `com.ibm.ejb.cb.` `runtime.CBCtxFactory`.

Listing 33-1
EJB acting as EJB client

```
package com.ticker;
import javax.ejb.*;
import java.rmi.*;
import javax.rmi.*;
import java.util.*;
import javax.naming.*;
import com.ticker.quote;

public class PortfolioBean extends EntityBean
{

    // OTHER METHODS

    public static int calculateValue(string tickerSym, int
quantity)
    {
      try {
        Properties p = new Properties();
        p.put(Context.INITIAL_CONTEXT_FACTORY,
            "com.ibm.ejs.ns.jndi.CNInitialContextFactory");

            p.put(Context.PROVIDER_URL,
                "iiop://your.server.name:9020");

        InitialContext ic = new InitialContext(p);
        Object homObj = ic.lookup("QuoteBean");
        QuoteHome home = (QuoteHome)
        javax.rmi.ProtableRemoteObject.narrow(
                HomObject, com.Ticker.QuoteHome.class);

        Quote quote = home.create();
        return quantity * quote.getPrice(tickerSym);
      }
      catch (Exception ex) {
            return 0;
      }
    }
  }
```

After the `InitialContext` object is ready, it is possible to perform the actual lookup using the JNDI name provided for the bean during deployment. The example shown in Listing 33-1 constructs the `InitialContext` object explicitly and assigns values to the individual properties. Because the client here is an EJB itself, this is not considered good EJB programming practice. Instead, these properties should be specified in the environment settings during bean deployment, as shown in Figure 33-1. This is especially important in order to allow for EJB portability (even between the WebSphere AE and CE version); that is, without recoding and recompilation. Listing 33-2 shows a revised version fragment of Listing 33-1 when assuming the environment variables are correctly set.

Figure 33-1
Setting JNDI
Environment
Properties in `jetace`

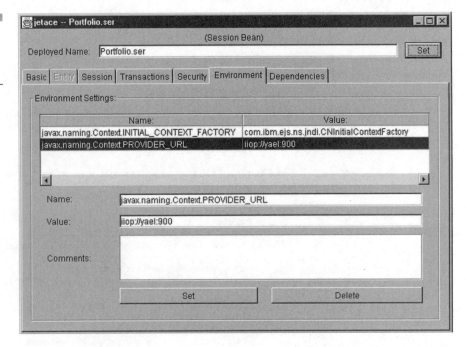

Listing 33-2
Revised example,
assuming that
properties are
externally set

```
package com.ticker;

import javax.ejb.*;
import java.rmi.*;
import javax.rmi.*;
import java.util.*;
import javax.naming.*;
```

```
import com.ticker.quote;

public class PortfolioBean extends EntityBean
{

    // OTHER METHODS

    public static int calculateValue(string tickerSym, int
quantity)
    {
      try {
        InitialContext ic = new InitialContext();
        QuoteHome home = (QuoteHome)
javax.rmi.ProtableRemoteObject.narrow(
                  HomeObject, com.Ticker.QuoteHome.class);
    Object homObj = ic.lookup("QuoteBean");

        Quote quote = incHome.create();
        return quantity * quote.getPrice(tickerSym);
      }
      catch (Exception ex) {
          return 0;
      }
    }
  }
```

The result of the lookup is converted into an EJB home object using the method `javax.rmi.PortableRemoteObject.narrow`. This method takes two parameters: the object to be narrowed and the class of EJB home object to be returned. The returned value of this method is cast to the home interface class.

Given the EJB home object, it is possible to create actual bean instances, as done in the examples shown in Listings 33-1 and 33-2. To complete the picture, recall that for stateful beans and entity beans, the create method might take some parameters. For entity beans, the `find` methods can be used to obtain EJBObject references and not only create methods.

One technicality relating to EJB clients, though not relevant to clients whom are EJB themselves, is that the CLASSPATH for the JVM should contain a few JAR files, which are provided under the lib directory in the WebSphere installation. These files are `ejs.jar`, `ujc.jar`, and `iioptools.jar`.

It makes sense for client code to store an EJB reference in a class variable after it is obtained to avoid repeatedly performing JNDI lookups and (in the case of session beans) bean creation. You should avoid doing that when coding a servlet because servlets should be able to support multiple clients. It is still possible to make the JNDI lookup in the servlet `init` method, and then use the home interface in the other servlet methods. Listing 33-3 shows a portion of the `PortfolioServlet`, which performs the lookup for the Portfolio bean home interface. The lookup is done in the `init` method, and the home interface obtained can be used in subsequent method invocations of the servlet.

Listing 33-3
Servlet client

```
package ticker.com;

import javax.servlet.*;
import javax.servlet.http.*;
import java.io.*;
import java.util.*;
import java.sql.*;
import java.text.*;
import com.ticker.portfolio;

public class PortfolioServlet extends HttpServlet {

  PortfolioHome home;

  // Other methods

  public void init(ServletConfig ps) throws ServletException {
      super.init(ps);
      try {
        Properties p = new Properties();
        p.put(Context.INITIAL_CONTEXT_FACTORY,
           "com.ibm.ejs.ns.jndi.CNInitialContextFactory");

            p.put(
          Context.PROVIDER_URL,"iiop://your.server.name:9020");

        InitialContext ic = new InitialContext();
        Object homObj = ic.lookup("PortfolioBean");
        home = (PortfolioHome)
                javax.rmi.ProtableRemoteObject.narrow(
                HomeObj, com.Ticker.PortfolioHome.class);

      catch (Exception ex) {
          // Handle exception
      }
  }


  public void doGet(HttpServletRequest request,
HttpServletResponse response) throws ServletException,
IOException {
//
// Extract customer name
//
```

```
// Create primary key for portfolio
PortfolioPK key = new PortfolioPK;
key.customerName = customerName;

try {
    Portfolio = home.findByPrimaryKey(key);

    } catch (Exception ex) {
        // Handle exception
    }
    // Use portfolio bean to present user with results
  }
}
```

Other Issues in Client Programming

In the following sections, we examine some of the other issues you may encounter in client programming. We discuss how to handle serialization, removing EJBObjects, and invalid session EJBObjects. The final section of this chapter covers transaction support in clients.

Invalid Session EJBObjects

As already discussed, one of the drawbacks of session beans is that they cannot survive a server crash, or even a session disconnection or timeout. This has some impact on client code. Namely, the client cannot depend on the EJBObject reference to remain valid. Whereas an EJBObject relating to session bean becomes invalid when the server crashes or if a timeout occurs, an EJBObject relating to an entity bean becomes invalid only when the object is removed from the server.

Given the likelihood of session bean objects getting invalidated, it is useful to place bean invocations within the scope of a try block that catches the `java.rmi.NoSuchObjectException`. This exception is the one thrown when an invalid EJBObject is used. Listing 33-4 shows a code fragment using the `Quote` bean which is ready to handle an invalid EJBObject.

```
Package com.ticker;

import javax.ejb.*;
import javax.transaction.*;
import com.ticker.quote;

class quoteUser {

  Quote quote;

  void getBean()
  {
          // Create instance of Quote and place in quote
  }

  int getHoldingValue(String ticker, int amount) {
     int value = 0;
     boolean done = false;
     do {
          try {
                value = amount* quote.getPrice(ticker);
                done = true;
          } catch(NoSuchObjectException ex) {
                getBean();
                sessionGood = false;
          } catch(Exception ex) {
                // Handle other problems

          }
     } while(!sessionGood);
     return value;
  }
}
```

Removing EJBObjects

The semantics of the remove operation are different for session beans
and entity beans. For session beans, the remove method should be
invoked whenever the client does not need the bean. This helps to reduce
memory consumption of the EJB server. Explicit removal is required
because standard approach of garbage collection provided by the JVM is
much more difficult to implement in an environment of distributed
objects.

For entity beans, activating the remove method causes the bean to be
removed from the underlying datastore along with the associated data.

Handle Serialization

A handle is a serializable reference to a bean. In other words, a handle can be obtained from a bean, and this handle can be serialized into a file or over the network. For example, if you have an EJBObject of type Quote that is called quote, you can obtain the handle with the statement:

```
Handle myHandle = quote.getHandle();
```

Later, you can retrieve the EJBObject:

```
Quote requote = (Quote) myHandle.getEJBObject();
```

Although that might not strike you as particularly impressive, the point is that the latter line of code could be run after retrieving the handle from some persistent storage or from another Java program.

Transactional Support in Clients

Although the EJB programming model allows for clients to take part in transaction management, this complicates client side programming. It also disagrees with the notion of a thin client that focuses on presentation.

Listing 33-5 shows a code fragment that illustrates how client-side transaction management is done. In the WebSphere environment, the transaction service of the server is contacted using the JNDI name jta/usertransaction. After a transaction context is obtained, the client code can initiate a transaction using the begin method, and EJB invocations can be done in the scope of the transaction.

Listing 33-5
Client side transaction management

```
import javax.ejb.*;
import javax.transaction.*;


class ClientCode {

    //
    //
    //
    void transactionMethod() {
```

continues

Listing 33-5
Continued

```
// Object EJB object references for later use

Context initialContext = new InitialContext();
UserTransaction tcon =
        (UserTransaction) initialContext.lookup(
                           "jta/usertransaction");

tcon.begin();

// Use EJB objects within the transaction scope

tcon.commit();
    }
}
```

An alternative to client-side transaction management is to "wrap" access to entity beans with session beans that do the transaction management. This approach places all transaction management in the middle tier and takes full advantage of the EJB container's transactional facilities.

34

Writing XML e-Business Applications

As we already mentioned, XML is quickly becoming the most important technology in developing e-business applications —both in the consumer space as well as in the business-to-business markets. XML is a fairly young technology, and as such, we believe that we have not yet seen all of the possible applications of this technology—nor has the industry managed to fully define the precise category(ies) in which this technology fits. Still, when we talk about applications that are making use of XML, there are some themes that are already common. These applications include the XML parser, DOM structures, and SAX. In this chapter, we develop a complete application that will exhibit the use of these themes and will illustrate how to use the XML tools that come bundled with WebSphere. As we have already seen with previous examples, the bundling of technologies with WebSphere is part of IBM's overall strategy. IBM is certainly one of the major e-business players (and perhaps the company that is most committed to e-business) and has a whole set of technologies enabling e-business. Because WebSphere is the primary deployment platform for e-business, it is only natural for WebSphere to become a technology bundle. XML is no exception. The primary XML-related technology is IBM's XML for Java Parser. In this chapter, we use this package extensively. Because the package is updated often on the AlphaWorks site, we chose to download the latest version (at this time, version 2.0.13) and use it instead of the default version that is supplied with the WebSphere release.

The Insider Trading Application

This chapter describes an application that we built to satisfy our new-found hobby of losing money on the stock market. Like many others, we have fallen for the fallacy that we can figure out which stock to purchase based on insiders' actions. Because there are many stock symbols, manually checking which stocks are being purchased by insiders is a difficult task. Therefore, our application performs an automated scan to determine in which companies insiders have decided to purchase company stock. Our assumption is that if insiders have decided to purchase stock using their own money, they must know something that we do not, and we should also purchase this stock.

The application works for companies that are listed on the *National Association of Securities Dealers Automated Quotation* (NASDAQ) stock exchange and makes use of two primary information sources. The first source is from the NASDAQ Web site (`http://www.nasdaq.com/`) and is used to determine all stock symbols on the exchange. Figure 34-1 shows an example of a typical Web page that lists NASDAQ companies. As you can see from the URL that we used (`http://www.nasdaqamex.com/dynamic/nnm_0.stm`), all stock symbols are listed on pages that have a URL with a suffix ranging from `nnm_0.stm` and `nnm_50.stm`. So, the first task our application needs to perform is to access the NASDAQ Web site, look up all the pages in this range, and extract from the site the stock symbols.

With all stock symbols in hand, we will access another data source. The Yahoo! Finance section lists insider trading information for any stock symbol. Figure 34-2 shows an example of the page that we want to find. Per stock symbol, the Yahoo! data sources list all insider trading (the page that we have chosen shows a number of insider buyers). As you can tell from the

Figure 34-1
Companies registered
on NASDAQ

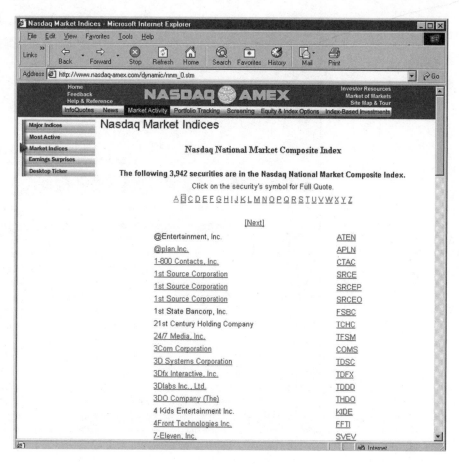

URL (`http://biz.yahoo.com/t/i/IACO.html`), when given a stock symbol such as MSFT, the URL we will need to access is `http://biz.yahoo.com/t/m/MSFT.html`. Therefore, with all of the stock symbols at hand (from the first stage), we can obtain access to all of these pages.

The final task is to parse these pages and look for entries in which the action is "Bought" or "Acquired," then extract the date when this action occurred and extract the price at which the stock was purchased. Then, all of the results are packaged and are written as an XML document that we can later view or can use from within yet another application. The fact that the generated file is in XML format makes it especially simple to use the file from another application. This feature is one of the primary benefits of XML over conventional formats.

Figure 34-2
Yahoo! Finance
insider trading
information

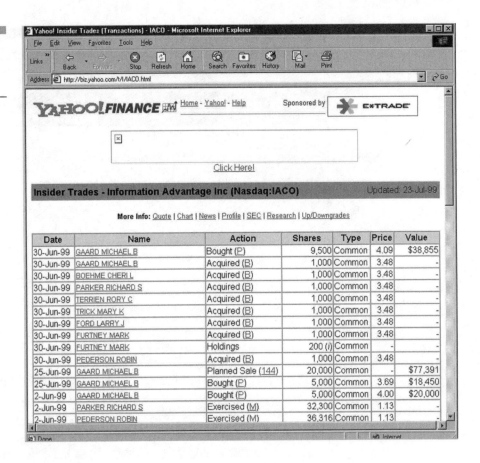

All parts of the application are written to be autonomous. Thus, the first module accesses the NASDAQ pages and outputs the symbols as an XML document. The second application module parses this document to find all of the symbols. Apart from the fact that this software is good for engineering practice, it gives us more opportunities to illustrate the use of the XML tools.

We use IBM's Java XML Parser to parse XML documents, to build DOM trees, and to access information. We also use the package to build DOM structures and output them as XML. The TreeViewer that comes bundled with the package (refer to Figure 34-3) is used to view XML documents for debugging purposes.

Figure 34-3
The TreeViewer
application

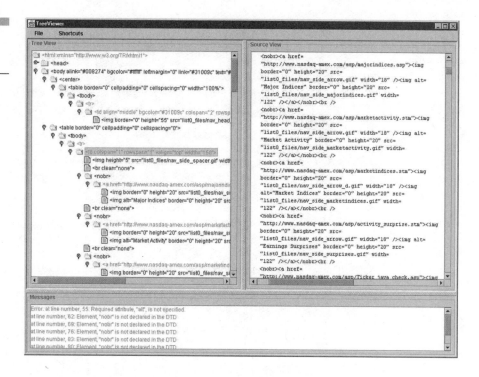

Generating the Stock Symbols

The first part of the application is simple enough and is shown in Listing
34-1. We iterate over the 50 pages that list all symbols on NASDAQ, and for
each one, we obtain the HTML page. We then look through the HTML for
the place where the `symbol` string occurs, and we extract the stock symbol.
We use a utility class called `HTMLFetcher`, which will come in handy in the
next module as well. The code for this class is shown in Listing 34-2. The
iteration places all symbols in one vector.

Listing 34-1
Extracting the stock
symbols

```
package book.websphere.chapter34;

import java.util.*;
import java.io.*;
import org.w3c.dom.*;
import org.xml.sax.helpers.ParserFactory;
import com.ibm.xml.parsers.*;
import org.xml.sax.*;
```

continues

Listing 34-1

Continued

```java
public class SymbolGenerator {

  public SymbolGenerator() {
  }

  public static void main(String[] args) {

    SymbolGenerator gen = new SymbolGenerator();

    Vector symbolVector = new Vector(1000);
    for (int i = 0 ; i <= 50 ; i++) {
      StringBuffer htmlText = HTMLFetcher.getHTMLFor(
        "http://www.nasdaq-amex.com/dynamic/nnm_" +
        Integer.toString(i) + ".stm");
      gen.extractSymbolInformationInto(htmlText, symbolVector);
    }
    gen.outputSymbolInformation(symbolVector);
  }


  void extractSymbolInformationInto(StringBuffer aBuf, Vector
symbolVector) {
    int index = 0;
    String str = aBuf.toString();
    while (index != -1) {
      index = str.indexOf("symbol=", index);
      if (index != -1) {
        int nextIndex = str.indexOf(">", index);
        String aSymbol = str.substring(index+7, nextIndex);
        symbolVector.addElement(aSymbol);
        index = nextIndex + 1;
      }
    }
  }

  void outputSymbolInformation(Vector symbolVector) {
    com.ibm.xml.parser.TXDocument myDocument =
      new com.ibm.xml.parser.TXDocument();

    try {
      ProcessingInstruction pi = myDocument.
        createProcessingInstruction("xml","version=\"1.0\"");
      myDocument.appendChild(pi);

      Element root = myDocument.createElement("stockSymbols");
      root.setAttribute("exchange", "NASDAQ");
      myDocument.appendChild(root);

      for (Enumeration e = symbolVector.elements() ;
e.hasMoreElements(); ) {
        String aSymbol = (String)e.nextElement();
        Element child = myDocument.createElement("symbol");
        Text t = myDocument.createTextNode(aSymbol);
        child.appendChild(t);
        root.appendChild(child);
      }
```

```
      FileWriter fw = new FileWriter("symbols.xml");
      myDocument.toXMLString(fw);
      fw.close();

    } catch (Exception e) {
        e.printStackTrace();
    }
  }
}
```

Listing 34-2

Fetching the HTML

```
package book.websphere.chapter34;

import java.net.*;
import java.io.*;

public class HTMLFetcher {
  static public StringBuffer getHTMLFor(String url) {
    try {
      URLConnection aConnection = (new URL(url)).openConnection();
      aConnection.setDoInput(true);
      aConnection.setDoOutput(true);
      aConnection.setUseCaches(false);
      InputStream inS = aConnection.getInputStream();
      StringBuffer buffer = new StringBuffer(4096);
      boolean atEnd = false;
      while (!atEnd) {
        int len = inS.available();
        byte[] buf = new byte[len];
        if (inS.read(buf, 0, len) == -1)
        atEnd = true;
        if (len > 0)
          buffer.append(new String(buf));
        Thread.sleep(10);
      }
      return buffer;
    } catch (Throwable ex) {
      ex.printStackTrace();
    }
    return null;
  }

}
```

The next step is to iterate over all of the symbols in the vector and construct the XML file. We use the DOM classes to build a document and then dump it to an XML file. Building the document is simple enough. You simply instantiate the nodes and create the relationships between them. Once the document has been created, we use the `toXMLString` method to create the XML string and write the document to a file. Figure 34-4 shows a segment of the resulting XML file.

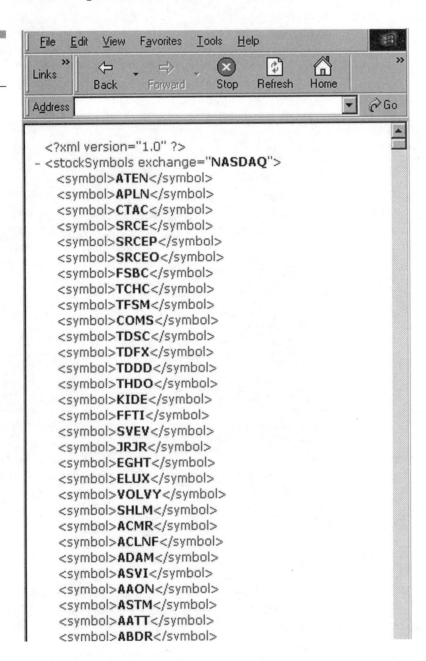

Figure 34-4
XML for stock symbols

```
<?xml version="1.0" ?>
- <stockSymbols exchange="NASDAQ">
    <symbol>ATEN</symbol>
    <symbol>APLN</symbol>
    <symbol>CTAC</symbol>
    <symbol>SRCE</symbol>
    <symbol>SRCEP</symbol>
    <symbol>SRCEO</symbol>
    <symbol>FSBC</symbol>
    <symbol>TCHC</symbol>
    <symbol>TFSM</symbol>
    <symbol>COMS</symbol>
    <symbol>TDSC</symbol>
    <symbol>TDFX</symbol>
    <symbol>TDDD</symbol>
    <symbol>THDO</symbol>
    <symbol>KIDE</symbol>
    <symbol>FFTI</symbol>
    <symbol>SVEV</symbol>
    <symbol>JRJR</symbol>
    <symbol>EGHT</symbol>
    <symbol>ELUX</symbol>
    <symbol>VOLVY</symbol>
    <symbol>SHLM</symbol>
    <symbol>ACMR</symbol>
    <symbol>ACLNF</symbol>
    <symbol>ADAM</symbol>
    <symbol>ASVI</symbol>
    <symbol>AAON</symbol>
    <symbol>ASTM</symbol>
    <symbol>AATT</symbol>
    <symbol>ABDR</symbol>
```

Getting the Insider Information

The second module is a bit more complex. The code is shown in Listing 34-3. First, we read in the XML file with the symbol information. This task is fairly straight-forward, because we know the structure of the XML file and simply cannot go wrong. Once we have the symbols, we iterate over all symbols. For each symbol, we open a connection to the Yahoo! site and obtain the HTML by using the HTMLFetcher class.

Listing 34-3
Extracting information about insider purchases

```
package book.websphere.chapter34;

import java.util.*;
import java.io.*;

import org.w3c.dom.*;
import org.xml.sax.helpers.ParserFactory;
import com.ibm.xml.parsers.*;
import org.xml.sax.*;

public class InsiderInspector implements ErrorHandler{

  public InsiderInspector() {
  }

  public static void main(String[] args) {

    InsiderInspector gen = new InsiderInspector();
    com.ibm.xml.parser.TXDocument myDocument =
      new com.ibm.xml.parser.TXDocument();

    try {
      ProcessingInstruction pi = myDocument.
        createProcessingInstruction("xml","version=\"1.0\"");
      myDocument.appendChild(pi);

      Element root = myDocument.createElement("insiderTrading");
      root.setAttribute("asOf", (new Date()).toString());
      myDocument.appendChild(root);

      Vector symbolVector = gen.retrieveAllSymbols();
      for (Enumeration e = symbolVector.elements() ;
e.hasMoreElements() ; ) {
        String aSymbol = (String)e.nextElement();
        StringBuffer htmlText = HTMLFetcher.getHTMLFor(
          "http://biz.yahoo.com/t/" + aSymbol.substring(0,1) +
          "/" + aSymbol + ".html");
        StringBuffer aBuf = HTMLTidier.tidyHTML(htmlText);
        if (aBuf != null) {
          Element symbolRoot = myDocument.createElement(aSymbol);
          root.appendChild(symbolRoot);
```

continues

Listing 34-3
Continued

```
            gen.extractInsiderInfo(aBuf, myDocument, symbolRoot);
        }
    }

    FileWriter fw = new FileWriter("insiderTrading.xml");
    myDocument.toXMLString(fw);
  com.ibm.xml.parser.TXDocument myDocument =
    new com.ibm.xml.parser.TXDocument();

  try {
    ProcessingInstruction pi = myDocument.
      createProcessingInstruction("xml","version=\"1.0\"");
    myDocument.appendChild(pi);

    Element root = myDocument.createElement("insiderTrading");
    root.setAttribute("asOf", (new Date()).toString());
    myDocument.appendChild(root);

    Vector symbolVector = gen.retrieveAllSymbols();
    for (Enumeration e = symbolVector.elements() ;
e.hasMoreElements() ; ) {
        String aSymbol = (String)e.nextElement();
        StringBuffer htmlText = HTMLFetcher.getHTMLFor(
          "http://biz.yahoo.com/t/" + aSymbol.substring(0,1) +
          "/" + aSymbol + ".html");
        StringBuffer aBuf = HTMLTidier.tidyHTML(htmlText);
        if (aBuf != null) {
          Element symbolRoot = myDocument.createElement(aSymbol);
          root.appendChild(symbolRoot);
          gen.extractInsiderInfo(aBuf, myDocument, symbolRoot);
        }
    }

    FileWriter fw = new FileWriter("insiderTrading.xml");
    myDocument.toXMLString(fw);
    fw.close();
  } catch (Exception ex) {
    ex.printStackTrace();
  }
}

Vector retrieveAllSymbols() {
  Vector symbols = new Vector(4096);
  BufferedReader br = null;
  try {
    br = new BufferedReader(new FileReader("symbols.xml"));
  } catch (Exception ex) {
    ex.printStackTrace();
    return null;
  }
  Parser parser = null;
  try {
    parser =
ParserFactory.makeParser("com.ibm.xml.parsers.NonValidatingDOMParse
r");
    parser.setErrorHandler(this);
  } catch (Exception ex) {
    ex.printStackTrace();
```

```
        return null;
      }
      try
      {
        parser.parse(new org.xml.sax.InputSource(br));

        org.w3c.dom.Document d =
((NonValidatingDOMParser)parser).getDocument();

        org.w3c.dom.Element rootElement = d.getDocumentElement();
        NodeList nodes = rootElement.getChildNodes();
        for (int i = 0 ; i < nodes.getLength() ; i++)
        {
          org.w3c.dom.Node aNode = nodes.item(i);
          if ((aNode instanceof org.w3c.dom.Element) &&
              aNode.getNodeName().equalsIgnoreCase("symbol")) {
            org.w3c.dom.Element aSymbolElement =
(org.w3c.dom.Element)aNode;
            String symbolName =
((org.w3c.dom.Text)aSymbolElement.getFirstChild()).getData();
            symbols.addElement(symbolName);
          }
        }
      } catch (Throwable ex) {
        ex.printStackTrace();
      }
      return symbols;
    }

  void extractInsiderInfo(
      StringBuffer aBuf,
      com.ibm.xml.parser.TXDocument myDocument,
      Element symbolRoot) {
    Parser parser = null;
    try {
      parser = ParserFactory.makeParser(
        "com.ibm.xml.parsers.NonValidatingDOMParser");
      parser.setErrorHandler(this);
    } catch (Exception ex) {
      ex.printStackTrace();
    }

    try {
      parser.parse(new org.xml.sax.InputSource(
        new ByteArrayInputStream(aBuf.toString().getBytes())));
      org.w3c.dom.Document d =
((NonValidatingDOMParser)parser).getDocument();
      org.w3c.dom.Element inputElement = d.getDocumentElement();
      recursivelyDescend(inputElement, myDocument, symbolRoot);
    } catch (Exception ex) {
      ex.printStackTrace();
    }
  }

  void recursivelyDescend(
      org.w3c.dom.Node aNode,
      com.ibm.xml.parser.TXDocument myDocument,
```

continues

Listing 34-3
Continued

```
            Element symbolRoot) {
    if (aNode instanceof org.w3c.dom.Text) {
        String theText = ((org.w3c.dom.Text)aNode).getData().trim();
        if (theText.length() >= 6) {
            String subS = theText.substring(0,6);
            if ((subS.compareTo("Bought") == 0) ||
                (subS.compareTo("Acquir") == 0)) {
                Node aParent = aNode.getParentNode().getParentNode();
                Element newElement =
myDocument.createElement("insiderPurchase");
                        try {
                    Node dateNode =
aParent.getFirstChild().getNextSibling().
                                getFirstChild();
                    newElement.setAttribute(
                        "date",
                        ((Text)dateNode).getData().trim());
                    Node priceNode =
aParent.getFirstChild().getNextSibling().
                        getNextSibling().getNextSibling().getNextSibling().
                        getNextSibling().getNextSibling().getNextSibling().
                        getNextSibling().getNextSibling().
                        getNextSibling().getNextSibling().getFirstChild();
                    newElement.setAttribute(
                        "price",
                        ((Text)priceNode).getData().trim());
                } catch (Throwable ex) {
                    newElement.setAttribute(
                        "error",
                        "There was an inside trade that could not be
parsed");
                }

                symbolRoot.appendChild(newElement);
            }
        }
    }
    NodeList nodes = aNode.getChildNodes();
    for (int i = 0 ; i < nodes.getLength() ; i++) {
        org.w3c.dom.Node subNode = nodes.item(i);
        recursivelyDescend(subNode, myDocument, symbolRoot);
    }
}

public void warning(SAXParseException exception) throws
SAXException {
    //do nothing
}

public void error(SAXParseException exception) throws
SAXException {
    //do nothing
```

```
    }

    public void fatalError(SAXParseException exception) throws
SAXException {
      //do nothing
    }


}
```

The next step is the interesting part. Instead of traversing the HTML source like we did in the previous section, we would like to view the HTML file as an XML document and actually traverse the XML document by using the document nodes. In time, this process will become more and more common, but at the moment, this action is difficult to perform. Most HTML pages on the Web are not well formed. Therefore, we start by converting the HTML page into a page that conforms to XML rules. We use a program called TIDY by Dave Raggett of Hewlett-Packard. The application can be downloaded from `http://www.w3.org/People/Raggett/tidy`. Among other features, the application can fix HTML documents so that they can be parsed by an XML parser. Listing 34-4 shows our utility class for performing this task (not a sophisticated way, but it gets the job done nevertheless).

Listing 34-4
Activating the TIDY program

```
package book.websphere.chapter34;

import java.io.*;

public class HTMLTidier {

  public HTMLTidier() {
  }

  public static StringBuffer tidyHTML(StringBuffer inBuf) {

    try {
      File outputFile = new File("insiders.html");
      FileWriter out = new FileWriter(outputFile);
      out.write(inBuf.toString());
      out.close();
    } catch (Throwable ex) {
```

continues

Listing 34-4
Continued

```java
        ex.printStackTrace();
        return null;
    }

    String[] cmdLine = {
        "tidy.exe", "-f", "errs.txt", "-im", "-asxml",
"insiders.html"};
    try {
        Runtime.getRuntime().exec(cmdLine);
        // Yes - it is ugly to just wait a few second
        // but its just a demo after all
        Thread.sleep(5000);
    } catch (Throwable ex) {
        ex.printStackTrace();
        return null;
    }

    String[] cmdLine = {
        "tidy.exe", "-f", "errs.txt", "-im", "-asxml",
"insiders.html"};
    try {
        Runtime.getRuntime().exec(cmdLine);
        // Yes - it is ugly to just wait a few second
        // but its just a demo after all
        Thread.sleep(5000);
    } catch (Throwable ex) {
        ex.printStackTrace();
        return null;
    }

    try {
        File inputFile = new File("insiders.html");
        FileReader in = new FileReader(inputFile);
        int justRead = 0;
        int index = 0;
        StringBuffer aBuf = new StringBuffer(4096);
        while(justRead != -1) {
            char[] buf = new char[1024];
            justRead = in.read(buf, index, 1024);
            aBuf.append(buf);
        }
        in.close();
        return aBuf;
    } catch (Throwable ex) {
        ex.printStackTrace();
    }
    return null;
    }
}
```

After we have a well-formed XML document, we can run the document through our parser and look for Text nodes that have the word "Bought" or

Figure 34-5
DOM structure with
text, date, and price
siblings

Figure 34-5
DOM structure with text, date, and price siblings

"Acquired." At this point, we look for the siblings that hold the date and the price information (remember, each node will have the structure as shown by the highlighted nodes in Figure 34-5) and append the information to the XML document. The result (after checking all possible stock symbols) is shown in Figure 34-6. Obviously, this process takes a long time to run, but we can run it all night and be ready for trading the next morning.

Figure 34-6

Insider trading XML

```xml
<?xml version="1.0" ?>
- <insiderTrading asOf="Fri Jul 23 00:00:00 GMT 1999">
  - <ODIS>
      <insiderPurchase date="30-Apr-99" price="3.05" />
      <insiderPurchase date="30-Apr-99" price="3.05" />
      <insiderPurchase date="30-Apr-99" price="3.05" />
      <insiderPurchase date="29-Apr-99" price="-" />
      <insiderPurchase date="9-Mar-99" price="6.56" />
      <insiderPurchase date="8-Mar-99" price="6.60" />
      <insiderPurchase date="5-Mar-99" price="6.63" />
      <insiderPurchase date="4-Mar-99" price="6.38" />
      <insiderPurchase date="3-Mar-99" price="6.63" />
      <insiderPurchase date="1-Mar-99" price="6.50" />
      <insiderPurchase date="26-Feb-99" price="6.50" />
      <insiderPurchase date="25-Feb-99" price="6.32" />
      <insiderPurchase date="24-Feb-99" price="6.13" />
      <insiderPurchase date="1-Feb-99" price="-" />
      <insiderPurchase date="7-Dec-98" price="6.25" />
      <insiderPurchase date="4-Dec-98" price="6.25" />
      <insiderPurchase date="3-Dec-98" price="6.25" />
      <insiderPurchase date="30-Oct-98" price="3.77" />
      <insiderPurchase date="30-Oct-98" price="3.77" />
      <insiderPurchase date="30-Oct-98" price="3.77" />
      <insiderPurchase date="26-Oct-98" price="4.69" />
      <insiderPurchase date="25-Sep-98" price="-" />
      <insiderPurchase date="28-Jul-98" price="-" />
  </ODIS>
  - <CBRL>
      <insiderPurchase date="14-Apr-99" price="17.88" />
      <insiderPurchase date="8-Mar-99" price="18.81" />
      <insiderPurchase date="4-Mar-99" price="18.69" />
      <insiderPurchase date="22-Feb-99" price="18.94" />
      <insiderPurchase date="18-Dec-98" price="21.98" />
      <insiderPurchase date="17-Dec-98" price="21.31" />
      <insiderPurchase date="16-Dec-98" price="21.63" />
      <insiderPurchase date="25-Sep-98" price="24.19" />
  </CBRL>
  - <HYSL>
```

35

Application of XSL Transformations

The central role that XML is beginning to play in e-business applications is augmented by the capabilities of XSL (and specifically, by the capabilities of XSLT). Recall that the XSL standard is really composed of two parts: one that defines how transformations from one XML dialect to another can be phrased, and one that defines formatting structures. Of the two, the definitions of transformation rules (XSLT) are of fundamental importance to the success of XML in e-business applications. Because different systems and different Web sites will ultimately end up with different XML structures, the capability to exchange information and bridge semantic mismatch is perhaps the primary issue that will determine the success or failure of XML. This bridging relies on the capability to define conversion rules in the form of XML transformations.

In this chapter, we will continue with the example from the previous chapter and will focus on the use of XSLT for processing XML documents as part of an e-business application. We use the LotusXSL package (version 0.17.4), which is available from AlphaWorks. The package has a full implementation of the XSLT specification from April 1999 and uses IBM's XML Parser for Java. The XSLT processor can be activated in one of three ways: by using a command-line interface, by using a servlet, or by using an applet to perform the processing. Each method is suitable for different operational scenarios.

Of these three scenarios, the most appropriate in the context of an e-business application is that of a servlet. This feature enables us to build applications that are flexible, where much of the processing takes place through a set of transformation rules. We will use the XSLT processor through a servlet that is supplied as part of the LotusXSL distribution. Depending on the version of WebSphere you have installed, the servlet, which is called DefaultApplyXSL, might already be installed on your servlet server. If not, you simply need to add this servlet to your servlet configuration (either by using the administration tool or by using an XML configuration file). If you have trouble installing the servlet, we suggest that you open the `lotus.` `xsl` JAR file under the servlets directory and then install the servlet into WebSphere.

The DefaultApplyXSL class inherits from an abstract class called ApplyXSL, which itself inherits from HttpServlet. When installing the servlet (which we called XSL so that our URL will be a bit shorter), there are a number of parameters you can set:

- `debug` A boolean value specifying whether the XSL processor should run in debug mode or not. We suggest that you always run in Debug mode until the final deployment stage, which will enable you to see what is going on and will save you a lot of time.

- `stripWhite` A boolean value specifying whether white spaces should be stripped from the XML and from the result

- `noConflictWarnings` A boolean value specifying whether conflict warning messages should be generated and passed through from the XSL processor

- `xslURL` The location of the default XSL file

- `mediaURL` The location (relative to the servlets directory) of the user agent mapping rules file. An example file—the one that is supplied by the default installation—is shown in Listing 35-1. The file enables the selection of transformation rules based on the user agent. Because the user agent information encapsulates the presentation capabilities of

```
# This property file is used by
# com.lotus.xsl.server.DefaultApplyXSL.
#
# Each line below specifies a mapping rule between a
# value contained in the HTTP request's user-Agent
# field and a value to be scanned for in XSL stylesheet(s)
# associated with the XML data. This mapping
# enables relationships to be defined between client
# capabilities and stylesheets capable of acting
# on these capabilities.
#
# The rules defined below are order-significant.  In
# other words, if the first rule is unsuccessful,
# the second rule will be tried, etc.  The media value
# "unknown" will be used when no rules are
# satisfied.
#
# Example:
#
# Mapping rules of...
#
#   MSIE=explorer
#   MSPIE=pocketexplorer
#
# ...and XML data that contains XSL stylesheet associations of...
#
# <?xml-stylesheet                 media="explorer"
# href="alldata.xsl"  type="text/xsl"?>
# <?xml-stylesheet alternate="yes" media="pocketexplorer"
# href="somedata.xsl" type="text/xsl"?>
#
# ...and an HTTP request that contains a user-Agent value of...
#
#   foo MSPIE bar
#
# ...will apply the XSL stylesheet somedata.xsl.
#
MSIE=explorer
MSPIE=pocketexplorer
HandHTTP=handweb
Mozilla=netscape
Lynx=lynx
Opera=opera
Java=java
AvantGo=avantgo
Nokia=nokia
UP.Browser=up
DoCoMo=imode
```

the client, it is almost always required to generate a different output from the servlet, based on the user agent. The properties file maps the values that will be in the User Agent field of the request to values used in the media attribute of the style sheet.

Listing 35-2
Mime Property file

```
# This property file is used by
# com.lotus.xsl.server.ApplyXSL.
#
# Each line below specifies a mapping rule between
# the result-ns attribute of an xsl:stylesheet element
# and the MIME type to be used in the HTTP response.
# A default MIME type of text/xml will be used
# when all mapping rules fail.
#
# Example:
#
# A mapping rule of . . .
#
#    http\://www.w3.org/TR/REC-html40=text/html
#
# ...and an XSL stylesheet that contains..
#
#    <?xml version="1.0" ?>
#    <xsl:stylesheet xmlns:html=
#        "http://www.w3.org/TR/REC-html40=text/html"
#        result-ns="html">
#
# ...will have its response MIME type set to text/html.
#
# PLEASE NOTE: Colons must be escaped.
#
http\://www.w3.org/TR/REC-xml=text/xml
http\://www.wapforum.org/WML/1.1=text/wml
http\://www.w3.org/TR/REC-html40=text/html
http\://www.w3.org/XSL/Transform/1.0=text/xsl
http\://www.w3.org/XSL/Transform/=text/xsl
http\://java.sun.com/JSML/0.5=text/jsml
http\://www.w3.org/TR/xhtml1=text/xml
http\://websphere/XSL/Jigsaw=application/vnd.wap.wml
```

■ mimeURL   This parameter points to another property file (an example
is shown in Listing 35-2) that is similar in nature to the Media
Property file but defines the content type that should be used when
creating the response by the servlet. Up to now, we have always used
text/HTML when generating a response from a servlet, because we
have always used a browser to activate the servlet. This situation is
not the only possible case, however. HTTP connections can be initiated
by devices that require different formats. An example that will become
more and more common as time goes on is the use of the *Wireless
Markup Language* (WML) for cellular phones. WML is a dialect of
XML that is being adopted by almost all cellular phone manufacturers,
and in the near future, such devices will connect to servers for
retrieving WML pages that will be displayed as shown in Figure 35-1.
While the XSL servlet can deliver output in any format, it needs to set
the correct content type for the response, because this information is

Figure 35-1
A display of WML on
a cellular phone

inserted into the HTTP response header. The last line in the property
file shown in Listing 35-2 is the one that is used to create the response
displayed in Figure 35-1.

Once the servlet is registered with WebSphere, we can go ahead
and invoke the XSL processor by entering a URL of the form `http://`
`websphere/servlet/XSL?URL=<source_xml_file>&xslURL=<xsl_`
`file>`.

Cutting Down on Size

Now that we have the infrastructure in place, we can turn to the task at
hand. In the last chapter, we ended by creating an XML file with a listing

of insider buyers. Unfortunately, the XML file is difficult to sift through because of its size (almost 2MB). The XML file is also not quite in the format that a typical user would like to see. In this section and in the following sections, we will provide a few XSLT examples showing how we process the data until the data is transformed into precisely the right format and content that we desire.

The first part is to strip out data that is useless. Data that is obviously useless includes XML nodes for stock for which the `insidePurchase` node has an error attribute (refer to Figure 35-2). The error attribute is generated whenever the parsing of node traversal fails in the last chapter's program. Because such nodes have no information in them, we can start by removing all such nodes.

Listing 35-3 shows the XSLT rules that are required for removing these nodes. Because the syntax and semantics of XSLT are non-trivial (to say the least), we will go over each rule at a detailed level and will explain as much as possible along the way. Every XSLT file is an XML file. As such, there is

Figure 35-2
Error attribute in the
`insiderPurchase`
node

```
  <insiderPurchase date="8-Oct-98" price="-" />
  </KIDE>
  <FFTI />
- <SVEV>
    <insiderPurchase error="There was an inside trade that could not be parsed" />
    <insiderPurchase error="There was an inside trade that could not be parsed" />
    <insiderPurchase error="There was an inside trade that could not be parsed" />
    <insiderPurchase error="There was an inside trade that could not be parsed" />
    <insiderPurchase error="There was an inside trade that could not be parsed" />
    <insiderPurchase error="There was an inside trade that could not be parsed" />
    <insiderPurchase error="There was an inside trade that could not be parsed" />
    <insiderPurchase error="There was an inside trade that could not be parsed" />
    <insiderPurchase error="There was an inside trade that could not be parsed" />
    <insiderPurchase error="There was an inside trade that could not be parsed" />
    <insiderPurchase error="There was an inside trade that could not be parsed" />
    <insiderPurchase error="There was an inside trade that could not be parsed" />
    <insiderPurchase error="There was an inside trade that could not be parsed" />
    <insiderPurchase error="There was an inside trade that could not be parsed" />
    <insiderPurchase error="There was an inside trade that could not be parsed" />
    <insiderPurchase error="There was an inside trade that could not be parsed" />
    <insiderPurchase error="There was an inside trade that could not be parsed" />
    <insiderPurchase error="There was an inside trade that could not be parsed" />
    <insiderPurchase error="There was an inside trade that could not be parsed" />
    <insiderPurchase error="There was an inside trade that could not be parsed" />
    <insiderPurchase error="There was an inside trade that could not be parsed" />
    <insiderPurchase error="There was an inside trade that could not be parsed" />
    <insiderPurchase error="There was an inside trade that could not be parsed" />
  </SVEV>
  <JRJR />
- <EGHT>
    <insiderPurchase date="1-Feb-99" price="3.40" />
    <insiderPurchase date="3-Aug-98" price="3.40" />
```

Listing 35-3
XSLT for removing error entries

```xml
<?xml version="1.0"?>

<xsl:stylesheet xmlns:xsl="http://www.w3.org/XSL/Transform/1.0">

   <xsl:template match="/">
        <insiderTrading example="1">
        <xsl:apply-templates/>
        </insiderTrading>
   </xsl:template>

   <xsl:template match="insiderTrading/*">
        <xsl:copy>
        <xsl:apply-templates/>
        </xsl:copy>
   </xsl:template>

   <xsl:template match="insiderPurchase[not(@error)]">
        <insiderPurchase date="{@date}" price="{@price}"/>
   </xsl:template>

</xsl:stylesheet>
```

a processing instruction that defines the XML version, followed by a single document root. The document root is an element of type <xsl:stylesheet>, and all of the other elements are embedded within the root element. The root element has a name space attribute that defines the URI to be used for all elements that belong to the XLS name space.

Next come the rules. The file has three rules, and each rule has a pattern that it attempts to match. Nodes will be processed once the pattern has been matched. The first rule in the file matches the root node of the source XML file only, and the root node is designated by a slash (/). The second rule matches any node that is a direct descendant of the insiderTrading node, and the syntax is similar to directory structures in Unix. The third and final node matches any insiderPurchase node that does not have an error attribute. In XSL, an attribute is designated by a preceding "at" symbol (@). Therefore, the pattern-match definition of the third rule should be read as "all insiderPurchase nodes such that there does not exist an attribute by the name of error."

The processing parts of the rules are fairly simple. For the root node, we create an XML element called *insiderTrading* with a single attribute called *example*. This element will form the root element in the result XML (see Figure 35-3). Then, we apply all of the rules for the rest of the document from the source file. The processing for the stock nodes is the simplest task. We simply copy the nodes over and continue processing the children. Finally, whenever we reach a purchase node that is not an error, we create

```
- <insiderTrading example="1">
  - <ATEN>
      <insiderPurchase date="27-Jan-99" price="-" />
      <insiderPurchase date="27-Jan-99" price="-" />
      <insiderPurchase date="27-Jan-99" price="-" />
      <insiderPurchase date="4-Nov-98" price="7.25 - 9.00" />
      <insiderPurchase date="2-Nov-98" price="7.25" />
      <insiderPurchase date="2-Nov-98" price="7.25" />
      <insiderPurchase date="22-Oct-98" price="3.94" />
      <insiderPurchase date="22-Oct-98" price="4.00" />
      <insiderPurchase date="21-Oct-98" price="4.25" />
      <insiderPurchase date="20-Oct-98" price="4.31 - 4.38" />
      <insiderPurchase date="19-Oct-98" price="4.63" />
      <insiderPurchase date="14-Oct-98" price="4.75" />
      <insiderPurchase date="15-Sep-98" price="10.38" />
      <insiderPurchase date="14-Sep-98" price="9.88" />
      <insiderPurchase date="4-Sep-98" price="9.19" />
      <insiderPurchase date="31-Aug-98" price="8.80" />
      <insiderPurchase date="31-Aug-98" price="8.63 - 8.75" />
      <insiderPurchase date="4-Aug-98" price="-" />
      <insiderPurchase date="4-Aug-98" price="-" />
      <insiderPurchase date="4-Aug-98" price="-" />
      <insiderPurchase date="4-Aug-98" price="-" />
      <insiderPurchase date="4-Aug-98" price="-" />
      <insiderPurchase date="4-Aug-98" price="-" />
    </ATEN>
    <APLN />
  - <CTAC>
      <insiderPurchase date="17-Mar-99" price="12.50 - 12.63" />
      <insiderPurchase date="30-Sep-98" price="5.94" />
      <insiderPurchase date="29-Sep-98" price="6.00" />
      <insiderPurchase date="9-Sep-98" price="6.50" />
      <insiderPurchase date="9-Sep-98" price="6.50" />
      <insiderPurchase date="26-Aug-98" price="5.75" />
      <insiderPurchase date="18-Aug-98" price="6.06" />
      <insiderPurchase date="14-Aug-98" price="6.00" />
      <insiderPurchase date="13-Aug-98" price="6.06" />
    </CTAC>
```

an appropriate node in the output. Note that the syntax for a calculated value embedded in a string is curly brackets.

Now we have managed to write our first XSLT file, and the file size is down to 1,316KB from 1,942KB—but we can do better. There are plenty of nodes with no inside trades at all (i.e., companies that follow the rules), and we can get rid of those as well. That task is simple enough. Listing 35-4 makes a small change to the pattern match of the second rule, stating that the rule is satisfied only for nodes that are child nodes of the insiderTrading nodes and have at least one insiderPurchase node. That worked, but it did not help much. We are only down to 1,306KB. Now, let's get rid of the nodes that have no price. If we do not know how much the insider spent, we cannot really tell whether the current price is high or low. Listing 35-5 shows the change to the XSLT file, which is down to 1,148KB.

Listing 35-4
XSLT for removing
nodes with no
purchases

```
<?xml version="1.0"?>

<xsl:stylesheet xmlns:xsl="http://www.w3.org/XSL/Transform/1.0">

    <xsl:template match="/">
        <insiderTrading example="2">
        <xsl:apply-templates/>
        </insiderTrading>
    </xsl:template>

    <xsl:template match="insiderTrading/*[insiderPurchase]">
        <xsl:copy>
        <xsl:apply-templates/>
        </xsl:copy>
    </xsl:template>

    <xsl:template match="insiderPurchase[not(@error)]">
        <insiderPurchase date="{@date}" price="{@price}"/>
    </xsl:template>

</xsl:stylesheet>
```

Listing 35-5
XSLT for removing
nodes with no price

```
<?xml version="1.0"?>

<xsl:stylesheet xmlns:xsl="http://www.w3.org/XSL/Transform/1.0">

    <xsl:template match="/">
        <insiderTrading example="3">
        <xsl:apply-templates/>
        </insiderTrading>
    </xsl:template>

    <xsl:template match="insiderTrading/*[insiderPurchase]">
        <xsl:copy>
        <xsl:apply-templates/>
        </xsl:copy>
    </xsl:template>

    <xsl:template match="insiderPurchase[not(@price='-')]">
        <insiderPurchase date="{@date}" price="{@price}"/>
    </xsl:template>

</xsl:stylesheet>
```

That is enough for cutting down the size. The next step is to look at sorting. In the next example, we sort the values by price. For each stock symbol, we want the inside trades to be listed with the price values determining the order. After all, we want the lowest possible price, so we might as well compare the current price to the lowest price bought by insiders. Listing 35-6

Listing 35-6
Sorting based
on price

```
<?xml version="1.0"?>

<xsl:stylesheet xmlns:xsl="http://www.w3.org/XSL/Transform/1.0">

  <xsl:template match="/">
     <insiderTrading example="4">
     <xsl:apply-templates/>
     </insiderTrading>
  </xsl:template>

  <xsl:template match="insiderTrading/*[insiderPurchase]">
     <xsl:copy>
     <xsl:apply-templates select="insiderPurchase">
         <xsl:sort select="@price" data-type="number"/>
     </xsl:apply-templates>
     </xsl:copy>
  </xsl:template>

  <xsl:template match="insiderPurchase">
     <insiderPurchase date="{@date}" price="{@price}"/>
  </xsl:template>

</xsl:stylesheet>
```

shows the XSLT file performing the sort. Note that the sort element has an optional data-type attribute for specifying how sorting should be performed. In our case, we do not want an alphanumeric sort—otherwise, a price of 10 will appear before a price of 3.

The next step is the really nice one (and the one that will have the most applications for e-business applications). We want to transform the XML file into HTML that will display all data in a table. This task sounds simple, and it should be. As things stand, however, there is a big problem. We cannot obtain the value of the actual tag in XSL. Because the XML is based on the fact that the stock symbols are tags instead of data, we certainly have a problem. This lesson is important, and we hope that after reading this chapter, you will learn to never use data as tags.

By changing the code for the servlet in the previous chapter (as shown in Listing 35-7) and running the XML generation again, we can change our XML source to look similar to Figure 35-4. This action enables us to use the XSLT code shown in Listing 35-8 to produce the end result shown in Figure 35-5. Finally, Listing 35-9 shows another XSLT file that can be used to transform the XML into WML that is shown in Figure 35-6. The model for WML is that of cards. The display of a cellular device displays one WML card at a time and enables moving between cards by using the phone's controls. Figure 35-7 shows the resulting display on the cellular phone—two cards and the screen being used to navigate between the cards. Note that

Listing 35-7
New-and-improved
XML generation code

```java
public static void main(String[] args) {

    InsiderInspector gen = new InsiderInspector();

    com.ibm.xml.parser.TXDocument myDocument =
      new com.ibm.xml.parser.TXDocument();

    try {
      ProcessingInstruction pi = myDocument.
        createProcessingInstruction("xml","version=\"1.0\"");
      myDocument.appendChild(pi);

      Element root = myDocument.createElement("insiderTrading");
      root.setAttribute("asOf", (new Date()).toString());
      myDocument.appendChild(root);

      Vector symbolVector = gen.retrieveAllSymbols();
      for (Enumeration e = symbolVector.elements() ;
                          e.hasMoreElements() ; ) {
        String aSymbol = (String)e.nextElement();
        StringBuffer htmlText = HTMLFetcher.getHTMLFor(
          "http://biz.yahoo.com/t/" + aSymbol.substring(0,1) +
          "/" + aSymbol + ".html");
        StringBuffer aBuf = HTMLTidier.tidyHTML(htmlText);
        if (aBuf != null) {
          Element symbolRoot = myDocument.createElement("stock");
          symbolRoot.setAttribute("symbol",aSymbol);
          root.appendChild(symbolRoot);
          gen.extractInsiderInfo(aBuf, myDocument, symbolRoot);
          System.err.println("Finished processing " + aSymbol);
        }
      }

      FileWriter fw = new FileWriter("insiderTrading.xml");
      myDocument.toXMLString(fw);
      fw.close();
    } catch (Exception ex) {
      ex.printStackTrace();
    }
  }
}
```

we have cheated a bit, because the WML file was only created for three stock symbols. Obviously, we would not want to move 1MB through a cellular connection—nor would we want thousands of cards on the device.

Figure 35-4
New and
improved XML

```
- <insiderTrading example="4">
  - <stock symbol="ATEN">
      <insiderPurchase date="22-Oct-98" price="3.94" />
      <insiderPurchase date="22-Oct-98" price="4.00" />
      <insiderPurchase date="21-Oct-98" price="4.25" />
      <insiderPurchase date="20-Oct-98" price="4.31 - 4.38" />
      <insiderPurchase date="19-Oct-98" price="4.63" />
      <insiderPurchase date="14-Oct-98" price="4.75" />
      <insiderPurchase date="4-Nov-98" price="7.25 - 9.00" />
      <insiderPurchase date="2-Nov-98" price="7.25" />
      <insiderPurchase date="2-Nov-98" price="7.25" />
      <insiderPurchase date="31-Aug-98" price="8.63 - 8.75" />
      <insiderPurchase date="31-Aug-98" price="8.80" />
      <insiderPurchase date="4-Sep-98" price="9.19" />
      <insiderPurchase date="14-Sep-98" price="9.88" />
      <insiderPurchase date="15-Sep-98" price="10.38" />
  </stock>
  - <stock symbol="CTAC">
      <insiderPurchase date="26-Aug-98" price="5.75" />
      <insiderPurchase date="30-Sep-98" price="5.94" />
      <insiderPurchase date="29-Sep-98" price="6.00" />
      <insiderPurchase date="14-Aug-98" price="6.00" />
      <insiderPurchase date="18-Aug-98" price="6.06" />
      <insiderPurchase date="13-Aug-98" price="6.06" />
      <insiderPurchase date="9-Sep-98" price="6.50" />
      <insiderPurchase date="9-Sep-98" price="6.50" />
      <insiderPurchase date="17-Mar-99" price="12.50 - 12.63" />
  </stock>
  - <stock symbol="SRCE">
      <insiderPurchase date="28-Aug-98" price="31.56" />
      <insiderPurchase date="25-Aug-98" price="34.00" />
      <insiderPurchase date="28-Jan-99" price="35.00" />
      <insiderPurchase date="1-Feb-99" price="36.00" />
  </stock>
  - <stock symbol="FSBC">
      <insiderPurchase date="27-Apr-99" price="19.00" />
      <insiderPurchase date="29-Apr-99" price="19.25" />
      <insiderPurchase date="26-Apr-99" price="19.38" />
```

Listing 35-8
XSLT for generating
HTML tabular display

```xml
<?xml version="1.0"?>
<xsl:stylesheet xmlns:xsl="http://www.w3.org/XSL/Transform/1.0">

  <xsl:template match="/">
    <HTML>
      <HEAD>
        <TITLE>
          Insider Buyer patterns
        </TITLE>
      </HEAD>
      <BODY>
        <H3>
          This table lists all insider purchases for Nasdaq stock.
        </H3>
        <TABLE BORDER="1" WIDTH="100">
          <xsl:apply-templates/>
        </TABLE>
      </BODY>
    </HTML>
  </xsl:template>

  <xsl:template match="stock">
    <TR>
      <TD>
        <xsl:value-of select="@symbol"/>
      </TD>
        <xsl:apply-templates/>
    </TR>
  </xsl:template>

  <xsl:template match="insiderPurchase">
      <TD>
        <xsl:value-of select="@date"/>
        <xsl:text>
          ;
        </xsl:text>
        <xsl:value-of select="@price"/>
      </TD>
  </xsl:template>

</xsl:stylesheet>
```

Figure 35-5
HTML display of insider buying patterns

ABGX	5-Mar-99 ; 14.50	14-Jun-99 ; 15.25	24-Jun-99 ; 15.31	15-Jun-99 ; 15.63								
AANB	30-Apr-99 ; 10.75	23-Apr-99 ; 11.00	30-Mar-99 ; 11.00	11-Feb-99 ; 11.75	22-Jun-98 ; 12.60	31-Aug-98 ; 13.75	14-Sep-98 ; 13.88	2-Dec-98 ; 14.80	1-Dec-98 ; 14.80	26-Aug-98 ; 15.13	24-Aug-98 ; 15.27	23-Oct-98 ; 17.63
ABBK	12-Apr-99 ; 14.86											
ABMD	5-Apr-99 ; 12.25	1-Apr-99 ; 12.25	29-Mar-99 ; 12.25	31-Mar-99 ; 12.50								
ABTE	3-Sep-98 ; 2.75 - 3.03	4-Sep-98 ; 2.88 - 3.38	2-Sep-98 ; 3.00	9-Sep-98 ; 3.25	1-Sep-98 ; 3.25 - 3.33	31-Aug-98 ; 4.53	11-Sep-98 ; 5.38 - 5.56	7-May-99 ; 7.00				
BOUT	24-Mar-99 ; 25.00	24-Mar-99 ; 25.00	24-Mar-99 ; 25.00	24-Mar-99 ; 25.00	24-Mar-99 ; 25.00	24-Mar-99 ; 25.00						
ABOV	15-Dec-98 ; 13.00	15-Dec-98 ; 13.00	15-Dec-98 ; 13.00	15-Dec-98 ; 13.00	11-Dec-98 ; 13.56							
ABRX	24-Dec-98 ; 16.77											
ACRI	20-Aug-98 ; 4.44	10-Aug-98 ; 4.63	10-Aug-98 ; 4.75	12-Aug-98 ; 5.00								

```
<?xml version="1.0"?>
<xsl:stylesheet xmlns:xsl="http://www.w3.org/XSL/Transform/1.0">

    <xsl:template match="/">
        <xsl:pi name="xml">
          version="1.0"
        </xsl:pi>
        <wml>
          <xsl:apply-templates/>
        </wml>
    </xsl:template>

    <xsl:template match="stock">
        <xsl:element name="card">
          <xsl:attribute name="id">
            <xsl:text>n</xsl:text>
            <xsl:number/>
          </xsl:attribute>
          <xsl:attribute name="title">
            <xsl:value-of select="@symbol"/>
          </xsl:attribute>
                <do type="options" label="First">
                <go href="#n1"/>
                </do>
                <do type="options" label="Second">
                <go href="#n2"/>
                </do>
              <p>
                <xsl:apply-templates/>
              </p>
        </xsl:element>
    </xsl:template>

    <xsl:template match="insiderPurchase">
        <xsl:value-of select="@date"/>
        <xsl:text>
              ;
        </xsl:text>
        <xsl:value-of select="@price"/>
        <br/>
    </xsl:template>

</xsl:stylesheet>
```

Figure 35-6
Resulting WM

```
<?xml version="1.0" ?>
- <wml>
  - <card id="n1" title="ATEN">
    - <do type="options" label="First">
        <go href="#n1" />
      </do>
    - <do type="options" label="Second">
        <go href="#n2" />
      </do>
    - <p>
        22-Oct-98 ; 3.94
        <br />
        22-Oct-98 ; 4.00
        <br />
        21-Oct-98 ; 4.25
        <br />
        20-Oct-98 ; 4.31 - 4.38
        <br />
        19-Oct-98 ; 4.63
        <br />
        14-Oct-98 ; 4.75
        <br />
        4-Nov-98 ; 7.25 - 9.00
        <br />
        2-Nov-98 ; 7.25
        <br />
        2-Nov-98 ; 7.25
        <br />
        31-Aug-98 ; 8.63 - 8.75
        <br />
        31-Aug-98 ; 8.80
        <br />
        4-Sep-98 ; 9.19
        <br />
        14-Sep-98 ; 9.88
        <br />
        15-Sep-98 ; 10.38
        <br />
```

Figure 35-7
WML display of
insider buying
patterns

Figure 35-7
WML display of insider buying patterns

36

IBM XML Tools

In this chapter, we provide an overview of a number of XML tools that we have found to be extremely useful in developing e-business applications. While these tools are not directly related to WebSphere and are not part of the WebSphere distribution, we feel that it is appropriate to broaden our horizons a bit. XML is simply a data format in many ways. Still, it is apparent today that XML will play a central role in anything that concerns applications of the future. Using bare XML is difficult. Therefore, many tools are quickly evolving that will help developers use XML. This chapter focuses on such tools. The other reason why we are including this chapter in our discussion here is because we believe that the technologies described in this chapter will find their way into WebSphere sooner or later. The tools we will discuss in this chapter are all from the IBM labs and are currently part of the AlphaWorks project. These are projects that are released to the industry at an alpha stage, to help them evolve into production-level software as quickly as possible. Once they evolve past this stage, they are removed from the Alpha-Works site and are either marketed as independent products or together with other product suites. Even at the time of this writing, we have two examples of such an upgrade. The IBM XML parser is part of the Web-Sphere distribution, and the TaskGuide XML wizard maker (one of the tools that we will describe in this chapter) is being used in VisualAge for Java. We believe that due to the overwhelming importance of XML, most of the tools described in this chapter will eventually find their way into the WebSphere distribution. Even if they do not, these tools are useful for building applications that are deployed using WebSphere.

Because we will be covering several tools in this chapter, we will not delve into details regarding each of them. We wish to provide you with an understanding of what the tools do and give simple examples to make the discussion concrete. If any particular tool sparks your interest or does something that resembles a task that you might need to perform, we suggest that you download the tool and examine it more closely. By the way, in one of the examples in this chapter we use XML and DTDs from Bluestone's XwingML package. We recommend that you should check out this product, too. XwingML enables you to define an XML document following a certain syntax that can be used to build fully functional Java Swing user interfaces. Thus, instead of building the code for the user interface, you can take a data-driven approach. While it is obviously simpler to build a user interface by using a GUI builder than by editing an XML file, many applications have the need to dynamically build a user interface (or at least some user interface components). In such cases, XwingML is highly useful.

XML Viewer

The first tool that is almost always necessary is some kind of viewer for XML documents. We actually use one of two viewers (everyone has different preferences). The first tool that you might find useful is an IBM Alpha-Works tool called XML Viewer, which is written in Java using the Swing libraries. The tool provides a hierarchical view of an XML document in the left pane, with a detailed view of the selected node in the right pane. Figure 36-1 shows an example of the tool. The tool is quite flexible in that you can set which elements of the XML are shown in each of the panes (refer to Figure 36-2a and Figure 36-2b). In addition, the tool can display the XML source (refer to Figure 36-3) and the DTD (as shown in Figure 36-4). These features make the viewer a convenient, one-stop viewer for all of the possible aspects of an XML document.

Figure 36-1
XML Viewer tool

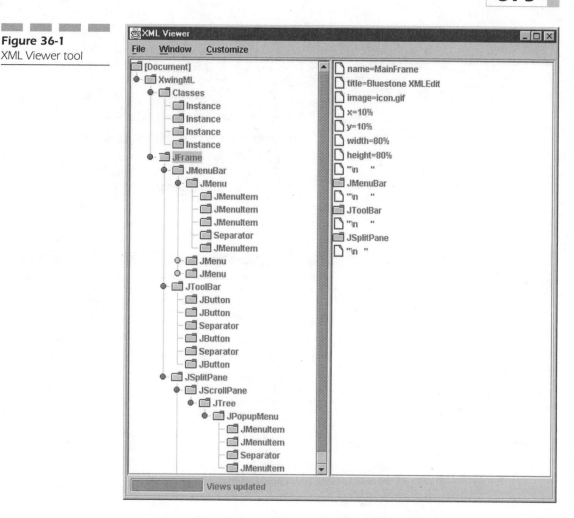

Figure 36-2a
Customize Tree View

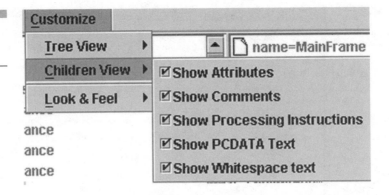

Figure 36-2b
Customize Children
View

ance

ance

ance

Figure 36-3
XML Source view

```
XML Source                                                              [X]
        <JMenu text="File" mnemonic="F">
            <JMenuItem icon="open.gif" text="Open..." mnemonic="0" accelerator="VK_0,CTRL_MA
            <JMenuItem icon="save.gif" text="Save" mnemonic="S" accelerator="VK_S,CTRL_MASK"
            <JMenuItem icon="save.gif" text="Save As..." mnemonic="a" actionCommand="saveas"
            <Separator/>
            <JMenuItem text="Exit" mnemonic="x" accelerator="VK_X,CTRL_MASK" actionListener=
        </JMenu>
        <JMenu text="Tools" mnemonic="T">
            <JMenuItem text="Parse" mnemonic="P" actionListener="ParseFile"/>
        </JMenu>
        <JMenu text="Help" mnemonic="H">
            <JMenuItem text="Contents" mnemonic="C"/>
            <JMenuItem text="Index" mnemonic="I"/>
            <JMenuItem text="Search" mnemonic="S"/>
            <Separator/>
            <JMenuItem text="About XMLEdit..." mnemonic="A" actionListener="About"/>
        </JMenu>
    </JMenuBar>
    <JToolBar orientation="HORIZONTAL" constraints="NORTH">
        <JButton icon="open.gif" actionListener="OpenFile"/>
        <JButton icon="save.gif" actionCommand="save" actionListener="SaveFile"/>
        <Separator/>
        <JButton icon="parse.gif" actionListener="ParseFile"/>
        <Separator/>
        <JButton icon="about.gif" actionListener="About"/>
    </JToolBar>
    <JSplitPane dividerSize="4" oneTouchExpandable="true" constraints="CENTER">
        <JScrollPane>
            <JTree name="FileTree" className="XMLTree" cellRenderer="XMLTreeCellRenderer">
                <JPopupMenu popupMenuListener="XMLPopupMenuListener">
```

The other alternative that we have found useful is to use Internet Explorer 5. This browser has built-in support for viewing XML files by using a predefined stylesheet that works with any XML document. The result is visually pleasing (refer to Figure 36-5), convenient to traverse, and fast. The source can be viewed by using the conventional View Source option, although that method opens Notepad (and is not too useful).

Figure 36-4
DTD view

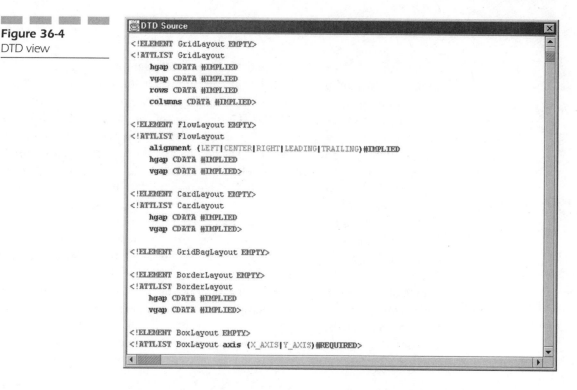

```
DTD Source                                                                    ×
<!ELEMENT GridLayout EMPTY>
<!ATTLIST GridLayout
    hgap CDATA #IMPLIED
    vgap CDATA #IMPLIED
    rows CDATA #IMPLIED
    columns CDATA #IMPLIED>


<!ELEMENT FlowLayout EMPTY>
<!ATTLIST FlowLayout
    alignment (LEFT|CENTER|RIGHT|LEADING|TRAILING)#IMPLIED
    hgap CDATA #IMPLIED
    vgap CDATA #IMPLIED>


<!ELEMENT CardLayout EMPTY>
<!ATTLIST CardLayout
    hgap CDATA #IMPLIED
    vgap CDATA #IMPLIED>


<!ELEMENT GridBagLayout EMPTY>


<!ELEMENT BorderLayout EMPTY>
<!ATTLIST BorderLayout
    hgap CDATA #IMPLIED
    vgap CDATA #IMPLIED>


<!ELEMENT BoxLayout EMPTY>
<!ATTLIST BoxLayout axis (X_AXIS|Y_AXIS)#REQUIRED>
```

Figure 36-5
Using Internet
Explorer 5 for
viewing XML
documents

```
File  Edit  View  Favorites  Tools  Help
Links  Back  Forward  Stop  Refresh  Home  Search  Favorites  History  Mail  Print
Address                                                              Go

        <JMenuItem icon="save.gif" text="Save As..." mnemonic="a"
          actionCommand="saveas" actionListener="SaveFile" />
        <Separator />
        <JMenuItem text="Exit" mnemonic="x" accelerator="VK_X,CTRL_MASK"
          actionListener="com.bluestone.xml.swing.XwingMLExit" />
      </JMenu>
-     <JMenu text="Tools" mnemonic="T">
        <JMenuItem text="Parse" mnemonic="P" actionListener="ParseFile" />
      </JMenu>
-     <JMenu text="Help" mnemonic="H">
        <JMenuItem text="Contents" mnemonic="C" />
        <JMenuItem text="Index" mnemonic="I" />
        <JMenuItem text="Search" mnemonic="S" />
        <Separator />
        <JMenuItem text="About XMLEdit..." mnemonic="A" actionListener="About" />
      </JMenu>
    </JMenuBar>
-   <JToolBar orientation="HORIZONTAL" constraints="NORTH">
      <JButton icon="open.gif" actionListener="OpenFile" />
      <JButton icon="save.gif" actionCommand="save" actionListener="SaveFile" />
      <Separator />
      <JButton icon="parse.gif" actionListener="ParseFile" />
      <Separator />
      <JButton icon="about.gif" actionListener="About" />
    </JToolBar>
-   <JSplitPane dividerSize="4" oneTouchExpandable="true" constraints="CENTER">
-     <JScrollPane>
-       <JTree name="FileTree" className="XMLTree"
          cellRenderer="XMLTreeCellRenderer">
-         <JPopupMenu popupMenuListener="XMLPopupMenuListener">
            <JMenuItem text="Expand" actionCommand="expand"
              actionListener="XMLTreeBranch" />
            <JMenuItem text="Collapse" actionCommand="collapse"
              actionListener="XMLTreeBranch" />
            <Separator />
Done                                                    My Computer
```

Task Guide

TaskGuide is a tool that supports the construction of wizards from XML files. The tool defines a XML syntax through which one can quickly and easily define the structure of multiple wizards and the navigation paths to be taken between the screens. TaskGuide is one of the most remarkable tools we have seen and is based on a simple idea that is amazingly powerful. TaskGuide is so easy to use that you can be up and running in less than 15 minutes. While TaskGuide is defined to be in an alpha state, it is of better quality than many production-level releases that we have had the misfortune to encounter.

A wizard is an application that has a strict user-interface paradigm. This paradigm consists of a set of simple steps that follow one another in a strict order. The wizard user has little navigation flexibility. Wizards are useful in cases where the process to be performed is not a daily activity, however, and instead of making the user learn a complex user interface, the application is designed in a way that is simple to use and does not leave many opportunities for errors.

Let's look at a simple example. Figures 36-6 through 36-8 show a simple wizard for setting up a profile for the Ticker.com example from Chapter

Figure 36-6
Setup Profile
Wizard—Step 1

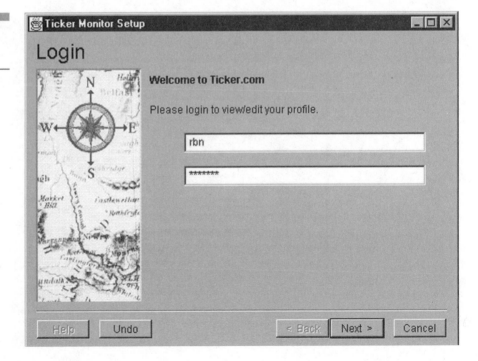

24, "Servlet Sessions." The wizard simply walks the user through a series of steps in a predefined order. Each panel performs a simple step and navigates to the next step, based on the selections made. For example, when viewing the profile and pressing the Add button, we navigate to the panel shown in Figure 36-7—where we enter values for the stock symbol and high and low thresholds. Then, when we press the Next button, we navigate back to the profile view (see Figure 36-8).

Putting together this wizard was a real no-brainer. In fact, we wrote little code in order to do so. Putting together the wizard requires no real coding. Instead, TaskGuide enables us to define the wizards by using an XML definition file. The source for our example is shown in Listing 36-1. As you can see, the XML code has three primary elements: the panel definition, the navigation definitions added to the panels, and a reference to Java code. Each panel describes the structure of a simple wizard, including its title, text messages, and the widgets that make up its user interface. Each panel can define which panel will be navigated to after pressing the Next button, the Previous button, etc. In addition, some user-interface elements (such as push buttons) can also be used for navigating. While the XML files are useful and TaskGuide has a rich set of widgets and navigation sequences, a real

Figure 36-7
Setup Profile Wizard
—Step 2

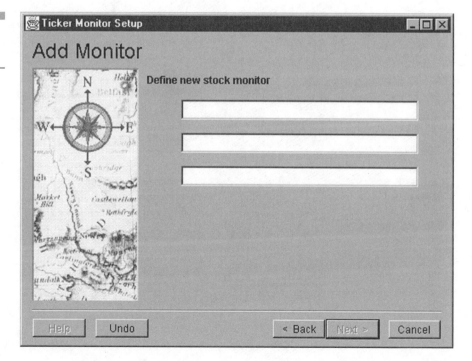

wizard will typically require access to information in a database or will require advanced widgets that are not provided by the tool. In such cases, the tool provides a simple way to call out to Java classes. Because TaskGuide itself is written in Java, the interaction between TaskGuide and Java extensions that are made by application programmers is simple—and the interfaces defined by the TaskGuide group are clear and easy to use. In addition, TaskGuide itself can be accessed through a set of well-documented interfaces. Even in this respect, the tool resembles a generally available product much more than a tool at an early stage.

Figure 36-8
Setup Profile Wizard
—Step 3

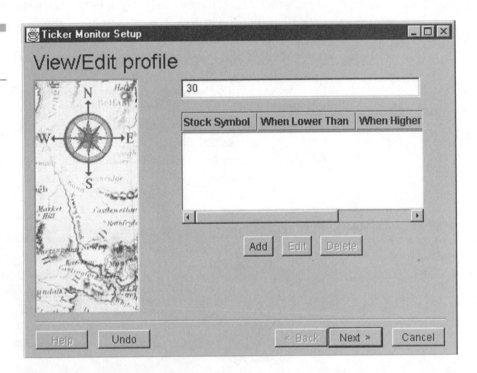

Listing 36-1
Setup Profile Wizard
XML source

```
<sguide high-res-size=(.5,.5)>
<title>Ticker Monitor Setup</title>
<panel name=login next="java com.ticker.Login">
        <title>Login</title>
        <p><b>Welcome to Ticker.com</b></p>
        <p>Please login to view/edit your profile.</p>
        <dataentry name=userName required/>
        <dataentry name=passwd password required/>
</panel>
<panel name=loginAgain next="java com.ticker.Login">
        <title>Login</title>
        <p><b>Welcome to Ticker.com</b></p>
        <p>Incorrect login or password; please try again.</p>
```

```
            <dataentry name=userName required/>
            <dataentry name=passwd password required/>
</panel>
<panel name=profile next=save>
        <title>View/Edit profile</title>
        <dataentry name=pollingFrequency format=integer init=30
required>
                Poll frequency (in minutes):
        </dataentry>
        <editlist
                name=monitors
                type="symbol(key), low, high"
                add=addMonitor
                edit=editMonitor
                separator="|"
                init="java com.ticker.GetProfile"
                reinit="java com.ticker.GetProfile"
                headers="Stock Symbol, When Lower Than, When Higher
Than"/>
</panel>
<panel name=save back=LAST-SEEN next="java
com.ticker.SaveMonitors">
        <title>Confirm</title>
        <p><b>Please confirm monitor definitions.</b></p>
        <p>Poll frequency (in minutes): %pollingFrequency%</p>
        <editlist
                name=monitors
                type="symbol(key), low, high"
                separator="|"
                init="java com.ticker.GetProfile"
                reinit="java com.ticker.GetProfile"
                headers="Stock Symbol, When Lower Than, When Higher
Than"
                no-add
                no-delete
                no-edit/>
</panel>
<panel name=addMonitor back=LAST-SEEN next="java
com.ticker.AddNewMonitor">
        <title>Add Monitor</title>
        <p><b>Define new stock monitor</b></p>
        <dataentry name=newMonitorSymbol required>Stock
symbol:</dataentry>
        <dataentry name=newMonitorLow>Notify when lower
than:</dataentry>
        <dataentry name=newMonitorHigh>Notify when higher
than:</dataentry>
</panel>
<panel name=editMonitor back=LAST-SEEN next=profile>
        <title>Edit Monitor</title>
        <p><b>Change Monitor Definition</b></p>
        <dataentry name=monitors.symbol>Stock symbol:</dataentry>
        <dataentry name=monitors.low>Notify when lower
than:</dataentry>
        <dataentry name=monitors.high>Notify when higher
than:</dataentry>
</panel>
</sguide>
```

Xeena

Xeena is another great tool with which you should be familiar. The more you use XML as a cornerstone technology for your e-business applications, the more XML files you will need to build. Building and editing XML files is fairly simple, but the task is certainly non-trivial. Up to now, you probably have been using your favorite text editor to build such files. This process is tedious and error-prone. Xeena provides an alternative.

Xeena is a general-purpose XML editor that can be used to build any XML document. Xeena starts by reading a DTD. Activating Xeena is done by using the command line xeena <dtd file name> <root element name>. The first argument passed to Xeena is the DTD filename. Xeena proceeds to read the DTD and constructs a palette that is based on the DTD. The palette is sensitive to the actual construction of the document. For example, if a certain element cannot be placed under the selected element, then that entry in the palette is grayed. The DTD is used to define the structure of the XML document, and Xeena does not permit the building of a document that does not fully conform to the DTD definition. In fact, whenever the user wants to edit a node, the options available at that node are enabled or disabled based on the DTD specification.

Figure 36-9 shows an example from the address book sample that comes with the Xeena distribution. The Xeena screen has four main areas (apart from a menu bar and a tool bar). At the top is the palette, which has a number of categories. In the address book sample, there is an address book category along with a general category for adding *Processing Instruction* (PI) nodes and comments. The center-left panel lists all possible elements in the XML document, and the center-right panel is the main area, which can hold a number of internal frames (MDI), each one being a separate document conforming to the same DTD. Each such frame displays the hierarchical structure of the XML document, and each node is displayed with its attributes. The bottom panel is used for messages.

Xeena uses XML files, saving the result of a session as an XML file and reading XML files. As such, Xeena is useful not only for when you need to build an XML file, but also in cases where you use XML in your application and need to provide your users with an XML editor. Because Xeena makes sure that the constructed XML fits the DTD, if you build your DTD carefully, Xeena can be an excellent tool for users because the validation is already built in.

Let's walk through an example of using Xeena. We use the address book sample, because it is simple and uses a model that is clear to everyone. We

Figure 36-9
Xeena address
book sample

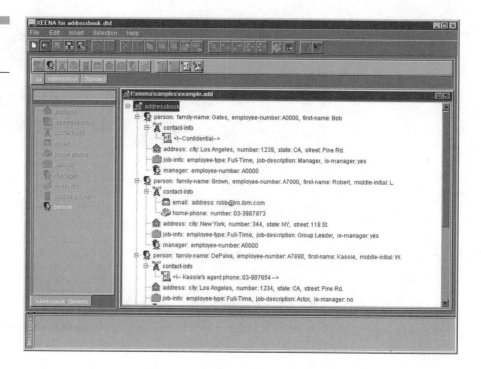

start Xeena and reach the main screen. We then open a new document from either the tool bar or the menu bar, as shown in Figure 36-10. Then, we proceed to add a new node under the root node. We can perform this action by either clicking the appropriate element in the center-left panel (refer to Figure 36-11), by clicking the element in the palette (as shown in Figure 36-12), or by selecting the root node and using the menu bar (refer to Figure 36-13). This action adds a node to the document object model. Now we have two nodes, as shown in Figure 36-14. Note that now the center-left pane and the palette highlight two elements as being active. In other words, according to the DTD, either a Person or a Contact-Info can be added somewhere in the document. The actions that can be performed in the context of a certain node are also dynamically adjusted by Xeena. For example, the menu that opens for the Person node (shown in Figure 3-14) shows that we can add another person either after or before the currently selected Person node, but not as a child of the selected node. According to the DTD, a Person node cannot have another person as a Child node). If we were to select the Contact-Info node, the menu would appear with only the *add as child* option active.

Figure 36-10
New XML document
in Xeena

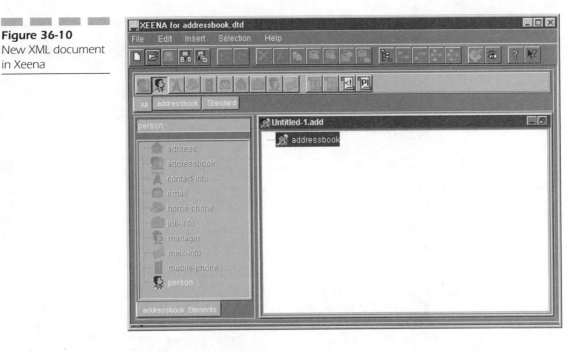

Figure 36-10
New XML document
in Xeena

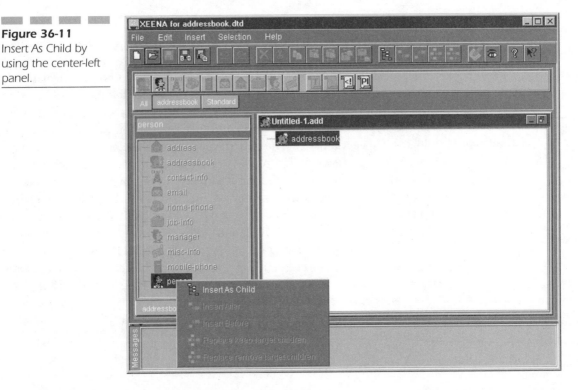

Figure 36-11
Insert As Child by
using the center-left
panel.

Figure 36-12
Insert As Child by
using the palette.

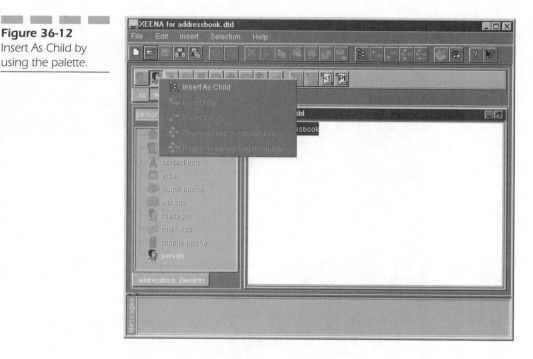

Figure 36-13
Insert As Child by
using the menu bar.

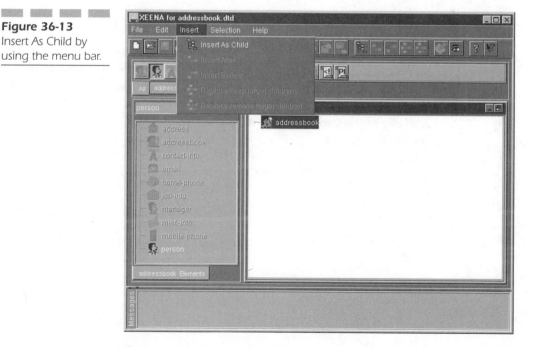

Figure 36-14
Inserting another
Person node

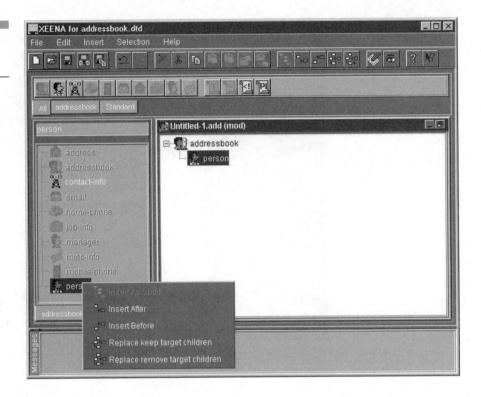

As we continue to build the XML document, Xeena guides us and stops us from making mistakes. At any point in time, we can receive help from Xeena in the form of a tool tip that tells us which elements can be added to this currently selected node (refer to Figure 36-15). We can also view the XML for any subtree of the XML document, based on the selected node (as shown in Figure 36-16). Finally, attributes can be edited by using the property editor, as shown in Figure 36-17.

Figure 36-15
Tool tip assistance

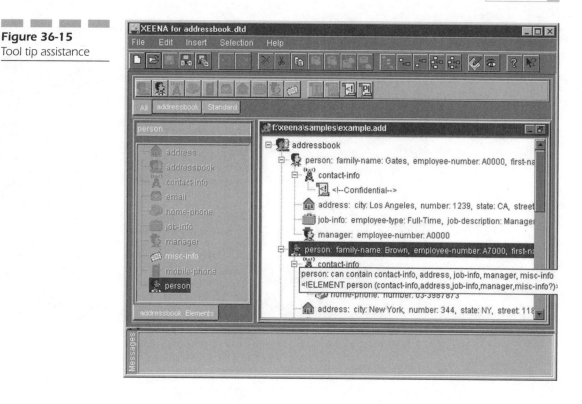

Figure 36-16
XML based on
selected node

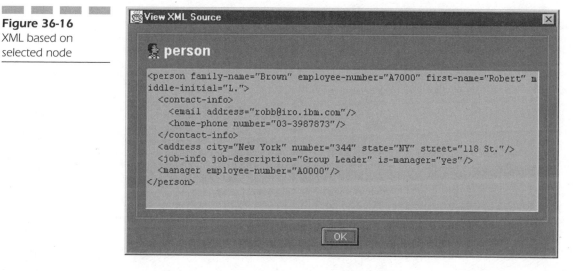

Figure 36-17
Editing attributes
in Xeena

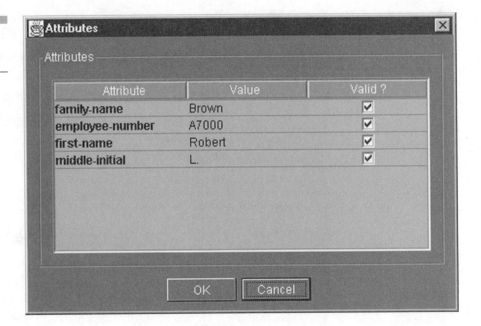

MQSeries Connectors

MQSeries is an IBM product that provides queue-based messaging services. This product blends flexibility and reliability. Flexibility is provided through a set of APIs that enable application programmers to specify any kind of messaging behavior that is required and that enable the support of a wide array of host platforms. MQSeries guarantees assured, once-only delivery of messages, and is robust enough to deal with cases in which a connection is currently not available.

Given the existing wide installation base of MQSeries, the motivation for having some sort of connectivity between WebSphere and MQSeries is obvious. Any enterprise that is currently using MQSeries-based applications would clearly prefer to reuse existing applications (or at least part of them) when moving to a Web-based solution.

When reusing MQSeries applications, the problem is that the basic abstractions in the WebSphere application server realm are somewhat different than the ones in MQSeries. The most common way to bridge such a gap between different abstractions or just different interfaces is to develop wrappers, which are also known as *adapters* [GoF] or connectors. As the name implies, the role of such wrappers is to wrap one kind of interface or abstraction and make it look like a different one. In our case, this procedure translates into taking MQSeries queues and providing an EJB interface for them by using an intermediate CORBA-based interface.

We should mention that at the time of this writing, IBM is supposed to release a version of MQSeries with *Java Messaging Service* (JMS) support. JMS is a Java-extension API that aims at simplifying the task of integration message systems with Java applications. JMS is an interface-based API that enables different vendors to provide their own implementation of a JMS service (similar to JDBC or JNDI). More details about JMS can be found at `http://java.sun.com/products/jms`.

Installation and Prerequisites

In order to use the MQSeries connector, you must have the WebSphere Application Server Enterprise Edition, which includes the *Component Broker* (CB). As part of the CB installation, you can specify the MQSeries Application Adaptor as one of the packages to install.

In addition, you must have VisualAge for Java and an installation of MQSeries. MQSeries must be installed on the same host on which the CB is running.

MQSeries-at-a-Glance

MQSeries is all about transporting messages. A message in MQSeries is an arbitrary stream of bytes, the format of which is application specific. In order to facilitate communication, messages are placed into queues. A queue enables an application to have a unidirectional information link to another application. In other words, the first application places messages in the queue, while the other application takes the messages from the queue. More formally, the first application uses a put operation, and the other application performs a get operation (which removes the message from the queue).

Queues in the same host machine can be grouped together and managed by queue managers. Queue managers in different machines can be linked so that some distinct queues are considered to be one logical queue.

The creation of queues and grouping them and linking them in this manner can be achieved by using the administration tools that are provided with MQSeries. In addition, new queues are to be created dynamically from within an application by using the MQSeries APIs.

The concept of message-based communication lends itself to a programming model based on asynchronous communication, in which the transmitting side does not need to wait for acknowledgment from the receiving side. Actually, the receiving side might be down or out of reach, and in this case, the message is kept in the queue and is sent later.

MQSeries can be used for synchronous or bidirectional communication by coupling two message queues. The first queue is used to send a message or a request from one application to another, and the second queue is used for sending an acknowledgment or reply in the opposite direction. Other models of communication, such as client-server, can be easily implemented by using the abstraction of a message queue.

Regardless of the communication model used, message-based programming can help promoting modularity. Different programmers can be in charge of developing different applications, and they have well-defined interfaces between them in the form of messages. While these well-defined interfaces are not as powerful as the ones that are offered by object-oriented object models (such as EJB or plain Java RMI), they did prove to be useful when developing large-scale distributed software.

MQSeries Message Queues in the Component Broker

MQSeries message queues are represented in the CB implicitly through messages. To this end, two interfaces are provided: *InboundMessage*, which represents an incoming message, and *OutboundMessage*, which represents an outgoing message. Invoking the respective get or put method performs an operation on the message queue.

Because the CB is essentially an object engine that supports the CORBA model, these interfaces are not Java language interfaces; rather, they are

CORBA interfaces. Both InboundMessage and OutboundMessage objects are managed by the CB and conform to its object model, and they provide full access to the MQSeries messaging system.

In virtually all non-trivial cases, InboundMessage and OutboundMessage objects are not used as is; rather, specialized forms of them are derived. CB provides a tool called Object Builder to build such specialized message types, but when using CB as part of WebSphere Enterprise Edition, it is possible to create such message types based on a Java property file (as explained in the next section).

Creating MQSeries EJBs

In order to use the CB objects, which encapsulate MQSeries functionality from a Java-based application, EJB support is provided. This support comes in the form of a tool called *MQ-Series Application Adaptor EJB* (mqaaejb). This tool generates a session bean that wraps a CB object, which in itself wraps an MQSeries queue.

In order to create a session bean, mqaaejb requires a Java properties file that specifies the type of message and its format. The type of message could be Inbound, Outbound, or InOut. The first two types correspond to Inbound-Message and OutboundMessage, as mentioned in the previous section—whereas the last one is a hybrid that pairs together an inbound queue and an outbound queue. Figure 37-1 depicts the flow of data in each of these message types. The message format is specified by a list of fields. Each field has a separate property, where the property name is the field name and the property value is the field type (which might look a little confusing at first glance).

For example, consider a message that contains four fields, as detailed in Table 37-1. The property file in Listing 37-1 can be used for creating a session bean for an outbound message with these fields.

Property fileThe usage of the mqaaejb command is as follows:

```
> mqaaejb -n baseBeanName -f propertiesFile [-p packageName] [-b
BOInterface]
```

The meaning of the arguments are summarized in Table 37-2. For instance, if the file InvPush.properties includes the properties that are listed in Listing 37-1, the following command can be used to create an session EJB for it:

```
> mqaaejb -n InvPush -f InvPush.properties -p book.ws.ch37
```

Figure 37-1
Illustration of different
message types: (a)
Inbound; (b)
Outbound; (c) InOut

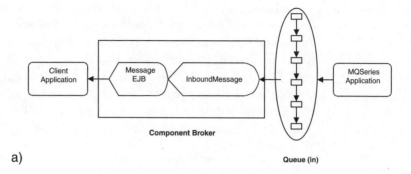

a)

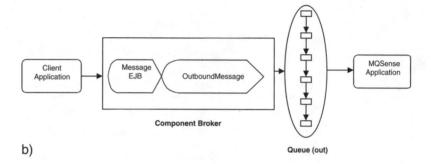

b)

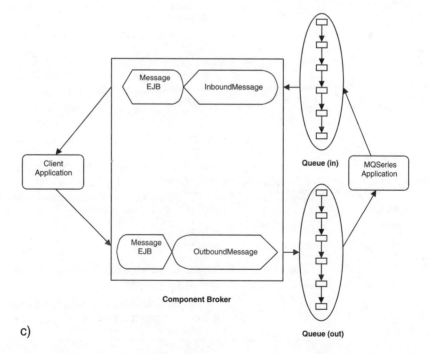

c)

The result would be that in the current directory, a subdirectory (or several nested subdirectories) would be created to correspond to the package name, and in this directory, the Java source files and a compiled class file would be placed. In addition, a JAR file containing these compiled Java class files and an XML file containing the EJB deployment descriptor are created, and both are placed in the current working directory. Once these files are created, it is possible to create an EJB JAR file by using the `jetace` tool. In our case, the command required would be as follows:

```
> jetace -f InvPush.xml
```

Finally, you can run the `cbejb` program to deploy the EJB.

Table 37-1

Sample Message Definition

Data Type	Field Name	Meaning
String	vehReg	Vehicle Registration #
String	owner	Owner of vehicle
String	newOwner	New owner of vehicle
Integer	price	Dollar amount for sale

Listing 37-1

Sample mqaaejb Properties File

```
vehReg=java.lang.String
owner=java.lang.String
newOwner=java.lang.String
price=int
```

Table 37-2

Arguments for the mqaaejb command

Argument	Meaning
baseBeanName	The name of the EJB to be created
propertiesFile	The properties file (like the one shown in Listing 37-1)
packageName	Optional package name for the EJB (if not specified, a default package name is given)
BOInterface	Optional specification of an existing CB object. This allows you to associate the EJB with that CB object, instead of creating a new one.

38

Tivoli
Enablement
Modules

Tivoli is a family of products aimed at simplifying the complex task of managing large distributed systems. It provides tools for the centralized control and monitoring of systems, and enables the automation of routine system administration tasks. Since Tivoli provides an easy-to-use graphical user interface for accessing remote machines and administering them, it goes without saying that Tivoli is a real time-saver when managing large enterprise networks. For more details about Tivoli, access Tivoli Systems Web site at www.tivoli.com.

With the ever-growing popularity of the Internet, it is difficult to imagine any serious enterprise network that does not include a Web server or, more likely, several of them. Once you have several Web servers, the problem of centralized control becomes critical, especially when you need to manage version updates for software or content, identify performance bottlenecks, and so on. For enterprise networks where Tivoli is used for management and monitoring, IBM (which incidentally is Tivoli Systems parent company) provides seamless integration with WebSphere.

In order to integrate Tivoli with the WebSphere Application Server (WSAS), IBM provides the WebSphere Application ServerPlus for Tivoli. This module enables centralized management of the WebSphere Application Server using Tivoli-based tools. A similar module is available for managing the HTTP server through Tivoli.

Installation and Prerequisites

In order to install the Tivoli enablement modules, you must have the *Tivoli Enterprise Console* (TEC) or the Tivoli Enterprise Management package installed along with the IBM WSAS (any edition). The software required for integrating the two products can be downloaded directly from the IBM Web site at www.ibm.com/software/webservers/management.

The installation itself is done through the TEC by selecting "Install Product..." under the Install menu. The resulting window is shown in Figure 38-1. The only thing you need to specify is which component you want to install. In our case, it is WebSphere Application ServerPlus for Tivoli. If you don't see it in the dialog that prompts you for the list of products to install, click the Select Media button and select the path to the installation files. You can also specify on which client machines the installation should take place.

Once you complete installation, the WebSphere Application ServerPlus icon is added to your TEC desktop under an icon called TivoliPlus. Double-click on the TivoliPlus icon and then on the WebSphere Application ServerPlus for Tivoli icon to get the window that includes the various tools and tasks available for managing WebSphere. These are detailed in the next section.

Figure 38-1
The Tivoli installation
window

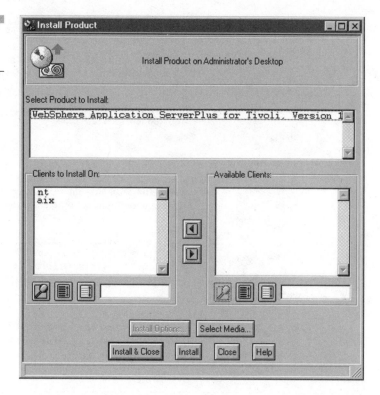

Using WebSphere ServerPlus for Tivoli

Tasks and resources related to the WebSphere application server are represented on the Tivoli console as icons, similar to the way other tasks and resources are represented in the Tivoli console. Table 38-1 lists the icons available under the WebSphere Application ServerPlus for Tivoli icon. Note that almost all these icons have a small plus sign on the upper right side, which indicates they belong to the ServerPlus module. The various icons enable you to do the following:

- View and edit server definitions
- View and edit monitoring definitions
- Perform monitoring
- Access log files
- Start or stop WebSphere services
- Perform routine management of WebSphere services

Table 38-1

WebSphere Application ServerPlus for Tivoli icons

Icon	Meaning
TivoliPlus	Folder icon under which TivoliPlus modules are located. The WebSphere enablement module is one of them.
WebSphere Application ServerPlus for Tivoli	Top icon for the WSAS icons
WSAS Indicator Collection	Visual indicator showing monitoring problems (the thermometer indicates problem severity)
NT WebSphere Application Servers	Icon representing the collection of NT-based WebSphere Application Servers (provided as a convenience to enable performing tasks on this collection)
Unix WebSphere Application Servers	Icon representing the collection of UNIX-based WebSphere Servers (provided as a convenience to enable performing tasks on this collection)
About WebSphere Application ServerPlus for Tivoli	Provides product information
Add Server Definition	Activates a task that adds a new IBM WSAS Server definition to the configuration file on target systems. This includes assigning an ID number for each server. This task requires the WebSphere installation directory, JDK installation directory, administration port, and administration user ID and password.
Remove Server Definition	Removes the server definition, hence disabling its management by Tivoli. This has no effect on the WebSphere Server execution.
List Server Definitions	Lists all server definitions for the different hosts managed

Icon	Meaning
Archive Server Logs	Performs a task of copying logs to an archive directory, possibly compressing them. This does not include truncating or deleting the current log files.
Dump Server	Dumps data about the current state of the server to a screen or a file (its name is user-specified)
Configure File Package	Configures the monitor scripts to be distributed to remote hosts (such as the path in which they should be placed)
WSAS_Monitors	Provides access to monitoring definitions
Monitors File Package	Installs monitoring scripts on remote hosts (which are in the subscription list)
WSAS Monitors	Review the status of monitored resources. The thermometer indicates the severity of problems, if there are any.
Start Servlet Service	Starts the servlet service on specified servers
Stop Servlet Service	Stops the servlet service on specified servers
Manage Servlet Service	Performs a certain operation in servlet service on specified servers. The operation can be **stop**, **start**, **restart**, **status**, or **statistics**.
Manage Servlets	Performs certain operations on single servlets (or on all servlets). Operations are **load**, **unload**, **status**, **stats**, or **statistics**. The servlet name (or "all") is user-specified.

continues

Table 38-1

Continued

Icon	Meaning
Manage EJS Service	Performs operations on EJS service (responsible for EJBs) in specified servers. Operations are **start**, **stop**, **status**, **containers**, **jars**, or **beans**. The last three provide a listing of the elements of the respective type.
Manage EJB Jar Files	Performs EJB file deployment operations on a specified set of servers. Operations are **deploy**, **deployable**, **deployed**, **undeploy**, **undeployed**, **beans**, or **status**. The EJB file is a user-specified parameter.
Show Server Status	Indicates current status of the server (that is, if the EJS and Servlet services are running)

Configuring Servers

Before anything else is done, you must first define the servers. This is a two-step process (not counting the WebSphere installation itself, which for our purpose we shall assume was already completed successfully). The first step is adding the machines that are WebSphere servers to the subscriptions lists of the ServerPlus module. There are two icons, one for NT servers and the other for UNIX servers. Right-clicking on either one will display a menu with the "Subscribers..." option. Selecting this option will enable you to define your subscriber list, which is the list of WebSphere servers of the respective kind. In the dialog that appears, you need to select the hosts from the list appearing on the right-hand side and transfer them to the list of current subscribers on the left-hand side. The next step is actually defining the settings for these servers. This is done by clicking the Add Server Definition icon, which brings up a dialog where you are required to provide the following configuration information:

- *WebSphere Application Server* (WSAS) *Installation Directory*   The root of the WebSphere installation (such as E:\WebSphere\Appserver)

- *JDK Home Directory*   The path for the JDK installation (such as C:\JDK1.1.7)

- *Admin Service Port*   The port number used for administrative tasks, which is 9527 by default

- *Administrator UserID and Password* The user ID and password for the administrator, as set during the installation. These are required for the various monitors and tasks to work correctly.

When adding the server definition, the server receives a server ID number.

Following the definition of servers, you need to distribute some monitoring scripts to the servers you have defined. This is again a two-phase process. First, you configure the package to be distributed using the Configure File Package icon. In the resulting dialog box, you enter the "Source Host Name," which basically is the Tivoli server host name (or wherever you have installed the TivoliPlus package) and the "Target Path," which is the path where the scripts are to be placed (any directory would do, as long as it is in the list of directories stored in the PATH environment variable on the remote machine).

After configuring the file package, you can distribute it. To do so, you need to define "subscribers" (which are host machines to which it will be distributed) by right-clicking the Monitors File Package icon and selecting "Subscribers..." from the menu. The selection process is identical to the one previously described for lists of application servers and consists of selecting the machines from the list on the right side and transferring them to the list on the left. After selecting the subscribers, you can immediately distribute the scripts by selecting Distribute from the menu displayed when right-clicking the Monitors File Package icon.

Monitoring

Using Tivoli ServerPlus, you can monitor various resources on the *WebSphere Application Server* (WSAS) host. This can help in accurate and timely identification of problems before they have a severe impact. Monitoring information is accessed through the WSAS Monitors icon. You can customize the thresholds used for the various resources and also the action triggered once a threshold is exceeded by selecting Properties from the WSAS Monitors icon menu. You can also determine how frequently (if at all) each monitor should be run. The resources that are monitored are as follows:

- *Logfile Entries* The number of lines in log file
- *Logfile Size* The size in bytes of the log file
- *Log Directory Free Space* Free space in the directory in which the log file resides

- *Server Status* Zero if all services are working properly; otherwise, it is a positive error code number

- *Current Server Memory in Use* Percentage of allocated server peak memory currently used

- *Server Memory Peak* The peak size of memory used by the server (in bytes)

- *Current Handler Pool in Use* Percentage of handler pool peak currently in use

- *Server Handler Pool Peak* The peak number of handlers concurrently used by the server

- *Server Requests Processed* The number of requests processed by the server (in the most recent monitoring interval)

- *Servlet Status* Returns 0 for a running servlet, 1 for one that is not (if several servlets are checked, the sum of these figures is provided)

- *Servlet Requests Processed* Number of requests processed by the servlet (in the most recent monitoring interval). If several servlets are checked, the sum of requests for all of them is provided.

- *Servlet Average Execution Time* Average execution time for the servlet calculated over its lifespan (since it was loaded)

- *Servlet Statistic* Monitors any statistic for the servlet (here you cannot check multiple servlets). The statistics are (with self-explanatory names) *Name, State, LoadedTime, TotExecTime, UserOrInternal, Local, AutoStart, AutoReload, Service, RealPath,* and *ClassName.*

- *Server Statistic* Check a statistic on a server. The available statistics repeat some of the aforementioned monitored values: *TotalRequests, TotalMemory, FreeMemory, TotalHandlerPool,* and *TotalExceptions.*

It is possible to run monitors on a set of servers, in which case each of the above measurements is the sum or average of the measurements for individual servers.

Invoking Other Tasks

The remainder of the icons available in the Tivoli ServerPlus window relate to various utility and control tasks. To invoke them, you need to double-click the corresponding icon and select the parameters in the dialog box that comes up. Most dialogs contain fields for user IDs and passwords, which are not required if they were defined in the Add Server Definitions entry. In addition, a Server ID List field is used to select which servers are to be included in a specific task. The default is "0", which means all servers. Alternatively, you can provide a list of colon delimited server ID numbers. Other fields vary with the task. For example, the Manage Servlet Service includes an entry for Server Request, which can be either **start**, **stop**, **restart**, **status**, or **statistics**.

CICS
Connectors

This chapter focuses on integrating WebSphere applications with CICS applications. CICS stands for *Customer Information Control System* and is IBM's online transaction processing product. CICS is essentially an application server providing transaction management. Although WebSphere is also an "application server," these two are world apart. In terms of the modern software world, CICS is prehistoric. It has been in use in the market for more than 30 years now, running on platforms such as MVS/ESA and OS/390. Because CICS has been around for such a long time, huge amounts of data are managed by CICS-based systems. In order to allow organizations to gradually migrate to newer technologies using an evolutionary approach, IBM has included into its CICS server some object-oriented capabilities. Actually, CICS TS 1.3 supports IIOP and allows writing server-side CICS applications in Java, which can easily invoke legacy CICS applications.

The approach you should take when seeking integration of CICS into WebSphere applications and servlets resembles the approach described in Chapter 37, *MQSeries Connectors*, for MQSeries integration. As with MQSeries, the challenge is "wrapping" abstractions from the CICS realm and giving them a Java interface. The problem here is a little more difficult because the mapping between abstractions is not so obvious. Whereas in the case of MQSeries the objective was to "wrap" queues that are simple and well-defined objects, in CICS, some of the data is not even stored in relational databases, so it is not so clear what the objects are.

IBM provides, as part of the *Component Broker* (CB) server, a special adapter called *Procedural Application Adapter* (PAA). The name emphasizes that it hooks in applications that are not object-oriented. Similar to the situation with MQSeries, the final step is creating an EJB to wrap the CB adapter object.

A completely different approach to connecting WebSphere with CICS is to use a Java library called JCICS directly from within servlets. We will not go into detail about this alternative, but it is important to note that this option has the advantage of not requiring CB (instead, the WebSphere Application Advanced Edition can be used). The disadvantage is that it requires more coding to do the mapping between the COMMAREA (that is, "communication areas") and Java objects. JCICS comes as part of the VisualAge for Java Enterprise Edition 3.0 distribution.

Procedural Application Adapter

The role of PAA is to translate data in procedural systems into objects. This is done by maintaining "proxy" objects that represent procedural data. These objects are referred to as *Procedural Adapter Objects* (PAO), and they have other functions besides being proxies. They also provide some caching functionality in order to improve overall performance. PAOs are created and updated as needed based on the data in the underlying database.

PAA provides a uniform way of doing the translation of data from procedural systems, but it does so while transparently using three different underlying technologies:

- *IBM Host-On-Demand* (HOD).   HOD allows the CB to simulate a user of a TN3270 terminal. This way the CB is able to access the screens of the CICS-based system.

- *External Call Interface* (ECI).   Using a pair of product called the CICS Transaction Gateway and the CICS Universal Client, the CB is able to generate requests to a CICS server in a manner that resembles RPC (or RMI).

- *Advanced Program to Program Communication* (APPC).   APPC is an implementation of the SNA LU 6.2 protocol, which allows CB to generate requests directly to the CICS server in a manner that resembles RPC (or RMI).

These three technologies are listed in an order that reflects the level of coupling and transactional support provided. HOD is the most loosely coupled solution and with the least transactional support (that is, operations done cannot be rolled back, but rather are immediately committed). The ECI solution provides improved transactional support (roughly the equivalent of a single phase commit transaction), and APPC goes beyond just providing a communication media and allows direct access to the transactional capabilities of the underlying CICS system.

Installation and Prerequisites

In order to use the CICS adapter, you must have the WebSphere Application Server Enterprise Edition, which includes the *Component Broker* (CB). As part of the CB installation, you can specify the CICS and IMS Application Adapter as one of the packages to install.

In addition, you must have VisualAge for Java Enterprise Edition, which includes the CICS Transaction Gateway and CICS Universal Client. VisualAge for Java Enterprise Edition include CICS connectors that are Java wrappers to CICS. These connectors allow you to connect to CICS system from within servlets, using the WebSphere Application Server *Advanced Edition* (AE).

If you intent to use HOD or APPC as the method of connectivity, you must have IBM eNetwork Communications Server installed. In addition, APPC might require other IBM communications products, depending on the platform on which CICS is running. In the following section, we will concentrate on connecting to CICS using ECI because this solution blends ease of use with enough power. If you are interested in using HOD or APPC, refer to the relevant IBM documentation.

Before starting the CICS Transaction Gateway, you must configure a file called `CICSCLI.INI` in the `BIN` directory under the installation of the CICS connectors. This file lists the CICS servers with which you may interact. Its format is quite simple and the initial version of the file includes a lot of explanatory comments. The file starts with identification of the client by a line of the following form:

```
Client = <client-name>
```

This line is followed by a sequence of attribute-value pairs specifying different aspects of the client configuration. Immediately after that, the servers are defined. The initial configuration file includes four server definitions (the last three of them are commented out). Each one starts with

```
Server = <server-name>
```

The predefined server names are:

- CICSTCP   Template for server for which TCP/IP communications are used
- CICSNETB   Template for server with NetBIOS communications
- CICSSNA   Template for server SNA communications
- CICST62   Template TCP62 communications (a hybrid of TCP/IP and SNA)

Based on the type of server you require, you should create a server entry (either by modifying the TCP/IP entry or uncommenting one of the others). In order to do that, you need to change the server-type to the server name and add the protocol parameters (for example, for TCP/IP the IP address and port). If you are not using TCP/IP communications, you should also uncomment the relevant driver definition at the end of the file.

In order to verify that the content of this file is correct, you can type `CICSTERM /S=<server-name>` at a command prompt. This should start a CICS terminal connected to the specified server. If unsuccessful, the error messages might help to find the problem. If this verification stage go smoothly, you can run the Transaction Gateway, either from the Start menu or by running `JGATE.EXE` in the same `BIN` directory.

Developing PAOs

PAOs are derived from `EntityProceduralAdapterObject` and are implemented as objects. In order to create such an object in VisualAge for Java, you need to enable the following features in your VisualAge for Java installation (this is done through the Add Feature option under QuickStart):

- CICS Connectors
- IBM Common Connector Framework
- IBM Component Broker Connectors
- IBM Enterprise Access Builder Library
- IBM Procedural Application Adapter

PAOs must implement four abstract methods—`create()`, `retrieve()`, `update()`, `delete()`—that should perform the interaction with their underlying persistent store (CICS, in our case). In addition, the PAO should have `get` and `set` methods for its fields.

PAOs extend the *Enterprise Access Builder* (EAB) library's notion of a "Business Object" and as such they neatly fit into the CB object model. Similar to EAB Business Objects, they also have "key" objects, derived from `BusinessObjectKey`, which are used to locate PAOs within the current object space. The name of a key object should be composed of the name of the PAO with "Key" appended to it.

The actual interaction with the CICS system is done by `Command` objects, which are used by the four PAO methods. These commands use special data beans that correspond to the data structure used for the CICS communication. ECI uses COMMAREAs, which are essentially data buffers used for CICS interprogram communication. Each data bean corresponds to a specific COMMAREA specification provided as a COBOL program, or alternatively as BMS or MFS maps (these two stand for *Basic Mapping Support* and *Message Format Service* respectively, and are two kinds of high-level screen definition languages for 3270 terminals). In order to create such beans, select the Tools option on the pop-up menu of the package in which the PAO is developed. The Records entry includes options for creating COBOL, BMS, and MFS records. (Figure 39-1 shows a sample dialog for creating a COBOL record; if there are several COMMAREA definitions in the file, you are prompted to select which one you want.)

Figure 39-1
Sample dialog for
creating COBOL data
record

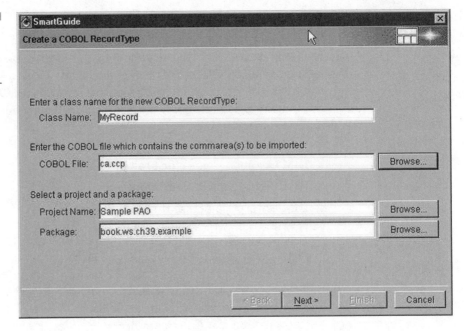

After the record is created, you can define a mapping between it and the PAO (using Create Mapper under Enterprise Access Builder entry in the same Tools menu). The mapping is a new class. To create it, select the PAO class and the data bean class and connect between attributes of the PAO and fields of the data record bean. You connect two fields by clicking the connect icon or using Connect from the Connections menu.

The implementation of "command" objects requires communicating with CICS. It is possible to automatically generate these comands using the Create Command option under the Enterprise Access Builder in the Tools menu of the package. To create a command, you must specify the mapper class, input bean, and output bean classes (you can also use the input bean for output). For each of these beans, select the fields that are to be communicated. The Create Command wizard lets you select the connectivity technique (HOD, ECI, or APPC).

Given the command object, the PAO four methods are easily implemented. The most common implementation would include creating a new command, setting its connection specification (using the method of setConnectionSpec, sending to it the PAO's this.getConnection-Spec()), and then setting all the input fields, calling the execute method of the command, and finally extracting the results.

Before developing your own PAOs, a good idea would be to take a look at some of the samples provided with VisualAge for Java. These should clarify some of the technicalities regarding the usage of the underlying communication mechanisms.

Note that PAOs can be imported into the Object Builder tool that is part of the CB, where its interaction with other CB objects can be specified.

Creating an EJB for a PAO

In order to have your WebSphere application interact with CICS applications, you need to create an appropriate EJB. To create an EJB out of a PAO, WebSphere provides the `paotoejb` tool (that is, PAO to EJB). The syntax of using this command is:

```
> paotoejb -name [ ejbName ] paoClass -hod | -eci | -appc
```

The `ejbName` parameter can include the desired name of the generated EJB. If not specified, the name of the PAO (or some shorthand form of it) will be used. The `paoClass` provides the fully qualified Java name for the PAO class (without the `.class` extension). The last option, coming after the PAO class, defined which kind of connectivity method is used: HOD, ECI, or APPC respectively.

After creating the EJB code, simply compile it using `javac` (using the command `javac ejbName*.java`) and place the compiled class files into a JAR file. Finally, in much the same way you deploy other EJBs, use the `jetace` tool to create an EJB JAR file and invoke the `cbejb` tool to do the deployment.

40

The WebSphere Administrative Console

The WebSphere Application Server is quite a complex product and, as such, requires a lot of configuration to work properly. In order to remedy this, IBM provided a user-friendly application called the WebSphere Administrative Console. This application is provided with WebSphere version 3.0 and later. In older versions, administration was conducted with an ordinary Web browser and a connection to port 9257.

The administration console is part of the WebSphere installation, but it can be installed separately. If you have WebSphere up and running, your installation should include the administration console under the `bin` directory in your WebSphere installation, in the file `adminclient.bat`. This batch file can be started with two optional arguments, which are the host name and port. These are useful for performing remote administration of a WebSphere server.

Using the Administrative Console

The administrative console, shown in Figure 40-1, is a typical Windows-based application. On the top of the window is a menu bar and below that are several command buttons. The middle part of the window is divided into two. On the left side is a "navigation area" that allows you to traverse through the different resources and tasks. When you focus on a specific resource or task, you get the relevant details on the right side, which is the work area. At the bottom of the window is a message area that indicates server activity, error messages, and the progress of commands initiated from the administration console.

Figure 40-1
The WebSphere Administrative Console

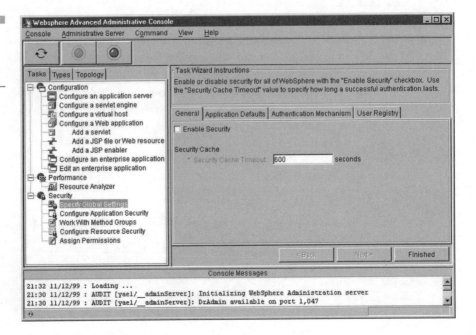

The menu bar includes lots of options:

- *Console*   General menu with three entries:
  - *Trace Enabled*   Allows enabling or disabling tracing
  - *Trace Settings*   Provides trace settings
  - *Serious Events*   A detailed listing of all serious events (an example shown in Figure 40-2), along with the capability to customize the definition of what a serious event is
- *Administrative Server*   Provides the capability to connect to and start a remote server. It is not relevant when using a local server.
- *Command*   Allows Undo, Redo, and History review. An example of the history review is shown in Figure 40-3.
- *View*   Provides capability to go into desktop mode, which allows displaying multiple views of the administration client work area and the capability to refresh the navigation area on the left side
- *Help*   Provides detailed help

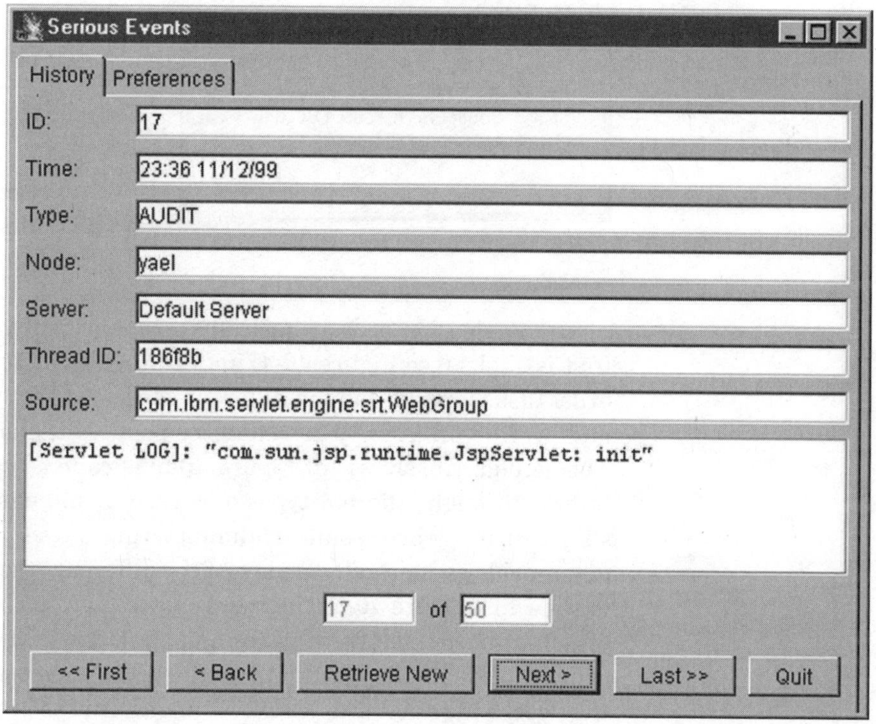

Figure 40-2
Serious Events listing

Figure 40-3
Recent Command
History listing

Command	Status	Completion Time	Result
Configure application security	Success	23:33:39 11/12/1999	Normal
Default Server.start	Success	23:37:44 11/12/1999	Normal
Deploy JarFile	Success	11:46:28 12/12/1999	Normal
EnterpriseBeans.create	Failed	11:49:16 12/12/1999	Exception
EnterpriseBeans.create	Failed	11:55:28 12/12/1999	Exception
Deploy JarFile	Success	12:12:55 12/12/1999	Normal
EnterpriseBeans.create	Success	12:13:27 12/12/1999	Normal

Recent Command History

Figure 40-4
Navigation area Tasks

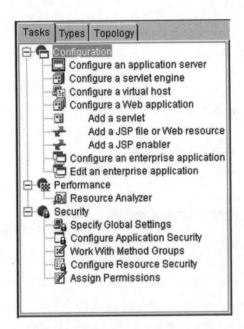

Tasks | Types | Topology

- Configuration
  - Configure an application server
  - Configure a servlet engine
  - Configure a virtual host
  - Configure a Web application
    - Add a servlet
    - Add a JSP file or Web resource
    - Add a JSP enabler
  - Configure an enterprise application
  - Edit an enterprise application
- Performance
  - Resource Analyzer
- Security
  - Specify Global Settings
  - Configure Application Security
  - Work With Method Groups
  - Configure Resource Security
  - Assign Permissions

The navigation area is basically a control tab with three options. The first is Tasks (see Figure 40-4) and it provides access to various task wizards. Tasks wizards help in different aspects of WebSphere administration and provide an activity-driven entry point to the administration process. The second tab, shown in Figure 40-5, is called Types and allows you to browse through different types of resources and entities, thus providing a subject-driven entry point to administering the server. The last tab, Topology, provides a hierarchical view of the different resources and entities and is shown in Figure 40-6. The hierarchy of the topology view is a hierarchy of containment; that is, the parent of an entity in the hierarchy tree corresponds to the directly containing entity. The topmost element of the tree is the WebSphere administrative domain. This is a group of one or more servers sharing the same administration definitions.

Figure 40-5
Navigation area
Types

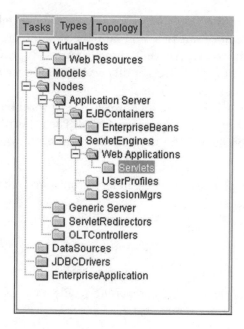

Figure 40-6
Navigation area
Topology

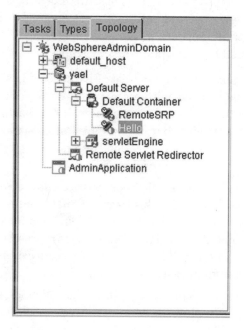

In general, the Topology view is more powerful because it usually allows editing attributes of the selected entity, whereas in the Types view, the display is organized as read-only tables. This is not to say that no operation can be made on the Types view. You can create new entities (for example, new EJBs), remove entities, and edit the default properties for a whole class of entities there. Another thing you can do in this view is set the default properties of all EJBs or all servlets. However, you may not modify properties of individual entities.

The toolbar below the menu bar provides several buttons, depending on the navigation area and resource selected. These buttons provide functionality that is available from the pop-up menu of the various resources. The buttons are

- *Refresh*   Refreshes the selection and contained entities
- *Start*   Starts a service
- *Stop*   Stops a service
- *Ping*   Checks if a service is running
- *Properties*   Opens a pop-up window with the properties of the resource
- *Default Properties*   Opens a pop-up window with the default properties of the resource type

Our discussion so far is a little obscure. Let's try to sort things out and list kinds of resources and entities we are dealing with here. (Some of the following material appears in the "Administering WebSphere Application Server Version 3 help file, published by IBM.)

- *Nodes*   A "node" in the administrative console is a physical machine, and it should coincide with an instance of the administrative server running on that machine (for example, if the machine is shown to be running, this implies that the administrative server is running on it). Nodes can contain application servers, generic servers, servlet redirectors, and OLT controllers.

- *Application Servers*   Application servers allow a Web server to support EJBs, servlets, and JSP. This term is a little confusing because the whole product is called WebSphere Application Server. You can use the product to install several application server processes on each node upon which you install it. Application servers contain EJB containers and servlet engines (one per server).

- *Generic Servers*   Generic servers are non-WebSphere processes managed from within the administrative console.

- *Servlet Redirectors*   Processes using RMI over IIOP to propagate servlet requests to remote nodes

- *OLT Controllers*   The *Object Level Trace* (OLT) and debug facility caters for debugging and tracing distributed applications.

- *Servlet Engine* A program running inside an application server that is in charge of executing servlets and JSP files

- *Web Application* A group of servlets, JSP, and HTML pages sharing the same servlet context. In the containment hierarchy, it is included in a servlet engine and contains servlets.

- *EJB Containers* These are EJB containers in the regular sense (that is, the one in the EJB specification). They contain EJBs and are contained in the application server.

- *EJBs* In the administrative console, EJBs are always deployed enterprise beans.

- *Enterprise Application* A grouping of servlets, JSP files, HTML pages, and EJBs. These creatures don't contain other resources because the resources used by them are dispersed all over the hierarchy and are not necessarily residing in the same node. For the same reason, enterprise applications appear directly under the whole administrative domain in hierarchical view.

- *Models* Models are templates used for creating clones of a server or another resource.

- *Data Sources* A data source corresponds to a JDBC-compliant database being used by EJBs to store persistent data.

- *JDBC Drivers* As the name implies, these represent the code for JDBC drivers. These must be managed (that is, the application server should be aware of them) so the corresponding database can be accessed.

- *Virtual Host* A servlet host that maintains a list of one or more Web applications to which it propagates HTTP requests from the servlet engine. This is useful for isolating applications on the same host.

- *Web Resources* "Served" paths for servlets, JSPs, and HTML pages (for example, URL). These are contained by virtual hosts.

- *Session Manager* A process that stores common servlet state information, thus promoting personalization. The session manager is contained in the servlet engine.

- *User Profile* A resource contained in the servlet engine, which allows it to record user-related information.

After reviewing the different kinds of resources, the following sections look at how to manipulate them. Note that during the WebSphere installation procedure, you are prompted to prepare a default configuration. If you selected this option, the installation procedure creates an application server, container, Web application, and servlet engine. This way, you can immediately play with WebSphere by configuring a servlet. If you did not go for the default configuration, you must manually create the various elements required before configuring a servlet or any other application resource.

In order to run simple applications, the default configuration is sufficient. You can add EJBs, servlets, and JSP pages into it quite easily using the respective task wizards. The remainder of this chapter details how you can configure your server in a partitioned manner, creating different instances of resources such as servlet engines and EJB containers. The motivation for doing so is twofold. One consideration is performance. By using multiple processors and multiple nodes, you are able to improve the performance of your system. The second issue is security: By defining multiple instances of a certain kind of resource, you are able to provide different access permissions to these resources.

The best way to get acquainted with WebSphere administration is to browse through the attributes of the default configuration and then add new elements using the task wizards detailed in Section 40.3.

Administrative Console Types

The administrative console Types navigation area allows the creation of new entities and resources and configuration of their default properties. We start our detailed treatment of the administration procedures with the Types because large portions of the task wizards simply concatenate several of the operations available in this navigation area.

The Types navigation area provides a view of the different types of resources with a hierarchy of folders that correspond to the containment rules for resources. Each folder represents a type of resource, and it includes folders for resource types that can be contained its type of resource. For example, the EJB container folder contains an EJBs folder. These folders provide access to a listing of all resources of the specific type, shown on the work area when selecting the folder. For example, Figure 40-7 shows the work area display when selecting the "Enterprise-Beans" folder, for a simple configuration based on the default one. It lists all the EJBs installed, as well as their name, container, state, JAR file, and start time if applicable.

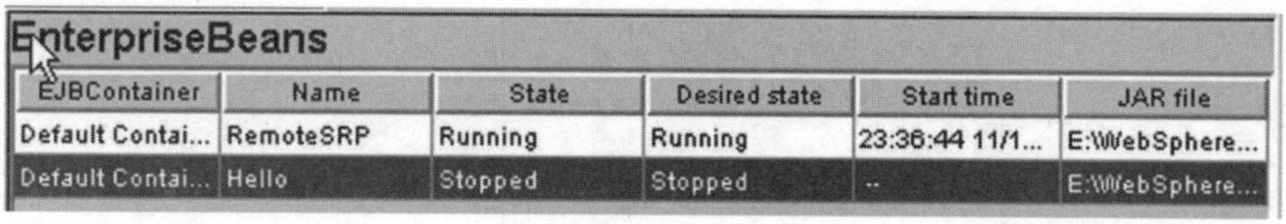

Figure 40-7

Work area display
for EnterpriseBeans
under types

EJBContainer	Name	State	Desired state	Start time	JAR file
Default Contai...	RemoteSRP	Running	Running	23:36:44 11/1...	E:\WebSphere...
Default Contai...	Hello	Stopped	Stopped	--	E:\WebSphere...

Each folder offers a pop-up menu that can be started by right-clicking it. The menu provides for creating and removing resources of the respective kind and setting default properties. Default properties are (obviously) the ones used as default when creating a new resource. In order to avoid repeating ourselves, we will not review the default properties because these are basically a subset of the properties you are able to set for each resource.

The first resource folder is VirtualHosts. When creating a new virtual host, you are prompted to provide for it a name, as well as name aliases. In addition, you can edit the list of MIME types supported. After you create a new host, it would appear in work area (for the Types navigation area) when selecting VirtualHosts. It will also appear under the topmost node in the Topology navigation area, called WebSphereAdminDomain. If you select the new host in this display, you can edit its properties with a dialog box identical to the one used when configuring it on the first time. By the way, when looking at the Topology, note that right-clicking resources allows you to remove them or create new ones. The creation procedure here is identical to the one in the Types area, except that if you create a new resource from the Topology area, you need not specify the containing resource (you already did that by double-clicking a resource).

For each of the different resources, a set of dialog boxes allows editing of its attributes. Table 40-1 summarizes the properties of each resource. These properties are required when creating a new instance of a resource and can be reviewed and edited when selecting an existing resource. If the resource is active (that is, is a process currently running), you might get two entries for a single property—one will show the value currently in use in the running process, the other will be an editable field for the property. Changing the value will not affect the running process unless it is restarted.

Table 40-1 Summary of resource properties

Resource Type	Property Group	Property	Meaning
Virtual Host	General	Name	Host name
	Advanced	Aliases	List of name aliases
		MIME Table	List of mime types and the corresponding extensions
Web Resources		Virtual Host	The host containing the resource
		Resource Name	Path to the resource
Models	General	Model Basis	Instance of resource to be used
	Model Properties	Name	Model name
		Make <Model Basis> a Clone	Checkbox allowing you to make the selected basis to be a clone of the model. This means changes to the model shall be propagated back to the basis.
		Recursively model all Instances under <Model Basis>	Checkbox allowing quick modeling of all sub-components of the model basis
	Resource-specific Properties	*(Set of properties to be used for the model. These are identical to the ones for a new instance of the same type as the model basis.)*	
Application Server	General	Name	Application server name
		Command line arguments	Command line arguments for the JVM process
		Environment	Environment setting (a set of properties each consisting of a pairing of name and value) for the JVM process
		Working directory	Working directory for the JVM process
		Standard input	Standard input for the JVM process
		Standard output	Standard output for the JVM process
		Standard error	Standard error for the JVM process
		Maximum startup attempts	The maximum number of times to restart the JVM if it fails to start
	EJBServer Properties	Workload management selection policy	Defines the method in which clients decide to which server to bind in case there is a workload mechanism at play

Resource Type	Property Group	Property	Meaning
Application Server	EJBServer Properties	Transaction timeout	Maximum duration for a transaction, after which the transaction is aborted
		Transaction inactivity timeout	Duration of transaction inactivity before it is aborted
		Trace specification	Trace specification string
		Trace output file	Output file for trace
		User ID	Operating system user ID under which to run
		Group ID	Operating system group ID under which to run
		Ping interval	Interval in which the admin-server samples this process
		Ping timeout	Duration of time after which the process is considered dead
		Ping initial timeout	Duration of time after which the process is considered failed
		Umask	Operating system umask for process (this an octal value used to mask the permissions placed for files created by the process)
		Process priority	Operating system process priority
		Thread pool size	Number of threads allocated to this server
		Security enabled	Is security enabled in the server (see Chapter 42)
	Parent	Node	Parent node containing the server
	Debug	Debug enabled	Is debug enabled (starting JVM with -debug, allowing to attach a debugger to the application server)
		OLT enabled	Is Object Level Trace enabled (if so, the server will send trace or debug information to OLT and OLD client interface)
EJB Container	General	Name	Container name
	Advanced	Cache size	Size of cache used for maintaining EJB instances
		Cache preferred limit	Number of bean instances the container attempts to keep in the cache
		Cache absolute limit	Maximum number of beans allowed in the cache

continues

Table 40-1 Continued

Resource Type	Property Group	Property	Meaning
EJB Container	Advanced	Cache clean-up interval	The frequency in which the container initiates a cleanup procedure for removing unused items in the cache (attempting to reach the preferred limit)
		Passivation directory	Directory for saving the persistent state of passivated session beans. Passivation takes place when beans must be removed from the cache. If required later, the bean instance is retrieved from a file in the passivation directory.
	Parent	Application server	The server in which the container resides
	DataSource	DataSource	Underlying datasource used for container-managed persistence
		User ID	Datasource user ID used for container-managed persistence
		Password	Datasource password used for container-managed persistence
Enterprise Java Bean	General	Name	EJB Name
		JAR file	Full path for the EJB JAR file
		Deployment descriptor	The deployment descriptor for the EJB
	Advanced	Minimum pool size	Minimum number of database connections the container can have for this bean
		Maximum pool size	Maximum number of database connections the container can have for this bean
		Find for update	Indicate whether the container should get an exclusive lock on the EJB when the findByPrimaryKey method is invoked
	Parent	EJB Container	The container in which the EJB resides
	DataSource	DataSource	Datasource for keeping persistent data
		User ID	Datasource user ID
		Password	Datasource password
		Create Table	Indicating whether a table should be created for persistent data
Servlet Engine	General	Name	Servlet engine name
	Parent	Application server	The containing server
	Advanced	Queue type	Defines the method of connectivity with the Web server—OSE, HTTP, or NONE (for OSE, addition settings are available)

Resource Type	Property Group	Property	Meaning
Servlet Engine	Advanced	Port	Port for connecting with the Web server
		Max. Connections	Maximum number of concurrent connections (with the Web server)
Web Application	General	Name	Web Application name
		Servlet Engine	The containing servlet engine
		Description	Free text description
		Virtual host	Virtual host used
		Full Web path	Web path to the application (excluding the host name)
	Advanced	Document root	File system directory on which the documents reside
		Classpath	Java classpath for the application
Servlet	General	Name	Servlet name
		Web Application	Containing application
		Description	Free text description
		Servlet Class Name	The Java class for the servlet
		Servlet Web Path List	One or more URLs for locating the servlet
	Advanced	Init Parameters	A set of initial parameters names and values to be used in the ServletConfig object provided to the servlet
		Debug Mode	Boolean indicating whether the servlet should run in debug mode
		Load at Startup	Boolean indicating whether to automatically load the servlet on startup
User Profile	General	Name	User profile name
		Servlet Engine	Containing servlet engine
	Enable	Enable User Profile	Indicates whether the user profile is active now
	DataSource	DataSource	The data source used
		UserID	Datasource user ID
		Password	Datasource password
	Classes		Set of attributes relating to the Java software implementation of user profiles. These can only modified through the WebSphere property files (see Chapter 41).
Session Manager	General	Name	Session Manager Name
		Servlet Engine	Containing servlet engine

continues

Table 40-1 Continued

Resource Type	Property Group	Property	Meaning
Session Manager	Enable	Enable Sessions	Indicates whether to enable session tracking
		Enable Cookies	Indicates whether to use cookies to track session IDs
		Enable URL Rewriting	Indicates whether to use rewritten URLs to track session IDs
		Enable Protocol Switch Rewriting	Indicates whether the session ID can be carried across protocol boundaries (that is, from HTTP to HTTPS and viceversa)
		Enable Persistent Sessions	Indicates whether session data should be stored in the datasource or only in memory
	Cookies	Cookie Name	Cookie used to store session IDs
		Cookie Comment	Free text cookie comment
		Cookie Domain	Specified the domain field for the session cookie (this can restrict destination to which the cookie is sent)
		Cookie Maximum Age	Maximum duration of time (in milliseconds) that the cookie will live on the client browser (−1 is only for this session).
		Cookie Path	The value of the path field sent for session cookies (forcing it to apply only to certain Web resources)
		Cookie secure	Indicates if cookies are to be used only over SSL
	Persistence	Persistence settings defined in the respective property file, along with a database user ID and password that can be set	
	Intervals	Invalidate Time	Length of time (in seconds) before cookie is invalidated
	Tuning	Using Multirow Sessions	Indicates whether each instance of application data is to be stored in a separate row (usually yielding better performance)
		Using Cache	Indicates whether a session cache should be used
		Using Manual Update	Indicates whether sessions are to be automatically sent to the data base, or only manually by servlet calling sync method
		Using Native Access	Specifies whether to use optimized SQL access based on a JNI interface written in C (this is relevant only for IBM's DB2)
		Allow Overflow	Whether the number of sessions in memory is allowed to exceed the value specified as the Base Memory Size
		Base Memory Size	The number of sessions to maintain in memory. If using persistence for sessions, this is the cache size, otherwise the maximum number of sessions allowed.

Resource Type	Property Group	Property	Meaning
Generic Server	General	Name	Server name
		Executable	Full path to the executable program
		Command line arguments	Command line arguments to the server program
		Environment	Environment setting (a set of properties each consisting of a pairing of name and value) for the server process
		Working directory	Working directory for the server process
		Standard input	Standard input for the server process
		Standard output	Standard output for the server process
		Standard error	Standard error for the server process
		Maximum startup attempts	Maximum restart attempts in case of failure to start
	Advanced	User ID	Operating system user ID under which to run
		Group ID	Operating system group ID under which to run
		Ping interval	Interval in which the admin-server samples this process
		Ping timeout	Duration of time after which the process is considered dead
		Ping initial timeout	Duration of time from startup after which the process is considered failed
		Umask	Operating system umask for process
		Process priority	Operating system process priority
	Parent	Node	Node on which the server runs
Servlet Redirector	General	Name	Servlet redirector name
		Node	Node on which the redirector runs
		Command line arguments	Command line arguments for the redirector
		Environment	Environment setting (a set of properties each consisting of a pairing of name and value) for the redirector process
		Working directory	Working directory for the redirector process
		Trace string	Trace directive for the servlet redirector

continues

Table 40-1 Continued

Resource Type	Property Group	Property	Meaning
Servlet Redirector	General	Trace log file	Log file to be used with servlet redirector
		Process Priority	Operating system priority for the servlet redirector process
		Maximum Startup Attempt	Number of attempts to restart in case of failure
	Advanced	User ID	Operating system user ID under which to run
		Group ID	Operating system group ID under which to run
		Standard output	Standard output stream for the redirector
		Standard error	Standard error stream for the redirector
		Port	Port used for the redirector
		Max. Connections	Maximal number of concurrent connections
OLT Controller	General	Name	OLT Controller name
		Node	Node on which the controller runs
		Trace Mode	Type of information to collect (0—Nothing, 1—Debugging, 2—Tracing, 3—Tracing and Debugging with prompt, 4—Tracing and debugging without prompt)
		Trace Host	Hostname on which OLT trace viewer is located
		Trace Port	Port on which OLT trace viewer is listening
		Home Directory	The directory in which OLT properties are held
		Driver Path	Full path to the binary executable for the OLT controller
		Debug Host	Hostname for the machine where the IBM Distributed Debugger is installed
		Debug Port	Port on which to contact the IBM Distributed Debugger on the Debug Host
		Process Priority	Operating system priority for the controller process
		Max Startup Attempts	Maximum number of times to attempt starting the process
	Advanced	Command Line Args	Command line arguments for the controller
		Environment	Environment settings for the controller

Resource Type	Property Group	Property	Meaning
		Working Directory	Working directory for the controller
		Umask	Operating system umask
		User ID	Operating system user ID under which to run
		Group ID	Operating system group ID under which to run
		Standard output	Standard output stream for the controller
		Standard error	Standard error stream for the controller
Data Source	General	Name	Data source name
		Database name	Database name
		Driver	JDBC driver
	Advanced (Connection Pooling Parameters)	Minimum connection pool size	Initial size of connections pool
		Maximum connection pool size	Maximum size of connections pool
		Connection timeout	Timeout for connection
		Idle timeout	Idle time before a connection is freed (removed from the pool)
		Orphan timeout	Duration of time a connection is not used before it is taken from the owner and returned to the pool
JDBC Driver	General	Name	JDBC driver name
		Implementation class	Fully qualified classname for the driver
		URL prefix	Common prefix for databases using the driver, usually of the form `jdbc:<database>`
		JTA-enabled	Indicates if the driver is JTA enabled
Enterprise Application (Can only be created and edited using the task wizards)	General	Name	Application Name
	Resources	Enterprise Beans	Enterprise beans contained in the application
		Web Applications	Web applications contained in the enterprise application
		Virtual Hosts	Virtual hosts used in the enterprise application

Administrative Console Tasks

The Tasks navigation area includes three categories of task wizards:

- *Configuration*   Allows quick configuration of new entities and resources
- *Performance*   Includes the Resource Analyzer, which allows monitoring the server and looking for performance bottlenecks
- *Security*   Allows administering server security. Security is a central issue in WebSphere administration and many of the resource definitions are made in order to serve as a platform for defining access permissions.

Configuration Tasks

The first configuration tasks are available. Configure an Application Server goes through the process of creating a new application server and continues to create the following components:

- EJB container and EJBs deployed in it
- Web application
- Servlet engine

The following tasks allow you to create a servlet engine, virtual host, Web application, and to configure a servlet, JSP file, or Web resource. These task wizards are guided walkthroughs through the set of attributes for the respective resource, as listed in Table 40-1.

The last two configuration tasks deal with configuring enterprise applications. These tasks allow you to create a new enterprise application or edit an existing one, by adding and removing resources from the application definition.

Performance

The resource analyzer provides an environment for profiling server activities. It contains entries for EJBs, Servlets, Sessions, Server resources, and DB pools. For each of these categories, it is possible to schedule the rate in which data is refreshed. The resource analyzer provides Start and Stop buttons to start and stop monitoring, and a Refresh button to force a refresh. For each category, the displayed data is resource-specific. For example, for servlets, you can see all the currently running servlets, as well as the number of requests, rate of requests (that is, requests per seconds), execution time, errors, idle time, and date and time of loading.

The resource analyzer provides a convenient point-and-click interface for generating real-time charts of the various resource usage parameters.

The main role of the resource analyzer is to allow you to identify performance problems. By pinpointing the problem and its source (for example, large CPU usage due to long execution time of a certain servlet), it allows you to either solve the problems or provide enough information to continue investigating them using other tools (for example, a Java code profiler).

Security

The security-related tasks allow you to enable WebSphere security and to configure the security-related behavior of applications and resources. These tasks are described in more detail in Chapter 42, "Administering Web-Sphere Security."

WebSphere Property Files

The WebSphere Administration Client, described in the previous chapter, allows the customization of the WebSphere installation according to your needs. In some cases, you might require direct access to WebSphere's configuration files, which are mostly Java property files. Such cases may occur if you enter the wrong parameters in the installation or if you change something in your setup. Obviously, editing these files is not recommended unless you are having trouble or you really know what you are doing.

Property files are concentrated in the `properties` directory under your WebSphere installation directory, except for `admin.config`, which is under the `bin` directory. In the WebSphere Application Server Standard Edition, the `was.prp` file is also under the `bin` directory.

Property Files

WebSphere property files are for the most part ordinary Java property files. In other words, they are composed of lines that have pairs of `property=value`, where the property is package-qualified. Listing 41-1 shows the `sas.server.props` file, which is representative of WebSphere's property files. The property files are as follows:

- `admin.config`   This file includes basic definitions for the WebSphere AdminServer. These might require some changes in case you change database settings or Java library locations. This file is used for "booting" the WebSphere Application Server admin-service. Here are some of the properties in this file:

  - `com.ibm.ejs.adminServer.nameServiceJar`   Naming Service JAR file

  - `com.ibm.ejs.adminServer.dbUrl`   Database JDBC URL

  - `com.ibm.ejs.adminServer.dbDriver`   Database driver class

  - `com.ibm.ejs.adminServer.classpath`   CLASSPATH to use when running the server

  - `com.ibm.ejs.adminServer.traceFile`   Trace logs

  - `com.ibm.ejs.adminServer.logFile`   Error logs

  - `com.ibm.ejs.adminServer.dbUser`   Database user

  - `com.ibm.ejs.adminServer.dbPassword`   Database password

  - `install.initial.config`   Boolean value indicating if the initialization of databases is required. This value should only be true the first time WebSphere Application Server is started.

- `was.prp`   This file contains paths and filenames of database-related files, which are used only when running the Standard Server Edition of WebSphere. In the Standard Edition, there is no repository such as DB2 or Oracle, and plain files are used instead.

- `sas.server.props`   This file contains some server-related properties, which include the user ID and password for running the server. Other properties in this file define security level and SSL parameters.

■ `sas.client.props` A subset of the definitions in the previous file

■ `bootstrap.properties` Configuration properties for JVM initialization, used for the server startup. These mainly include paths to various libraries and files.

■ `media.properties` This property file is used for mapping client capabilities and XSL stylesheets, required as part of the process of converting an XML document using the Lotus XSL processor (a set of APIs for formatting and converting XML documents). The file is composed of a sequence of rules, each on a separate line. A rule has the form `<user-agent>=media`. Given XML data with XSL stylesheets associations, these rules are used to determine which XSL stylesheet to apply, based on the user-agent value in the HTTP request.

■ `nameservice.config` Includes definitions for the naming service, including its container definitions.

■ `queues.properties` Includes some definition relating to queues used for internal communication in the WebSphere application server.

■ `rules.properties` This file includes translation rules for mapping virtual paths to servlets or sequences of servlets. The format for this file is `<virtual-path>=<servlet-name>` (the right-hand side can be replaced by a series of comma-separated servlet names).

■ `servlet_engine.properties` Includes definitions for the servlet engine of the server, including its container definitions.

■ `version.properties` This isn't really a properties file; it contains a text string that holds the full name of the product, including the version, edition, and platform.

■ `com\ibm\websphere\product.properties` Properties that include the product name, edition, version, build number, and build date.

Listing 41-1
File `sas.
server.props`

```
#SAS Properties - Editable
#Wed Jun 16 17:27:51 EDT 1999
com.ibm.CORBA.loginUserid=admin
com.ibm.CORBA.loginPassword=galahad
com.ibm.CORBA.securityEnabled=false
com.ibm.CORBA.authenticationTarget=LOCALOS
com.ibm.CORBA.delegateCredentials=methodDefined
com.ibm.CORBA.principalName=shakshuka/admin
#SAS Properties - DO NOT EDIT
#Wed Jun 16 17:27:51 EDT 1999
com.ibm.CORBA.SSLKeyRing=com.ibm.websphere.DummyKeyring
com.ibm.CORBA.SSLKeyRingPassword=WebAS
```

continues

## Chapter 41

Listing 41-1
Continued

```
com.ibm.CORBA.SSLClientKeyRing=com.ibm.websphere.DummyKeyring
com.ibm.CORBA.SSLClientKeyRingPassword=WebAS
com.ibm.CORBA.SSLTypeIServerAssociationEnabled=true
com.ibm.CORBA.SSLTypeIClientAssociationEnabled=true
com.ibm.CORBA.SSLV3SessionTimeout=9600
com.ibm.CORBA.standardClaimQOPModels=integrity
com.ibm.CORBA.standardPerformQOPModels=confidentiality
com.ibm.CORBA.loginTimeout=30
com.ibm.CORBA.loginSource=properties
com.ibm.CORBA.LTPAServerAssociationEnabled=true
com.ibm.CORBA.LTPAClientAssociationEnabled=false
com.ibm.CORBA.keytabFileName=f:/WebSphere/AppServer/etc/keytab5
com.ibm.CORBA.securityDebug=no
com.ibm.CORBA.securityTraceLevel=none
com.ibm.CORBA.bootstrapRepositoryLocation=f:/WebSphere/AppServer/
etc/secbootstrap
com.ibm.CORBA.disableSecurityDuringBootstrap=false
LOCALOS.server.id=admin
LOCALOS.server.pwd=galahad
```

XML Configuration Files

The following configuration files are XML files. Although they are not property files per se, they act as property or configuration files. Using XML, it is easier to express the structure of data types, which is useful for session data and user profiles.

- `initialEJSSetup.xml` Includes the initial configuration for the EJB server and containers.

- `olt.xml` Configuration related to the Object Level Trace and Debugging product (OLT and OLD). This file determines which servlet events are traced and debugged when using OLT/OLD.

- `session.xml` Defines what session data is (in the context of session management) and to which database it should be stored.

- `userprofile.xml` This file is intended to store the user profile definition.

42

Administering WebSphere Security

This chapter reviews the WebSphere Administriative Console that enables the administrator to control the various security settings. All security-related settings are accessible from the Tasks navigation area and are concentrated under the Security entry.

WebSphere security revolves around authentication and authorization. You can define the authentication mechanism to be used as well as define the authorization policies, that is, grant permissions to different users to perform actions on resources. Resources in this context are Web-resources of the kind discussed in Chapter 40. In order to simplify the description of permissions, the concept of *method groups* is introduced. Method groups are essentially collections of methods treated uniformly for authorization purposes. The remainder of this chapter reviews the various security tasks available in the administrative console.

Global Security Settings

Global security settings focus on aspects that are common to all applications. Figure 42-1 shows the "Specify Globals Setting" task.

The following properties can be set:

- **General**
  - *Enable Security*   Indicates whether security is enabled at all (if not on, all other security settings are ignored).
  - *Security Cache Timeout*   Determines the duration of time (in seconds) a server can cache security information, thus avoiding repeated access to a user registry lookup (which might be expensive).

- **Application Defaults**   Default settings for applications (which can be overridden when defining the application-specific settings, as detailed in the next section)

Figure 42-1
The Specify Global Settings window

- *Realm Name*   The security realm to which the application belongs
- *Challenge Type*
  - *None*   No authentication takes place (consequently, protected resources cannot be accessed)
  - *Basic*   User ID and password (usually using HTTP)
  - *Certificate*   Indicates that clients need to provide a digital certificate for authentication
  - *Custom*   Sets tailor-made authentication mechanisms by specifying a URL of a servlet that takes over the responsibility for authentication
  - *Use SSL*   Specifies that an SSL connection is required (does not apply if the challenge type is "none")

- **Authentication Mechanism**
  - *Local Operating System*   Indicates that the underlying operating system's users database is used for authentication (such as the /etc/passwd database in UNIX systems)
  - Lightweight Third-Party Authentication (*LTPA*)   Specifies that authentication is done using an LDAP service. This requires the following additional properties:
    - *Token expiration*   Time in minutes before an LTPA token is invalidated (then authentication is required again)
    - *Generate Keys*   Causes the LTPA mechanism to generate new encrypted keys. Requires a password for use by the key-generating mechanism. Note that keys are automatically generated, and this button is used for replacing them.
    - *Import from file*   Imports a file with encrypted keys (useful for sharing keys with other security-related products)
    - *Export to file*   Saves your encryption keys to a file
    - Enable Single Sign On (*SSO*)   Stores extra information in LTPA tokens so that other applications accept clients already authenticated by the application server. This means clients will not be required to repeat the authentication process when entering a new application. This includes the following:
      - *Shared Name*   The name of a cookie used to share SSO information
      - *Domain*   Restricts SSO to a given domain
      - *Import from file*   Loads SSO token information from a file

- *Export to file*   Saves SSO token information to a file
- *Limit to SSL connections only*   Indicates the token information must be used only for SSL (to avoid having it go over non-secure connections)

- **User Registry**   If using "Local Operating System" as the authentication mechanism, the User Registry requires a security server ID and password. If using LTPA, you need to define the LDAP server settings. These include the LDAP server hostname, port, ID and password, directory type, base DN, bind DN, and bind password.

Application Security

The Configure Application Security task enables you to determine the security settings for a specific application. The application-specific information includes the user ID under which the application will run and the password for this ID. This determines which permissions the application will have when running. You can look for users using a special search dialog box, which integrates with the underlying LDAP service or operating system registry. The search options are as follows:

- *Search for*   Indicates whether to search for users, groups, or roles (the latter can be searched only if the directory allows it)
- *Search filter*   A pattern to be matched (possibly using (*) as a wildcard character)
- *Everyone, All Authenticated Users, or Selection*   The domain of the search (what to search for)

Once you perform the search, the Search Results list at the bottom fills up, and you can select an individual user, as shown in Figure 42-2.

Other properties that can be set per application are Realm, Challenge Type, and Use SSL. All have the same meaning as in the application defaults entry, mentioned in the previous section.

Method Groups

Method groups are sets of methods grouped for the sole purpose of assigning them to permissions. The Work with Method Groups task enables you to

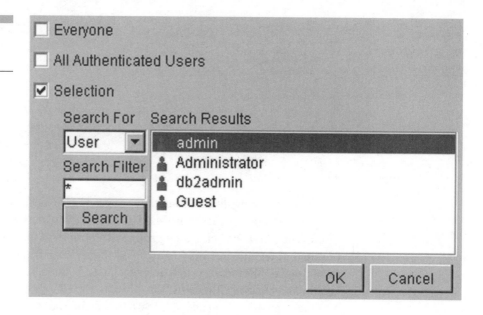

Figure 42-2
The User Search
Dialog window

specify which method groups are used. It supports two operations: adding new method groups and removing existing method groups. Method groups are used when setting resource security, as detailed in the next two sections.

Resource Security

The "Configure Resource Security" option enables you to define the security-related settings of a Web resource, such as a servlet, HTML page, or JSP. The first stage in such a definition is selecting the resource to configure out of the selection tree provided by the administration console (see Figure 42-3).

Figure 42-3
The Resource
Selection window

Figure 42-4

Associating methods
to method groups

Next, you can define the method groups to be associated with each method, as shown in Figure 42-4 (alternatively, you can use the default group settings). Associating a group with a method is done by selecting the method, then clicking "Add," and selecting a group from the pop-up window that appears. Removing such an association is done by selecting the method group and clicking "Remove."

Once you have method groups defined for the resource, you can define other security properties for the resource, but these are relevant only to EJBs:

- *Run-As Mode* This mode is specified in the deployment descriptor of the bean, either SYSTEM, CLIENT, or SPECIFIED. In Websphere Application Server version 3, the SPECIFIED method maps a bean method to application identities rather than a Run-As identity (that's why you can't select the Run-As identity during deployment with jetace).

- *Run-As Identity* Theoretically, this shows the security identity under which the bean method is to be executed if the Run-As mode is set to SPECIFIED. Again, this is not used in WebSphere Application Server version 3.

- *Mapped Application Identity* This specifies the application identity to be assumed by the bean or bean method when selecting the Run-As mode to be SPECIFIED. The application identity is specified through the Configure Application Security task discussed previously.

- *Specific Methods Settings* This enables you to set the previous three properties on a per-method basis (define the Run-As Mode, Run-As Identity, and Mapped Application Identity for each method).

Assigning Permissions

The last task related to security is "Assign Permissions." This task enables you to associate user registry entries with a *permission*. A permission is a pairing of an application with a method group. For example, the pairing of the ReadMethods group with an application called Ticker would read Ticker-ReadMethods. The purpose of this task is to associate users with permissions. The effect of that is that once the user is authenticated by the authentication mechanism, he is authorized to access all method groups he is associated with. The mechanics of associating permissions to users are similar to the way methods are assigned to method groups using the Add and Remove buttons. When adding a user, you are provided with the user search dialog box of the kind shown in Figure 42-2. Figure 42-5 shows an example of setting permissions.

Setting permissions is the essence of the security setup of an application, since it is where the resource security configuration along with the method groups are associated with users from the underlying registry. In a sense, all the definitions detailed in the previous sections are made in order to allow assigning permissions.

Figure 42-5
Associating
permissions

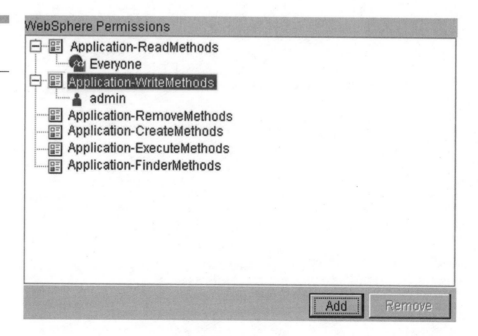

The effect of these permissions is that any requests by non-authorized users will be rejected, resulting in an exception of some sort on the client side. Although this bottom line is very simple, some effort must be made in order to achieve it, in terms of making the correct definitions. The reason the process of definitions might be tricky is that it is application-dependant. And in this case, mistakes can be costly, as placing too many restrictions will prevent legitimate users from working with the application, while granting more permissions than needed could lead to malicious actions by non-authorized users.

43

WebSphere Performance Pack

One of the main reasons for using the WebSphere application server is conducting business over the Internet (or e-business, as IBM likes to call it). While the advantages of using the Internet as a vehicle for doing business are quite obvious and exciting, the Internet has some inherent drawbacks that limits its applicability to business applications. These drawbacks relate mainly to its reliability and performance problems, which are due to network congestion. These performance limitations of Web sites are not theoretical but are rather quite practical. A Web site that is not designed with special care and consideration of these issues might not have the capability to provide continuous service for large quantities of users. Rather, the site might instead crash or return some cryptic HTTP error to users (such as "File Not Found" or "Access Forbidden: Too many users").

IBM WebSphere Performance Pack is a collection of tools that provide an Internet infrastructure software. This infrastructure attempts to address the strict performance and reliability requirements that are imposed by business applications. Through capabilities such as caching, file management, and load balancing, WebSphere Performance Pack tries to boost the performance of Internet applications so that they can meet the challenges posed by the current demanding business environment.

This chapter gives an overview of the tools that are offered as part of the WebSphere Performance Pack. The following chapters address in more detail the application's individual components.

WebSphere Performance Pack Components

The WebSphere Performance Pack consists of three main components:

- *File sharing*   The IBM AFS Enterprise File System enables a set of cooperating hosts to share file systems across LAN and WAN boundaries. This file sharing makes use of data replication in order to increase the availability of data throughout the system. This component is explored in detail in Chapter 44, "IBM AFS Enterprise File System."

- *Caching and filtering*   IBM WebTraffic Express is a caching proxy server that facilitates a significant reduction in bandwidth requirements and response time. IBM WebTraffic is the subject of Chapter 45, "IBM WebTraffic Express."

- *Load balancing*   IBM SecureWay Network Dispatcher is capable of dynamically load-balancing TCP servers. The application reduces the load on a Web site by linking several servers to the site and by dispatching data from the Web site to users through these servers. IBM SecureWay is described in detail in Chapter 46, "IBM SecureWay Network Dispatcher."

Each of these components operates in an independent fashion, yet they complement each other.

AFS Enterprise File Systems

The AFS file system originates from the Andrew File System project, which was initiated at Carnegie Mellon University (Pittsburgh, Pennsylvania). This project focused on implementing a truly distributed file system. Some individuals who were involved in this research project formed Transarc Corporation and continued developing this file system into a commercial product called AFS. Later, Transarc was acquired by IBM.

AFS was originally used for reducing the burden of managing large shared-file systems by using a system-wide virtual logical name space and directory structure that was unrelated to the actual physical location of files and directories. AFS is essentially based on the client-server paradigm. AFS clients access files using the virtual logical name space, while AFS servers are in charge of the actual physical files. AFS found its niche in the world of HTTP servers as a tool for reducing the amount of effort required for maintaining the relationship between URLs and actual files. In other words, HTTP servers used AFS clients so that they could become oblivious to the actual directory structure and file location. Furthermore, the use of AFS improves the efficiency of access to both local and remote data. The secret of this improvement is that AFS clients perform local caching of remote files when these files are accessed. Unlike other systems (such as NFS), caching here is not limited to memory caching. If needed, files are cached on the local disk. In most cases, this technique would still prove to be much faster than performing network access over the Internet or over a WAN. While caching usually means extra work for checking updates to the original file, AFS servers keep track of clients that are performing caching and informs them of these file changes.

AFS also provides increased availability and performance through file replication. Files that are frequently accessed yet are infrequently modified are replicated in several file servers. When a client requires such a file, the client might access each one of the servers that is holding the file replica (hence, reducing the load on servers). If the server is down or is unreachable, the file can be retrieved elsewhere (hence, boosting data availability).

Special consideration was made for issues of system administration. AFS includes several management utilities that are intended to simplify the tasks of managing the distributed file system. These utilities deal with backup, reconfiguration, and other maintenance tasks and do these jobs with minimal or no system down time by creating on-line replications of data.

AFS makes use of powerful lower-level layers for its work. Kerberos-based authentication is used to guarantee data security. Under this authentication scheme, users must prove their identities before accessing any network services. Following identity authentication, AFS still maintains ACLs and implements a strict policy for file access permission for different users and groups of users. AFS also makes use of *Remote Procedure Call* (RPC) for lower-level communication. RPC has numerous advantages in terms of performance, and with RPC, administrative commands can be issued from any client workstation when given the right permissions.

WebSphere Traffic Express

WebSphere Traffic Express performs two roles in the WebSphere Performance Pack: acting as a caching proxy server and as a content filter. Successful caching of data means less network communication, which in turn reduces the delay time for requests made by users. Content filtering is not a performance issue per se, but a WebSphere Traffic Express feature introduced to ensure effective filtering. Content filtering can be viewed as somehow reducing network congestion, because it avoids servicing some requests. Obviously, this method is not a user-friendly way of reducing network load. The main motivation for content filtering is probably protecting children who have access to the Internet, but you can also use this filtering to block access to specific sites for whatever reason.

Similar to any other proxy server, WebSphere Traffic Express acts as a middle man—taking requests from clients, forwarding them to a Web server, and responding to the clients as if it were a Web server. Taking advantage of this positioning, Websphere Traffic Express can boost performance through caching and at the same time perform filtering for blocking forbidden sites or offensive content.

WebSphere Traffic Express provides the following caching capabilities:

- Caching of HTTP requests served
- Support for extremely large caches
- Caching of pages whose header information indicated that they should be fetched each time

- Optional capacity for automatically refreshing the cache with updated versions of the most frequently accessed pages

- Periodic garbage collection, ensuring that old data is not cached indefinitely

- Remote cache access, enabling several machines to share the same cache by using AFS

The following filtering capabilities are also provided:

- *Platform for Internet Content Selection* (PICS) rules guiding the use of rating labels that are placed in HTML or HTTP headers

- Lists of URLs for which access is blocked

- APIs for flexible filtering definitions (using programming)

SecureWay Network Dispatcher

The most critical problem for widely used Internet sites is the problem of slow response or no response at all. Such difficulties are often encountered when a large amount of users attempt to access the same resources at the same time. For example, when Kenneth Starr's Independent Counsel report to the House of Representatives was posted on the Web, the report could hardly be accessed due to the huge demand for the information.

While this situation might not pose a problem for governmental institutions that are only interested in promoting the public's right to knowledge (and possibly entertainment), commercial and business applications must maintain high availability and reliability in order to provide services to customers and prevent the loss of credibility.

The SecureWay Network Dispatcher addresses the need for quick routing of Internet traffic by using three different functions: Dispatcher, Interactive Session Support, and Content-Based Routing. These functions can be deployed separately or together to suit the specific requirements for your site. The three functions complement each other and ensure that Web traffic is smoothly routed to reduce network congestion. These functions also increase availability and fault tolerance.

The Dispatcher is used to balance the load on a server by using a several parameters, all of which can be dynamically set. Using these parameters, which represent various weights and measurements, the Dispatcher balances the load both locally (on the LAN) and remotely (over the WAN).

The Interactive Session Support is a DNS-based daemon that is responsible for load monitoring. This daemon can be installed on each of your servers. Once running, these daemons elect one daemon as their leader, and this daemon represents the other daemons to the outside world. The Interactive Session Support periodically monitors the level of activity on the servers in which the daemons reside; therefore, it can detect the least heavily loaded server. You can then use a simple round-robin approach or a more sophisticated user-specified approach to relieve the load from other servers and place it on the least heavily loaded server. The Interactive Session Support provides an observer interface to enable other applications to make use of the load-monitoring data collected. Specifically, data can be passed to the Dispatcher by using the Dispatcher observer. The Dispatcher can then utilize these reports when executing its load-balancing policies.

Content-Based Routing can be used to balance Web traffic by inspecting the content of a URL request originating at the client. This component enables you to define rules that determine which server is used for which kind of content. Content-Based Routing works in conjunction with the Web-Traffic Express component.

WebSphere Performance Pack Scenario

Figure 43-1 shows a possible schematic layout of a WebSphere Performance Pack network.

The flow of data in such a network is as follows:

- Client requests reach the local WebSphere Traffic Express through local (client-side LAN) Network Dispatcher.
    - The local Network Dispatcher distributes the load between multiple WebSphere Traffic Express servers (where applicable). This way, client requests are forwarded to the least-loaded proxy server.
    - The local Network Dispatcher is backed up by the backup Dispatcher machine, which provides increased fault tolerance.
- WebSphere Traffic Express performs Web content caching and immediately serves the client request if already cached. In addition, it declines the request if the content does not meet the specified filter criteria. Caching is performed by using AFS for improved reliability and performance.

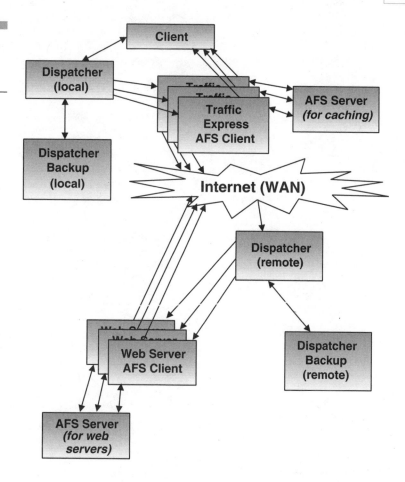

Figure 43-1
WebSphere
Performance Pack
network

- If a request over the WAN is made, it is serviced by the remote (server-side LAN) Network Dispatcher.

  - The remote Network Dispatcher distributes the load between multiple Web servers and selects the least-loaded Web server to service the incoming request.

  - Here, too, the Network Dispatcher has a backup machine for improved reliability.

- Once the request reaches the Web server, it is serviced by accessing the requested file. The file is accessed through the AFS, which boosts performance and reliability.

- The response to the client can be returned on a separate high-speed connection (and not necessarily via the same route).

IBM AFS Enterprise File System

AFS is a distributed file system. In other words, it facilitates the sharing of files over a network in a manner that is transparent to users. As detailed in the previous chapter, AFS is part of the WebSphere Performance Pack and is used to boost performance and increase availability for large-scale Web sites and proxy servers. Its main advantages are its high scaleability, ease of sharing data, and reliable access to replicated data. Other strong points are simplified administration and built-in security features. All these enable easy mirroring of content on multiple servers, as well as updating of software when required, without any security or performance drawbacks.

This chapter delves into the details of AFS installation, configuration, and management. It is worth pointing out that AFS is a general-purpose product, not originally intended to support Web-based applications. However, as already mentioned in the scenario laid out in the previous chapter, AFS it perfectly suited to the needs of high-performance Web sites. Such sites require the high availability and performance offered by AFS. In many cases replication can be useful as well, especially when employing the SecureWay Network Dispatcher, that allows clustering servers holding identical content.

AFS Terms

This section defines some of the terms and concepts used in the context of AFS. Because AFS and distributed file systems are inextricably linked, some file storage must be part of the game. The set of machines on which file storage is provided is called *file server machines*. In contrast, *client machines* are machines that are used to access data on file server machines.

On the AFS servers, some processes are responsible for handling the various aspects of AFS request (for example, handling file requests, managing security, mapping logical names to physical locations, and so on). These processes are called *server processes*.

The *AFS database server* is one designated machine maintaining AFS databases. These databases include:

- *Authentication database*   Storing accounts, passwords, and other security information
- *Volume location database*   Holds the mapping between volumes and actual physical locations
- *Protection database*   Contains information about AFS users and groups
- *Backup database*   Contains backup information (for example, backup frequency)

In order to store this complex configuration, the *AFS system control machine* is responsible for maintaining master copies of AFS system configuration files. These contain information about each machine's local cell and the names of database servers in the cell.

An important abstract is the *AFS cell*. Essentially, this is a collection of client machines and server machines that together form an administrative unit. The cell is considered to encompass the machines, the AFS data stored on file server machines, the AFS internal databases (along with the Database servers), and the accounts created to access the machines and their resources. The cell name is the second element in the fully qualified path of an AFS data item. Such a path is of the form `/afs/<cellname>/filename`. Each AFS user account and each single AFS machine belongs to exactly one cell, which is referred to as the *local cell*. A user may access other cells, referred to as foreign cells.

AFS files are grouped into *AFS volumes*. A volume is essentially a container for a set of related files, and it resides on a single partition. A volume corresponds to a part of the directory tree. Volumes can vary in size, but are usually expected to be less than a partition size.

AFS support *replication*. It allows system administrators to replicate volumes that are frequently accessed but seldom updated. This effectively means a read-only copy of the same volume is located on a different machine. This, in turn, improved availability (that is, if one machine holding this volume crashes, it is still accessible) and performance (this volume can be accessed on one of several servers, reducing the load on each individual server).

AFS uses *caching* on client machines to boost performance. When a request is issued on a client machine to access a certain file, the request is forwarded to the respective file server, but the result is cached in the client machine memory or disk space. Subsequent requests can be serviced from the cache. In order to ensure data consistency, the File server notifies all client machines using a file after the file is modified. In this case, all cached copies of the file are invalidated and it must be fetched from scratch.

AFS support *backup* of data to create old versions of volumes. These versions can be used to have a "hot backup" accessible by users (for example, for the purpose of retrieving mistakenly deleted files).

AFS security requires *mutual authentication* on the part of both client machines and file server machines. The authentication procedure is based on Kerberos, which is an authentication technique originally developed at the *Massachusetts Institute of Technology* (MIT), but now commonly found in many UNIX flavors. In addition to authentication, AFS utilizes *access control lists*, which essentially determines for each directory what access rights each other (or group of users) has. Table 44-1 summarizes the seven different access rights you can assign on an ACL.

Permission	Short Form	Meaning
Lookup	(l)	Grants permission to list the contents of a directory
Read	(r)	Grants access to read files in a directory
Insert	(i)	Grants permission to create new files and subdirectories in a directory
Write	(w)	Grants permission to modify a file (and modify its UNIX permissions)
Delete	(d)	Grants permission to remove a file
Lock	(k)	Grants permission to lock a file
Administer	(a)	Grants access to modify the ACL on the directory

Table 44-1

Summary of ACL access modes

AFS Installation and Configuration

Our discussion focuses on the installation of AFS on Windows NT. Before you start the installation, you should verify that you have at least 50MB of free space on the default system drive, plus one complete NTFS disk partition that will be allocated for storing AFS data (such a partition can be created using the Windows NT Disk Administrator tool). Obviously, you require administrator privileges for this installation. AFS installation also requires having JRE version 1.1.6 or later (which shouldn't be a problem if you have *WebSphere Application Server* [WSAS] installed). One last consideration is that you should have network connections between clients and servers, and that the clocks in these machines should be roughly synchronized. For this purpose, you can use the Windows NT Time Service (TimeServ).

Now we're ready to start the installation. Run the `setup.exe` program in the WebSphere Performance Pack distribution (if you have multiplatform CD, look under the NT directory). The installation program is a standard Windows installation. The first window welcomes you to the installation; click Next to continue. Next appears the README file for the IBM WebSphere Performance Pack. Click Next to continue. Now a dialog box is shown to select the installation location. Select a location and click Next.

The installation program now prompts you to select the components of the Performance Pack you want to install, as shown in Figure 44-1. Select the File Sharing component. From the subcomponents appearing in the right window, you must select File Sharing Client. If the machine is

Figure 44-1
WebSphere
Performance Pack
installation

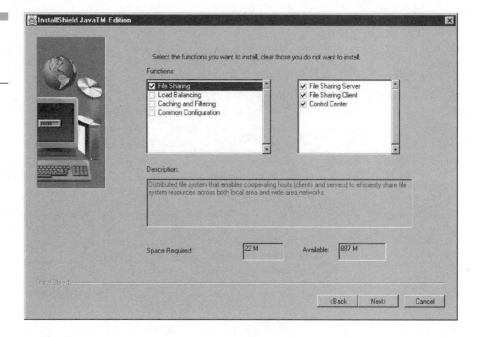

intended to be an AFS server, you also must select the File Sharing Server subcomponent. The Control Center subcomponent should be selected if you are installing AFS on a machine that is intended to serve as an AFS Control Center. After you click Next, you are prompted to replace any existing copies of WebSphere Performance Pack (that is, if you have any previous installations). Finally, click Install to commence the actual installation process. A dialog box shows the progress of the installation. After all files are successfully copied, you are informed that the installation is complete. Now click Finish and reboot the machine.

After it is installed, the AFS appears as a program group under Performance Pack, which in turn is under IBM WebSphere. The installation program creates AFS Server Configuration, AFS Client Configuration, and AFS Control Center Configuration icons (as required by the roles of this machine) in the Windows NT Control Panel. The installation program also creates entries for AFS server and AFS client in the Services Control Panel.

To proceed with AFS configuration, start the AFS Server Configuration Wizard (under the Server entry in the AFS group, which is in Performance Pack group mentioned earlier). This wizard guides you through the configuration process. Following the initial welcome window, you are prompted with a dialog box (shown in Figure 44-2) requesting the name of the cell, along with the AFS principal and principal password. You must specify in

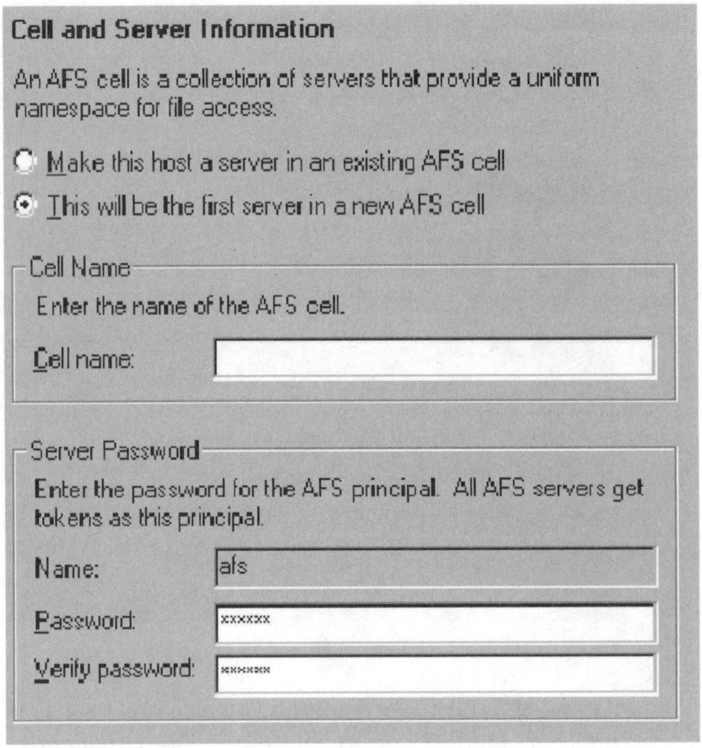

Figure 44-2
AFS Server
Configuration
Wizard: Cell Name
selection

Cell and Server Information

An AFS cell is a collection of servers that provide a uniform namespace for file access.

○ Make this host a server in an existing AFS cell

◉ This will be the first server in a new AFS cell

┌─Cell Name──────────────────────────────────────┐
│ Enter the name of the AFS cell.   │
│   │
│ Cell name: [   ] │
│   │
└───┘

┌─Server Password────────────────────────────────┐
│ Enter the password for the AFS principal. All AFS servers get │
│ tokens as this principal.   │
│   │
│ Name: [afs   ] │
│   │
│ Password: [xxxxxx   ] │
│   │
│ Verify password: [xxxxxx   ] │
└───┘

this dialog box whether this is the first server in a new cell or if you are connecting to an existing cell. Click Next to proceed to the next window, shown in Figure 44-3. Here, select the password for the AFS administrator account and the AFS ID for this account. The next phases are configuring the file service and the database service. These are done automatically for the first AFS machine in the cell. Next, select whether the machine can serve as a backup machine (default is yes). Finally, select the AFS partition out of the available disk partitions. The Configuration Wizard the drives that cannot be selected as AFS partitions. You can only configure partitions containing no data as AFS partitions. The next steps are creating the root volumes and defining the replication; both are automatic for the first AFS machine. Next you can select whether the machine should be configured as the cell's system control server. Now the Configuration Wizard recaps the list of operations to be performed. After you click the Configure button, the actual configuration takes place.

AFS client configuration is much simpler, and it requires opening the AFS Client Configuration under the Control Panel. In this window (shown

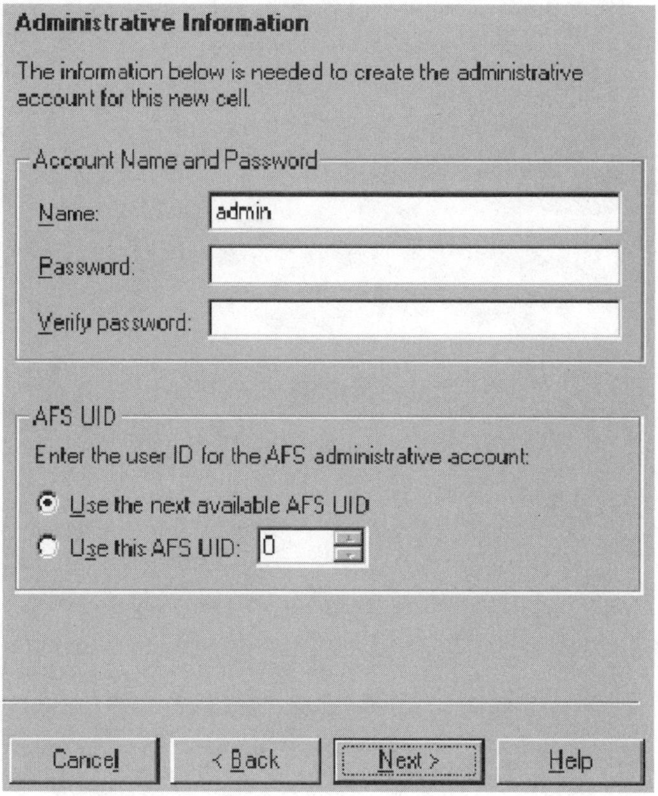

Figure 44-3
AFS Server
Configuration
Wizard:
Administrative
Information

Administrative Information

The information below is needed to create the administrative account for this new cell.

─Account Name and Password─────────────────

Name: admin

Password:

Verify password:

─AFS UID─────────────────────────────

Enter the user ID for the AFS administrative account:

⦿ Use the next available AFS UID

○ Use this AFS UID: 0

| Cancel | < Back | Next > | Help |

in Figure 44-4), you specify the default AFS cell name for this machine. (Under the AFS cells tab, you can see all available cells, or add new cells if they do not appear there.)

After configuring the AFS client, you can start the AFS client service. Now map AFS paths to Windows NT logical drive names. This can be done from the AFS Client Configuration window.

Managing AFS Volumes

For AFS file systems, it is possible to retrieve the mount point and volume or partition properties through the AFS menu under the NT Explorer popup menu. This AFS menu is available in the right-click popup menu and AFS file directory. In this same menu, it is also possible to set *Access Control Lists*

Figure 44-4
AFS Client
Configuration

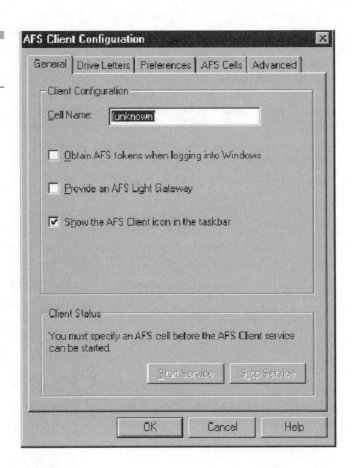

(ACLs). Setting ACLs includes setting permission entries, as shown in Figure 44-5. Each entry is keyed into a window of the form shown in Figure 44-6.

To manipulate volumes, you can use the AFS Server Manager (under Server in the AFS program group). This program allows you, among other things, to create new volumes and view all currently available volumes, partitions, and services.

Managing AFS Accounts

The AFS Account Manager Program, shown in Figure 44-7, can be invoked by selecting Account Manager under Control Center in the AFS program

Figure 44-5
ACL setting window

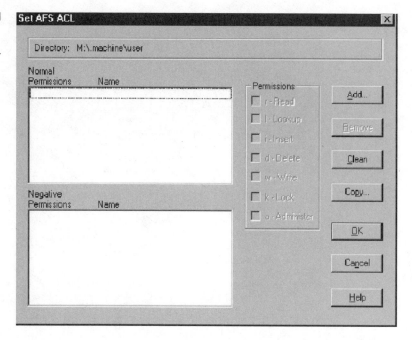

Figure 44-6
ACL Entry window

group. This application allows you to create new users (as shown in Figure 44-8) and edit user properties (as shown in Figure 44-9). You can create groups and edit their properties as well.

Another feature of this program is that you can control access to AFS directory on a per-machine basis. These machines can be assigned to groups

Figure 44-7
AFS Account
Manager—Users
view

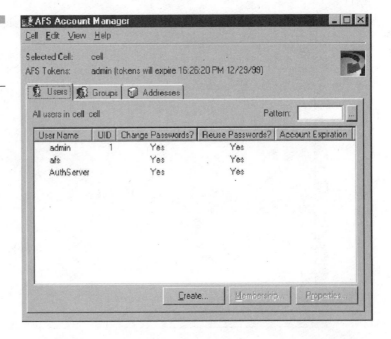

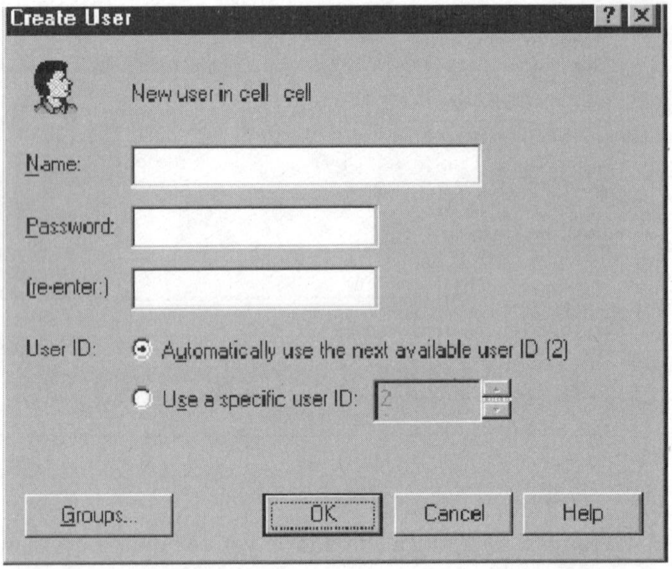

Figure 44-8
AFS Account
Manager—Create
User window

that in turn can have ACLs associated with them. Machines are assigned to groups by the IP address, and you can use 0 as a wildcard (that is, X.Y.0.0

Figure 44-9
AFS Account
Manager—User
Properties window

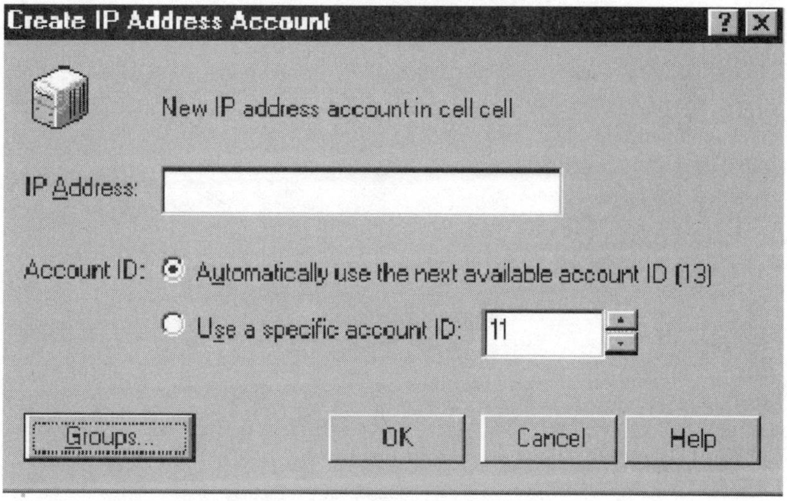

Figure 44-10
Create IP Address
Account

would be all machines with any address X.Y.W.Z). Figure 44-10 shows an example of defining such a machine account.

IBM WebTraffic Express

Continuing our discussion of the IBM WebSphere Performance Pack, this chapter examines IBM WebTraffic Express. This product is essentially a proxy server with some extra functions for filtering that have been added.

Installation and Startup

The installation of WebTraffic Express is quite simple. Once you obtain the WebSphere Performance Pack CD-ROM—or download the program from IBM's Web site at www.software.ibm.com/webservers/cahceman or www.software.ibm.com/webservers/wte—you just run the installation program that guides you through the steps, which includes the selection of the installation directory and administrator username and password. Once the installation process is complete, you need to reboot your machine.

To verify the installation, look at the Services control panel (shown in Figure 45-1). Once you select the Web Traffic Express entry, you can start the application by pressing the Start button. If desired, you can make the application start automatically every time you boot your machine by pressing the Startup button and modifying the Startup Type in the services dialog that appears.

An alternate method to start WebTraffic Express is to run the whttpg program, which resides in the Bin directory under the Installation directory. Once you run this program (by either using Run in the Windows Start menu or using a command prompt), you get the GUI shown in Figure 45-2.

Figure 45-1
Services control panel

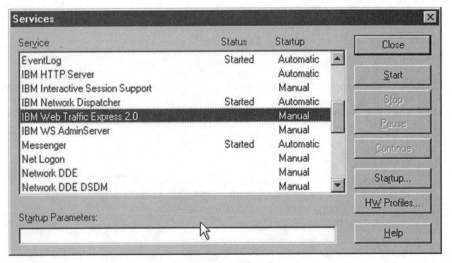

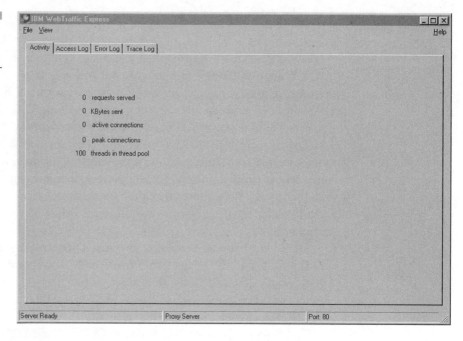

Figure 45-2
IBM WebTraffic
Express console GUI

This GUI can come in handy when you need to monitor the status and activity of the WebTraffic Express server. Note that under the File menu, you can stop and restart the server. The View menu enables you to change between the different views, which is just the same as using Tab+Control.

The different views available are as follows:

- *Activity*   A summary of server activity, including the amount of requests and a count of outgoing traffic
- *Access Log*   Log of proxy requests made (these are stored in a log file, which is by default Logs\http-proxy under your WebTraffic Express Installation directory)
- *Error Log*   Log of run-time errors
- *Trace Log*   Log of trace messages

Using this GUI is not crucial, because you can connect to the server by using any Web browser (as explained in the next section).

WebTraffic Express Configuration

Because WebTraffic Express is a proxy server, it is intended to interact with Web browsers. Therefore, the most natural way to access the server and to configure it is by connecting to the server. To perform that action, open your Web browser and connect to `http://your-machine` by keying the address, as you would do for any URL. The WebTraffic Express main page loads.

The first item to verify is that your browser is correctly set. If not, you are advised to "Tune your browser first." The most common reason for needing to tune your browser is if you are using an out-of-date browser (or one without Java support installed). Java support is a must for using Web-Traffic Express (and is quite useful regardless), so you need to install this application.

Once your browser problems are settled (that is, if you had any problems in the first place), you can configure WebTraffic Express. Before going into the details of performing that task, notice that the WebTraffic Express main page provides links to the IBM WebTraffic Express Web site and to the IBM documentation for this product.

To configure your server, click the CONFIGURATION AND ADMINIS-TRATION FORMS link. Your browser prompts you for the administrator's username and password before continuing. The username and password are configured during installation but can also be set by using the `htadm` program, which resides in the Bin directory of your WebTraffic Express installation. The parameters for this program are the password file, user-name, requested password, and the user's real name and are presented as follows:

```
htadm -adduser password-file username password real-name
```

The password file is `admin.pwd` by default, under your NT installation directory.

After verifying your password, your browser should show you the Web-Traffic Express Configuration Page. Through this page, you will be able to configure your server. The configuration is stored in the `ibmproxy.conf` file under your Windows NT Installation directory. You can directly edit the file if you want, but all configuration details can be edited through the administration forms in your Web browser. In the following section, we shall focus on editing the different configuration parameters through the graphic interface that is provided by the configuration pages. The configuration file is quite simple to understand and essentially resembles the Web server `http.conf` file.

Proxy Configuration

The configuration page is divided into two parts, as you can see in Figure 45-3. On the left side, there is a frame that is used for navigating around the different configuration categories. Once you select a specific category, the configuration details for this category appear on the right side. For example, select Proxy Settings under Proxy Configuration. The resulting window is shown in Figure 45-3. Here, you can select the protocols for which the server acts as a proxy. The available protocols are HTTP, FTP, Gopher, and SSL tunneling, and all protocols are selected by default. Next, you can select the proxy buffer size. The buffer allocated here is used for buffering data that comes from dynamic components, such as servlets. Finally, there is an entry for the proxy access log file.

Figure 45-3
Proxy Settings page

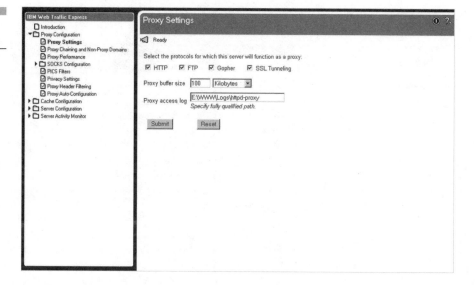

If you make any changes to the form, you should click the Submit button to save them. If you want to make the changes effective immediately, you need to click the Reset button. Clicking this button causes the server to reread the configuration file.

The next entry under Proxy Configuration deals with proxy chaining. Proxy chaining enables you to use several proxies. To use chaining, you must define for a server a different server that is next on the chain. Once a request is made that cannot be served (i.e., the file is not cached), the server goes to the next server along the chain, rather than looking for the file over the Internet in the actual content server. The advantage of chaining proxies is in their capability to support a large network of users. If you have a large organization in which several LANs are hooked up, you can have one proxy on each LAN, then chain them to one central proxy that connects to the Web. Chaining proxy servers has some obvious advantages, such as reducing the load on proxy servers and enabling you to place the proxy server near users. This technique does, however, introduce latency to the process of serving requests, so you would not want to overdo it. Each request potentially has to traverse the whole chain before being served.

Proxy chaining can be set independently for different protocols. The Proxy Chaining setup page is shown in Figure 45-4. You can set the next server along the chain for HTTP, FTP, or Gopher requests. In addition, this

Figure 45-4
Proxy Chaining page

page enables you to provide a list of domains for which you do not want to use a proxy at all. For any servers or domains that you specify here, requests will not be cached.

The next configuration page, called Proxy Performance, is shown in Figure 45-5. With this page, you can determine whether your server should run as a pure proxy (in other words, that it will only perform caching and will not be a content server itself). You can also determine whether persistent connections to clients should be enabled. Such a connection reduces the time for serving a client's request but requires network bandwidth and a dedicated thread on your server. The other options in this page deal with whether you want your server to read the SOCKS configuration file, whether you need to send HTTP/1.0 to downstream servers (this action is required only if you have downstream servers that cannot take HTTP/1.1 requests), and whether FTP URLs should be absolute or relative.

The next two pages deal with SOCKS configuration. You should use these pages if you have a SOCKS server on your firewall. On the Direct Connections page (refer to Figure 45-6), you should specify addresses for requests that do not need to pass through the SOCKS server. On the SOCKS Connections page (refer to Figure 45-7), you specify the ones that should pass through the SOCKS server. In both pages, the list of addresses

Figure 45-5
Proxy Performance
page

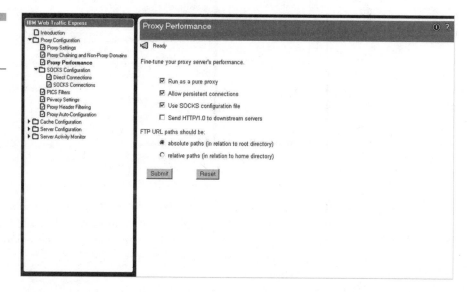

Figure 45-6
SOCKS configuration
Direct Connections
page

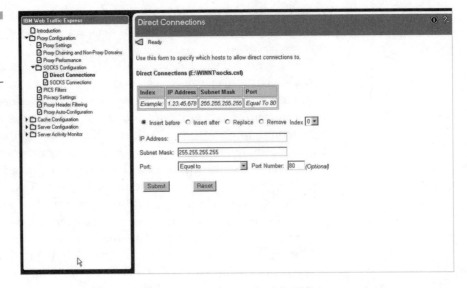

Figure 45-7
SOCKS configuration
SOCKS Connections
page

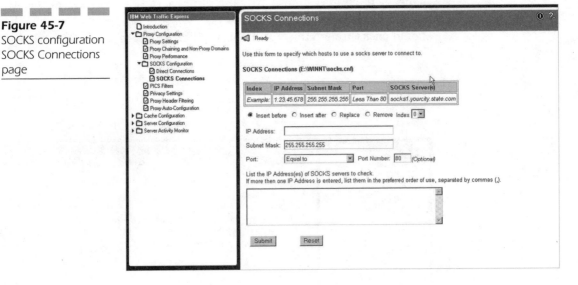

(including IP address and port) are organized in a table, and you can indicate whether you want to insert before, insert after, replace, or remove a specific entry. On the SOCKS connections page, you also need to specify the IP addresses of the SOCKS servers.

The next page deals with PICS filtering. PICS stands for *Platform for Internet Content Selection* and is a protocol for filtering Web information through labeling content. On the PICS Filters page, shown in Figure 45-8, you can determine the PICS filtering rules to use on your proxy server. Similar to the previous couple of pages, you have a table of entries —each corresponding to one filter. You can create a new filter, copy an existing one (for editing), edit an existing filter, and delete a filter. For each filter, you can edit the detailed information, which includes its name and when it should be active (refer to Figure 45-9). Once you submit this information, you can edit the actual filtering criteria, that includes the following components:

- The users to whom the rule should apply (leaving this table empty makes the rule apply to all users)

- The PICS rating services to use (refer to Figure 45-10). See the URL www.w3.org/PICS for more details about PICS concepts for PICS-server URLs.

- URLs to always pass (a list of URLs for which requests are always served under this rule)

Figure 45-8
PICS Filters page

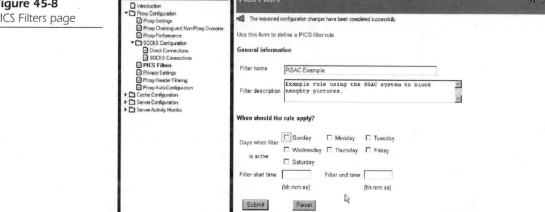

Figure 45-9
PICS Filters page
continued

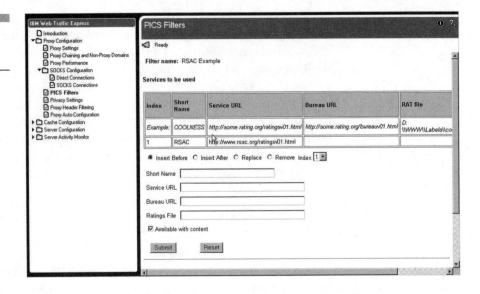

Figure 45-10
PICS filters definition

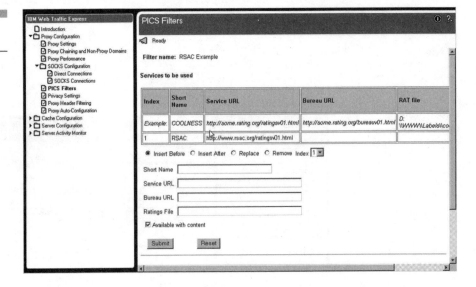

- URLs to always fail (a list of URLs for which requests are rejected under this rule)

- Conditional filtering to be used. Here, you can do your own filtering based on PICS rating-information data. The form of the conditional filter is `Filter(Pass( ' <condition>' )` or `Filter(Fail`

Figure 45-11
Privacy Settings page

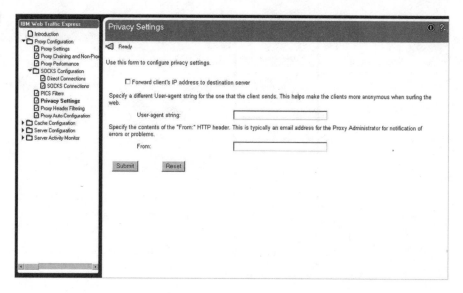

('<condition>')), where <condition> is a logical expression containing PICS rating-information attributes.

The next item on the Proxy Configuration list deals with privacy settings and is shown in Figure 45-11. This item enables you to indicate whether you want to forward your client's IP address to content servers and to specify a different User-agent string than the one the client sends. These two features are useful for masking the identity of clients. HTTP requests inherently include the requesting client IP address plus a user-agent identification, which includes the browser type and the operating system. If you type Proxy Server in the User-agent string field, all requests forwarded to content servers will not include the actual browser and operating system of clients. The last field on this page enables you to specify the proxy administrator e-mail address. This field is used when presenting error messages to the user. To mask user information, you can also use the next page, which is called Proxy Header Filtering. On this page, you can specify HTTP headers that will be blocked by the server (i.e., will not be forwarded to the Web server contacted). For example, the User-agent header can be blocked, meaning that it will not be sent at all (in other words, whatever you specified in the User-agent string field in the previous page is ignored, of course).

Figure 45-12
Proxy Auto-
Configuration page

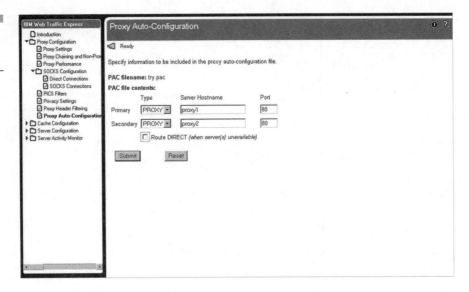

The last entry in the Proxy Configuration section deals with Proxy auto-configuration. In this section, you can create and edit *Proxy Auto Configuration* (PAC) files. These are JavaScript files that are used in conjunction with a specific request, to determine whether a proxy server, SOCKS server, or direct connection should be used. When editing a PAC file, you are provided with the page shown in Figure 45-12. You can provide a primary and a secondary PROXY/SOCKS server and also indicate whether you will enable direct routing if the servers are not available.

Note that once you configure this feature, the Web browsers on the client side must be configured to read the PAC file.

Cache Configuration

The Cache Configuration folder includes the pages for cache configuration. The first page, Cache Settings, is shown in Figure 45-13. Here, you indicate whether caching should be used and whether you want aggressive caching. You can also ask to override client reload requests (meaning that when the user on the client side asks for a reload in his or her browser, you do not contact the content server if you have the data cached) and to perform caching based on incoming URLs. This page also enables you to specify the cache

Figure 45-13
Cache Settings page

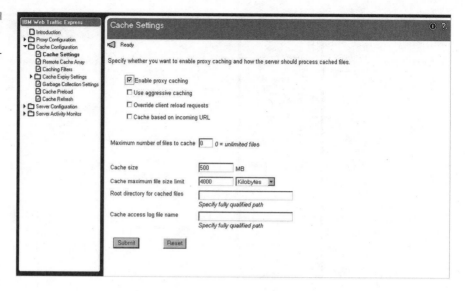

size in megabytes, the maximum number of files to cache, the maximum file size to cache, the cache location on the disk, and the cache access log file. The next entry, Remote Cache Array, enables you to set a shared cache for several proxies. The following entry, Caching Filters, enables you to determine whether or not you want filtering of local domain files and query responses and enables you to specify URLs upon which you specifically want or do not want caching to be performed.

The Cache Expiry Settings entries enable you to control how the cache is managed. The first page is Garbage Control Settings, which is shown in Figure 45-14. Here, you can determine whether you want to have garbage collection at all. The purpose of garbage collection is to free space in the cache. If you want garbage collection, you can select the amount of memory that will be available for this task, when to perform the task (this job is CPU intensive, so you better choose a time when the system is not loaded), the amount of cache to be used once garbage collection is finished (zero means empty), and the kind of algorithm to use (minimizing bandwidth utilization, response time, or a blend of both). This page also enables you to perform garbage collection at will. The next two pages, Cache Preload (Figure 45-15) and Cache Refresh (Figure 45-16) enable you to indicate whether you want the cache refreshed (i.e., whether you want files to be reloaded from Web servers) and the details and limits for this refresh.

Figure 45-14
Garbage Collection
Settings page

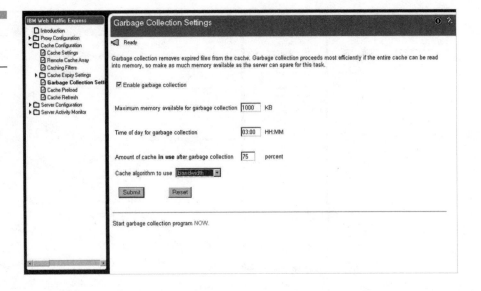

Figure 45-15
Cache Preload page

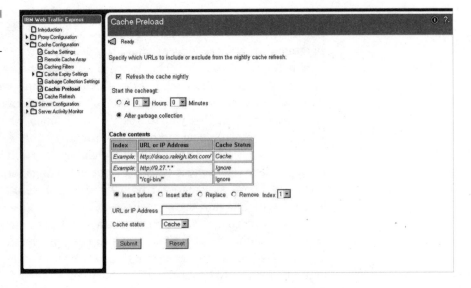

Server Configuration

As the name suggests, the Server Configuration folder enables you to configure the server. The Basic Settings page enables you to set the host name and

Figure 45-16
Cache Refresh page

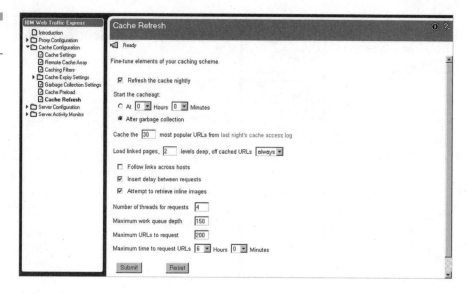

Figure 45-17
Document Protection
page

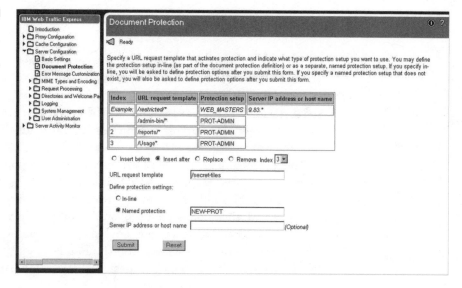

port number and to configure the use of server-side includes. The Document Protection page (refer to Figure 45-17) enables you to set up protection for specific pages or page templates. As shown in Figure 45-18, you need to specify the Protection realm (shown to the user when prompting for the password), the password file and groups file, and the different permissions.

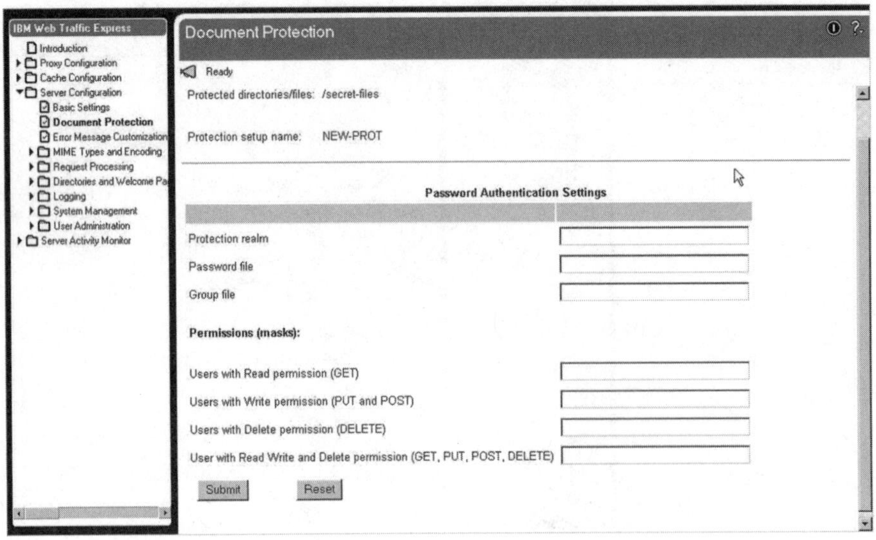

Figure 45-18
Document Protection
definition

The Error Message Customization shows the message file for each kind of error. If you want to change a message, you can either specify a new file or just edit the message file.

Next is the MIME types and MIME encoding settings, which usually should be kept alone unless you have a special kind of file that you want to introduce at that location.

The pages under Request Processing enable you to determine how requests are processed. The API Request Processing page enables you to define external applications to be invoked during request processing, and the HTTP Methods page enables you to control which HTTP requests are served. The User Methods page enables you to define user-specific HTTP requests that are to be served, and the Request Routing page enables you to define specific treatment for specific URLs or URL templates.

The Directories and Welcome Page folder enables you to set the server welcome page (which is used in case the user does not specify a specific file in the URL and instead specifies only the host address), the way directory listings are provided, and directory icons settings.

The Logging folder enables you to set the log files, to determine the log archiving method (which could be either purge or compress and is applied to files that are older than a certain time period or larger than a certain size). You can also indicate exclusions to the access log—i.e., URLs for which access requests will not be logged.

The System Management folder enables you to set the maximum number of threads and the timeout and maximum number of requests on a persistence connection with a client, under the Performance page. The timeouts shown on the Timeouts page (refer to Figure 45-19) are used to control server processing time. The input timeout field is used to set the time permitted for a client to send a request after making a connection to the server. The output timeout determines the maximum time permitted for the server to send output to a client. This limit does not apply to requests that require a local CGI-bin program. For these, the Script Timeout field is used. The last entry in this folder enables you to activate *Simple Network Management Protocol* (SNMP).

The last entry under Server Configuration enables you to add and remove users and change passwords. These users and passwords are to be used for document protection, as explained in the previous section.

Figure 45-19
Timeouts page

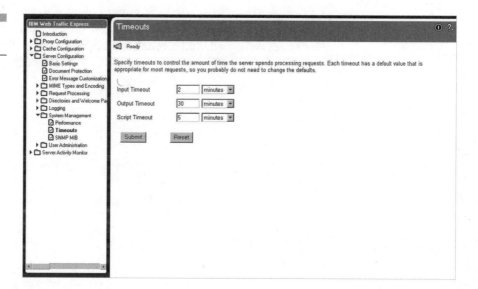

Server Activity Monitor

The last folder on the left frame enables you to monitor the server activity and provides the following entries:

- *Activity Statistics*   Information regarding the number of threads used and available, server response time, number of requests processed, and number of errors

- *Network Statistics*   Information regarding the number of bytes sent and received and the transmission rate

- *Access Statistics*   Includes information about client accesses made to the proxy, including users and passwords (where applicable) and the HTTP method

- *Proxy Access Statistics*   Includes information about proxy activity, such as which URLs were provided from the cache and which were requested from the Web server

- *Cache Statistics*   Includes information about the status of the cache, such as whether caching is activated and whether garbage collection is in progress

- *Garbage Collection Summary*   Summary of the last garbage collection process, including start time, end time, number of files removed, and number of files after completion

- *Cache Refresh Summary*   Summary of information relating to cache refresh, including start time and end time for last refresh, number of pages refreshed, and a breakdown of the reasons for refresh (e.g., specified in configuration file, accessed in the previous night's access log)

46

IBM SecureWay Network Dispatcher

The last component of the WebSphere Performance Pack is the SecureWay Network Dispatcher. This is a crucial ingredient in guaranteeing the responsiveness and availability of your Web services. The Network Dispatcher includes three different components aimed at load-balancing: the network dispatcher, *interactive session support* (ISS), and *content-based routing* (CBR).

Installation and Startup

The installation of the network dispatcher is quite simple. Once you obtain the WebSphere Performance Pack CD or download it from the IBM Web site at www.software.ibm.com/network/dispatcher, you only need to run the installation program. This program guides you through the steps, which include the selection of the installation directory and administrator username and password. Once the installation process is complete, you need to reboot your machine. The installation process creates an icon for SecureWay network dispatcher either on the start menu (if you install just the dispatcher product) or under the Performance Pack entry in the WebSphere group. Once you start the program, you get the network dispatcher main window, as shown in Figure 46-1.

In order for the network dispatcher program to work, you need to have the network dispatcher service up. By default, it is started automatically when you boot the system. If not, you can start it through Services in the control panel.

Network Dispatcher Configuration

In order to configure the network dispatcher, select the Dispatcher icon under Network Dispatcher on the left side of the window and then select "Start Configuration Wizard" under Dispatcher (or from the pop-up menu available by right-clicking).

Figure 46-1
Network dispatcher
GUI

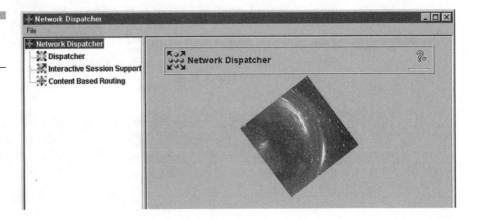

The configuration wizard takes you through the process of configuring a cluster of servers. The goal here is to set up several servers working on the same LAN and to provide access for remote clients to these servers. This setup is done in a manner that the server content is identical and any incoming requests are routed to an arbitrary server in an attempt to minimize server load. Prior to configuring the dispatcher, you need to have the servers all set up and working. It is advised to check connectivity between all nodes (using ping, Telnet, or just a Web browser).

The configuration wizard takes you through the following steps:

- *Selecting an IP address for the cluster* This should be an IP address or a recognized hostname on the same LAN as the servers.

- *Selecting a port for the service to be load-balanced* The dispatcher software is oblivious to the actual application. It could be HTTP, Telnet, FTP, or any other TCP/IP application.

- *Selecting servers to be load-balanced* You can add servers to a list and remove them if needed.

- *Starting an advisor* The dispatcher makes use of "advisor" processes to collect server information, which is used as input to the load-balancing algorithm. You are prompted to start an advisor for the port you selected.

- *Configuring the servers to receive packets addressed to the cluster* On UNIX systems, this is done using `ifconfig`. For example, in Solaris the command is `ifconfig lo0:1 <cluster-address> 127.0.0.1 up`. In Windows NT, you need to add a new network adapter called MS Loopback Adapter and set its IP address to the cluster address. After rebooting, you should remove the duplicate route entries to the cluster IP address. To do that, type `route print`, which shows the routing table. Look for a duplicate entry for the cluster IP address under Gateway Address and delete the redundant entry (which should be the one whose IP address starts with a different number from the one used for your LAN) with `route delete <network-address> <gateway-address>`.

Once you complete the definition of clusters, the dispatcher creates a hierarchy of icons in the navigation area on the left side (see Figure 46-2). The different kinds of icons represent different types of entities:

Figure 46-2
The Network
Dispatcher
Navigation area

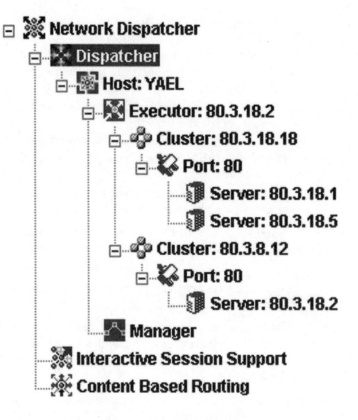

- *Host*   This represents the host on which the network dispatcher service is running.

- *Executor*   A component in charge of routing TCP and UDP connections to servers based on the type of request (that is, based on the port). This component is always active when the dispatcher is being used.

- *Manager*   A component that considers inputs for advisors and from ISS monitoring (if ISS is used for monitoring), weighs them together, and determines how to load-balance requests. If no manager is used, load balancing is performed using weighted round-robin scheduling (where the weights are current server loads).

- *Advisor*   This sends dummy requests to servers in order to measure their response time. These results are provided to the manager as input to the load-balancing process. Advisors are protocol-dependent and are available for HTTP, FTP, SSL, SMTP, NNTP, POP3, and Telnet.

- *Cluster*   A set of servers operating together with a designated IP address

■ *Port*   A certain TCP/IP port associated with a cluster IP address

■ *Server*   A single server (sometimes referred to as back-end server, which actually provides a service). An example is a Web server (an HTTP server) or the WebSphere application server.

The hierarchy of entities is such that the "executor" contains clusters, which contain ports, which contain servers, and the manager contains advisors.

Selecting an entity icon will bring up its details for the work area. In addition, you can right-click the icon to get a pop-up menu, which allows the reconfiguration or addition of new subcomponents. Selecting the executor provides general packet statistics and error statistics, as shown in Figure 46-3. In addition, it is possible to provide some configuration settings, pertaining mainly to the limits on the number of ports, clusters, and servers.

In the same spirit, selecting a cluster shows the current statistics and configuration settings, along with the list of servers (see Figure 46-4). It shows the weights of the servers (which measures their respective capacities). Selecting a server shows the current statistics, which are merely the

Figure 46-3
The executor status window

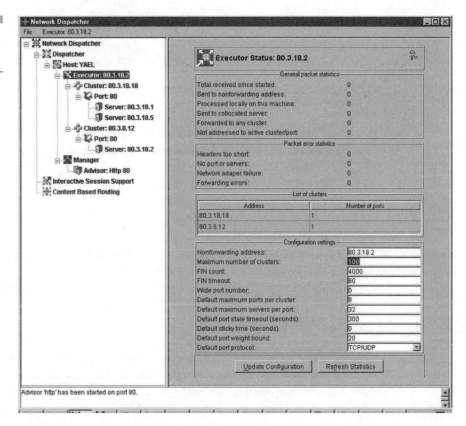

Figure 46-4
The cluster window

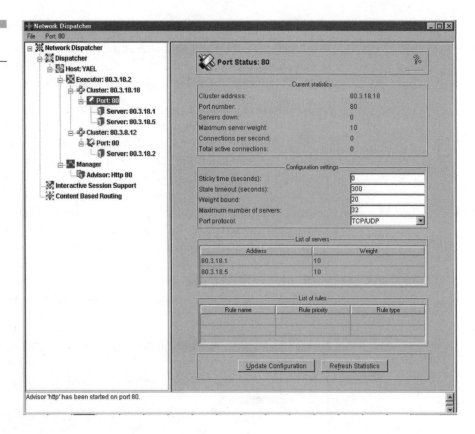

IP addresses of the cluster and server along with the port number. The configuration settings include the server weight.

Advisors show their names, port number, and log file name, along with a list of connected servers. It is possible to configure the detail level of logs and the frequency of updates.

The most complex interface belongs to the manager, as shown in Figure 46-5. In addition to showing the file and port used, it is possible to configure the relative importance of different load-balancing inputs. You can set the weights given to new connections, old connections, advisor input, and ISS inputs. It is also possible to apply smoothing to the weights given to servers. This can be useful to reduce the effect of rapid and short-lived fluctuations in server load.

One last feature offered by the dispatcher is rule-based load-balancing. You can add "rules" under the "Port" entity in a cluster. A rule provides the capability to determine which servers can handle certain requests. This provides additional flexibility in load balancing. The dispatcher offers several different kinds of rules, each of which define when the rule should be applied:

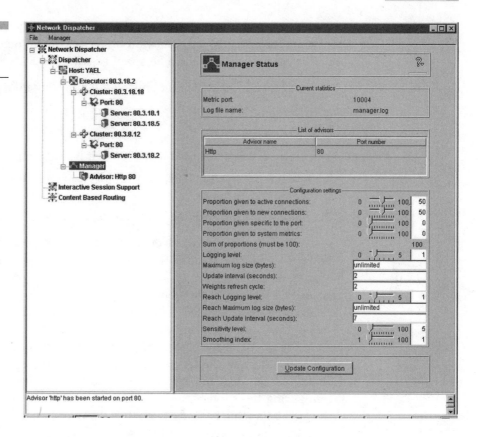

Figure 46-5
The Manager window

■ *Client IP address*   Enables you to discriminate between clients based on their IP addresses.

■ *Time of day*   Enables you to route traffic to different servers at different times of day.

■ *Connections per second on a port*   Enables you to use different sets of servers given the current rate of requests.

■ *Total connections on a port*   Enables you to use different sets of servers given the total load.

■ *Client port*   Enables you to discriminate between clients based on ports (for example, you can provide better service on a specific port).

■ *Content*   Enables you to discriminate between requests based on their content. This is used only by the CBR component discussed previously.

■ *Always true*   Enables you to specify rules that are always valid as long as the relevant servers are not down. This is useful in situations where a certain set of servers is supposed to handle requests, but when they're all down, you want other servers to handle traffic (and this contingency plan can be specified with other kinds of rules).

When specifying rules, you provide the following information:

- Rule name
- Type of rule
- Priority, a positive number (the lower it is, the higher the priority)
- Optional parameters (such as the start and end times for time-of-day rules and port numbers)
- List of servers associated with the rule

During runtime, rules are evaluated one by one, based on their priority. When a "valid" rule is found (that is, the specified rule is matched and some of the associated servers are running), the list of servers associated with it is used for load-balancing requests.

To summarize, let's look at a simple example. Say you have four servers called `www1.shiok.com`, `www2.shiok.com`, `www3.shiok.com`, `www4.shiok.com`, all on the same LAN. Using the dispatcher configuration wizard, you add a new cluster called `www.shiok.com` (you should assign a free IP address on the same LAN to this name) and set port 80 for HTTP. After configuring the servers to receive packets addressed to `www.shiok.com`, the load balancing is ready to go. It is quite easy to see it at work; all you need to do is to start a Web browser and point to your cluster address (in this example, `www.shiok.com`). The HTTP request will be referred to one of the four servers, and a subsequent request will be spread between them in an attempt to balance the load. You can see which server gets which request both by using the network dispatcher statistics mentioned earlier or just by looking at the activity logs of your HTTP server.

Interactive Session Support

The *interactive session support* service (ISS) goes one step further in allowing the setup of a large cluster of servers operating together while ensuring load balancing and high availability.

ISS introduces the concept of a *cell*. An ISS cell is a group of servers managed together and in some sense is an extension of the dispatcher notion of a cluster. A cell is composed of nodes (which are servers) that provide services. A service is essentially a type of protocol (such as HTTP) and each node can be associated with one or more services.

Before stating ISS, you need to set up a configuration file called `iss.cfg`. The minimal configuration file should contain the following two lines:

```
cell <cell-name> local
node <hostname> 1
```

Once this file is ready, you can start the ISS (by starting the service in the Services window under the control panel). Next, you can use the Network Dispatcher interface to connect to the ISS service by providing the host on which it is running.

Once you connect, you get an icon for the ISS host under the ISS icon and, below it, an icon corresponding to the cell. Selecting it shows the cell attributes on the work area on the right side. These attributes include the heart beat interval. This attribute determines the frequency at which ISS contacts ensure they are still alive (such a contact is referred to as a "heartbeat"). Other attributes specify once in how many heartbeats a dispatcher update is made and how many "missing" heartbeats constitute a network or node failure. The Authentication Key attribute is used to provide authentication between cell members. Under the cell, you can add nodes (by right-clicking the cell icon). Nodes are identified by a name and ID number. Once the nodes are added, you need to specify one node as the "monitor" and the rest as ISS agents.

The next step is adding resources (again, right-click the cell icon). Resources are identified by a user-defined name. The resource is associated with a metric that measures the amount of load on that resource. A metric can be internal or external. An internal metric is one specified by ISS (one of `CPULoad` and `FreeMem`, indicating the load on the CPU and the free physical memory respectively, both in terms of percentage). An external metric is associated with an arbitrary program that, when executed, returns a measurement number as a result. For the resource metric, you can specify the following:

- *The metric range*   The upper and lower limits on values for the metric
- *Fail limit*   At what value is it considered "failed" (that is, it should not be used for new requests)
- *Recover limit*   At what value is the node considered useful again (after failing)
- *Policy*   What is the objective, minimizing or maximizing the metric

Once resources and nodes are defined, we can specify the services. Services are added again under the associated node and need to be identified by a port (the dialog asks for a DNS server, but it is not required when working with the dispatcher). To the service, we add resources and nodes. A typical configuration would include a "Web service" on port 80 with a node list containing the servers and a resource list.

Finally, you need to add the "observer." Observers are in charge of collecting load-balancing information. ISS provides three kinds of observers, but the kind relevant here is the Dispatcher observer (other observers can be used to perform load-balancing using the mapping provided by a DNS name server, which is not usually practical for Web-based applications). The port number is selected to the default dispatcher port once you select the Dispatcher observer, so the only selection required is the node on which the observer runs. To the observer, you add the list of services it is monitoring, such as a Web service.

Once the observer and agents are all operational, the dispatcher can be configured to use ISS information in making its load-balancing decisions by setting the respective weights that are part of the dispatcher manager attributes.

Content-Based Routing

The last piece in the load-balancing puzzle is *content-based routing* (CBR). Essentially, CBR enables Web Traffic Express to proxy requests to specific servers based on the content of the specific URL request (that is why it is called *content*-based routing). How is this actually done? Well, CBR matches the URL to a user-specified rule and a set of candidate servers is given to the network dispatcher, which selects the server most suited to serve the request.

Note that when using the dispatcher for CBR, it does not forward packets to other servers, but rather implements the user-provided rules in order to select servers. The rules are allowed to use the information provided in the HTTP request (that is, server IP address, client IP address, path, and possibly HTTP headers).

To configure CBR, select the Content-Based Routing icon in the network dispatcher interface and then select "Connect to Host" from the pop-up menu. You are prompted to connect to the host, which is required to be running WTE.

The technique used to configure and manage the CBR hierarchy is similar to the one used with the dispatcher. The difference is that you can add cluster rules that determine how to handle packets. These are rules that have a special type called "Content." For these rules, it is possible to specify a pattern that is matched against the request URLs. Using this pattern, it is possible to let specific servers handle different requests based on the URL path. The pattern is specified as a Boolean expression using * as a wildcard and &, |, and ! for logical AND, OR, and NOT, respectively. In the expression, the following keywords are available:

- `client` Client IP address
- `url` Request URL
- `protocol` Protocol prefix of the URL
- `path` Path of the URL
- `refer` Referred URL
- `user` User ID section of URL

For example, a rule could be `(client=128.2.*) & (path=*.avi)`, meaning that this rule focuses on requests coming from clients whose IP address starts with 128.2 and are requesting AVI files.

Another parameter for content-based rules enables you to set "cookie affinity," which means that once a server is selected for our requests, the same requests shall use the same server for a certain period of time. The period of time is set in the "sticky time" field of the rule specification dialog. The net effect of using CBR rules is load balancing different Web servers based on URL content.

INDEX

ABOUT THE AUTHOR

Ron Ben-Natan is Chief Technology Officer and Senior Vice President of Engineering at ViryaNet—a software provider of B-to-B Internet solutions for service communities (www.viryanet.com). Prior to that he has worked for companies such as Intel, AT&T Bell Laboratories, Merrill Lynch and as a consultant at J.P. Morgan. He has a Ph.D. in Computer Science from the Hebrew University of Jerusalem in the field of distributed computing and has authored four books titled "CORBA," "Objects on the Web," "CORBA on the Web," and "The SanFrancisco Developer's Guide," all published by McGraw-Hill.

Ori Sasson is the co-founder and CEO of KS Software in Tel-Aviv, Israel. He has 13 years of experience in object-oriented technology, and extensive experience relating to Java and Internet computing. He has a M.Sc. in Computer Science from the Hebrew University of Jerusalem, and is currently in the process of obtaining a Ph.D. in theoretical Computer Science at the same university.

ABOUT THE CD

The CD-ROM contains an evaluation version of the WebSphere Application Server, Standard Edition. In addition, it includes the entry version of VisualAge for Java version 3.0, and of WebSphere Studio version 3.0. Installation walkthroughs for all three products are provided as part of the discussion in the book. The book and the software provided on this CD-ROM (both the development tools and the runtime environments) allow you to build and deploy WebSphere-based e-Business applications within a matter of a few days!

In case you are prompted for a product serial number or key during the installation process, just type in any number.

ABOUT THE CODE SAMPLES

The code samples for the book *WebSphere Starter Kit* provide ready-to-run e-Business applications written in Java for the WebSphere application server. These examples highlight various aspects of server-side programming, such as *JavaServer Pages* (JSP), *Enterprise Java Beans* (EJB), and Servlet programming. The code samples are grouped by chapter, and each chapter has one ZIP file that includes the relevant Java and HTML source files. These code samples can be found at www.mcgraw-hill.com.

SOFTWARE AND INFORMATION LICENSE

The software and information on this diskette (collectively referred to as the "Product") are the property of The McGraw-Hill Companies, Inc. ("McGraw-Hill") and are protected by both United States copyright law and international copyright treaty provision. You must treat this Product just like a book, except that you may copy it into a computer to be used and you may make archival copies of the Products for the sole purpose of backing up our software and protecting your investment from loss.

By saying "just like a book," McGraw-Hill means, for example, that the Product may be used by any number of people and may be freely moved from one computer location to another, so long as there is no possibility of the Product (or any part of the Product) being used at one location or on one computer while it is being used at another. Just as a book cannot be read by two different people in two different places at the same time, neither can the Product be used by two different people in two different places at the same time (unless, of course, McGraw-Hill's rights are being violated).

McGraw-Hill reserves the right to alter or modify the contents of the Product at any time.

This agreement is effective until terminated. The Agreement will terminate automatically without notice if you fail to comply with any provisions of this Agreement. In the event of termination by reason of your breach, you will destroy or erase all copies of the Product installed on any computer system or made for backup purposes and shall expunge the Product from your data storage facilities.

LIMITED WARRANTY

McGraw-Hill warrants the physical diskette(s) enclosed herein to be free of defects in materials and workmanship for a period of sixty days from the purchase date. If McGraw-Hill receives written notification within the warranty period of defects in materials or workmanship, and such notification is determined by McGraw-Hill to be correct, McGraw-Hill will replace the defective diskette(s). Send request to:

Customer Service
McGraw-Hill
Gahanna Industrial Park
860 Taylor Station Road
Blacklick, OH 43004-9615

The entire and exclusive liability and remedy for breach of this Limited Warranty shall be limited to replacement of defective diskette(s) and shall not include or extend any claim for or right to cover any other damages, including but not limited to, loss of profit, data, or use of the software, or special, incidental, or consequential damages or other similar claims, even if McGraw-Hill has been specifically advised as to the possibility of such damages. In no event will McGraw-Hill's liability for any damages to you or any other person ever exceed the lower of suggested list price or actual price paid for the license to use the Product, regardless of any form of the claim.

THE McGRAW-HILL COMPANIES, INC. SPECIFICALLY DISCLAIMS ALL OTHER WARRANTIES, EXPRESS OR IMPLIED, INCLUDING BUT NOT LIMITED TO, ANY IMPLIED WARRANTY OF MERCHANTABILITY OR FITNESS FOR A PARTICULAR PURPOSE. Specifically, McGraw-Hill makes no representation or warranty that the Product is fit for any particular purpose and any implied warranty of merchantability is limited to the sixty day duration of the Limited Warranty covering the physical diskette(s) only (and not the software or information) and is otherwise expressly and specifically disclaimed.

This Limited Warranty gives you specific legal rights; you may have others which may vary from state to state. Some states do not allow the exclusion of incidental or consequential damages, or the limitation on how long an implied warranty lasts, so some of the above may not apply to you.

This Agreement constitutes the entire agreement between the parties relating to use of the Product. The terms of any purchase order shall have no effect on the terms of this Agreement. Failure of McGraw-Hill to insist at any time on strict compliance with this Agreement shall not constitute a waiver of any rights under this Agreement. This Agreement shall be construed and governed in accordance with the laws of New York. If any provision of this Agreement is held to be contrary to law, that provision will be enforced to the maximum extent permissible and the remaining provisions will remain in force and effect.